T0332777

Handbook of Research on Cybersecurity Issues and Challenges for Business and FinTech Applications

Saqib Saeed
Department of Computer Information Systems, College of Computer Science and Information Technology, Imam Abdulrahman Bin Faisal University, Dammam, Saudi Arabia

Abdullah M. Almuhaideb
Department of Networks and Communications, College of Computer Science and Information Technology, Imam Abdulrahman Bin Faisal University, Dammam, Saudi Arabia

Neeraj Kumar
Thapar Institute of Engineering and Technology, India

Noor Zaman
Taylor's University, Malaysia

Yousaf Bin Zikria
Yeungnam University, South Korea

A volume in the Advances in Information Security, Privacy, and Ethics (AISPE) Book Series

Published in the United States of America by
IGI Global
Business Science Reference (an imprint of IGI Global)
701 E. Chocolate Avenue
Hershey PA, USA 17033
Tel: 717-533-8845
Fax: 717-533-8661
E-mail: cust@igi-global.com
Web site: http://www.igi-global.com

Library of Congress Cataloging-in-Publication Data

Names: Saeed, Saqib, 1980- editor.
Title: Handbook of research on cybersecurity issues and challenges for
  business and FinTech applications / Saqib Saeed, Abdullah M. Almuhaideb,
  Neeraj Kumar, Noor Jhanjhi, and Yousaf Bin Zikria, editors.
Description: Hershey, PA : Business Science Reference, an imprint of IGI
  Global, [2023] | Includes bibliographical references and index. |
  Summary: "This book offers high-quality original research contributions
  on the specialized theme of cybersecurity challenges in diverse business
  areas, disseminating theoretical foundations and empirical studies by
  researchers and practitioners to realize dependable technological
  systems"-- Provided by publisher.
Identifiers: LCCN 2022016694 (print) | LCCN 2022016695 (ebook) | ISBN
  9781668452844 (h/c) | ISBN 9781668452868 (ebook)
Subjects: LCSH: Financial engineering--Data processing--Security measures.
  | Computer networks--Security measures. | Computer security.
Classification: LCC HG104 .H36 2023 (print) | LCC HG104 (ebook) | DDC
  332.0285/41--dc23/eng/20220623
LC record available at https://lccn.loc.gov/2022016694
LC ebook record available at https://lccn.loc.gov/2022016695

This book is published in the IGI Global book series Advances in Information Security, Privacy, and Ethics (AISPE) (ISSN: 1948-9730; eISSN: 1948-9749)

British Cataloguing in Publication Data
A Cataloguing in Publication record for this book is available from the British Library.

For electronic access to this publication, please contact: eresources@igi-global.com.

Advances in Information Security, Privacy, and Ethics (AISPE) Book Series

Manish Gupta
State University of New York, USA

ISSN:1948-9730
EISSN:1948-9749

MISSION

As digital technologies become more pervasive in everyday life and the Internet is utilized in ever increasing ways by both private and public entities, concern over digital threats becomes more prevalent.

The **Advances in Information Security, Privacy, & Ethics (AISPE) Book Series** provides cutting-edge research on the protection and misuse of information and technology across various industries and settings. Comprised of scholarly research on topics such as identity management, cryptography, system security, authentication, and data protection, this book series is ideal for reference by IT professionals, academicians, and upper-level students.

COVERAGE

- Internet Governance
- Cyberethics
- Data Storage of Minors
- Device Fingerprinting
- Privacy Issues of Social Networking
- Privacy-Enhancing Technologies
- Security Classifications
- Computer ethics
- Information Security Standards
- Network Security Services

IGI Global is currently accepting manuscripts for publication within this series. To submit a proposal for a volume in this series, please contact our Acquisition Editors at Acquisitions@igi-global.com or visit: http://www.igi-global.com/publish/.

Titles in this Series

For a list of additional titles in this series, please visit: http://www.igi-global.com/book-series/advances-information-security-privacy-ethics/37157

Cybersecurity Issues, Challenges, and Solutions in the Business World
Suhasini Verma (Manipal University Jaipur, India) Vidhisha Vyas (IILM University, Gurugram, India) and Keshav Kaushik (University of Petroleum and Energy Studies, India)
Information Science Reference • © 2023 • 325pp • H/C (ISBN: 9781668458273) • US $265.00

Handbook of Research on Technical, Privacy, and Security Challenges in a Modern World
Amit Kumar Tyagi (Vellore Institute of Technology, Chennai, India)
Information Science Reference • © 2022 • 474pp • H/C (ISBN: 9781668452509) • US $325.00

Applications of Machine Learning and Deep Learning for Privacy and Cybersecurity
Victor Lobo (NOVA Information Management School (NOVA-IMS), NOVA University Lisbon, Portugal & Portuguese Naval Academy, Portugal) and Anacleto Correia (CINAV, Portuguese Naval Academy, Portugal)
Information Science Reference • © 2022 • 271pp • H/C (ISBN: 9781799894308) • US $250.00

Cross-Industry Applications of Cyber Security Frameworks
Sukanta Kumar Baral (Indira Gandhi National Tribal University, India) Richa Goel (Amity University, Noida, India) Md Mashiur Rahman (Bank Asia Ltd., Bangladesh) Jahangir Sultan (Bentley University, USA) and Sarkar Jahan (Royal Bank of Canada, Canada)
Information Science Reference • © 2022 • 244pp • H/C (ISBN: 9781668434482) • US $250.00

Methods, Implementation, and Application of Cyber Security Intelligence and Analytics
Jena Om Prakash (Ravenshaw University, India) H.L. Gururaj (Vidyavardhaka College of Engineering, India) M.R. Pooja (Vidyavardhaka College of Engineering, India) and S.P. Pavan Kumar (Vidyavardhaka College of Engineering, India)
Information Science Reference • © 2022 • 269pp • H/C (ISBN: 9781668439913) • US $240.00

Information Security Practices for the Internet of Things, 5G, and Next-Generation Wireless Networks
Biswa Mohan Sahoo (Manipal University, Jaipur, India) and Suman Avdhesh Yadav (Amity University, India)
Information Science Reference • © 2022 • 313pp • H/C (ISBN: 9781668439210) • US $250.00

Global Perspectives on Information Security Regulations Compliance, Controls, and Assurance
Guillermo A. Francia III (University of West Florida, USA) and Jeffrey S. Zanzig (Jacksonville State University, USA)
Information Science Reference • © 2022 • 309pp • H/C (ISBN: 9781799883906) • US $240.00

701 East Chocolate Avenue, Hershey, PA 17033, USA
Tel: 717-533-8845 x100 • Fax: 717-533-8661
E-Mail: cust@igi-global.com • www.igi-global.com

List of Contributors

Abaid, Zainab / *National University of Computer and Emerging Sciences, Islamabad, Pakistan* 65

Abbas, Naveed Naeem / *Department of Computing, School of Electrical Engineering and Computer Science, National University of Sciences and Technology, Islamabad, Pakistan* 1, 174, 192, 225

Ahmad, Rizwan / *National University of Sciences and Technology, Islamabad, Pakistan* 174, 225, 266

Ahmad, Tahir / *Center for Cybersecurity, Bruno Kessler Foundation, Trento, Italy* 266

Ahmed, Waqas / *Pakistan Institute of Engineering and Applied Sciences, Pakistan* 174, 225

Aigbefo, Queen / *Macquarie University, Australia* 243

Alabbad, Dina A. / *Imam Abdulrahman bin Faisal University, Dammam, Saudi Arabia* 91

Almuhaideb, Abdullah M. / *Department of Networks and Communications, College of Computer Science and Information Technology, Dammam, Saudi Arabia & Imam Abdulrahman bin Faisal University, Dammam, Saudi Arabia* 91

Anttiroiko, Ari-Veikko / *Tampere University, Finland* 388

Arshad, Razi / *Department of Computing, School of Electrical Engineering and Computer Science, National University of Sciences and Technology, Islamabad, Pakistan* 1, 192, 314

Asghar, Muhammad Ibtisam / *BARANI Institute of Sciences, Pakistan* 364

Aslam, Mudassar / *Department of Cybersecurity, FAST School of Computing, Pakistan & FAST National University of Computer and Emerging Sciences, Islamabad, Pakistan* 266

Azizi, Neda / *Torrens University, Australia* 21

Bello, Abubakar / *Western Sydney University, Australia* 243

Bettaswamy, Manasa / *PES University, Bengaluru, India* 208

Booshan, Bharath / *Acharya Institute of Graduate Studies, India* 208

Booshan, Shabista / *ISBR Business School, Bengaluru, India* 208

Bose, Vijay / *Vaagdevi College of Engineering, India* 208

Chaudhry, Usama Habib / *Department of Computing, School of Electrical Engineering and Computer Science, National University of Sciences and Technology, Islamabad, Pakistan* 1, 192

Cheng, Haw Yih / *University of Technology Sarawak, Malaysia* 112

Çubuk, Ecem Buse Sevinç / *Adnan Menderes University, Turkey* 410

Dawar, Prince / *Poornima Group of Colleges, Jaipur, India* 449

Dawar, Sunny / *Faculty of Management and Commerce, Manipal University Jaipur, India* 449

Demirdöven, Burcu / *Pamukkale University, Turkey* 410

Ekaputra, Irwan Adi / *Universitas Indonesia, Indonesia* 426

Gull, Hina / *Imam Abdulrahman bin Faisal University, Dammam, Saudi Arabia* 91

Haass, Omid / *RMIT University, Australia* 21

Hasan, Anum / *Department of Computer Science, National University of Modern languages, Rawalpindi, Pakistan* 130

Husodo, Zaäfri Ananto / *Universitas Indonesia, Indonesia* 426

Hussain, Khalid / *Department of Computer Science, Superior University, Islamabad, Pakistan* ... 364

Idrees, Sarmad / *Department of Information Security, College of Signals, Pakistan & National University of Sciences and Technology, Islamabad, Pakistan* 146

Iqbal, Sardar Zafar / *Imam Abdulrahman Bin Faisal University, Dammam, Saudi Arabia* 91

Jhanjhi, N. Z. / *Taylor's University, Malaysia* 49

Khan, Fawad / *Department of Information Security, College of Signals, Pakistan & National University of Sciences and Technology, Islamabad, Pakistan* 288

Khan, Md. Abir Hasan / *Tampere University, Finland* 388

Khan, Muhammad Sohaib / *Department of Information Security, College of Signals, Pakistan & National University of Sciences and Technology, Islamabad, Pakistan* 146

Kudal, Pallavi / *Dr. D.Y. Patil Institute of Management Studies, Pune, India* 449

Laddunuri, Madan Mohan / *Malla Reddy University, India* 208

Laraib, Areeba / *Mehran University of Engineering and Technology, Pakistan & Shaheed Zulfiqar Ali Bhutto Campus, Pakistan* 49

Latif, Rana Muhammad Amir / *Department of Computer Science, COMSATS University Islamabad, Sahiwal, Pakistan* 338, 364

Lau Hui Yi, Adrian / *University of Technology Sarawak, Malaysia* 112

Mariana, Christy Dwita / *Bina Nusantara University, Indonesia* 426

Mirza, Baria Mubashar / *National University of Sciences and Technology, Islamabad, Pakistan* ... 65

Naeem, Noshaba / *Department of Information Security, College of Signals, Pakistan & National University of Sciences and Technology, Islamabad, Pakistan* 288

Nasir, Tooba / *Beaconhouse International College, Islamabad, Pakistan* 91

Nazir, Saqib / *Department of Information Security, College of Signals, Pakistan & National University of Sciences and Technology, Islamabad, Pakistan* 146

Oulasvirta, Lasse O. / *Tampere University, Finland* 388

Qazi, Shams / *National University of Sciences and Technology, Islamabad, Pakistan* 174, 225

Rai, Rashmi / *School of Business and Management, Christ University, Bangalore, India* 449

Riaz, Muhammad Usama / *BARANI Institute of Sciences, Pakistan* 338

Riaz, Qaiser / *Department of Computing, School of Electrical Engineering and Computer Science, National University of Sciences and Technology, Islamabad, Pakistan* 314

Saadat, Ahsan / *National University of Sciences and Technology, Islamabad, Pakistan* 65

Saeed, Saqib / *Department of Computer Information Systems, College of Computer Science and Information Technology, Imam Abdulrahman Bin Faisal University, Dammam, Saudi Arabia* 91

Sanyal, Shouvik / *Dhofar University, Oman* 208

Saqib, Madeeha / *Imam Abdulrahman bin Faisal University, Dammam, Saudi Arabia* 91

Shah, Imdad Ali / *Taylor's University, Malaysia* 49

Shivaram, Chethan / *Acharya Institute of Graduate Studies, India* 208

Sriram V. P. / *Acharya Bangalore B School, Bengaluru, India* 208

Subramanian, Mathiraj / *Alagappa University, India* 208

Tahir, Hasan / *Department of Information Security, School of Electrical Engineering and Computer Science, Pakistan & National University of Sciences and Technology, Islamabad, Pakistan* 130

Tahir, Shahzaib / *Department of Information Security, College of Signals, Pakistan & National*

University of Sciences and Technology, Islamabad, Pakistan 130, 146, 288

Tamara, Dewi / *Bina Nusantara University, Indonesia* 426

Thangam, Dhanabalan / *Presidency Business School, Presidency College, Bengaluru, India* 208

Ullah, Subhan / *Department of Cybersecurity, FAST School of Computing, Pakistan & FAST National University of Computer and Emerging Sciences, Islamabad, Pakistan* 266

Umer, Muhammad / *Department of Computer Science, COMSATS University Islamabad, Sahiwal, Pakistan* 364

Yaqoob, Tahreem / *Department of Information Security, College of Signals, Pakistan & National University of Sciences and Technology, Islamabad, Pakistan* 288

Zaman, Tariq / *ASSET, University of Technology, Sarawak, Malaysia* 112

Zeerak, Adeel Ahmed / *Department of Computing, School of Electrical Engineering and Computer Science, National University of Sciences and Technology, Islamabad, Pakistan* 1, 192

Zeren, Halim Emre / *Aydın Adnan Menderes University, Turkey* 410

Table of Contents

Preface xxv

Acknowledgment xxix

Chapter 1
Digital Transformations in Business and FinTech 1

Adeel Ahmed Zeerak, Department of Computing, School of Electrical Engineering and Computer Science, National University of Sciences and Technology, Islamabad, Pakistan
Razi Arshad, Department of Computing, School of Electrical Engineering and Computer Science, National University of Sciences and Technology, Islamabad, Pakistan
Naveed Naeem Abbas, Department of Computing, School of Electrical Engineering and Computer Science, National University of Sciences and Technology, Islamabad, Pakistan
Usama Habib Chaudhry, Department of Computing, School of Electrical Engineering and Computer Science, National University of Sciences and Technology, Islamabad, Pakistan

Chapter 2
Cybersecurity Issues and Challenges 21

Neda Azizi, Torrens University, Australia
Omid Haass, RMIT University, Australia

Chapter 3
Cybersecurity and Blockchain Usage in Contemporary Business 49

Imdad Ali Shah, Taylor's University, Malaysia
N. Z. Jhanjhi, Taylor's University, Malaysia
Areeba Laraib, Mehran University of Engineering and Technology, Pakistan & Shaheed Zulfiqar Ali Bhutto Campus, Pakistan

Chapter 4
The Insider Threat Landscape and the FinTech Sector: Attacks, Defenses, and Emerging Challenges65

Zainab Abaid, National University of Computer and Emerging Sciences, Islamabad, Pakistan

Ahsan Saadat, National University of Sciences and Technology, Islamabad, Pakistan

Baria Mubashar Mirza, National University of Sciences and Technology, Islamabad, Pakistan

Chapter 5

E-Commerce and Cybersecurity Challenges: Recent Advances and Future Trends 91
Hina Gull, Imam Abdulrahman bin Faisal University, Dammam, Saudi Arabia

.Dina A. Alabbad, Imam Abdulrahman bin Faisal University, Dammam, Saudi Arabia

Madeeha Saqib, Imam Abdulrahman bin Faisal University, Dammam, Saudi Arabia

Sardar Zafar Iqbal, Imam Abdulrahman Bin Faisal University, Dammam, Saudi Arabia

Tooba Nasir, Beaconhouse International College, Islamabad, Pakistan

Saqib Saeed, Department of Computer Information Systems, College of Computer Science and Information Technology, Imam Abdulrahman Bin Faisal University, Dammam, Saudi Arabia

Abdullah M. Almuhaideb, Department of Networks and Communications, College of Computer Science and Information Technology, Dammam, Saudi Arabia & Imam Abdulrahman bin Faisal University, Dammam, Saudi Arabia

Chapter 6

Scaffolding Undergraduate Students' Ethical Cyber Behaviour With Philosophy and Theory.......... 112
Tariq Zaman, ASSET, University of Technology, Sarawak, Malaysia

Adrian Lau Hui Yi, University of Technology Sarawak, Malaysia

Haw Yih Cheng, University of Technology Sarawak, Malaysia

Chapter 7

Security and Privacy Guidelines for IT Operations Under Pandemics and Epidemics 130
Hasan Tahir, Department of Information Security, School of Electrical Engineering and Computer Science, Pakistan & National University of Sciences and Technology, Islamabad, Pakistan

Shahzaib Tahir, Department of Information Security, College of Signals, Pakistan & National University of Sciences and Technology, Islamabad, Pakistan

Anum Hasan, Department of Computer Science, National University of Modern languages, Rawalpindi, Pakistan

Chapter 8

Cloud Ecosystem-Prevalent Threats and Countermeasures..146

Sarmad Idrees, Department of Information Security, College of Signals, Pakistan & National University of Sciences and Technology, Islamabad, Pakistan

Saqib Nazir, Department of Information Security, College of Signals, Pakistan & National University of Sciences and Technology, Islamabad, Pakistan

Shahzaib Tahir, Department of Information Security, College of Signals, Pakistan & National University of Sciences and Technology, Islamabad, Pakistan

Muhammad Sohaib Khan, Department of Information Security, College of Signals, Pakistan & National University of Sciences and Technology, Islamabad, Pakistan

Chapter 9

Investigation of Trust Models to Alleviate the Authentication Challenge in FinTech........................174

Naveed Naeem Abbas, National University of Sciences and Technology, Islamabad, Pakistan

Rizwan Ahmad, National University of Sciences and Technology, Islamabad, Pakistan

Shams Qazi, National University of Sciences and Technology, Islamabad, Pakistan

Waqas Ahmed, Pakistan Institute of Engineering and Applied Sciences, Pakistan

Chapter 10

Data Leakage in Business and FinTech 192

Usama Habib Chaudhry, Department of Computing, School of Electrical Engineering and Computer Sciences, National University of Sciences and Technology, Islamabad, Pakistan

Razi Arshad, Department of Computing, School of Electrical Engineering and Computer Sciences, National University of Sciences and Technology, Islamabad, Pakistan

Naveed Naeem Abbas, Department of Computing, School of Electrical Engineering and Computer Sciences, National University of Sciences and Technology, Islamabad, Pakistan

Adeel Ahmed Zeerak, Department of Computing, School of Electrical Engineering and Computer Sciences, National University of Sciences and Technology, Islamabad, Pakistan

Chapter 11

Enhancing Cybersecurity Through Blockchain Technology 208

Sriram V. P., Acharya Bangalore B School, Bengaluru, India

Shouvik Sanyal, Dhofar University, Oman

Madan Mohan Laddunuri, Malla Reddy University, India

Mathiraj Subramanian, Alagappa University, India

Vijay Bose, Vaagdevi College of Engineering, India

Bharath Booshan, Acharya Institute of Graduate Studies, India

Chethan Shivaram, Acharya Institute of Graduate Studies, India

Manasa Bettaswamy, PES University, Bengaluru, India

Shabista Booshan, ISBR Business School, Bengaluru, India

Dhanabalan Thangam, Presidency Business School, Presidency College, Bengaluru, India

Chapter 12

Impact of Deepfake Technology on FinTech Applications 225

    Naveed Naeem Abbas, National University of Sciences and Technology, Islamabad, Pakistan

    Rizwan Ahmad, National University of Sciences and Technology, Islamabad, Pakistan

    Shams Qazi, National University of Sciences and Technology, Islamabad, Pakistan

    Waqas Ahmed, Pakistan Institute of Engineering and Applied Sciences, Islamabad, Pakistan

Chapter 13

Organisational and Individual Behavioural Susceptibility and Protection Approach for
Ransomware Attacks 243

    Abubakar Bello, Western Sydney University, Australia

    Queen Aigbefo, Macquarie University, Australia

Chapter 14

Prevention of Cryptojacking Attacks in Business and FinTech Applications 266

    Subhan Ullah, Department of Cybersecurity, FAST School of Computing, Pakistan & FAST
        National University of Computer and Emerging Sciences, Islamabad, Pakistan

    Tahir Ahmad, Center for Cybersecurity, Bruno Kessler Foundation, Trento, Italy

    Rizwan Ahmad, School of Electrical Engineering and Computer Science, National University
        of Sciences and Technology, Islamabad, Pakistan

    Mudassar Aslam, Department of Cybersecurity, FAST School of Computing, Pakistan &
        FAST National University of Computer and Emerging Sciences, Islamabad, Pakistan

Chapter 15

Privacy-Preserving Computing via Homomorphic Encryption: Performance, Security, and
Application Analysis 288

    Noshaba Naeem, Department of Information Security, College of Signals, Pakistan &
        National University of Sciences and Technology, Islamabad, Pakistan

    Fawad Khan, Department of Information Security, College of Signals, Pakistan & National
        University of Sciences and Technology, Islamabad, Pakistan

    Tahreem Yaqoob, Department of Information Security, College of Signals, Pakistan &
        National University of Sciences and Technology, Islamabad, Pakistan

    Shahzaib Tahir, Department of Information Security, College of Signals, Pakistan &
        National University of Sciences and Technology, Islamabad, Pakistan

Chapter 16

Quantum and Post-Quantum Cybersecurity Challenges and Finance Organizations Readiness 314

    Razi Arshad, Department of Computing, School of Electrical Engineering and Computer
        Science, National University of Sciences and Technology, Islamabad, Pakistan

    Qaiser Riaz, Department of Computing, School of Electrical Engineering and Computer
        Science, National University of Sciences and Technology, Islamabad, Pakistan

Chapter 17
A Secure Distributed System for the Electronic Voting System Using Blockchain Technology 338
Rana Muhammad Amir Latif, Department of Computer Science, COMSATS University Islamabad, Sahiwal, Pakistan
Muhammad Usama Riaz, BARANI Institute of Sciences, Pakistan

Chapter 18
Blockchain-Based Secure and Efficient Ride Sharing System 364
Rana Muhammad Amir Latif, Department of Computer Science, COMSATS University Islamabad, Sahiwal, Pakistan
Muhammad Ibtisam Asghar, BARANI Institute of Sciences, Pakistan
Muhammad Umer, Department of Computer Science, COMSATS University Islamabad, Sahiwal, Pakistan
Khalid Hussain, Department of Computer Science, Superior University, Islamabad, Pakistan

Chapter 19
Open Governance in Budgeting and Financial Reporting: A Case Study on the Local Governance of Bangladesh 388
Md. Abir Hasan Khan, Tampere University, Finland
Lasse O. Oulasvirta, Tampere University, Finland
Ari-Veikko Anttiroiko, Tampere University, Finland

Chapter 20
The Role of Data Governance in Cybersecurity for E-Municipal Services: Implications From the Case of Turkey 410
Ecem Buse Sevinç Çubuk, Adnan Menderes University, Turkey
Halim Emre Zeren, Aydın Adnan Menderes University, Turkey
Burcu Demirdöven, Pamukkale University, Turkey

Chapter 21
Re-Thinking Cryptocurrencies as Safe-Haven Investment: Evidence in the U.S. and Emerging Countries 426
Christy Dwita Mariana, Bina Nusantara University, Indonesia
Irwan Adi Ekaputra, Universitas Indonesia, Indonesia
Zaäfri Ananto Husodo, Universitas Indonesia, Indonesia
Dewi Tamara, Bina Nusantara University, Indonesia

Chapter 22
Perceived Cyber Security Challenges in Adoption and Diffusion of FinTech Services in India 449
Pallavi Kudal, Dr. D.Y. Patil Institute of Management Studies, Pune, India
Sunny Dawar, Faculty of Management and Commerce, Manipal University Jaipur, India
Rashmi Rai, School of Business and Management, Christ University, Bangalore, India
Prince Dawar, Poornima Group of Colleges, Jaipur, India

Compilation of References 466

About the Contributors 538

Index 549

Detailed Table of Contents

Preface xxv

Acknowledgment xxix

Chapter 1
Digital Transformations in Business and FinTech 1

    Adeel Ahmed Zeerak, Department of Computing, School of Electrical Engineering and
        Computer Science, National University of Sciences and Technology, Islamabad, Pakistan
    Razi Arshad, Department of Computing, School of Electrical Engineering and Computer
        Science, National University of Sciences and Technology, Islamabad, Pakistan
    Naveed Naeem Abbas, Department of Computing, School of Electrical Engineering and
        Computer Science, National University of Sciences and Technology, Islamabad, Pakistan
    Usama Habib Chaudhry, Department of Computing, School of Electrical Engineering and
        Computer Science, National University of Sciences and Technology, Islamabad, Pakistan

The ever-growing technological innovations and inventions are reshaping businesses at external and internal levels. Digital transformation is the process that integrates technologies in business processes and strategies. This transformation is mostly dependent on data and is driven by evolving technologies, rapid growth in competition, and shift in consumer behavior. It enables a business to be more agile and productive and to provide a better customer experience. This chapter discusses the impact of digital transformation in business and the fintech industry by highlighting the modern technologies used in transformation, the effect on business, the fintech industry, and their current trends. Furthermore, it elaborates on how digital transformation affects businesses at different levels. Lastly, it discusses the challenges faced by businesses in the process of digital transformation and recommends solutions for them.

Chapter 2
Cybersecurity Issues and Challenges 21

    Neda Azizi, Torrens University, Australia
    Omid Haass, RMIT University, Australia

Interest in study about cybersecurity and related security topics has grown dramatically in recent years. This interest has been motivated by a number of elements, two of which stand out: 1) In this business world, information systems, databases, and distributed internet-based systems and communications become significantly universal. Hence, organizations recently recognize the requirements for a fundamental security strategy because of increasing intensity and complexity of security-related attacks and risks. This strategy may be considered as the use of authorised hardware and software and skilled and trained personnel to meet the requirements. 2) Cybersecurity education has developed as a national objectives/ strategy in most of the countries. Further, a number of frameworks and standards is designed and developed for computer security education. Accordingly, the number of fields and subjects offered at universities, education colleges, and other institutions in terms of cybersecurity and related fields has increased.

Chapter 3

Cybersecurity and Blockchain Usage in Contemporary Business...49

Imdad Ali Shah, Taylor's University, Malaysia
N. Z. Jhanjhi, Taylor's University, Malaysia
Areeba Laraib, Mehran University of Engineering and Technology, Pakistan & Shaheed Zulfiqar Ali Bhutto Campus, Pakistan

The use of computers is becoming more and more common. The power and maliciousness of powerful attackers are increasing. Organizations must improve their ability to mitigate information security threats. Adequate protection is more critical than ever. With websites and social media platforms holding a wealth of personal information and potentially damaging content, attackers use the internet's sophisticated hacking tools to cause harm to individuals and organizations. Attacks have become stealthier, with more significant economic damage and broader damage. Blockchain must be the solution to the security problem of financial transactions. However, judging from the results and expected answers from the industry and organization, it is crucial to understand how financial institutions deal with these issues by looking at blockchain deployments in cybersecurity. A blockchain is a digital database that records all mentoring transactions. This technology supports many different exchanges that are currently in use. The authors also believe that blockchain should be integrated into many parts of cybersecurity. The primary goal of this chapter is to review relevant research papers and book chapters over the past 10 years to understand how successful cybersecurity and blockchain implementations have been in the enterprise and to identify the different challenges and concerns that enterprise personnel face. They also provide suggestions and solutions to problems.

Chapter 4

The Insider Threat Landscape and the FinTech Sector: Attacks, Defenses, and Emerging Challenges65

Zainab Abaid, National University of Computer and Emerging Sciences, Islamabad, Pakistan
Ahsan Saadat, National University of Sciences and Technology, Islamabad, Pakistan
Baria Mubashar Mirza, National University of Sciences and Technology, Islamabad, Pakistan

The increased reliance on online services during the recent pandemic has compelled businesses and operations to make a major technological shift to ensure online presence. However, this online paradigm shift has also attracted malicious agents who aim to benefit from vulnerabilities in the cyber world. These attackers target a wide spectrum of sectors including healthcare, government agencies, education, and financial services. In this chapter, the impact of insider security attacks on FinTech applications is discussed. A detailed account of insider attacks applicable on FinTech applications is provided. Moreover, solutions and recommendations are provided to make FinTech applications more secure by preventing and defending against insider attacks benefitting from emerging fields like crypto-currency, micro-finance, and robo-advisors. Successful prevention and defense against these attacks will ensure that the FinTech industry can be secure and can contribute in, as laid out in UN's Sustainable Development Goals, decent work and economic growth for the masses.

Chapter 5

E-Commerce and Cybersecurity Challenges: Recent Advances and Future Trends 91

Hina Gull, Imam Abdulrahman bin Faisal University, Dammam, Saudi Arabia

Dina A. Alabbad, Imam Abdulrahman bin Faisal University, Dammam, Saudi Arabia

Madeeha Saqib, Imam Abdulrahman bin Faisal University, Dammam, Saudi Arabia

Sardar Zafar Iqbal, Imam Abdulrahman Bin Faisal University, Dammam, Saudi Arabia

Tooba Nasir, Beaconhouse International College, Islamabad, Pakistan

Saqib Saeed, Department of Computer Information Systems, College of Computer Science and Information Technology, Imam Abdulrahman Bin Faisal University, Dammam, Saudi Arabia

Abdullah M. Almuhaideb, Department of Networks and Communications, College of Computer Science and Information Technology, Dammam, Saudi Arabia & Imam Abdulrahman bin Faisal University, Dammam, Saudi Arabia

COVID-19 has accelerated the digital transformation in the business sector as many business organizations adopted electronic commerce to keep their operations running. Business organizations have also increased their participation on social networking applications to attract customers. Due to huge presence of users, social networking sites have also evolved into an emerging marketplace, which is referred as social commerce. There are many security issues involved in technological adoption in different business processes. On the other hand, social media is extensively used for product marketing, so fake information and fake product reviews can also influence consumers purchasing decision, so providing accurate marketing information is also a challenge for business organizations. In this chapter, the authors conduct a systematic literature review to understand the cybersecurity issues faced by business organizations and customers and how recent advances such as fintech, etc. provide additional cybersecurity challenges for business organization to protect themselves and their customers.

Chapter 6

Scaffolding Undergraduate Students' Ethical Cyber Behaviour With Philosophy and Theory 112

Tariq Zaman, ASSET, University of Technology, Sarawak, Malaysia

Adrian Lau Hui Yi, University of Technology Sarawak, Malaysia

Haw Yih Cheng, University of Technology Sarawak, Malaysia

Due to the growing challenges of cyber security, accreditation agencies demand computing ethics and professionalism as part of the computer science undergraduate curriculum. Many professional bodies developed codes of ethics and professional conduct, providing fundamental principles and letting the professional "decide" their response to face ethical dilemmas. The ethical codes rarely provide examples from real life. Therefore, in a six-month semester, the authors developed a teaching and learning module simulating real-life conflicting scenarios to enable students to participate in ethical and philosophical argumentation. They also target to demonstrate how storytelling, conflicting scenarios, and comics can be used to enhance computer science students' engagement in theoretical and philosophical discussions related to ethical cyber behaviour. Two assignments were part of the students' evaluation. They need to develop textual and visual conflicting scenarios for co-distributed clauses of the ACM code of ethics and then test those scenarios with users.

Chapter 7

Security and Privacy Guidelines for IT Operations Under Pandemics and Epidemics 130

Hasan Tahir, Department of Information Security, School of Electrical Engineering and Computer Science, Pakistan & National University of Sciences and Technology,

Islamabad, Pakistan

Shahzaib Tahir, Department of Information Security, College of Signals, Pakistan &
*   National University of Sciences and Technology, Islamabad, Pakistan*
Anum Hasan, Department of Computer Science, National University of Modern languages,
*   Rawalpindi, Pakistan*

Deteriorating health conditions under a pandemic force governments and authorities to consider enforcing lockdown protocols to limit the spread of a disease. Once a lockdown protocol is enforced, many verticals are instantly impacted by the lack of available workforce and other issues. Critical infrastructures, information systems, integrated IT systems cannot be administered using existing guidelines/standards under a pandemic. Thus organizations, governments, enterprises, and economies are ill equipped to deal with IT and economic issues emerging as a result of a pandemic. This chapter explores the impact of the COVID-19 pandemic on IT systems, IT operations, and security. This chapter calls attention to the lack of preparedness, absence of standards and protocols that deal with epidemics and pandemics. Thus, considering the changing organizational posture, this chapter brings to light opportunities for redressal, and recommendations have been made to ensure better preparation in the future.

Chapter 8

Cloud Ecosystem-Prevalent Threats and Countermeasures.. 146
Sarmad Idrees, Department of Information Security, College of Signals, Pakistan & National
*   University of Sciences and Technology, Islamabad, Pakistan*
Saqib Nazir, Department of Information Security, College of Signals, Pakistan & National
*   University of Sciences and Technology, Islamabad, Pakistan*
Shahzaib Tahir, Department of Information Security, College of Signals, Pakistan &
*   National University of Sciences and Technology, Islamabad, Pakistan*
Muhammad Sohaib Khan, Department of Information Security, College of Signals, Pakistan
*   & National University of Sciences and Technology, Islamabad, Pakistan*

Cloud-based services are in high demand because they give consumers and businesses a lot of flexibility in employing new applications and high-end infrastructure at a low cost. Despite the increased activity and interest, there are still worries about security vulnerabilities with cloud computing, resulting in hurdles for both consumers and service providers in terms of data protection, privacy, and service availability. As a result, cloud service providers and consumers must ensure that the cloud environment is secure from both external and internal threats. This chapter provides a comprehensive overview of key components of the cloud computing ecosystem and security concerns encompassing its impact on businesses. It focuses on understanding cloud computing technology, deployment environments, services, and usage considerations. The chapter identifies the most common security risks, allowing both end users and providers to identify the risks connected with the technology. Finally, different countermeasures to important security and privacy issues are presented.

Chapter 9

Investigation of Trust Models to Alleviate the Authentication Challenge in FinTech........................ 174
Naveed Naeem Abbas, National University of Sciences and Technology, Islamabad, Pakistan

Rizwan Ahmad, National University of Sciences and Technology, Islamabad, Pakistan
Shams Qazi, National University of Sciences and Technology, Islamabad, Pakistan
Waqas Ahmed, Pakistan Institute of Engineering and Applied Sciences, Pakistan

FinTech applications are increasingly vulnerable to cyber-attacks (identity theft, data breaches, distributed denial of service attacks, phishing attacks, insider threats), which have become a threat to many firms. These threats against FinTech services have the potential to wreak enormous societal, economic, and organizational harm. It is noted that various proposed methods failed to address the fundamental FinTech security issues of scalability, privacy, and trust distribution. Various well-known compliances of all FinTech are being adopted by developed countries to counter these cyber-attacks. Blockchain arouses increasing interest in different economic sectors, with confidentiality, availability, and integrity being fundamental factors. The study shows that the mass adoption of blockchain-based trust models has accelerated in the financial industry with private permissioned blockchain. The primary goal of these trust models is to assure the security, reliability, trustworthiness, and implementation of FinTech compliance.

Chapter 10
Data Leakage in Business and FinTech 192
Usama Habib Chaudhry, Department of Computing, School of Electrical Engineering and Computer Sciences, National University of Sciences and Technology, Islamabad, Pakistan
Razi Arshad, Department of Computing, School of Electrical Engineering and Computer Sciences, National University of Sciences and Technology, Islamabad, Pakistan
Naveed Naeem Abbas, Department of Computing, School of Electrical Engineering and Computer Sciences, National University of Sciences and Technology, Islamabad, Pakistan
Adeel Ahmed Zeerak, Department of Computing, School of Electrical Engineering and Computer Sciences, National University of Sciences and Technology, Islamabad, Pakistan

With the advent of the internet and day-by-day advancement in technology, traditional services started to utilize technology to offer better, digitized, cutting-edge services. Financial services called FinTech are one such example of the adoption of cutting-edge technologies. On the other hand, with the adoption of technologies comes to the cybersecurity risks associated with them. Data leakage is one big issue in FinTech and business-related applications and services. The main aim of this chapter is to identify different ways and methods by which data leakage occurs and its adverse effects on organizations providing FinTech services. Furthermore, this chapter explores the various solutions and challenges in their implementation. It is concluded that no single solution can handle data leakage from all perspectives. Multiple solutions need to be combined and utilized to handle all scenarios.

Chapter 11
Enhancing Cybersecurity Through Blockchain Technology 208

Sriram V. P., Acharya Bangalore B School, Bengaluru, India
Shouvik Sanyal, Dhofar University, Oman
Madan Mohan Laddunuri, Malla Reddy University, India
Mathiraj Subramanian, Alagappa University, India
Vijay Bose, Vaagdevi College of Engineering, India
Bharath Booshan, Acharya Institute of Graduate Studies, India
Chethan Shivaram, Acharya Institute of Graduate Studies, India
Manasa Bettaswamy, PES University, Bengaluru, India
Shabista Booshan, ISBR Business School, Bengaluru, India
Dhanabalan Thangam, Presidency Business School, Presidency College, Bengaluru, India

Blockchain technology ensures data security through an integrated system whereby it collects, arranges, stores, and disseminates information in different blocks. This technology thus enables adding the data to the network. Once data has been added to the network, no one can alter the data set either by adding or deleting it. Further, this technology also helps to track and check the changes if anything is made to a blockchain, as the changes remain in the database forever. Since this technology uses lots of systems in a blockchain, it will regularly download its data, arranging, and keeping the copy locally. Locating the data errors and cyberattacks in advance by analyzing the data documented, it employs the consent of various participants and accomplishments in cryptography. With this backdrop, the chapter has attempted to disclose the basics of blockchain technology in data security, why blockchain in cybersecurity, how it ensures cybersecurity, its benefits, its innovative uses, and the future of cybersecurity in the online business platforms.

Chapter 12

Impact of Deepfake Technology on FinTech Applications.. 225
Naveed Naeem Abbas, National University of Sciences and Technology, Islamabad, Pakistan
Rizwan Ahmad, National University of Sciences and Technology, Islamabad, Pakistan
Shams Qazi, National University of Sciences and Technology, Islamabad, Pakistan
Waqas Ahmed, Pakistan Institute of Engineering and Applied Sciences, Islamabad, Pakistan

The distribution of fabricated disinformation through deliberate manipulation of audio/video content by imposters with the intent to affect organization is deepfake. The "infodemic" that spread alongside the COVID-19 pandemic also increased cyber risk in financial technology (FinTech) applications. The continuous evolution of cybercrime has culminated with deepfakes which severely magnify the threats of traditional frauds. Recent evidence indicates that deepfake videos are mainly created with the help of artificial intelligence (AI) or machine learning (ML) techniques. This results in creation of fake videos by merging, superimposing, and replacing actual video clips and images with other videos. There are a lot of people who accept deepfake videos as actual videos without any doubt. The use of AL and ML techniques have made video/image forgery difficult to identify with the help of existing deepfake detection techniques. Deepfake technology is becoming more and more sophisticated, and detection of fake videos is relatively challenged for quite some time.

Chapter 13

Organisational and Individual Behavioural Susceptibility and Protection Approach for
Ransomware Attacks... 243

Abubakar Bello, Western Sydney University, Australia
Queen Aigbefo, Macquarie University, Australia

Ransomware attacks have become complex due to the ability of networked-systems constantly used as attack-vectors for propagating the ransomware payload to victims. The threat is socially engineered, making it difficult for victims to protect their data. Confidential information resources and assets are lost and rarely recovered in an attack resulting in financial losses amounting to millions of dollars. Ongoing research is exploring avenues to solve this problem including cybersecurity awareness and training from a singularised perspective, not pluralistic, to educate users of the consequences of their actions. The purpose of this study is to gain perceptions of several industries to develop insights on how to protect organisations from becoming victims of socially engineered ransomware attacks. Using a qualitative approach, critical themes on behavioural susceptibility to socially engineered ransomware were obtained, as well as the demand for applying behavioural theories and technical controls to develop effective training and education initiatives for resisting these attacks.

Chapter 14

Prevention of Cryptojacking Attacks in Business and FinTech Applications..................................... 266

Subhan Ullah, Department of Cybersecurity, FAST School of Computing, Pakistan & FAST National University of Computer and Emerging Sciences, Islamabad, Pakistan
Tahir Ahmad, Center for Cybersecurity, Bruno Kessler Foundation, Trento, Italy
Rizwan Ahmad, School of Electrical Engineering and Computer Science, National University of Sciences and Technology, Islamabad, Pakistan
Mudassar Aslam, Department of Cybersecurity, FAST School of Computing, Pakistan & FAST National University of Computer and Emerging Sciences, Islamabad, Pakistan

More than 2000 different cryptocurrencies are currently available in business and FinTech applications. Cryptocurrency is a digital payment system that does not rely on banks to verify their financial transactions and can enable anyone anywhere to send and receive their payments. Crypto mining attracts investors to mine and gets some coins as a reward for using the cryptocurrency. However, hackers can exploit the computing power without the explicit authorization of a user by launching a cryptojacking attack and then using it to mine cryptocurrency. The detection and protection of cryptojacking attacks are essential, and thus, miners are continuously working to find innovative ways to overcome this issue. This chapter provides an overview of the cryptojacking landscape. It offers recommendations to guide researchers and practitioners to overcome the identified challenges faced while realizing a mitigation strategy to combat cryptojacking malware attacks.

Chapter 15

Privacy-Preserving Computing via Homomorphic Encryption: Performance, Security, and Application Analysis 288

Noshaba Naeem, Department of Information Security, College of Signals, Pakistan &
National University of Sciences and Technology, Islamabad, Pakistan
Fawad Khan, Department of Information Security, College of Signals, Pakistan & National
University of Sciences and Technology, Islamabad, Pakistan
Tahreem Yaqoob, Department of Information Security, College of Signals, Pakistan &
National University of Sciences and Technology, Islamabad, Pakistan
Shahzaib Tahir, Department of Information Security, College of Signals, Pakistan &
National University of Sciences and Technology, Islamabad, Pakistan

In the era of IoT and big data, an enormous amount of data being generated by various sensors and handheld devices and for sectors not limited to healthcare, commerce, smart driving, smart grids, and fintech requires privacy and security. Although security can be ensured once the data is in transit or at rest, for certain application domains need to ensure privacy computations over encrypted data. Homomorphic encryption (HE) is one mechanism that allows parties to compute any arbitrary functions in an encrypted domain. Homomorphic encryption schemes have been employed in various applied sectors for privacy preservation; however, the limiting factor of these schemes is the computational and communication overhead and associated security. This chapter reviews the types of HE schemes, the application domains, and the associated costs for privacy preserving computing and discusses the underlying mathematical hardness problems, security in the classical and post quantum era, and challenges and recommendations for tradeoff in applied domains.

Chapter 16

Quantum and Post-Quantum Cybersecurity Challenges and Finance Organizations Readiness 314

Razi Arshad, Department of Computing, School of Electrical Engineering and Computer
Science, National University of Sciences and Technology, Islamabad, Pakistan
Qaiser Riaz, Department of Computing, School of Electrical Engineering and Computer
Science, National University of Sciences and Technology, Islamabad, Pakistan

Cryptography is used to protect sensitive information, but it is also required in many applications to ensure secure functionality and availability. The 100-year-old principles of physics are becoming industrially controllable, which leads to the era of the industrial quantum revolution. Products and applications such as quantum sensors, quantum simulators, quantum computers, and quantum cryptography are developing, which will affect the design of secure cryptographic systems. Post-quantum cryptography is a new field of research developing parallel to the progress in quantum technologies. Post-quantum cryptography deals with the development and investigation of algorithms that are assumed to be unbreakable even with quantum computers. This chapter will discuss the quantum and post-quantum cryptographic algorithms in detail and the migration strategies from classical asymmetric algorithms to post-quantum algorithms. This chapter also discusses the finance organization's readiness and recommendation for the replacement of vulnerable asymmetric algorithms with post-quantum algorithms.

Chapter 17

A Secure Distributed System for the Electronic Voting System Using Blockchain Technology 338

Rana Muhammad Amir Latif, Department of Computer Science, COMSATS University Islamabad, Sahiwal, Pakistan

Muhammad Usama Riaz, BARANI Institute of Sciences, Pakistan

Traditionally, electronic voting has relied on a centralized method of administration. The database and the system are both under the jurisdiction of the system's central administration, which oversees the voting process. As a result, issues like database manipulation and duplicate voting may arise, whether accidentally or purposefully. Permissionless blockchain technology has helped overcome many of these issues; however, since the basic consensus technique of such blockchains demands particular computer resources for each voting operation, they are not ideal for new voting systems. Power consumption, efficiency, and system latency all suffer as a result. These issues may be alleviated in part if electronic voting technologies are used. By using corporate blockchain technology, this research presents an electronic voting system that is very reliable and secures the secret vote. It also discusses some of the frequent security and dependability challenges of electronic voting system solutions, such as a flexible network setup.

Chapter 18

Blockchain-Based Secure and Efficient Ride Sharing System 364

Rana Muhammad Amir Latif, Department of Computer Science, COMSATS University Islamabad, Sahiwal, Pakistan

Muhammad Ibtisam Asghar, BARANI Institute of Sciences, Pakistan

Muhammad Umer, Department of Computer Science, COMSATS University Islamabad, Sahiwal, Pakistan

Khalid Hussain, Department of Computer Science, Superior University, Islamabad, Pakistan

The attractive advantages of ridesharing include reduced traffic congestion and shared travel costs for users and drivers. However, most existing rideshare systems rely on an intermediary to coordinate the service, creating a single point of failure and raising privacy issues about exposure through internal and external assaults. The suggested approach allows drivers to provide ridesharing services directly to riders without needing a central hub or reliable intermediary. Sharing trips may teach passengers and drivers about transportation logistics without requiring them to change their plans or costs. The suggested system employs a time-locked technique to solve these problems. A membership deposit system for ridesharing services uses smart contracts and zero-knowledge evidence gathering. In short, the driver and the passenger need to put up some deposit to prove they are serious about using the blockchain. Later, a driver must show the blockchain that he or she was at the agreed-upon pick-up location at the appointed time.

Chapter 19

Open Governance in Budgeting and Financial Reporting: A Case Study on the Local Governance

of Bangladesh... 388

Md. Abir Hasan Khan, Tampere University, Finland
Lasse O. Oulasvirta, Tampere University, Finland
Ari-Veikko Anttiroiko, Tampere University, Finland

This chapter discusses the adoption of open governance in public finance with a particular view to citizen-friendly budgeting and consistent financial reporting in local government in the developing country context. The authors are interested in how a concept that was developed in the Western world is adopted in developing countries. The objective is to shed light on local councilors' understanding of the conditions and development needs of open governance in budgeting and financial control in Bangladeshi municipalities. According to our survey conducted in 2018 with municipal managers and councilors, the key institutional actors consider that the conditions of open governance in local public finance are fairly good, financial information is provided systematically, and the competence level is sufficient among both citizens and representatives of local government. However, participatory methods and the utilization of digital tools in budgeting and financial reporting are still in their infancy.

Chapter 20

The Role of Data Governance in Cybersecurity for E-Municipal Services: Implications From the

Case of Turkey 410

Ecem Buse Sevinç Çubuk, Adnan Menderes University, Turkey
Halim Emre Zeren, Aydın Adnan Menderes University, Turkey
Burcu Demirdöven, Pamukkale University, Turkey

The "e-Municipality Project" in Turkey has developed information systems (IS) for electronic municipal services since May 2017. This chapter discusses the role of data governance in relation to implementing an effective cybersecurity strategy for the project. Data were collected using a workshop with information technology (IT) officials of municipalities and semi-structured interviews with eight information IS managers about their experiences in the project. The research revealed that good data governance has been a prerequisite for any organization focused on its potential to transform processes, decision making and performance. Data governance delivers the insights that organizations need to identify their high-value and high-risk data sets and allocate additional or specific resources to protect this data. Good data governance for secured municipal services is related to a number of trade-offs between the different actors and their responsibilities. The dichotomy between centralization and decentralization of data governance can help to understand the management of cyber risks.

Chapter 21
Re-Thinking Cryptocurrencies as Safe-Haven Investment: Evidence in the U.S. and Emerging
Countries 426
    Christy Dwita Mariana, Bina Nusantara University, Indonesia
    Irwan Adi Ekaputra, Universitas Indonesia, Indonesia
    Zaäfri Ananto Husodo, Universitas Indonesia, Indonesia
    Dewi Tamara, Bina Nusantara University, Indonesia

This chapter investigates the global crisis's impact on the safe-haven role of the two most significant cryptocurrencies based on their market capitalizations: Bitcoin and Ethereum. This study compares the volatility transmission between the Bitcoin and stock markets in four emerging countries: Indonesia, Malaysia, Nigeria, and South Africa. This study follows the framework of volatility transmission of Diebold and Yilmas. This research also investigates the safe-haven role of cryptocurrencies using the safe-haven regression analysis and decoupling hypothesis. Overall results support the notion of cryptocurrencies as alternative investments. On average, the pairwise volatility spillover between Bitcoin and stock market in Indonesia, Malaysia, Nigeria, and South Africa reverted back to half of its mean in about 2-3 days. This result suggests on the choice of short-term investment for investors in the Bitcoin market. This study contributes to the discussion of cryptocurrencies as safe haven.

Chapter 22
Perceived Cyber Security Challenges in Adoption and Diffusion of FinTech Services in India 449
    Pallavi Kudal, Dr. D.Y. Patil Institute of Management Studies, Pune, India
    Sunny Dawar, Faculty of Management and Commerce, Manipal University Jaipur, India
    Rashmi Rai, School of Business and Management, Christ University, Bangalore, India
    Prince Dawar, Poornima Group of Colleges, Jaipur, India

FinTech is a term that refers to a new type of digital technology that intends to build up and automate the distribution and management of financial services. FinTech is an abbreviation for "financial technology." FinTech, or financial technology, assists companies, business holders, and consumers in managing their financial procedures and methods. The high adoption rate of fintech services creates a whole ecosystem of looters and hackers. This indeed is scary, and this chapter makes an attempt to understand the adoption rate of fintech services and diffusion challenges at the same time.

Compilation of References 466

About the Contributors 538

Index 549

Preface

Digital transformation within organizations leads to optimization of business processes and bringing additional challenges in the form of security threats and vulnerabilities. Cyber-attacks incur financial losses for victim organizations and affect their reputation; therefore, cybersecurity has become very critical for business enterprises. Extensive technological adoption in businesses and the evolution of Fintech applications require reasonable cybersecurity measures to protect organizations from security threats, both internal and external. Recent advances in the cybersecurity domain such as zero trust architecture, applications of machine learning, and quantum and post-quantum cryptography have an immense potential to be utilized in securing technological infrastructures. In this book, we have documented high-quality original research contributions on theoretical foundations and empirical studies of cybersecurity implications in digital transformation globally.

Digital transformation requires a well thought out strategy to benefit the organization in question. In the first chapter, the authors have highlighted how digital transformation makes an organization more agile, competitive and customer centric. The chapter outlines the impact of digital transformation on the fintech industry and highlights current tools and trends along with associated challenges and improvement recommendations.

In the second chapter, Neda Azizi and Omid Haass provide an in-depth introduction of cyberthreats and attacks posing a cybersecurity threat. The chapter also lists different countermeasures that could improve resilience against potential cyber threats. Furthermore, the chapter documents real-time cyber threats detection and mitigation challenges as well as privacy and ethical aspects relevant to cybersecurity.

Chapter 3 provides a comprehensive literature to highlight the adoption of blockchain in business organizations. Authors have outlined the challenges faced by business organizations and recommended solutions to benefit business organizations in their journeys of fintech adoption.

Chapter 4 presents a discussion on how the increase in digital transformation of business domains may result in vulnerabilities that could be exploited by hackers. The discussion then expands on the impact of insider threat attacks in fintech applications. The authors highlight shielding such insider threats could help in fostering sustainable technological infrastructures.

In Chapter 5, Hina Gull and her colleagues discuss e-commerce growth rising more since COVID-19 and how critical it is to ensure that e-commerce applications are secure enough to have a pleasurable, as well as reliable, user experience while shopping. Authors have carried out a literature review to document challenges faced by business organizations and security risks faced by businesses and customers especially due to recent advancements in fintech technologies.

Chapter 6 presents a detailed discussion on growing cybersecurity challenges and the importance of undergraduate programs to include ethical cyber behavior courses in the curriculum to make future professionals aware of potential threats . Tariq Zaman and their colleagues provide case studies on how they employed storytelling, conflicting scenarios, and comics in the course delivery.

In Chapter 7, Hasan Tahir and his colleagues evaluate the impact of pandemics and epidemics on IT operations. The authors discuss current guidelines to administer IT infrastructure were lacking at the time of the pandemic, for instance unpreparedness, absence of standards and protocols dealing with epidemics and pandemics require major attention, so a set of recommendations have been designed to make IT operations efficient in the future.

Chapter 8 presents a discussion on the demand for cloud-based services being on the rise due to flexibility and provision of affordable quality infrastructures, by Sarmad Idrees and his colleagues. The authors put forth their ideas about the innate need to ensure security in cloud-based services from internal as well as external threats. They then discuss key components of the cloud ecosystem and associated security risks along with recommendations to counter security and privacy challenges.

In Chapter 9, the authors discuss the increasing vulnerability of fintech applications as a major threat to business continuity. They further discuss the excessive use of blockchain technologies in different business domains leading to enhanced adoption of blockchain-based trust models in financial industry bringing forth trustworthiness and reliability as well as aiding in compliance of policies.

Technology adoption is a complex process that requires not only financial resources but also human resources and technological infrastructure. In Chapter 10, Usama Habib Chaudhry and his colleagues discuss the critical issues related to adopting fintech technologies such as data leaks. In this chapter, they document challenges and make recommendations to address these challenges. They stress upon a single uniform solution not being feasible due to organizational and user diversity and that organizations must try to adopt multiple approaches in order to optimally control data leaks.

Chapter 11 presents a discussion on blockchain technology enhancing security resulting in secure data availability over the network, by Sriram et al. The updates in the blockchain are systematically recorded and the adoption of cryptographic algorithms to encrypt user consent further strengthens security. The chapter further provides an in-depth discussion on how cybersecurity is achieved with blockchain and the future of online businesses in achieving optimal security.

In Chapter 12, Naveed Abbas, et al. discuss how manipulated audio and video content based on deep fake technology can adversely affect fintech applications. The use of artificial intelligence and machine learning techniques to merge, impersonate, and replace video content makes it difficult to distinguish between real and fabricated content. In addition, the authors present the challenges posed by deep fake technologies in these fintech applications.

Chapter 13 presents an elaborated account on how socially engineered ransomware attacks make data protection difficult by Abubakar Bello and Queen Aigbefo. The authors discuss how different industries improve their resilience against ransomware attacks and how the adoption of behavioral theories to shape user behavior, awareness training regarding such attacks and employing technical controls are among the effective strategies adopted in the industry to tackle ransomware attacks.

In Chapter 14, Subhan Ullah and colleagues discuss critical security breaches brought about by crypto jacking attack by hackers to mine cryptocurrency without authorization. This chapter further presents a detailed background of crypto jacking and recommendations to mitigate crypto jacking malware attacks.

Noshaba Naeem and her colleagues focus on homomorphic encryption in Chapter 15. The authors highlight different types of homomorphic encryption schemes, their associated advantages, disadvantages, and challenges of adopting such encryption mechanisms within the business domain.

Chapter 16 presents a discussion on how quantum and post-quantum cryptography will bring more security to business applications by Razi Arshad and Qaiser Riaz. The authors discuss different quantum and post-quantum cryptographic algorithms and financial organizations' readiness to deploy such algorithms in their business applications.

In Chapter 17, Muhammad Amir Latif and Muhammad Usama Riaz explore how blockchain technology can aid in securing electronic voting systems to avoid data manipulation, be it accidental or intentional. They discuss how permission less blockchain can solve these issues, but power consumption, efficiency and system latency then pose a problem. The authors have deployed corporate blockchain technology to develop a secret voting system that has improved security and flexible network setup.

Chapter 18's authors present a proposal on a blockchain ride sharing application. Ride sharing applications are being widely used but traditional systems require an intermediary platform. In the approach adopted by the authors, however, a blockchain approach is used where the membership deposit system employs smart contracts for both the driver and passenger. At the designated time the driver presents the passenger with the blockchain component which includes conditions already agreed upon.

Abir Hasan Khan and his colleagues carried out an empirical study in Bangladesh to understand the adoption of open governance perspective in the public finance sector. They present this study and their findings in Chapter 19. The study collected data from municipal managers and councilors and found that use of advanced tools for budgeting and financial reporting have not been used as widely, however, open governance standards were adopted and systematic perseverance of financial information is sustained for citizens as well as local government representatives.

In Chapter 20, Ecem Sevinç Çubuk and her colleagues present results from the "e-Municipality Project" in Turkey. Authors have used a mix of quantitative and qualitative data to understand the role of data governance in implementing a cybersecurity strategy. The findings show data governance is critical in transforming organizational processes and identifying high risk data to adopt more strict cybersecurity measures. They also found that segregation of responsibilities among different stakeholders helped in securing municipal services for this project.

Christy Mariana and her colleagues explore the safe-haven role of Bitcoin and Ethereum cryptocurrencies in Chapter 21. The authors compared bitcoin with stock markets in Indonesia, Malaysia, Nigeria, and South Africa and found that the bitcoin market is the choice of investors for short-term investments.

In the final chapter, Pallavi Kudal and her colleagues highlight the underlying cybersecurity challenges in the adoption of fintech services in India. The advancements of organizational processes by adopting fintech technologies benefit organizations and expose their vulnerabilities to hackers. The authors relate the adoption rates of fintech and associated challenges in this chapter.

The book is comprised of theoretical foundations and empirical studies by researchers and practitioners to provide a nice balance in theory and practice. The book will be useful to academics from a range of fields including, information systems, cybersecurity, organizational science and government officials and organizations. This book will also be helpful for students that want to learn about the insights of security implications of digital transformation processes to achieve business continuity.

Saqib Saeed
Department of Computer Information Systems, College of Computer Science and Information Technology, Imam Abdulrahman bin Faisal University, Dammam, Saudi Arabia

Abdullah M. Almuhaideb
Department of Networks and Communications, College of Computer Science and Information Technology, Imam Abdulrahman Bin Faisal University, Dammam, Saudi Arabia

Neeraj Kumar
Thapar Institute of Engineering and Technology, India

Noor Zaman
Taylor's University, Malaysia

Yousaf Bin Zikria
Yeungnam University, South Korea

Acknowledgment

We would like to thank Saudi Aramco Cybersecurity Chair, Imam Abdulrahman Bin Faisal University, Saudi Arabia for its support in completing this book.

Chapter 1
Digital Transformations in Business and FinTech

Adeel Ahmed Zeerak

Department of Computing, School of Electrical Engineering and Computer Science, National University of Sciences and Technology, Islamabad, Pakistan

Razi Arshad

Department of Computing, School of Electrical Engineering and Computer Science, National University of Sciences and Technology, Islamabad, Pakistan

Naveed Naeem Abbas

Department of Computing, School of Electrical Engineering and Computer Science, National University of Sciences and Technology, Islamabad, Pakistan

Usama Habib Chaudhry

Department of Computing, School of Electrical Engineering and Computer Science, National University of Sciences and Technology, Islamabad, Pakistan

ABSTRACT

The ever-growing technological innovations and inventions are reshaping businesses at external and internal levels. Digital transformation is the process that integrates technologies in business processes and strategies. This transformation is mostly dependent on data and is driven by evolving technologies, rapid growth in competition, and shift in consumer behavior. It enables a business to be more agile and productive and to provide a better customer experience. This chapter discusses the impact of digital transformation in business and the fintech industry by highlighting the modern technologies used in transformation, the effect on business, the fintech industry, and their current trends. Furthermore, it elaborates on how digital transformation affects businesses at different levels. Lastly, it discusses the challenges faced by businesses in the process of digital transformation and recommends solutions for them.

DOI: 10.4018/978-1-6684-5284-4.ch001

INTRODUCTION

The term *Digital Transformation* was coined by the consulting firm **Capgemini** in late 2011 (Holotiuk & Beimborn, n.d.) (A Companion to Film Theory, n.d.). Digital Transformation is the wide transformation process that embraces the whole organization including processes and employees with the help of modern technologies (Ebert & Duarte, 2018a) (Gong & Ribiere, 2021). The digital transformation uses technology as strategic competency and not as a support function. It entails the creation of new business models which are driven by technology to create and increase business value for an organization (Bohnsack et al., 2021). Digital Transformation depends mostly on data-driven technologies (e.g., data analytics, Artificial Intelligence). Data regarding consumers, competitors, markets, etc. is collected, stored, analyzed, and utilized to enhance customer experience and business processes in an organization (Gölzer & Fritzsche, 2017).

The process of digital transformation is driven by three major factors: i.e., evolving technologies, rapid growth in competition & shift in consumer behavior (Osmundsen et al., 2018). Evolving technologies have not only enabled businesses to cross borders but also enabled SMEs (Small to Medium Enterprises) to compete with large-scale enterprises. The swift growth in the Information Technology industry has given rise to the development of many technologies enabling organizations to improve their businesses (Hsu et al., 2018). Consumers can actively shape market trends by demanding products and services that are suited to their wants and preferences (Rawat & Matter Expert, 2016). This diversity and globalization of businesses accelerate competition in businesses. Technological advancements have also affected society which in turn drives businesses to realign their strategies with the digital world.

Digital modernization in the financial sectors has led to the dawn of new financial services known as fintech. Financial Technology or Fintech is the consolidation of two terms i.e., finance and technology, and can be described as innovations in financial services made possible by technology that might lead to new business models, applications, processes, or products and have an impact on financial markets and institutions as well as the delivery of financial services (Feyen et al., 2021a) (Galchenkova & Chupsa, 2020). It uses technologies including blockchain, artificial intelligence, big data, etc. to provide banking services efficiently. It also expands to the development and use of cryptocurrencies e.g., Bitcoin (I. Lee & Shin, 2018) (Puschmann, 2017).

Digitization, Digitalization, Digital Transformation

Digital transformation is normally confused with the terms 'Digitization' & 'Digitalization' which are necessary steps to achieve digital transformation, not the complete process (Contributor, n.d.) (Zhao et al., 2020). Figure 1 summarizes the digitization, digitalization, and digital transformation which are detailed below:

Digitization

Digitization is the process of converting physical/analog information into digital (binary) information e.g., storing physical financial records into excel sheets. It is mainly concerned with the transformation of information and not the processes thus not altering activities that generate business value (Liao et al., 2020).

Digitalization

Digitalization can be described as the use of digital technologies to change a business model and provide new revenue and value-producing opportunities e.g., the use of an online communication process for complaints thus reducing processing time and increasing value. The business process can be improved by the inclusion of digital technology which results in more efficient and well-coordinated processes hence enhancing customer experience. Digitalization leverages the digitization process to change a business model (Imgrund et al., 2018).

Digital transformation

Digital Transformation can be best described as the impact caused by digitalization and is the most widespread phase encompassing the whole organization i.e., stakeholders, business process, strategic goals, and organizational structure. It changes the existing business models or adds new ones to create and enhance the business value of the organizations. Examples of Digital Transformation can include an introduction to new business models like platform as a service or the use of digital platforms (Liao et al., 2020).

Figure 1. Phases of Digital Transformation

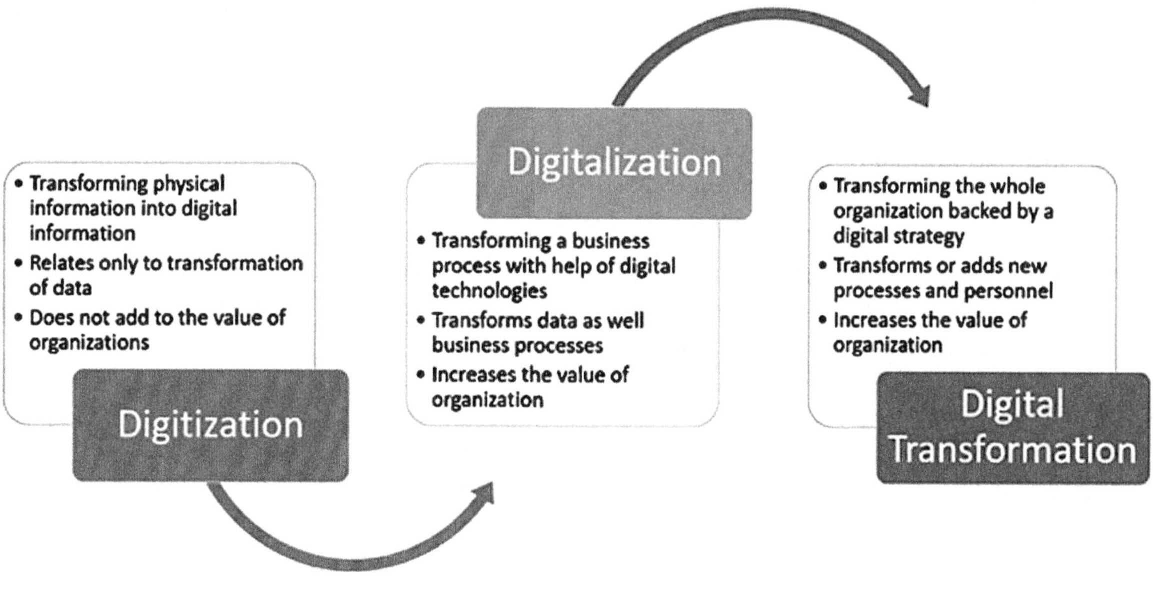

Strategic Direction of Digital Transformation

The different phases of digital transformation affix multiple changes in an organization affecting digital resources, the structure of the organization, growth strategies, and goals. To effectively compete in the digital world, businesses need digital assets like data storage, information, communication infrastructure, and supporting technology. Digital agility, Digital networking, and big data analytics are also a necessity in the digitization process. The digitization process results in the inclusion of new digital resources. The business processes are redesigned to align with the digital resources including, mostly agile and modular processes. Agile methods, modular business units, and digital functional units are being adopted in the business industry at a faster rate. This transition in business processes leads to changes in organizational structure and modification or addition of strategies (Warner & Wäger, 2019). These modified or new strategies add new performance indicators and goals in the business which helps businesses to grow in a competitive market.

Advantages of Digital Transformation

Agility

The use of digital technology directs most of the work to computer systems which takes a lot less time as compared to the manual effort and removes any chance of human errors thus making the business processes more agile and less error-prone (Li et al., 2021).

Better Customer Experience

The vast amount of data regarding customer preferences & trends can be analyzed using Big Data and Artificial Intelligence (AI) techniques which result in a better and smooth user experience. By tracing the digital footprints and extracting information about their need and preferences, businesses can better customize products that tend to the preferences of the customer, thus, enhancing customer experience (Abuhasan & Moreb, 2021)

Increased Productivity

With the agile business processes and better customer experience mentioned above, digital transformation increases business productivity which inevitably leads to a rise in business value. Digital Transformation boosts productivity in a variety of including automated routines, improving the production process, and improving customer relations with businesses (Kostić, 2018).

Faster Time to Market

One of the key benefits of digital transformation is faster and more targeted market reach. Businesses can use online platforms to market their products which enables them to reach the customer at a faster pace. Digital platforms can also improve customer engagement and provide better services.

Digital Technology has prevailed in almost every aspect of the business industry. The introduction of new technologies is revolutionizing business and will continue to do so in the future. It is very important to learn about these new technologies and how it is reshaping our business. This chapter emphasizes the importance of digital transformation by discussing the latest technologies, their impact, and trends. The rest of the chapter is organized as follows: Section 2 discusses the latest digital technologies, their impact on business and fintech, and current trends. Sections 3 and 4 outline the challenges that are faced by digital transformation and their recommendations. In the end, section 5 concludes the chapter.

LITERATURE REVIEW

Modern Digital Transformation Technologies

The digital world is currently going through innovations and inventions at a very fast pace which affects the process of digital transformation. The technology adopted today for digital transformation might become out-of-date, hence it is very important to choose the best-suited technology for any organization. Following are some digital technologies that are currently used across various organizations and are considered to expand in near future in relevance to business and fintech (Zaki, 2019).

1. Big Data

Big Data or Big Data analytics can be defined as the use of analytical procedures for a large volume of data sets that are used to extract market trends, customer preferences, and patterns. Organizations and businesses use historical as well as current data combined with big data analytics which enables them to make optimal decisions that result in effective marketing, customer personalization, and improved operational efficiency (Miklosik & Evans, 2020).

2. Blockchain

Blockchain provides a method of storing data amongst multiple parties that ensure data integrity. It provides a decentralized model with immutability. The immutable nature of blockchain makes secure any malicious data modification. Other benefits associated with the use of blockchain are efficiency, speed, transparency, and traceability. Blockchain is widely used across public and private sector organizations including healthcare, finance, etc. Some applications of blockchain include electronic voting, cryptocurrencies, etc. (Shukla et al., n.d.).

3. Artificial Intelligence

Artificial Intelligence (AI) is the ability of digital systems and technologies to imitate human intelligence and behaviors. AI has spanned across most of the IT fields and is developed through machine learning and deep learning. The business industry is using the potential of AI for improving productivity and efficiency while at the same time reducing the potential for human error. Some applications of AI in business include market prediction, virtual assistants, targeted marketing, etc. (Miklosik & Evans, 2020)

4. Cloud Computing

Cloud Computing is a model of computing in which dynamically scalable and usually virtualized resources are provided as a service over the internet. The resources may include servers, databases, networking, or storage resources. No additional setup is required to access these resources except for an active internet connection. Organizations, especially SMEs use cloud computing models due to their higher availability, scalable nature, low cost, and less manual effort required to manage their infrastructure. In the business industry, it is used for hosting applications, agility improved productivity, disaster recovery, low-cost maintenance, etc. (Clohessy et al., 2017)

5.   Internet of Things

The Internet of Things (IoT) can be defined as a system of interconnected, sometimes heterogenous, devices having unique identifiers with the ability to sense, collect, and send data over a network. These devices work together to achieve a desired goal over a small or large area. The use of these IoT devices and networks in business can help to gain a competitive advantage and better consumer experience. IoT applications in business include, but are not limited to, Livestock tracking & smart greenhouses in agriculture, parking solutions & traffic monitoring in smart cities, and smart grid systems (Zimmermann et al., 2015)

Digital Transformation in Business

The active and brisk developments in the field of information technology have created the need for digital transformation in businesses affecting all parts of society from changes in individual lifestyles to changes in business environments. Digital transformation has become a fundamental requirement in current business conditions affecting all personnel and processes within an organization which brings about substantial modifications in the business models & processes occasionally resulting in a change in organization activities (Pereira et al., 2022) Agile & continuous developments have become one of the key features of modern organizations which is possible only employing technology (Schwertner, 2017).

Traditional business models have become obsolete making themselves unable to provide sustainability in a competitive environment. The businesses and organizations that rely on the practice of the internet, technologies, and digital business models differ substantially from organizations relying on traditional models. Digital business models make the resources of an organization more modular and efficient(Vučeković & Gavrilović, n.d.). Digitally transformed businesses are 26 percent more profitable than traditional businesses according to a study by the Massachusetts Institute of Technology in 2013. Hence, the lack of adaptation to digital transformation might result in business closure(Loonam et al., 2018) (Leão & da Silva, 2021).

Digital transformation varies notably across different organizations. Since each organization has its organizational structure, business processes, and strategies, it is difficult to provide a single digital transformation strategy that applies to every organization. which implies complications of the digitization of different organization sectors resulting in significant change across these sectors (Faraz Mubarak et al., 2019)(Yucel, 2018).

Case Study: Netflix and Blockbuster

The importance of digital transformation in the business sector can further be elaborated with help of a case study of Netflix & Blockbuster. Both Blockbuster & Netflix were videotape & DVD rental companies that worked by purchasing movies & video publishing licenses from producers & copyright owners and renting the movies to the public at a much cheaper rate with Blockbuster holding the major share of the market in 2000.

Due to its lack of understanding of the impact of digital technologies on the business, Blockbuster went out of business. Even though it had enough resources and time to develop a new digital transformation of its business processes, Blockbuster hesitated to adapt to the latest technologies in Video & DVD industry. This led to the complete closure of its operation in 2010. On the other hand, Netflix evolved its business models to include digital technologies and align them with customer needs which makes it one of the leading video streaming & rental giants in the 21ˢᵗ century. This indicates the fact that how digital transformation can help to enhance operations, improve customer experience, compete in the market, and make businesses future-proof (Lacity et al., 2022) (Widia et al., 2021).

Recent Trends of Digital Transformation in Business

Digital transformation is one of the integral components of the sustainability of businesses across the globe. The COVID-19 pandemic which resulted in major disruptions in businesses has made us realize the importance of digital transformation for businesses. Digital transformation ensured continuous functioning, growth, and sustenance of the majority of businesses by enabling remote work during the COVID-19 pandemic. (Horgan et al., 2020) Organizations and businesses are moving towards a digital approach for business to counter the effects of the pandemic. Most businesses and industries have realized the prominence of digital transformation and have started the process of digital transformation. Now, businesses are more inclined toward investments in digital technology including AI, blockchain, IoT, etc. (Fernández-Rovira et al., 2021). According to Gartner, 91% of businesses are engaged in the process of digital transformation. Global GDP is expected to be digitalized by 65% by 2022. Cloud-driven IT resources are majorly being utilized across businesses with a Global Cloud Revenue of $474 billion in 2022. An amount of $58.3 billion has been invested in Artificial Intelligence in 2021 which is expected to rise to $309.6 billion by 2026. As reported by Prophet, 54% of transformation efforts continue to focus on modernizing customer experience. These statistics highlight the fact that most businesses and industries are driven by digital technology and others are moving toward the process of digital transformation.

Current businesses reinforced with digital transformation have adopted or adopted hybrid working environments and distributed and modular business models. On the technology side, Cloud Computing, Blockchain, Artificial Intelligence (Machine Learning), and Big Data are gaining more attention in the industrial sectors (C. H. Lee et al., 2021).

FUTURE DIRECTION

The business industry is employing digital transformation at a very fast pace. Digital transformation is anticipated to grow from $469.8 billion to $1009.8 billion with a Compound Annual Growth Rate (CAGR) of 16.5%. According to International Data Corporation (IDC), investments in digital transformation will rise to $7 trillion with a CAGR of 18%. The World Economic Forum states that $100 trillion will be added to the world economy by 2025 through digital transformation (Zachariadis & Ozcan, 2017).

Digital Transformation in Fintech

Digital transformation has become a fundamental requirement in every industry including the fintech industry as well. This transformation has enabled Fintech to become more customer-centric and advanced by utilizing modern technologies(Gomber et al., 2018) (Naz et al., 2022). Using digital platforms, financial services have become more effective, and customer-friendly, resulting growth of the fintech market. Fintech also provides an organization with a competitive edge in the market through its agility and efficiency. (Mavlutova & Volkova, n.d.)The financial services industry has also been modernized by digital transformation leading to the introduction of a new class of business firms i.e., Fintech. These fintech firms have introduced new business functions in finance which include digital payment services (Mobile Banking, Peer to Peer (P2P) payments, e-wallets), Credit and Lending, Insurance Services, and Investment Management (Mobile Trading, Online Brokerage). Overall, the emergence of fintech companies has increased economic development and financial stability(Boratyńska, 2019) (Suryono et al., 2020) (Suryono et al., 2020)

Fintech has improved the finance industry in a variety of ways with the ability to reconstitute the business's nature with technologies and following trends, including building a better relationship between the industry and customers. Business managers are advised to apply fintech culture in their business models, which will future of the finance industry (Diener & Špaček, 2021). Apart from modernizing and pacing up the functioning of the financial industry, fintech has also introduced a new set of financial services which include, but are not limited to, Personal Banking, flexible lending capabilities, Online trading, Digital Payments, and Cryptocurrency (Senyo et al., 2022) (Feyen et al., 2021b).

1. Personal Banking

The extensive use of mobile phones in daily routines has mostly become the first choice to avail of banking services like instant transfers. As reported by Deloitte, 72% of people use their mobile phones to access banking. Mobile banking is gaining more attention day by day by offering a quick, easy, and efficient way to streamline and optimize financial operations (Dhanalakshmi et al., n.d.).

2. Flexible lending capabilities

Fintech has broadened the adoption of online lending by facilitating lenders and borrowers with digital platforms. This enables lenders to reach out to more audiences at a faster cadence with simplified processes. Fintech financing also makes use of these cutting-edge technologies to provide customers more control over their financial flows enabling borrowers to apply for credit facilities anywhere across the globe, encouraging a proactive and active strategy for financial management (Eça et al., n.d.) (Rishabh & Schäublin, n.d.).

3. Online Trading

Fintech has enabled traders to execute their transactions without any financial institution using online platforms. With the availability of abundant information available, fintech can provide real-time estimates regarding the trading market enabling traders to invest their assets more efficiently. Cryptocurrency and the introduction of robot advisors have also introduced new modes of trading (Senyo et al., 2022).

4. Digital Payments

The process of digital payments has also been modernized by fintech. Fintech has introduced new methods of payment, including cryptocurrencies, e-wallets, etc. Inter-currency digital payments can be made across the globe within a matter of seconds including a variety of payment methods such ApplePay, AliPay, WeChatPay, etc. different from traditional payment options (Poerjoto et al., 2021) (F. Chen & Chen, 2021).

5. Cryptocurrency

A cryptocurrency is a form of digital currency which supports transactions (often anonymous) executed, verified, and maintained by a decentralized system. Cryptocurrencies are becoming a significant part of the fintech industry by providing efficient money transfers and reducing the risk of fraudulent activity (Allen et al., 2022) (Elsaid, 2021). As of the year 2022, the total number of cryptocurrencies has risen to around 12,000 with Bitcoin and Ethereum on top.

6. Robo-Advisors

Financial advising services are gaining popularity at a rapid rate which provides insight into investments, credits, and insurance. Robo-advisors (automated services that provide information on investments without the intervention of a human). By presenting clients with a specific set of questions, these advisors provide the most optimal plans for investment, credit, or insurance. But it's not quite clear that these Robo-advisor questions adequately collect the data required to serve the customer's "best interest,". Algorithms are under the focus of regulators and politicians since they won't act for the ultimate objective of the customer. However, financial advisors speed up the investing process, resulting in cheaper costs and higher speed while avoiding conflicts of interest, assuming honesty and openness are expected.

Traditional Banking vs. Digital Banking

Digital banks (financial service organizations) are more advanced offering better services, low costs, and less processing time. These banks function differently from traditional banks in terms of work ethic, structure, consumer experience, and adaptability (Kitsios et al., 2021) (Manser Payne et al., 2021). Table 1 highlights the differences between both models. Digital banking provides a distributed, yet collaborative environment centered around customer experience and with more inclination towards change with ease. Traditional models, on the other hand, have a hierarchical structure with an isolated environment and are less inclined to change. These models also rely on customer data to improve customer experience but do not involve any real-time data and customer involvement (*Digital Transformation in Financial Services A Report from the Deloitte Center for Financial Services*, n.d.).

Table 1. Traditional vs. Digital Banking Model

Organization Traits	Traditional Banking Model	Digital Banking Model
Work Ethic	Isolated & fixed team structures Isolated operations Geographically bounded	Collaborative & dynamic team structure No geographical boundaries
Structure	Hierarchical Goals determined top level personnel	Distributed Flattening and changing hierarchy Ongoing shifts in decision rights and power Changing mix of traditional and nontraditional stakeholders
Customer experience	Customer-focused using analytics with past customer data with no customer involvement	Customer-centric using analytics with real-time data including customer involvement
Adaptability	Less adaptable to change with a slow change process	Highly adaptable to change with an agile change process

Levels of Digital Transformation in Finance and Fintech

Digital transformation influences the finance and fintech industry on different levels majorly spanning across the internal, network, and external levels. It improves the models and processes within the firm, improves the interaction between the firm and its stakeholders, and regulates changes to meet external transformation needs (Alt et al., 2018).Figure 2 Levels of Digital Transformation. Figure 2 summarizes the three transformation levels that are discussed in detail as follows:

1.   Internal Transformation

At the internal level, FinTech entails a shift in corporate attention focus away from internal business procedures toward adopting a consumer-centered perspective. Several integrated digital platforms and channels have partially replaced traditional business, and the core capabilities have shifted from products and services to online channels, digital analytics, and platforms (Alt et al., 2018). This is accompanied by an increase in digitalized (automated) operations that are loosely coupled with core banking systems but are frequently developed internally using agile development approaches and predefined API interfaces (Mhlungu et al., 2019).

2.   Networking Transformation

At the network level, businesses in the FinTech spectrum are better networked with specialized external partners, and competition is typically stronger with reduced profit margins. Moreover, the competitive environment of FinTech currently contains new start-ups and lateral entrants in the established financial services industry. These industries have fundamentally different business cultures than traditional financial services firms (Gimpel et al., 2018) The reduced switching cost among Fintech suppliers has increased customer switching easier thus making the retention of customers difficult.

3.   External Transformation

Outside the boundaries of the business, regulation shifts from tougher standards for held equity, more international oversight, and lower protection provided by national laws to stricter regulations for held equity, more international supervision, and higher protection provided by national law. (Malenkov et al., 2021) This is also necessary because key infrastructures, such as central banks and payment services, will no longer be provided by centralized national entities or focal firms but rather by digital systems governed by different network partners for specialized purposes (such as payments, investment, and financing), or even operate entirely decentralized (e.g., blockchains). Digital infrastructures are widely used, which enables low-cost operations and the transition to a cashless society (Tarutė et al., 2018).

Figure 2. Levels of Digital Transformation

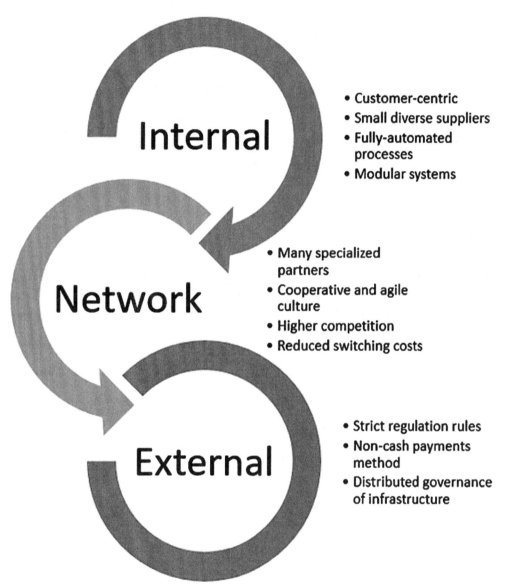

- Customer-centric
- Small diverse suppliers
- Fully-automated processes
- Modular systems

- Many specialized partners
- Cooperative and agile culture
- Higher competition
- Reduced switching costs

- Strict regulation rules
- Non-cash payments method
- Distributed governance of infrastructure

Case Study: Toyota Financial Services

Toyota Financial Services (TFS) is a global organization that provides retail and dealer financing. In 2009, TFS faced a major downfall in demand due to fewer sales of automobiles and endured a rise in payment defaults. This made the company officially realize that they need to have a digital approach to solve its problems. Using data analytics technologies, TFS divided its customer base into low-risk and high-risk. The high-risk customers were monitored closely and frequently as compared to low-risk customers. Because of this analytic-driven strategy, the loan application in FSI grew by nine percent with a customer base of 50,000 (*Digital Transformation in Financial Services A Report from the Deloitte Center for Financial Services*, n.d.) (Westerman, n.d.)

Recent Trends of Digital Transformation in Fintech

The evolution of technology is also contributing to rapid changes in Fintech technology. The major technologies that are used in the Fintech industry include Blockchain, Artificial Intelligence, the Internet of Things (IoT) & Cloud Computing (Restoy, n.d.). Table 2 enlists a few use cases of these technologies in the fintech industry. Blockchain is playing the most significant role in the fintech market with an investment of $425.5 million only in Europe (Crunchbase, 2021). Artificial intelligence (AI) and machine learning (ML) have induced rapid growth in the global financial technology or fintech industry with a market share of $9.13 billion in 2022 (The Business Research Company, 2022). Cloud & IoT are also rising in the fintech industry due to their high availability, scalability, and distributed environment (Matt et al., 2015) (Werth et al., 2020).

FUTURE DIRECTIONS

The FinTech blockchain market is expected to grow from USD 370.3 Million in 2018 to USD 6,228.2 Million by 2023, at a Compound Annual Growth Rate (CAGR) of 75.9% during the forecast period. Industry data suggests that by 2026, the global market size for AI in fintech will account for an astonishing USD 26.67 billion while maintaining a CAGR of 23.17% from 2021 through 2026.

Table 2. Application to Modern Technologies in Fintech

Technology	Applications
Block Chain	Banking and P2P payments Cryptocurrency Smart Contracts
Artificial Intelligence	Smart decision making Predictive Analytics Robo Advisors Fraud Detection
Cloud Computing	Enhanced Data Management Open banking Risk Management
Internet of Things	IoT-enabled Smart Contract Dedicated Smart wallets Peer-to-peer assets

Digital Transformation Challenges and Recommendations

As digital transformation adds to the productivity and efficiency of a business, adopting digital transformation comes with its own set of various challenges. Understanding these challenges and providing solutions has become an area of interest (Mićunović & Srića, n.d.). Digital transformation statistics indicate that only 16% of digital transformation adds to the performance or sustainability of the business(Pelletier & Martin Cloutier, n.d.) (Saarikko et al., 2020).

Inadequate Change Management Plans

Businesses that lack profound change management plans are not able to shift their business models with dynamic trends and constantly changing technologies failing to meet their digital transformation objectives. On other hand, businesses with a profound change management plan have more tendency to meet the digital transformation objectives. A lack of a change strategy sets up any new project or implementation plan up for failure (Rodríguez-Abitia & Bribiesca-Correa, 2021)

Cross-functional teams driven by innovation can help define a better change management plan allowing businesses to take a proactive approach to digital transformation and focus on customer needs (Pelletier & Martin Cloutier, n.d.) (Bullock & Sullivan, 2022)(Ghavifekr & Fung, 2021).

Inadequate Digital Transformation Strategy

As each business functions differently enforced with a unique set of strategic goals and directions, digital transformation strategy varies for each business. Before implementing a digital transformation process, a business must understand its structure and processes, areas of improvement, latest technologies, and market trend which helps in forming the optimal digital transformation strategy. This strategy can help in choosing the most suitable set of technology required for the digital transformation of a business. For example, just because blockchain has gained more attention in technological advancements, it must be appropriate for every business (Ebert & Duarte, 2018b).

Recommendations

The digital transformation strategy can be optimized by hiring a consultant who can help in selecting the digital technologies and models which are best suited to the business needs and help in increasing the productivity of the business.

Lack of IT Expertise

A skilled IT team is a significant component of the transformation process and plays a major role in its success. Most business organizations lack IT expertise resulting in a failed or inefficient digital transformation process. The gaps that are faced by businesses mostly consist of a lack of skills in software integrations, data analytics, data migrations, and cybersecurity (Fischer et al., 2020). An enterprise study states that 54% of business organizations are not able to meet digital transformation goals due to a lack of IT experts.

Recommendations

Outsourcing this process to consultants and digital transformation experts can help overcome this challenge (Werth et al., 2020). Businesses are incorporating new digital awareness policies and procedures to help their staff get better acquainted with dynamic technology.

Security Constraints

Privacy and cybersecurity concerns are one of the challenges that many businesses face, especially data-sensitive businesses. The majority of digital transformation solutions entail moving the data away from on-premises systems to cloud-based storage and consolidating all of a company's data into a single central location. It introduces the heightened risk of hackers stealing client information and business secrets. Cyberattacks can target flaws in the system design, and workflow to breach the data. Hence, it is very important to protective measures for the security of your data (Mendhurwar & Mishra, 2021)

Recommendations

Cybersecurity experts can help mitigate these challenges by scanning your systems for any weaknesses or vulnerabilities and applying appropriate defensive measures. Cloud should also provide complete security details and policies to customers outsourcing data to the cloud.

The Constant Change in Customer Needs

The process of digital transformation is quite complex, and rigorous and can span over months. The incessant shift in customer needs and behavior affects the transformation significantly because of customer-centric approaches. The transformation process might be required to change during the implementation of the transformation. This acts as a barrier to digital transformation or results in inefficient digital transformation.

Recommendations

Businesses must address this challenge while designing the digital transformation strategy by applying the agile methodology. Agile methodology benefits from the new surfacing opportunities by adapting to new tools & processes and modernizing traditional practices(von Leipzig et al., 2017). Big data analytics and different machine learning models are also utilized to keenly observe the shift in the customer and propose strategies based on these observations.

Adoption of New Technologies

The precipitous rise of new technologies is contributing to the evolution of digital transformation. Although these technologies make business processes efficient and effective, business organizations often face difficulty in adopting the new technologies due to a lack of documentation or training in getting hands-on practice with new systems. The adoption also stopped the fact that businesses believe that there is nothing wrong with the current processes and technologies. (C. L. Chen et al., 2021).

Recommendations

The challenges in the adoption of new technologies can be oppressed by extensive use of documentation and thorough onboarding training which will improve employee performance resulting in the productivity of the business. Businesses are advised to invest in digital adoption platforms (DAP). DAP provides an interactive walkthrough, user flows, product tours, onboarding experiences, and embedded knowledge bases to improve the adoption processes. They also provide insight into the most used features of the tool and how that tool can help enhance your business (van Dyk & van Belle, 2019).

CONCLUSION

The innovation and inventions of digital technologies are growing at a faster pace which has embedded technology in almost every aspect of society. In business, traditional business models are becoming outdated unable to compete with digitally transformed models. Digital transformation is one of the major requirements for business sustainability and growth and is driven by evolving technologies, rapid growth in competition & shifts in consumer behavior. Blockchain, AI, ML, Big Data & Cloud are major contributors to the transformation of businesses leading to increased productivity, better customer experience, and faster processes. Digital transformation has also introduced hybrid working models and distributed and modular business models. It varies greatly across the business due to the diverse structure of business models and processes. It is anticipated to grow at a CAGR of 16.5% in the coming years. Digital transformation has established its roots in the finance industry leading to the emergence of fintech. Fintech offers standard financial services through technology and introduces new finance models in the finance industry. Through the process of digital transformation, fintech has presented mobile banking, digital payments, e-wallets, P2P trading, flexible lending, cryptocurrencies, and much more. The fintech industry is evolving at a faster pace and is replacing with more streamlined and accessible financial services. Even though digital transformation is an essential process, it comes with its fair share of challenges including insufficient change management, incapable digital strategy, embracing new technologies, and lack of IT expertise and security. These challenges slow down or stop the process of digital transformation in business and fintech and might result in inefficient digital transformation. Hence, it is very important to address these challenges during the process of digital transformation.

REFERENCES

A Companion to Film Theory. (n.d.). Academic Press.

Abuhasan, F., & Moreb, M. (2021). The Impact of the Digital Transformation on Customer Experience in Palestine Banks. *2021 International Conference on Information Technology, ICIT 2021 - Proceedings*, 43–48. 10.1109/ICIT52682.2021.9491744

Allen, F., Gu, X., & Jagtiani, J. (2022). Fintech, Cryptocurrencies, and CBDC: Financial Structural Transformation in China. *Journal of International Money and Finance*, *124*, 102625. Advance online publication. doi:10.1016/j.jimonfin.2022.102625

Alt, R., Beck, R., & Smits, M. T. (2018). FinTech and the transformation of the financial industry. In Electronic Markets (Vol. 28, Issue 3, pp. 235–243). Springer Verlag. doi:10.100712525-018-0310-9

Bohnsack, R., Kurtz, H., & Hanelt, A. (2021). Re-examining path dependence in the digital age: The evolution of connected car business models. *Research Policy*, *50*(9), 104328. Advance online publication. doi:10.1016/j.respol.2021.104328

Boratyńska, K. (2019). Impact of Digital Transformation on Value Creation in Fintech Services: An Innovative Approach. *Journal of Promotion Management*, *25*(5), 631–639. Advance online publication. doi:10.1080/10496491.2019.1585543

Bullock, M., & Sullivan, M. (2022). *Change Management During Digital Transformation Projects: How to Overcome Barriers Using an Agile Approach and Modern Change Models*. Academic Press.

Chen, C. L., Lin, Y. C., Chen, W. H., Chao, C. F., & Pandia, H. (2021). Role of government to enhance digital transformation in small service business. *Sustainability (Switzerland)*, *13*(3), 1–26. doi:10.3390u13031028

Chen, F., & Chen, X. (2021). How Does FinTech Affect Consumer Non-cash Payment Satisfaction? The Moderating Role of Financial Knowledge. *South Asian Journal of Social Studies and Economics*, 217–231. doi:10.9734/sajsse/2021/v12i430329

Clohessy, T., Acton, T., & Morgan, L. (2017). The Impact of Cloud-Based Digital Transformation on IT Service Providers. *International Journal of Cloud Applications and Computing*, *7*(4), 1–19. doi:10.4018/IJCAC.2017100101

Contributor, J. B. (n.d.). *Digitization, Digitalization, And Digital Transformation: Confuse Them At Your Peril I write and consult on digital transformation in the enterprise.* https://www.forbes.com/sites/jasonbloomberg/2018/04/29/digitization-digitalization-and-digital-transformation-confuse-them-at-your-peril/#78e677fd2f2c

Dhanalakshmi, A., Prema Rajan, R. K., & Hui, X. (n.d.). *An Empirical Study on the Adoption Intention of Financial Technology (FinTech) Services among Bank Users*. Academic Press.

Diener, F., & Špaček, M. (2021). Digital transformation in banking: A managerial perspective on barriers to change. *Sustainability (Switzerland)*, *13*(4), 1–26. doi:10.3390u13042032

Digital transformation in financial services A report from the Deloitte Center for Financial Services. (n.d.). www.deloittedigital.com

Ebert, C., & Duarte, C. H. C. (2018). Digital Transformation. *IEEE Software*, *35*(4), 16–21. doi:10.1109/MS.2018.2801537

Eça, A., Ferreira, M., Prado, M., & Rizzo, A. E. (n.d.). *The Real Effects of FinTech Lending on SMEs: Evidence from Loan Applications*. www.cepr.org

Elsaid, H. M. (2021). *A review of literature directions regarding the impact of fintech firms on the banking industry*. Qualitative Research in Financial Markets. doi:10.1108/QRFM-10-2020-0197

Faraz Mubarak, M., Zulfiqar Ali Bhutto, S., Ali Shaikh, F., Mubarik, M., Ahmed Samo, K., & Mastoi, S. (2019). The Impact of Digital Transformation on Business Performance A Study of Pakistani SMEs. In *Technology & []*. www.etasr.com]. *Applied Scientific Research*, *9*(6).

Fernández-Rovira, C., Álvarez Valdés, J., Molleví, G., & Nicolas-Sans, R. (2021). The digital transformation of business. Towards the datafication of the relationship with customers. *Technological Forecasting and Social Change*, *162*, 120339. Advance online publication. doi:10.1016/j.techfore.2020.120339

Feyen, E., Frost, J., Gambacorta, L., Natarajan, H., & Saal, M. (2021). *BIS Papers No 117 Fintech and the digital transformation of financial services: Implications for market structure and public policy.* www.worldbank.org

Fischer, M., Imgrund, F., Janiesch, C., & Winkelmann, A. (2020). Strategy archetypes for digital transformation: Defining meta objectives using business process management. *Information & Management*, *57*(5), 103262. Advance online publication. doi:10.1016/j.im.2019.103262

Galchenkova, E., & Chupsa, P. (2020). Introduction of fintech companies and their impact on the financial market. *Business Strategies*, *8*(6), 157–159. doi:10.17747/2311-7184-2020-6-157-159

Ghavifekr, S., & Fung, H. Y. (2021). Change Management in Digital Environment Amid the COVID-19 Pandemic: A Scenario from Malaysian Higher Education Institutions. In S. Saeed, M. P. R. Bolívar, & R. Thurasamy (Eds.), *Pandemic Lockdown, and Digital Transformation.* doi:10.1007/978-3-030-86274-9_8

Gimpel, H., Rau, D., & Röglinger, M. (2018). Understanding FinTech start-ups – a taxonomy of consumer-oriented service offerings. *Electronic Markets*, *28*(3), 245–264. doi:10.100712525-017-0275-0

Gölzer, P., & Fritzsche, A. (2017). Data-driven operations management: Organisational implications of the digital transformation in industrial practice. *Production Planning and Control*, *28*(16), 1332–1343. doi:10.1080/09537287.2017.1375148

Gomber, P., Kauffman, R. J., Parker, C., & Weber, B. W. (2018). On the Fintech Revolution: Interpreting the Forces of Innovation, Disruption, and Transformation in Financial Services. *Journal of Management Information Systems*, *35*(1), 220–265. doi:10.1080/07421222.2018.1440766

Gong, C., & Ribiere, V. (2021). Developing a unified definition of digital transformation. *Technovation*, *102*, 102217. Advance online publication. doi:10.1016/j.technovation.2020.102217

Holotiuk, F., & Beimborn, D. (n.d.). *Critical Success Factors of Digital Business Strategy.* Academic Press.

Horgan, D., Hackett, J., Westphalen, C. B., Kalra, D., Richer, E., Romao, M., Andreu, A. L., Lal, J. A., Bernini, C., Tumiene, B., Boccia, S., & Montserrat, A. (2020). Digitalisation and COVID-19: The Perfect Storm. *Biomedicine Hub*, *5*(3), 1–23. doi:10.1159/000511232 PMID:33564668

Hsu, C. C., Tsaih, R. H., & Yen, D. C. (2018). The evolving role of IT Departments in digital transformation. *Sustainability (Switzerland)*, *10*(10), 3706. Advance online publication. doi:10.3390u10103706

Imgrund, F., Fischer, M., & Winkelmann, A. (2018). *Approaching Digitalization with Business Process Management.* https://www.researchgate.net/publication/323665985

Kitsios, F., Giatsidis, I., & Kamariotou, M. (2021). Digital transformation and strategy in the banking sector: Evaluating the acceptance rate of e-services. *Journal of Open Innovation*, *7*(3), 204. Advance online publication. doi:10.3390/joitmc7030204

Kostić, Z. (2018). Innovations and digital transformation as a competition catalyst. *Ekonomika (Nis)*, *64*(1), 13–23. doi:10.5937/ekonomika1801013K

Leão, P., & da Silva, M. M. (2021). Impacts of digital transformation on firms' competitive advantages: A systematic literature review. *Strategic Change*, *30*(5), 421–441. doi:10.1002/jsc.2459

Lee, C. H., Liu, C. L., Trappey, A. J. C., Mo, J. P. T., & Desouza, K. C. (2021). Understanding digital transformation in advanced manufacturing and engineering: A bibliometric analysis, topic modeling and research trend discovery. *Advanced Engineering Informatics*, *50*, 101428. Advance online publication. doi:10.1016/j.aei.2021.101428

Lee, I., & Shin, Y. J. (2018). Fintech: Ecosystem, business models, investment decisions, and challenges. *Business Horizons*, *61*(1), 35–46. doi:10.1016/j.bushor.2017.09.003

Li, H., Wu, Y., Cao, D., & Wang, Y. (2021). Organizational mindfulness towards digital transformation as a prerequisite of information processing capability to achieve market agility. *Journal of Business Research*, *122*, 700–712. doi:10.1016/j.jbusres.2019.10.036

Liao, H.-T., Zhao, M., & Sun, S.-P. (2020). *A Literature Review of Museum and Heritage on Digitization*. Digitalization, and Digital Transformation.

Loonam, J., Eaves, S., Kumar, V., & Parry, G. (2018). Towards digital transformation: Lessons learned from traditional organizations. *Strategic Change*, *27*(2), 101–109. doi:10.1002/jsc.2185

Malenkov, Y., Kapustina, I., Kudryavtseva, G., Shishkin, V., & Shishkin, V. I. (2021). Digitalization and strategic transformation of retail chain stores: Trends, impacts, prospects. *Journal of Open Innovation*, *7*(2), 108. Advance online publication. doi:10.3390/joitmc7020108

Manser Payne, E. H., Dahl, A. J., & Peltier, J. (2021). Digital servitization value co-creation framework for AI services: A research agenda for digital transformation in financial service ecosystems. *Journal of Research in Interactive Marketing*, *15*(2), 200–222. doi:10.1108/JRIM-12-2020-0252

Matt, C., Hess, T., & Benlian, A. (2015). Digital Transformation Strategies. In Business and Information Systems Engineering (Vol. 57, Issue 5, pp. 339–343). Gabler Verlag. doi:10.100712599-015-0401-5

Mavlutova, I., & Volkova, T. (n.d.). *Digital Transformation Of Financial Sector And Challenges For Competencies Development*. Academic Press.

Mendhurwar, S., & Mishra, R. (2021). Integration of social and IoT technologies: Architectural framework for digital transformation and cyber security challenges. *Enterprise Information Systems*, *15*(4), 565–584. doi:10.1080/17517575.2019.1600041

Mhlungu, N. S. M., Chen, J. Y. J., & Alkema, P. (2019). The underlying factors of a successful organisational digital transformation. *South African Journal of Information Management*, *21*(1). Advance online publication. doi:10.4102ajim.v21i1.995

Mićunović, N., & Srića, V. (n.d.). *Digital Transformation in Montenegro-opportunities, challenges, and recommendations for improvement? Building elite (excellence in leadership, innovattion and technology) network*. doi:10.9790/0661-2301021018

Miklosik, A., & Evans, N. (2020). Impact of Big Data and Machine Learning on Digital Transformation in Marketing: A Literature Review. In *IEEE Access* (Vol. 8, p. 101284–101292). Institute of Electrical and Electronics Engineers Inc. doi:10.1109/ACCESS.2020.2998754

Naz, F., Karim, S., Houcine, A., & Naeem, M. A. (2022). Fintech Growth during COVID-19 in MENA Region: Current Challenges and Future prospects. *Electronic Commerce Research*. Advance online publication. doi:10.100710660-022-09583-3

Osmundsen, K., Iden, J., & Bygstad, B. (2018). *Association for Information Systems AIS Electronic Library (AISeL) Digital Transformation: Drivers, Success Factors, and Implications Recommended Citation*. https://aisel.aisnet.org/mcis2018/37

Pelletier, C., & Martin Cloutier, L. (n.d.). *Challenges of Digital Transformation in SMEs: Exploration of IT-Related Perceptions in a Service Ecosystem*. https://hdl.handle.net/10125/59934

Pereira, C. S., Durão, N., Moreira, F., & Veloso, B. (2022). The Importance of Digital Transformation in International Business. *Sustainability (Switzerland)*, *14*(2), 834. Advance online publication. doi:10.3390u14020834

Poerjoto, J. I., Gui, A., & Deniswara, K. (2021, February 16). Identifying Factors Affecting the Continuance Usage Intention of Digital Payment Services among Millennials in Jakarta. *2021 25th International Conference on Information Technology, IT 2021*. 10.1109/IT51528.2021.9390125

Puschmann, T. (2017). Fintech. *Business & Information Systems Engineering*, *59*(1), 69–76. doi:10.100712599-017-0464-6

Rawat, A., & Matter Expert, S. (2016). *Achieving Customer-Centricity Through Digital Transformation Anubhav RawaT Subject Matter Expert*. www.cmo.com

Restoy, F. (n.d.). *Regulating fintech: what is going on, and where are the challenges?* Bank for International Settlements. www.suerf.org/policynotes

Rishabh, K., & Schäublin, J. (n.d.). *Fintech Lending and Sales Manipulation*. Academic Press.

Rodríguez-Abitia, G., & Bribiesca-Correa, G. (2021). Assessing digital transformation in universities. *Future Internet*, *13*(2), 1–17. doi:10.3390/fi13020052

Saarikko, T., Westergren, U. H., & Blomquist, T. (2020). Digital transformation: Five recommendations for the digitally conscious firm. *Business Horizons*, *63*(6), 825–839. doi:10.1016/j.bushor.2020.07.005

Schwertner, K. (2017). Digital transformation of business. *Trakia Journal of Sciences*, *15*(Suppl.1), 388–393. doi:10.15547/tjs.2017.s.01.065

Senyo, P. K., Gozman, D., Karanasios, S., Dacre, N., & Baba, M. (2022). Moving away from trading on the margins: Economic empowerment of informal businesses through <scp>FinTech</scp>. *Information Systems Journal*, isj.12403. Advance online publication. doi:10.1111/isj.12403

Shukla, B., Khatri, S. K., & Kapur, P. K. (n.d.). *2017 6th International Conference on Reliability, Infocom Technologies and Optimization (ICRITO) (Trends and Future Directions)*. Amity University.

Suryono, R. R., Budi, I., & Purwandari, B. (2020). Challenges and trends of financial technology (Fintech): A systematic literature review. In Information (Switzerland) (Vol. 11, Issue 12, pp. 1–20). MDPI AG. doi:10.3390/info11120590

Tarutė, A., Duobienė, J., Klovienė, L., Vitkauskaitė, E., & Varaniūtė, V. (2018). Identifying factors affecting digital transformation of SMEs. ICEB.

van Dyk, R., & van Belle, J. P. (2019). Factors influencing the intended adoption of digital transformation: A South African case study. *Proceedings of the 2019 Federated Conference on Computer Science and Information Systems, FedCSIS 2019*, 519–528. 10.15439/2019F166

von Leipzig, T., Gamp, M., Manz, D., Schöttle, K., Ohlhausen, P., Oosthuizen, G., Palm, D., & von Leipzig, K. (2017). Initialising Customer-orientated Digital Transformation in Enterprises. *Procedia Manufacturing*, *8*, 517–524. doi:10.1016/j.promfg.2017.02.066

Vučeković, M., & Gavrilović, K. (n.d.). *Digital Transformation and Evolution ofBusiness Models*. Academic Press.

Warner, K. S. R., & Wäger, M. (2019). Building dynamic capabilities for digital transformation: An ongoing process of strategic renewal. *Long Range Planning*, *52*(3), 326–349. doi:10.1016/j.lrp.2018.12.001

Werth, O., Schwarzbach, C., Rodríguez Cardona, D., Breitner, M. H., & Graf von der Schulenburg, J. M. (2020). Influencing factors for the digital transformation in the financial services sector. *Zeitschrift Fur Die Gesamte Versicherungswissenschaft*, *109*(2–4), 155–179. doi:10.100712297-020-00486-6

Westerman, G. (n.d.). *The Questions Leaders Should Ask in the New Era of Digital Transformation*. Academic Press.

Widia, F., Rosanensi, M., & Rahmawati, L. (2021). Netflix's Strategy to Dominate the World's Entertainment Media Market After the Death of Blockbuster. *JBTI : Jurnal Bisnis : Teori Dan Implementasi*, *12*(3), 155–171. doi:10.18196/jbti.v12i3.13396

Yucel, S. (2018). Estimating the benefits, drawbacks and risk of digital transformation strategy. *Proceedings - 2018 International Conference on Computational Science and Computational Intelligence, CSCI 2018*, 233–238. 10.1109/CSCI46756.2018.00051

Zachariadis, M., & Ozcan, P. (2017). *The API economy and digital transformation in financial services: The case of open banking*. Academic Press.

Zaki, M. (2019). Digital transformation: Harnessing digital technologies for the next generation of services. *Journal of Services Marketing*, *33*(4), 429–435. doi:10.1108/JSM-01-2019-0034

Zhao, M., Liao, H.-T., & Sun, S.-P. (2020). *An Education Literature Review on Digitization*. Digitalization, Datafication, and Digital Transformation.

Zimmermann, A., Schmidt, R., Sandkuhl, K., Wißotzki, M., Jugel, D., & Möhring, M. (2015). Digital enterprise architecture-transformation for the internet of things. *Proceedings of the 2015 IEEE 19th International Enterprise Distributed Object Computing Conference Workshops and Demonstrations, EDOCW 2015*, 130–138. 10.1109/EDOCW.2015.16

Chapter 2
Cybersecurity Issues and Challenges

Neda Azizi

https://orcid.org/0000-0001-5651-4869
Torrens University, Australia

Omid Haass
RMIT University, Australia

ABSTRACT

Interest in study about cybersecurity and related security topics has grown dramatically in recent years. This interest has been motivated by a number of elements, two of which stand out: 1) In this business world, information systems, databases, and distributed internet-based systems and communications become significantly universal. Hence, organizations recently recognize the requirements for a fundamental security strategy because of increasing intensity and complexity of security-related attacks and risks. This strategy may be considered as the use of authorised hardware and software and skilled and trained personnel to meet the requirements. 2) Cybersecurity education has developed as a national objectives/strategy in most of the countries. Further, a number of frameworks and standards is designed and developed for computer security education. Accordingly, the number of fields and subjects offered at universities, education colleges, and other institutions in terms of cybersecurity and related fields has increased.

1. CYBER THREATS AND ATTACKS

This section provides an overview of cybersecurity issues and challenges. We begin with an introduction to cybersecurity and develop a discussion of computer-related assets that are subject to a variety of cyber threats and risk analysis. Accordingly, the section provides an overview of the classifications of cyber threats and attacks that users and managers wish to identify and manage them, and a look at the security engineers to protect computer assets and networks and track incidents. However, the focus of

DOI: 10.4018/978-1-6684-5284-4.ch002

this section, is on four fundamental topics including introduction to cyber Security, the challenges of cybersecurity, various cyber threats, and security engineering and risk analysis.

1.1 Introduction to Cyber Security

The NISTIR 7298 report (Glossary of Key Information Security Terms, July 2019) defines the cybersecurity concept as measures used to protect confidentiality, integrity, and availability of system, and data (such as software, hardware, network), and information being processed, stored, and communicated.

This definition represents the concepts of confidentiality, integrity, and availability that build what is merely referred to as the CIA triad. These three concepts are at the heart of cybersecurity and include security goals for information and computer systems. The FISMA (Standards for Security, Categorization of Federal Information and Information Systems, February 2004) defines three security goals for information and computer systems:

- **Confidentiality:** Considering permissible limits on access and disclosure of information, including tools to protect sensitive personal information and proprietary information.
- **Integrity:** Protection against correction or destruction of false information, including ensuring non-repudiation and accuracy of information.
- **Availability:** Ensuring timely and reliable access of authorized users to resources when needed.

Depending on an organization's security objectives and their regulatory requirements, one of these three concepts (confidentiality, integrity, and availability) might take precedence over another. For example, confidentiality is critical for certain government agencies; integrity is vital for financial sector; and availability is important in both the ecommerce and the healthcare sector (Dalziel, 2014). An organization could decide how to use these three concepts given their specific requirements, balanced with their goals to develop a seamless and safe user experience. An organisation that requires high confidentiality and integrity might sacrifice lightning-speed performance that other organisations might value more highly.

1.2 The Challenges of Cybersecurity

Computer and network security is both interesting and complex (Al Obaidan & Saeed, 2021; Stallings & Brown 2018). Some of the reasons are as follows:

- Cybersecurity seems simple to the beginner at first. In fact, the main requirements for security systems can be self-explanatory such as confidentiality, integrity, and availability. Although the approaches applied to meet these requirements can be complex completely, and understanding them may require some fairly sophisticated reasoning.
- Providing a comprehensive security approach, one could consider possible attacks on those security characteristics. In essence, successful attacks are developed with a completely different perspective of the problem, thus exploiting an unexpected weakness in the exploitation approach.
- Due to point 2, the approaches applied to develop certain services are quite contradictory. Therefore, a security approach isn't simple, and it is not clear from the statement of a specific requirement that such detailed measures are required. Instead the various threats are considered that detailed security requirements make sense.

- As you design different security approaches, you need to decide where to apply them. This is true both in a physical placement and logical sense concept.
- Security services often involve more than one specific protocol. Thus, it may also rely on communication protocols whose processes can complicate the development of a security approach.
- Cybersecurity is considered as a battle of wits between a criminal who trying to find holes and a designer who trying to solve them. The advantage that the attackers have is that they only need to find one weak point, while the designer need to find and mitigate all the weak points to achieve successful security.
- Managers and developers must realize some advantages of a security investment until a security breach occurs.
- Managers and developers require to monitor and control of computer security continuously and regularly and is complex in today's short-term and dynamic environment.
- Security is often an issue that is considered in a computer system after the system is developed, instead of an integral part of the system process.
- Many developers and managers consider a comprehensive security as an obstacle to the efficient and user-friendly performance of a computer system.

The challenges just listed are addressed in multiple ways with different threats and security approaches throughout this chapter. We now turn to investigate the various threats and attacks that must be dealt with, and then give some ideas of the types of threats that apply to various categories of computer systems.

1.3 Various Cyber Threats

Businesses are significantly affected by malicious cyber-attacks. Former Cisco CEO John Chambers once said, "There are two types of companies: those that have been hacked, and those who don't yet know they have been hacked." According to report of the Cisco Annual Cybersecurity Report (2021), the volume of events has almost quadrupled since 2016. Therefore, cybercrime has increased increasingly as people try to take advantage of vulnerable business systems.

Risk

In the context of cybersecurity, risk is often defined as an "equation"— *Vulnerabilities * Threats = Risk*—as if vulnerabilities are something you can multiply by threats to arrive at risk, thereby, risk is considered as probability that a specific threat using a specific exploit can take advantage of a particular vulnerability (Clark et al. 2015).

Vulnerability

The most common software security vulnerabilities include:

- **Injection:** Attacker sends simple text-based attacks that exploit the syntax of the targeted interpreter-APIs, SQL statements, and LDAP queries
- **Broken Authentication and Session Management**: Attacker gains illegal system access via stolen, exposed credentials and password, on session IDs

- **Cross-site Scripting (XSS):** Hacker sends message-based attack scripts that exploit the translator in the Web browser
- **Insecure Direct Object Reference:** Authorized system user (insider attacker), alters a parameter value that directly refers to an unauthorized system object to attempt unauthorized access
- **Security Misconfiguration:** Attacker accesses default accounts, unused pages, unpatched flows, unprotected files and directories to gain unauthorized access to or knowledge of the system
- **Buffer overflow:** Attacker infuses the input memory stack with a system compromising directive
- **Sensitive Data exposure:** Encryption key theft, MitM attacks, theft of clear data assets at rest or in transit
- **Missing functional level access control:** Insider threat, where a user changes the URL or a parameter to a privileged function. In addition, rogue users gain access to unprotected functions or data assets
- **Cross-site Request Forgery (CSRF):** User of forged HTTP needs that trick a victim into submitting them through image tags (XSS) or other approaches where the user is authenticated, the attack succeeds
- **Using known vulnerable components:** Customizes the exploit to attack a discovered weakness
- **Unchecked redirects and forwards:** The targeting of unsafe forwards to bypass security checks and redirect to rogue website
- **DNS poisoning:** The attacker introduces rogue data into a DNS resolver's cache, causing the name server to return an incorrect IP address, thus diverting traffic to the attacker's computer

Threats

Threats is defined as a circumstance or state with the potential to adversely impact on computer system, users, organisational performances, and even other entities whin organisations through unauthorized access, destruction, disclosure, changes of information systems or denial of system services (Bonneau, 2012). Consequence, cyber threats and attacks consist of the accessible and exploitable vulnerabilities in the system, so they are deliberate unauthorized actions on the system. A systematic and fundamental analysis of key factors of vulnerability makes users, developers and security managers aware of where security approaches are required. Common types of cyber-attacks includes Malware, Phishing, Man-in-the-middle (MitM), Denial-of-service (DDoS), Structured Query Language (SQL) web, Zero-day and DNS. However, threats can be categorized in the following way:

- Software threats
- Web attacks
- Network attacks
- Hardware attacks

Software Threats

Software threats are malicious factors of computer applications that might offend the computer and steal sensitive personal information. In this light, the malicious programs are mostly called malware. Malware is a software developed intentionally to illustrate malicious factors, including spyware, Trojan horse, rootkit, ransomware, viruses, and worms (Almashhadani et al. 2022; Almuhaideb & Saeed, 2020). It might infect computer applications, networks and is developed to harm those applications and networks in some way (Luk, 2007). Depending on the type of gaols of malware, this malicious can show itself differently to the user or developer. Sometimes, the malware has relatively mild and benign effects, while sometimes it might be disastrous (Enoch et al 2022). No matter the approach, all types of malware are developed to exploit computer applications and devices at the expense of the user, developer and to the benefit of the hacker -- the people who has designed the malware (De Carvalho et al. 2022). Malware programs develop a diversity of physical and virtual means to extend malware that infects computer applications, devices or networks. For example, malicious authors might be delivered to a system with a USB device, via popular communication tools and by drive-by downloads, which automatically download malicious programs to systems without the user's approval (Bloom, 1970).

Figure 1. Software threats

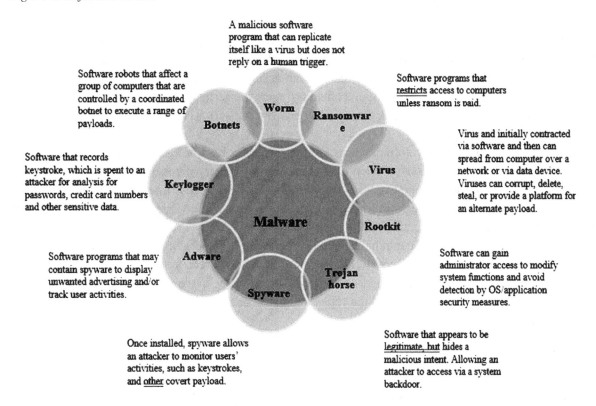

As a result, the software attacks are much harder to defend against due of some specific targeting and persistence. It requires a combination of technical countermeasures as well as awareness training to assist people to prevent these types of threats.

Web Attacks

Web applications do raise a number of security concerns arising from inappropriate coding. Serious weaknesses/ vulnerabilities can permit attacker to obtain direct access to databases - sensitive data -

known as a web attack. As stated, websites depend on databases to transfer valuable information to actors, then vulnerable to at least one of the diverse ways of hacking techniques; can put at serious risk your sensitive information- web attack. Current research noticed that 75% of cyber-attacks are done at the web application level.

- Cross Site Request Forgery
- Cross-Site Scripting Attack
- Structured Query Language injection Attack

Cross-site request forgery and Cross-Site Scripting Attack:

Cross-site request forgery (also known as CSRF) is a kind of web attack that allows a hacker to make users to perform some actions that they do not want to perform. CSRF permits an attacker to partially circumvent the principles and policies, which are developed to prevent various websites from interfering with each other, in essence, attacker tries to control what the client bowser sent to the website.

Cross-Site Scripting (also known as XSS) attacks are a form of injection where malicious scripts are injected into otherwise safe and trusted websites. XSS attacks often occur when an attacker applies a web application to send malicious code, in essence, attacker tries to control what the website sends to the client browser, typically in the form of a client browser side script, to another end user

The vulnerabilities of Cross-Site Scripting are typically more serious than Cross-site request forgery:

- Cross-site request forgery normally uses to a sub-process of actions that a user is capable of performing. Many applications develop Cross-site request forgery defences in general, but ignore one or two practices that are exposed. Therefore, a successful Cross-Site Scripting exploit might typically force a user to perform some actions that the user will be able to perform, regardless of the function in which the vulnerability arises.
- Cross-site request forgery could be defined as a "one-way" vulnerability, in that while an attacker might force the victim to subject an HTTP request, they didn't recover the reply from that request. Reciprocally, Cross-Site Scripting is "two-way" vulnerability, in that the attacker's injected script might subject ideal requests, read the reply, and extracting the data to an external domain of the attacker's selecting.

Structured Query Language (SQL)

Structured Query Language (also known as SQL) injection can happen when a criminal inserts malicious code into a server that uses Structured Query Language and tries to access vulnerable information it mostly would not. It is a programming language that is generally applied in relational database or data stream information systems. In essence, a criminal might perform a Structured Query Language injection simply via delivering malicious code into a website service box.

Network Attack

A Network attack is defined as attempt to achieve unauthorized access to computer systems and assets, with the purpose of stealing valuable information or fulfil other malicious performances. Network security attacks can be considered as a passive attacks, attackers attempt to learn or apply information from the system, but does not affect system resources; and an active attack, and attackers attempt to change system resources or affect the system operation.

Network attacks can be classified in the following way:

- **Packet Sniffing**: Sniffing is a data interception technology. It is the act of collecting and recording some or all packets that pass through a computer network, regardless of how the packet is addressed. In this light, any packet, or a defined subset of packets will be collected for a comprehensive analysis. Thus managers can apply the collected data for different purposes such as bandwidth and traffic controlling and monitoring.
- **Packet Spoofing**: Spoofing is an intruder imitates another legitimate device or user to launch an attack against the network. It is the creation of Internet Protocol (IP) packets with the source Internet Protocol address intended to disguise the identity potential network trouble spots or criminal activity on networks
- **Attacks on Transmission Control Protocol (TCP) protocol:** TCP RST (Rest) attack is the most common attack on the Internet in which attackers send forged TCP RST packets to the host.
- **DNS Attacks**: A DNS attack is an exploit in which an attacker benefits from vulnerabilities in the domain names so that they are rerouted to a new IP address.
- **Heartbleed Bug and Attack:** The Heartbleed bug is a serious vulnerability in open source software (OpenSSL) cryptographic software library. Anyone with an internet connection is able to extract this bug to track or read the memory of vulnerable systems, leaving no evidence of the compromised system.
- **Denial-of-service (DDoS):** A DDoS attack floods systems or servers with traffic to shut down a network, resources and bandwidth, thereby the system will not be able to operate requested activities. DDoS includes Smurf attacks, Tribe Flood Network attack and Stacheldraht attacks.

Hardware Attack

A hardware attack is defined as an exploitable vulnerabilities in the computer system that may cause attack via a remote as well as physical computing device that safeguards and manages digital keys for a comprehensive authentication and provides cryptoprocessing. There are four types of hardware attacks based on the awareness of the attack including information system hardware, physical facility, supporting facilities, and personnel. Therefore hardware attacks have various capabilities and objectives, some use hardware Trojans that are introduced during construction, while others monitor system releases. Thus, managers often employ mitigation techniques to protect the system when a hardware attack has been identified.

In sum, hardware attacks can be categorised in the following way:

- **Environmental threats** such as Natural disasters, fire smoke, water, lightning and hazards
- **Technical threats** such as electrical power, electromagnetic inference and HSM design
- **Human-caused threats** such as Unauthorized physical access, theft and vandalism

Corresponding to the different vulnerabilities to an information systems are threats that can exploit those vulnerabilities. Therefore, a countermeasure is an operation taken to prevent a security attack. Generally, a countermeasure may be considered to mitigate or prevent a specific attack from succeeding (Frahim, 2015). Once mitigations or prevention fail in some reasons, the purpose is to discover the attack then recover from the impacts of the attack. A countermeasure can introduce some other vulnerabilities. Thus, some vulnerabilities might remain after countermeasures are applied. In this case, the vulnerabilities may be exploited by threat agents representing a high level of risk to the systems, thereby, users require to mitigate those risk given other constraints.

Table 1. Computer and Network threats, attacks and assets

Attacks/Threats	Confidentiality	Integrity	Availability
Software	An unauthorized copy of the software has been made.	A work program is tailored, either to cause it to fail during execution or cause to do an unwanted thing	Programs are removed and user access is denied.
Hardware	Not encrypted the USB drive has been stolen.		Stolen equipment or it becomes inactive, thus denying service.
Web	Unauthorized reading of data is done.	Existing files are modifying or new files are built.	Files are deleted and user access is prohibited.
Network	Messages are read, thus the traffic pattern of messages is explored.	Messages are changed, delayed, rearranged, or repeated. False messages are made.	Messages are lost or deleted. Relationship lines or networks become unavailable.

Considering a fundamental defence requires understanding the offense. We reviewed the 4 most common cybersecurity attacks (software, hardware, web and network) that hackers apply to disrupt and compromise assets. In addition, attackers have other options to gain unauthorized access to critical infrastructures and valuable personal information including initialization vector (IV) attack, bluesnarfing, phishing, DoS, and OS vulnerabilities.

There are numerous approaches may be applied to eliminate vulnerabilities and prevent threats to computer system (Ali et al, 2022). These approaches can be provided in the following in terms of functional requirements:

- Access Control, Awareness and Training
- Audit and Accountability
- Certification, Accreditation, Security and Risk Assessments
- Configuration Management and Contingency Planning
- Identification and Authentication
- Incident Response and Maintenance
- Media, communication, Physical, and Environmental Protection
- Personal security
- System and services Acquisition
- System and Information Integrate

This section reflects the need to focus on both technical and managerial perspectives to achieve Web service, Network, software and Hardware security in that regards.

1.4 Security Engineering and Risk Analysis

System engineer is something things happen as intended, but security engineer is something things don't happen. Security engineering is about building systems to remain dependable in the face of malice, error, or mischance. Similar to other systems engineering activities in that its primary motivation is to support the delivery of engineering solutions that satisfy pre-defined functional and user requirements, but it has the added dimension of preventing misuse and malicious behaviour.

Security engineers build the systems used to protect computer systems and networks and track incidents. Security Engineering is important because of nuclear safety control systems, medical equipment, automatic driving cars, ATM machines, aeroplane controls, banking systems, and transportation control systems, however, and failure of these systems may lead to death, injury, or serious harm (Jan et al., 2021). Therefore, failure of those systems may lead to death, injury, or serious harm. In 2017, National Institute of Standards and Technology (NIST) published some critical mechanisms for security engineering such as authentication (password, biometrics), authorisation (access control), cryptography (encryption, hashing, digital signature, etc), secure coding (input validation, session management, etc), redundant and fault-tolerant systems, and risk/security assessment. These mechanism includes supporting activities and specific focus area analysis on key topics within user-access management.

A cybersecurity frameworks, standards, guidelines provide a common language and set of processes for security managers within organisations and business to understand their security postures and those of their vendors. In essence, with these frameworks, standards, guidelines in place it becomes much easier to define the processes and procedures that the organization can take to assess, monitor, and minimize risk (Hanif et al. 2022). They can be categorised in the following way:

1. Domain-agnostic such as ISO/ IEC Standards, NIST, SANS 20 Critical Control, COBIT Security Baseline, Information Security Standard of Good practice, Cyber Resilience Framework and CMM, Shared Assessment Model/ SIG
2. Domain, technology or sector – specific such as NERC CIP, NIST800-82, NISTIR 7628, 3GPP (wireless telecommunications)
3. Other domain–specific standards bodies & Industry for a such as ATIS in a telecommunication domain

National Institute of Standards and Technology (NIST)

NIST was founded in 1901 and is now part of the U.S. Department of Commerce. NIST is one of the nation's oldest physical science laboratories which established the agency to eliminate some risks and uncertain evets to U.S. industrial competitiveness at the time (Özkan et al. 2021). It is an organization with strong values which managers and employees uphold these values via following its processes and procedures to achieve high performing environment that is safe and respectful of all. Particularly, this framework has been specifically designed with baseline approach for achieving security, 33 principles in total, technology agnostic, guideline for engineering secure systems and maps to stages of development, for businesses to understand security foundation and mitigating risks based rules and their increase resilience and reduce vulnerabilities.

NIST guidance:

- Security Foundation
- Risk Based Rules
- Ease of Use
- Increase Resilience
- Reduce vulnerabilities
- Design with Network in mind

Figure 2. Stages of SDLC Development

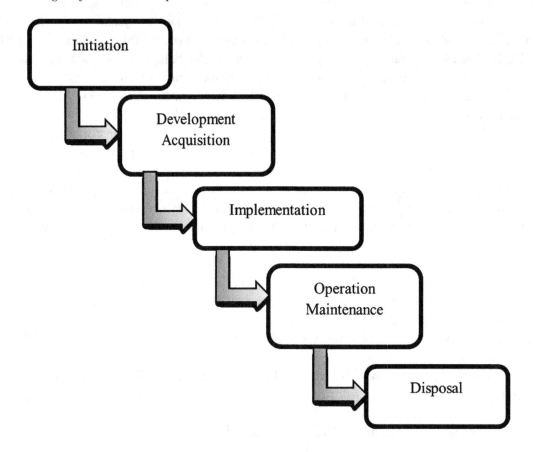

Security Foundation

- Step 1. Establish a sound 1 security policy
- Step 2. Treat security as an integral part of the overall security design
- Step 3. Clearly delineate the physical and logical security boundaries governed by associated security policies
- Step 4. Ensure that developers are trained in how to develop secure software

Risk Based Rules

- Step 5. Reduce risk to an acceptable level
- Step 6. Assume that external systems are insecure
- Step 7. Identify…trade-offs between reducing risk and increased costs and decrease in other aspects of operational effectiveness.
- Step 8. Implement tailored system security measures to meet organizational security goals.
- Step 9. Protect information while being processed, in transit, and in storage.
- Step 10. Consider custom products to achieve 10 adequate security
- Step 11. Protect against all likely classes of "attacks."

Ease of Use

- Step 12. Where possible, base security on open standards for portability and interoperability.
- Step 13. Use common language in developing security requirements.
- Step 14. Design security to allow for regular adoption of new technology, including a secure and logical technology upgrade process.
- Step 15. Strive for operational ease of use.

Increase Resilience

- Step 16. Implement layered security (Ensure no single point of vulnerability).
- Step 17. Design and operate an IT system to limit damage and to be resilient in response.
- Step 18. Provide assurance that the system is, and continues to be, resilient in the face of expected threats.
- Step 19. Limit or contain vulnerabilities
- Step 20. Isolate public access systems from mission critical resources (e.g., data, processes, etc.).
- Step 21. Use boundary mechanisms to separate computing systems and network infrastructures.
- Step 22. Design and implement audit mechanisms to detect unauthorized use and to support incident investigations.
- Step 23. Develop and exercise contingency or disaster recovery procedures to ensure appropriate availability.

Reduce Vulnerabilities

- Step 24. Strive for simplicity.
- Step 25. Minimize the system elements to be trusted.
- Step 26. Implement least privilege.
- Step 27. Do not implement unnecessary security mechanisms.
- Step 28. Ensure proper security in the shutdown or disposal of a system.
- Step 29. Identify and prevent common errors and vulnerabilities.

Design With Network in Mind

- Step 30. Implement security through a combination of measures distributed physically and logically
- Step 31. Formulate security measures to address multiple overlapping information domains.
- Step 32. Authenticate users and processes to ensure appropriate access control decisions both within and across domains.
- Step 33. Use unique identities to ensure 33 accountability

Therefore, a fundamental security engineering and analysis is any means taken to deal with a security threats, risks and attack. Ideally, we only need to know the attacker, built-in a comprehensive security,

2. CYBER ATTACK COUNTERMEASURES

A cyber countermeasure is defined as an action, process, system, facilitators, mechanism or technology that serves to prevent or eliminate the effects of a cyber-attack against a user, victim, computer, web, server, network or associated device. However, the focus of this section, is on four fundamental topics including security assessment and safeguards, cryptography, authentication protocols, and access control.

2.1 Security Risk Assessment and Safeguards

We now turn to the critical risk management factors of the IT security process. This stage is important, because without it there is any chance that resources cannot be deployed where they are most effective. Therefore, some risks are not addressed and leave the organization vulnerable, while other safeguards may be applied without wasting money, resources and time. Generally, every organizational asset is investigated and every imaginable risk is assessed for it. If a risk is assessed as too high, appropriate corrective controls and responses are implemented to mitigate the risk to an appropriate level. In practice, this is simply not possible. The time and effort required, for all type of organisations, is typically neither achievable nor affordable. Even if possible, the rapid rate of change in technologies (implementing new IT technologies) and the wider threat environment (risks) means that any assessment will become outdated as soon as it is completed, if not sooner! Generally, some sort of compromise assessment is required.

In addition, we have to make decision as to what constitutes to mitigate the risk to an acceptable level. In an ideal world, the aim is to completely mitigate risks. Again, this is clearly impossible. A more realistic alternative is to allocate some resources to risk mitigation commensurate with the potential costs to the organization if that risk were to happen. This process should also consider the likelihood of the hazard occurring. Determining an acceptable level of risk is simply prudential management and means that the resources expended are rational within the organization's available budget, time, and resources. The purpose of the risk management process is to provide management with the valuable information they require to make right decisions about where to apply resources.

All type of organisations, from small/medium organisations to national governments, there is simply a need for a range of alternatives to carry out this process. As mentioned in previous section, there are a range of frameworks, standards and guidelines that provide appropriate IT security risk assessment processes, including ISO/ IEC Standards, NIST, SANS 20 Critical Control, COBIT Security Baseline.

Particularly, ISO 13335 recognizes four approaches to identifying and minimising risks within an organization:

- Baseline approach
- Informal approach
- Detailed risk analysis approach
- Combined approach

Choosing among these is determined by the available resources and from a basic high-level risk analysis of how reasonable the IT systems are and how vital to the organizational business goals. Regulatory limitations can also need special approaches. This information should be distinguished when developing the Cybersecurity policies and strategies.

Baseline Approach

The goal of the baseline approach to risk management is to implement a basic level of security controls on information systems using baseline documentation, codes of practice, and industry best practices. The benefits of the baseline approach are that it does not require additional resources to perform a comprehensive risk management, and the same actions can be repeated across a wide range of systems. The main benefit is that special attention is not given to the changes at risk of the organisation based on who they are and how their systems are applied. Furthermore, it is a possibility that the baseline can be set too high, leading in costly security measures that may not be warranted, or may be set too low, leading in inadequate security and leaving the organization makes vulnerable.

Therefore, the baseline approach to risk management aims is to implement ideally agreed controls to develop protection against the most common risks. Thus, the baseline approach builds a right base from which further security measures may be organised. Appropriate baseline recommendations can be achieved from a wide range of organizations, including:

- Different national and international frameworks and standards
- Cybersecurity-related organizations such as the CERT, NSA, and so on
- Industry sector councils

Using a baseline approach is generally only recommended for small organizations without the resources to implement more formal approaches, at least it ensures that a basic level of security is applied, which is not guaranteed by the default settings of many systems.

Informal Approach

The goal of the informal approach to risk management is to conduct an informal and hands-on risk analysis for the organizational information systems. The risk analysis does not involve the use of organised and structured processes, but rather benefits from the tacit/explicit knowledge and expertise of the employees performing the risk analysis. These can either be internal consultations/experts or external experts/consultations. A major benefit of the formal approach is that the people performing the analysis need no additional skills. Therefore, an appropriate and informal risk management may be deployed partially quickly and cheaply. However, as the information technology systems are being determined, judgments may be made about too high vulnerabilities and risks to information systems that may the baseline approach could not address. Thus, in this approach, there is a possible that some vulnerabilities cannot be addressed properly and the results may be skewed by people's views and perceptions of the performing the analysis. It can thus lead to inadequate justification for recommended controls, resulting to questions over whether the proposed costs is clearly justified.

Hence, the informal approach might typically be suggested for small to medium scale organizations where the information systems are not required to meeting the organizational goals, and where additional costs cannot be justified.

Detailed Risk Analysis Approach

The fundamental approach is to conduct a detailed risk analysis of the information systems, applying a formal process. This approach provides the greatest degree of assurance that all main risks have been identified and their implications addressed. This process includes various steps including identifying assets, identifying threats and vulnerabilities to those assets, determining the likelihood of the risk occurring and its consequences for the organization if it occurs, and thus the risk the organization is exposed. With this information, suitable controls may be selected and implemented to address the identified risks. The benefits of this approach are that it provides the most accurate assessment of an organization's IT system security risks and provides a strong justification for the costs of proposed controls.

The detailed risk analysis approach also provides the comprehensive information for ongoing to manage risks as they evolve and change. The main disadvantage is the expenditure, experienced and skilled human resources, and the time taken to perform this risk analysis. Hence, the detailed risk analysis might generally recommended to large organizations with IT systems critical to their business objectives, some government organizations or businesses providing key services to them or key national infrastructure. For such organizations, there is no choice but to apply the detailed risk analysis approach.

Combined Approach

The combined approach components of the baseline, informal, and detailed risk analysis approaches. The goal of this approach is to provide acceptable levels of protection as much as possible then to determine and provide the protection controls applied on key information systems over time. The combined approach begins with the implementation of appropriate baseline security recommendations on all systems processes. Next, systems either subjected to high risk levels or keys to the organization's business goals are identified in the high-level risk analysis. Then a decision will be made to possibility fulfil an immediate informal risk management on critical systems, with focusing on the quickly modifying controls to more properly reflect their needs. Hence, a structured process of performing detailed risk analyses of these information systems may be established. This may conclude in the most suitable and cost-effective security controls being selected and implemented on these systems over time. The combined approach has a significant number of benefits. The utilization of the initial risk analysis to determine where further resources require to be considered, instead of facing a full detailed risk analysis of all information systems, can sell to management more easily. Furthermore, it can results in the development of a strategic management to identify where too high risks are likely to occur. It may provide an accurately planning aid in the subsequent management of the cybersecurity. Consequently, ISO 13335 standard considers for most organizations, in most circumstances as this standard is the most cost effective.

Security Safeguards

A risk assessment process within an organization identifies areas needing action. Thus organisations need to select appropriate controls to apply in this action. An IT security safeguard can help to mitigate/minimize risks. Stallings and Brown' model (2018) proposed three steps to implement IT security management controls including step 1: prioritize risks, step 2: respond to risks, and step 3: monitor risks. In the security context, control is defined as an action, process, or procedure that mitigates risk by preventing a security attack, by eliminating the harm it may cause, or by identifying and reporting risks to select corrective responses. The IT security management controls shown in Figure 3 include steps of implementation process of controls.

Figure 3. IT Security Management Controls and Implementation
(Stallings and Brown 2018, page 491)

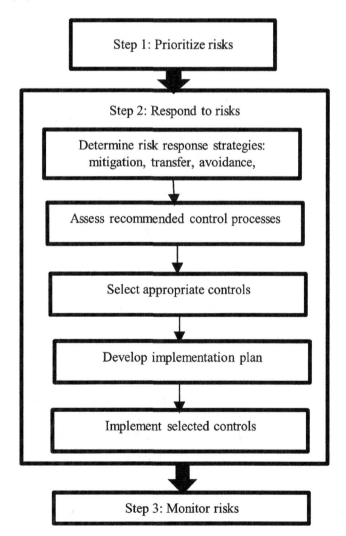

Some IT security management controls reduce multiple risks at the same time, thereby selecting suitable controls may be very cost effective. Controls will be categorised as the following mechanisms:

- **Management controls:** These controls refer to issues and procedures that management requirements to address such as security policies, principles, frameworks, and standards that influence the selection of both operational and technical controls to eliminate the risk and to protect the organizational objectives.
- **Operational controls:** These controls relate to mechanisms and processes that are primarily implemented by individuals instead of systems to address the implementation process. People use security policies, principles, frameworks, and standards ensuring consistency in security performances and correcting identified operational deficiencies.
- **Technical controls:** These controls relate to correct use of hardware and software security mechanisms in information systems. These simple and complex technical controls measures work together to secure key and sensitive information, and IT systems functions.

In turn, each of these control classes may include supportive controls (i.e. underlying technical IT security mechanisms), preventative controls (i.e. preventing security breaches from vulnerabilities), detection and recovery controls (i.e. providing means to restore the resulting lost computing resources).

2.2 Cryptography

A critical mechanism in many computer security applications is the utilization of Cryptography algorithms. This section provides an overview of use cryptography to secure communications and understand the role of cryptography in ensuring the integrity and authenticity of data. This section also focus on symmetric encryption as conventional encryption, or single-key encryption, was the only type of encryption in use prior to the implementation of public-key encryption in the late 1970s. This will enable us to understand the context within which the algorithms are used. Then, we look at some important block encryption algorithms to introduce a symmetric stream encryption and the widely used stream cipher RC4.

We focus on the application of encryption scheme to achieve confidentiality including five ingredients:

- **Plaintext:** This is an encrypted message, document or file that is fed into the cryptography algorithm as input.
- **Encryption algorithm:** The encryption algorithm refers to different sub-processes and transformations on the plaintext.
- **Secret key:** The secret key refers as an input to the cryptography algorithm. The exact sub-processes and transformations performed by the algorithm depend on the Secret key.
- **Ciphertext:** This is encrypted message transformed from plaintext and the secret key using an encryption algorithm as output. For a given message, two different keys can produce two different cipher messages including Substitution Transposition ciphers.
- **Decryption algorithm:** This algorithm type is used for encrypting data to encrypt and decrypt different parts of the texts, however, it takes the ciphertext and the same secret key and produces the plaintext.

Cryptographic systems are ideally categorised in following three independent factors:

1. **The way in which the plaintext transform into ciphertext.** The algorithms are considered as substitution principles, in which each factor in the plaintext is planned into another factor, and transposition principles, in which factors in the plaintext are redeveloped. The point is that no fundamental information be lost.
2. **The number of keys applied.** If both sender and receiver apply the same key, the cryptographic system is referred to as conventional encryption, symmetric, secret-key, or single-key. If the sender and receiver each use a different key, the cryptographic system is referred to as public-key encryption, asymmetric, or two-key.
3. **The processes used for plaintext.** A block ciphertext processes the input one block of factors continuously, producing output a block at a time, as it goes along.

The process of trying to explore the plaintext or key is known as cryptanalysis. The strategy applied by the cryptanalyst process relies on both the concept of the encryption algorithm and the information available to the cryptanalyst. In some cases, not even the encryption scheme is known, but typically, we presume the opponent does know the scheme applied for encryption. One type of the attacks under these conditions is the brute-force method of testing all possible keys. This becomes impractical if the key space is too large. Therefore, the opponent need to focus on an analysis of the ciphertext itself, generally applying various statistical tests to it. To use this approach, the opponent must have some general idea of the type of plaintext that is concealed, such as a message, an Excel file, and a Java source listing, so on. A ciphertext-only attack is the easiest to defend against because the adversary has the least amount of information to work with. Therefore, the analyser is able to gain one or more plaintext texts as well as their encryption algorithms as well as the analyser know that original plaintext patterns appear in a text.

Table 2. Types of Attacks on Encrypted Messages (Stallings and Brown, 2018)

Type of Attack	Known to Cryptanalyst
Ciphertex	• Encryption algorithm • Ciphertext to be decoded
plaintext	• Encryption algorithm • Ciphertext to be decoded • One or more plaintext–ciphertext pairs formed with the secret key
Chosen plaintext	• Encryption algorithm • Ciphertext to be decoded • Plaintext message chosen by cryptanalyst, together with its corresponding ciphertext generated with the secret key
Chosen ciphertext	• Encryption algorithm • Ciphertext to be decoded • Purported ciphertext chosen by cryptanalyst, together with its corresponding • decrypted plaintext generated with the secret key
Chosen text	• Encryption algorithm • Ciphertext to be decoded • Plaintext message chosen by cryptanalyst, together with its corresponding ciphertext generated with the secret key • Purported ciphertext chosen by cryptanalyst, together with its corresponding decrypted plaintext generated with the secret key

Hence, if the adversary is looking for some very specific data or information, parts of the message may be known. For example, if a complete accounting file is being transmitted, an adversary may know the placement of certain keywords in the file header. In addition, if the analyst can somehow force the source system to inject the message chosen by the analyst into the system, then a chosen plaintext attack is possible. Generally, if the analyst can select messages to encrypt, the analyst can intentionally select patterns that are expected to reveal the structure of the key.

As shown in Table 2, two other types of attack including chosen ciphertext and chosen text, are less dramatically used as cryptanalytic techniques but are nonetheless possible avenues of attack. Only relatively weak algorithms are not able to withstand a plaintext attack. In general, an encryption algorithm is developed to resist a plaintext attack. An encryption algorithm is computationally secure if the ciphertext produced by the algorithm meets some criteria including the cost of breaking the password is greater than the value of the encrypted information, and the time required to break the password is greater than the useful life of the information.

Unfortunately, it is not easy to estimate the amount of effort required to achieve successful analyse the ciphertext. Hence, presuming there are no essential mathematical weaknesses in the scheme, a brute-force approach is indicated, and here we can make rational estimates of costs and time. The brute-force method involves following every possible key until an apprehensible translation of the ciphertext into plaintext is achieved. In general, half of the possible keys can be tried to achieve success.

More cryptographic methods can be listed as following way:

- Mathematical rigour (definition of secrecy, PRNG)
- MAC (Message Authentication Code) using Symmetric Cipher
- Modern ciphers – Elliptic Curve, Lattice-Based Cryptography
- Quantum crypto
- Generating Keys from passwords (PBKDF, etc)
- Hashing passwords, salting, and attacks of password hashes

2.3 Authentication Protocols

Authentication is defined as the process of validating a reported identity that a user is who that person claims to be. An authentication protocol is the approach we use to perform that task. An authentication protocol authorize a receiving party to verify the identity of another person. All information systems apply some form of network authentication to authenticate users. As more sensitive information is stored electronically and as attackers become more adept at stealing it, authentication becomes more important, thus without authentication, losses may be significant.

The ten most popular authentication approaches organisations use include the following:

- **Kerberos:** If we work in a Windows environment, we have used the Kerberos protocol. This protocol relies on symmetric keys drawn from a central key distribution centre. Kerberos protocol is not complete, although the protections are significant.
- **LDAP:** LDAP is an open, vendor-neutral protocol for accessing and maintaining that static data such as usernames, passwords, email addresses, printer connections.

- **OAuth 2.0:** we applied OAuth 2.0 protocol, if we have ever applied a login from another site to get into a new site. In essence, an application pulls resources on behalf, and we don't have to share credentials.
- **RADIUS (Remote Access and Dial-in User Service):** RADIUS protocol verifies the information by comparing it to data in a database when we provide a username and password.
- **SAML:** SAML protocol exchanges authentication data between ID PS and service providers.
- **CHAP (Challenge-Handshake Authentication Protocol):** This protocol authenticates users periodically, even within the same session.
- **DIAMETER:** This system provides a guideline for authentication messages. It's derived from RADIUS, and it's provided a development upon RADIUS protocol.
- **EAP (Extensible authentication protocol):** Wireless networks and some connections mainly lean on EAP.
- **PAP (Password authentication protocol):** A sender submits a password, which the system compares to a database.
- **TACACS (Terminal Access Controller Access- Control System):** Accomplish IP-based authentication through this protocol, it includes encryption in last version.

2.4 Access Control

We focus on two definitions of access control in this section.

- NISTIR 7298 (Glossary of Key Information Security Terms, July 2019) defined access control as the process of presenting or denying specific requests to achieve and apply data/information and related data/information processing services as well as enter special physical mechanisms.
- RFC 4949 (Internet Security Glossary) defined access control as a procedure by which use of information system is regulated according to a specific security policy and is allowed just by authorized entities including users, programs, processes, or other systems according to that policy.

Therefore, we may consider access control as a central factor of IT security. The principal objectives of It security are to eliminate unauthorized users from obtaining access to information systems to eliminate legitimate users from accessing information systems in an unauthorized behaviour, and to enable legitimate users to access resources in an authorized behaviour.

Figure 4 shows a relationship between access control and IT security functions. Access control context involves the following principles and functions:

- Authentication: Verify that the credentials of a user or other system resources are credible.
- Authorization: This authorization function determines who is trusted for accessing a system resource.
- Audit: A comprehensive review and audition of system activities due to system controls, to ensure align with written policy and process, to eliminate breaches in security, and to suggest any modification in control, policy, and process.

Figure 4. Relationship between access control and IT security functions
Source: Based on [SAND94]

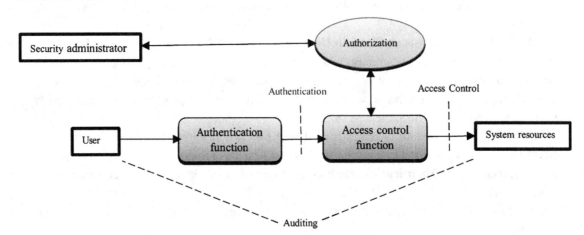

An access control function mediates between a user and system entity, such as applications, information systems, firewalls, files, storages, and databases. The system need to validate a system resource seeking access. Generally, the authentication function determines if the user is authorized to access the system at all. Hence, the access control function determines whether the especial requested access by the user is authorized. A security administrator sustains an authorization database that specifies what kind of access control function to which entity is permitted for this user. The access control function assists this database to assign whether to grant access. An auditing action controls, monitors and keeps a record of user accesses to system entity.

An access control function can be embodied in an authorization database, however, it can determine what kind of access are authorized, under what conditions, and by whom. Access control policies can be grouped into the following classifications:

- **Discretionary access control (DAC):** This access control is designed based on the identity of the requestor and on access authorizations indicating what users are permitted to do. The DAC is subjected optional as a resource may have access permissions that allow the resource, by its own volition, to enable another resource to access some entities.

- **Mandatory access control (MAC):** This access control is developed based on comparing critical system resources with security clearances. The MAC is assumed mandatory as a resource that has clearance to access an entity might not, just by its own volition, enable another resources to access that entity.

- **Role-based access control (RBAC):** This access control is designed based on the policies that requestors have within the system and on policies indicating what accesses are permitted to requestors in specific policies.

- **Attribute-based access control (ABAC):** This access control is developed based on attributes of the requestors, the entity to be accessed, and current environmental situations.

Discretionary access control is the traditional methodology of developing access control policy. Mandatory access control is a concept that evolved out of needs for military computer security and is best covered in the context of cybersecurity. Both Role-based access control and Attribute-based access control have become significantly popular. These four access control mechanisms are not mutually exclusive, an access control policy may apply two or even all three of these mechanisms to cover different policies of security system resources.

3. REAL-TIME CYBER THREAT DETECTION AND MITIGATION

This section looks at some of the most widely used and important Internet security protocols and standards. We focus on understanding the basic operation of data networked communications and investigating protocols network operations such as DKIM, IPs, DNS, TCP/TLS, HTTP and etc. However, the focus of this section, is on three fundamental topics including network security, web security, secure sockets layer and transport layer security, and legal and ethical aspects.

3.1 Network Security and Web Security

Domain keys identified mail (DKIM) is a determination for cryptographic signing of email messages that allows a signing domain to take responsibility for a message in an email flow. Recipients of a message may verify the signature by investigating the signing domain immediately to recover the suitable public key, however verifying that the message was authenticated by the party holding the signing domain's private key. DKIM is widely used by a wide range of email providers, including corporations, government agencies, Gmail, Yahoo and many ISPs (Saeed et al. 2021).

To understand how DKIM works, it's helpful to have a basic understanding of the Internet email architecture currently defined in RFCs 5598 (Internet Mail Architecture, 2009). Internet mail architecture fundamentally is defined as a user world in the form of MUAs (Message User Agents) component as well as a transport world in the form of MHS (Message Handling Services) component that includes MTA (Message Transfer Agents). The MHS generally adopts a message from a person and delivers it to another, building a virtual MUA-to-MUA dynamic environment. This architecture includes three types of interoperability including: interoperability requirements between users that messages can be formatted by the MUA that the message must be displayed by the destination MUA to the recipient of the message, interoperability requirements between the MUA and the MHS components that messages are posted from an MUA to the MHS first, then they are delivered from the MHS to the destination MUA and interoperability is required between the MTA elements along the transfer path through the MHS.

Figure 5 shows the critical components of the Internet mail architecture, which include the following:

- **Message User Agent (MUA):** This component focuses on user actors and user applications which it can be considered as their representative within the e-mail service. Generally, this function might be located on the user's computer and is defined as an e-mail client program or a local network e-mail server. The author MUA component creates a message and enforces initial submission into the MHS through a MSA. The receivers MUA processes the mail for storing or displaying.
- **Mail submission agent (MSA):** this component adopts the submitted mail by author MUA and performs the policies and principles of the requirements of Internet standards. This function is housed in the MUA or as a separate model. In some case, the Simple Mail Transfer Protocol (SMTP) is applied between the MUA and the MSA components.

- **Message transfer agent (MTA):** This components relays mail simply for an application-level, that is similar with a packet switch for moving the message closer to the receivers.
- **Mail delivery agent (MDA):** this components is responsible for moving the message from the MHS to the message store.
- **Message store (MS):** This component might be located on a machine as the MUA or a remote server. Clearly, an MUA retrieves messages from a remote server including Post Office Protocol (POP) and Internet Message Access Protocol (IMAP).

Figure 5. Key components and Protocols in the Internet Mail Architecture
(Stallings and Brown 2018, Page 688)

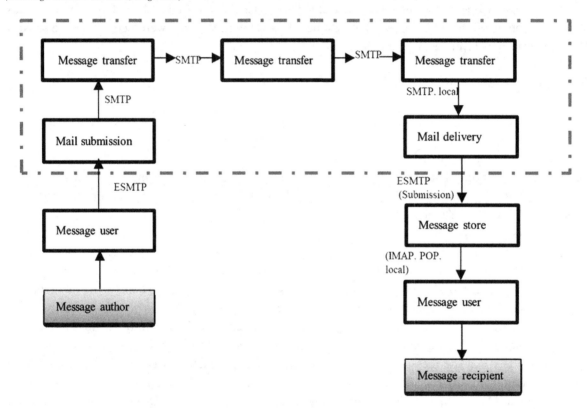

3.2 Secure Sockets Layer (SSL) and Transport Layer Security (TLS)

One of the most popular security services is the Secure Sockets Layer (SSL) and the follow-on Internet standard RFC 4346 (The Transport Layer Security Protocol Version 1.1, 2006). Transport Layer Security (TLS) has greatly supplanted fundamentally SSL implementations (Hansman, 2004). Typically, TLS is defined as a general-purpose service including a set of protocols that rely on TCP. At the fundamental level, TLS can be considered as kind of the underlying protocol suite and thus may be transparent to applications (Schreider & Noakes-Fry, 2017). Further, TLS may be embedded in some special packages. In general, TLS is developed to make use of TCP to deliver a reasonable end-to-end security service. TLS is not only a security protocol, instead it can considered as a two layers of protocols, as shown in Figure 6.

Figure 6. Secure sockets layer and Transport layer security Protocols
(Stallings and Brown 2018, Page 690)

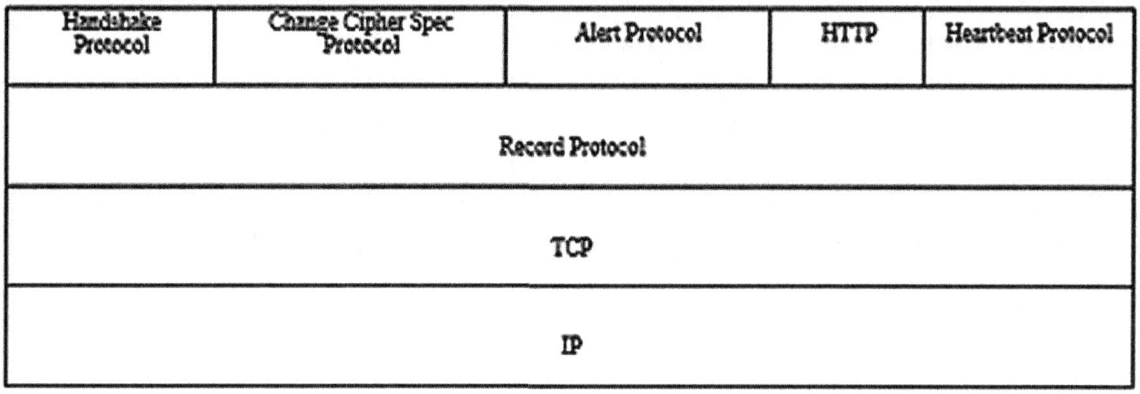

Handshake Protocol	Change Cipher Spec Protocol	Alert Protocol	HTTP	Heartbeat Protocol
Record Protocol				
TCP				
IP				

The Record Protocol is define as a fundamental security services to different higher-layer protocols. In general, the Hypertext Transfer Protocol (HTTP) can act on top of TLS. HTTP provides the transfer service for Web client/server interaction. In addition, three higher-layer protocols are considered as part of TLS including the Alert Protocol, the Change Cipher Spec Protocol, and the Handshake Protocol that they are used in the management of TLS exchanges.

SST and TLS Attacks

Since the introduction of SSL in 1994 and the subsequent standardization of TLS, a number of attacks against these protocols have been devised. The identification of each attack requires changes in the protocol through encryption tools or some mechanisms of the SSL and TLS implementation to counter these attacks.

However, threats can be categorized in the following way:

- **Attacks on the Handshake Protocol**: A method is developed to compromise the Handshake Protocol based on exploiting the RSA encryption scheme implementation (countermeasures implementation). Thus the attack was reformed and adjusted to not only thwart the countermeasures, but also to speed up the attack.
- **Attacks on the record and application data protocols:** Some vulnerabilities or risks have been identified in the record and application data protocol, leading to patches to counter the new risks/ threats.
- **Attacks on the PKI:** Investigating the validity of X.509 certificates is a learning activity into a variety of attacks, both in the concepts of SSL/TLS and elsewhere. The users identified issues in the source code of OpenSSL, GnuTLS, JSSE, ApacheHttpClient, Weberknecht, cURL, PHP, Python, and applications build upon or with these products.

However, the history of attacks and countermeasures for SSL/TLS is representative of that for other Internet-based protocols. A "perfect" protocol and a "perfect" implementation strategy will never be achieved. The constant trade-off between threats and countermeasures determines the evolution of Internet-based protocols.

Hypertext Transfer Protocol Secure (HTTPS)

Hypertext Transfer Protocol Secure (HTTPS) is defined as a protocol to implement secures communication and data transfer between a user's Web browser and Web server (Shafi et al. 2019). The HTTPS mechanism is created into all Web browsers, the use of which relies on the Web server protecting HTTPS communication. Hence, the following factors of the communication are encrypted once HTTPS is used:

- URL of the requested document
- Contents of the document
- Contents of browser forms (filled in by browser user)
- Cookies sent from browser to server and from server to browser
- Contents of HTTP header

HTTPS is documented in RFC 2818, however there is no major change in using HTTP over either SSL or TLS, and both security protocols are considered as a HTTPS.

3.3 Legal and Ethical Aspects

An issue that overlaps significantly with computer security is privacy. Concerns about the extent to which personal privacy is compromised may lead to a variety of legal and technical approaches to strengthen privacy rights. Therefore, a number of organizations or governments have adopted policies and regulations to protect the privacy of individuals (Reuvid, 2018).

Cybersecurity researcher has suggested a definition of a set of functional requirements in a privacy class, which may be implemented in a trusted system. The aim of the privacy functions is to protect a user against disclosure and misuse of identity by other users.

Privacy can be grouped into the following classifications:

- Anonymity
- Pseudonymity
- Unlinkability
- Unobservability

Nevertheless, the importance of information systems within organisations lead to emerge many potential misuses and abuses of information and electronic communication that create privacy and security problems. In addition, issues of legality, misuse and abuse raise concerns of ethics (Zulkifl et al. 2022). Ethics is defined as a system of moral policies that relates to the benefits damages of special actions, and to the rightness and wrongness of motives and ends of those actions. Stallings and Brown (2018) pointed out that computer have become the primary repository of both personal information and negotiable assets, so these assets can merely be viewed, created, and altered by technical and automated means. Those who can figure out and exploit the technology as well as those who have achieved access permission, have power related to those assets.

Furthermore, it has always been the case that those with special knowledge or special skills have additional ethical obligations beyond those common to all humanity. Figure 7 illustrated an ethical hierarchy, at the top of the hierarchy are the ethical values professionals share with all human beings, such as integrity, fairness, and care. Ay the middle level of the hierarchy are general principles applicable to all professionals, being a professional with specific training imposes additional ethical obligations with respect to those affected by their work. Finally, each profession has associated with it specific ethical values and obligations related to the specific knowledge of those in the profession and the powers that they have to affect others (Khadam et al. 2021; Villalón-Fonseca, 2022).

Figure 7. The Ethical Hierarchy
(Stallings and Brown 2018, Page 619)

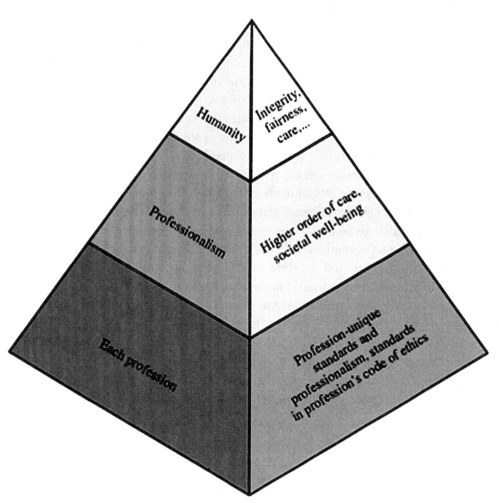

However, a classic article on security and ethics noticed that ethical issues arises as results of the principles of computer science, such as the following:

- **Repositories and processors of information:** Unauthorized use of computer services without use or information storage on computers raises questions of appropriateness or fairness.
- **Producers of new forms and types of assets:** computer systems are completely new kind of systems, possibly not purpose to the same contests of ownership as other systems.
- **Instruments of acts:** Computer services and users and developers must be responsible for the integrity and appropriateness of computer assets.
- **Symbols of intimidation and deception:** A computer system is a machine, absolute truth producer, not subject to blame, and as anthropomorphic replacements of human resources who err could be carefully considered.

4. SUMMARY OF THE CHAPTER

Many computer security researchers have discussed that security research or implementations are crucial to the clear understanding and addressing of cybersecurity issues and challenges. Without standards, it may be difficult for organisations to understand some of the basic concepts and interactions among security functions. The overview of cybersecurity issues reinforce the security concepts introduced in the chapter, give the organisations a greater appreciation of how a cryptographic or security function works, and can motivate users and managers and give them confidence that they are capable of not only exploring but implementing the details of a security capability.

In this chapter, we have tried to present the concepts of cybersecurity as clearly as possible and have provided numerous cyber threats and attacks to understand those concepts. However, many organisations will wish to identify and manage those threats and attacks and analyse risks. This chapter also provides some frameworks and guidelines and describes security protocols available in that regard. Finally, two concepts: security awareness program and security training program can facilitate managers and users within an organisation to protect their valuable and sensitive information/ data. **Security awareness program** refers to inform and focus a users' attention on issues related to security within the organization. Such programs includes security basics and literacy factors, given the widespread utilisation of information systems in organizations. Therefore, users are aware of their responsibilities for securing data and the restrictions on their activities in the interests of security, and are motivated to act accordingly. Employees understand the significance of security for the well-being of the organization. **Security training program** refers to teach employees the skills to operate their IT related actions more securely. Depending on the role of the user, training teaches what they should do and how they should do it.

REFERENCES

Al Obaidan, F., & Saeed, S. (2021). Digital Transformation and Cybersecurity Challenges: A Study of Malware Detection Using Machine Learning Techniques. In Handbook of Research on Advancing Cybersecurity for Digital Transformation (pp. 203-226). IGI Global. doi:10.4018/978-1-7998-6975-7.ch011

Ali, S., Hafeez, Y., Bilal, M., Saeed, S., & Kwak, K. S. (2022). Towards Aspect Based Components Integration Framework for Cyber-Physical System. *Computers Materials & Continua*, *70*(1), 653–668. doi:10.32604/cmc.2022.018779

Almashhadani, A. O., Carlin, D., Kaiiali, M., & Sezer, S. (2022). MFMCNS: A multi-feature and multi-classifier network-based system for ransomworm detection. *Computers & Security, 121*, 102860. doi:10.1016/j.cose.2022.102860

Almuhaideb, A. M., & Saeed, S. (2020). Fostering sustainable quality assurance practices in outcome-based education: Lessons learned from ABET accreditation process of computing programs. *Sustainability, 12*(20), 8380. doi:10.3390u12208380

Bloom, B. (1970, July). Space/time Trade-offs in Hash Coding with Allowable Errors. *Communications of the ACM, 13*(7), 422–426. doi:10.1145/362686.362692

Bonneau, J. (2012). The Science of Guessing: Analyzing an Anonymized Vorpus of 70 Million Passwords. *IEEE Symposium on Security and Privacy.* 10.1109/SP.2012.49

Clark, K., Duckham, M., Guillemin, M., Hunter, A., McVernon, J., O'Keefe, C., Pitkin, C., Prawer, S., Sinnott, R., Warr, D., & Waycott, J. (2015). *Guidelines for the Ethical use of Digital Data in Human Research.* The University of Melbourne.

Dalziel, H. (2014). *Introduction to US Cybersecurity Careers.* Syngress.

De Carvalho, A. F. P., Saeed, S., Reuter, C., Rohde, M., Randall, D., Pipek, V., & Wulf, V. (2022). Understanding Nomadic Practices of Social Activist Networks through the Lens of Infrastructuring: the Case of the European Social Forum. *Computer Supported Cooperative Work (CSCW),* 1-39. 10.100710606-022-09442-7

Enoch, S. Y., Moon, C. Y., Lee, D., Ahn, M. K., & Kim, D. S. (2022). A practical framework for cyber defence generation, enforcement and evaluation. *Computer Networks, 208*, 108878. doi:10.1016/j.comnet.2022.108878

Frahim, J. (2015). *Securing the Internet of Things: A Proposed Framework.* Cisco White Paper.

Hanif, M., Ashraf, H., Jalil, Z., Jhanjhi, N. Z., Humayun, M., Saeed, S., & Almuhaideb, A. M. (2022). AI-Based Wormhole Attack Detection Techniques in Wireless Sensor Networks. *Electronics (Basel), 11*(15), 2324. doi:10.3390/electronics11152324

Hansman, S., & Hunt, R. (2004). A Taxonomy of Network and Computer Attacks. *Computers & Security.*

Jan, S. U., Abbasi, I. A., & Algarni, F. (2021). A key agreement scheme for IoD deployment civilian drone. *IEEE Access: Practical Innovations, Open Solutions, 9*, 149311–149321. doi:10.1109/ACCESS.2021.3124510

Khadam, U., Iqbal, M. M., Saeed, S., Dar, S. H., Ahmad, A., & Ahmad, M. (2021). Advanced security and privacy technique for digital text in smart grid communications. *Computers & Electrical Engineering, 93*, 107205. doi:10.1016/j.compeleceng.2021.107205

Luk, M. (2007). MiniSec: A Secure Sensor Network Communication Architecture. *International Conf. on Information Processing in Sensor Networks.* 10.1109/IPSN.2007.4379708

Özkan, E., Azizi, N., & Haass, O. (2021). Leveraging smart contract in project procurement through dlt to gain sustainable competitive advantages. *Sustainability, 13*(23), 13380. doi:10.3390u132313380

Reuvid, J. (Ed.). (2018). *Managing Cybersecurity Risk: Cases Studies and Solutions.* Legend Press Ltd.

Saeed, S., Almuhaideb, A. M., Bamarouf, Y. A., Alabaad, D. A., Gull, H., Saqib, M., Iqbal, S. Z., & Salam, A. A. (2021). Sustainable Program Assessment Practices: A Review of the ABET and NCAAA Computer Information Systems Accreditation Process. *International Journal of Environmental Research and Public Health, 18*(23), 12691. doi:10.3390/ijerph182312691 PMID:34886417

Schreider, T., & Noakes-Fry, K. (2017). *The manager's guide to cybersecurity law: essentials for today's business.* Academic Press.

Shafi, A., Saeed, S., Bamarouf, Y. A., Iqbal, S. Z., Min-Allah, N., & Alqahtani, M. A. (2019). Student outcomes assessment methodology for ABET accreditation: A case study of computer science and computer information systems programs. *IEEE Access: Practical Innovations, Open Solutions, 7,* 13653–13667. doi:10.1109/ACCESS.2019.2894066

Stallings, W., & Brown, L. (2018). *Computer security: principles and practice* (4th ed.). Pearson Education Limited.

Villalón-Fonseca, R. (2022). The nature of security: A conceptual framework for integral-comprehensive modelling of IT security and cybersecurity. *Computers & Security, 120,* 102805. doi:10.1016/j.cose.2022.102805

Zulkifl, Z., Khan, F., Tahir, S., Afzal, M., Iqbal, W., Rehman, A., Saeed, S., & Almuhaideb, A. M. (2022). FBASHI: Fuzzy and Blockchain-Based Adaptive Security for Healthcare IoTs. *IEEE Access: Practical Innovations, Open Solutions, 10,* 15644–15656. doi:10.1109/ACCESS.2022.3149046

Chapter 3
Cybersecurity and Blockchain Usage in Contemporary Business

Imdad Ali Shah
Taylor's University, Malaysia

N. Z. Jhanjhi
 https://orcid.org/0000-0001-8116-4733
Taylor's University, Malaysia

Areeba Laraib
Mehran University of Engineering and Technology, Pakistan & Shaheed Zulfiqar Ali Bhutto Campus, Pakistan

ABSTRACT

The use of computers is becoming more and more common. The power and maliciousness of powerful attackers are increasing. Organizations must improve their ability to mitigate information security threats. Adequate protection is more critical than ever. With websites and social media platforms holding a wealth of personal information and potentially damaging content, attackers use the internet's sophisticated hacking tools to cause harm to individuals and organizations. Attacks have become stealthier, with more significant economic damage and broader damage. Blockchain must be the solution to the security problem of financial transactions. However, judging from the results and expected answers from the industry and organization, it is crucial to understand how financial institutions deal with these issues by looking at blockchain deployments in cybersecurity. A blockchain is a digital database that records all mentoring transactions. This technology supports many different exchanges that are currently in use. The authors also believe that blockchain should be integrated into many parts of cybersecurity. The primary goal of this chapter is to review relevant research papers and book chapters over the past 10 years to understand how successful cybersecurity and blockchain implementations have been in the enterprise and to identify the different challenges and concerns that enterprise personnel face. They also provide suggestions and solutions to problems.

DOI: 10.4018/978-1-6684-5284-4.ch003

1. INTRODUCTION

As businesses begin to reshape their futures, they may investigate how blockchain technology can help them grow. While blockchain has the potential to benefit every sector, there are some misconceptions about the technology that could hinder businesses from implementing it. Blockchain database technology is known for supporting and securing Bitcoin transactions, but its applicability to more considerable cybersecurity challenges is just beginning. The genius of blockchain technology lies in its ability to verify transactions between parties and then keep a permanent record of those transactions on a decentralized network. Due to its nature, falsifying records in a blockchain ledger is extremely difficult at best. The technological world is accelerating. Technology has exploded, enabling companies to reach new heights of profitability and survival Nguyen, D. C, (2020). Artificial intelligence and machine learning have revolutionized the business environment, not just in terms of innovative commodities and technologies. Blockchain technology is disrupting banking procedures and allowing business leaders to elevate lawyers to do more for corporate goals Hassan, M. U (2019). While technological advancements, especially blockchain technology, have allowed the accounting profession to advance and establish itself, we also expressed concerns about the general cybersecurity of various businesses. When a new technology is implemented within a company or department, it affects most different levels of accounting. Relatively successful technology is being implemented in the accounting industry and cybersecurity Siegfried, N. (2020), Michelin, R. A. (2018), Yu, Y (2018). This study aims to fill in gaps in the literature and contribute to previous research that provides a broad perspective on the impact of blockchain technology on accounting Huang, J 2019. From a local or centralized accounting system, the software gradually evolved to a decentralized system using the Internet in the early stages of its use Ray, B. C. (2019), De Filippi (2020) This also reduces errors in the middle, the number of middlemen, and the need to pay royalties and other secondary activities to others. Everyone can see what action is happening; thousands of computers are entirely transparent and constantly verified Uddin, Ozyılmaz, K. R. (2017), Uddin, M. A. (2019). Financial service companies and technology-based organizations are essential contributors to the explosive growth of blockchain technology Dhar Dwivedi, A (2019). The company's cybersecurity has always been an issue due to hacking. Many large corporations' future success and wealth now depend on their ability to withstand this external risk Fujimura, S., (2015). Most of these attacks have always been aimed at obtaining sensitive information about transactions and financial resources held by businesses, basic blockchain mechanisms in fig 1.

Figure 1. Overview of basic blockchain mechanisms
ResearchGate, 2022

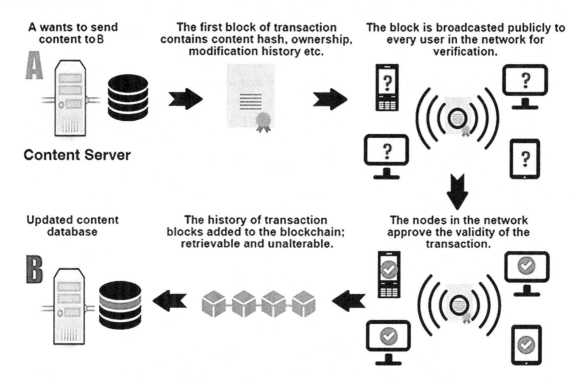

The following points have been discussed in this chapter:

1. We focused on the blockchain and its role in business activities.
2. We focused on security issues and challenges in the business environment.
3. We focused on business applications in the context of past research articles and book chapters in the last ten years.
4. We provided recommendations and solutions to issues and challenges.

2. LITERATURE REVIEW

Today's technological capabilities mean many data systems, including almost all accounting systems, utilize the concept of a centralized database. A closed system database with a single administrator is called a "centralized database". Even though data is collected from multiple sources and locations, it is stored on a single controller server. It gives businesses complete control over their data systems, including access points and data governance Gao, F., (2018). Blockchain technology is becoming more and more well-known. Cryptocurrency is a digital currency with no tangible exchange form, only electronic transactions Gazali, H. M, (2017). The fact that the government does not currently regulate cryptocurrencies will be explored in depth later in this article. Despite the authorities' interest in blockchain, the US has no accounting laws. For example, the U.S. government prints and manages the U.S. dollar and controls the currency's circulation. The trading and digital circulation of cryptocurrencies are controlled by computer algorithms. Purchase orders, invoices, and payment receipts are examples of these documents. When an electronic funds transfer is initiated, funds are sent from the originator's bank to the recipient's bank. After that, the recipient will confirm the payment with the sender. Due to its decentralized structure, transactions can take place on the blockchain network, and if all requirements are met, data miners will verify and complete the transaction Herian, R. (2017), Ishmaev, G., (2017). Businesses that rely on a centralized architecture to deliver secret information and meet customer needs are vulnerable to cyber-attacks and incur higher operational costs. This is because centralized systems only need one entry point to be provoked. To achieve the effectiveness of the IoT, a blockchain approach would be a better choice Huckle, S, (2016). It's a distributed network with encrypted data, nodes that can't be hacked, and a consensus process that prohibits hostile actors from meddling with the system Kewell, B., (2021). IoT works with cloud servers, and as the number of people using these networks grows daily, there are some worries about how to keep up with the demand. The more users are involved, the more capacity must be built for them, just like with any other continuously developing program or platform, blockchain Distributed Databases in fig 2.

Figure 2. Overview of blockchain Distributed Databases
Lee, B 2017.

Distributed ledger technology (DLT) based on peer-to-peer networks isn't new, but it's difficult to grasp for the public. Some have also been hailed as the most innovative technological development of the new century. How they vary makes blockchains appealing for a wide range of industrial applications.

3. EVALUATION OF BLOCKCHAIN IN CYBERSECURITY, FOR NOW, A DAYS BUSINESS

Blockchain is quickly establishing itself as one of the most reliable and robust methods of cybersecurity available. Regarding information exchange, the current rules we have been working on for years will use trusted intermediaries. The intermediary is responsible for securing the transaction and any difficulties that may arise along the way, such as security breaches. Commercial blockchain technology is helpful for entities that transact with each other. Permissioned users can use distributed ledger technology to simultaneously access the same information, increasing efficiency, building trust, and reducing friction. Blockchain can also quickly adjust the size and scale of solutions, and many solutions can be customized to do many jobs across sectors. The benefits of blockchain for businesses are based on four characteristics unique to the technology. Blockchain is transforming businesses in all walks of life around the world. More trust can increase efficiency by avoiding duplication of work, and blockchain technology is transforming supply chains, food delivery, financial services, government, retail and other industries. When a block of an event record is accepted, it is immediately generated across all ledgers for all participants in that channel. Each network partner can access a single "trusted reality" of transactions, which they may see and share. More blocks can be added but not withdrawn, ensuring a permanent record of all transactions and increasing stakeholder trust. Blocks can only be created and accessed by authorized entities. Access is granted only to trusted parties. There is no need to establish such a central authority between two parties due to the ability to take advantage of the blockchain's clean, trustworthy, and decentralized public ledger

Lee, S. H., (2018). Blockchain security is significantly higher than previous solutions, and a company's investment in the blockchain technology should be a strategic decision. The middleman: Blockchain provides a secure solution that allows these transactions to happen while eliminating the middleman Li, X. (2020). A blockchain is an excellent tool for cybersecurity and reliability. At all times, blockchain can ensure anonymity and security O'Leary, K (2017). This shows that the industry must be checked to ensure blockchain is the right technology to implement,

Shah, I. A., (2022). Its permanency, authenticity, and blockchain technology can help businesses enhance their operations Tosh, D., (2017). Although most big firms accept blockchain as a reality, many doubt its practicality as an option for improving their business operations. The expense and difficulty of implementation are the primary reasons why businesses Conoscenti, M., (2016). Blockchain technology rapidly advances in various fields, but CEOs lack sufficient experience in making business choices based on Zhao, J. L (2016). Thanks to the way blockchain operate, it is feasible to increase the security of both forward and backward links in supply chains. Every link in the supply chain can be tracked, and the sources of vulnerability may be identified. Given the public availability of blockchain, it may be assumed that it might be used to hunt down recalled items rather than the current approach that firms use when a product appears to be more susceptible to viral issues. Many of the primary supply chain security concerns may be addressed by utilizing the blockchain Journal of Management Analytics techniques Karafiloski, E., (2017). This can be an example of what a blockchain can accomplish when fully exploiting its capabilities as a security framework. After discussing the application of blockchain in cybersecurity, it is easy to see its value in the accounting industry. Accounting requires secure record-keeping and the implementation of proper processes. While blockchain remains the basic purpose it exhibits when used for higher levels of cybersecurity, these same uses are also used for accounting Karafiloski, E., (2017). The invention and implementation of blockchain technology make the preparation and evaluation of annual financial statements unnecessary. Accounting and a range of other applications can benefit from using blockchain to record and report transactions and other financial statements Sengupta, J., (2020). Many of the goals that auditors and other accountants want to achieve with their information and data are met by blockchain technology. To some extent, the accuracy of the information verified after the audit can be guaranteed, but it can never be guaranteed that it is error-free. Therefore, after an audit is completed, it is risk-rated based on the independent auditor's judgement. The concept with proven accurate data Miglani, A., (2020), Alladi, T., (2020). To improve regulation and prevent financial fraud, a blockchain is being used. Financial misbehaviour is a problem that emerges in the corporate world. This misconduct might arise because of unethical acts by a corporation Hassija, V., (2019). This shows serious concerns about the lack of communication between countries. This is where blockchain technology might come in handy in the accounting field. If these organizations use blockchain, it proposes a way to "aggregate misconduct complaints without relying on a single party" Shah, I. A., (2022). Humayun, M., (2020). All parties involved can clearly and transparently observe any misconduct related to the various IDs. This service is almost free and provides a more efficient program to protect the entire company, blockchain Distributed ledger types in fig 3.

Figure 3. Overview of blockchain Distributed ledger types
Euromoney, 2022.

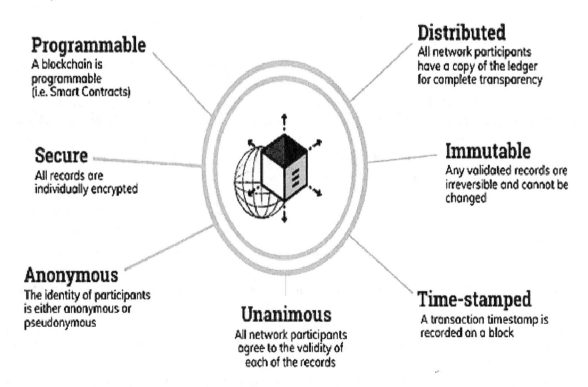

Due to their data structure, sequencing, power requirements, real-world implementation, and usage of currency, blockchains differ from other distributed ledger formats. While consensus is a crucial feature of DLT, developers can utilize a variety of approaches to achieve it, including proof of stake (PoS) and proof of work (PoW) (PoW). A DLT does not necessitate the construction of a blockchain from a structural standpoint.

3.1 When Blockchain and Cybersecurity Meet

The cybersecurity triangle highlights the importance of confidentiality, integrity, and availability for any network. While blockchains provide integrity through a decentralized validation network and accessibility through the public display of block transactions, they do not offer secrecy Singh, A. P., (2020). On the other hand, data stored on blockchains should only be information that businesses are ready to make public.

3.2 Protecting Our Secrecy of Information

Because of the variable rights, and restrictions, network managers are increasingly struggling to secure critical assets and resources. Unlike data for a conventional network, which might be separated and stored in-house, blockchains are public, networked, and distributed over an external network of nodes.

4. BLOCKCHAIN APPLICATIONS FOR THE BUSINESS

Although blockchain technology emerged with Bitcoin, blockchain has far-reaching potential beyond today's cryptocurrencies. Beyond cryptocurrencies, blockchain offers a variety of applications in financial services, supply chains, and the public sector Kumar, M. S., (2021). Below are some blockchain applications that help industries and business activities become more efficient and faster figure 4.

Figure 4. Overview of blockchain application for business

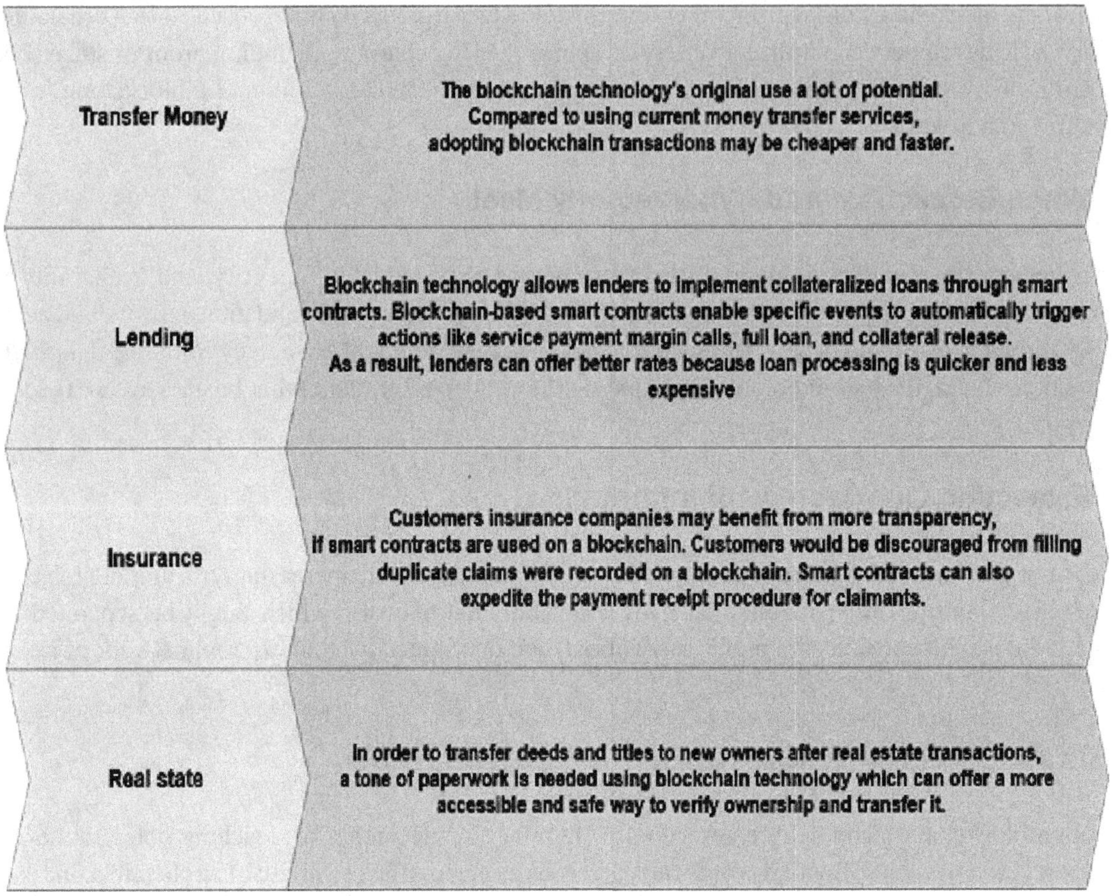

Transfer Money	The blockchain technology's original use a lot of potential. Compared to using current money transfer services, adopting blockchain transactions may be cheaper and faster.
Lending	Blockchain technology allows lenders to implement collateralized loans through smart contracts. Blockchain-based smart contracts enable specific events to automatically trigger actions like service payment margin calls, full loan, and collateral release. As a result, lenders can offer better rates because loan processing is quicker and less expensive
Insurance	Customers insurance companies may benefit from more transparency, if smart contracts are used on a blockchain. Customers would be discouraged from filling duplicate claims were recorded on a blockchain. Smart contracts can also expedite the payment receipt procedure for claimants.
Real state	In order to transfer deeds and titles to new owners after real estate transactions, a tone of paperwork is needed using blockchain technology which can offer a more accessible and safe way to verify ownership and transfer it.

5. BUSINESS EXECUTION ON BLOCKCHAIN

Blockchain may be customized to meet the demands of every enterprise. There are four primary types of blockchain choices that businesses may pick from Gill, S. H., (2022). each with its advantages.

5.1 Semi-private

The blockchain-based concept is comparable to the semi-private blockchain. Regarding the number of checks in place, this blockchain concept falls between permission and permissionless. One firm sets the requirements for access to the net, and as long as the conditions are met, that user is authorized to see and transact on the network Saeed, S., (2020). This form of blockchain, according to SAP, is "appealing for business-to-business use cases and systems integration."

5.2 Private

A private blockchain is like a centralized internal ERP system. It may be controlled and managed by an administrator who authorizes users. Users can be granted either read-only or update access to the blockchain, allowing users to trade. This sort of blockchain, according to SAP, is not suitable for use in production situations Muzammal, S. M., (2021). Because this is a centralized database, outsider organizations can only do business and access the register if they can connect to the organization's network remotely. This negates the point of blockchain because many advantages acquired via external connections are unavailable.

5.3 Public

The public blockchain is the most well-known blockchain, as it is used by cryptocurrencies like bitcoin for their peer-to-peer network. Anyone with an internet connection and a server may use the blockchain to read and conduct transactions Muzammal, S. M., (2020). Because this sort of blockchain has no regulatory authority, it operates in a permissionless environment. Because of the network's architecture, all users may remain anonymous in their transactions. Businesses, particularly substantial multinational corporations, are continually improving their operations. Software and technical innovations are heavily linked with operational improvements in today's technological environment. To guarantee that there are no threats to the segregation of tasks, management, internal audit, and external auditors must rigorously examine the software. Conflicts in the segregation of tasks represent a significant danger to an external auditor Ullah, A. (2020), Shah, I. A. (2022). While analyzing the segregation of duties concerns, according to a senior auditor at a big four accounting firm, it must be confirmed that only the proper people have access to edit any component of the company's ERP system. Any detected conflicts must be resolved quickly to prevent unauthorized system usage.

6. DISCUSSION

Though limited, existing research on blockchain and its usage in business, particularly in the accounting field, provides us with insights into the future of blockchain technology and its application in accounting. It is undeniable that blockchain will have a significant impact on accounting and all its related professions. Because of the never-ending growth of technology, predicting what blockchain will do in future generations is challenging Shah, I. A., (2021). The technologies listed below are almost guaranteed to be currently affecting accounting or will be shortly for various corporations and firms. Because of all these rising technologies, the traditional accounting job will face a slew of changes in the coming years. Although these changes will be disruptive, they will also open a slew of possibilities in the industry Ujjan, R. M. A., (2021). It can significantly influence a company's cyber security system in business or accounting. As a result, we demonstrate that enterprises must consider their main activities to ensure a healthy and safe future for blockchain accounting in the face of cybercrime.

A blockchain is an excellent tool for cybersecurity and reliability. At any time, blockchain can provide anonymity and security Al-Jaroodi, J., (2019). This suggests that the industry must be checked to ensure blockchain is the right technology to implement Demirkan, S. (2020),

Barzilay, O. (2017). Its permanence, authenticity, and blockchain technology can help businesses enhance their operations. While most large corporations have embraced blockchain as a reality, many doubt its utility as an option to improve business operations. The cost and difficulty of implementation are the main reasons for enterprises T. Aste., (2017). Every link in the supply chain can be traced, and the source of the vulnerability can be identified. Given the public availability of blockchain, it can be assumed that it may be used to hunt down recalled items rather than the current method companies use when products appear more susceptible to virus issues. Many major supply chain security issues can be addressed by using blockchain management analytics techniques Nguyen, D. C. (2020), Hassan, M. U. (2019), Khan, M. A. (2018). This can serve as an example of what a blockchain can accomplish when it takes full advantage of its capabilities as a security framework. After talking about blockchain applications in network security, it is not difficult to see their value in the accounting industry. Accounting requires secure record-keeping and the implementation of appropriate processes. While blockchain remains the fundamental purpose, it exhibits Siegfried, N. (2020). The invention and implementation of blockchain technology make the preparation and evaluation of annual financial statements unnecessary. Accounting and various other applications can benefit from using blockchain to record and report transactions and other financial statements. Blockchain technology can meet many goals auditors and other accountants hope to achieve with their information and data, blockchain in IoT application in fig 5.

Figure 5. Overview of adopting blockchain in IoT application
Uddin, M. A, 2021

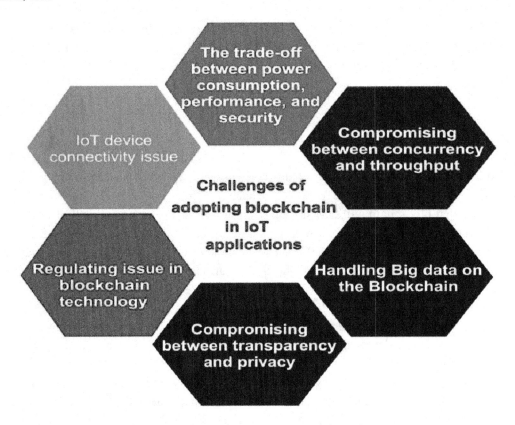

DISCUSSION CHAPTER CONTRIBUTION

Our contribution in this chapter is that, in the last ten years, related research articles and book chapters have been peer-reviewed for the title of the book chapter. A blockchain is a distributed and decentralized ledger system that allows many transactions to be recorded on computers. The blockchain was created to power money. Because of its ability to detect any misconduct and establish confidence in transactional integrity, modern technology is dubbed a "trusted security system. Transparency is built into the blockchain technology. Any transactions done on the blockchain are not protected by privacy. When a transaction is described as "secure, blockchain may be employed in a variety of ways. One of the best uses of its integrity assurance is to create security measures for various technologies. Several recent attacks have occurred on social media sites such as Twitter and Facebook. These attacks compromised millions of accounts, and user information fell into the wrong hands. Businesses, particularly substantial multinational corporations, are continually improving their operations. Software and technical innovations are heavily linked with operational improvements in today's technological environment. To guarantee that there are no threats to the segregation of tasks, management, internal audit, and external auditors must rigorously examine the software. Conflicts in the segregation of duties represent a significant danger to an external auditor. Blockchain is quickly establishing itself as one of the most reliable and robust methods of cybersecurity available. Regarding information exchange, the current rules that we have been working on for years will use trusted intermediaries. The intermediary is responsible for securing the transaction and any difficulties that may arise along the way, such as security breaches. Commercial blockchain technology is helpful for entities that transact with each other. Further hacking can be avoided if blockchain technology is deployed correctly in these messaging systems. The rapid development of current technology is giving birth to cyberattacks, which makes them more sophisticated and executable. The dynamic nature of the business environment in today's global economy is increasing the need for business professionals to keep up with current market conditions. The blockchain market is expected to grow from $4.8 billion in 2021 to $68.5 billion in 2027, a CAGR of 69.5%

7. CONCLUSION AND FUTURE WORK

The use of computers is becoming more and more common. The power and maliciousness of powerful attackers are increasing. Organizations must improve their ability to mitigate information security threats. With websites and social media platforms holding a wealth of personal information and potentially damaging, adequate protection is more critical than ever. Attackers make extensive use of the Internet's sophisticated hacking tools to cause harm to individuals and organizations. Attacks have become stealthier, with more significant economic damage and broader damage. Blockchain must be the solution to the security problem of financial transactions. However, judging from the results and expected answers from the industry and organization, it is crucial to understand how financial institutions are dealing with these issues by looking at blockchain deployments in the context of cybersecurity. A blockchain is a digital database that records all mentoring transactions. This technology supports many different exchanges that are currently in use. The rapid development of current technology is giving birth to cyberattacks, which makes them more sophisticated and executable. The dynamic nature of the business environment in today's global economy is increasing the need for business professionals to keep up with current market conditions. The blockchain market is expected to grow from $4.8 billion in 2021 to $68.5 billion in 2027, a CAGR of 69.5%. We also believe that blockchain should be integrated into many parts of cybersecurity. Hackers use modern techniques to obtain malicious objects, steal personal information, and attack financial institutions. From this perspective, we need to continue to work on security issues.

REFERENCES

Al-Jaroodi, J., & Mohamed, N. (2019). Blockchain in industries: A survey. *IEEE Access: Practical Innovations, Open Solutions*, *7*, 36500–36515. doi:10.1109/ACCESS.2019.2903554

Alladi, T., Chamola, V., Sahu, N., & Guizani, M. (2020). Applications of blockchain in unmanned aerial vehicles: A review. *Vehicular Communications*, *23*, 100249. doi:10.1016/j.vehcom.2020.100249

Amir Latif, R. M., Hussain, K., Jhanjhi, N. Z., Nayyar, A., & Rizwan, O. (2020). A remix IDE: Smart contract-based framework for the healthcare sector by using Blockchain technology. *Multimedia Tools and Applications*, 1–24. https://link.springer.com/article/10.1007/s11042-020-10087-1

Aste, T., Tasca, P., & Di Matteo, T. (2017). Blockchain technologies: The foreseeable impact on society and industry. *Computer*, *50*(9), 18–28. doi:10.1109/MC.2017.3571064

Barzilay, O. (2017). *3 ways blockchain is revolutionizing cybersecurity*. Retrieved from www. forbes. com: https://www.forbes.com/sites/omribarzilay/2017/08/21/3-ways-blockchain-is-rev olutionizing-cybersecurity/#77dc34b12334

Buterin, V. (2014). *A Next-Generation Smart Contract and Decentralized Application Platform*. Etherum. Available: http://buyxpr.com/build/pdfs/Ethe reumWhitePaper.pdf

Conoscenti, M., Vetro, A., & De Martin, J. C. (2016, November). Blockchain for the Internet of Things: A systematic literature review. In *2016 IEEE/ACS 13th International Conference of Computer Systems and Applications (AICCSA)* (pp. 1-6). IEEE. https://ieeexplore.ieee.org/abstract/document/7973732

De Filippi, P., Mannan, M., & Reijers, W. (2020). Blockchain as a confidence machine: The problem of trust & challenges of governance. *Technology in Society*, *62*, 101284. doi:10.1016/j.techsoc.2020.101284

Demirkan, S., Demirkan, I., & McKee, A. (2020). Blockchain technology in the future of business cyber security and accounting. *Journal of Management Analytics*, *7*(2), 189–208. doi:10.1080/23270012.20 20.1731721

Dhar Dwivedi, A., Malina, L., Dzurenda, P., & Srivastava, G. (2019). *Optimized Blockchain Model for Internet of Things based Healthcare Applications*. arXiv e-prints, arXiv-1906.

Ellul, J., Galea, J., Ganado, M., Mccarthy, S., & Pace, G. J. (2020, October). Regulating Blockchain, DLT and Smart Contracts: a technology regulator's perspective. In *ERA Forum* (Vol. 21, No. 2, pp. 209-220). Springer Berlin Heidelberg. https://link.springer.com/article/10.1007/s12027-020-00617-7

Euromoney. (n.d.). *Learning*. Available at https://www.euromoney.com/learning/blockchain-explained/what-is-blockchain

Fujimura, S., Watanabe, H., Nakadaira, A., Yamada, T., Akutsu, A., & Kishigami, J. J. (2015, September). BRIGHT: A concept for a decentralized rights management system based on blockchain. In *2015 IEEE 5th International Conference on Consumer Electronics-Berlin (ICCE-Berlin)* (pp. 345-346). IEEE. https://ieeexplore.ieee.org/abstract/document/7391275/

Gao, F., Zhu, L., Shen, M., Sharif, K., Wan, Z., & Ren, K. (2018). A blockchain-based privacy-preserving payment mechanism for vehicle-to-grid networks. *IEEE Network, 32*(6), 184–192. doi:10.1109/MNET.2018.1700269

Gazali, H. M., Hassan, R., Nor, R. M., & Rahman, H. M. (2017, May). Re-inventing PTPTN study loan with blockchain and smart contracts. In *2017 8th international conference on information technology (ICIT)* (pp. 751-754). IEEE. 10.1109/ICITECH.2017.8079940

Gill, S. H., Razzaq, M. A., Ahmad, M., Almansour, F. M., Haq, I. U., Jhanjhi, N. Z., . . . Masud, M. (2022). Security and Privacy Aspects of Cloud Computing: A Smart Campus Case Study. *Intelligent Automation & Soft Computing, 31*(1), 117-128. https://iopscience.iop.org/article/10.1088/1742-6596/1979/1/012035/meta

Hassan, M. U., Rehmani, M. H., & Chen, J. (2019). Privacy preservation in blockchain-based IoT systems: Integration issues, prospects, challenges, and future research directions. *Future Generation Computer Systems, 97*, 512–529. doi:10.1016/j.future.2019.02.060

Hassija, V., Chamola, V., Saxena, V., Jain, D., Goyal, P., & Sikdar, B. (2019). A survey on IoT security: Application areas, security threats, and solution architectures. *IEEE Access: Practical Innovations, Open Solutions, 7*, 82721–82743. doi:10.1109/ACCESS.2019.2924045

Herian, R. (2017). Blockchain and the (re) imagining of trusts jurisprudence. *Strategic Change, 26*(5), 453-460.

Huang, J., Kong, L., Chen, G., Wu, M. Y., Liu, X., & Zeng, P. (2019). Towards secure industrial IoT: Blockchain system with credit-based consensus mechanism. *IEEE Transactions on Industrial Informatics, 15*(6), 3680–3689. doi:10.1109/TII.2019.2903342

Huckle, S., Bhattacharya, R., White, M., & Beloff, N. (2016). Internet of things, blockchain and shared economy applications. *Procedia Computer Science, 98*, 461–466. doi:10.1016/j.procs.2016.09.074

Humayun, M., Jhanjhi, N. Z., Hamid, B., & Ahmed, G. (2020). Emerging smart logistics and transportation using IoT and blockchain. *IEEE Internet of Things Magazine, 3*(2), 58-62. https://ieeexplore.ieee.org/abstract/document/9125435

Ishmaev, G. (2017). Blockchain technology as an institution of property. *Metaphilosophy, 48*(5), 666-686.

Karafiloski, E., & Mishev, A. (2017, July). Blockchain solutions for big data challenges: A literature review. In *IEEE EUROCON 2017-17th International Conference on Smart Technologies* (pp. 763–768). IEEE. doi:10.1109/EUROCON.2017.8011213

Kewell, B., Adams, R., & Parry, G. (2017). Blockchain for good? *Strategic Change, 26*(5), 429-437.

Khan, M. A., & Salah, K. (2018). IoT security: Review, blockchain solutions, and open challenges. *Future Generation Computer Systems, 82*, 395–411. doi:10.1016/j.future.2017.11.022

Kumar, M. S., Vimal, S., Jhanjhi, N. Z., Dhanabalan, S. S., & Alhumyani, H. A. (2021). Blockchain based peer to peer communication in autonomous drone operation. *Energy Reports*, *7*, 7925–7939. doi:10.1016/j.egyr.2021.08.073

Lee, B., & Lee, J. H. (2017). Blockchain-based secure firmware update for embedded devices in an Internet of Things environment. *The Journal of Supercomputing*, *73*(3), 1152–1167. doi:10.100711227-016-1870-0

Lee, S. H., & Yang, C. S. (2018). Fingernail analysis management system using microscopy sensor and blockchain technology. *International Journal of Distributed Sensor Networks, 14*(3).

Li, X., Jiang, P., Chen, T., Luo, X., & Wen, Q. (2020). A survey on the security of blockchain systems. *Future Generation Computer Systems*, *107*, 841–853. doi:10.1016/j.future.2017.08.020

Michelin, R. A., Dorri, A., Steger, M., Lunardi, R. C., Kanhere, S. S., Jurdak, R., & Zorzo, A. F. (2018, November). SpeedyChain: A framework for decoupling data from the blockchain for smart cities. In *Proceedings of the 15th EAI international conference on mobile and ubiquitous systems: Computing, networking and services* (pp. 145-154). 10.1145/3286978.3287019

Miglani, A., Kumar, N., Chamola, V., & Zeadally, S. (2020). Blockchain for Internet of Energy management: Review, solutions, and challenges. *Computer Communications*, *151*, 395–418. doi:10.1016/j.comcom.2020.01.014

Muzammal, S. M., Murugesan, R. K., & Jhanjhi, N. Z. (2020). A comprehensive review on secure routing in internet of things: Mitigation methods and trust-based approaches. *IEEE Internet of Things Journal*, *8*(6), 4186–4210. doi:10.1109/JIOT.2020.3031162

Muzammal, S. M., Murugesan, R. K., & Jhanjhi, N. Z. (2021, March). Introducing mobility metrics in trust-based security of routing protocol for internet of things. In *2021 National Computing Colleges Conference (NCCC)* (pp. 1-5). IEEE. https://ieeexplore.ieee.org/abstract/document/9428799

Nguyen, D. C., Pathirana, P. N., Ding, M., & Seneviratne, A. (2020). Integration of blockchain and cloud of things: Architecture, applications and challenges. *IEEE Communications Surveys and Tutorials*, *22*(4), 2521–2549. doi:10.1109/COMST.2020.3020092

O'Leary, K., O'Reilly, P., Feller, J., Gleasure, R., Li, S., & Cristoforo, J. (2017, August). Exploring the application of blockchain technology to combat the effects of social loafing in cross functional group projects. In *Proceedings of the 13th International Symposium on Open Collaboration* (pp. 1-8). 10.1145/3125433.3125464

Ozyılmaz, K. R., & Yurdakul, A. (2017, October). Integrating low-power iot devices to a blockchain-based infrastructure: work-in-progress. In *Proceedings of the thirteenth acm international conference on embedded software* (p. 13). ACM.

Ravi, N., Verma, S., Jhanjhi, N. Z., & Talib, M. N. (2021, August). Securing VANET Using Blockchain Technology. In *Journal of Physics: Conference Series* (Vol. 1979, No. 1, p. 012035). IOP Publishing. https://iopscience.iop.org/article/10.1088/1742-6596/1979/1/012035/meta

Ray, B. C., Chowdhury, S. D., & Khatun, A. (2019). Productive performance and cost effectiveness of broiler using three different probiotics in the diet. *Bangladesh Journal of Animal Science*, *48*(2), 85–91. doi:10.3329/bjas.v48i2.46761

ResearchGate. (n.d). Available at https://www.researchgate.net/figure/Overview-of-the-blockchain-working-principle_fig1_319128148

Saeed, S., Jhanjhi, N. Z., Naqvi, M., Humayun, M., & Ahmed, S. (2020, October). Ransomware: A framework for security challenges in internet of things. In *2020 2nd International Conference on Computer and Information Sciences (ICCIS)* (pp. 1-6). IEEE. https://ieeexplore.ieee.org/abstract/document/9257660

Sengupta, J., Ruj, S., & Bit, S. D. (2020). A comprehensive survey on attacks, security issues and blockchain solutions for IoT and IIoT. *Journal of Network and Computer Applications*, *149*, 102481. doi:10.1016/j.jnca.2019.102481

Shah, I. A. (2022). Cybersecurity Issues and Challenges for E-Government During COVID-19: A Review. *Cybersecurity Measures for E-Government Frameworks*, 187-222. https://www.igi-global.com/chapter/cybersecurity-issues-and-challenges-for-e-government-during-covid-19/302729

Shah, I. A., Habeeb, R. A. A., Rajper, S., & Laraib, A. (2022). The Influence of Cybersecurity Attacks on E-Governance. In *Cybersecurity Measures for E-Government Frameworks* (pp. 77–95). IGI Global. doi:10.4018/978-1-7998-9624-1.ch005

Shah, I. A., & Rajper, S., & ZamanJhanjhi, N. (2021). Using ML and Data-Mining Techniques in Automatic Vulnerability Software Discovery. *International Journal (Toronto, Ont.)*, *10*(3).

Shah, I. A., Wassan, S., & Usmani, M. H. (2022). E-Government Security and Privacy Issues: Challenges and Preventive Approaches. In *Cybersecurity Measures for E-Government Frameworks* (pp. 61-76). IGI Global. https://www.igi-global.com/chapter/the-influence-of-cybersecurity-attacks-on-e-governance/302722

Sharma, P. K., Kumar, N., & Park, J. H. (2020). Blockchain technology toward green IoT: Opportunities and challenges. *IEEE Network*, *34*(4), 263–269. doi:10.1109/MNET.001.1900526

Siegfried, N., Rosenthal, T., & Benlian, A. (2020). Blockchain and the Industrial Internet of Things: A requirement taxonomy and systematic fit analysis. *Journal of Enterprise Information Management*.

Singh, A. P., Pradhan, N. R., Luhach, A. K., Agnihotri, S., Jhanjhi, N. Z., Verma, S., Kavita, Ghosh, U., & Roy, D. S. (2020). A novel patient-centric architectural framework for blockchain-enabled healthcare applications. *IEEE Transactions on Industrial Informatics*, *17*(8), 5779–5789. doi:10.1109/TII.2020.3037889

Tosh, D. K., Shetty, S., Liang, X., Kamhoua, C. A., Kwiat, K. A., & Njilla, L. (2017, May). Security implications of blockchain cloud with analysis of block withholding attack. In *2017 17th IEEE/ACM International Symposium on Cluster, Cloud and Grid Computing (CCGRID)* (pp. 458-467). IEEE. 10.1109/CCGRID.2017.111

Uddin, M. A., Stranieri, A., Gondal, I., & Balasubramanian, V. (2019, February). An efficient selective miner consensus protocol in blockchain oriented IoT smart monitoring. In *2019 IEEE International Conference on Industrial Technology (ICIT)* (pp. 1135-1142). IEEE. 10.1109/ICIT.2019.8754936

Uddin, M. A., Stranieri, A., Gondal, I., & Balasubramanian, V. (2021). A survey on the adoption of blockchain in iot: Challenges and solutions. *Blockchain: Research and Applications*, 2(2), 100006. doi:10.1016/j.bcra.2021.100006

Ujjan, R. M. A., Khan, N. A., & Gaur, L. (2022). E-Government Privacy and Security Challenges in the Context of Internet of Things. In *Cybersecurity Measures for E-Government Frameworks* (pp. 22–42). IGI Global. doi:10.4018/978-1-7998-9624-1.ch002

Ullah, A., Azeem, M., Ashraf, H., Jhanjhi, N. Z., Nkenyereye, L., & Humayun, M. (2021). Secure Critical Data Reclamation Scheme for Isolated Clusters in IoT enabled WSN. *IEEE Internet of Things Journal*. https://ieeexplore.ieee.org/abstract/document/9491079

Yu, Y., Li, Y., Tian, J., & Liu, J. (2018). Blockchain-based solutions to security and privacy issues in the internet of things. *IEEE Wireless Communications*, 25(6), 12–18. doi:10.1109/MWC.2017.1800116

Zhao, J. L., Fan, S., & Yan, J. (2016). Overview of business innovations and research opportunities in blockchain and introduction to the special issue. *Financial innovation, 2*(1), 1-7.

Zheng, Z., Xie, S., Dai, H., Chen, X., & Wang, H. (2017). An overview of blockchain technology: architecture, consensus, and future trends. *2017 IEEE International Congress on Big Data (BigData Congress)*. 10.1109/BigDataCongress.2017.85

Chapter 4
The Insider Threat Landscape and the FinTech Sector:
Attacks, Defenses, and Emerging Challenges

Zainab Abaid

 https://orcid.org/0000-0003-0402-3712

National University of Computer and Emerging Sciences, Islamabad, Pakistan

Ahsan Saadat

National University of Sciences and Technology, Islamabad, Pakistan

Baria Mubashar Mirza

 https://orcid.org/0000-0002-0486-6974

National University of Sciences and Technology, Islamabad, Pakistan

ABSTRACT

The increased reliance on online services during the recent pandemic has compelled businesses and operations to make a major technological shift to ensure online presence. However, this online paradigm shift has also attracted malicious agents who aim to benefit from vulnerabilities in the cyber world. These attackers target a wide spectrum of sectors including healthcare, government agencies, education, and financial services. In this chapter, the impact of insider security attacks on FinTech applications is discussed. A detailed account of insider attacks applicable on FinTech applications is provided. Moreover, solutions and recommendations are provided to make FinTech applications more secure by preventing and defending against insider attacks benefitting from emerging fields like crypto-currency, micro-finance, and robo-advisors. Successful prevention and defense against these attacks will ensure that the FinTech industry can be secure and can contribute in, as laid out in UN's Sustainable Development Goals, decent work and economic growth for the masses.

DOI: 10.4018/978-1-6684-5284-4.ch004

INTRODUCTION

The modern era is characterized by rapid technological development that directly impacts lives in many domains, ranging from home life to business to healthcare. The advancement in technology and the global move towards digitization has helped various countries in their economic growth. This technology development and associated economic growth is in line with the UN's sustainable development goals, *decent work* and *economic growth.*

Global trends are usually driven by financial and business motivations. It was inevitable that the rapid advancement in technology would also find its application in the financial world. In this regard, the term *FinTech* was recently coined. FinTech covers cutting-edge technological solutions applied to the field of finance and related services such as banks, financing companies and insurance companies. FinTech has become one of the fastest growing and most lucrative technological fields in the modern era due to the potential gains involved. A combination of factors has contributed to its prolific growth: technological advancements, the intense business competition and high customer expectations characteristic of capitalist markets (which in turn triggers innovation), and inflation-driven requirements to save on costs and maximize profits. According to Statista (Statista, 2022) the global Fintech market is anticipated to grow at a Compound Annual Growth Rate (CAGR) of around 20% over the next four years.

Like any emerging field, FinTech faces challenges in several domains, such as data management, hardware and infrastructure requirements, and the complexity of interaction among loosely connected or disparate systems. The work presented in (Gai, 2018) ranks security and privacy among the top five crucial aspects of FinTech developmental challenges. This is not surprising, given the sensitivity of financial data, both from a privacy perspective as well as the potential for misuse. The more widespread any technology becomes, the more lucrative it becomes for cybercriminals to attack, as they stand to gain more profit from successful attacks. In this respect, FinTech is among the most high-risk domains that attract malicious actors and must be systematically and thoroughly secured. Given the growing interest of hackers in this field, coupled with financial stress and layoffs in the uncertain economic situation globally, there is increased motivation for cyber-attacks, including *insider attacks*, which are the primary focus of this chapter.

The Covid-19 pandemic turned the world upside down. During this pandemic, digitization became the reason for the survival of many businesses, contributing to the survival of a crumbling global economy. A large proportion of businesses shifted either entirely online or at least had to maintain an online presence for some operations. Due to the never-ending lockdowns and social distancing restrictions, in-person visits to financial institutions such as banks were reduced. To overcome these challenges, multiple countries facilitated their citizens and introduced measures which could encourage the users to use FinTech services remotely. For instance, in Pakistan the online transaction fee was waived for inter-bank transactions to encourage bank customers to restrict movement to halt the spread of the virus. Similarly, account opening and registration processes for various financial services were offered remotely via web or phone. This online nature of FinTech services, even though it provided convenience to customers, also opened opportunities for malicious actors. Increased financial transactions online also gave rise to online frauds which included hacking into personal accounts for money withdrawals or phone call-based scams for getting access to confidential information. Overall, the vastly increased online attack surface, coupled with the fact that many households lost their jobs and struggled financially, resulted in a massive rise in cybercrime after the pandemic.

A broad spectrum of attacks targets FinTech organizations and services. For example, denial of service attacks, data destruction or tampering, data exfiltration and espionage, ransomware and myriad other attacks target FinTech. Many of these attacks are common with other domains, such as healthcare, but as discussed above, FinTech applications are particularly attractive to cyber attackers. As the field of FinTech grows, new trends and technologies have also emerged, such as microfinance and cryptocurrency, which bring their own unique security and privacy challenges. The speed of their adoption and the rapid move to shift existing services into cyberspace has surpassed the speed of development of appropriate security standards and technologies for FinTech. Hence, these new technologies remain ripe for attackers to profit from.

In this chapter, we focus on one particularly challenging class of attacks, namely *insider attacks*, which are hard to detect and defend against and have perhaps the greatest potential for damage. Insider attacks are defined as threats to an organization that originate from within, for example from its employees, ex-employees or contractors. Insider attacks have not been limited to digital scenarios but have always existed in the sense that ill-intended insiders, using their higher access and trusted status, have often misused their privileges for carrying out harm. However, recently they have been gaining increasing attention in cybersecurity. These attacks have become more prevalent due to easy availability of tools that allow for privilege escalation, social engineering and network-based man-in-the-middle attacks and are facilitated by new classes of malware such as ransomware and wiper malware.

According to Verizon's Data Breach Investigations Report (Verizon, 2022), 27% (i.e., nearly one-third) of threat actors in data breaches seen in financial services organizations in 2022 were insiders. At the same time, organizations lack the ability to effectively defend against insider threats. 63% of organizations surveyed by Cybersecurity Insiders (Insiders, 2021) in 2021 felt that they could not effectively "monitor, detect, and respond to insider threats", and 49% of organizations could not detect insider threats before data left the organization.

The bottom line is that with the high sensitivity and increasing online presence of financial service companies, as well as new technologies in FinTech, guarding against insider attacks is just as important, if not more, than guarding against external threats. The well-known "castle" model of security, where an organization prioritizes guarding its perimeter (much like an ancient fort wall), assuming the inside to be safe, is no longer applicable to modern day cybersecurity. There is a global move towards the "city" model, where the entrance protocol is not assumed to be perfectly capable of filtering out malicious entrants, and security must be applied inside as much as on the perimeter (Leuprecht, 2016).

In the remaining sections of this chapter, we provide details of the insider threat landscape, identifying attackers, their motivations, and their techniques. We then discuss how FinTech applications are vulnerable to these attacks. We also propose solutions and the way forward for how FinTech applications can be made more secure by preventing and detecting insider attacks, and specifically discuss emerging applications like crypto-currency and micro-finance. Finally, we conclude our work by emphasizing the importance of successful prevention of these attacks for the stability and growth of the FinTech sector.

BACKGROUND: THE INSIDER THREAT LANDSCAPE

In cybersecurity, insider threats are considered very challenging as the attack originates from within the apparently safe bounds of the organization, while traditionally the "castle" model of cyber defense mechanisms (Leuprecht, 2016) views attacks as coming from the outside world. According to recent surveys, a significant percentage of total cybercrimes globally involve insiders. Moreover, since insiders have first-hand access to sensitive information, the damage caused by their actions is more severe compared to an outside attacker who might acquire access only for a short duration and via discreet (and hence limited functionality) channels. The total cost of insider attacks is hard to determine and depends on the particular attack and the duration of the incident. The Ponemon Institute reported that the average time to contain an insider attack was 85 days in 2022, and incidents that took over 90 days to contain cost an organization an average of $17 million annually (Ponemon Institute, 2022).

Insider attacks are not only causing increased damage but also showing an alarming growth rate. A Cybersecurity Insiders' survey conducted in 2021 found that 57% of organizations felt that the insider threat had grown over the past 12 months (Insiders, 2021). According to research conducted by the Ponemon Institute (Ponemon Institute, 2022), insider-led cybersecurity incidents have increased by 44% from 2020 to 2022, while the total cost of these incidents has also risen by 34% (since 2016, this number is up by 60%). Many factors have played a role in this increase. For instance, the move towards the Bring Your Own Device (BYOD) culture has increased insider threats greatly in the last couple of years; BitGlass found in 2020 that 82% of organizations cannot detect insider threats from their employees' personal devices.

Having described the enormous impact of insider threats, we now present an overview of the insider threat landscape, and identify threat actors, their motivations, and the types of attacks they may carry out. Insider attacks, as introduced earlier, are those that originate from within the organization. Thus, the perpetrators of these attacks can be either purely within the organization, somehow affiliated to it, or purely outside the organization but have somehow gained access to the internal network.

Figure 1. Classification of Insider Threat Actors

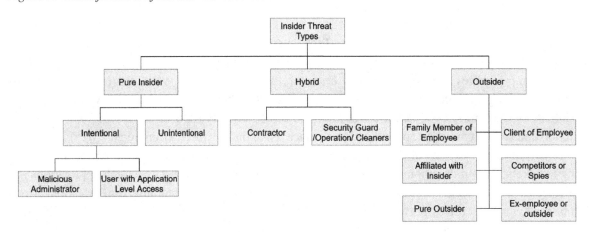

Threat Actors

Figure 1 presents a categorization of typical inside threat actors. Each category is described below.

Pure Insider

Pure insiders are threat actors that are permanent employees of the organization, for example, IT staff, managers, and operational teams. As Figure 1 shows, these insiders may either intentionally or unintentionally carry out attacks. *Intentional* attackers can either be malicious users who have only application-level, limited access, but carry out privilege escalation attacks (Rangwala, 2014) to temporarily gain higher privileges needed to act on their objectives, or malicious administrators who have administrative or root-level access. Recent surveys (Cybersecurity Insiders, 2020) report that 63% of insider attacks are carried out by employees with privileged access; hence the remaining attacks are likely to require some form of privilege escalation. Section 2.3 outlines some technical details of privilege escalation and privileged user attacks.

Unintentional attacks are an unfortunate reality of today's cybersecurity landscape, where an insider completely inadvertently causes a security breach, through actions such as:

- Opening an apparently legitimate email attachment (which installs a keylogger virus)
- Clicking a phishing link leading to theft of credentials, which the attacker can then use to enter the organizations' systems
- Accidentally exfiltrating data to an attacker in response to a *spoofed* email from a team member (i.e., the email is actually from someone pretending to be the team member).

The interested reader may refer to (Abulencia, 2021) for a detailed look at the human factors that influence unintended insider threats.

Outsider

Outsiders are actors entirely outside of an organization who are neither their long-term employees nor temporary contractors or business affiliates. One sub-category of these may be *pure outsiders* who have absolutely nothing to do with anyone in an organization. The reason we mention these in insider attacks is that by definition, insider attacks are those that originate from within an organization, so by this definition, outside attackers that have somehow gained access to the organization's internal network will also cause an insider attack. Other sub-categories as seen in Figure 1 are actors who are somehow or the other related to the organization, although they are not themselves part of it. For example, they may be family members of employees, clients of employees, ex-employee, spies of a competitor, or someone otherwise affiliated with an insider.

Hybrid Actors

These actors are neither purely part of an organization nor can be classified as outsiders; either the nature of their engagement with the organization is temporary (say, an auditor temporarily given access to accounting and finance information) or their jobs are not the core operations of the company but other housekeeping sort of tasks such as security, cleaning, mail delivery and so on. Oftentimes these hybrid actors have been used to accomplish something on the inside; a famous example is Stuxnet, the malware that damaged Iran's nuclear centrifuges (Edwards, 2014). The nuclear facility was air-gapped to ensure strict control over what entered the computer systems, but an infected USB stick was brought into the facility by an insider and plugged in, from where the malware then spread over the internal network. Likewise, cleaners can eavesdrop on conversations, read screen displays, socially engineer employees to obtain Wi-Fi access and so on, potentially leading to serious security breaches.

Cole and Ring (Cole, 2005) suggest that inside attackers may be *self-motivated* (acting on their own will, decision and objectives), *recruited* (i.e. a previously innocent employee hired by an outside attacker to achieve some objective by facilitating or carrying out an attack within an organization), *or planted* (someone who is especially trained and then joins an organization with the express purpose of carrying out an attack). This categorization can apply to any of the threat actors within our taxonomy, i.e. inside, outside or hybrid.

Motivations

Insider threats may be motivated by a wide variety of factors. We summarize the main motivations in Figure 2. It is important to understand the motivations of threat actors when a threat landscape is to be fully understood, as the threat actors and their motivation often together determine the amount of resources that will be used in an attack and accordingly, the attack vectors an attacker may be able to use or the arsenal of tools the attacker will have access to. As Figure 2 shows, insider attacks may be motivated by profit, destruction, espionage, a personal vendetta or ideological differences.

Profit

A large majority of attacks are done for personal benefit or profit. Cybersecurity Insiders' 2019 report cited that fraud (55%) and monetary gain (49%) were the biggest factors that drive malicious insiders, followed by theft of intellectual property (44%) (Cybersecurity Insiders, 2019). This can include breaching databases to sell data on the black market or discovering and selling knowledge of vulnerabilities in company systems on the black market. Another category of this is modifying software to earn cash – for example, a bank's web developer inserts a web exploit into the bank's online banking website that runs a malicious script in the victim's browser for stealing their credentials or initiating money transfers to the attacker's account (this is a stored XSS attack as described in (Hydara, 2015)). Countless fraud cases have also been reported where the perpetrator is an insider. A CERT Insider Threat Center study funded by the Department of Homeland Security in the U.S.A reports several such cases, for example, an accountant who created a fake employee profile and used it to pay herself for six years before being detected (Cummings, 2012).

Figure 2. Motivations of Inside Threat Actors

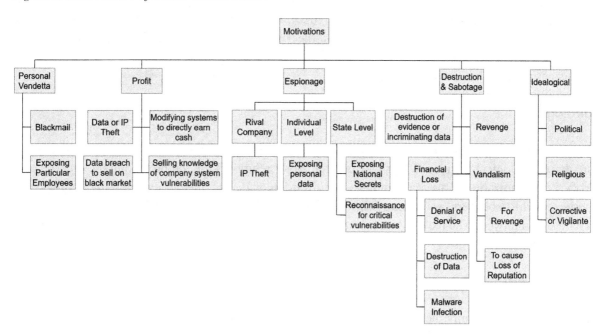

Destruction and Sabotage

This motive can be simply for vandalism, where the objective is to halt or disturb the daily functioning of an organization (e.g. for revenge, by an ex-employee), or for causing financial loss. The latter is more common in today's intensely competitive scenario. One recent incident is the May 2021 ransomware attack on U.S.A's Colonial Pipeline (Smith, Stephanie, 2022), where an employee's remote desktop sharing credentials were leaked. The attackers used the employee's machine to enter the network, where they then launched a series of ransomware attacks that resulted in the pipeline's operations being halted for several days, fuel shortages across the East Coast, and a state of emergency being declared by the U.S. President. Other similar attacks have used Wiper malware, a class of malware that has the core objective of destroying files and halting systems. A famous example is the Shamoon malware that was used to overwrite the master boot records of thousands of machines of Aramco, the Saudi state-owned oil company, making them unusable (Bronk, 2013). Both attacks are examples of *unintentional* (but avoidable, as we discuss in Section 4) insider involvement; a weak password in the former case, and a phishing link followed by an employee in the latter.

Espionage

It is no secret that rival companies, and sometimes nation states, initiate insider attacks for spying on their rivals, to steal state secrets or intellectual property. According to a PricewaterhouseCoopers study (PricewaterhouseCooper (PwC), 2019), in some sectors (primarily manufacturing, followed by finance, healthcare and ICT), corporate espionage is said to constitute 94% of all cybercrime. State level espionage is seen as a critical threat to modern national security. As early as 2015, Chinese hackers were deemed responsible for breaking into US government computers and accessing the data of 4 million current and former federal employees. In 2020, Enisa reported that 38% of malicious actors involved in cyber espionage were nation state actors (Enisa ETL, 2020). Espionage may also be *individual* level, where an individual who wishes to expose a secret of another (perhaps based on some personal vendetta, or for blackmail), inserts spyware into the victim's machine (e.g. that performs keylogging or takes screenshots) or engages in any other form of spying.

Ideological

Whistleblowers and *hacktivists*, individuals who hack into organizations' systems for political activism, have ideological motives (which may be political or religious) for compromising the security and privacy of organizations. Chelsea Manning and Edward Snowden are famous examples of ideologically motivated whistleblowers, as is Julian Assange of WikiLeaks (Touchton, 2020).These are usually high-privileged employees who have access to sensitive documents and can leak them to the public via email and other channels.

Personal Vendetta

An employee, their family member or client, or anyone associated with the employee may have a personal vendetta against the organization or against a particular employee in the organization, due to which they may engage in finding information to harm them or use malware or other techniques to discredit the individual or business. For example, healthcare systems are heavily targeted by attacks where the private health data of public personalities, e.g. celebrities or politicians, is made public, and insiders are involved in many of these attacks. In 2013, the Cedars-Sinai Medical Center in Los Angeles reported that 6 workers were fired over a celebrity data breach when they made her health records public; the story was reported by the LA Times (Los Angeles Times, 2013).

Techniques

Now we delve a little deeper into the technicalities of insider attacks and discuss what methods and attack vectors are used by the perpetrators. From a defense perspective, this is perhaps the most important to know, as mitigation techniques will depend directly on the specific intrusion techniques used by the attackers. Figure 3 summarizes some of the common attack vectors involved in past insider attacks. This is not an exhaustive list, as the actual attack vectors vary widely and are very difficult to enumerate in the scope of this chapter. However, it covers most of the main techniques that have been seen in recent attacks.

Figure 3. Common attack vectors used by inside threat actors

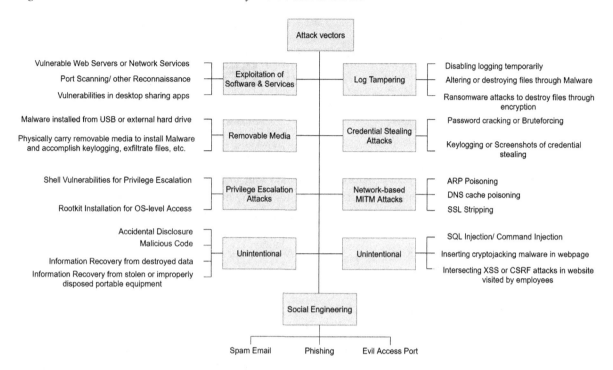

The most common, by far, is *social engineering*. This is often the entry point for outside attackers to get inside an organization so that they can launch attacks from within. Many attacks begin with an employee clicking on a seemingly innocuous link that launches a vicious malware, or a spam or phishing email that leads to a page that captures the visitor's credentials. An attacker in the proximity of an organization can launch an Evil Twin Access Point (Agarwal, 2018) and trick an employee into revealing the Wi-Fi password. *Credential stealing* can also be accomplished, as Figure 3 shows, by password-cracking approaches (e.g., using readily available software like John The Ripper (John the Ripper password cracker, n.d.) or more advanced custom software) or deploying keylogger malware in the target's machine. Social engineering and credential stealing are closely related in the sense that they ultimately achieve the same objective: compromise an insider's identity to gain access into the internal network. A pure outsider can, in this way, launch their attacks from within the network.

The second most common way for outsiders to enter an organization is via *remote exploitation* of vulnerable software and services running on the organization's public-facing systems. This necessarily follows an information gathering or probing stage where the attacker queries the targeted systems for running services, open ports and installed software on public-facing servers to find one or more vulnerabilities that can be targeted. For instance, a webserver hosting an HTTPS website that allows backward compatibility with HTTP may be targeted by an SSL stripping attack, where an attacker downgrades a client's HTTPS communication to HTTP to be able to read private information in cleartext (that HTTPS would otherwise have encrypted). Together, social engineering, credential stealing and probing for remote exploitation represent the first stage of the well-known Lockheed Martin Cyber-Kill Chain (Mihai, 2014) as shown in Figure 4.

Figure 4. The Cyber-Kill Chain

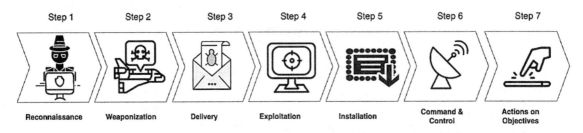

Reconnaissance is a necessary step before the attacker can formulate the appropriate exploit code (*Weaponization*) to target a particular vulnerability. Insiders may be instrumental in the reconnaissance stage of remote exploitation; for example, an IT technician may reveal knowledge of legacy code on a server that has not been updated and is hence vulnerable to a buffer overflow exploit.

Privilege escalation attacks (Rangwala, 2014) allow under-privileged users to either elevate their privilege to administrative levels, or to access a higher-privileged service, which then allows them to bypass the original restrictions placed on them. For example, universities typically do not allow student accounts to install or remove software in lab machines, but a student who successfully gains root access to a machine can bypass this limitation. This can be done by using vulnerabilities in system tools like Windows SysInternals or using slightly more advanced tools like Metasploit that can automatically generate exploits that result in opening a shell with root access on a vulnerable machine. It is beyond the scope of this chapter to detail all possible methods of performing privilege escalation. Several surveys, for example (Rangwala, 2014) taxonomize privilege escalation techniques that the interested reader may refer to.

Network based man-in-the-middle (MITM) attacks (Conti, 2016) can allow an attacker to insert himself in the middle of an ongoing, even apparently secured session, such as the SSL stripping attack referred to earlier. An insider who is already on the organization's local network can perform several different attacks that require the attacker to be on the local network, such as ICMP redirection, DNS cache poisoning (Nachreiner, 2003), and ARP poisoning (Man, 2020) to effectively insert himself in the middle of any two hosts and intercept (or even redirect) their communications. The captured messages can be copied and sent out to a malicious actor, or they can be *sink-holed,* or sent to a non-existent address, to effectively perform a denial-of-service attack on the communicating users.

Inside actors may insert *web exploits* (e.g., cross-site scripting or cross-site request forgery) into the organization's websites, or else they may use web exploits (such as SQL injection or command injection) to steal data from the databases linked to the organizations' websites.

Figure 5. SQL Injection to read or alter database linked to website

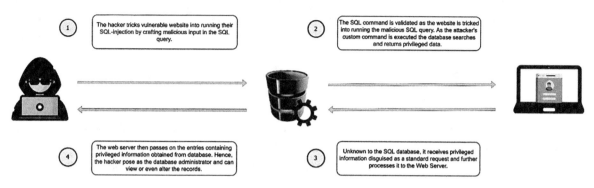

Figure 5 shows an SQL injection exploit where a user who is aware of an SQL vulnerability in a sensitive website (for example, a payroll system that can only be accessed from the local network) can input a cleverly formatted string into one of the input fields on the website and read arbitrary data from the backend database or even make changes such as changing another user's salary, attendance record or password. Naturally, because of having access to the local network, even low-privileged users can carry out such exploits if there are vulnerabilities in the organization's websites. IT staff or other technically savvy users may be able to perform reconnaissance for such vulnerabilities, and web developers may be able to intentionally leave vulnerabilities in websites to create backdoors for enabling later exploits.

Unintentional attacks have their own unique vectors. According to (Greitzer, 2014), unintentional insider threats can be categorized into four types. The first is threats posed by malicious code, where an employee inadvertently launches malware in the organization, through an infected USB device, laptop, phone or by visiting an unsafe website from the organization's local network. In this case, sensitive or private data can be accessed by unauthorized users via social engineering. Another is threats posed by disclosure, where sensitive data gets accidentally disclosed to malicious agents via web, fax, email, or mail. The third is threats posed by improper disposal of physical records, where Standard Operating Procedures (SOPs) are not followed while disposing off physical records and attackers retrieve records from either digital or physical garbage (e.g., lost or discarded documents in paper form). The last is threats posed by not-in-possession portable equipment or *removable media* (another attack vector in Figure 3), where lost or stolen data storage devices, or even phones or laptops, can end up in criminals' hands and sensitive data is recovered from them. With increased usage of portable devices such as phones and tablets, this threat is significant.

Finally, *log tampering* is another common insider attack vector that organizations should watch out for. This can be a post-attack indicator if it can be flagged. Most organizations use some form of auditing where logs of employee actions are maintained, e.g., server logs, network traffic logs or operating system event logs. Insiders with high privileges, for example server admins, can alter these log files or even overwrite them to hide trails of malicious actions. Logs may be read-only, in which case more advanced attacks, such as ransomware-enabled encryption of files in secondary storage or wiper malware to destroy the files entirely, may be used.

Summary: In summary, this section gave a broad overview of the insider threat landscape, beginning with the types of threat actors (insider, outsider, or hybrid) and their motivations (sabotage, profit and so on) and their techniques (privilege escalation, social engineering and so forth). This shows the broad scope and targets of inside attackers as well as the variety of techniques that are available to them. In the next section, we look at FinTech applications and specifically outline their vulnerabilities to insider threats.

INSIDER ATTACKS IN FINTECH APPLICATIONS

FinTech has since its inception attracted the particular interest of inside threat actors. Verizon reported in their 2021 Breach Investigations Report that the finance and healthcare industries experienced the most incidents where employees misused their privileged access (Verizon, 2022). The Ponemon Institute also found that financial services companies bear the highest cost of protecting against or responding to insider threats, estimated on average at $25 million in 2022, which also represents an increase of 47% compared to the average spending in 2020 (Ponemon Institute, 2022).

In this section, we identify how the inside threat actors listed in the previous section can impact FinTech services. We also highlight the motivation behind insider attacks on FinTech services.

Inside Threat Actors Involved in FinTech Attacks

Below we highlight some common attack scenarios that inside threat actors may be involved in when targeting FinTech companies.

Pure Insider

For the case of *pure insider (intentional attack)*, an employee working in any financial service company may become the perpetrator of an insider attack. Consider an example of a transaction initiated for an online purchase by a customer. If the customer decides to pay online, via a debit or credit card or by simply using his online banking app, his credentials may be available to an insecurely implemented web service (one that does not hash or salt the password, for example). A malicious system administrator or an employee having admin level access to the sensitive information of customers can pass it on to other cyber criminals. In terms of employees having application-level access to customer information, we can consider an example of an insurance company where the customers usually submit their history and financial information at the time of registration for the service. The customer service representative gets access to the customer's sensitive information, which he can leak for malicious purposes. Moreover, once all sensitive data becomes available in the databases of the company, an insider system administrator acting as a malicious administrator can extract relevant information from the customer and pass it on to cybercriminals, who can use it for identity stealing, fraud or blackmail.

For the case of *pure insider (unintentional attack)*, an employee becomes the source of providing a vulnerability to another attacker outside the organization. As an example, if proper authentication mechanisms and verification processes are not in place, then impersonation in person or over the phone or internet may result in a scenario where an employee ends up leaking information to the attacker out of goodwill or negligence. These attacks usually fall into the social engineering category described earlier. Similarly, an employee might open an email which looks legitimate but ends up installing a keylogger virus, leading to leakage of authentication credentials which could then be used to access sensitive financial information. Similar damage can be done if an employee ends up clicking a phishing link. Another common unintentional action from an employee can be accidental exfiltration of data to an attacker in response to a spoofed email from a team member.

Outsider

Outsider attackers, as mentioned in previous section, can be categorized into six types of attackers: pure outsider, affiliated with insider, employee family member, employee client, ex-employee and competitors.

A *pure outsider* will need to break into the security landscape of an organization linked with a FinTech service. Typically, attackers falling into this category will use technological means such as hacking, malware etc. to access sensitive data.

An *attacker affiliated with an insider* is one of the most common type of facilitator observed in cyber-fraud cases, and includes family members or clients of an employee. Attacks carried out by this category of attackers may be intentional or unintentional. In case of intentional, the employee can use his affiliate to enable the actual attacker to succeed by passing sensitive information. In case of unintentional, sensitive information can be leaked to the actual attacker via the affiliate if the employee ends up sharing sensitive information with the affiliate during informal interaction.

Another attacker category which contributes significantly in the outsider attacker landscape is the ex-employee category. Ex-employees can either have sensitive information learnt during their stay at the organization, or still have access to the information if the exit policies of the organization are not secure. This can include being able to access company resources via remote login or data stored on a storage device. Drivers behind such attacks may be grievances experienced during the stay at the firm or monetary incentives from competitors. Lastly, another important category is the attacks originated by competitors via planted spies within another rival firm, to get access to sensitive information.

To summarize, we conclude that the outsider attacks are either facilitated by a remote attack on the target system or due to lack of security policies and mechanisms, including robust exit processes of employees or background-checked onboarding of new employees.

Hybrid Attacker

Hybrid actors might provide specialized services to a firm, for example an auditor temporarily given access to accounting and finance information. However, their engagement with the firm is temporary. This category also includes contractors and/or staff hired to carry out day-to-day activities in a firm to support maintenance or operations. For example, a security guard or a cleaner at firm should not have access to any sensitive information, as information handling responsibilities are beyond the job description of these employees. However, a lapse in following standard operating procedures may leak financial information which may become accessible to the hybrid attacker (guard or cleaner). Disposal of information and records (in paper or disk form) without following the standard procedures can become a contributor in this type of information leakage.

Inside Attacker Motivations for Targeting FinTech Services

As discussed in the previous section, the motivation behind insider attacks depends on a variety of factors. In the FinTech industry, money is a key factor: financial gain and causing financial damage to rivals are heavily at play in insider attacks. Malicious attackers can use a relevant type of inside attacker to cause a data breach for a FinTech service, and then sell the information in black market. Moreover, in case the attacker is able to acquire knowledge of vulnerabilities in a finance related firm, he can sell the knowledge further to rival firms or exploiters. The most common motivation to exploit a vulnerability in an organization providing FinTech services is to get access to funds and make withdrawals or payments. Moreover, once an attacker gets inside a firm's system, committing a financial fraud become easier, for example using a bank's email server to send fake emails to scam customers into fraudulent transfers.

For rival companies or competitors who attempt to access another firm's sensitive data, direct financial loss is not the only agenda. A competitor could be interested in ensuring that a target firm's system is attacked (e.g., denial of service) to prevent the target firm from competing in an auction or bid. Similarly, financial loss can be caused to the target firm when an insider attack leads to destruction of data or disruption of service due to a malware infection. In the business world, reputation is more important than a one-time financial loss so a target firm's system can be intruded via an inside attack to malign the reputation of the firm. A bank going offline for even an hour or two would cause major customer inconvenience and thousands of dollars' loss of business to the bank.

While we have covered the aspects of rivals or ex-employees, another motivation to intrude into a FinTech service provider's security system is for the benefit of an individual. For instance, a person who is likely to receive a penalty from a bank or insurance company due to his actions (such as non-payment, accident history, frauds etc.) would be motivated to breach into the firm's records to cause destruction of evidence or incriminating data.

Lastly, the motivation behind an inside attack can be to access private information of managers or decision-makers in a firm providing FinTech services, to influence their decisions or policies. The private information can be used for personal vendetta such as for blackmail or threatening to publicly malign their reputation.

EXISTING SOLUTIONS: DEFENDING AGAINST INSIDER THREATS

In this section we discuss existing solutions for defending against insider threats. These are not specific to the FinTech domain but nonetheless are all applicable to it. In the next section we specifically discuss security recommendations for FinTech.

We group approaches for defending against insider attacks into three chronologically ordered stages: *deterring* (preventing) attacks from occurring, *detecting* them when they do occur and *responding* to them after they are detected (attack containment and response procedures). We categorize defence techniques into these three major groups as shown in Figures 6 and 7.

Deterrence

Deterrence refers to all policies and technical controls for preventing insider attacks from happening at all. We split deterrence approaches into five further categories.

The first of these is *psychological factors* or approaches that consider the human element. All these focus on the human factors that cause employees to behave maliciously. For instance, (Moore et al., 2016) suggest prioritizing employee satisfaction and minimizing their stress level. Stressed employees are more likely to be careless and make mistakes that lead to unintentional attacks, while dissatisfied and disgruntled employees who do not feel valued by the company are a prime target for recruiters who wish to hire insiders to carry out attacks such as theft of trade secrets. Recommended approaches for increasing employee satisfaction with a view to minimizing insider threat include:

- Mandatory vacation
- Workplace facilities such as gyms and break rooms
- Retreats and social events

(Sarkar, 2010) suggest careful involvement of Human Resources (HR) in employee exit, such as exit interviews and debriefing for employees that are leaving, so that they do not unintentionally reveal trade secrets or become instruments to an attack. Part of exit policy is succession planning, i.e., training replacements for employees that leave, particularly those in leadership positions. New employees are not very familiar with security procedures and are much more likely to commit unintentional errors that lead to attacks, and to fall prey to social engineering. If someone pretending to be IT calls a new employee and asks for their credentials to grant access to a restricted service, the employee may not yet know that this is not part of routine procedures. Even employees who take up a new higher role within the same organization may not have enough training for that role and may not use unfamiliar products optimally or in a secure way. Succession planning involves careful documentation and procedure development for training of new employees that succeed a previous employee in a leadership position.

Employee profiling is critically important and often yields useful results in controlling insider threats. An organization should maintain a *profile* of every employee that can include, depending on the organization, their usual day to day activities, responsibilities, and habits. Social media and emails can also be mined for profile building. A deviation from an employee's normal behaviour profile can flag either (1) that the employee is being impersonated by an outsider who has gained access to the employee's credentials or (2) that the employee is showing signs of turning malicious. For example, (Okolica, 2007) showed that it was possible to predict upcoming whistleblowing based on the last few months of emails of the whistle-blowers.

Figure 6. Deterring insider attacks

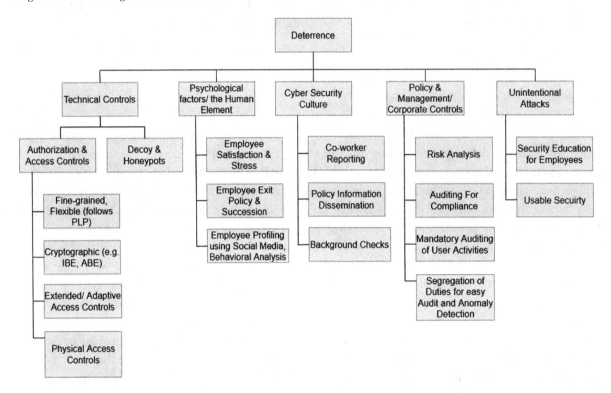

Cybersecurity culture development is another effective way of deterring insider attacks. The idea is to systematically build a culture that revolves around prioritizing cyber security. Primarily this begins with cybersecurity education, so that ideally all employees equally recognise the importance of cybersecurity in the organization. Disseminating security policy information effectively, through talks and trainings, is part of developing this culture. This also includes encouraging co-worker reporting if an employee is noticed as, for example, acting unusually, threatening to harm the company, or attempting to recruit colleagues to collude in an attack. Background checks before an employee is hired can also indicate if the employee is likely to be a good fit in the company's security culture.

Next up are measures to reduce *unintentional attacks*. Some of these, such as minimizing employee stress and providing security education, are covered above. Importantly, *usable security* should be prioritized. Usable security, by definition, is security with a human-centric focus, i.e., developing security systems from the ground up by considering the nature of the humans who use them. Security should be as convenient and easy as possible and should not require the user to remember a lot of information or go through complicated procedures. Hence, security principles such as the KISS (Keep it Simple, Stupid!) principle (Singer, 2014) should be considered in all security systems. If security is not usable, users tend to find ways to circumvent it, which results in security loopholes and breaches and invites cyberattacks.

Policy and corporate controls refer to defining enterprise-wide policies and putting procedures in place that are designed to deter insider attacks. Many of these are general security policies, such as performing *risk analysis* exercises to identify vulnerable assets and determine which assets should be prioritized for protection (in most modern organizations, data or IP has the highest value). Defining auditing and log monitoring procedures is also important so that employees know that their actions are monitored and that insider attacks can be caught; for log auditing to be effective, segregating employee duties and banning account-sharing is also important, so that employee actions can be separated. Finally, prior research has also suggested mandatory logging of all user activity for the first 60 days of joining the workplace, to aid with behavioural profiling and minimizing the risk from a new employee.

The way that most of the above policies are implemented is through *technical controls*, which refer to the actual tools and technologies that are used to achieve authorization, access control and other insider threat management objectives. Strong *access control* is critical to any organization that has sensitive data and resources. Early models of access control were not very flexible, for example, role-based access control which defines access rules for each role in an organization (e.g. all managers have a certain access level). This leads to many instances of over-privilege where a particular employee does not in fact need access that some other employees in that role need. Managing access entirely per-individual is also not scalable and is prone to errors and inconsistencies. Cryptographic access control is one solution where cryptography is used to restrict access to content, by simply encrypting data and ensuring that only authorized individuals possess the keys to decrypt a particular data item. This form of access control is flexible, as keys can be changed quickly or re-encryption can be done, as well as fine-grained, because encryption is attribute-based (Qiao, 2014), i.e., depending on several attributes of a user (e.g., role, department, or even the time of day) instead of just a role. With attribute-based encryption, it is easier to follow the principle of least privilege, which states that each user should only be given the minimum access that they need. Ganiyu et. al (Ganiyu, 2021) also introduced the notion of extended access control for a bring-your-own-device scenario where access is based on a risk assessment process; when there is higher risk, access becomes more restricted. Finally physical access control policies should also be designed to ensure safety of sensitive equipment (e.g., old or backup secondary storage devices, servers etc.) and discourage snooping, shoulder-surfing, and desk-searching. Another rather interesting idea in technical controls is to use decoys (Bowen, 2009) or honeypots, i.e., apparently sensitive documents left deliberately open or intentionally vulnerable machines placed in the network to attract and eventually expose malicious users.

Figure 7. Detecting and responding to insider threats

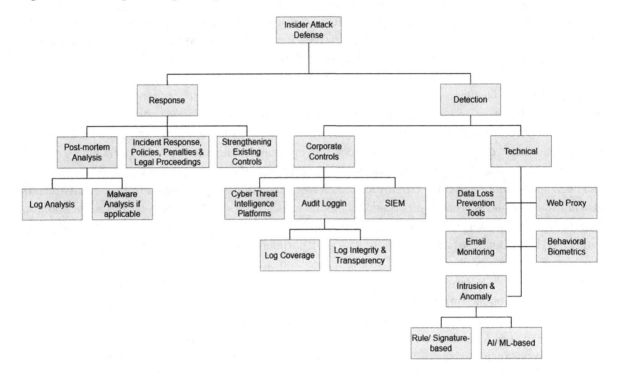

Detection

We now come to a discussion of detection approaches. As opposed to deterrence, which deals with preventing attacks altogether, detection approaches focus on discovering attacks that are ongoing. As insider attacks tend to be very stealthy, the average time to detect insider attacks is 77 to 85 days (Ponemon Institute, 2022), which is a very long period of time in which significant damage can be sustained by the organization, for example in terms of slowly stolen data or discreet fraud payments transferred to an attacker. We discuss detection approaches in two main categories, i.e., technical controls and corporate controls.

Technical Controls

In this category we discuss modern technology that can be used for detecting ongoing attacks. The first such technology is *data loss prevention* (Liu, 2010). Data loss prevention deals with both exfiltration and infiltration of data (although generally exfiltration is a bigger concern when considering insider threats). Data loss prevention defines a set of tools and processes to prevent data leakage. It includes classifying data into different levels to identify the most critical data, such as personally identifiable information and IP, and then implementing controls to protect data at rest, data in use and data in motion, for securing endpoints, and for detecting leaks so that the attack can be quickly contained.

Email monitoring and web proxy are related technologies in that they both inspect otherwise private outgoing or incoming communication of employees. The former, as the name suggests, is simply passing all incoming and outgoing emails through a filter which uses algorithms such as keyword matching and other natural language processing techniques (Salloum, 2021) to discover an illicit activity, such as sending out private files from the organization or communicating with suspicious outsiders. Web proxy involves passing all a user's web traffic through a middle point (the proxy, which is effectively a legitimate MITM) which then passes it on to the destination.

Behavioural biometrics (Ellavarason, 2020) is a relatively recent field whose main premise is continuous authentication, i.e., to detect if an employee's account or session has been hijacked or the employee is being impersonated by someone else. The idea is to build a profile of the normal behaviour (e.g. typing speed, mouse movement pattern, usual activities) of a user, and then look for anomalies in that profile during use. This is promising for the detection of credential sharing or credential stealing scenarios where a malicious actor is impersonating another employee by using their account or a previously established web session.

Intrusion detection systems (IDS) and anomaly detection, which can be either rule or signature based (looking for particular signatures or behavioural patterns), or more recently, machine learning or deep learning based, is a generic solution for cybersecurity which can be specifically adapted to look for insider attacks. A very simple example is flagging failed logon attempts as a possible privilege escalation attack indicator. SIEM systems do similar monitoring and generate intrusion alerts and can similarly be tuned to look for indicators of insider threats.

Corporate Controls

Similar to deterrence, detection also needs some corporate controls in addition to technical controls. Audit logging is important both in the deterrence and the detection stage. For detection, it is particularly important that logging systems cover the whole range of actions that may be part of or indicate an insider attack (for example, all stages of the Cyber-Kill Chain, which represents the typical lifecycle of an advanced attack, should be captured). Log integrity (i.e. logs being tamper-proof) and transparency (some part of it being public, so that insiders are deterred by the fear of being exposed publicly) are also important properties to ensure. Recently, blockchain-based solutions have been proposed that hold these properties (Ahmad A. S., 2019), as blockchains are both transparent and reliably tamper-proof.

Response

Incident response procedures dictate how ongoing attacks should be responded to, i.e., what to do if an attack, and possibly its perpetrator, is discovered. For example, what should an organization do if its customers' data is breached? Legal procedures for disclosing a breach to the public, for penalizing perpetrators and for crime reporting must be documented and communicated in advance. Similarly, policies and procedures for post-mortem analysis of an attack should be defined, i.e., how can log analysis be done most efficiently, and if necessary, how will any malware used in the attack be analysed (to prevent the same being used in future). The most important step in the response is closing the loop, i.e., plugging the insights learned from the attack back into strengthening policies and existing controls.

OVERALL RECOMMENDATIONS FOR SECURING FINTECH

Protection from FinTech-focused cybercrime is not a one-dimensional task. Responsibility lies with both the organizations involved in FinTech operations and the users who use related financial services. In this section we first discuss some general principles for securing FinTech organizations against insider attacks, and then specifically present recommendations for securing emerging FinTech domains with unique challenges.

General Recommendations for FinTech Security Against Insider Threat

The primary onus is on the organizations involved in FinTech business. As discussed throughout this chapter, the nature of insider threats and attacks makes it essential for an organization to have robust security policies in place for all operations. To reduce the risks of insider threats, multiple risk mitigation practices can be implemented.

The concept of non-overlapping duties and defining scope can ensure that every employee only has access to relevant information and not to any information which is beyond the domain of his job responsibilities. This will help to investigate the right person in case of any breach and any employee would know that his actions cannot stay undiscovered. The concept of mandatory vacation (Kaur, 2021) helps to improve the mental health of employees which reduces the intensity of grievances employees may hold during their stay at the firm. This can help in maintaining a trust-based relationship with the employees even when they exit the firm. Similarly, introduction of robust employee related security policies such as acceptable use policy (detailing each inductee about the risks involved) and employee exit policy can help in mitigating the risks. Regular awareness workshops need to be conducted for employees where best practices need to be emphasized to create awareness, which could prevent unintentional information leakage leading to an attack. Moreover, policies need to be implemented at company level and efforts need to be made at social level for creating a legislation to punish cyber criminals.

The most critical role in minimizing the vulnerabilities which can be exploited by the attackers is if the employees working at the FinTech service provider firms. These employees need to demonstrate responsible behavior to ensure that their actions do not cause any unintentional damage to the firm's reputation or services. Taking precautionary measures such as not revealing credentials to any affiliate, not clicking on any irrelevant link on their phones or computers, using updated anti-virus software, and following best practices for password protection can reduce the vulnerability points.

Emerging Domains: Cybercrime and Insider Threat

In this section, we turn our attention to some of the most recent developments in FinTech and discuss how these technologies, whose very inception comes at a time rife with cybercrime, should be standardized and designed to minimize the risk of exploitation and compromise.

Blockchain and Crypto-Currency

The advent of blockchain and crypto-currency has marked a major shift in the financial world. Crypto-currency provides transparency and decentralization on the one hand (Joo, 2019) but also anonymity on the other hand, as the identity of blockchain users is not tied to their real world identity. This anonymity aids cybercriminals in earning through cryptocurrency; for example, most ransomware seen so far demand ransom in Bitcoins. Crypto-jacking malware (Eskandari, 2018) is another menace of the post-blockchain world, where unsuspecting users' processing power is used in crypto-mining to earn crypto-currency profit for criminals. Blockchain is seen as secure and tamper-proof but is not without its security issues. For example, if private keys are stolen or disclosed via unintentional errors (e.g. phishing), the security of the whole system falls apart. Private key leakage was behind some of the recent blockchain hacks; for example, Binance, operator of a major crypto-currency exchange, lost about $40 million in Bitcoins following a leak of private keys via phishing and other attack vectors (Techcrunch, 2019).

On the other hand, blockchain technology itself can be a strong tool in securing against insider attacks. As blockchains can be used to maintain tamper-proof records, they can be used for audit logging, as proposed in (Ahmad A. a., 2018), to guard against log-tampering attacks, for securing supply chain data or any other data that is to be stored both transparently and in an integrity-preserving manner.

AI and Robo-Advisors in FinTech

FinTech has greatly adopted Artificial Intelligence, for example Erica, Bank of America's well-known chatbot who answers banking queries (Erica, 2022). Deep learning has been proposed for credit scoring, and machines can decide whether to give a customer a loan (Gunnarsson, 2021). While this technology is tremendously helpful and cost-saving for FinTech organizations that benefit from it, it brings its own security issues. Machine learning can be fooled, and small perturbations in inputs can sometimes lead to vastly different (and wrong) decisions (Ingle, 2021). A credit risk classifier that has been poisoned or mis-trained can issue wrong decisions, directly impacting human lives. For insiders who may have access to the trained model, it is easier to glean information to fool the classifiers, and perhaps even to make it learn inaccurate patterns. Robo-advisors, in the same vein, are bots who assist with investment management (Sironi, 2016). They may or may not be AI-based. Once again, because of the use of artificial intelligence, a robo-advisor may be poisoned or input data can be modified such that the output goes against a particular person or the organization in general – this is the sort of attack that an individual with a vendetta against the organization or an employee may engage in.

Micro-finance

Another recent development in FinTech is micro-finance. Micro-finance is defined as the provision of financial services such as loans, saving accounts and other banking services to low-income or remote populations traditionally unable to access conventional banking services (Ashta, 2021). It is a relatively recent technology but is gaining popularity very fast globally, especially in developing countries where a large segment of the population fits the target audience description. Micro-finance faces more cyber-threats simply because of being a new entrant in the market, and particularly because its users are often lower-income groups with little to no technical or security expertise, and in developing countries, often also lacking basic education.

Overall, we recommend that as these technologies are relatively new and mostly lacking standardization, they actually present a golden opportunity to build security *into* the design, rather than adding it on as accidents occur. This should both prevent and manage to quickly isolate and detect threats, even when they originate from inside the network.

CONCLUSION

In this chapter, we presented an overview of insider threats and possible attacks which relate to FinTech. Advancement in technology and its application in financial services has resulted in an increased attack surface in this domain, attracting the interest of cyber-attackers coming with a variety of motivations. These attacks can result in damage to FinTech organizations' assets or their reputation, as well as direct loss of privacy and financial losses to their customers. Robust cyber-defense policies which can prevent insider attacks are essential to minimize the risks associated with insider threats. However, since the rapid transition to cyberspace in recent years has outpaced corresponding cyber-defense mechanisms, there is a need for increased awareness and adaptation to environments for improving the existing defense mechanisms. We also provided brief use cases to build a case that prevention is the best form of defense against insider attacks. Benefitting from past experiences and case studies, the number of insiders contributing to this cybercrime can be reduced. Responsible work practices by the employees and stakeholders across the board will minimize the room available for exploitation of the vulnerabilities. Efforts must be made to create awareness about cybercrime laws which could prevent most of the attackers fearing the consequences. Finally, it is critically important to ensure that the protocols and standards that are being designed for emerging domains such as cryptocurrency, micro-finance and AI-based decision making are designed from the ground up with security in mind, i.e. security by design rather than security as an after-thought. This will ensure that the future of FinTech remains as stable as possible and losses to FinTech organizations and their customers can be minimized.

REFERENCES

Abulencia, J. (2021). Insider attacks: Human-factors attacks and mitigation. *Computer Fraud & Security*, *2021*(5), 14–17. doi:10.1016/S1361-3723(21)00054-3

Agarwal, M., Biswas, S., & Nandi, S. (2018). An efficient scheme to detect evil twin rogue access point attack in 802.11 Wi-Fi networks. *International Journal of Wireless Information Networks*, *25*(2), 130–145. doi:10.100710776-018-0396-1

Ahmad, A. a. (2018). Towards blockchain-driven, secure and transparent audit logs. In *Proceedings of the 15th EAI International Conference on Mobile and Ubiquitous Systems: Computing, Networking and Services* (pp. 443-448). 10.1145/3286978.3286985

Ahmad, A. S., Saad, M., & Mohaisen, A. (2019). Secure and transparent audit logs with BlockAudit. *Journal of Network and Computer Applications*, *145*, 102406. doi:10.1016/j.jnca.2019.102406

Ashta, A., & Herrmann, H. (2021). Artificial intelligence and fintech: An overview of opportunities and risks for banking, investments, and microfinance. *Strategic Change*, *30*(3), 211–222. doi:10.1002/jsc.2404

Bowen, B. M. (2009). Baiting inside attackers using decoy documents. In *International Conference on Security and Privacy in Communication Systems* (pp. 51--70). Springer.

Bronk, C. R., & Tikk-Ringas, E. (2013). The cyber attack on Saudi Aramco. *Survival*, *55*(2), 81–96. doi:10.1080/00396338.2013.784468

Cole, E. a. (2005). *Insider threat: Protecting the enterprise from sabotage, spying, and theft*. Elsevier.

Conti, M., Dragoni, N., & Lesyk, V. (2016). A survey of man in the middle attacks. *IEEE Communications Surveys and Tutorials*, *18*(3), 2027–2051. doi:10.1109/COMST.2016.2548426

Cummings, A. a. (2012). *Insider threat study: Illicit cyber activity involving fraud in the US financial services sector*. Carnegie-Mellon Univ.

Edwards, C. A. (2014). An analysis of a cyberattack on a nuclear plant: The stuxnet worm. *Critical Infrastructure Protection, 59*.

Ellavarason, E. R., Guest, R., Deravi, F., Sanchez-Riello, R., & Corsetti, B. (2020). Touch-dynamics based behavioural biometrics on mobile devices–a review from a usability and performance perspective. *ACM Computing Surveys*, *53*(6), 1–36. doi:10.1145/3394713

Enisa, E. T. L. (2020). *Cyber Espionage; From January 2019 to April 2020*. Retrieved September 22, 2022, from https://www.enisa.europa.eu/topics/threat-risk-management/threats-and-trends/etl-review-folder/etl-2020-cyberespionage

Erica. (2022). Retrieved September 22, 2022, from https://promotions.bankofamerica.com/digitalbanking/mobilebanking/erica

Eskandari, S. a. (2018). A first look at browser-based cryptojacking. In *2018 IEEE European Symposium on Security and Privacy Workshops (EuroS&PW)* (pp. 58--66). 10.1109/EuroSPW.2018.00014

Fruhlinger, J. (2020). *What is phishing? How this cyber attack works and how to prevent it*. Retrieved from CSO Online: https://www.csoonline.com/article/2117843/what-is-phishing-how-this-cyber-attack-works-and-how-to-prevent-it.html

Gai, K., Qiu, M., & Sun, X. (2018). A survey on FinTech. *Journal of Network and Computer Applications*, *103*, 262–273. doi:10.1016/j.jnca.2017.10.011

Ganiyu, S. O. (2021). *Extended Risk-Based Context-Aware Model for Dynamic Access Control in Bring Your Own Device Strategy. In Machine Learning and Data Mining for Emerging Trend in Cyber Dynamics*. Springer.

Greitzer, F. L. (2014). *Analysis of unintentional insider threats deriving from social engineering exploits. IEEE Security and Privacy Workshops*. doi:10.1109/SPW.2014.39

Gunnarsson, B. R., vanden Broucke, S., Baesens, B., Óskarsdóttir, M., & Lemahieu, W. (2021). Deep learning for credit scoring: Do or don't? *European Journal of Operational Research*, *295*(1), 292–305. doi:10.1016/j.ejor.2021.03.006 PMID:34955589

Homoliak, I. E. (2018). *Insight into insiders and it: A survey of insider threat taxonomies, analysis, modeling, and countermeasures*. Academic Press.

Hydara, I., Sultan, A. B. M., Zulzalil, H., & Admodisastro, N. (2015). Current state of research on cross-site scripting (XSS)–A systematic literature review. *Information and Software Technology*, *58*, 170–186. doi:10.1016/j.infsof.2014.07.010

Ingle, G. B. (2021). *Adversarial Deep Learning Attacks—A Review*. Information and Communication Technology for Competitive Strategies. doi:10.1007/978-981-16-0882-7_26

Insiders, C. (2019). *Insider Threat Report, 2019*. Retrieved September 21, 2022, from https://www.cybersecurity-insiders.com/portfolio/insider-threat-report/

Insiders, C. (2020). *Insider Threat Report*. Retrieved September 22, 2022, from https://www.cybersecurity-insiders.com/wp-content/uploads/2019/11/2020-Insider-Threat-Report-Gurucul.pdf

Insiders, C. (2021). *2021 Insider Threat Report*. Retrieved September 21, 2022, from https://www.cybersecurity-insiders.com/portfolio/2021-insider-threat-report-gurucul/

John the Ripper password cracker. (n.d.). Retrieved September 22, 2022, from https://www.openwall.com/john/

Joo, M. H. (2019). Cryptocurrency, a successful application of blockchain technology. *Managerial Finance*.

Kaur, G. Z. (2021). *Understanding Cybersecurity Management in FinTech. Springer International Publishing, 2021*. Springer International Publishing.

Leong, K. (2018). FinTech (Financial Technology): What is it and how to use technologies to create business value in fintech way? *International Journal of Innovation, Management and Technology*, 74–78. doi:10.18178/ijimt.2018.9.2.791

Leuprecht, C. D., Skillicorn, D. B., & Tait, V. E. (2016). Beyond the Castle Model of cyber-risk and cyber-security. *Government Information Quarterly*, *33*(2), 250–257. doi:10.1016/j.giq.2016.01.012

Littell, J. (2019). *Don't Believe Your Eyes or Ears: The Weaponization of Artificial Intelligence, Machine Learning, and Deepfakes*. Retrieved from War on the Rocks: https://warontherocks.com/2019/10/dont-believe-your-eyes-or-ears-the-weaponization-of-artificial-intelligence-machine-learning-and-deepfakes/

Liu, S., & Kuhn, R. (2010). Data loss prevention. *IT Professional*, *12*(2), 10–13. doi:10.1109/MITP.2010.52

Los Angeles Times. (2013). *Six people fired from Cedars-Sinai over patient privacy breaches*. Retrieved September 22, 2022, from https://www.latimes.com/local/la-xpm-2013-jul-12-la-me-hospital-security-breach-20130713-story.html

Man, K. a. (2020). Dns cache poisoning attack reloaded: Revolutions with side channels. *Proceedings of the 2020 ACM SIGSAC Conference on Computer and Communications Security*, 1337-1350. 10.1145/3372297.3417280

Mihai, I.-C. D. (2014). Cyber kill chain analysis. *Int'l J. Info. Sec. & Cybercrime*, *3*, 37.

Moore. (2016). *The Critical role of positive incentives for reducing insider threats*. Carnegie Mellon University.

Nachreiner, C. (2003). *Anatomy of an ARP poisoning attack*. Academic Press.

Najaf, K. M. (2021). *Fintech firms and banks sustainability: Why cybersecurity risk matters?* Academic Press.

Okolica, J. S. (2007). Using Author Topic to detect insider threats from email traffic. *Digital Investigation*, *4*, 158–164.

Ponemon Institute. (2022). *Cost of insider threats global report*. Retrieved September 21, 2022, from https://www.bloomberg.com/press-releases/2022-01-25/global-cybersecurity-study-insider-threats-cost-organizations-15-4-million-annually-up-34-percent-from-2020

PricewaterhouseCooper (PwC). (2019). *Study on the Scale and Impact of Industrial Espionage and Theft of Trade Secrets through Cyber*. Retrieved September 22, 2022, from https://www.pwc.com/it/it/publications/docs/study-on-the-scale-and-Impact.pdf

Qiao, Z. a. (2014). Survey of attribute based encryption. *15th IEEE/ACIS International Conference on Software Engineering, Artificial Intelligence, Networking and Parallel/Distributed Computing (SNPD)*, 1-6.

Rangwala, M. e., Zhang, P., Zou, X., & Li, F. (2014). A taxonomy of privilege escalation attacks in Android applications. *International Journal of Security and Networks*, *9*(1), 40–55. doi:10.1504/IJSN.2014.059327

Salloum, S., Gaber, T., Vadera, S., & Shaalan, K. (2021). Phishing email detection using natural language processing techniques: A literature survey. *Procedia Computer Science*, *189*, 19–28. doi:10.1016/j.procs.2021.05.077

Sarkar, K. R. (2010). Assessing insider threats to information security using technical, behavioural and organisational measures. *Information Security Technical Report*, *15*(3), 112–133. doi:10.1016/j.istr.2010.11.002

Singer, A. a. (2014). *Keep it Simple, Stupid: Why the Usual Password Policies Don't Work, and What to Do About It*. Academic Press.

Sironi, P. (2016). *FinTech innovation: from robo-advisors to goal based investing and gamification*. John Wiley & Sons. doi:10.1002/9781119227205

Smith, S. (2022). Out of Gas: A Deep Dive Into the Colonial Pipeline Cyberattack. In *SAGE Business Cases*. SAGE Publications.

Statista. (2022). *Fintech – Worldwide*. Retrieved September 21, 2022, from https://www.statista.com/outlook/dmo/fintech/worldwide

Techcrunch. (2019). *Binance pledges to 'significantly' increase security following $40M Bitcoin hack*. Retrieved September 22, 2022, from https://techcrunch.com/2019/05/10/binance-security-hack/

Touchton, M. R. (2020). Whistleblowing or leaking? Public opinion toward Assange, Manning, and Snowden. *Research & Politics, 7*(1).

Verizon, B. (2022). *2022 Data Breach Investigations*. Retrieved September 21, 2022, from https://www.verizon.com/business/resources/reports/dbir/2022/financial-services-data-breaches

KEY TERMS AND DEFINITIONS

Blockchain: A distributed ledger that maintains records of digital transactions (e.g., money transfer events, sale or service events, etc.) using a peer-to-peer network of user machines rather than relying on a central authority or server, and which uses cryptography for security.

Crypto-Currency: A digital currency that is not centrally managed by any government or any other authority, in which transaction records are verified and maintained essentially by the public, through a completely decentralized system based on cryptography.

FinTech: Financial technology, a term that covers the use of technology in financial services organizations to reduce costs, increase efficiency, improve customer service, or automate and facilitate routine procedures.

Insider: Someone who is either permanently or temporarily affiliated with the organization (e.g., a permanent employee or a temporary contractor), affiliated with someone in the organization, e.g., an employee's family member or client, or has gained temporary access to the organization's internal network, e.g., a remote attacker who has obtained an employee's credentials to remotely log into an internal system.

Insider Attack: An attack that originates from within the organization's internal network.

Phishing: Fake communication that pretends to be from a legitimate source and intends to trick the receivers into divulging private information (e.g., a fake email pretending to be from a bank, intended to trick bank customers into sharing their online banking credentials).

Privilege-Escalation: The steps through which a lower-privileged user is able to temporarily elevate privileges and carry out actions that are only permitted to higher-privileged users; for example, an IT employee may not ordinarily be privileged to disable a firewall but is able to do so by exploiting some vulnerability.

Social Engineering: Tricking human users and relying on their actions to gain access to restricted information or systems, e.g., calling an employee pretending to be the human resource department and getting them to grant access to their private documents.

Chapter 5
E-Commerce and Cybersecurity Challenges:
Recent Advances and Future Trends

Hina Gull

Imam Abdulrahman bin Faisal University, Dammam, Saudi Arabia

Dina A. Alabbad

(iD) https://orcid.org/0000-0001-7624-8924

Imam Abdulrahman bin Faisal University, Dammam, Saudi Arabia

Madeeha Saqib

Imam Abdulrahman bin Faisal University, Dammam, Saudi Arabia

Sardar Zafar Iqbal

Imam Abdulrahman Bin Faisal University, Dammam, Saudi Arabia

Tooba Nasir

Beaconhouse International College, Islamabad, Pakistan

Saqib Saeed

(iD) https://orcid.org/0000-0001-7136-3480

Department of Computer Information Systems, College of Computer Science and Information Technology, Imam Abdulrahman Bin Faisal University, Dammam, Saudi Arabia

Abdullah M. Almuhaideb

Department of Networks and Communications, College of Computer Science and Information Technology, Dammam, Saudi Arabia & Imam Abdulrahman bin Faisal University, Dammam, Saudi Arabia

ABSTRACT

COVID-19 has accelerated the digital transformation in the business sector as many business organizations adopted electronic commerce to keep their operations running. Business organizations have also increased their participation on social networking applications to attract customers. Due to huge presence of users, social networking sites have also evolved into an emerging marketplace, which is referred as social commerce. There are many security issues involved in technological adoption in different business processes. On the other hand, social media is extensively used for product marketing, so fake information and fake product reviews can also influence consumers purchasing decision, so providing accurate marketing information is also a challenge for business organizations. In this chapter, the authors conduct a systematic literature review to understand the cybersecurity issues faced by business organizations and customers and how recent advances such as fintech, etc. provide additional cybersecurity challenges for business organization to protect themselves and their customers.

DOI: 10.4018/978-1-6684-5284-4.ch005

INTRODUCTION

Electronic Commerce (E-commerce) has been inextricably linked to the Internet from its initial launch in 1991. E-commerce can be described as a process that includes the purchasing and selling of goods and services over the internet just with the tap of a finger. According to Investopedia, it is a 'business model' that makes sure that the purchase can be made over computers, cellphones, and other smart devices making it convenient for both the consumer and the business company by offering a large selection of products as well as advanced shipment, payment, and delivery methods. By offering these services, this technology has brought the seller and marketplace closer together. The development and widespread use of the World Wide Web has led to an exponential increase in e-commerce, and as a result, it has become a vital component of business policy and processes across the world. This elevated use of e-commerce has resulted in the latest advancements in industries. Because of the rapid growth of e-commerce, more computer professionals have chosen to dedicate their skills to developing applications that improve computer-assisted transactions over the internet. Most current businesses prefer payments made straight through their own banking channels or through a mediator payment system. In this instance, the buyer is required to disclose their private bank account information to the mediator. There is usually no physical contact between the two parties.

The unique approach of e-commerce has made it popular among people of all age groups. It has been recognized globally thanks to platforms such as Amazon and eBay, which have increased the influx of users, including penetration from both mobile and desktop browsers, together with a rise in the company sales (Junadi & Sfenrianto, 2015). In addition to this, when the pandemic shattered normal life and lockdowns were imposed around the globe in 2020, remote transactions gained even more appeal because of their web-based business viewpoint. It allowed small businesses to thrive and survive during the tough times. According to Digital Commerce 360's study of US Department of Commerce data, e-commerce spending in the first half of 2020 reached $347.26 billion, up 30% each year. In comparison, e-commerce sales climbed by only 12.7 percent in the first half of 2019 (Ali, 2021). Furthermore, Etsy, a rapidly growing website, processed $10.28 billion in gross item sales in 2020. That's a 106.84 percent rise since the previous year. Figure 1 depicts the merchandise sales of Etsy (Dean, 2021) since its launch in 2005.

Figure 1. Merchandise sale of Etsy
(Dean, 2021)

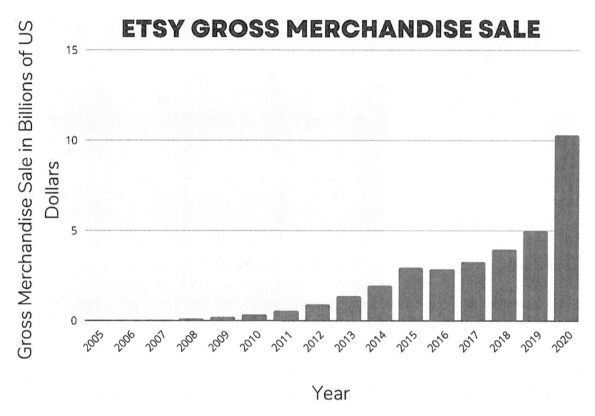

The e-commerce industry, like many other industries, has evolved over a period of time Saeed et al., (2013), Saeed, (2019). It has modified itself to keep up in this era of electronic payment with the latest financial technology (FinTech). This term has originated from the contraction of the two terms Financial and Technology (Gai et al., 2018, p. 262). Electronic payment systems, often known as paperless money transfers, are used by e-commerce businesses (S Fatonah et al, 2018). By decreasing paperwork, transaction expenses, and additional labor expenses, it has changed commercial operations. (Hami & Cheng, 2013). E-commerce processing is easier to use, and it consumes less time than manual processing. In addition, it allows a company to broaden its market reach (Qatawneh et al, 2016). Most popular FinTech applications in the world include Robinhood, MoneyLion, Chime and many more. Table 1 portrays top FinTech apps, the country they are based in and their valuation in 2021 (The Fintech 50 2021).

Table 1. FinTech Companies and their Valuation

	FinTech App	Country	Valuation
1	Coinbase	USA	$85.7 Billion
2	Revoult	UK	$33 Billion
3	RobinHood	USA	$32 Billion
4	Nubank	Brazil	$30 Billion
5	N26	Germany	$3.5 Billion
6	Tellus	USA	$265 Million
7	Chime	USA	$25 Billion
8	MoneyLion	USA	$2.9 Billion
9	Finch	USA	$15 Million
10	Mint	USA	$103 Million

Mobile banking, cryptocurrency, block-trading, and marketplace lending are just a few features that are usually auto-associated with e-commerce. It has undergone significant development not simply to remain relevant, but also to guarantee secure customer transactions. FinTech is driven by technology-enabled innovation that not only enhances existing financial services, but also provides a way for those who do not have a bank account to get money. One aspect of FinTech is electronic payment transactions, sometimes known as e-payment (Hassan et al, 2020). A service based on mobile banking is a type of payment FinTech service (Kim et al, 2016). Mobile banking and e-banking are examples of e-payment systems (Yaokumah, 2017). Figure 2 shows the top 100 FinTech applications by category (Koetsier, 2021).

Figure 2. Top 100 FinTech Apps by Category
(Koetsier, 2021)

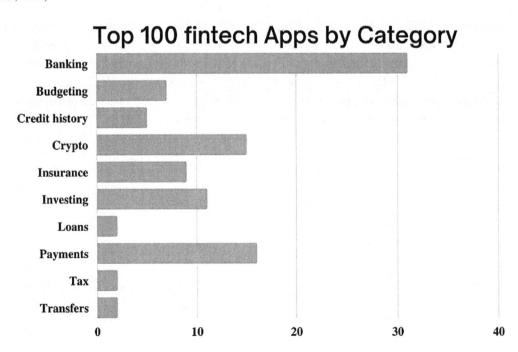

Despite all the accomplishments that e-commerce has achieved in the online world, there are security issues that sometimes cause harm to online shoppers and, as a result, harm business owners as well. Just like any other domain (Naeem et al., 2020; Khadam et al., 2021; Shahid et al., 2022; Zulkifl et al.,2022), security breach occurs in the e-commerce space as well (Waseem, 2020). Cybercrimes are computer-based or internet-based criminal activities that damage concerned parties. Cybercrimes are categorized as cyber-dependent crimes, for instance, hacking, viruses, etc., and cyber-enabled crimes, such as phishing, identity theft, and other frauds, etc. The elevation in cyber-crimes by anonymous assailants is due to the belief that they might not get caught (Buil-Gil et al., 2021). The tremendous global expansion of financial technology organizations and commercial centers has increased the exposure of weaknesses within the FinTech infrastructure, making it a target for cybercriminals and hackers. Likewise, concerns about network security within FinTech businesses have gradually grown (Choo, K. K. R., 2011). According to a definition by Cisco, cybersecurity is "an approach that includes several levels of protection." It is no surprise that entrepreneurs are increasingly strengthening cybersecurity. Developed countries such as the United States and Australia are more vulnerable to sophisticated cyberattacks because of the vast advancement in their information technology (IT) sector. According to Juniper Research (2021), global e-commerce losses due to online payment fraud were predicted to be $20 billion in 2021. This represents an increase of nearly 14% above the previous year's figure of $17.5 billion.

In this chapter we explore the state of the art to provide a concise reference to trust issues, cybercrimes, legal implications of e-commerce, and usage of machine learning to foster security in e-commerce. Rest of the chapter is structured as follows: Section 2 provides a detailed background and related work followed by solutions and recommendations to the trust issues related to e-commerce in section3. Section 4 portrays possible future research directions, followed by conclusions in section 5.

BACKGROUND AND RELATED WORK

In this chapter we have mainly explored trust issues, cybercrimes, legal implications of e-commerce and usage of machine learning to foster security in e-commerce.

Trust and Security in E-Commerce

There are many studies focusing on trust and security aspects related to e-commerce. Ali et al., (2016) conducted an empirical study in Malaysia and highlighted that customers' trust is a crucial factor in online business and personal security, financial security, system security, privacy and cybercrime are key components in fostering customer trust. Stewart and Jürjens (2018) explored key factors affecting the adoption of financial technologies in Germany and found that intuitive interface, customer trust, and security as key factors that encourage people to shop online. Choi and Mai (2018) carried out an empirical study in Vietnam to investigate the relationship between customer loyalty and e-service quality and concluded that promoting trust is vital for the growth of e-commerce. Lee et al.,(2018) found that customer trust positively influence purchase intention and distrust impacts customers' risk perception, whereas website quality positively influences buyer's trust in an intermediary positively affected their trust in the seller and intention to purchase. Based on an empirical study with Korean customers, Kim (2020) highlighted that motivational factors positively contribute to perchance intention of customers and prior positive experience with online vendors results in enhanced purchase intention from same e-commerce vendors.

Pabian et al. (2020) highlighted that e-commerce security is a living issue, therefore, e-commerce security requires sustainable efforts to foster security in terms of security of payment methods, personal information, and purchased good. Customer security depends upon the security of the e-portal, which could face security issues due to negligence or lack of technical staff. D'Adamo et al., (2021) carried out an empirical study in order to understand European customers' security perception of e-commerce in post-COVID scenario. They found varying levels of sensitivity to the cybersecurity issues of e-commerce. Their investigation further showed customers from Denmark, Sweden and Netherlands were more open to e-commerce compared to customers from other European countries. Gull et al. (2022) carried out an empirical study on mobile commerce applications in Saudi Arabia and found that customers perceive the need for security enhancement of mobile commerce applications there.

Cybercrimes and E-Commerce

Numerous studies have highlighted cybercrimes targeting e-commerce and ways to enhance e-commerce security. Katherine Smith (Smith, 2011) investigated the origin of e-commerce and associated risks. She also discussed types of cybercrime that impede e-commerce and that e-commerce is one of the most important aspects of corporate globalization. Reduced business obstacles, globalization of capital markets, the drive toward International Financial Reporting Standards (IFRSs), and internet financial reporting are all contributing factors. Smith referred to e-risks as a possibility of financial and technological issues related to conducting business online. The businesses face new obstacles as economic, industrial, and regulatory situations change.

Cyberspace is open to criminals looking to abuse computer networks (Smith, 2011). Some people attempt to enter a company's computer system simply to see if they might be able to. When hackers get access to a system, they could potentially cause serious difficulties by removing or altering data. Some hackers wreak havoc by writing programs that duplicate themselves and occasionally carry out destructive programming instructions such as random file deletion. Some noteworthy risks include: i) change in the e-commerce landscape replacing outdated solutions; ii) the volume and scope of hazards could grow due to international company operations; iii) computing power, connectivity, and speed could propagate viruses more efficiently, compromising systems within entire networks, compound errors, and harming interconnected parties; iv) hackers are always coming up with new hacking tech, which means new refined risks for businesses. Smith further investigated the studies related to cybercrime (Smith, 2011). Another very common cybercrime is a computer virus that may attach itself to other programs and then activates itself at a later time, and could cause significant damage to computer systems or files, not necessarily to steal data through phishing, but only to cause general disorder within an organisation(Smith, 2011). In addition, Botnet are setup by hacker with directions to monitor the computer systems, and or networks, they have been leashed upon. Cyberterrorism is another cybercrime used by terrorists that inflict damage to online computer systems, such as shutting down e-commerce websites and/or erasing files.

Chevers (Chevers et. al. 2019) studied the impact of cybercrimes on the e-banking sector and proposed a model to assess the role of cybercrime in preventing financial institutions from using e-banking. They suggested a greater understanding of cybercrimes could lead to more effective prevention and detection measures. Their study gave way to 3 hypotheses Their first hypothesis is based on phishing, where it is supposed to have an adverse effect on the acceptance of e-banking. Phishing is very widespread on websites that ask for credit card information. These actions are prevalent on websites such as banking and sites that employ online payment systems. Assailants create phony clones of official bank websites to convince potential victims to access their accounts and maintain sensitive information such as bank account numbers, passwords, and security question answers in this way. A phishing target might also fall victim to hacking or identity theft since the information obtained on the victim can be used in different unlawful ways.

This leads to the formulation of Chevers's second hypothesis, (Chevers et. al. 2019), that identity has a potentially damaging impact on e-banking. A phishing attacker might consider hacking as a destination. It is a criminal activity of entering into a computer by intentionally deceiving protection procedures to steal information normally done through a trojan horse. White, black, and grey hats are commonly used terms that describe different types of hackers. Black hat hackers make up the mainstream of hackers and enter networks without permission and with harmful intent and steal information. Chevers's third hypothesis, (Chevers et. al. 2019), is hacking has an adverse effect on e-banking. All three hypothesis were tested through a survey which proved all three hypotheses to be true.

Digital forensics, which deals with obtaining data and examining crime events and tools to present them in court as evidence, has evolved into a critical tool and software application in the battle against cybercrimes. Fianyi (Fianyi, 2016) studied the steps taken to detect and prevent cyber-attacks through digital forensic techniques to help clients decrease their susceptibility to fraudulent transactions and in turn reduce fraud-related business losses. Since conducting business online, as well as other related online activities, have become inextricably intertwined with our daily lives, this research investigated the risks, damages, and expenses that cybercrimes pose to individuals and businesses when they are targetted. Amazon and eBay were used as case studies for respondents who utilize these well-known e-commerce sites for a variety of transactions. A total of 60 volunteer respondents were chosen at random to participate in the study. The data was examined using descriptive-analytical techniques which revealed three basic findings. First, it was discovered that the majority of respondents paid for their online purchases with a visa debit card, indicating that the money is in their account. The use of American Express was the minimum informed method of online payment, implying that few people utilize it. Second, many respondents encountered several forms of cybercrimes including phishing vishing, spoofing, e-theft, cyberterrorism, malware, and spam.

Setiawan et al., (2018) studied the effects of cybercrimes on e-business and trust. They investigated the adoption of a development model for consumers and setup cybercrime definition as cyber scam, privacy violation, and the usage of personal data without consent. Online shoppers are frequently exposed to risks such as credit card fraud and acquiring items they did not seek. This is an illustration of how online shopping has a detrimental impact on consumer perceptions. As an outcome, it was determined that cyber security could influence customers' attitudes toward online stores.

Furthermore, they stated that business analysts are optimistic about the future of the internet site when it comes to digital purchasing of products (B2C) and company-to-company dealings (B2B). The elements of an online business, on the other hand, are more likely to fail to retain their customers. This is not restricted to the internet expansion strategy alone; the company must also pay attention to its current customers and find ways, trust building for instance, in order to retain them in the long run. This concludes to the fact that building trust with the customers is very important for customer retention. They noted three main effects of cybercrimes on customers' purchasing behavior. The option to repurchase online, or signup for repeated orders for a set period of time, is gradually becoming a marketing tool for consumers, and cybercrime has the power to depreciate the information provided on the internet. Setiawan claim that online security issues, such as unsafe online transactions, are driven by a lack of awareness of online deception, which can happen through direct contact and using, and believing information on, social media Setiawan et al., (2018).

Apau & Koranteng (2019) studied the impact of cybercrime and trust on e-commerce technologies in Ghana. They used an online questionnaire survey approach, and data was thoroughly examined using Partial Least Square Structural Equation Modelling. The Theory of Planned Behavior (TPB) was employed on the hypothetical grounds for this investigation which is an expansion of other well-known theories. The TBP has been used to describe the correlation between human approach and conduct, as well as to anticipate how people might behave based on data on their attitudes and intentions. They identified three basic constructs within the original theory: i) attitude; ii) subjective norm; and iii) received behavioral control which make intent and ultimately behavior. Apau & Koranteng (2019), in addition, proposed a conceptual model that combines cybercrime insights, internet medium believe, and trader believes with the Theory of Planned Behavior. This model suggests perception toward conduct and intention to buy products using e-commerce websites are directly influenced by cybercrime insights, trader believes, and internet medium believes. Apau & Koranteng (2019) formulated some basic hypothesis: trust on e-commerce sellers and internet medium positively affects e-commerce consumers' purchase, consumer's attitude towards behavior. Moreover, cybercrime perceptions have a negative impact on attitude towards behavior and consumer's intention to make online purchases. The data collected for the study showed that trust in internet media, attitude toward behavior, subjective norms, perceived behavioral control, and cybercrime beliefs are all significant determinants of online purchase intention. These findings clarify the effects of trust and cybercrime perceptions on users' purchasing intentions for businesses and stakeholders. It also emphasizes the importance of including security elements that lessen risks of using e-commerce platforms. The collection of data through a non-probabilistic approach limited the research. As a result, the study's conclusions cannot be applied to the full population. In addition, study did not consider demographic details of respondents.

Fahlevi et al., (2019) studied the impacts of cybercrime on digital business in Indonesia. They employed interview methodologies and descriptive data from research sources of digital business to investigate cybercrime in Indonesia. They found, based more on past research, while cybercrime is a worldwide concern, some of the wealthier nations with significant global corporations, particularly e-commerce firms, have become the world's greatest crime market. Cybercrime assaults are more common in developed countries than in undeveloped countries, prompting several countries to enact unlawful legislation as part of preventative measures. Because cybercrime creates a genuine overhead for organizations, the resolution of cluster security in digital business is taken extremely seriously and cautiously as published statistics suggest the total deficit triggered by crime extends to $ 1.5 Trillion per year in Indonesia.

Legal Implications of E-Commerce

Busy lifestyles and convenience of home delivery have played major roles in the rise of e-commerce Wong and Choi (2022). When the pandemic sent the world to a total halt in 2020, everyone turned to their trusted steed in the dark, dire, and testing times of global lockdowns, the internet. While large businesses were already thriving with their online dealings such as Amazon, eBay, Netflix, and Etsy, the pandemic nudged small businesses toward e-commerce as well Saeed et al., (2013), Saeed, (2019), Caplan (2021), Mckinsey (2020). The lockdowns saw a lot of business losses and some claimed bankruptcy. The lockdowns did, however, bring in more profits for small online businesses Fairlie and Fossen (2022), Masterson (2020).

E-commerce has led many a business to exponential growths and turning over revenues worth billions. With all of its success e-commerce has always faced more than its fair share of threats of cybercrimes including identity theft, hacking, and payment fraud Fianyi (2016). Cybercrime threats have increased in both the number and the intensity of attacks, evolving into elusive polymorphic malware that changes the code within itself Webroot Inc (2021). Ransomware attacks have also grown phenomenally since the COVID-19 lockdowns as the world shifted to online learning and work-from-home, SonicWall (2022).

People's hesitation to make online purchases stem from the fear of all the looming threats related to online shopping, such as online payment and credit card fraud; and buying goods that they haven't seen or examined physically. In the name of safeguarding public interest government bodies around the globe have imposed regulations and laws concerning e-commerce. These laws include restrictions of buyers' age, client data protection, licences and permits, inclusion of taxes, security of payment gateways, and shipping restrictions for substances such as liquids and medications Estay (2022). Contractual laws for online transactions follow the traditional principles of commerce, in addition it is important to consider different international laws given how online trade involves products and services moving across international borders, Zottola (2014).

Different countries have imposed their own set of laws and regulations on e-businesses. China has imposed regulations on e-commerce that ensure online platforms provide comprehensive information about the sellers and the products, safeguard customer rights, offer strong customer data protection, network operation security, clear e-contracts, proper restrictions on offering only bundled goods as the default purchase option.

Pakistan's legal framework for e-commerce is based on three statues: the Electronic Transaction Ordinance of 2002 ETO (2002), the Payment Systems and Electronic Fund Transfers Act, 2007 (PSEFT 2007), and Pakistan Electronic Crimes Act, 2016 (PECA 2016) which streamlined offences and penalties regarding e-commerce (MoC, 2019). In addition to the existing acts the State Bank of Pakistan imposed further regulations on e-commerce. These regulations include Regulations for Payment Card Security (2016), Regulations for Security of Internet Banking (2015), Regulations for Electronic Money Institutions (2019), Branchless Banking Regulations (2016), and Regulations for Prevention against cyber-attacks (2016).

E-commerce regulations in India include Consumer Protection Act of 2019 which states the e-businesses must clearly publish their business policies, including the regular clauses of client data protection contracts, possible jurisdiction matters, returns and exchanges, types of payment options they offer, and delivery, shipment, and receiving charges, Mir (2022), Singh (1999), Shah & Nagree (2002).

Internet of Healthcare Things (IoHT) has also been a major target of cybercrime attacks in recent years. A set of suitable regulatory framework is essential for the safe working of IoHT, the framework must include secure healthcare related data, Shahid et al. (2022).

With countries enforcing their own, and some unique, laws and regulations on e-commerce and online platforms, conflicts arise when goods move across borders. For instance, European Union only allow their citizen's data to be used outside of the EU borders presenting extra challenges for developing countries with their Standard Contractual Clauses (SCC) and Binding Corporate Rules (BCR), which are cost more money and time, Mattoo and Meltzer (2022).

USA trading laws, imposed by the Federal Trade Commission, treat e-commerce similar to regular trade with some further regulations imposed such as clear privacy policy disclosure before collection of customer data, children's online privacy protection, FDC (2017, 2022). The FTC have further been working on safeguarding public interest, more to do with e-commerce, through innovations technology, enforcing more transparency and accountability through legislation in collection and use of consumer data, protection against bias introduced through 'algorithmic harms', where AI influences public decisions.

Machine Learning in E-Commerce

ML techniques play an important role in discovering underlying patterns and difficult to detect information within large datasets. This consequently leads to empower the decision-making processes within businesses and applications. Applications of ML usually involve prediction, classification, feature extraction, prescriptive analysis, and optimization. There are three basic ML models: supervised, unsupervised, and reinforcement. The supervised model works by improving the algorithm performance by practice as it learns from experience to improve the performance on new data by using labelled examples. This process involves comparing the output of prediction with the expected results. The unsupervised models work with unlabeled and unclassified data, this helps in exploring data patterns and hidden structures. The reinforcement model utilizes trial and error method to find out the correct behavior by interacting with the environment (Kaur, 2021).

Due to the huge benefits of ML, its techniques were adopted widely in e-commerce areas starting with inventory management and this later expanded to customer experience. ML applications have been replacing humans in many domains specifically in operational tasks that consume human resources with low margin profits such as the industry sector. This has led to many retail companies adopting technologies for their processing (Makers 2021).

E-commerce companies have multiple reasons for taking an interest in ML techniques, for instance, using ML aids in focusing on the most important information within their business by analysing huge amounts of organizational data. e-commerce Another reason is increasing the conversion rate to empower on-site search engines by analysing user's search with the previously analysed data to improve the recommendation process for customers based on their interest and suggest similar products that matches their need. Stock management, competing products management, synchronizing the stock level and supply chain with the website recommendations, running marketing campaigns relevant to the customers are more benefits that the use of ML bring to businesses. Moreover, ML techniques are used to improve the efficiency of the business operations and predictions for future demands, to take decisions based on solid grounds extracted from data, and to enhance the process of business by improving the efficiency of fraud detection and prevention (Bawack, 2022).

Based on an investigation conducted in (Weber, 2019) the use of ML in retail companies aimed at supporting various marketing critical decisions, replacing high-cost human resources, and to optimize low-margin business activities. Their study has categorized the ML initiatives adopted in ten largest retail companies worldwide as: classification, prediction, clustering, optimization, anomaly detection, ranking, and recommendation. Literature review shows evidence that the largest retail companies around the world are using applications to manage and place orders, provide online customers service to automate the regular activities, transporting and delivering goods, and for financial accounting.

One of the main fields in employing ML in e-commerce is for products categorization and classification, for this purpose, the research conducted in (Pawłowski, 2021a) have utilized ML algorithms to categorize products with their taxonomy labels to ease the process of products search and listing. To achieve their intended goal, different methods were utilized: Single Classifier, Top-Down Classifier, and

CNN + Glove pre trained word embedding. The results showed that the state-of-the-art SVM classifier combined with TF-IDF feature extraction techniques provided the best text classification result for the e-commerce environment for the challenges faced.

Pawłowski et. al. (Pawłowski, 2021a) has applied machine learning techniques to solve the issue of products classification in the e-commerce systems due to its important role during searching and browsing which influence customers' decisions and shopping experience. The used method involved using Bag-of-word natural language processing technique for text classification. The dataset obtained from Polish industry website included products information, such as name and category, and the search log file was used to train and test the ML model. Shrivastava et. al (Shrivastava 2017) have developed a predictive model to predict product category in e-commerce using Multiclass Decision Forest' ML algorithm that was deployed on Microsoft's Azure which is a public cloud service platform. The developed model was trained on dataset of nine categories and ninety-three features. The obtained results are promising in terms of the achieved model accuracy and can be used for the purpose of analyzing e-commerce data with cloud platform for product categorization. In order to determine the best model for the classification process, twelve different ML classifiers were used for training and testing. Their research findings prove the validity of their hypothesis that classification accuracy is expected to be improved by supplying textual names of products that reflect its real features along with user's content. Machine learning techniques were used for the purpose of online consumer conversion by Lee et. al. (Lee, 2021). In their work, they studied the performance of eight major machine learning algorithms that could potentially be used in e-commerce activities. An approximation of about 374,749 different behaviors of online consumers was collected from different platforms such as Google Merchandise and online shopping stores to investigate the best ML algorithm to predict online consumer. By applying 5-fold cross validation, the results showed that the XGB model was found to be the best technique for the intended goals of predicting online customers' conversion.

Several works understood the importance of identifying the relations between users and products in the e-commerce environment and how to better promote their products to the users, which helps in improving the business based on customer's interest. Those works also address a number of other issues as well. They have reviewed different ML techniques applied in the field of online products recommendation. The findings of the review study confirm the importance of such systems in e-commerce applications (Zhang, 2020) Machine learning techniques were employed in e-commerce for the task of recommending products to users based on their interests, the recommender system relies mainly on textual or image information for customer's search and purchase. The published work on by (Zhang, 2020) proposed a ML approach for similar image-based recommender system with applying Principal Component Analysis (PCA) for dimensionality reduction. A similar image was found by applying the K-Mean++. The approach provided superior performance and helped in improving the process of e-commerce product recommendation.

In the context of predicting e-commerce customer churn, the study presented in (Matuszelański, and Kopczewska 2022), focused on analyzing transaction datasets for a number of e-commerce retail companies in Brazil. For their study, they collected 100,000 orders data on store transactions from the Kaggle.com public repository. The collected data included: orders numerical data such as the number of items bought, data on customers' textual reviews after purchase, and socio-geo-demographic data. Two ML algorithms were employed for the modelling stage: the XGBoost and Logistic Regression. The findings of their study were the number of characteristics that indicates customer's tendency to churn which was summarized as: the amount paid in the first purchase, how many items were purchased and their delivery costs, and the demographic environment and location. Customers' reviews for companies' services and products were a main source of useful information which helps in business improvement and identification of strengths and weaknesses.

In this context, the research conducted by Hong et. al. (Hong et. al., 2019) analyzed the textual information on online customer reviews for fresh e-commerce market using Neural Networks to measure customer's satisfaction logistics. The study focused on China's largest fresh market. They found that the main factors contributing to customer satisfaction include ease of communication, reliability, convenience, and responsiveness.

Product reviews play an important role in customer's decisions, especially on e-commerce platforms where customers cannot view and examine products as they would in real life. ML techniques are widely used in analyzing sentiment product reviews which aid in customers' decision making. The work presented in (Le et. al. 2021) applied RNN ML algorithms to improve customer service by exploiting emotional words from customer reviews for sentiment evaluation for Vietnamese language. The system aggregates data from the e-commerce websites, then classifies the reviews by exploiting features extracted from customer's feedback. They used a dataset of 30,000 records with 80% and 20% split for training and testing. The results showed that the top five features affecting customers reviews were: price, shipment, product quality, the design, and customer satisfaction with the shopping experience. Their work was also advanced by developing and connecting a web-app with the server to visualise the research results.

Another work that used ML techniques for customers review sentiment analysis was for mobile e-commerce application (Olagunju et. al., 2021) where seven top African mobile e-commerce applications were included in the study. Five supervised ML algorithms were used: Stochastic Gradient Descent (SGD), Logistic Regression (LR), Support Vector Machine (SVM), Multinomial Naïve Bayes (MNB), and Random Forest (RF), besides Linguistic Inquiry Word Count (LIWC), to build a sentiment analysis model that predicted and classified customer reviews in to positive and negative. The obtained results showed that the best ML algorithm to be used for the purpose of classifying e-commerce customers reviews is the MNB. Results also showed that customers' positive reviews depended mostly on some factors including user friendliness, fast delivery, offers and discounts, and offering affordable products. The negative reviews were mainly motivated by bad customer service and return policy, shipping costs, packaging, mistakes with delivery, unreliable sellers and poor-quality products, and other technological issues such as payment platforms.

Other efforts in using ML in the field were made to improve security and fraud detection in the online business environment. In the work presented in (Wu et. al., 2018), a model for classifying websites into counterfeit and legitimate was built in order to improve customer experience and to increase awareness on how to identify and avoid fraudulent websites. For training the model, 400 legitimate websites were collected using Google search engine, where 400 counterfeit ones were collected from Fraudulent fan page ranking, Whoscall, and Google search engine. Three classifiers were used: Logistic Regression (LR), Decision tree (DT), and Support vector machine (SVM). The work identified the characteristics of fraudulent websites by the length of the URL as those tends to be shorter, the content element as huge saving ads appears and there are no links to social media or mobile apps, and by the content structure.

In (Xu et. al. 2019), an evaluation of credit risks was conducted. They implemented a user-friendly system for e-commerce sellers' credit risk evaluation by using ANN, logistic regression, and dynamic Bayesian network. The dataset for training included 609 sellers' credit cases taken from Taobao. The results suggested using ANN provided the highest accuracy in offering a secure and fast method for online transactions.

Secure Payment in E-Commerce

Cybercriminals frequently steal sensitive personal and financial information from millions caught unawares. With resources and skills required to hack into a vast number of databases, cybercriminals have rendered the black market as a multibillion-dollar business. According to a report (Gai et al, 2017), some of the threats covered in digital businesses are narrowed down as the following:

1. Business operations
2. Butsourcing

The main focus here, however, is on the security and privacy issues that arise during the payment process according to the customer and merchant perspectives.

Verizon published the Data Breach Investigations Report in 2018 (Verizon, 2018, p. 4), which disclosed there had been over 53,000 information security related incidents. The report elaborated further that 36% of the data breaches had been caused either during or after online payment transactions.

Enterprise owners ought to be more cautious and aware of suspicious activities within the company to minimize risks. Identity fraud is one of the major forms of deceit and cause of financial loss in e-commerce. Electronic payment methods that have been in frequent use over the last two decades include credit cards, debit cards, card fees and e-money (Hami & Cheng, 2002). A fraudster can make multiple purchases from a single IP address using various cards and dodge the security check. To seem like a real customer, a scammer can setup fake emails, usernames, and addresses. Internet fraud might also take place due to internal threats if an employee leaks the data and breaches the company's confidentiality regulations. Offenders have used some of the stolen information to open bank accounts, acquire credit cards, and open telephone or utility accounts, converting the relevant data they managed to steal into cash. In 2020, the Federal Trade Commission of USA (FTC) received 4.8 million reports of identity theft and credit card fraud, totaling $4.5 billion in losses. The number of incidents and loss in income in 2019 increased by 45%.

In addition to this, credit cards are one of the most famous targets for fraud and theft (Delamaire et al, 2009). Various studies have been carried out to figure out the root cause for this infringement. The first technique has been widely used by black-hat hackers who use modern software to generate fake credit card numbers along with their expiry dates. This is accomplished through the use of the Luhn algorithm, which is used by credit card companies to assign a credit card number to a customer. Another approach is infecting a computer by keylogger programs that can retrieve sensitive details. Spam mail is used by cybercriminals to affect web users by asking them to download free games or software, and when these mails are launched and downloaded, sniffers and key loggers are automatically downloaded alongside, installed, and run on the users' computer. Finally, professional hackers can clone banking websites, which have more frequent user visits, and send it to the users with the intent of extracting private or personal information.

Email phishing, the first type of phishing, is carried out through email messages, its primary being persuasion of the receiver to willingly reveal their username and password or any other sensitive information that the phisher may require. Vishing, the second type of phishing, is based upon the same principle as phishing but over voice calls. The customer can be asked to reveal their bank ID and other financial details. And the third and final type of phishing, smishing, uses short message service (SMS) to prey upon the individuals. The phisher convinces the recipient that their account (PayPal, bank etc) has been compromised and they must share their current login information in order to gain access to the system. Once the fraudster has obtained the login information, they can change the password and prevent the victim from gaining access to their own account.

Merchant identity fraud is similar to the consumer identity fraud but here the scammer sets up a con website after gaining illegal access to the original one. The fake site provides cheap products to users thereby asking them for payment through credit cards. The user credit card is stolen when the payment is made and the conman uses this newly founded "business" to charge customers' credit cards repeatedly, then closes the account and walks away with money, having left the real business to deal with several recurring billing, consumer complaints, and forgery reports.

SOLUTIONS AND RECOMMENDATIONS

Various cybercrimes, such as data theft, malware attack, phishing emails, etc. attacking e-commerce websites have become all too common in recent years, with increased costs for businesses and downstream impacts that enable various sorts of frauds. Security control measures cannot only become a preventive shield against these crimes within the organization but can also help customers to become the prey of these attacks. In the light of the expanding threat landscape, implementing and incorporating security mechanisms is critical to appropriately addressing risks more specifically related to the e-commerce sector. Multifaceted preventive controls help to foster creativity, an increase in revenue, and improved customer trust. Risk evaluations also provide awareness of cyber risk management methods, which produce practical benefits, and assist business executives and security professionals in identifying and prioritizing essential assets. In addition, integrating threat modeling at the developmental stages, before the software goes in for production and to public-facing settings, can help to mitigate the risks introduced by unsafe coding techniques. Because of their general populace architecture, e-commerce companies are particularly vulnerable to threats. Regular monitoring of these external systems helps with the detection of key vulnerabilities in online applications, such as unsafe code, old or unsupported versions, and known but unpatched flaws. These tools are used to enhance targeted protection methods and improve patch management procedures. Furthermore, strong authentication management methods are an important part of cybercrime prevention strategies. Similar methods, such as use of digital forensic techniques, zero trust adoption, arranging security awareness programs for employees, and keeping an eye on external engagements, can help organizations deal with cybercrimes.

To make the e-payment secure, business owners have prioritized payment security to detect and block internal and external cyber threats. Consequently, cybersecurity is now more vital than entrepreneurial digitalization. During transmission, the data must be securely encrypted, and any saved payment information must be safeguarded as the fraudulent activities have been on a rise. Top-notch quality payment gateways have become mandatory. A payment gateway acts as an entrance point to the national banking system. (Masihuddin et al, 2017). It is linked to consumers, banks, and traders through the Internet and is responsible for the speed, reliability, and safety of all transactions (Hassan et al, 2020). Businesses should apply for SSL (Secure Server Layer) certification which makes the site data difficult to hack and the customer data will not leak. Some of the more common SSL certificates include extended validation, wildcard SSL certificates, AMT SSL certificates, and general-purpose SSL certificates. Redirecting the payment to platforms such as PayPal, Amazon Pay etc. adds extra layers of protection which ensures any threats posed would be tackled efficiently. These apps usually employ tokenization, which allows the user to pay without revealing their credit card number. So, even if their transaction information is compromised, their actual credit card number is safe. Asking for Card Verification Codes (CVV) at checkout prevents fraudulent transactions. The merchant can confirm that the owner of a credit card is the one making the purchase with the user by verifying the three or four-digit number on the back of the card.

FUTURE RESEARCH DIRECTIONS

Quality of system design is an important trust enabler, so there is a need for adoption of user centric system design approaches to align technological artifacts with user needs, which will, in turn, enhance customer trust (Saeed et al., 2013, AlGothami & Saeed,2021). As far as secure e-payment is concerned, E-commerce enterprises can aid their clients by reminding them of official channels, websites, and payment platforms on a consistent basis. Enterprises ought to inform individuals about any fraudulent websites that may try to extract their information. While the main responsibility to ensure their client data and transactions are secure falls on online businesses, the customers are also liable to carefully inspect internet sites before entering delicate information such as bank account details, credit card numbers, and online wallet information. Customers can check for a trust seal or for any suspicious URLs that do not have the same credentials as the original site.

Using a secure password, which contains a different array of characters, numbers, and symbols, is one of the best e-commerce payment fraud prevention techniques to avoid password or code hacking. Using secure password storage apps, such as Lastpass, NordPass, and PassCamp etc. to jumble or mix up passwords can also prove to be helpful in ensuring payment safety. Furthermore, it is instrumental that e-commerce sites do their part by joining hands with a payment provider that is coherent with an upper echelon of data security.

CONCLUSION

The Internet has effectively, and successfully, opened up new market opportunities while also ensuring it has a positive influence on established firms. On the other hand, it has come across an enormous number of security challenges. It is the main source of fraud including payment frauds as well as fake products with fake reviews. It is very interesting scientifically to understand which security challenges are addressed by business organisations in securing their technological infrastructure, and how customers perceive these security concerns while engaging in online business, and how much trust they might be willing to put in the marketing information presented on social commerce sites. Making secure transactions may appear to be an insurmountable effort in this Web-savvy era, but by taking essential precautions, both the merchant and the consumer might be able to reap the benefits of a safer environment free of scammers. The only way to combat the payment fraud threat is through effective fraud management, which includes regular monitoring and updating of prevention setups on constant basis as transaction scam schemes evolve gradually and constantly.

REFERENCES

AlGothami, S. S., & Saeed, S. (2021). Digital Transformation and Usability: User Acceptance of Tawakkalna Application During Covid-19 in Saudi Arabia. In *Pandemic, Lockdown, and Digital Transformation* (pp. 95–109). Springer. doi:10.1007/978-3-030-86274-9_6

Ali, F. (2021, February 19). *Ecommerce trends amid coronavirus pandemic in charts*. Digital Commerce 360. Available online: https://www.digitalcommerce360.com/2021/02/19/ecommerce-during-coronavirus-pandemic-in-charts/

Ali, N. I., Samsuri, S., Sadry, M., Brohi, I. A., & Shah, A. (2016, November). Online shopping satisfaction in Malaysia: A framework for security, trust and cybercrime. In *2016 6th International Conference on Information and Communication Technology for The Muslim World (ICT4M)* (pp. 194-198). IEEE. 10.1109/ICT4M.2016.048

Apau, R., & Koranteng, F. N. (2019). Impact of cybercrime and trust on the use of e-commerce technologies: An application of the theory of planned behavior. *International Journal of Cyber Criminology*, *13*(2), 228–254. doi:10.5281/zenodo.3697886

Bawack, R. E., Wamba, S. F., Carillo, K. D. A., & Akter, S. (2022). Artificial intelligence in E-Commerce: A bibliometric study and literature review. *Electronic Markets*, *32*(1), 297–338. doi:10.100712525-022-00537-z PMID:35600916

Bhatia, N. L., Shukla, V. K., Punhani, R., & Dubey, S. K. (2021, June). Growing Aspects of Cyber Security in E-Commerce. In *2021 International Conference on Communication information and Computing Technology (ICCICT)* (pp. 1-6). IEEE. 10.1109/ICCICT50803.2021.9510152

Bhatt, C. (2022, May 17). *10 Best Fintech Apps You Should Look Up to In*. Techtic Solutions. Available online: https://www.techtic.com/blog/best-fintech-apps/

Bhowmik, A., & Karforma, S. (2021). Linear feedback shift register and integer theory: A state-of-art approach in security issues over e-commerce. *Electronic Commerce Research*, 1–21. doi:10.100710660-021-09477-w

Buil-Gil, D., Miró-Llinares, F., Moneva, A., Kemp, S., & Díaz-Castaño, N. (2021). Cybercrime and shifts in opportunities during COVID-19: A preliminary analysis in the UK. *European Societies*, *23*(S1), S47–S59. doi:10.1080/14616696.2020.1804973

Caplan, J. (2021). *E-Commerce Has Been A Lifeline For Small Businesses During The Pandemic. Where Do They Go From Here?* Available at: https://www.forbes.com/sites/johncaplan/2021/05/03/ecommerce-has-been-a-lifeline-for-small-businesses-during-the-pandemic-where-do-they-go-from-here/?sh=45570e4a3587

Chen, C. M., Cai, Z. X., & Wen, D. W. M. (2021). Designing and Evaluating an Automatic Forensic Model for Fast Response of Cross-Border E-Commerce Security Incidents. *Journal of Global Information Management*, *30*(2), 1–19. doi:10.4018/JGIM.20220301.oa5

Chen, J., Chen, J., & Xue, Z. (n.d.). *Chinese e-commerce law: new challenges and new opportunities.* Spring 2019 Legal Briefing. Available at: https://www.inhouselawyer.co.uk/legal-briefing/chinese-e-commerce-law-new-challenges-and-new-opportunities/

Chevers, D. A. (2019). The impact of cybercrime on e-banking: A proposed model. *International Conference on Information Resources Management*, 10.

Choi, Y., & Mai, D. Q. (2018). The sustainable role of the e-trust in the B2C e-commerce of Vietnam. *Sustainability*, *10*(1), 291. doi:10.3390u10010291

Choo, K. K. R. (2011). The cyber threat landscape: Challenges and future research directions. *Computers & Security*, *30*(8), 719–731. doi:10.1016/j.cose.2011.08.004

What Is Cybersecurity? (2022, May 12). Cisco.

D'Adamo, I., González-Sánchez, R., Medina-Salgado, M. S., & Settembre-Blundo, D. (2021). E-commerce calls for cyber-security and sustainability: How european citizens look for a trusted online environment. *Sustainability*, *13*(12), 6752. doi:10.3390u13126752

Dean, B. (2021). *Etsy User and Revenue Stats: How Many People Shop on Etsy in 2022.* Available online: https://backlinko.com/etsy-users

Delamaire, Abdou, & Pointon. (2009). Credit card fraud and detection techniques: A review. *Banks and Bank Systems, 4*(2).

Electronic Commerce (e-commerce). (2021, September 17). *Investopedia.* Available online: https://www.investopedia.com/terms/e/ecommerce.asp

Estay, B. (2022). *How to (Realistically) Start an Online Business That (Actually) Grows in 2022.* Available at: https://www.bigcommerce.com/blog/how-to-start-online-business/

Fahlevi, M., Saparudin, M., Maemunah, S., Irma, D., & Ekhsan, M. (2019). Cybercrime Business Digital in Indonesia. *E3S Web of Conferences, 125*, 1–5. doi:10.1051/e3sconf/201912521001

Fairlie, R., & Fossen, F. M. (2022). The early impacts of the COVID-19 pandemic on business sales. *Small Business Economics*, *58*(4), 1853–1864. doi:10.100711187-021-00479-4

Fatonah, S., Yulandari, A., & Wibowo, F. W. (2018). A Review of E-Payment System in E-Commerce. *Journal of Physics: Conference Series, 1140*, 012033. doi:10.1088/1742-6596/1140/1/012033

Fianyi, I. (2016). *Curbing cyber-crime and Enhancing e-commerce security with Digital Forensics.* https://arxiv.org/abs/1610.08369

FTC. (2017). *Text of the Federal Trade Commission Enforcement Policy Statement.* https://www.ftc.gov/legal-library/browse/federal-trade-commission-enforcement-policy-statement-regarding-applicability-childrens-online

FTC. (2022). *Policy Statement on Education Technology and the Children's Online Privacy Protection Act.* https://www.ftc.gov/legal-library/browse/policy-statement-federal-trade-commission-education-technology-childrens-online-privacy-protection

FTC. (2022). *Combatting Online Harms Through Innovation: A Report to Congress*. https://www.ftc.gov/reports/combatting-online-harms-through-innovation

Fuscaldo, D. (2021, November 19). Everything You Need to Know About E-Commerce. *Business News Daily*. Available online: https://www.businessnewsdaily.com/15858-what-is-e-commerce.html

Gai, K., Qiu, M., & Sun, X. (2018). A survey on FinTech. *Journal of Network and Computer Applications*, *103*, 262–273. doi:10.1016/j.jnca.2017.10.011

Gull, H., Saeed, S., Iqbal, S. Z., Bamarouf, Y. A., Alqahtani, M. A., Alabbad, D. A., Saqib, M., al Qahtani, S. H., & Alamer, A. (2022). An Empirical Study of Mobile Commerce and Customers Security Perception in Saudi Arabia. *Electronics (Basel)*, *11*(3), 293. doi:10.3390/electronics11030293

Hami, A. N. R., & Cheng, A. Y. (2013). *A Risk Perception Analysis on the use of Electronic Payment Systems by Young Adult*. Academic Press.

Hassan, M. A., Shukur, Z., Hasan, M. K., & Al-Khaleefa, A. S. (2020). A Review on Electronic Payments Security. *Symmetry*, *12*(8), 1344. doi:10.3390ym12081344

Hong, W., Zheng, C., Wu, L., & Pu, X. (2019). Analyzing the Relationship between Consumer Satisfaction and Fresh E-Commerce Logistics Service Using Text Mining Techniques. *Sustainability*, *11*(13), 3570. doi:10.3390u11133570

JRana, P., & Baria,. (2015). A Survey on Fraud Detection Techniques in Ecommerce. *International Journal of Computers and Applications*, *113*(14), 5–7. doi:10.5120/19892-1898

Junadi & Sfenrianto. (2015). A Model of Factors Influencing Consumer's Intention To Use E-payment System in Indonesia. *Procedia Computer Science, 59*, 214–220. doi:10.1016/j.procs.2015.07.557

Kaur, S., Gupta, S., Singh, S., & Arora, T. (2021). A Review on Natural Disaster Detection in Social Media and Satellite Imagery Using Machine Learning and Deep Learning. *International Journal of Image and Graphics*, 2250040. Advance online publication. doi:10.1142/S0219467822500401

Khadam, U., Iqbal, M. M., Saeed, S., Dar, S. H., Ahmad, A., & Ahmad, M. (2021). Advanced security and privacy technique for digital text in smart grid communications. *Computers & Electrical Engineering*, *93*, 107205. doi:10.1016/j.compeleceng.2021.107205

Kim, S. S. (2020). Purchase intention in the online open market: Do concerns for e-commerce really matter? *Sustainability*, *12*(3), 773. doi:10.3390u12030773

Kim, Y., Choi, J., Park, Y., & Yeon, J. (2016). The Adoption of Mobile Payment Services for "Fintech". *International Journal of Applied Engineering Research: IJAER*, *11*(2), 1058–1061.

Koetsier, J. (2021). *Fintech 2021 top 100 apps: who's winning, emerging players, where it's all going*. Singular. https://www.singular.net/blog/top-fintech-apps-2021/

Le, N. B. V., & Huh, J. H. (2021). Applying Sentiment Product Reviews and Visualization for BI Systems in Vietnamese E-Commerce Website: Focusing on Vietnamese Context. *Electronics (Basel)*, *10*(20), 2481. doi:10.3390/electronics10202481

Lee, J., Jung, O., Lee, Y., Kim, O., & Park, C. (2021). A Comparison and Interpretation of Machine Learning Algorithm for the Prediction of Online Purchase Conversion. *Journal of Theoretical and Applied Electronic Commerce Research, 16*(5), 1472–1491. doi:10.3390/jtaer16050083

Lee, S. J., Ahn, C., Song, K. M., & Ahn, H. (2018). Trust and distrust in e-commerce. *Sustainability, 10*(4), 1015. doi:10.3390u10041015

M. (2020). *The History of Ecommerce: How Did It All Begin?* Miva Blog. Available online: https://blog.miva.com/the-history-of-ecommerce-how-did-it-all-begin

Makers, P. (2021). *Artificial Intelligence, Machine Learning and Big Data in Finance.* OECD.

Masihuddin, M., Islam Khan, B. U., Islam Mattoo, M. M. U., & Olanrewaju, R. F. (2017). A Survey on E-Payment Systems: Elements, Adoption, Architecture, Challenges and Security Concepts. *Indian Journal of Science and Technology, 10*(20), 1–19. doi:10.17485/ijst/2017/v10i20/113930

Masterson, V. (2020). *6 ways the pandemic has changed businesses.* Available at: https://www.weforum.org/agenda/2020/11/covid-19-innovation-business-healthcare-restaurants/

Mattoo, A., & Meltzer, J. P. (2018). International data flows and privacy: The conflict and its resolution. *Journal of International Economic Law, 21*(4), 769–789. doi:10.1093/jiel/jgy044

Matuszelański, K., & Kopczewska, K. (2022). Customer Churn in Retail E-Commerce Business: Spatial and Machine Learning Approach. *Journal of Theoretical and Applied Electronic Commerce Research, 17*(1), 165–198. doi:10.3390/jtaer17010009

McKinsey & Company. (2020). *How COVID-19 has pushed companies over the technology tipping point—and transformed business forever.* Available at: https://www.mckinsey.com/business-functions/strategy-and-corporate-finance/our-insights/how-covid-19-has-pushed-companies-over-the-technology-tipping-point-and-transformed-business-forever

Mir, F. A. (2011). Emerging Legal Issues Of E-Commerce In India. *International Journal of Electronic Commerce Studies.* Available at: http://academic-pub.org/ojs/index.php/ijecs/article/view/976

MoC, Ministry of Commerce, Pakistan. (2019). *E-Commerce Policy of Pakistan.* https://www.commerce.gov.pk/content/uploads/2019/11/e-Commerce_Policy_of_Pakistan_Web.pdf

Nabi, F., Tao, X., & Yong, J. (2021). Security aspects in modern service component-oriented application logic for social e-commerce systems. *Social Network Analysis and Mining, 11*(1), 1–19. doi:10.100713278-020-00717-9

Naeem, H., Ullah, F., Naeem, M. R., Khalid, S., Vasan, D., Jabbar, S., & Saeed, S. (2020). Malware detection in industrial internet of things based on hybrid image visualization and deep learning model. *Ad Hoc Networks, 105*, 102154. doi:10.1016/j.adhoc.2020.102154

Olagunju, T., Oyebode, O., & Orji, R. (2020). Exploring Key Issues Affecting African Mobile eCommerce Applications Using Sentiment and Thematic Analysis. *IEEE Access: Practical Innovations, Open Solutions, 8*, 114475–114486. doi:10.1109/ACCESS.2020.3000093

Pabian, A., Pabian, B., & Reformat, B. (2020). E-Customer Security as a Social Value in the Sphere of Sustainability. *Sustainability*, *12*(24), 10590. doi:10.3390u122410590

Pawłowski, M. (2021a). Machine Learning Based Product Classification for eCommerce. *Journal of Computer Information Systems*, 1–10. doi:10.1080/08874417.2021.1910880

Qatawneh, A. M., Aldhmour, F. M., & Aldmour, L. T. (2016). The Impact of Applying the Electronic Cheque Clearing System on Employees' Satisfaction in Accounting Departments' of Jordanian Islamic Banks. *International Business Research*, *9*(2), 137. doi:10.5539/ibr.v9n2p137

Saeed, S. (2019). Digital Business adoption and customer segmentation: An exploratory study of expatriate community in Saudi Arabia. *ICIC Express Letters*, *13*, 133–139.

Saeed, S., Khan, M. A., & Ahmad, R. (Eds.). (2013). *Business strategies and approaches for effective engineering management*. IGI Global. doi:10.4018/978-1-4666-3658-3

Saeed, S., Wahab, F., Cheema, S. A., & Ashraf, S. (2013). Role of usability in e-government and e-commerce portals: An empirical study of Pakistan. *Life Science Journal*, *10*(1), 8–13.

Setiawan, N., Emia Tarigan, V. C., Sari, P. B., Rossanty, Y., Putra Nasution, M. D. T., & Siregar, I. (2018). Impact of cybercrime in e-business and trust. *International Journal of Civil Engineering and Technology*, *9*(7), 652–656.

Shah, A., & Nagree, P. (n.d.). *Legal Issues in E-Commerce*. Nishith Desai Associates. Available at: http://www.nishithdesai.com/fileadmin/user_upload/pdfs/Legal_issues_in_eCommerce.pdf

Shahid, J., Ahmad, R., Kiani, A. K., Ahmad, T., Saeed, S., & Almuhaideb, A. M. (2022). Data protection and privacy of the internet of healthcare things (IoHTs). *Applied Sciences (Basel, Switzerland)*, *12*(4), 1927. doi:10.3390/app12041927

Shakya, V., Chatterjee, J. M., & Thakur, R. N. (2021). Network Security and Its Impact on Business Strategy: A Case Study on E-Commerce Site Daraz. Com. *Network Security*, *3*(1).

Shrivastava, A., Sondhi, J.S., & Kumar, B. (2017). *Machine learning technique for product classification in e-commerce data using Microsoft Azure cloud*. Academic Press.

Singh, D. (1999). *Electronic Commerce: Issues for the South*. Trade-related Agenda, Development and Equity. Working Paper, South Centre.

Smith, K. T. (2011). An Analysis of E-Commerce: E-Risk, Global Trade, and Cybercrime. SSRN *Electronic Journal*. doi:10.2139/ssrn.1315423

SonicWall. (2022). *SonicWall Cyber Threat Report*. Available at: https://www.sonicwall.com/2022-cyber-threat-report/

Stewart, H., & Jürjens, J. (2018). *Data security and consumer trust in FinTech innovation in Germany*. Information & Computer Security. doi:10.1108/ICS-06-2017-0039

Taneja, B. (2021). The Digital Edge for M-Commerce to Replace E-Commerce. In Emerging Challenges, Solutions, and Best Practices for Digital Enterprise Transformation (pp. 299-318). IGI Global.

The Fintech 50 2021. (n.d.). *Forbes*. Retrieved May 30, 2022, from https://www.forbes.com/fintech/2021/#170f1f1f31a6

Verizon. (2018). *Data Breach Investigations Report*. Available online: https://www.verizon.com/about/sites/default/files/2018-Verizon-Annual-Report.pdf

Vinoth, S., Vemula, H. L., Haralayya, B., Mamgain, P., Hasan, M. F., & Naved, M. (2022). Application of cloud computing in banking and e-commerce and related security threats. *Materials Today: Proceedings*, *51*, 2172–2175. doi:10.1016/j.matpr.2021.11.121

Wang, M., & Choi, J. (2022). How Web Content Types Improve Consumer Engagement through Scarcity and Interactivity of Mobile Commerce? *Sustainability*, *14*(9), 4898. doi:10.3390u14094898

Waseem, A. (2020). Analysis of Factor Affecting e-Commerce Potential of any Country using Multiple Regression. *Jinnah Business Review*, *8*(1), 1–17. doi:10.53369/YONH5168

Weber, F., & Schütte, R. (2019). A Domain-Oriented Analysis of the Impact of Machine Learning—The Case of Retailing. *Big Data and Cognitive Computing*, *3*(1), 11. doi:10.3390/bdcc3010011

Webroot Inc. (2021). *Webroot BrightCloud Threat Report 2021*. Available at: https://community.webroot.com/news-announcements-3/the-2021-webroot-brightcloud-threat-report-54-of-phishing-sites-use-https-to-trick-users-347178

Wu, K., Chou, S., Chen, S., Tsai, C., & Yuan, S. (2018). Application of machine learning to identify Counterfeit Website. *Proceedings of the 20th International Conference on Information Integration and Web-Based Applications & Services*. 10.1145/3282373.3282407

Xu, Y. Z., Zhang, J. L., Hua, Y., & Wang, L. Y. (2019). Dynamic Credit Risk Evaluation Method for E-Commerce Sellers Based on a Hybrid Artificial Intelligence Model. *Sustainability*, *11*(19), 5521. doi:10.3390u11195521

Yaokumah, W., Kumah, P., & Okai, E. S. A. (2017). Demographic Influences on E-Payment Services. *International Journal of E-Business Research*, *13*(1), 44–65. doi:10.4018/IJEBR.2017010103

Zhang, M., Lin, L., & Chen, Z. (2021). Lightweight security scheme for data management in E-commerce platform using dynamic data management using blockchain model. *Cluster Computing*, 1–15. doi:10.100710586-021-03373-6

Zhang, Q., Lu, J., & Jin, Y. (2020). Artificial intelligence in recommender systems. *Complex & Intelligent Systems*, *7*(1), 439–457. doi:10.100740747-020-00212-w

Zottola, A. J. (2014). *Legal Considerations for E-Commerce Businesses*. Available at: https://www.venable.com/insights/publications/2014/04/legal-considerations-for-ecommerce-businesses

Zulkifl, Z., Khan, F., Tahir, S., Afzal, M., Iqbal, W., Rehman, A., Saeed, S., & Almuhaideb, A. M. (2022). FBASHI: Fuzzy and Blockchain-Based Adaptive Security for Healthcare IoTs. *IEEE Access: Practical Innovations, Open Solutions*, *10*, 15644–15656. doi:10.1109/ACCESS.2022.3149046

Chapter 6
Scaffolding Undergraduate Students' Ethical Cyber Behaviour With Philosophy and Theory

Tariq Zaman
https://orcid.org/0000-0001-6957-3710
ASSET, University of Technology, Sarawak, Malaysia

Adrian Lau Hui Yi
University of Technology Sarawak, Malaysia

Haw Yih Cheng
University of Technology Sarawak, Malaysia

ABSTRACT

Due to the growing challenges of cyber security, accreditation agencies demand computing ethics and professionalism as part of the computer science undergraduate curriculum. Many professional bodies developed codes of ethics and professional conduct, providing fundamental principles and letting the professional "decide" their response to face ethical dilemmas. The ethical codes rarely provide examples from real life. Therefore, in a six-month semester, the authors developed a teaching and learning module simulating real-life conflicting scenarios to enable students to participate in ethical and philosophical argumentation. They also target to demonstrate how storytelling, conflicting scenarios, and comics can be used to enhance computer science students' engagement in theoretical and philosophical discussions related to ethical cyber behaviour. Two assignments were part of the students' evaluation. They need to develop textual and visual conflicting scenarios for co-distributed clauses of the ACM code of ethics and then test those scenarios with users.

DOI: 10.4018/978-1-6684-5284-4.ch006

INTRODUCTION

Malaysia has become one of the most popular destinations for higher education in the last decade. However, the Malaysian Education Blueprint (MEB) 2015-2025 acknowledges the lack of requisite knowledge skills and attitude in Malaysian graduates, which is getting wider because of the uncertain future and technological disruption. The blueprint highlights the six primary attributes, including ethics and spirituality, that lead the graduates' aspirations in Malaysian Higher Education (Ministry of Education Malaysia, 2015). Therefore, all the undergraduate programmes integrate a course on ethics to address the student's needs and satisfy the programme's accreditations requirements. In the last two decades, computing technologies have been deeply integrated and touched the lives of everyone. The applications and algorithms also resulted in unintended but harmful consequences along with positive impacts (O'Neil, 2016). Significant concerns emerged about the efficacy of the courses on ethics in computer science education. Kugler (2022) argues to ask, reflect, and initiate philosophical discussion on big-picture questions related to technology and morality in cyberspace before the technology is developed. The topic of morality and technology is not new in the field of Philosophy, and the Philosophy of science has developed tools to discuss the fundamental questions about technology and where responsibility would lie in case of any harm caused by the technologies. Previous researchers also discussed the strong relationship between the thinking process in the human brain, moral behaviour and the influence of technology on a user's neurochemistry (Sherman et al., 2018; Crone and Konijn, 2018). The algorithms motivate users to make positive moral decisions and reward them for making bad ones. One solution designed by Harvard University is to integrate topics of ethics across the curriculum and engage faculty from the Philosophy department to co-teach the course (Grosz et al., 2019). This should instigate the students' thinking process not just on technology development but also on the technology needs, impact, and design. Teaching and learning of ethics in computer science are now a day considered a trans-disciplinary domain for exploration by not just positioning it within the hardcore technical computer science. In this book chapter, we will share the process of designing, developing and facilitating ethics and professionalism course in a computer science programme. The course aims to develop the students' understanding of ethical and structural challenges when dealing with emerging issues, such as cyber security, misinformation, and algorithm biases. In the following sections, first, we will provide the literature review and background, followed by the course contents and methodology. In the methodology section, we will provide details of the course design, and in the following section, we will provide the structure of students' assignments and assessments with a few examples. The chapter will end with a discussion and conclusion section.

LITERATURE REVIEW

Integrating Ethics in Computer Science Curriculum

In 1985 in his landmark article, Moor (1985) provided a pivotal definition of ethics within the domain of computer science, which laid down the foundation of ethics education in computer sciences. The definition describes computer ethics as *"the analysis of the nature and social impact of computer technology and the corresponding formulation and justification of policies for the ethical use of such technology."* However, later on, because of the diverse nature of education in computing ethics, the definitions are further supported by explicit codes of conduct and checklists. The ACM's Code of Ethics is amongst the examples of top-down guidelines that have been highly cited and adapted as a formality by the computer-related industries and academic programs (Gotterbarn et al., 2017; Anderson, 1992). Initially, the usual practice was to introduce Ethics and Professionalism as a standalone course in the second or the third year of computer science degree programs. These specialised courses provide opportunities for detailed and comprehensive approaches to ethics education in computer science and information technology fields. However, the students considered ethical challenges as a separate domain for debate than their technical computing-generated challenges. However, the students' evaluation results show a close relationship between age, exposure to the technologies, experience and the student's performance in the courses (Kink and Nolen, 1985; Epstein, 1995). In their survey of 115 such technology ethics courses from 94 universities worldwide, Fiesler et al. (2020) presented recommendations for effectively integrating topics of ethics across the computer science curriculum. Their recommendations include ethics pedagogy, appropriateness of integrating ethics into purely technical programming courses and the lack of standardisation of the course contents as a positive breathing space for educators. Slager et al. (2021) presented outcomes of the Computing Ethics Narratives (CEN) project, which provides active learning material such as fiction and non-fiction narratives, provocative simulations, video content, and personal reflection exercises. These materials are easily accessible across computer science courses and programs and can be delivered in online or face-to-face teaching and learning environment.

With the growth of computer science as a field of research and development, new subfields and specialisations are emerging, such as Artificial intelligence, augmented reality, and now metaverse therefore the practitioners are looking for specialised courses of Ethics education within their field, such as Saltz et al. (2018) emphasised the need for ethics in data science and highlighted twelve key ethics areas that should be included within ethics curriculum for data science. They also posit the lack of any existing code which covers all the identified themes. Antoniou et al. (2021) argued the need for an explicit discussion on the ethical use and design of technology in cultural heritage institutions and training technologists in understanding the ethical dilemmas within the cultural heritage domain. In terms of institutional approaches, Stanford university introduced a multidisciplinary course taught and facilitated by the faculty of philosophy and social science besides computer science (Reich et al. 2020). Ferreira & Vardi (2021) reported the efficacy of the newly designed Ethics and Accountability course, which incorporates elements from the philosophy of computer science, critical media theory, and society, science, and technology studies. The course aimed to encourage a deep engagement of the students in discussions and reflections on issues related to social justice and computer science. These courses usually adopted a diverse range of teaching and learning methods, including field visits, writing reflective journals, and attending guest lectures. However, previous studies (such as Gardner, 1991 and Antoniou et al., 2021) postulate that learning outcomes of ethics courses rarely turn into actions outside the classroom setting. Therefore, many questions are still remaining on how to make the contents and methodologies of teaching ethics in computer science to achieve the goals. Dean and Nourbakhsh (2022) reported a study of designing, developing, and testing ethics modules for instructors of 11 computer science courses at the university. Some of their suggestion include extending the duration of pedagogy learning, relaxed participation requirement and enhancing peer interaction.

Visual Communication in Educational Setting

Within the field of psychology, social competence trainings focus on improving social behaviors, social perception, reducing inappropriate responses, self-regulation, and social problem-solving skills (Spence,2003). Amongst many other methods, assessment and trainings include the discussion of pictorial vignettes that depict challenging social scenarios, interpersonal cartoon scenarios and comics with blank speech bubbles that need to be filled in (Spence, 2003). Drawings and visual methods have also been used in cross-cultural communication in a variety of research disciplines. Wain et al. (2013) compiled videos of indigenous narratives of healthcare, using them to trigger classroom discussions to enhance students' empathy; thereby enabling future health providers to improve their management of indigenous patients. Even photography has been proposed as a method for non-verbal communication in cross-cultural settings (Weiser, 1988). Emme et al. (2006) report on the method of producing visual narratives in the form of fotonovela to assist new immigrant children to explore non-verbal strategies of communication. Community drawing sessions have also proven to be useful in communicating concept representations and perceptions (Winschiers-Goagoses et al., 2012).

Pictorial representation and Comics of the case can attract users' attention and facilitate them in creating their own understanding of the setting of the text (McVicker, 2007; Toh et al., 2017). Van Gevelt et al. (2017) used pictorial representations of a choice experiment to rank the community's preference for electricity services in remote Sarawak, Malaysia. Zaman et al. (2016b) used drawings and sketches to explore the local indigenous community's representation of Oroo', a forest sign language of the Penan community. Akcanca (2020) also claimed that comics could relay abstract concepts to learners excitedly. The claim was further supported by Sentruk and Simsek (2021) with a study conducted to assess the effect of educational comics and educational cartoons on students' academic achievement. Sentruk and Simsek (2021) reported that educational comics positively impacted student academic achievement. The study also showed that the educational comics favoured educational cartoons in the perspective of repeatability, where educational cartoons will halt the learning process when it is stopped while students can return to the point where they want to focus during their learning process on comics (Sentruk and Simsek, 2021).

While images are without doubt very successful in triggering emotional responses, less obvious has been their adequacy in communicating very specific messages, especially across cultures. The myth of the universality of pictures and their perceptual processes has been disproved by numerous researchers (Nisbett & Miyamoto, 2005; Keith, 2011; Davidoff, Fonteneau, & Goldstein,2008). The interpretation of pictures has been found to be culturally dependent, with each unique community relying on their familiar context (Winschiers-Goagoseset al.,2012).

BACKGROUND

For the last decade, the Advanced Centre for Sustainable Socio-Economic and Technological Development (ASSET) engaged with the indigenous communities in Borneo in service-learning and participatory design projects. Meanwhile, the research team published several research publications highlighting the ethical dilemmas faced by the students and researchers when designing technologies for and with local and indigenous communities (Zaman, 2016b). Also, it is acknowledged that several professional bodies and institutions have codes of ethics (such as ACM and IEEE); however, the concepts are hard to internalise and operationalise in associated ethical behaviours. Therefore, we explored a more holistic approach to address the issues and restructured an undergraduate course, Ethics and Professionalism (CSS3613), by integrating components from "Responsible Research and Innovation" (RRI). RRI is an approach that considers various environmental, societal, social and economic concerns throughout the innovation process to create value for society while respecting the environment (Owen, Macnaghten and Stilgoe, 2020). This approach questions the process of ethical governance and research integrity in technology and innovation design. It extends the discussion to encompass questions of uncertainty (in its multiple forms), purposes, motivations, social and political constitutions, trajectories, and directions of innovation that are taking place in any proximity. The newly designed course aims to provide the students with an understanding of responsibilities and ethical issues in the working environment, risks and liabilities, and intellectual property to develop software and deal with the challenges responsibly, ethically and professionally. The course was facilitated by a lecturer and a teaching assistant who is a student in Masters in Computing programme.

COURSE CONTENTS

Ethics and Professionalism (CSS 3663) course is a core subject compulsory for undergraduate students in the School of Computing and Creative Media, University of Technology Sarawak, during the first semester of their second year of study. The course contents are divided into three parts; in the first part, students were exposed to theoretical and philosophical discussions comprises discussions on ethics, right vs wrong, belief vs knowledge, responsibility and reflexivity, the challenges of social media, misinformation, and racial and gender biases in algorithms design. The second part of the course deals with the specific codes of ethics. We selected the Association for Computing Machinery (ACM) Code of Ethics as a reference for this course. As developed by the ACM COPE (Committee on Professional Ethics), the ACM Code of Ethics guides the members' ethical and professional conduct. The code highlights fundamental considerations for contributing to societal and human well-being. The code comprises 7 general ethical principles, 9 professional responsibilities, 7 professional leadership principles, and 2 articles on members' compliance with the code. To provide students with a better understanding of complex ethical issues in computer science, the third part of the course includes case studies on emerging issues such as cyber security, misinformation and algorithm biases in social media and search engines.

METHODOLOGY

Teaching and Learning Context

To develop the students' ethical reasoning and understanding of the complex challenges of the software world, we used misinformation and fake news on social media as a teaching and learning context. Multiple case studies have been provided to the students for discussion and reflection on the role and approaches of big tech companies, including social media giants and search engines, and how they tackle the challenges of fake news. The causes and failure in controlling fake news and misinformation on social media have been discussed within the first and second order of reflexivity (Golob et al., 2021).

Reference Material for Theoretical Understanding

Ethics is a sub-field of philosophy. In computer science, much focus is on "solving problems" but not on the consequences of adopting a specific approach to solve that problem. Additional reading materials scaffold the three parts of the course contents. The students' theoretical understanding has been directed with the help of Crowell et al. (2004) article on moral psychology and information ethics. The chapter describes a "Four-Component Model" of moral behaviour. Based on the two technology-mediated domains, electronic communications and digital intellectual property, it has been illustrated how technology can impact each of the four components: sensitivity, judgment, motivation, and action. To better understand the challenges of misinformation and fake news spread in online media, Cusumano's (2021) article has been referred for reading and discussion. The article revolves around Section 230 of the U.S. Communications Decency Act of 1996, regulating social media and the Internet. Cusumano (2021) highlights the dilemma of social media platforms which struggle between platform neutrality, cyber security, and protection of revenue streams. A question, "can we sue a social media company, rather than the creator of the post, for spreading fake news?" was posed to the students. Two other reading materials were provided to the students; Epstein and Robertson (2015) and Kirkpatrick (2020), which highlight the effect of search engine manipulation and its impacts on the outcomes of elections. Also, students have been suggested to watch The Great Hack and The Social Dilemma documentaries. The Great Hack highlights a case of big data manipulation to influence the voters' decisions and outcomes of key elections such as the Brexit referendum and the 2016 US presidential race. The students have been reminded that the film provides a best case of good journalism than scholarly analysis. The documentary also establishes the historical, political, and technical context and tries to answer the question: How dangerous was Cambridge Analytica? Students have been guided to discuss questions such as "under what circumstances can personal information be shared on social media, and who should be the gatekeeper?"

The Social Dilemma uncovers the secret face of social media platforms, warns about the precarious impact of social networking and illustrates how the users trust are deceived by the social media platforms. The documentary features interviews and narration of the former employees of the big social media platforms (such as Google, Facebook, Twitter) who went public at great personal risk. The documentary presents the issues of a teenager's social media addiction and how companies collect information about the users by using algorithms to influence the human decisions. The documentary educates the society about the harms of social media, but it lacks providing a tangible solution (Barnet et al., 2020).

For a group presentation, Benjamin et al. (2007) case study has been provided, so the students critically reflect on the role of technology and discuss how the data divide, a breach in data security and politics of meta-data empower the rich than those in need. These materials helped the computer science students develop a broader understanding of their technology choices. Software developers usually focus on developing the best application to solve a problem; here, "the best" is defined in terms of speed, storage and usability, and do not thoroughly reflect and include the consequences and impacts of their choice of technology. Besides reading material, online platforms such as whitesave.me (https://whitesave.me) and rentaminority (https://rentaminority.com) were used for students' exercise to prompt the potential for misuse of technologies.

Stories and Reflection

Artz (1998) argued that three characteristics make the teaching of ethics in computer science difficult; 1): the consequences and impacts of new technologies cannot be known in advance; 2): the behaviour of the user (human) is complex to predict and 3): absence of consensus on standards of ethical behaviour. Therefore, the author suggested using storytelling for the moral sense development in individuals. Stories integrate the contextual ambiguity in exploring issues in computer ethics and developing the students' moral and logical judgment to address the emerging issues (Korhonen & Vitvitsou, 2019). We used multiple stories and scenarios to initiate the discussions and prepare the students to deal with the ambiguities in ethical phenomena and technology design processes, such as understanding the imprecise representation of reality in the digital world or the thin layers of responsibility between designers, developers and users when technologies go wrong. An example of the story is as below, adapted from Toyama (2017);

"Imprisoned in a tower with his son, Icarus, Daedalus fashioned wings out of feathers and wax. As they planned their escape, he warned Icarus not to fly too close to the sun for fear that the wax would melt. Once they were in the air, though, Icarus ignored his father's warnings. He soared exuberantly into the sky. His wings fell apart, and Icarus fell to his death."

Further questions were given to direct the students' deeper understanding of the issues surrounding technology design, the role of the designers and developers, and the responsibilities of the users. As Toyama (2017) mentioned, the real lesson in the story is not just about technology but about the right heart, mind, and will of the human involved.

Conflicting Scenario

According to Donnelly and Fitzmaurice (2005), scenarios are usually used in problem-based learning, where students are first introduced to complex cases to solve or learn from them. Elliot-Kingston et al. (2016) explained scenario-based learning (SBL) to stir students into recalling prior "existing knowledge", researching "missing knowledge", evaluating "new knowledge" that applies to the given scenario before assimilating new and existing knowledge to come out with learning outcomes finally. Callanan and Peri (2010) used a scenario-based approach in teaching conflict management to compare the differences in students' responses between scenario-based learning and standardised assessment instrument. As mentioned above, the ethics classes were formulated by giving students several case studies and scenarios based on real-life experiences related to the ethical issues students may face when they embark on their professional journey. In addition, to design new scenarios, some of the scenarios, including the below, have been used from the previous work (Winschiers-Theophilus et al., 2015).

"The community has a long term established relationship with UNIMAS and has accommodated a number of researchers in the past. As the activities are infringing in their socio-economic activities, compensation rates have been determined by the community and been mutually agreed on. For example, a half-day session is compensated with RM 45.00 per person and a full day with RM 90.00.

The researcher has scheduled a half-day session with ten community members as per his approved budget of RM 450.00. Once the session started in the community hall, a number of other community members joined and two of them stayed all the way through, making extremely valuable contributions to the session. After the session, three people stayed on engaging in some interesting conversation with the researcher for one hour. The purpose of the research and discussions was to find ways on how to improve community income with tourist stays.

Decide on how you will pay each community member. Motivate your decision"

Another conflicting scenario is to highlight the challenges of managing expectations of the participants in a study, which is as follows;

"Delta Soft has been hired to develop a Management Information system (MIS) for a newly built oil refinery. The project's cost is RM 5 Million, and the delivery timeline is six months. This is the last project to be executed by Mr Kasper (the Project Lead) before leaving Delta Soft for good. After the first three months, Mr Kasper realised that the project was behind the timeline. He requested immediate feedback from the team members, and Mr Chin, the Project Scheduler, suggested increasing the working time with extra time allowances for the team members. After two weeks, it was realised that the measure was not effective, and there was a need for additional measures. Based on the effective practice in other companies, some of the staff members suggested providing an extra financial incentive to those team members who complete their tasks within the allocated timeframe, and another option is to give additional financial incentives to those who meet the maximum number of tasks each day.

You are one of the team members, and the company asked for your opinion before making any decision; so, what do you think, which option the company should choose? Support your answer with logical arguments.

Comics and Visual Communication of Ethical Challenges

Visual communication is a method of teaching and learning that has been adapted in numerous fields for different purposes, including training and enhancement of learning. To assess the effectiveness of the ACM code of ethics, we developed comics based on a conflicting scenarios and then tested on computer science students. The students' feedback on the effectiveness of comics was also recorded. Below is an example of the comic (see Figure 1) that we integrated into the course. The designed comic is based on a conflicting scenario developed by Winschiers-Theophilus et al. (2015).
Conflicting Scenario:

A long-planned trip to the jungle to collect some research data has just started. A local Penan guide, a foreign inhabiting researcher and a group of UNIMAS research students took off early in the morning. The local Penan, who is very knowledgeable, explains plants and practices on the way, especially about their relationship with birds as their guides in the forest. Suddenly, a specific bird crosses their path. The Penan guide becomes all agitated and tells the group to turn back to the village as danger is ahead, as announced by this bird. The group returns to the village. It was their last day in the village and there are no more opportunities to collect this data during this trip. The foreign researcher who has been living with the Penans over the last 4 months and has gone many times to the forest offers the UNIMAS students to take them to the jungle.

What would be your action?

Resolve the matter within your group, exploring the consequences.

Figure 1. Comic designed and used in the course.

In the course, we also used the sketches developed by the indigenous Penan community to communicate interaction guidelines to visiting researchers during their research trips (Goagoses et al., 2020; Zaman et al., 2016a).

STUDENTS ASSIGNMENT AND SEMESTER PROJECT

The students' assessments have two key components; a group assignment to create conflicting scenarios for a better understanding of the articles of the ACM code of ethics and a group project to develop pictorial comic stories for reflection and internalising the code of ethics. Cantered around the code of ethics, each group of students targeted creating 5 scenarios and comics based on the cases and designed evaluation sessions with users (their fellow undergraduate students). Each case presents a scenario where a principle of ethics is discussed and followed by an open-ended question to describe the phenomenon's ambiguity and advance the target user's reasoning and critical thinking. In their reflection, students highlighted the challenge of their own conformity biases, reflected in their designed scenarios. An example of the students'' created scenario is as follows;

Joseph and his team have developed an online software system called SEED that offers better medication administration, patient-doctor online private conversation, swift transactions, inventory management, patient monitoring and more to hospitals. For years, SEED has its ground in almost every hospital in the world, including some under-developed countries.

During scheduled maintenance, Joseph discovered a vulnerability breach and almost leaked confidential data of every hospital. It could potentially lock the system down from the developers themselves. This vulnerability is fatal and must be fixed immediately, but because of the dependencies of the hospital on the system, this situation is very time-sensitive; therefore, Joseph only has two options.

The first option is to contact every hospital and other stakeholders using SEED, which could take days to verify and confirm, risking malicious attackers attacking the system and taking control of it to do more harm. Pulling the system offline without contacting the hospitals is the second option. The system downtime will not be specified, and the system will not be working for any hospital at all. Complications might happen during the downtime, and patients may be affected.

In the project, the same scenarios were translated into pictorial comics (see Figure 2). The effectiveness of the scenarios and comics was tested with groups of users, and the students presented the results in the final group project presentation.

Figure 2. An example of the students'' created comic

At the end of the course, the students submitted a written reflective journal based on What? So What? and Now What? (Rolfe et al. 2001) to evaluate their shared experience of the course and to improve and identify ways to act ethically when facing an ethical and professional conflict. In the reflective journal, students highlighted the course contents' novelty and the time limitation for internalising the course's key messages. For many of the students, the course was "unique" because of its contents and teaching methodologies, such as the context; misinformation and fake news on social media.

For the students, the course contents included topics from law and discussion on technical issues such as Search Engine Optimisation from political and ethical perspectives were new. Initially, they were baffled by the complexity of the problem, but after the deep guided discussion and critical reflection exercises, they could explore the relationship and connect the lessons learned with their personal experiences.

DISCUSSION AND CONCLUSION

The Consequences

All the professional bodies face a significant challenge in enforcing the ethical codes; in case of violation, the enforcement options are only limited to expulsion from the professional society. Suppose the violator is not a member of the community, then they are not even bound to this condition. In June 2011, ACM Council (and IEEE), on the recommendations of the Committee on Professional Ethics (COPE), expelled and revoked membership of Professor Tao Li, of the University of Florida. The violation has been reported for Prof. Li's undue influence and breaching the peer review in two conferences in 2017 and 2019. However, Prof Li has already resigned from University of Florida in April 2021 against investigation of his graduate student's suicide. The conclusions of the committee confirm two important accusation of the graduate student's suicidal note. The ACM imposed a penalty of a 15-year ban on Prof Li's participation in any ACM Conference or Publication. The President of ACM also wrote a letter to the family of the deceased student to let them know the investigation result and their decision. However, friends and fellows of the deceased student accused the process and the academic structure as "A Dishonest, Indifferent, and Toxic Culture" (Chawla, 2021)

The Internationalisation Processes

An alternative to deal with the challenge of addressing computer scientists' behaviour is to train and educate them at the individual level. Although the ethical and professional codes of the professional bodies are written carefully but without integrating them into the graduate student's training, they will be just unread appendices in the books. The training includes a combination of individualised learning methods and scaffolding tools such as course contents and learning process, instructional tools, and pace of learning based upon the abilities and interest of each learner. Goagoses et al. (2020) reported that just a sketch book is ineffective, without scaffolding it with more information or human guidance, to communicate cultural guidelines to novice researchers.

Discussion Around Philosophy and Values

In addition, the ethical standards are not an isolated mechanism but part of the larger social and societal values and are based on the historical experiences of the scientific community; therefore, learning within the framework of philosophical thinking and theoretical underpinning empowers students to recognise when they are making ethical and technical choices. Pardoux (2022) reported the challenges of translating theoretical ethical frameworks into practices and emphasised on the need to understand the ethical infrastructures in which ethical frameworks are developed and deployed. Pardoux broaden the discussion to understand the production processes and biases embedded in the Artificial Intelligence based Systems (AIS) and the biases and the ethical frameworks in which their use is integrated. A recommendation of the research is to add philosophical considerations regarding the design methodologies of AIS.

Designing and Application in the Wild

Computer Science is considered an applied discipline and, nowadays, designing and developing computer applications is not bound to the lab environment but preferred to be designed and developed in the sild local contexts. Interaction within the wild contexts, engagement with actors (beyond humans), and freedom from time and space are the factors that advocate for integrating knowledge from diverse fields such as social sciences and psychology. Computer sciences students are very comfortable designing hardcore technical systems and technologies; however, predicting and handling the unforeseen challenges before the technology deployment is difficult for them. Blumenthal et al (2020) created a stakeholder impacts visualisation and reported that "all people are stakeholders in computing". The visualisation is developed on the CARE process (Consider, Analyze, Review, and Evaluate) and is providing additional scaffolding to the learners in order to engage them in considering the holistic societal context in which design and development decisions of computing algorithms are made.

Multiplicity and Peer Support

In Malaysia the computer science curriculum usually allows one single course focused on computing ethics during the whole degree program. The course covers various topics from hardcore computer programming languages to human-computer interactions; therefore, digging deeply into specific ethical issues and learning the core technical content is challenging (Hollander et al., 2009). As Grosz et al (2019) reported teaching standalone ethics course in computer science program and the lesson learned are easy to forget when engaged in a technical design task. Therefore, the authors also suggested collaboration with colleagues and doctoral students, from philosophy and science and society programs which will benefit in integrating the ethical reasoning into the technical course more easily and more expertly. We offered the newly designed course for the first time in this session, and we have many potential areas for improvement which will be exercised in the upcoming sessions. As Dean and Nourbakhsh (2022) reported, peer learning brings multiple perspectives to the discussion and immerses positively and constructively therefore, we will engage the existing students as mentors in the upcoming sessions. It will enhance the learning experience with peer support in side and offline discussions.

ACKNOWLEDGMENT

We thank all the students for taking part in the project. This work was carried out with the aid of a grant from the University of Technology Sarawak. We are also thankful to the authors and Skechers of Penan community interaction protocols for sharing and allowing us to use the material in our classroom teaching and learning.

REFERENCES

Akcanca, N. (2020). An alternative teaching tool in science education: Educational comics. *International Online Journal of Education & Teaching*, 7(4), 1550–1570.

Anderson, R. E. (1992). ACM code of ethics and professional conduct. *Communications of the ACM*, *35*(5), 94–99. doi:10.1145/129875.129885

Antoniou, A., Vayanou, M., Katifori, A., Chrysanthi, A., Cheilitsi, F., & Ioannidis, Y. (2021). "Real Change Comes from Within!": Towards a Symbiosis of Human and Digital Guides in the Museum. *ACM Journal on Computing and Cultural Heritage*, *15*(1), 1–19.

Artz, J. M. (1998). The role of stories in computer ethics. *ACM SIGCAS Computers and Society*, *28*(1), 11–13. doi:10.1145/277351.277354

Barnet, B., & Bossio, D. (2020). Netflix's The Social Dilemma highlights the problem with social media, but what's the solution? *The Conversation, 6.*

Benjamin, S., Bhuvaneswari, R., & Rajan, P. (2007). Bhoomi:'E–governance'', or, an anti–politics machine necessary to globalize Bangalore? *CASUM–m Working Paper.*

Blumenthal, R., & Blumenthal, J. (2020). Consider Visualizing Society within the ACM Code of Ethics. In *Proceedings of the 51st ACM Technical Symposium on Computer Science Education* (pp. 1292-1292). 10.1145/3328778.3372587

Callanan, G. A., & Perri, D. F. (2010). Teaching conflict management using a scenario-based approach. *Journal of Education for Business*, *81*(3), 131–139. doi:10.3200/JOEB.81.3.131-139

Chawla, D. S. (2021, April 15). *Research misconduct findings, 15-year publishing ban in graduate student suicide case.* Nature news. Retrieved August 16, 2022, from https://www.nature.com/nature-index/news-blog/research-misconduct-publishing-ban-graduate-student-suicide-case

Crone, E. A., & Konijn, E. A. (2018). Media use and brain development during adolescence. *Nature Communications*, *9*(1), 1–10. doi:10.103841467-018-03126-x PMID:29467362

Crowell, C. R., Narvaez, D., & Gomberg, A. (2004). Moral psychology and information ethics. *Information Ethics: Privacy and Intellectual Property: Privacy and Intellectual Property*, 19.

Cusumano, M. A. (2021). Section 230 and a tragedy of the commons. *Communications of the ACM*, *64*(10), 16–18. doi:10.1145/3481354

Davidoff, J., Fonteneau, E., & Goldstein, J. (2008). Cultural differences in perception: Observations from a remote culture. *Journal of Cognition and Culture*, *8*(3-4), 189–209. doi:10.1163/156853708X358146

Dean, V., & Nourbakhsh, I. (2022). Teaching Ethics by Teaching Ethics Pedagogy: A Proposal for Structural Ethics Intervention. In *Proceedings of the 53rd ACM Technical Symposium on Computer Science Education* (pp. 272-278). 10.1145/3478431.3499319

Donnelly, R., & Fitzmaurice, M. (2005). Collaborative Project-based Learning and Problem-based Learning in Higher Education: a Consideration of Tutor and Student Role in Learner-Focused Strategies. In G. O'Neill, S. Moore, & B. McMullin (Eds.), *Emerging Issues in the Practice of University Learning and Teaching* (pp. 87–98). AISHE/HEA.

Elliott-Kingston, C., Doyle, O. P. E., & Hunter, A. (2016). Benefits of scenario-based learning in university education. *Acta Horticulturae*, (1126), 107–114. doi:10.17660/ActaHortic.2016.1126.13

Emme, M., Kirova, A., Kamau, O., & Kosanovich, S. (2006). Ensemble research: A means for immigrant children to explore peer relation- ships through fotonovela. *The Alberta Journal of Educational Research*, *52*, 160–181.

Epstein, R., & Robertson, R. E. (2015). The search engine manipulation effect (SEME) and its possible impact on the outcomes of elections. *Proceedings of the National Academy of Sciences of the United States of America*, *112*(33), E4512–E4521. doi:10.1073/pnas.1419828112 PMID:26243876

Epstein, R. G. (1995). Latest developments in the "killer robot" computer ethics scenario. *ACM SIGCSE Bulletin*, *27*(1), 111–115. doi:10.1145/199691.199746

Ferreira, R., & Vardi, M. Y. (2021). Deep tech ethics: an approach to teaching social justice in computer science. In *Proceedings of the 52nd ACM Technical Symposium on Computer Science Education* (pp. 1041-1047). 10.1145/3408877.3432449

Fiesler, C., Garrett, N., & Beard, N. (2020, February). What do we teach when we teach tech ethics? a syllabi analysis. In *Proceedings of the 51st ACM Technical Symposium on Computer Science Education* (pp. 289-295). 10.1145/3328778.3366825

Gardner, H. (1991). The tensions between education and development. *Journal of Moral Education*, *20*(2), 113–125. doi:10.1080/0305724910200201

Goagoses, N., Winschiers-Theophilus, H., & Zaman, T. (2020). Community protocols for researchers: Using sketches to communicate interaction guidelines. *AI & Society*, *35*(3), 675–687. doi:10.100700146-019-00914-x

Golob, T., Makarovic, M., & Rek, M. (2021). Meta-reflexivity for resilience against disinformation. *Comunicar*, *29*(66), 107–118. doi:10.3916/C66-2021-09

Gotterbarn, D., Bruckman, A., Flick, C., Miller, K., & Wolf, M. J. (2017). ACM code of ethics: A guide for positive action. *Communications of the ACM*, *61*(1), 121–128. doi:10.1145/3173016

Grosz, B. J., Grant, D. G., Vredenburgh, K., Behrends, J., Hu, L., Simmons, A., & Waldo, J. (2019). Embedded EthiCS: Integrating ethics across CS education. *Communications of the ACM*, *62*(8), 54–61. doi:10.1145/3330794

Hollander, R., & Arenberg, C. R. (2009). *Ethics Education and Scientific and Engineering Research: What's Been Learned? What Should Be Done? Summary of a Workshop. National Academy of Engineering*. The National Academies Press.

Keith, K. D. (Ed.). (2019). *Cross-cultural psychology: Contemporary themes and perspectives*. John Wiley & Sons. doi:10.1002/9781119519348

Kirkpatrick, K. (2020). Deceiving the masses on social media. *Communications of the ACM*, *63*(5), 33–35. doi:10.1145/3386375

Korhonen, A., & Vivitsou, M. (2019). Digital storytelling and group work. *Annual Conference on Innovation and Technology in Computer Science Education*. 10.1145/3304221.3325528

Kugler, L. (2022). Technology's impact on morality. *Communications of the ACM, 65*(4), 15–16. doi:10.1145/3516516

McVicker, C. J. (2007). Comic strips as a text structure for learning to read. *The Reading Teacher, 61*(1), 85–88. doi:10.1598/RT.61.1.9

Ministry of Education Malaysia. (2015). Malaysia education blueprint 2015–2025 (higher education). *Ministry of Education Malaysia, 2025*, 40.

Moor, J. H. (1985). What is computer ethics? *Metaphilosophy, 16*(4), 266–275. doi:10.1111/j.1467-9973.1985. tb00173.x

Nisbett, R. E., & Miyamoto, Y. (2005). The influence of culture: Holistic versus analytic perception. *Trends in Cognitive Sciences, 9*(10), 467–473. doi:10.1016/j.tics.2005.08.004 PMID:16129648

O'Neil, C. (2016). *Weapons of math destruction: How big data increases inequality and threatens democracy.* Broadway Books.

Owen, R., Macnaghten, P., & Stilgoe, J. (2020). Responsible research and innovation: From science in society to science for society, with society. In *Emerging technologies: ethics, law and governance* (pp. 117–126). Routledge. doi:10.4324/9781003074960-11

Pardoux, É. (2022). Ethical Design for AI in Medicine. In *Proceedings of the 2022 AAAI/ACM Conference on AI, Ethics, and Society* (pp. 907-907). 10.1145/3514094.3539564

Reich, R., Sahami, M., Weinstein, J. M., & Cohen, H. (2020, February). Teaching computer ethics: A deeply multidisciplinary approach. In *Proceedings of the 51st ACM Technical Symposium on Computer Science Education* (pp. 296-302). 10.1145/3328778.3366951

Rolfe, G., Freshwater, D., & Jasper, M. (2001). *Critical reflection for nursing and the helping professions: a user's Guide.* Palgrave Macmillan.

Senturk, M., & Simsek, U. (2021). Educational comics and educational cartoons as teaching material in the social studies course. *American Educational Research Journal, 9*(2), 515–525. doi:10.30918/ AERJ.92.21.073

Sherman, L. E., Greenfield, P. M., Hernandez, L. M., & Dapretto, M. (2018). Peer influence via Instagram: Effects on brain and behavior in adolescence and young adulthood. *Child Development, 89*(1), 37–47. doi:10.1111/cdev.12838 PMID:28612930

Slager, K., Nunez, R., Short, W., & Doore, S. A. (2021, March). Computing Ethics Starts on 'Day One' Ethics Narratives in Introductory CS Courses. In *Proceedings of the 52nd ACM Technical Symposium on Computer Science Education* (pp. 1282-1282). 10.1145/3408877.3439648

Spence, S. (2003). Social skills training with children and young peo- ple: Theory, evidence and practice. *Child and Adolescent Mental Health, 8*(2), 84–96. doi:10.1111/1475-3588.00051 PMID:32797550

Toh, T. L., Cheng, L. P., Ho, S. Y., Jiang, H., & Lim, K. M. (2017). Use of comics to enhance students'' learning for the development of the twenty-first-century competencies in the mathematics classroom. *Asia Pacific Journal of Education, 37*(4), 437–452. doi:10.1080/02188791.2017.1339344

Toyama, K. (2017). Geek Heresy: Rescuing Social Change from the Cult of Technology. *Innovations in Teaching & Learning Conference Proceedings*, (9). 10.13021/itlcp.2017

Van Gevelt, T., Holzeis, C. C., George, F., & Zaman, T. (2017). Indigenous community preferences for electricity services: Evidence from a choice experiment in Sarawak, Malaysia. *Energy Policy*, *108*, 102–110. doi:10.1016/j.enpol.2017.05.054

Winschiers-Goagoses, N., Winschiers-Theophilus, H., Rodil, K., Kapuire, G., & Jensen, K. (2012). Design democratization with communities: Drawing toward locally meaningful design. *International Journal of Sociotechnology and Knowledge Development*, *4*(4), 32–43. doi:10.4018/jskd.2012100103

Winschiers-Theophilus, H., Zaman, T., & Yeo, A. (2015, June). Reducing "white elephant" ICT4D projects: a community-researcher engagement. In *Proceedings of the 7th International Conference on Communities and Technologies* (pp. 99-107). 10.1145/2768545.2768554

Zaman, T., Winschiers-Theophilus, H., George, F., Wee, A. Y., Falak, H., & Goagoses, N. (2016a). Using sketches to communicate interaction protocols of an indigenous community. In *Proceedings of the 14th Participatory Design Conference: Short Papers, Interactive Exhibitions, Workshops-Volume 2* (pp. 13-16). 10.1145/2948076.2948088

Zaman, T., Yeo, A. W., & Jengan, G. (2016b). Designing digital solutions for preserving Penan sign language: A reflective study. *Advances in Human-Computer Interaction*, *2016*, 1–9. Advance online publication. doi:10.1155/2016/4174795

ADDITIONAL READING

Connolly, R. W. (2011, June). Beyond good and evil impacts: rethinking the social issues components in our computing curricula. In *Proceedings of the 16th annual joint conference on Innovation and technology in computer science education* (pp. 228-232). 10.1145/1999747.1999812

Couldry, N., & Mejias, U. A. (2020). *The costs of connection: How data are colonizing human life and appropriating it for capitalism*. Stanford University Press. doi:10.1515/9781503609754

Ethics4EU. (2021). *Existing competencies in the teaching of ethics in computer science faculties*. Erasmus+ Project. http://ethics4eu.eu/outcomes/existing-competencies-in-the-teaching-of-ethics-in-computer-science-faculties-research-report/

Forester, T., & Morrison, P. (1994). *Computer ethics: Cautionary tales and ethical dilemmas in computing*. MIT Press.

HortonD.McIlraithS. A.WangN.MajediM.McClureE.WaldB. (2022, February).

Knight, W. (2017) Biased algorithms are everywhere, and no one seems to care. *Technology Review*. Retrieved Aug. 16, 2022 from https://bit.ly/2tIh1EX

Köbis, N., Bonnefon, J. F., & Rahwan, I. (2021). Bad machines corrupt good morals. *Nature Human Behaviour*, *5*(6), 679–685. doi:10.103841562-021-01128-2 PMID:34083752

McDonough, S., & Brandenburg, R. (2019). Who owns this data? Using dialogic reflection to examine an ethically important moment. *Reflective Practice*, *20*(3), 266–355. doi:10.1080/14623943.2019.1611553

Purewal, T. S. Jr, Bennett, C., & Maier, F. (2007). Embracing the social relevance: Computing, ethics and the community. *ACM SIGCSE Bulletin*, *39*(1), 556–560. doi:10.1145/1227504.1227496

Stavrakakis, I., Gordon, D., Tierney, B., Becevel, A., Murphy, E., Dodig-Crnkovic, G., Dobrin, R., Schiaffonati, V., Pereira, C., Tikhonenko, S., Gibson, J. P., Maag, S., Agresta, F., Curley, A., Collins, M., & O'Sullivan, D. (2022). The teaching of computer ethics on computer science and related degree programmes. a European survey. *International Journal of Ethics Education*, *7*(1), 101–129. doi:10.100740889-021-00135-1

Topi, H., Kaiser, K. M., Sipior, J. C., Valacich, J. S., Nunamaker, J. F. Jr, de Vreede, G. J., & Wright, R. (2010). Curriculum guidelines for undergraduate degree programs in information systems. *Communications of the AIS*, *26*(18), 359–428.

Wain, T., Sim, M., Hayward, C., Coffin, J., Mak, D., & Rudd, C. (2013). Creating cultural empathy and challenging attitudes through indigenous narrative project. *Eculture*, *5*, 18–26.

Weiser, J. (1988). See what I mean? Photography as nonverbal com- munication in crosscultural psychology. In F. Poyatos (Ed.), *Cross- cultural perspectives in nonverbal communication* (pp. 240–290). Hogrefe Publishers.

Chapter 7
Security and Privacy Guidelines for IT Operations Under Pandemics and Epidemics

Hasan Tahir

*Department of Information Security, School of Electrical Engineering and Computer Science,
Pakistan & National University of Sciences and Technology, Islamabad, Pakistan*

Shahzaib Tahir

*Department of Information Security, College of Signals, Pakistan & National University of Sciences
and Technology, Islamabad, Pakistan*

Anum Hasan

Department of Computer Science, National University of Modern languages, Rawalpindi, Pakistan

ABSTRACT

Deteriorating health conditions under a pandemic force governments and authorities to consider enforcing lockdown protocols to limit the spread of a disease. Once a lockdown protocol is enforced, many verticals are instantly impacted by the lack of available workforce and other issues. Critical infrastructures, information systems, integrated IT systems cannot be administered using existing guidelines/standards under a pandemic. Thus organizations, governments, enterprises, and economies are ill equipped to deal with IT and economic issues emerging as a result of a pandemic. This chapter explores the impact of the COVID-19 pandemic on IT systems, IT operations, and security. This chapter calls attention to the lack of preparedness, absence of standards and protocols that deal with epidemics and pandemics. Thus, considering the changing organizational posture, this chapter brings to light opportunities for redressal, and recommendations have been made to ensure better preparation in the future.

DOI: 10.4018/978-1-6684-5284-4.ch007

INTRODUCTION

A pandemic is an epidemic disease that spreads rapidly to engulf countries, continents and eventually the world. Historically, the human race has faced many deadly pandemics like bubonic plague, Spanish flu, etc. A pandemic that has devastated the world in the 21st century is the Coronavirus Disease 2019 (COVID-19). At the end of January 2020 the World Health Organization (WHO) classed the situation as a Public Health Emergency of International Concern (PHEIC). Owing to COVID-19 rapid spread and the number fatalities, the characterization of the situation was declared pandemic on 11 March 2020. The COVID-19 is a highly infectious respiratory disease that spreads through touching contaminated surfaces, respiratory droplets, etc. Common symptoms of the disease include but are not limited to breathing difficulty, throat pain, flu, fever, cough, muscle aches, loss of taste/ smell etc. The origins of the virus are somewhat unclear but it spread globally with Italy, India, Spain, US, France, UK, Iran, being the most effected.

International efforts are mostly geared towards reducing the spread of disease, establishing quarantine centers, limiting economic impact, creating awareness, ensuring availability of medical supplies, vaccination research, providing optimized care of infected patients, enforcing travel restrictions and methods of enforcing lockdown protocols etc. Clearly these methods fall in the defensive strategy and often put into practice due to lack of preparedness. As the world grapples with the human impact of the virus there are numerous areas of the society, economy, industry, services, government that are being effected and largely overlooked. When the virus began to spread in China, a lockdown protocol was enforced (23 January,2020) owing to which people were restricted to their home thus industries were closed leading to disruption of the international supply chain. Educational institutions were shut down and air traffic was reduced to limit movement of individuals who may be carriers of the COVID-19 virus. Numerous projects have also been put on hold as the international economy is significantly impacted by the global financial recession caused as a result of the virus. Now that the world is experiencing the third wave of COVID-19 the above protective measures have been enforced globally. Given in table 1 are the statistics from the WHO weekly epidemiological report (WHO, 2022) dated 22 February 2022 of WHO regions under the COVID-19 pandemic.

Table 1. WHO regions and the cumulative deaths to date

WHO Region	Cumulative Deaths
Europe	1843169 (31%)
Americas	2600596 (44%)
Western Pacific	176613 (3%)
South-East Asia	757525 (13%)
Eastern Mediterranean	329934 (6%)
Africa	168916 (3%)

The National Strategy for Pandemic Influenza Implementation plan for National Security Council 2006 has identified the impact a pandemic influenza could have on IT systems (House, n.d.). An excerpt from the document highlights this as follows:

"Unlike many other catastrophic events, an influenza pandemic will not directly affect the physical infrastructure of an organization. While a pandemic will not damage power lines, banks, or computer networks, it has the potential ultimately to threaten all critical infrastructure by its impact on an organization's human resources by removing essential personnel from the workplace for weeks or months. Therefore, it is critical that organizations anticipate the potential impact of an influenza pandemic on personnel and, consequently, the organization's ability to continue essential functions."

Models, standards, guidelines, frameworks specific to IT governance generally target value delivery, strategic alignment, performance management, resource management and risk management at various depths. While healthcare standards/ guidelines exist that assist the healthcare sector for the management of pandemic the same cannot be said for the IT sector and its many verticals. IT specific standards, by design are either descriptive or prescriptive but they do not address emergent scenarios like those related to the spread of pandemic. Thinking beyond an individual's health these standards should include what needs to be done to ensure continuity of IT services, protection of IT resources, information management, risk management under emergent scenarios, etc (Shahid et al., 2022). Studies that discuss contingency planning in the event of a natural disaster are not applicable to a pandemic because natural disasters are limited in geographical coverage and are mostly in the form of fire, earthquake, flooding, etc. A pandemic on the other hand is a disease that can spread rapidly within the human population and could have no direct impact on the IT infrastructures and implementations.

This chapter for the first time brings to light IT and cyber security related issues that have emerged as a result of the spread of the COVID-19 pandemic. The chapter then explores the primary reason why IT systems were ill prepared for dealing with a pandemic and its many effects. Thus the need for creation of standards or guidelines that come into effect under emergent conditions (including pandemic spread and other extraordinary scenarios) has been highlighted. It has also been felt that while planning for business continuity, risk management (particularly acceptance and transference), contingency planning the appropriate C-level executive (CEO, CTO, CFO, CISO, etc) should consider the possibility of emergent scenarios by allocating higher probability to pandemics and epidemics.

The remaining chapter first explores the core problem that has caused widespread disruptions and losses to the IT industry and those associated with it. The concept of IT security is studied further with a detailed discussion on the impact of COVID-19 on the attack surface. Guidelines and standards play a crucial part in IT management and governance therefore it has been shown that existing guidelines do not appropriately deal with the issue of a pandemic. The chapter shows the impact of a lockdown on IT systems and project management failures. Changed environmental circumstances can lead to capacity planning failures of various nature which has been shown later on. The chapter closes with a set of recommendations for future preparedness and conclusions.

UNDERSTANDING THE PROBLEM

In an extensive survey (ISACA, n.d.) incorporating 3700 individuals from 123 countries, it has shown that organizations have had to face the negative impact of the pandemic. A deeper investigation of the problem reveals that the impact on organizations is not just limited to financial. Moreover study has shown varying extent of impact on various industries like tourism, healthcare, education, etc (Xiang et al., 2021). A breakdown of seen adverse effects is as follows:

- An overall decrease in revenue and sales
- Supply chain disruptions
- Irregularities in business operations
- Reduction in budgets
- Reduction in business productivity

The spread of the COVID pandemic has had significant impact on many verticals incorporating IT. The problem of reduced service provisioning, lack of workforce availability, capacity planning failures, risk management failures under an epidemic and pandemic requires a holistic solution. The above problems combined with inadequacy of existing standards, adhoc policy making, ill preparedness, confusion, pronounced attack surface, human factors needs to be acknowledged and an expedited action is needed to address the issues faced by the IT industry under a pandemic. A deeper analysis of the above confirms that the IT industry was never prepared to face a pandemic. COVID is not the first pandemic and isn't the most devastating pandemic known to man. Despite this the IT industry was never prepared and is still not prepared to face pandemics and epidemics. The availability of internet, cloud, communication software enabled limited continuation of services. Despite this fact there have been notable losses and failures at all levels. The COVID pandemic has presented unique opportunities for public administrations, NGO and enterprises of all sizes (Saeed et al., 2021).

What is particularly worrying is the fact that COVID is not the first pandemic to have hit the human population in recent history. More deadly pandemics have been recorded that have caused fatalities at a scale much higher as compared to COVID. Despite this fact industries, healthcare, education, aviation, etc remined largely unprepared which resulted in unprecedented losses. What is even more worrying is the fact that officially reported figures cannot be fully trusted. A detailed study has reported that the actual deaths could be double or even quadruple of the reported deaths (Adam, 2022). This is even more troubling in developing countries where the healthcare infrastructure is not well established. Thus decision making at all levels is being done with inaccurate figures.

When dealing with pandemics one must note that their scale can be unprecedented with significant impact on social, economic and environmental factors. As guidelines are limited and data both scarce and contradictory, organizations seek advice but are unable to decide the right set of actions needed (Boiral et al., 2021).

A survey (Zou et al., 2020) was recently conducted that incorporating 524 organizations in China. 18% of the total organization were related to IT. The study shows that most IT companies confirmed delays in product launch. Moreover IT companies have also had to seek loans to support their ongoing business. The survey confirms that large organizations were relatively well positioned to deal with the pandemic. Smaller organizations required subsidies to operate while larger organizations requested for loan repayment extensions in light of problems they faced due to the pandemic.

To summarize, the chapter explores the following questions related to the pandemic and the IT industry:

- Are organizations prepared to deal with outbreaks like pandemics and epidemics?
- Are there any readily available guidelines for organization and enterprises to deal with IT challenges that are presented in the wake of a pandemic or epidemic?
- Do pandemics present any particular cyber security related challenges?

SAFETY VS. IT SECURITY MEASURES

Organizations large and small enforce guidelines and policies with varying levels of repercussions ranging from advisory to strict compliance. These guidelines and standards are enforced for a range of reasons, but a prominent reason is to ensure compliance with recommendations during a disruption like a pandemic, natural disaster etc. Hence safety measures are enforced to ensure protection and limit adverse impact on humans. Conventionally, safety measures have been associated with physical workers and those who work under dangerous conditions. Security measures particularly those associated with IT are designed to ensure delivery of security services like confidentiality, integrity and availability. Secondary security services may be provisioned depending on the application at hand and compliance needs. Safety and security measures are two sides of the same coin. So it could be speculated that a safety breach can lead to a security breach and vice versa. Whenever there is a breach of any kind it can be traced to multiple failures of various nature.

Adoption of IoT, industry 4.0, bring your own device policies mandates the need for stringent measures that compliment both safety and security measures. When considering a pandemic it must be emphasized that increased connectedness can heighten both the risk and impact of a pandemic. For instance, networked biometric devices are installed for automated employee attendance. These devices could become a source of virus spread as multiple users come into close contact with the device.

PRONOUNCED ATTACK SURFACE

The attack surface is a study of the possible exploitation points in a larger system(Bellovin, 2016). Effort needs to be made to ensure that the attack surface is as small as possible. Under the spread of the pandemic a unique situation is created where the attack surface can be inflamed thus leading to privacy and security compromise. Presented below are common attack vectors that have evolved due to the current pandemic.

Remote-work Environment

As increasing number of employees are encouraged to work from home, this dramatically increases the attack surface. This trend has been observed internationally as part of lockdown protocol enforcement. This could be a necessity or out of choice. Regardless, employees access remote services from conventional home networks with limited to no security provisions. Also when working remotely staff will create shadow IT solutions that are not necessarily in line with the organizations policies. This increases the chances of a security incident. Thus organizations must determine which critical functions remain onsite and which remain offsite.

Skeleton Staff

Skeleton staff is the minimum number of essential staff that is required for business operations. The use of skeleton staff is essential particularly in distressing times. Under the COVID pandemic temporary workforce, workplace and HR reshaping exercises were conducted to limit employee exposure to the pandemic. When there is reduced availability of staff and the environment is under special conditions this dramatically increases the attack surface as opportunistic actors are presented with the ideal situation for committing a crime. Quarantined staff members who are otherwise key members of the team are not available when required. The use of skeleton staff is purely a quality versus quantity balance. To be effective departments must ensure the right combination incorporating both quality and quantity in their staff presence. With no precise formula the number of skeleton staff is a function of organization size, shifts, department size (and subdepartments), service sector and regulatory requirements (including health and safety). Recommendations (Dongrie et al., 2020) regarding organizational behavior and leadership qualities throws light on improvements at many levels of the organization.

Rising Phishing Attacks

Phishing is an attack that aims to obtain sensitive information particularly login credentials like username, passwords, pin codes etc. When employees login to the corporate network from remote locations they do so with a variety of devices with varying platforms. Many of these devices have never been logged and used to access services. This provides attackers the opportunity to employ phishing techniques thereby gaining illegitimate access to user credentials. The use of social engineering to exploit the emergent scenario is also worth noting (Ghafir et al., 2016).

Rising Email Based Attacks

The spread of COVID-19 has also shown a sharp increase in email-based attacks. Mostly these attacks exploit the natural curiosity associated with the spread of a pandemic. Thus the emails sent by attackers are crafted to look like informative bulletins from renowned organizations like the World Health Organization (WHO). The attack vector breakdown shows that 32% macro based weaponized documents were shared, 12% were office exploits, 35% of the total attack vector was related to malicious links placed in emails and 21% of the attacks were due to emails embedded with malicious executables (*The Coronavirus Is Already Taking Effect on Cyber Security– This Is How CISOs Should Prepare | Threatpost*, n.d.). It is worth noting that the attack surface could be even worse for organizations that have weaker security posture. The above statistics have been depicted in the graph below.

Figure 1. Statistics of heightened attacks of various types under the COVID-19

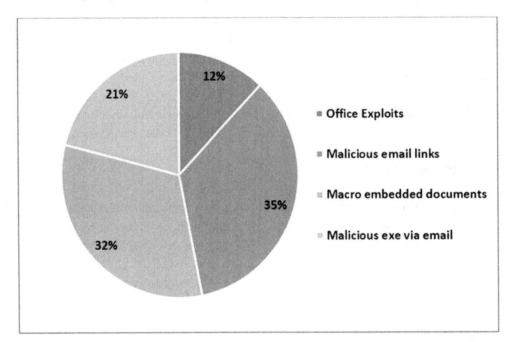

Malicious Smartphone Applications

Under normal circumstances the attack surface puts a moderate emphasis on malicious smartphone applications, but considering the emergent circumstances a large number of COVID-19 themed applications have been emerged. These applications target one or more of the following areas associated with the pandemic:

- Pandemic dashboard application with live statistics
- COVID-19 self-screening/ scoring application
- News sharing/ information dissemination

The applications are phishing oriented and some may even be designed to conduct espionage operations. Rather than relying on ill motivated sources of information an intelligence baseline can be defined. This should include consistent and trusted sources of information like the WHO and offices of the local government.

Resurrection of Outdated Systems

The replacement and update of IT equipment is a necessary step that needs to be regularly taken to ensure consistent, improved and reliable service. Cyber security incidents are known to emerge from the use of outdated systems that have inherent vulnerabilities. Use of operating systems that are beyond the end of support period, out of date firmware, non-updated browsers, antivirus software can allow attackers to exploit inherent vulnerabilities with little effort. These concerns are particularly valid when staff work from home and manage with whatever equipment is at hand since offices do not have a large enough pool of devices to distribute among employees. Similarly, as hospitals are put under increased load; obsolete equipment and systems may need to be resurrected. This has the potential to increase the attack surface under special circumstances.

A similar concern seen here is the disruption of equipment supply chain. As international supplies are greatly impacted, the result is a reduction in production. When a lockdown protocol is initiated, people purchase IT equipment in an effort to support their work from home environment. IT equipment manufacturers cannot keep up with the huge demands. During the COVID pandemic a shortage of semi conductors has been seen that is attributed to low manufacturing capacity and increased global demand.

INADEQUACY OF EXISTING GUIDELINES/ STANDARDS

Based on the measures adopted to combat COVID and the many methods of attacks it is quite clear that C-levels, system managers, policy makers were ill prepared from various perspectives. This lead to the enforcing of adhoc, unplanned and unrealistic policies that perhaps further worsened an already critical situation. The source of the problem lies in the fact that existing IT guidelines/ standards on contingency planning under special circumstances do not adequately address the spread of pandemic. A reason for the lack of policy in this regard could possibly stem from the assumption that it the probability of a life threatening pandemic is very low. This could explain the limited preparation at a global scale thus leading to significant losses. As shown in Table 1, a careful investigation of various organizational plans throws light on the effectiveness of the individual plans in light of their purpose but one immediately notes that there is no plan in place for pandemics and epidemics. Moreover none of the existing plans incorporate activities or guidelines related to pandemics and epidemics.

Table 2. A comparison of various plans, their purpose and scope

Plan	Purpose	Scope
Business Continuity Plan	Provides procedures for sustaining essential business operations while recovering from a significant disruption	Addresses business processes: IT addressed based only on its support for business process
Business Recovery Plan	Provides Procedures for recovering business operations immediately following a disaster.	Addresses Business processes: Not IT focused: IT addressed based only on its support for business process
Continuity of Operations Plan	Provides procedures and capabilities to sustain and organizations essential strategic functions at an alternate site for up to 30 days	Address the subset of an organization's missions that are deemed most critical: Usually written at headquarter level: not IT focused
IT Contingency Plan	Provides procedures and capabilities for recovering a major application of general support system	Same as IT contingency plan: Addresses IT system disruptions: Not business process focused
Crisis Communications Plan	Provides procedures for disseminating status reports to personnel and the public	Addresses communications with personnel and the public; not IT focused.
Cyber Incident Response Plan	Provides strategies to detect, respond to and limit consequences of malicious cyber incident	Focuses on Information Security responses to incidents affecting systems and/or networks
Disaster Recovery Plan	Provides detailed procedure to facilitate provision of capabilities at an alternate site	Often IT focused: limited to major disruptions with long term effects.

Risk management is a comprehensive study of identifying, controlling, mitigating and documenting risks being faced by an organization and its assets. Risk management is a fully functional discipline that addresses many risks ranging from theft to act of God. There is no known method that is able to incorporate pandemics into the risk management life cycle. To do so mathematical models need to be created that are able to predict annualized rate of occurrence and also the cost impact of a pandemic.

A popular framework that targets IT management and governance is COBIT (ISACA, 2018). The framework created by ISACA has been updated in 2019 but incorporates no guidelines for dealing with pandemics and epidemics. While the framework incorporates many praiseworthy design factors that deal with risks, people, organizational structure, governance, technology, threat landscape etc, there are no guidelines related to pandemics and epidemics. COBIT is a descriptive model and does not prescribe what steps need to be taken. This fact can be seen with concern because with the onset of COVID organizations needed guidelines and assistance with their operations and staff which were entirely missing. However, it can be speculated that those organizations that had a strong governance placed at their core were in a better position to deal with emerging scenarios like those in COVID. The COBIT 2019 incorporates a design factor called Future Factors. This was done so that the framework evolves with the underlying organizations and their technology. It can be predicted that the next incarnation of the COBIT framework may incorporate guidelines related to pandemics.

NIST special publication 800-34, Rev. 1, addresses the issue of contingency planning in federal information systems but the standard outlines principles for only handling disruptions to information systems. Furthermore, the guidelines are applicable to service resumption after a disruption. A pandemic is a unique scenario because it is always unclear when regular services can resume as the pandemic continues to spread globally. The standard does not address individual incident types and the associated counter measures. Further the standard only provides guidelines for client/ server systems, telecommunication systems and mainframe systems. The standard needs thorough revision to incorporate areas such as cyber security and other modern infrastructures like the cloud.

Considering the relevance, similar observations have been made when considering the superseded NIST IT Contingency Planning Guide for Information Technology Systems (Swanson et al., 2002) (currently replaced with NIST special publication 800-34 Rev 1 (Swanson et al., 2010)). The document provides recommendations for the establishment of a contingency plan but does not consider pandemic and its rapid spread. Although the standard addresses seven IT platforms but does not consider security infrastructure and systems as an essential part of contingency planning. A concern with this standard is that it suggests common recovery strategies, but does not suggest a set of services that are required to ensure minimum service continuity for essential IT platforms.

The ISO standard 22313:2020 (*ISO 22313:2020(En), Security and Resilience — Business Continuity Management Systems — Guidance on the Use of ISO 22301*, n.d.) has successfully delineated a business continuity management system. The standard suggests introducing a controlled and gradual disruption of service via a controlled response. The standard also highlights the importance of a business continuity and its positive impact on services. The standard suggests that with a business continuity management system in place the services can be brought back to an acceptable level considerably faster. The standard has also provided tasks relevant to leadership, planning, support, operations, performance evaluation, improvement. Although this seems like a holistic addressal of the situation, it is not readily applicable to IT systems and critical infrastructure. IT systems, their security and availability need to be addressed via a specific standards or guidelines.

ISO is in the process of making a dedicated standard for contactless delivery services. The standard aims to cover principles, responsibilities, delivery methods, service processes, quality control and improvements that can be incorporated to effectively implement contactless delivery services. This is a much needed area that interestingly is unregulated and has played a significant role in limiting the impact of the COVID pandemic.

The Health Insurance Portability and Accountability Act (HIPAA) (PF et al., 2018) is a US legislation that provides guidelines for privacy and security of medical information. The act has been waived under the COVID-19 pandemic (Office for Civil Rights et al., 2020). This has primarily been done to facilitate hospitals and healthcare givers while there is a disaster protocol in place or for a limited time when hospitals initiate a disaster protocol. When public health is compromised under the spread of a pandemic, the healthcare providers are under immense pressure to respond to queries and must respond to public demand for information. The HIPAA reiterates the importance of patient privacy but allow certain relaxations for wider convenience. For example telehealth staff are able to provision services to patients beyond what was permitted under standard circumstances. Similarly certain patient rights are relaxed from being mandatory to minimum thus facilitating information sharing but at the same time enforcing user centric design (Saeed et al., 2016). Two important lessons are learnt from the reduced enforcements of the HIPAA.

- HIPAA was not readily applicable to the spread of a large scale pandemic like the COVID-19.
- The HIPAA facilitates patients from urban and rural areas to use video communication software to connect to their physician. While this is a much needed service it could give rise to a range of attacks like impersonation and identity theft if the system is poorly designed or tested.

When considering the EU General Data Protection Regulation (GDPR) (*General Data Protection Regulation (GDPR) Compliance Guidelines*, n.d.) under the spread of the pandemic, different countries following the regulation responded differently. Their very response is an indication that the regulation adds to the complexity and makes it difficult to provide rapid health services in testing times. For instance, Germany took the stance that the health of individuals is of importance and that this should not be hindered by privacy laws. Ireland noted the unprecedented challenge and suggested a proportionate regulatory approach. A statement by the UK (no longer part of EU) information commissioners office said that it would be considering COVID-19 outbreak when looking into data privacy violations (*Coronavirus Pandemic Changes How Your Privacy Is Protected - CNET*, n.d.). This shows that public health in a pandemic has precedence over privacy regulations. A praise worthy quality of GDPR is that it does not prohibit remote-work and also obligates minimum non-identifiable data archiving to ensure user privacy. The later could prove to be detrimental as authorities try to determine who one has been in physical contact with in weeks running to the infection.

Technological advancements have played a major role in controlling the spread of the COVID pandemic. Many smartphone applications aimed at flattening the curve have been developed for tracing the contacts made with a covid positive individual. These apps have been effective at the cost of the security and privacy of the individuals. These apps not only trace the contacts made but also keep track of personal identifiable information. This gives rise to the need of privacy-preserving contact tracing applications. Many researchers have proposed privacy-preserving contact tracing apps that are based on blockchain, anonymization and machine learning techniques (Tahir et al., 2021). As mentioned earlier, contact tracing applications have been made possible due to flexibilities and exemptions issued in light of the spread of the pandemic.

Many standards and recommendations need to be revised to incorporate latest technologies and methods. An opportunity that has emerged from the spread of the COVID-19 pandemic is the need to revisit protocols and standards to incorporate new forms of essential infrastructures/ technologies that have emerged since the creation of the standard. Standard defining organizations must take the initiative to create standards or family of standards that are dedicated to IT, epidemics and pandemics. While researching the lack of policy regarding pandemics and their impact on governance, IT systems; user privacy and security has become very obvious and is a point of grave concern. Here, one must note that limited guidelines that do exist are not being followed due to insufficient publicity and implementation. Since organization are unaware of the guidelines therefore practical and immediate actions cannot be implemented for the control of pandemics and its impact on IT systems and organization.

IMPACT OF LOCKDOWN/SKELETON STAFF

A government handles a pandemic through different methods. An effective method of limiting the spread of a pandemic is through the enforcement of a lockdown protocol. There can be various forms of lockdown protocols ranging from moderate to very strict. Reduced availability of staff means a significant upstream and downstream impact for service consumers. Some services will be in high demand while others are not available. There are numerous IT specific services that are monitored round the clock for safety, security and quality reasons. A Cyber Security Operating Center (CSOC) is a comprehensive network monitoring solution that can be programmed to take certain actions automatically; but this cannot be said for all possible attack use cases. There can be many scenarios particularly those related to zero day attacks that require extensive user/administrative intervention. Similar impact can be observed on network operating center and broadcast operations control center. Unavailability of sufficient staff to run essential monitoring systems can compound the security posture.

The enforcement of a lockdown protocol presents the opportunity to establish a comprehensive work from home policy. Also practice runs can be performed to assess the organizations posture with reduced staff availability. It must be stressed that this should be done while considering standards and relevant case studies.

INFORMATION SECURITY PROJECT MANAGEMENT FAILURES

Under the pandemic large scale management issues (Mannebäck & Padyab, 2021) were seen that emerged due to a change in environment and a lack of experience in the emergent circumstances. While, the use of adhoc procedures and policies is discouraged; under the pandemic organizations and leaders were forced to make decisions on incomplete, incorrect and unreliable information. This has the potential of causing failures and having long term negative impact on the organization. This can be improved by incorporating AI and business analytics into the decision making process (Einhorn et al., 2019).

The purpose of information security project management is to incorporate security practices into the project management life cycle while also ensuring projects are within scope, schedule and budget. When requirements are gathered, possible delays to the project are identified and their impact on scope and budget is also identified. While the common reasons for delays in projects is known and documented, the effects of pandemic on project management SDLC is quite unclear. A lesson learnt here is that under the spread of the COVID-19 there will be project delays of various degrees. Project overruns, budget revision, schedule adjustments and negotiations will be required on a wide scale.

Pandemic related project management concerns have emerged owing to lack of consideration that a pandemic could be wide spread to the extent that it negatively impacts IT projects from various perspectives. This creates an opportunity for project managers to create buffer zones in the timelines and also redefine contracts to incorporate emergent scenarios related to pandemics.

CAPACITY PLANNING FAILURES AND SLOWING OF IT PRODUCTION

With the spread of a pandemic, increasing number of employees and staff have been given instructions to work remotely. Thus there is reduced traffic on the corporate network and an increased load on conventional home networks. This has put unprecedented load on the IT and communications infrastructure. Telecom service providers under standard conditions are not able to perform capacity planning to accommodate extended durations of lockdown, particularly if it is unclear when regular services will resume. A similar concern that stems from inability to perform capacity planning is not being able to predict the impact of patient influx on healthcare systems. As the number of infected people reaches counts of thousands, the standard healthcare information systems are under immense pressure from various perspectives. This creates the case for thorough stress testing of IT systems both within and outside the healthcare domain. Using modern simulation tools and Artificial Intelligence (AI) algorithms complex networks can be studied with reference to increased loads and also the possibility of security attacks can be studied.

During a pandemic, governments consider enforcing a lockdown to limit the spread of the virus. This has a mentionable impact of production thus disrupting supply and demand of raw materials, components, parts, etc. IT equipment manufacturers and purchasers are among the first to feel the impact of a disrupted supply chain. Increase in prices and reduced availability has a significant impact on IT service providers. The need for essential components is not addressed which can make service provision impossible. For example, Wuhan where the COVID-19 virus originated is touted as the worlds largest production hub of fiber optics. As the entire city is vacated or placed under lockdown the manufacturing of fiber optic equipment is disrupted. Similar outcomes can be seen and predicted across the world.

The slowing of IT production has presented an opportunity to explore alternate supply channels from multiple continents. Backup suppliers and manufacturers need to be identified for resilience and business continuity during varying geographic spread of a pandemic. Various e-commerce channels can continue providing services to specific business types (B2B, B2C, C2B, C2C).

Here it must be mentioned that scarcity of materials and commodities is a real concern (The One Brief, n.d.) . Businesses will feel that there is scarcity of certain materials due to disruption in supplies and often because of inflated prices. A relevant example to consider is the global shortage of semiconductor silicon chips. The reduced availability is attributed to increased demand on electronic devices while there is limited production capacity available in the world.

IMPLICATIONS FOR EMPLOYEES

The above mentioned issues have a significant impact on both the employers, employees and customers. Similar issues are also faced by the employees who work under circumstances that are different from the conventional. Employees face the issue of reduced productivity and are unable to focus as their environment has changed and is no longer conducive to office work. A similar issue that has been brought to light is that employers will install surveillance software on devices they provide to their employees. This class of software is designed to track location, web browsing history and also transmit a screen shot at regular intervals. This way the employers can track their employees and their productivity when they are operating remotely. Monitoring employees this way is a violation of individuals security, privacy and confidentiality.

RECOMMENDATIONS/ACTIONS FOR MITIGATION

Analysis of the COVID pandemic and its impact on widespread IT services can be used as an inspiration for devising a recommendation for the way forward. A point here is that there is no single action/procedure that can be taken in place of a detailed standard that deals with pandemics and epidemics.

- Leading standard setting organizations like IEEE, NIST, Chertoff Group, ISO need to constitute committees that present an RFC for the wider audience. This cannot be done by individuals due to lack of mandate.
- Identify platforms and websites that are well trusted for information concerning the pandemic/emergent situation.
- Large enterprises particularly those that work with critical infrastructure should constitute a command and control center supported by cross functional teams to monitor and act in extreme circumstances.
- The created command and control center should implement a pandemic management plan when the first signs of a pandemic/ epidemic are seen. A proactive role is suggested to limit spread of diseases as frequent as the common flu, etc.
- Business leaders/ champions should start early preparation and monitor absenteeism in relation to providing essential business functions. Establishing a trigger based escalation matrix can add clarity and strength in decision making.
- Identify single point of failure (people, process, function, supplier, customers etc). Identify alternate channels of service delivery to ensure possibility of services with minimum possibility of exposure to the employees.
- Establish a communication channel for emergent situations thus ensuring contact and knowledge dissemination.
- Follow best practices/ recommendations made by experts and community planners. One may consider using probabilistic tools/ analytical tools to determine pandemic risk and impact (Sun et al., 2020).
- Research is needed to incorporate pandemics in risk management strategies.
- A pandemic needs to be considered when planning for business continuity. Also apply appropriate controls to limit effects and gain senior management approval.

- Anticipate and plan for supply chain disruption particularly when a pandemic lingers..
- Install end-point protection systems to facilitate work from home employees.
- Plan for the impact of a pandemic while defining capacity, project timelines and costing.
- Adopt policies for remote-work, BYOD, attendance, collaborations and skeleton staff.
- Disable or raise precautions about systems that require physical interaction for example biometric, pin inputs terminals, ATM machines, lift buttons etc.

Here it must be emphasized that the best way forward is to put into practice dedicated standard/ family of standards for dealing with pandemics. This has been mentioned in point one of this section. Until this is done organizations and IT managers should adopt the remaining points from the above list to the best of their abilities. Obviously an industry standard will incorporate all the above points and possibly many more as comments from experts are received. The adoption of a standard of this nature cannot be limited to a single organization because that would have no impact on a wider scale. To be fully effective a standard will need to defined by an organization that possesses the expertise and the mandate to take on the activity otherwise the outcome will not be adopted by the wider industry. The ideal outcome of the exercise would be better preparedness (reduced disruption, service continuity and making effort to reduce exposure to disease) once an epidemic starts to take hold. Here it pertinent that under distressing times it is important to eliminate sources of confusion and rumors.

CONCLUSION

The COVID-19 is a pandemic that has impacted global operations across all verticals of the society. It can be said that this is the first pandemic that has spread to engulf the entire world. With the third wave and more than 180 nations effected by the disease, it has brought life to a stand still in many modern nations. Governments and community leaders are making impact by creating awareness and ensuring that healthcare services are able to deal with the high number of patients being put into care. Once an individual is diagnosed with COVID-19 they are put into quarantine for a period. Anybody who may have been exposed to the pandemic is also placed in isolation to limit its spread. This creates an emergent scenario where essential services have been disrupted. This chapter has explored the many areas of IT that have been impacted by the pandemic from various perspectives. Study of the emerging situation has shown that as services are compromised the cyber attack surface has been pronounced. Attackers have created seemingly meaningful but malicious applications and websites for smartphone and computers that have rapidly spread with the help of social media. To make the situation worst there is little to no guidance/ standards that address IT systems, operations, preparedness and pandemics. Detailed study of existing standards and protocols has shown that organizations regardless of size and service type were poorly prepared for disruptions caused by a pandemic. This is precisely where the problem lies and needs stakeholder input at a large scale to be fully addressed.

This chapter has thus explored some opportunities that have arisen with the emergent scenario. Also recommendations have been made to conclude with what could be done in future pandemics and emergent situations with particular focus on preparedness and service continuity. The suggestions can enable us to be better prepared for future pandemics and possibly reduce the impact on the world economies.

REFERENCES

Adam, D. (2022). The pandemic's true death toll: Millions more than official counts. *Nature*, *601*(7893), 312–315. doi:10.1038/d41586-022-00104-8 PMID:35042997

Bellovin, S. M. (2016). Attack Surfaces. *IEEE Security and Privacy*, *14*(3), 88. doi:10.1109/MSP.2016.55

Boiral, O., Brotherton, M.-C., Rivaud, L., & Guillaumie, L. (2021). Organizations' Management of the COVID-19 Pandemic: A Scoping Review of Business Articles. *Sustainability*, *13*(7), 3993. doi:10.3390u13073993

Coronavirus pandemic changes how your privacy is protected - CNET. (n.d.). Retrieved February 27, 2022, from https://www.cnet.com/health/coronavirus-pandemic-changes-how-your-privacy-is-protected/

Dongrie, V., Sharma, A., & Choudhary, R. (2020). *Workforce, workplace and HR reshaping - During COVID-19 Pandemic*. Academic Press.

Einhorn, F., Marnewick, C., & Meredith, J. (2019). Achieving strategic benefits from business IT projects: The critical importance of using the business case across the entire project lifetime. *International Journal of Project Management*, *37*(8), 989–1002. doi:10.1016/j.ijproman.2019.09.001

General Data Protection Regulation (GDPR) Compliance Guidelines. (n.d.). Retrieved February 27, 2022, from https://gdpr.eu/

Ghafir, I., Prenosil, V., Alhejailan, A., & Hammoudeh, M. (2016). Social Engineering Attack Strategies and Defence Approaches. *2016 IEEE 4th International Conference on Future Internet of Things and Cloud (FiCloud)*, 145–149. 10.1109/FiCloud.2016.28

House, W. (n.d.). *The national strategy for pandemic influenza*. Academic Press.

ISACA. (2018). *Introduction and Methodology*. http://linkd.in/ISACAOfficial

ISACA. (n.d.). *ISACA Survey Cybersecurity Attacks Are Rising During COVID 19*. Retrieved April 25, 2022, from https://www.isaca.org/why-isaca/about-us/newsroom/press-releases/2020/isaca-survey-cybersecurity-attacks-are-rising-during-covid-19

ISO 22313:2020(en), Security and resilience — Business continuity management systems — Guidance on the use of ISO 22301. (n.d.). Retrieved February 27, 2022, from https://www.iso.org/obp/ui/#iso:std:iso:22313:en

Mannebäck, E., & Padyab, A. (2021). Challenges of Managing Information Security during the Pandemic. *Challenges*, *12*(2), 30. doi:10.3390/challe12020030

Office for Civil Rights, T., Department of Health, U., & Services, H. (2020). *COVID-19 & HIPAA Bulletin Limited Waiver of HIPAA Sanctions and Penalties During a Nationwide Public Health Emergency*. Author.

PF, E., P, A., & MJ, H. (2018). Health Insurance Portability and Accountability Act. Encyclopedia of Information Assurance, 1299–1309. doi:10.1081/E-EIA-120046838

Saeed, S., Bamarouf, Y. A., Ramayah, T., & Iqbal, S. Z. (2016). Design Solutions for User-Centric Information Systems. *Design Solutions for User-Centric Information Systems*. doi:10.4018/978-1-5225-1944-7

Saeed, S., Rodríguez Bolívar, M. P., & Thurasamy, R. (Eds.). (2021). Pandemic, Lockdown, and Digital Transformation. doi:10.1007/978-3-030-86274-9

Shahid, J., Ahmad, R., Kiani, A. K., Ahmad, T., Saeed, S., & Almuhaideb, A. M. (2022). Data Protection and Privacy of the Internet of Healthcare Things (IoHTs). *Applied Sciences (Basel, Switzerland)*, *12*(4), 1927. doi:10.3390/app12041927

Sun, X., Chung, S., & Ma, H. (2020). Operational Risk in Airline Crew Scheduling: Do Features of Flight Delays Matter? *Decision Sciences*, *51*(6), 1455–1489. doi:10.1111/deci.12426

Swanson, M., Bowen, P., Phillips, A. W., Gallup, D., & Lynes, D. (2010). *Contingency planning guide for federal information systems*. doi:10.6028/NIST.SP.800-34r1

Swanson, M., Wohl, A., Pope, L., Grance, T., Hash, J., & Thomas, R. (2002). *Contingency planning guide for information technology systems*. doi:10.6028/NIST.SP.800-34

Tahir, S., Tahir, H., Sajjad, A., Rajarajan, M., & Khan, F. (2021). Privacy-preserving COVID-19 contact tracing using blockchain. *Journal of Communications and Networks (Seoul)*, *23*(5), 360–373. doi:10.23919/JCN.2021.000031

The Coronavirus is Already Taking Effect on Cyber Security– This is How CISOs Should Prepare | Threatpost. (n.d.). Retrieved February 27, 2022, from https://threatpost.com/cynet-the-coronavirus-is-already-taking-effect-on-cyber-security-this-is-how-cisos-should-prepare/153758/

The One Brief. (n.d.). *2021's Top 10 Risks: The Pandemic Shines a Spotlight on Interconnected Risks - The One Brief*. Retrieved April 25, 2022, from https://theonebrief.com/2021s-top-10-risks-the-pandemic-shines-a-spotlight-on-interconnected-risks/

WHO. (2022). *COVID-19 Weekly Epidemiological Update*. WHO.

Xiang, S., Rasool, S., Hang, Y., Javid, K., Javed, T., & Artene, A. E. (2021). The Effect of COVID-19 Pandemic on Service Sector Sustainability and Growth. *Frontiers in Psychology*, *12*, 1178. doi:10.3389/fpsyg.2021.633597 PMID:34025507

Zou, P., Huo, D., & Li, M. (2020). The impact of the COVID-19 pandemic on firms: A survey in Guangdong Province, China. *Global Health Research and Policy*, *5*(1), 1–10. doi:10.118641256-020-00166-z PMID:32885048

Chapter 8
Cloud Ecosystem–Prevalent Threats and Countermeasures

Sarmad Idrees

Department of Information Security, College of Signals, Pakistan & National University of Sciences and Technology, Islamabad, Pakistan

Saqib Nazir

Department of Information Security, College of Signals, Pakistan & National University of Sciences and Technology, Islamabad, Pakistan

Shahzaib Tahir

Department of Information Security, College of Signals, Pakistan & National University of Sciences and Technology, Islamabad, Pakistan

Muhammad Sohaib Khan

Department of Information Security, College of Signals, Pakistan & National University of Sciences and Technology, Islamabad, Pakistan

ABSTRACT

Cloud-based services are in high demand because they give consumers and businesses a lot of flexibility in employing new applications and high-end infrastructure at a low cost. Despite the increased activity and interest, there are still worries about security vulnerabilities with cloud computing, resulting in hurdles for both consumers and service providers in terms of data protection, privacy, and service availability. As a result, cloud service providers and consumers must ensure that the cloud environment is secure from both external and internal threats. This chapter provides a comprehensive overview of key components of the cloud computing ecosystem and security concerns encompassing its impact on businesses. It focuses on understanding cloud computing technology, deployment environments, services, and usage considerations. The chapter identifies the most common security risks, allowing both end users and providers to identify the risks connected with the technology. Finally, different countermeasures to important security and privacy issues are presented.

DOI: 10.4018/978-1-6684-5284-4.ch008

INTRODUCTION

Cloud computing is a relatively new topic in the IT industry, and it is rapidly expanding. It contains benefits and weaknesses that vary depending on client needs, thus they have not been well investigated, recorded, or tested yet. This chapter explains how and when cloud computing is an effective platform for gaining access to shared computing resources such as applications, servers, storage, and networks. The goal of cloud computing is to allow people to benefit from modern technologies without having to be knowledgeable about each one. This field tries to lower the upfront cost of setting up the entire infrastructure and allow computer users to focus on their tasks rather than being distracted by IT issues. So, nowadays, a computer user does not need to know JavaScript to create a web site; instead, apps can be subscribed to, through the internet (cloud computing) and then launched.

Whether you realize it or not, cloud computing has played a role in your lives in some manner. We use cloud computing services on daily basis, through applications like Microsoft Office 365 or storage spaces as services (Dropbox, OneDrive, Google Drive/ photos, etc.), web-based email systems, or social networking sites (Facebook, LinkedIn, Myspace, and Twitter). Businesses use cloud computing as well; firms rent services from cloud computing service providers to cut operational expenses and enhance cash flow, among other things.

With all internet users using the cloud in some fashion, most of us do not realize it since we are using the free services only and are not bothered to look into the back-end technology. This is where most of the data breaches also occur which gives raise to security and privacy concerns pertaining to cloud computing. Authors of Grobauer, Walloschek, and Stocker (2010, pp. 50–57) have defined four indicators of cloud-specific vulnerabilities, introduced a security-specific cloud reference architecture, and provided examples of cloud specific vulnerabilities for each architectural component. Suryateja (2018, pp. 297–302) gave a guideline to organizations who wanted to shift to Cloud Computing but did not mention what are the possible solutions to the threats / vulnerabilities and how can they be covered in SLA (Service Level Agreement). Authors of Alouffi, Hasnain, Alharbi, Alosaimi, Alyami, and Ayaz (2021, pp. 57 792– 57 807) presented a systematic literature review (SLR) and aimed to review the existing research studies on Cloud Computing security, threats, and challenges, again without mentioning the possible solutions. T.-S. Chou (2013, p. 79) demonstrated Real world cloud attacks techniques that hackers used against Cloud Computing systems and presented the countermeasures to only those attacks.

This chapter provides a holistic view of cloud computing, its vulnerabilities, threats and then elaborates upon counter measures to all of them. In this chapter we shall cover following:

- Gather the latest trends and techniques in cloud computing technologies and present them in an understandable pattern.
- We have listed and identified most of, if not all, security issues of cloud services so that an organization wanting to shift to cloud computing can have an overview of the risks they will be having after taking their decision to shift to cloud.
- Businesses are rapidly expanding, and the impact of technology on them cannot be denied. Cloud computing has becoming increasingly important for corporate growth, a section of the chapter focuses on impact of cloud computing on businesses.
- Separate cloud vulnerabilities from security issues are spelled out and various cloud computing vulnerabilities are categorized since most of the authors are unable to distinguish them for com-

mon users like B. Grobauer, T. Walloschek, and E. Stocker (2010, pp. 50–57) and P. S. Suryateja (2018, pp. 297–302).

- Countermeasures to various threats are appropriately catered and spelled out their appropriate countermeasures. Our proposed approach will help in following manner:
- Help developers to have a holistic approach while developing services basing on cloud.
- Help the cloud users to identify any of the threat pertaining to them, and if so, what they can do to mitigate the threat.
- Help enterprises in compiling their SLA with the cloud service providers so to not miss out any countermeasure for security related aspect.

CLOUD COMPUTING ENVIRONMENT

Cloud computing can be defined in many ways, yet there is no universal definition for it. NIST's (National Institute of Standards and Technology) definition of cloud computing is considered as the de facto definition. NIST defines cloud computing as "cloud computing is a model for enabling ubiquitous, convenient, on demand network access to a shared pool of configurable computing resources that can be rapidly provisioned and released with minimal management effort or service provider interaction" Badger, Grance, Patt-Corner, and Voas (2012). We define it as "A cloud system is a collection of network accessible computing resources that customers (i.e., cloud consumers) can access over a network". The term cloud computing includes a variety of systems, mechanism and technologies along with services and deployment models.

Fig 1 shows how a cloud system relates to its consumers in which a modular system has been created without its operational visibility to the users. A cloud service provider manages its hardware and virtual machines on their datacenters as and when required without customers knowledge. The users are also virtually separated from each other and have no knowledge of other users using the cloud. A bird eye view on cloud computing deployment models and their features is given in Table 1.

Figure 1. Cloud relation with consumers – Overview

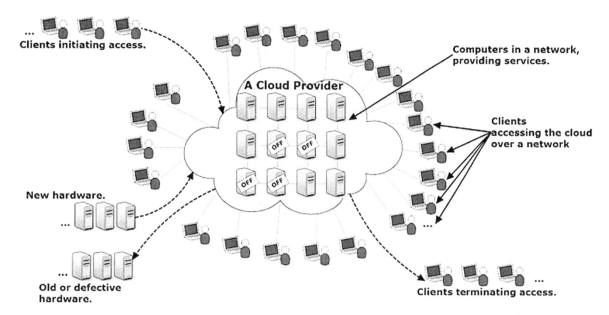

There can be following cloud deployment environments based on different scenarios.

ON SITE PRIVATE CLOUD SCENARIO

This cloud environment is used to access computing resources at the customer location. The private cloud can be centralized for a single user or distributed among multiple users. The security perimeter in this type of cloud scenario encompasses both client and private cloud resources. Consider the following factors when building a private cloud scenario: -

- **Network dependency**: The network dependency is limited to the local area network, which is used by on site clients to access computing resources. If the corporation wants its various sites to use the same cloud, it must use regulated communication means to avoid any security breaches.
- **IT skills**: In this type of cloud scenario, the consumer company will need IT skills not just to manage the user devices that will access the private cloud, but also to deploy and manage the cloud.
- **Hardware resource management**: Users' workloads must be able to be moved between computers in the private cloud without causing any disruption. Furthermore, to avoid failure or malfunction at any time, it is vital to build redundancy by deploying the cloud in multiple locations. Individual clients will not be aware of the placement of hardware in the infrastructure of the consumer organization at any one time, but the consumer organization will have complete control and visibility over the workloads.
- **Access policies**: Client workloads are shared on the same cloud hardware and local network but are separated by cloud provider access control. Any error or flaw in the policies that have been implemented may jeopardize the workload. Techniques like logical segregation, which incorporates VPN routing and forwarding, will help to limit the danger. Furthermore, because private clouds

are subject to attack by authorized users of consumer organizations as well as malicious insiders, risk can be managed by restricting the possible attackers.

- **Data import / export**: Because of network constraints, large data imports and exports are typically constrained in an on-premises private cloud system. This stumbling block can be overcome by implementing a high performance, dependable network architecture.
- **Security from external threats**: In this type of cloud situation, consumer organizations can use strong security measures to ensure cloud resources are protected to the same level as non-cloud resources. Firewalls, multi factor authentication, intrusion detection systems, encryption, and physical security are all examples of security methods.
- **High up-front cost**: On-premises cloud computing necessitates the purchase of hardware and software, such as high end computers, computing resources, operating system and storage requirements etc., resulting in a high initial cost for the consumer. The following are some strategies for reducing upfront costs:
  - **Converted data centers**: Customers can convert a portion of their existing data center to a cloud environment, lowering their cloud implementation costs.
  - **Sharing of hardware resources**: cloud computing can be done with existing machines in the enterprise. In this case, the cloud system will share hardware resources with the user, resulting in a lower upfront cost.
- **Limited resources**: On-site private cloud have restricted storage and computing capacity, which were developed based on the needs of the company and the cost benefit ratio in mind. If more cloud computing resources are required at any moment, additional costs will be incurred to satisfy the exact requirement.

Fig 2 shows a cloud model connected with its subscriber within an organization; this cloud is usually not connected to the internet; however, a boundary controller is configured to connect legitimate users remotely.

Figure 2. On site private cloud

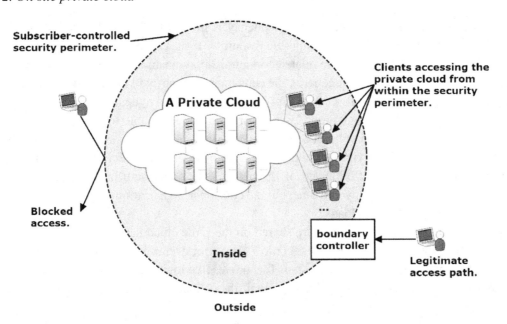

Table 1. Cloud deployment models and salient features

Deployment Model	Features	Description
On site private cloud	Network dependency	Network dependency limited to LAN to access computational resources
	IT skills	Requires IT skills to manage user devices
	Hardware resource management	Creates redundancy by implementing cloud at geographically diverse locations
	Access policies	Workload separated by access policies employed by cloud provider
	Performance limitation	Huge import / export of data due to network limitation
	Security from external threats	Organization can employ strong security measure to protect the cloud resources
	High up-front cost	Requires hardware resource and software for installation which causes high upfront cost
	Limited resources	Limited resources in terms of storage space and computing resources
Outsourced private cloud environment	Network dependency	Consumer must establish communication link with the provider
	Hardware resources	Cloud must have the ability to transfer client's workload within the machine
	Performance limitation	Network limitation may hinder data import / export
	Security from external threats	security must be implemented on provider and consumer perimeter
	Computing resources	Greater as compared to on site cloud computing
On site community cloud computing	Network dependency	Dual communication link is necessary among community members
	IT expertise	Good quality of IT skills is required
	Workload location / positioning	Configuration of outsourcing must be discussed prior to joining
	Security internal / external threats	Security is essential both on provider organization and participant organization perimeter
	Performance limitation	Network limitation may hinder the data import / export
	Upfront cost	Upfront cost varies for consumer and provider
	Resource limitation	Resource limitation will remain there have to analyze cost vs benefit ratio

Continued on following page

Table 1. Continued

Outsourced community cloud	Network dependency	Like outsourced private cloud where a communication link with provider is required
	Workload location / positioning	Provider who implements necessary security and visibility perimeters
	Security internal / external threats	Security perimeters are as same as in on-site community cloud
	Performance limitation	High performance, dedicated link and reliable connectivity can minimize network overload
	Upfront cost	vary from organization to organization
Public cloud	Network dependency	Users / consumers are connected to cloud resources via public internet
	Workload location / positioning	Can carry out shifting of data or processing depending upon efficiency and performance
	Risk factor / security risk	Workload of competitors co-exist; provider must ensure precautions to avoid any breach
	Consumer control over workload	Do not have any tangible way to monitor workload regarding unauthorized access or copying
	Upfront cost	Pay only for what you need to use in cloud environment
Hybrid cloud scenario	Combination of two or more private, community or public clouds.	Two or more private, community or public clouds can be combined to achieve the efficiency and workable environment as per requirements of the organization
	Workable and efficient environment	
	Design and implement extremely efficient system	

OUTSOURCED PRIVATE CLOUD ENVIRONMENT

In this scenario, an organization accesses the required cloud resources from vendor. The vendor does not deploy cloud environment within the premises of organization instead it extends the required resources to organization. Outsourced cloud environment has two separate security parameters, one is implemented by cloud provider and the other is implemented by organization who intends to get cloud resources outside his premise. Secure communication link and security parameter are important for data storage and processing conducted in outsourced cloud scenario. Thus, it is the provider who takes the responsibility to establish security parameters and avoid merging of extended private cloud resources with other cloud resources which is within the same environment. Fig 3 shows a cloud model connected with its subscribers. Organization must consider following before outsourcing the computational resources in outsourced private cloud: -

- **Network dependency**: In outsourced private cloud, consumer must establish communication link with the provider, and this is unavoidable. So, consumer must implement and adopt dedicated secure and reliable link with the provider.

- **Hardware resources**: Outsourced private cloud must have the ability to transfer client workload within the machine without creating any inconvenience for the consumer i.e without the consumer being aware of migration. In this case, the provider must provide some visibility and control to consumer pertaining to their workload location. Moreover, as per the consumer requirement the provider will employ requisite security perimeter and the workload will be transferred within the agreed security platform.
- **Data import / export**: Network limitation may hinder the data import / export between the consumer and the provider. Network capacity limitation can be adjusted but cannot be eliminated therefore high performance and reliable connectivity be establish between consumer and the provider to minimize network overload.
- **Security from external threats**: In outsourced private cloud, it is imperative that security must be implemented on provider and consumer perimeter to avoid any security breach. Most importantly, in this type of cloud scenario the communication link is vital which merits protection from malicious attempt.
- **Computing resources**: As compared to on site cloud computing, the amount of computing resources and data storage in outsourced private cloud is greater. Therefore, this scenario is elastic in nature for provision of facilities to the clients.

Figure 3. Outsourced Private Cloud

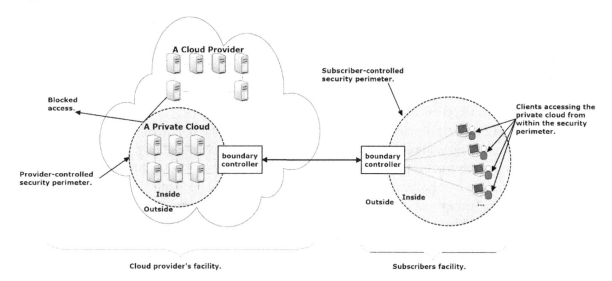

ON SITE COMMUNITY CLOUD COMPUTING

A community can be defined as a collection of organizations, each of which performs a certain task to meet a specific requirement. Now, it is possible that any organization will need to use cloud computing to meet their needs. On site community cloud computing is a solution in which a community member implements a cloud environment. Clients from many participating organizations use a common pool of computing resources, necessitating sharing solutions. For a community cloud to function, at least one member of the community must install cloud services. Each participant organization will have its own security perimeter and will be connected through a secure communication link in terms of security. Graphical representation of onsite community cloud is represented in Fig 4. Following are important factors to consider:

- **Network dependency**: Clients must access cloud resources, which necessitates careful network design. In the on-site community cloud scenario, it is consequently critical that communication channels meet the requirements for dependability and security. A dedicated leased network can be employed in this case for security, dependability and efficiency. Furthermore, a dual communication link is required among community members in order to understand the services that they provide or require from one another.

- **IT expertise**: There are two types of participant organization in this type of cloud scenario. The first group consists of people who extend cloud services, while the second group consists of those who merely use these services or resources. As a result, the member business that is providing cloud services is expected to have more polished and high-quality IT skills than those who simply use the facility. To put it another way, a cloud provider should have a high degree of IT experience, but a client who is not involved in cloud installation can rely on a lower level of IT expertise. In any event, IT skills are required in the cloud computing environment.

- **Workload positioning**: Clients are always worried about the location of their workload, as well as its security and visibility. Workload remains inside the participant company in this sort of cloud scenario. If a member organization wants to extend cloud services, it may choose to outsource cloud services; as a result, an organization concerned about the location of its workload must explore outsourcing configurations before entering the community cloud environment.

- **Security from internal / external threats**: To avoid a security breach, security is required on both the provider and participating organization perimeters. To eliminate conflicts of interest inside the company, communication ties within the organization are essential. Requisite services must reach their target client.

- **Data import / export**: Because enterprises are employing cloud resources and each member organization has a large number of customers, network overload is a possibility. As a result, network constraints may obstruct data import/export, which must be modified and handled accordingly. Network overload may be reduced with high performance and consistent connectivity.

- **Upfront cost**: The upfront cost differs in this sort of cloud scenario; those that wish to supply cloud services will have to spend more, while users will have to spend less.

- **Resource limitation**: In on site private cloud scenario, resources are pooled locally for the on site community cloud. While a result, resource constraints will persist as community groups evaluate the cost benefit ratio.

Figure 4. On-Site Community Cloud

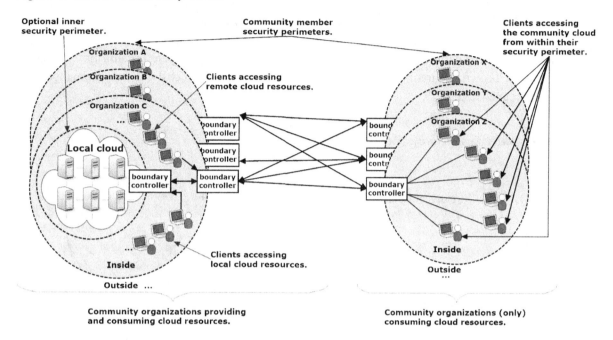

OUTSOURCED COMMUNITY CLOUD SCENARIO

This cloud environment is very similar to outsourced private cloud scenario but here a vendor is responsible for provisioning and management of cloud services and resources. Organizations access the cloud resource as per their requisite need. It is the cloud provider who implements the security perimeter and ensures the interchange mingling of community cloud resources with other cloud resources. Moreover, cloud provider must enforce sharing policies among the participant organization within the community cloud. Graphical representation of outsourced community cloud scenario is given in Fig. 5. Important considerations are as under: -

- **Network dependency**: Network dependency pertains to this type of cloud scenario is similar to outsourced private cloud scenario where a communication is link is required to be established with provider. Primary difference is that multiple secure communication links must be established from community organization to vendor facility. Secure and reliable network is the backbone of this cloud environment.
- **Workload positioning**: Security and requisite visibility of workload bears the credibility on cloud environment. Consumers are always concerned about the confidentiality and integrity of their workload. It is the provider who implements necessary security and visibility perimeters; therefore, participant organization must consider all related aspect pertaining to workload location.
- **Security from internal / external threats**: Security perimeters are as same as in on site community cloud scenario. Security services are imperative and needs to be implemented with great care which includes confidentiality, integrity, and availability.
- **Performance limitation due to data import / export**: Network overload may cause network connectivity problem. As organizations needs to access cloud resources and each organization has

numerous users utilizing the facility thus performance limitation can occur. High performance, dedicated link and reliable connectivity can minimize network overload.

- **Upfront cost**: In this type of cloud environment, participant organizations are accessing the cloud resources over the network which is provided by vendor. Each participant organization in a community has its own requirement for cloud resources therefore upfront cost will vary from organization to organization.

Figure 5. Outsourced community cloud

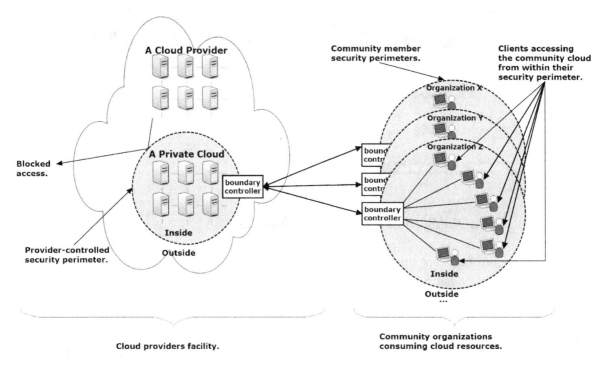

PUBLIC CLOUD SCENARIO

In this case, the provider sets up a cloud environment on a wider scale, allowing clients from all over the world to use cloud computing services over the internet. The public cloud scenario, like other cloud settings, is not client specific, such as a collection of individuals, a community, or an organization. To service a varied pool of customers, this form of cloud environment has massive processing and storage capabilities, as well as communication links that are largely via the public internet. Fig 6 shows a cloud model connected with its subscriber. The following are the most important points to consider before moving to public cloud:-

- **Network dependency**: Consumers connect to cloud resources over the public internet in a public cloud environment. As a result, establishing a connection is extremely reliant on internet infrastructure, and any defect can lead to concerns with dependability. When operating in a cloud environment, consumers must also consider the security of the established connection. To avoid a security breach, both the supplier and the consumer must take all necessary precautions.

- **Workload positioning**: In a public cloud situation, the provider can transfer client data or processing at any moment to the cloud data center, based on the efficiency and performance of the cloud infrastructure. Furthermore, the supplier must provide a task shifting policy that ensures the workload integrity is not jeopardized. Clients, on the other side, can either enable or disallow the cloud provider to move workloads, and this must be expressly agreed upon.

- **Risk factor**: In a public cloud situation, several users use the cloud resource, resulting in a single system being shared by a large number of users. In practice, it is fair to assume that opponents workloads will coexist in the same system. Confidentiality, integrity, and availability are all security services that are required. A prospective attacker can exploit any failure or weakness; thus, the provider must take all required efforts to prevent a breach.

- **Consumer control over the workload**: Cloud providers handle the specifications and system setup, and they normally do not share this information with customers. Similarly, software used in a cloud environment is not accessible to clients for evaluation. As a result, users have no real means to keep track of their workload in terms of unwanted access or copying. In this case, the customer must assume and trust the provider's security and auditing capabilities. Furthermore, the supplier must have a method in place to guarantee data integrity to its consumers.

- **Upfront cost**: In this scenario, clients only pay for the services they require in a cloud environment. In other words, users do not need to invest in expensive systems and software for their specific needs when the same service can be obtained for a fraction of the cost through cloud computing. On the other side, the provider will have to spend a significant amount of money to set up a cloud infrastructure.

Figure 6. Public cloud environment

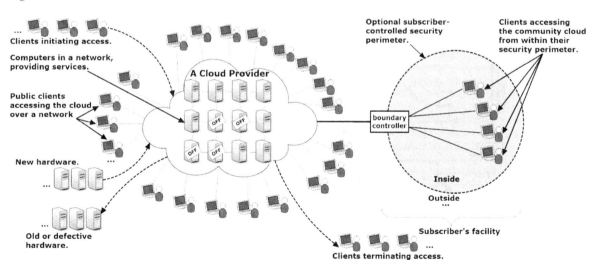

HYBRID CLOUD SCENARIO

The integration of two or more private, communal, or public cloud creates this cloud environment shown in Fig 7. The requirements of the customer lead the vendor to a specific combination of cloud scenarios in order to accomplish the required results. Second, the cloud provider provides a usable and efficient environment that considers all probable circumstances. Furthermore, because the cloud provider is operating a business and wants it to be lucrative, the vendor will always design and operate a highly efficient hybrid system. It is possible that a client uses a private cloud for typical workloads, but accesses one or more external cloud as needed for high demand jobs. Similarly, one of the hybrid possibilities is to use one type of cloud to offer resource backup to other processes/ data. The nature and kind of task creates opportunities for customers to use different cloud scenarios; for example, a business may use an outsourced private cloud to manage sensitive data such as payroll information but use a public cloud for software development and testing.

SECURITY ISSUES OF CLOUD SERVICES

Software as a Service (SaaS) – Security Issues

Clients utilize apps that are hosted on the vendor's cloud infrastructure in this situation. The user uses a thin client interface, such as a web browser, to access the desired program, as well as web-based emails. SaaS provides on-demand application services such as email, conferencing, and business apps. It is emphasized that the user has no influence over them, and that the supplier is in charge of all elements of the given services. A holistic view is represented in Fig 8. Following are security concerns present in it:

Figure 7. Hybrid Cloud Scenario

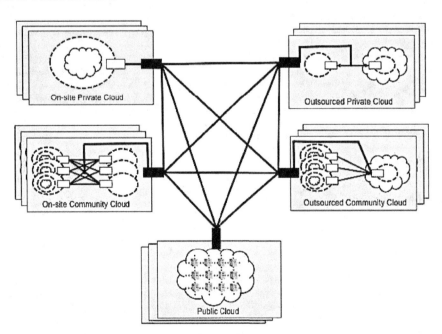

- **Application security**: Cloud apps are accessed over a public network, such as the internet, which is vulnerable to malware. Any flaw in a web application creates a vulnerability that an attacker can exploit to steal information or inflict other harm. Injection, cross-site scripting (XSS), security misconfiguration, sensitive data disclosure, and other important web application vulnerabilities are just a few.
- **Multi tenancy**: Because data from several clients is kept in the cloud, there is a risk of data leakage among the customers. Customers' data must be kept separate by enforcing strict security measures such as virtualization management etc.
- **Data security**: Every user is concerned about the security of their data. When SaaS users are forced to rely on the cloud provider, the difficulty becomes enormous. The complete duty for data security, privacy, and segregation while data is processed or stored rests with the SaaS provider.
- **Accessibility**: Accessing cloud applications via the public network is significantly easier using a public computer or mobile device. However, information-stealing mobile malware, unsecured Wi-Fi networks, and OS flaws make it a security concern.

Figure 8. Security Issues in cloud computing - broad overview

Platform as a Service (PaaS) – Security Issues

Users are given a platform and environment to build apps and services in this category of cloud computing. PaaS services are hosted in the cloud and accessed over the internet by users. This category allows users to avoid purchasing and maintaining expensive hardware and software by using PaaS services for their needs at a lower cost. PaaS is primarily reliant on a secure and stable network, as well as web browser security. The following are some of the security concerns: -

- **Third party relationship**: PaaS expands not just programming languages and needed services, but also third party services. When a PaaS provider additionally extends services from third parties, network and data security become top priorities.
- **Development life cycle**: Users use PaaS services for application development, and the vendor may update or upgrade the components of hosted services. As a result, any change in PaaS component will not only influence the system development life cycle (Z Mahmood, 2013) (S Saeed, 2013), but it may also jeopardize the security of the application on which a user is working. In this context, PaaS must provide a means for informing users of any changes or upgrades that may have an impact on the user development process. Furthermore, users must maintain their development

process agile in order to stay up with vendor changes. Similarly, to minimize any difficulty, users must store their data in many locations.

- **Infrastructure security**: Users have security control over their own applications being developed, but they have no assurances about the PaaS services and components provided to them. In a clod environment, the PaaS application and user workload are both hosted on the same server, hence any security compromise in the PaaS application exposes the user workload to risk. As a result, the provider is solely responsible for the security of data connected with user applications that is sent, processed, and stored.

Infrastructure as a Service (IaaS) – Security Issues

IaaS is a self-service paradigm that allows users to access and administer a remote data center architecture, including computing, storage, networking, and other services. Instead of investing a lot of money on hardware and software, users may get IaaS services at a much lower price. As a result, IaaS is a pool of resources made available by a provider in the form of a virtualized system that can be accessed through the internet. In contrast to SaaS and PaaS, IaaS is managed by the user, giving them control over security as long as the virtual machine is not vulnerable. The virtual machine's security is managed by the user, while the provider controls the underlying computing, data storage, and network. In this instance, the user need assurance from the vendor regarding the essential security, particularly with regard to virtual computers. The following are some of the security risks with virtual machines:

- **Virtual Machine Monitor (VMM)**: It is a piece of code or software that controls and manages the virtual machine, and it, like any other piece of software, has problems such buffer overflow and API vulnerabilities etc. Furthermore, an attacker can compromise the VMM during virtual machine migration and transfer the target virtual machine to a hostile server.
- **Resource sharing**: Sharing resources may compromise the virtual machine's security (VM). As a result, a malicious VM can obtain information without the VMM's knowledge.
- **Repository of VM image**: In this case, a valid user can download or upload a virtual machine image. An attacker with a legitimate account can upload a malicious VM that, if used mistakenly, will infect the system and potentially expose data.
- **Roll back of VM**: VM can be rolled back to its prior scheduled time in case a user encounters a critical configuration error or other such problems. However, this rollback feature may cause issues such as the loss of corrected vulnerabilities or re-enabling previously deactivated accounts.
- **Virtual networks**: It is a cost-effective and reliable technique of VM interconnection; however, it poses a security risk in cloud computing such as script injection or XSS.

IMPACT OF CLOUD COMPUTING ON BUSINESSES

Cloud Computing Technology (CCT) facilitates dynamic connection amongst workers in a highly competitive small business environment. Organizations can utilize web-based software to facilitate communication between suppliers, customers, and distributors, as well as to make decisions about the firm's external environment. CCT has the potential to transform accuracy and dependability, improve service, and lower costs if effectively implemented. Large corporations have hopped on board the cloud computing bandwagon swiftly. CCT is especially useful for businesses because it cuts down IT resources and time spent managing them. Businesses may take advantage of CCT's availability, reliability, security, scalability, flexibility, and more instead of depending on expensive hardware, software, and personnel to maintain them. Receiving new software applications sooner, decreasing IT effort, and boosting IT collaboration are all key benefits of switching to CCT by organizations. Making a big shift to a cloud-based infrastructure is a means for enterprises to significantly reduce hardware costs. CCT streamlines processes and shortens development cycles for others. CCT can dramatically enhance operational efficiency if properly planned and implemented. Nonetheless, there are several issues to consider and overcome, as with any new technology rollout. Successful deployments necessitate a systematic examination of users, as well as the targeted business results (cost savings, faster time to market, and higher service standards) and services required.

CCT's Benefits and Drawbacks for Enterprises

CCT democratizes IT advantages for businesses in the following ways: -

- It is less expensive and easier to start and grow a business.
- Reduces costs by using variable rather than fixed costs.
- Increases workplace flexibility.
- Collaboration at work is improved.
- Provides scalable resources and improves data security.
- Customer acquisition, service, and support are improved.
- Allows for the purchase of resources with operating money rather than capital funds.
- Allows small enterprises to cut delivery times and begin operations sooner.
- Makes resources that were previously only available to large corporations accessible and inexpensive.
- Allows a business to move its operations to a vendor that offers a better cloud service or a lower price.

Accelerated time to market and greater business agility are two primary areas of business and technological efficiency that cloud computing helps enterprises achieve. These growing cloud technological approaches, on the other hand, can lead to security flaws and human blunders. Platform inconsistency, network vulnerability, data unreliability, and business discontinuity are among potential downsides of cloud technology use in enterprises.

The Impact of Cloud Computing in FINTECH

The significant impact cloud computing is having on meeting many of the financial sector's requirements is driving an accelerating trend in fintech. Security, service, innovation, and scalability are just a few of the benefits that the cloud has to offer to the banking sector. Fintech startups and major financial institutions are competing to offer their consumers and end users faster, more reliable, and always-on digital products and services. All of this is possible with cloud computing, which is both cost effective and secure in an age where regulatory compliance is becoming increasingly severe.

Critical Trends and Benefits of Cloud Computing in Fintech

- **Advanced data management**: The financial services business relies heavily on data. It is required for a wide range of tasks, including routine account management, user identity verification, balance display, and spending analysis. Fintech organization may use cloud technology to store, manage, and access large amounts of data securely, cost effectively, and independently, from anywhere and at any time.
- **Accelerated innovation**: The fintech industry innovation has been boosted by the agility that cloud computing has provided to the sector. Cloud computing enables financial institutions to develop and market products more quickly while also allowing them to respond fast to shifting demands and emerging trends. The COVID-19 outbreak posed numerous hurdles for the fintech industry, which cloud computing has aided financial services organization in quickly and easily overcoming (Hind Naser,2020).
- **Enhanced security**: Customers are becoming increasingly mindful of how their personal data is safeguarded in the age of high-profile data breaches and cyber security threats. The financial services industry has a responsibility to protect its customer data, and the cloud is helping them do so more effectively. Many of the vulnerabilities that traditional on-premises IT infrastructures provide are being reduced by cloud computing in financial services, from data encryption to zero trust verification and access control.
- **Greater scalability**: Fintech companies frequently experience rapid growth, and these organization require infrastructure that supports rather than hinders their expansion. Financial institutions can grow up rapidly and easily with cloud infrastructure. Financial businesses frequently need to store additional resources in the cloud, which is far more cost-effective than upgrading or expanding traditional on premises infrastructure. This is due to a variety of factors, including rapidly growing customer bases and the digitization of traditional banking services.

Best Practices for Cloud Computing in Financial Services

There are several things that businesses should keep in mind if they want to get the most out of cloud computing in fintech. Here are a few critical points to keep in mind for financial services stakeholders on the road to cloud adoption: -

- **Demonstrable compliance**: Cloud providers should give proof of compliance to financial institution stakeholders, such as ISO 27001: Information Security Management System certification, ISO 22301: Business Continuity Management System certification, and PCI: DSS Payment Card Industry Attestation certification (telehouse, 2021).
- **Access control and encryption**: When it comes to cloud computing in financial services, the cloud provider you choose should be able to provide you with strong access control and data encryption regulations. Before choosing a provider based on these rules, make sure to inquire about how they will apply to your unique use cases to verify that any financial data is properly protected.
- **Disaster recovery**: A solid disaster recovery plan is required for any cloud system. Any cloud provider worth dealing with will have a disaster recovery strategy in place, so it is crucial to know how it works once your company has one.

Briefly, cloud computing is a critical enabler for financial organization. It enables financial sector organizations of all sizes and types to incorporate scalability and flexibility into their business models, allowing them to achieve agility and remain competitive in a continuously changing market. Cloud computing may also help finance companies increase security, comply with tight regulatory requirements, and simplify their typically complicated infrastructures.

The Impact of Cloud Computing on Healthcare

Health insurance companies, hospital and physician networks, laboratories, pharmacies, patients, and other entities make up the healthcare ecosystem, which is huge, diverse, and highly complicated. It is crucial that some important information is transmitted rapidly and accurately across various businesses in a discreet and secure manner for this ecosystem to function effectively and promptly. In healthcare, securing patient information is regarded extremely sensitive, as are privacy concerns, probably one of the factors that has decelerated the adoption of cloud computing in the healthcare industry. When it comes to cloud computing, it must be managed using modern technology and techniques. Data, information and services, on the other hand, can surely benefit from cloud collaboration because they can potentially span cities, states, and even countries. In the current context, private clouds appear to be implemented first due to security concerns, followed by public infrastructure. It could be a good idea to sketch out the healthcare industry's key priorities first, and then assess which cloud computing components might be efficiently utilized to help them. Rising healthcare expenses, the quality of services offered to patients and customers, privacy, data security and integrity, and disaster recovery appear to be leading considerations. Some of the inherent features, such as scalable infrastructure, data centers for persistent data, security models, and quick access to information, can be used to address some of these needs.

CCT's Benefits for Healthcare

Some of the key benefits of implementing cloud computing in healthcare encompass following: -

- **Infrastructure and dynamic scalability**: As the number of customers in the healthcare industry grow, so does the number of healthcare solution providers, and so does the business. As a company grows, it invests extensively in additional processing capacity and IT resources to meet the expanding demand. These computing resources are set up to handle a complex and changing environment. Organizations now have a way to deal with this problem, thanks to cloud computing. Infrastructure-as-a-Service (IaaS) and Platform-as-a-Service (PaaS) are cloud-based business models that allow companies to use existing infrastructure or tailor it to their own needs. In a short period of time, more servers can be added or deleted as needed. Rather than keeping data such as hospital information, physician networks, pharmacies and their locations on private on-site computers, they can store it in cloud-based data centers. The seller will also be in charge of keeping up with software updates. This will eventually free up various resources and lower the cost of maintaining them for providers of healthcare solutions. Organizations may be able to better alter and optimize their resource capacity planning thanks to the scalable architecture of cloud. Cloud computing, with its cost-effective price structure and low-cost maintenance, can be a huge benefit to small to medium-sized clinics that cannot afford large IT investments and staff. Amazon's S3, which provides scalable storage architecture, is an example.

- **Information sharing**: Healthcare organization do not work in isolation; they must continually communicate with other groups. To process claims, provide customer support services, new member acquisitions, and fulfil provider requests, a lot of data is provided and received. Electronic Medical Records (EMRs) are now stored in providers own databases. If part of this data can be moved to the cloud and shared across these businesses and platforms, it could result in better and faster service coordination and ultimately, higher customer satisfaction. Some patient information, such as Electronic Health Records (EHRs), Electronic Medical Records (EMRs), Personal Health Records (PHRs), Payer Based Health Records (PBHRs), and so on, can be moved to the cloud and shared with hospitals and physicians in different states or countries with explicit customer consent (Ahuja, Sanjay & Mani, Sindhu & Zambrano, Jesus. (2012)). With the same information, there will be less errors. This has a lot of potential in terms of offering better service at a lower cost. Some of these advantages can be seen in Microsoft's HealthVault. HealthVault was created with the goal of creating a centralized location to keep health information such as medical photograph, doctor's fax notes, and converting them to digital formats. It can also assist pharmacies, labs, hospitals, clinics, and other healthcare providers in retrieving and applying health information to their specific needs, allowing them to provide better and faster services to patients. Consumers can use the HealthVault connection center to integrate data from their fitness and health equipment, such as heart rate monitors and blood pressure monitors, to their health records.

- **Availability**: Cloud services with high availability can only assist healthcare companies to provide un-interrupted services with minimal downtime. Cloud may be operated programmatically to obtain near real time scalability capabilities. To ensure high availability, clusters with several nodes can be established. Furthermore, because the resources are fixed at the start of the calculation, the applications can be scaled up or down as the workload changes. Managing healthcare applications on the cloud is also expected to make them more widely available and accessible at all times. Maintenance costs could be dramatically reduced as a result of this. Understanding the security and privacy risks in healthcare could be the first step toward moving healthcare apps to the cloud.

Challenges of Cloud Computing in Healthcare

The delayed adoption of the cloud computing concept in the health care profession is mostly owing to major security and interoperability concerns. Those concerns must be addressed to eliminate uncertainties about shifting to the cloud and reaping the benefits of all the solutions and enhancements it offers. Unlike other types of data, healthcare data is subject to rigorous confidentiality, privacy, and security considerations. When it comes to migrating medical records to the cloud, HIPAA compliance is the most important need. Migrating whole data storages to a third party company is a difficult undertaking, especially when sensitive data like healthcare is involved. Because more problems will arise with access controls, audit controls, authentication, authorization, transmission security, and storage security to avoid exposing the information to unauthorized individuals, even more robust security should be ensured. These challenges have hampered cloud adoption and must be solved for cloud technologies to be trusted. Fortunately, several cloud providers, such as Microsoft, Google and Amazon, have pledged to adopt the strongest rules and processes to protect customer data and privacy.

- **Interoperability**: When it comes to migrating healthcare systems to the cloud, interoperability is one of the most difficult issues to overcome. It is because different healthcare organization use a variety of protocols, operating systems, programming languages, platforms, data formats, databases, and methodologies. Currently, healthcare systems are not built using standard data modelling constructs, resulting in disparate database architectures and incompatible systems. Interoperability of healthcare systems must occur at various levels: provider, software, computer, data, and system integration. Incompatibility of healthcare systems has made cross institutional use difficult. Health businesses must combine their old systems with new web and cloud-based technologies to adopt the cloud. Furthermore, they should standardize operations such as obtaining patient information and saving it to cloud storage. Developers of computer software must not only collaborate, but also share a similar data model and create products that can communicate with one another. Furthermore, they must adhere to regulatory frameworks and standards to comply with HIPAA regulations. Another challenge when creating cloud apps is data standardization and formatting. Furthermore, there is currently nothing that connects healthcare data in a consistent and uniform manner, which is costly, redundant, and insufficient. As a result, universal standards can be used to provide integration and interoperability, making management, upgrading, and maintenance easier. To design more interoperable systems, a new approach to developing healthcare systems is required. The health community will reap numerous and significant benefits as a result of this transformation. It appears that integrating current healthcare systems and making them interoperable with the latest cloud-based technologies will be a difficult undertaking. Although, by establishing adaptable and scalable standards and integrating medical data, the various caregivers will tremendously benefit.

In a nutshell, cloud computing introduces a new business paradigm that provides various benefits to the healthcare sector as a whole. Patients and healthcare organization would gain greatly from using the cloud in medical services, since it would improve patient quality of service, collaboration amongst healthcare institutions, and lower IT costs. Through sharing information across healthcare companies, this collaborative strategy allows healthcare services to interoperate in order to provide faster and more efficient response, hence improving patient service quality. As a result, hospitals, clinics, imaging centers, pharmacies and insurance companies can easily communicate patient medical data, prescription information, X-rays, test results, physician references, physician availability, and other information that authorized organizations can access from anywhere. All of this information would be utilized to make decisions, gain better diagnoses and treatments to produce better results, schedule physician appointments, expedite insurance acceptance, and so on, all of which would greatly improve the quality of service provided to patients. When it comes to migrating to the cloud, one of the most important benefits for healthcare organizations is the reduction in IT expenditures. All IT processes will be relocated to a remote cloud computing infrastructure, where they will be executed and stored, if the cloud model is adopted.

VULNERABILITIES IN CLOUD COMPUTING

Understanding the vulnerabilities in the cloud environment assists both the provider and the user in developing efficient security rules and mechanisms. A comprehensive overview of threat spectrum is given in Fig 9. The following is a list of cloud computing vulnerabilities: -

- **Insecure application program interface (API)**: APIs allow users to interact with the cloud environment. Correct APIs are critical to cloud computing security. Weak credentials, poor authorization checks, and insufficient input data validation are all security flaws in the API. This issue affects all three types of cloud computing services: SaaS, PaaS, and IaaS.
- **Vulnerabilities related to data**: Data from other users, who may be invaders or rivals, can coexist with yours in cloud computing. If data separation is ineffective, it may result in privacy breach. Furthermore, putting data in plain language increases the risk value multifold. If this vulnerability exists, SaaS, PaaS, and IaaS are all vulnerable to this attack. Security and service capabilities that customers can utilize to help them meet data privacy and data security requirements under Family Educational Rights and Privacy Act (FERPA) (20 U.S.C. § 1232g; 34 CFR Part 99) and other student data privacy laws and regulations by utilizing A. W. Services. (2021).
- **Virtual machine (VM) vulnerabilities**: Any inside attacker can target VMs with malicious attempts since they have IP addresses and are accessible within the cloud. Not only that, but uncontrolled migration, possibly hidden routes, and uncontrolled rollback might expose the cloud and its users to security risks. Because of this flaw, IaaS can be hacked.
- **Virtual machine images**: The public collection of VM images is insecure because an attacker might infect his virtual image with malware. The users who use the compromised photos are vulnerable to assault. This vulnerability in IaaS can be exploited.
- **Hypervisor**: The hypervisor's complexity presents a vulnerability that can be exploited. Because the IaaS platform makes use of virtual computers, it is vulnerable to attack. This vulnerability in IaaS necessitates security.
- **Virtual networks**: Many virtual machines sharing virtual connections create a security weakness that may be exploited by an attacker. IaaS is a platform that is vulnerable to attacks owing to flaws in virtual networks.

Threats and Countermeasures

Any flaw in the cloud computing system poses a risk to the user. Appropriate security is required in the cloud environment to protect both providers and users from loss. Summary of threats and counter measures is given in Table 2. The following is a detailed list of dangers to the cloud environment and countermeasures: -

- **Hijacking of account or service**: The takeover is caused by social engineering and poor credentials. Once the account has been hacked, the attacker has access to sensitive data or services and can engage in nefarious behaviours such as data tampering, limiting access to desired services, and redirecting transactions. The following is a list of the threat's vulnerability and countermeasures:

  Causes: This danger to SaaS, PaaS, and IaaS is caused by an unsecure and faulty API.
  Countermeasure: Identity and access management prevents account or service hijacking. Introduction to aws security (2021) provides guidelines for identity and access management integration and API integration with any of your own applications or services.

- **Data hunting**: Because data can only be erased from a system if the hardware is destroyed altogether. The lost data might be recovered by an attacker and used for any harmful purpose.

The following are the causes and countermeasures: -

Causes: This danger to SaaS, PaaS, and IaaS is caused by two vulnerabilities.

- Data sharing and coexistence
- Data separation is inefficient or non-existent

   Countermeasure: Both the supplier and the user must have a technique in place to specify the destruction of the SLA. Protection to ensure the confidentiality, integrity, and availability of your systems and data is hallmark and necessary steps mentioned in best practices for designing amazon api gateway private apis and private integration (2021) must be adopted to ensure these features.

- **Data leakage**: An attacker can get access to data while it is being stored, transferred, or processed. The following are the causes and countermeasures: -

Causes: The following are the vulnerabilities that lead to data leaking on SaaS, PaaS, and IaaS platforms:

- Data from many users is grouped together in a single location.
- Separation of stored data is not done properly.
- Data is stored in plain text format.
- IP address visibility for virtual machines.
- Failure to follow required VM migration and roll-back procedures.
- Virtual connections are shared.

Countermeasures: The following are the salient features: -

- **Fragmentation, redundancy and scattering technique**: The goal of this technology is to provide intrusion prevention and hence secure storage. Because little fragments of data have no meaningfull value, this strategy entails breaking down the data into small fragments. The fragmented data is then disseminated over the distributed system in a redundant manner after fragmentation.
- **Digital signatures**: The RSA algorithm (Rivest-Shamir-Adleman) can be used to encrypt data sent over the internet. The RSA algorithm is well-known and commonly utilized in cloud computing.
- **Homomorphic encryption**: It is a type of encryption in which cypher text is used to perform computations without being decoded. Moreover, searches can also be performed while data still being encrypted S. Tahir and M. Rajarajan (2018, pp. 1628–1633). This method protects data not just when it is being stored, but also while it is in transit or being processed.
- **Encryption**: For data security, a strong encryption technology such as AES (Advance Encryption Standard can be utilized.
- **Denial-of-Service (DoS)**: Cloud computing resources may be denied to legitimate users, which might harm SaaS, PaaS, and IaaS customers. The following are the causes and countermeasures:

Causes: The following flaws cause a denial-of-service attack in a cloud environment:
DoS can be caused by inadequate credentials, poor authorizations checks, and insufficient input validation.

Countermeasures: To supply effective and necessary computing resources, cloud providers must enforce regulations. Furthermore, having multiple data centers in different countries with a good load balancing system to distribute traffic between them is a reasonable action to take to prevent DoS attacks. Additionally, network firewalls and more specialized web application firewalls can be used to prevent DoS attacks Tabrizchi and Rafsanjani (2020, pp. 9493–9532).

- **Manipulation of data**: An attacker can employ SQL injection, cross-site scripting, and command injection against a web application to modify data transmitted from the user application to the server application. This threat is directed at SaaS users Krishnaveni, Prabakaran, and Sivamohan (2016). The following are the causes and countermeasures: -

Causes: Default passwords, weak credentials, and inappropriate access controls can all be used by attackers to obtain access to data.

Countermeasures: Because web apps are available to the general public through the internet, they are an easy target. Any flaw in a web application's security will result in data modification or loss. As a result, a web application scanner may be used to discover the security flaw. Furthermore, against possible dangers, a web application firewall is quite effective.

- **VM escape**: It is the use of a hypervisor to gain control of the infrastructure beneath it. This attack might harm IaaS users and providers. The following are the causes and countermeasures: -

Causes: The risk of VM escape is created by complex hypervisor code and flaws.

Countermeasures: The countermeasures are as follows:

- **Hyper safe**: This method ensures the integrity of hypervisor control flow. Memory pages are protected, and control data is converted into pointer indexes, using this approach. Experts carried out four sorts of assaults, including modifying the hypervisor code, executing injection code, modifying the page table, and tampering with the return table, but hyper safe effectively countered all of them.
- **Trusted cloud computing platform (TCCP)**: The two cornerstones of TCCP are the trusted virtual machine monitor and trusted coordinator. This allows the provider to create an environment in which the user may assess whether or not the environment is secure prior to launching the VM.
- **Trusted virtual datacenter**: This solution enforces obligatory access control, hypervisor based isolation, and secured communication routes to achieve workload separation.
- **Making of malicious VM**: A bad user can develop a harmful VM, such as a Trojan horse, and put it in the VM repository. IaaS is a platform that might be harmed by this issue. The following are the causes and countermeasures:

Causes: The vulnerabilities that have become a source of this danger are as follows:

- Placing the virtual machine in the public repository.
- VM images are not patched.

Countermeasures: Access control, image filtering, and repository maintenance services harden the VM and make the attacker's job more difficult.

- **Insecure VM migration**: During a live network migration, the contents of VM files might be exposed. The attacker can use this exposed VM content to get unauthorized access to data, move the VM to an untrusted host, and construct and transfer several VMs, causing disruption or DoS. This threat may be directed towards IaaS.

Causes: A virtual machine may be duplicated, which enables flexibility but also compromises security.
Countermeasures: The preventative measures to avert this hazard are as follows:

- **Protection of VM migration**: One of the approaches for protecting VM during and after migration is the "Protection Aegis for Live Migration of VM (PALM)" framework by authors F. Zhang, Y. Huang, H. Wang, H. Chen, and B. Zang (2008, pp. 9–18).
- **Virtual network services (VNSs)**: It is a framework that lets you set security policies for each virtual machine and provide continuous protection when migrating by authors L. Gupta, T. Salman, R. Das, A. Erbad, R. Jain, and M. Samaka (2019, pp. 141–147).

Further techniques for secure migration of VM can be implemented via Efficient VM migrations using forecasting techniques in cloud computing as by E. Zharikov, S. Telenyk, and P. Bidyuk (2020, pp. 149–168).

- **VM sniffing or spoofing**: The attacker may be able to monitor the network or divert the VM as a result of this. Because VMs are part of IaaS, this vulnerability jeopardizes the security of this domain.

Causes: This vulnerability is exacerbated by the sharing of virtual bridges.
Countermeasures: To counter this threat, virtual network security is the way to go.

Figure 9. Cloud Computing Threat Spectrum

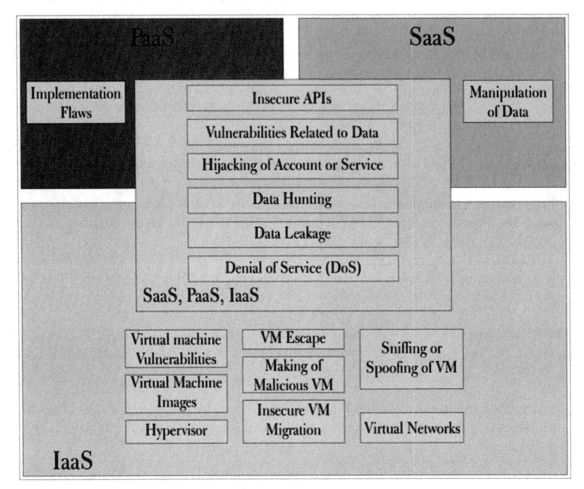

Table 2. Threats and Countermeasures

Threat	Causes	Countermeasure
Hijacking of Account or Service	An insecure and flawed API	Identity and access management
Data Hunting	Co-existence of data Inefficient / weak separation of data.	Specify destruction in SLA
Data Leakage	Various users' data is gathered in one place. There is no proper data separation. Plain text is used to place and store data. IP address visibility for virtual machines Migrating and rolling back virtual machines without following the required protocol. Connections between computers are shared.	Fragmentation, Redundancy and Scattering technique Digital Signatures Homomorphic Encryption Encryption
Hijacking of Account or Service	An insecure and flawed API	Identity and access management
Data Hunting	Co-existence of data Inefficient / weak separation of data.	Specify destruction in SLA
Data Leakage	Various users' data is gathered in one place. There is no proper data separation. Plain text is used to place and store data. IP address visibility for virtual machines Migrating and rolling back virtual machines without following the required protocol. Connections between computers are shared.	Fragmentation, Redundancy and Scattering technique Digital Signatures Homomorphic Encryption Encryption
Denial of Service (DoS)	Weak credentials, insufficient authorization checks, and weak input validation Ineffective allocation of resources	Multiple data centers in different countries with a good load balancing system
Manipulation of Data	Passwords that aren't changed, credentials that aren't strong, and access policies that aren't appropriate	Web application scanner can be employed to identify security vulnerability Hyper Safe
VM Escape	Complex hypervisor code	Trusted cloud computing Platform Trusted Virtual Datacenter
Making of Malicious VM	Placing the VM in public repository Non-patching of VM images.	Access control, image filtering and repository maintenance
Insecure VM Migration	A virtual machine (VM) may be duplicated, which enables flexibility but also compromises security	Protection of VM Migration Virtual Network Services (VNSs)
Sniffing/ Spoofing of VM	Sharing of virtual bridges	Virtual network security

CONCLUSION

Cloud computing is an IT technology that offers various advantages to its customers; nonetheless, it is plagued by security problems, slowing down its adoption. Understanding the types of security issues that exist in cloud computing will aid organizations and users in making the switch to cloud computing. Furthermore, the provisioning of countermeasures against potential threats will aid the user in placing a high level of trust in cloud computing. Many academics, IT specialists, organizations, and cloud providers have put in significant effort to minimize the security threat and related security vulnerabilities. This article presents a comprehensive picture as well as countermeasures to assist developers, users, or enterprises who rely or desire to rely on cloud services. Moreover, using cloud computing appropriately and efficiently in a business can help not only to enhance revenue by allowing fewer staff to work remotely, but also enhance productivity. In a nutshell, cloud computing provides consumers with the services they require to be successful, inventive, and competitive.

REFERENCES

Ahuja, S., Mani, S., & Zambrano, J. (2012). A Survey of the State of Cloud Computing in Healthcare. *Network and Communication Technologies.*, *1*. Advance online publication. doi:10.5539/nct.v1n2p12

Alouffi, Hasnain, Alharbi, Alosaimi, Alyami, & Ayaz. (2021). A systematic literature review on cloud computing security: Threats and mitigation strategies. *IEEE Access, 9*(57), 792–807.

Badger, M. L., Grance, T., Patt-Corner, R., & Voas, J. M. (2012). Cloud computing synopsis and recommendations. National Institute of Standards & Technology.

Best practices for designing amazon api gateway private apis and private integration. (2021). Available: https://docs.aws.amazon.com/whitepapers/latest/best-practices-api-gateway-private-apis-integration/best-practices-api-gateway-private-apis-integration.html

Chou, T.-S. (2013). Security threats on cloud computing vulnerabilities. *Inter-national Journal of Computer Science & Information Technology, 5*(3), 79–88. doi:10.5121/ijcsit.2013.5306

Grobauer, B., Walloschek, T., & Stocker, E. (2010). Understanding cloud computing vulnerabilities. *IEEE Security and Privacy, 9*(2), 50–57. doi:10.1109/MSP.2010.115

Gupta, L., Salman, T., Das, R., Erbad, A., Jain, R., & Samaka, M. (2019). Hyper-vines: A hybrid learning fault and performance issues eradicator for virtual network services over multi-cloud systems. In *2019 International Conference on Computing, Networking and Communications (ICNC)*. IEEE.

Krishnaveni, S., Prabakaran, S., & Sivamohan, S. (2016). Automated vulnera-bility detection and prediction by security testing for cloud saas. *Indian Journal of Science and Technology, 9*(1).

Mahmood, Z. (2013). *Software engineering frameworks for the cloud computing paradigm* (S. Saeed, Ed.). Springer.

Naser, H. (2020). The Impact Of Cloud Computing In Fintech. *VEXXHOST*. https://vexxhost.com/blog/cloud-computing-in-fintech/

Saeed, S. (Ed.). (2013). *Knowledge-based processes in software development*. IGI Global.

Services, A. W. (2021). *Ferpa and student data privacy compliance on aws*. Available: https://d1.awsstatic.com/whitepapers/compliance/AWS-ferpa-whitepaper.pdf

Suryateja, P. S. (2018). Threats and vulnerabilities of cloud computing: A review. *International Journal on Computer Science and Engineering, 6*(3), 297–302.

Tabrizchi, H., & Rafsanjani, M. K. (2020). A survey on security challenges in cloud computing: Issues, threats, and solutions. *The Journal of Supercomputing, 76*(12), 9493–9532.

Tahir, S., & Rajarajan, M. (2018). Privacy-preserving searchable encryption framework for permissioned blockchain networks. In *2018 IEEE International Conference on Internet of Things (iThings) and IEEE Green Computing and Communications (GreenCom) and IEEE Cyber, Physical and Social Computing (CPSCom) and IEEE Smart Data (SmartData).* IEEE.

The impact of cloud computing in fintech. (2021). *TELEHOUSE.* https://www.telehouse.net/blog/the-impact-of-cloud-computing-in-fintech/

Zhang, F., Huang, Y., Wang, H., Chen, H., & Zang, B. (2008). Palm: security preserving vm live migration for systems with vmm-enforced protec-tion. In *2008 Third Asia-Pacific Trusted Infrastructure Technologies Conference.* IEEE.

Zharikov, E., Telenyk, S., & Bidyuk, P. (2020). Adaptive workload forecasting in cloud data centers. *Journal of Grid Computing, 18*(1), 149–168.

Chapter 9
Investigation of Trust Models to Alleviate the Authentication Challenge in FinTech

Naveed Naeem Abbas

National University of Sciences and Technology, Islamabad, Pakistan

Rizwan Ahmad

(iD) https://orcid.org/0000-0002-4758-7895

National University of Sciences and Technology, Islamabad, Pakistan

Shams Qazi

National University of Sciences and Technology, Islamabad, Pakistan

Waqas Ahmed

Pakistan Institute of Engineering and Applied Sciences, Pakistan

ABSTRACT

FinTech applications are increasingly vulnerable to cyber-attacks (identity theft, data breaches, distributed denial of service attacks, phishing attacks, insider threats), which have become a threat to many firms. These threats against FinTech services have the potential to wreak enormous societal, economic, and organizational harm. It is noted that various proposed methods failed to address the fundamental FinTech security issues of scalability, privacy, and trust distribution. Various well-known compliances of all FinTech are being adopted by developed countries to counter these cyber-attacks. Blockchain arouses increasing interest in different economic sectors, with confidentiality, availability, and integrity being fundamental factors. The study shows that the mass adoption of blockchain-based trust models has accelerated in the financial industry with private permissioned blockchain. The primary goal of these trust models is to assure the security, reliability, trustworthiness, and implementation of FinTech compliance.

DOI: 10.4018/978-1-6684-5284-4.ch009

INTRODUCTION

The word FinTech originated from "financial technology" and it was initially used in the early 1990s by Citicorp's chairman John Reed (P. S. Wu, 2017) (Puschmann et al., 2020). It has come to be a common terminology in recent years that refer to novel technologies and encourages the improvement of financial industry structure incorporation of the financial industry, mutual promotion, and interaction (Shin, 2019). Most banks are now adopting FinTech due to personalizing offerings, generating new income streams, improving customer service, and targeting cross-selling (Kumari & Devi, 2022) (Aaron et al., 2017). Now digital banking is moving towards credit brokerage, video consultancy services, and the incorporation of social media. Approximately 75% of customers globally utilize at least one FinTech service, and this number is anticipated to grow as more individuals use mobile banking, contactless payments, online lending, micro-investing, and other FinTech-powered financial activities (Oladapo et al., 2021) (Abdillah, 2020). Companies across the Middle East are moving to digitization fast, putting customers at the forefront of their focus using technologies such as voice, data, and Artificial Intelligence (AI). According to (COMTEX, 2022) prediction, there will be a $306 billion projected value of the global FinTech market by 2023 and Islamic FinTech is projected to grow to $128 billion by 2025. Figure 1 presents the evolution of FinTech from generation 1.0 to 3.5. **FinTech 1.0 (1886 – 1967):** This phase of FinTech evolution includes the growth of infrastructure to enable multinational financial services. In the year 1886 by implementing technologies like Morse code and telegraph, the United States introduced the first electronic financial transfer system to the world (Helleiner, 1998). Today these are simple standards, but it was revolutionary at that time when infrastructure was being expanded to increase the financial transactions and services over greater distances. **FinTech 2.0 (1967 – 2008):** The very first Automated Teller Machine (ATM) was developed by Barclays in 1967 (Bátiz-Lazo, 2009), and it was the opening of this new phase, in which the move from analog to the digitization of funds was performed. In the 1980s, with the advancement of the banking sector due to mainframe computers and the expansion of online banking. The 1990s witnessed the start of digital banking, in this era customers started to manage their money in various ways. **FinTech 3.0 (2008-Current):** Lack of faith in banking sectors create the financial crisis, along with the legislative reforms, exposing the market to new providers. As smartphones become more popular, they will become the primary way for consumers to access the internet and other financial services. Bitcoin was introduced in 2009 followed by other cryptocurrencies based on blockchain technology (Phillip et al., 2018). **FinTech 3.5:** can be considered as the main reason for changes in customers' behavior and the way people more rapidly approach the banking sector in developing countries. In China and India people are the highest Fintech applications users in the world because they did not feel overburdened with banking infrastructure and services like Western countries people feel, and hence have been able to implement innovative solutions more rapidly than their Western counterparts. (Arner et al., 2018) (Sorongan et al., 2021) (Ashta & Biot-Paquerot, 2018).

On the other side, FinTech applications are facing tremendously increased cyber-attacks that have become a challenge for many organizations (Nayak & Singh, 2021). These cyber-attacks against FinTech services might cause significant social, economic, and organizational damage (Berg et al., 2020). In 2021 the average cost of a data breach in the banking sector is $5.72 million (Kost, 2022). FinTech applications are the primary target of many modern cyber-attacks. Besides the attacks, FinTech applications have made waves and disrupted the finance industry. They come with lots of challenges but the biggest issue is authentication. Gaining customer trust and loyalty takes a lot of hard work especially when money is involved. It has been seen that most people lack trust and are skeptical while switching to something new such as FinTech, to make their financial operations simpler. It can be observed that most of the attacks get successful after compromising the authentication and other verification methods of FinTech applications. To combat these threats and protect users' information, there is a need to implement strong authorization and authentication mechanisms as part of the FinTech application security policy (Gocer & Bahtiyar, 2019) (Stoica & Sitea, 2021).

In the prior studies, different ways have been introduced to prevent authentication and authorization attacks in FinTech applications. **1) Multi-factor authentication (MFA):** It is a process where online users make two or more claims to prove their identity. Using such an authentication process in the FinTech application verifies all these claims, and only then does it let the users utilize a given service. An MFA system can use a combination of passwords, the specific identifier of a device, fingerprint, etc. (Ometov et al., 2018) (Bhargav-Spantzel et al., 2007). **2) Data Encryption:** Encryption in FinTech applications to protect sensitive data at rest or in transition must be a high-priority consideration for the organization. Many legacy technology solutions did not include data encryption; therefore, it is not possible to match up with modern security standards (Das, 2019) (Meng et al., 2021). **3) Firewall and Antivirus solutions:** A combination of robust firewalls and antivirus solutions is being used as a key building block toward securing FinTech applications. **4) Regulatory Compliance:** FinTech applications need to comply with different regulations Payment Card Industry/Data Security Standard (PCI/DSS), General Data Protection Regulation (GDPR), etc. Complying with these can be challenging since organizations have silos between their information security, development, and operations teams. Most organizations are integrating compliance and auditing directly into their DevOps processes to maintain the security of the application (Treleaven, 2015) (Bu et al., 2021).

MAJOR FINTECH REGULATIONS AND POLICIES

The presence of rules and laws for the establishment and operation of financial systems is obvious. The advancement of technology in hardware/software platforms has a significant influence on the stability, correct performance, efficiency, and energy consumption of blockchain systems (Branch, 2022). The most well-known compliance of all FinTech rules is, apparently, PCI DSS (Working & Series, 2019). The Gramm-Leach-Bliley Act (GLBA) of the United States mandates financial firms to protect sensitive client data (Ryle et al., 2022). To be GLBA-compliant, FinTech must notify customers about how they will use their sensitive data. The EU applies the Revised Directive on Payment Services across the Atlantic (PSD2). In addition to measures like its US equivalent, it requires FinTech businesses to identify security-related Key Performance Indicators (KPIs), reviews risks regularly, and create new safety safeguards, with a specific focus on mobile apps. Additionally, it is also compulsory for any FinTech company that uses data on EU people must comply with the General Data Protection Regulation (GDPR), even if they are not headquartered in the EU (Hoofnagle et al., 2019). FinTech companies that provide financial services in Australia must have an Australian financial services license or obtain a direct exemption from having one. The Corporation Act of Australia is the enabling legislation. The Australian Transactions Reports and Analysis Center (AUSTRAC): rules governing FinTech in general and online transactions. Second, the Australian Prudential Regulation Authority governs FinTech activity in banking and insurance.

Figure 1. Evolution of FinTech

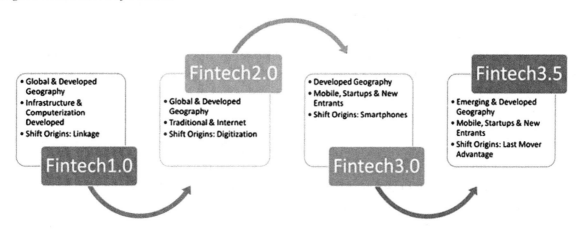

The following threats are related to FinTech applications security:

1. Identity Theft: Most hacks into FinTech applications try to steal sensitive personal data and money by using stolen usernames and passwords to impersonate users and access accounts. According to a 2021 global study of financial institutions, account hacking attempts increased by 282% between 2019 and 2020 (Najaf et al., 2021) (Hammood et al., 2020).

2. Data Breaches: All the amount of personal and financial data exists in FinTech applications. Cybercriminals are more interested in sensitive data because they can commit financial fraud and make money by selling it to others. This happens by exposing API endpoints without proper access controls, launching various phishing attacks, and sneaking in malware (Suseendran et al., 2020) (Morufu Olalere1, Juliana Ndunagu2, Shafi'i M. Abdulhamid3, 2019).

3. DDoS Attacks: Distributed Denial of Service (DDoS) attacks are a major security risk to FinTech applications (Kaur et al., 2021b). In DDOS attacks, hackers flood an application with traffic to break down applications' security in the process. Unfortunately, most FinTech applications do not have the resource restrictions or rate limitations to counter these types of targeted attacks (Y. Lu, 2018) (Saad et al., 2020).

4. Phishing Attacks: According to (Kerner, 2022), 36% of data breaches happen through a phishing attack. Recently, in many phishing attacks, cybercriminals masquerade as government sector, company CEO, banks, and other legitimate bodies to trap customers to reset their passwords or share sensitive financial information over the phone (Nikkel, 2020). The effects of phishing attacks are high; once cybercriminals have access, they can use ransomware or other malware and cause a data breach and identity theft. It is difficult to distinguish Phishing emails from legitimate emails, which can create a major security risk to FinTech apps and users (Kaur et al., 2021c) (Mehrban et al., 2020).

5. Insider Threats: Sometimes, an employee falls for a phishing trick and accidentally provides access to your system to cybercriminals. Reports (Https://www.idwatchdog.com, 2022) indicate that 60% of security breaches are created by insider threats from employees within the company.

Recently, some researchers suggested implementing of Blockchain based trust model as a solution to mitigate cyber-attack threats in FinTech applications. Blockchain is a technology that makes it almost hard to change or break into a system by allowing the recording of information in a very secure manner. Transactions between two persons or the tracking of the custody of couriers may be carried out using blockchain. The platforms, which were built to provide "accurate reporting, monitoring, and analysis of all forms of digital financial transactions", are an intriguing use of blockchain technology. There are several key areas where companies can use the Blockchain-based trust model in financial software and systems e.g., payments, remittances, trade finance, and improving record keeping (Lukonga, 2018). Finally, banks can overcome the problem of verifying their customers' identities through a Blockchain-based trust model. It has been noticed in literature that very few trust models have been proposed for authentication mechanisms in FinTech applications. The main objective of our study is to comprehensively examine the different trust models that help to alleviate the authentication challenge in FinTech.

The chapter is planned as follows. A literature review is discussed in Section 2. After that, Section 3, and Section 4 present the security challenges and prevention techniques of FinTech applications. Section 5 contains the major FinTech regulations and policies. In the end, Section 6 concludes.

LITERATURE REVIEW

The creation of the ATM was the biggest financial industry breakthrough (Al-Ashban & Burney, 2001). Since 1838, Financial transactions have been conducted over telegraphs. After the banking sector has moved towards the IT industry to improve its procedures (Wilson, 2017) (Rauniyar et al., 2021). For the financial services business, analog technology was turned into digital technology in the early 1990s (Gomber et al., 2018a) (Pisano, 2006). In the systematic literature review, (Xavier, 2017) asserted that FinTech is more than just the use of IT technology in the financial sector. FinTech companies have made significant advances in a variety of areas, for example, mobile networking, big data, cloud computing, trust management, and mobile embedded systems, (Omarini, 2018) (Gomber et al., 2018b). In the last few years, it has been observed that traditional financial institutions and FinTech firms have enhanced their collaboration in many areas (Suprun et al., 2020) (Navaretti et al., 2018) (Hornuf et al., 2021). The cyber-breach of FinTech businesses enhances traditional banks' susceptibility and fraud risk. (Lewis & Baker, 2013) imply that the amount of cybercrimes has increased since the financial inclusion of FinTech businesses. (Emanuel Kopp, Lincoln Kaffenberger, 2017) mentioned that data breaches cause damage to an organization's reputation, revenue, customers, brand, and huge operational costs for FinTech firms. According to the research, cybercrime may have a detrimental impact on the financial performance of FinTech businesses as well as partner firms (Kovalchuk et al., 2021) (Najaf et al., 2020). A wide range of different products and services have been introduced recently, like smartphones, various mobile banking services, Internet of Things (IoT) devices, and intelligent vehicles have been introduced as a result of the rapid development of new technologies. As a result, improved security mechanisms, computation modes, and trust evaluation mechanisms are rapidly required to increase the reliability and security of FinTech terminal equipment (Zhang & Zhou, 2020) (Bellini et al., 2020). Blockchain-based trust model already has been introduced by researchers for security purposes in different applications. (Al-Rakhami & Al-Mashari, 2021) suggested a simplified trust architecture for IoT-based supply chain management that streamlines data exchange and decreases computational, storage, and latency needs while boosting security. (Bendiab et al., 2018). introduced a novel trust and identity management model to overcome the poor trust management in the field of federated identity management system, which consists of many security-related issues, like force organizations to move their sensitive identity data to the cloud. Novel model is based on Blockchain with improved security measures. (Moinet et al., 2017) worked on a model based on Blockchain data structure to store decentralized authentication and node trust information. For data security transmission in air traffic management networks, (Y. Wu et al., 2021) present a novel model BlockTrust, that is based on Blockchain trust model which consists of cryptographic algorithms to form a trust chain in the airspace ground integrated network. (Urien, 2021) introduced a new IoT Trust Model that is based on two secure elements TLS-IM, which is used on the client side, and TLS-SE is used on the server side to enforce Pre-Shared Key (PSK) security against eavesdroppers to avoid device cloning or illegitimate use. (Rahmani et al., 2022) worked on cloud-based environment and try find out possible use cases based on Blockchain to mitigate different challenges of trust issues.

According to (Rasheed et al., 2022) Blockchain's feature, traceability based on a decentralized network achieves security and privacy services by utilizing the hashes of a previous transaction attached with the time stamp and making it public for rejection of any adversary attack. Conventional security algorithms for IoT rely on trustworthy third parties, therefore (S. B. Goyal (City University, Malaysia), Pradeep Bedi (Galgotias University, India), Anand Singh Rajawat (Shri Vaishnav Vidyapeeth Vishwavidyalaya, India), and Divya Prakash Shrivastava (Higher Colleges of Technology, Dubai, 2022) used Blockchain technology for secure authentication in various wireless sensor networks (WSNs). (Z. Lu et al., 2018) proposed a Blockchain-based Anonymous Reputation System (BARS) to determine a privacy-preserving trust model for vehicular ad hoc networks (VANETs) to counter the tracking attacks against the privacy of VANETs. (Li et al., 2022) developed a trust management algorithm capable of detecting harmful activities while creating anonymous zones and removing dangerous users from the system. It has been discovered that the requirement for information exchange among vehicles network introduced vulnerabilities and threats that cybercriminals might exploit. To overcome the vulnerabilities, (Singh et al., 2022) worked on a trust-driven privacy approach for the Internet of Vehicles (IoV) that employs both encryption and steganography. It is based on an Efficient Algorithm for Secure Transmission (EAST) that integrates steganography and encryption algorithms. Recently, The Wireless Sensor Internet of Things (WSIoTs) had several issues, like fewer security risks, cost efficiency, unreliable data communication, and high energy consumption. To overcome these issues, a novel trust model based on Blockchain for WSIoTs is suggested by (Javaid, 2022). (Keshavarz et al., 2020) worked on a UASTrustChain, which is a Blockchain-based trust management framework. The framework's major goal is to differentiate unusual behaviors generated by real attacks from those induced by severe environmental circumstances. To achieve security and trust in the financial sector, (Song et al., 2022) worked on the multidimensional trust evaluation mechanism of FinTech. (Yuen, 2020) presents novel work based on authenticated, private auditable consortium blockchain and its implementation. This prohibits a malicious user from misusing the privacy attribute, only authorized parties may be involved in the transaction, and auditors or law enforcement authorities can expose the entire transaction data (Kabra et al., 2020) demonstrate a Blockchain-based architecture for automated check clearing in financial organizations to overcome the cheque truncation system limitation like illegal duplication of cheque images, invisible ink usage, visibility issues in beneficiary name, and amount on the cheque. It has been concluded from literature, that blockchain has emerged as a new technology that presents distributed immutable ledger with time stamps. Being immutable, forgeries are not possible in records, and this provides trust and consensus among all participating entities in the network. Moreover, it is also noticed that blockchain-based trust model is being used in many real-world applications (IoT, IoV, WSNs, cloud computing) for security purposes, but there are very few researchers that have proposed trust model for FinTech applications security. Our aim in conducting this study is to investigate an efficient and effective trust model for FinTech applications.

SECURITY CHALLENGES OF FINTECH APPLICATIONS

According to (Sokolov, 2020), 97% of FinTech application analysis outcomes show that lacked sufficient security, and when decompiled or reverse-engineered various vulnerabilities have been discovered. Cyberattacks cost the banking industry an average of $18.3 million per organization each year. Security challenges of FinTech applications are the following:

1. Cloud Computing Security Issues

Now a day financial services e.g., digital wallets, payment gateways, banking services, and others rely on cloud-based platforms. The advantages of cloud computing are scalability, accessibility, speed, and many more (Verma & Adhikari, 2020).

2. Malware Attacks

Newer FinTech is moving away from Society for Worldwide Interbank Financial Telecommunication (SWIFT) and into blockchain-based payment protocols, but the malware attacks are still having their impact (Dias & Vieira, 2022). Malware has unique features to use multiple entry points from various sources: malicious websites, emails, third-party software, pop-ups, and so on. FinTech applications can be protected from malware threats using solutions such as automatic real-time malware detection and periodical VAPT (Kaur et al., 2021a).

3. Application Breaches

FinTech firms rely significantly on applications that allow end customers to enter sensitive information and transfer money with a few clicks. Applications can be one of the main attack vectors. Unfortunately, once cybercriminals have access to your application, they can easily obtain access to the rest of your network. Therefore, it is compulsory to scan vulnerabilities on daily basis for any mobile or web application to avoid any type of cyber-attack (Universities, 2021).

4. Money Laundering and Cryptocurrency-Related Risks

In previous years cryptocurrencies have grown in popularity, but they have also established themselves as a key security concern for FinTech (Basir et al., 2020). The anonymity feature of cryptocurrency is also being used for money laundering (Faccia et al., 2020). For this purpose, FinTech companies that deal with cryptocurrencies should only use secure trading platforms.

5. Digital Identity

One major FinTech security challenge is protecting users from digital identity theft (Jibril et al., 2020). Mobile applications allow FinTech companies to offer a seamless experience of multiple financial operations such as wealth management, online payments, etc. in one place. Advanced digital identification methods such as biometrics sensors, One-Time Password (OTP) generation, and code-generating applications have improved FinTech security to a great extent as compared to the traditional methods of passwords and Personal identification numbers (PINs). However, given the advancements in software technology, these security techniques are not considered much safer now. To avoid the risk of identity theft and replication, FinTech companies need to invest in measures like adaptive authentication, also called risk-based authentication. These security techniques analyze user behavior before granting access.

6. Meeting Compliance Requirements

A financial institution such as an electronic money Institution, payment institution, or specialized bank, must comply with different standards related to data privacy, security, and failure to satisfy compliance rules can result in significant penalties as well as severe security problems (Acar & Çitak, 2019).

7. Financial Challenges

Another challenge will be securing FinTech infrastructure, which may quickly become prohibitively expensive. Regardless of the matter how scalable the application design is, there is a need to alter or upgrade the infrastructure regularly (Ignatyuk et al., 2020) (Bernards, 2019).

8. Mobile Platforms and IoT Devices

Today FinTech applications have made it easier to access sensitive financial information anytime, from anywhere through mobile devices. However, the more devices that are used to access a certain account, the more likely it is that the account will be compromised. While speed is essential in FinTech in today's world, it is also prudent to introduce new supported platforms only after extensive security testing (Dapp, 2015) (Hwang et al., 2021).

EFFICIENT AND EFFECTIVE TRUST MODEL AND PREVENTIONS TECHNIQUES FOR FINTECH APPLICATIONS

1. **Artificial Intelligence (AI):** In terms of automated fraud detection, AI has come a long way. Machine learning algorithms can learn how to forecast user behavior and detect anything deemed strange by a thorough analysis of the huge amount of big data generated by FinTech businesses (Giudici, 2018) (Ashta & Herrmann, 2021).
2. **Multi-cloud storage -** Cloud-based services are regarded as secure. Businesses are establishing a private cloud as a backup plan, which is a legitimate strategy for protecting your organization from security breaches and data loss.

3.   **Blockchain -** Most of the system breaches are almost impossible to penetrate due to the decentralized structure of Blockchain. Between hybrid, private, and public, depending on the needs of FinTech, blockchain networks might make trade-offs between privacy, trustworthiness, and speed (Fosso Wamba et al., 2020). Table 1 presents various Blockchain-based trust models that have been proposed for the prevention of cyber-attacks in FinTech applications.

The rate of cybercrime has risen steadily with each passing year (OGBENIKA et al., 2000). Because traditional banks that use FinTech businesses are more exposed to cyber-attacks, cyber security is becoming the key worry for FinTech firms (Tang, 2021). Secure and reliable management of FinTech applications has become one of the major challenges faced by industries and banking sectors. The main reason is due to the huge number of customers/ users, which means more user accounts, their passwords, and sensitive information to provision monitor and secure. Therefore, FinTech applications security must ensure the entire requirement including Privacy, Compliance, Encryption, and Anonymity for the protection of customer's sensitive information. Collaboration with FinTech businesses provides several benefits, including lower client costs, lower operational costs, and rapid service (Tapanainen, 2020).

Table 1. Comparison of Blockchain-based Trust Model

Paper	Type	Consensus	(Self-Sovereign Identities) SSI	Privacy	Compliance	Encryption	Anonymity
(Yuen, 2020)	Consortium	PBFT	No	Yes	No	Yes	Yes
(Kabra et al., 2020)	Consortium	PoA	No	Yes	No	Multiple	Yes
(Liu et al., 2021)	Public	DPoS	Yes	Yes	No	Yes	No
(Song et al., 2022)	Private	PoS	No	Yes	No	Yes	No
(Liao et al., 2022)	Consortium	PoA	Yes	Yes	GDPR	No	Yes

Distributed Ledger Technology is altering the FinTech and forcing the current banking system forward (Du et al., 2019) (Ullah et al., 2022). Different Blockchain-based trust model has been compared in Table 1 to identify the better trust model framework for FinTech applications. In 2020 (Yuen, 2020) worked to trace the malicious user in the system who can perform malicious activities. The main purpose of the framework is to verify all the transactions without disclosing any sensitive detail details about users, like their identity, the amount being transferred, etc. It has two drawbacks as compared to another trust model it does not meet any compliance requirements of FinTech and SSI is not supported in this model. After that (Kabra et al., 2020) introduced a framework named MudraChain for automated cheque clearance, where clearance operations are handled by the blockchain network. This framework is based on consortium Blockchain that used PoA consensus and implements the encryption multiple times for more security. As a drawback, it does not support any FinTech-related compliance. (Song et al., 2022) proposed a private Blockchain based framework that is built on a multi-dimensional trust index system and evaluation mechanism (MDTEM). The main purpose of this framework is to ensure the trustworthiness of financial services, security and reliability of sensitive information. But the drawback of this framework seems to be it does not meet any FinTech compliance and SSI. Recently, identity management and access control framework built on blockchain for the open banking ecosystem is introduced by (Liao et al., 2022). This framework applies a stateless authentication mechanism and smart contracts that offers such functionalities as decentralized third-party login (TPL), like the ability to data authorization, open bank accounts online, integrated payouts, and TSP access monitoring. As compared to other trust model it has GDPR compliance for FinTech applications, but it does support encryption mechanism (Ferrari, 2022).

According to the research on the security of FinTech applications (Matsuura, 2019) (Mosteanu & Faccia, 2021), the most appropriate Blockchain for security purposes is Consortium, and Proof of Authority (PoA) consensus may be suggested for better implementation of various trust models for FinTech (Eyal, 2017) (Pompella & Costantino, 2021).

CONCLUSION

It is concluded that Blockchain can improve the implementation of FinTech in a secure and verifiable decentralized manner. The creation of various trust models for FinTech applications has significantly aided in the incorporation of Blockchain with FinTech. In this chapter, the FinTech evolution phase and trust models related to FinTech application security have been discussed. These trust models help to counter the tremendously increased cyber-attacks on FinTech applications and assure the security, reliability, and trustworthiness of the sensitive customer's data. It is also noted that the advancement of regulatory methods in the field of FinTech can help to minimize challenges such as tax collection, money laundering, trade monitoring, and terrorist financing activities and will have a significant impact on future development.

REFERENCES

Aaron, M., Rivadeneyra, F., & Samantha, F. (2017). *Fintech: Is this time different? A framework for assessing risks and opportunities for central banks. Bank of Canada Staff Discussion Paper, No. 2017-1.* Bank of Canada. https://www.banqueducanada.ca/wp-content/uploads/2017/07/sdp2017-10.pdf

Abdillah, L. A. (2020). *FinTech E-Commerce Payment Application User Experience Analysis during COVID-19 Pandemic.* doi:10.15294/sji.v7i2.26056

Acar, O., & Çitak, Y. E. (2019). Fintech Integration Process Suggestion for Banks. *Procedia Computer Science, 158*, 971–978. doi:10.1016/j.procs.2019.09.138

Al-Ashban, A. A., & Burney, M. A. (2001). Customer adoption of tele-banking technology: The case of Saudi Arabia. *International Journal of Bank Marketing, 19*(5), 191–201. doi:10.1108/02652320110399683

Al-Rakhami, M. S., & Al-Mashari, M. (2021). A blockchain-based trust model for the internet of things supply chain management. *Sensors (Basel), 21*(5), 1–15. doi:10.339021051759 PMID:33806319

Arner, D. W., Barberis, J. N., & Buckley, R. P. (2018). FinTech and RegTech in a Nutshell, and the Future in a Sandbox. SSRN *Electronic Journal*. doi:10.2139/ssrn.3088303

Ashta, A., & Biot-Paquerot, G. (2018). FinTech evolution: Strategic value management issues in a fast changing industry. *Strategic Change*, *27*(4), 301–311. doi:10.1002/jsc.2203

Ashta, A., & Herrmann, H. (2021). Artificial intelligence and fintech: An overview of opportunities and risks for banking, investments, and microfinance. *Strategic Change*, *30*(3), 211–222. doi:10.1002/jsc.2404

Basir, I. N., Alwi, S., Salleh, M. N. M., Aslam, S. N. A. M., & Abdullah, S. M. M. (2020). The occurrence of FinTech: The insight into the world of cryptocurrency from a Chinese investment perspective. *Test Engineering and Management, 83*(1089), 1089–1100. https://www.scopus.com/inward/record.uri?eid=2-s2.0-85082778628&partnerID=40&md5=b540e68af95d809171b94bd1e79a53d5

Bátiz-Lazo, B. (2009). Emergence and evolution of ATM networks in the UK, 1967-2000. *Business History*, *51*(1), 1–27. doi:10.1080/00076790802602164

Bellini, E., Iraqi, Y., & Damiani, E. (2020). Blockchain-Based Distributed Trust and Reputation Management Systems: A Survey. *IEEE Access: Practical Innovations, Open Solutions*, 8, 21127–21151. doi:10.1109/ACCESS.2020.2969820

Bendiab, K., Kolokotronis, N., Shiaeles, S., & Boucherkha, S. (2018). WiP: A novel blockchain-based trust model for cloud identity management. *Proceedings - IEEE 16th International Conference on Dependable, Autonomic and Secure Computing, IEEE 16th International Conference on Pervasive Intelligence and Computing, IEEE 4th International Conference on Big Data Intelligence and Computing and IEEE 3, 2018*, 716–723. 10.1109/DASC/PiCom/DataCom/CyberSciTec.2018.00126

Berg, G., Guadamillas, M., Natarajan, H., & Sarkar, A. (2020). Fintech in Europe and Central Asia. *Fintech in Europe and Central Asia*, *4*. Advance online publication. doi:10.1596/33591

Bernards, N. (2019). The poverty of fintech? Psychometrics, credit infrastructures, and the limits of financialization. *Review of International Political Economy*, *26*(5), 815–838. doi:10.1080/09692290.2019.1597753

Bhargav-Spantzel, A., Squicciarini, A. C., Modi, S., Young, M., Bertino, E., & Elliott, S. J. (2007). Privacy preserving multi-factor authentication with biometrics. *Journal of Computer Security*, *15*(5), 529–560. doi:10.3233/JCS-2007-15503

Branch, T. (2022). International Journal of Research in Industrial Engineering Paper Type : Original Article Identifying key indicators for developing the use of blockchain technology in financial systems 1 | Introduction 2 | Literature review. *International Journal of Research in Industrial Engineering*, *x*(x).

Bu, Y., Li, H., & Wu, X. (2021). Effective regulations of FinTech innovations: The case of China. *Economics of Innovation and New Technology*. Advance online publication. doi:10.1080/10438599.2020.1868069

COMTEX, A. N. (2022). *Global Fintech Market 2022 Industry Overview, New Market Opportunities and Statistics Research Report 2030*. Author.

Dapp, T. (2015). Fintech reloaded – Traditional banks as digital ecosystems With proven walled garden strategies into the future. *Deutsche Bank Research Management*, 1–27.

Das, S. R. (2019). The future of fintech. *Financial Management, 48*(4), 981–1007. doi:10.1111/fima.12297

Dias, M. D. O., & Vieira, P. (2022). Are the Russian Banks Threatened with Removal from SWIFT? A Multiple Case Study on Interbank Financial Messaging Systems. *International Journal of Scientific Research and Management, 10*(March), 3137–3144. Advance online publication. doi:10.18535/ijsrm/v10i3.em1

Du, W., Pan, S. L., Leidner, D. E., & Ying, W. (2019). Affordances, experimentation and actualization of FinTech: A blockchain implementation study. *The Journal of Strategic Information Systems, 28*(1), 50–65. doi:10.1016/j.jsis.2018.10.002

Eyal, I. (2017). Blockchain Technology: Transforming Libertarian Cryptocurrency Dreams to Finance and Banking Realities. *Computer, 50*(9), 38–49. doi:10.1109/MC.2017.3571042

Faccia, A., Narcisa, P., Moşteanu, R., Mintoff, T. D., Pio, L., Cavaliere, L., Foggia, U., Caggese, V. R., Fg, F., & Mataruna-dos-santos, L. J. (2020). Electronic Money Laundering, The Dark Side of Fintech. An Overview of the Most Recent Cases. *ICIME 2020: Proceedings of the 2020 12th International Conference on Information Management and Engineering*, 29–34. 10.1145/3430279.3430284

Ferrari, M. V. (2022). The platformisation of digital payments: The fabrication of consumer interest in the EU FinTech agenda. *Computer Law & Security Review, 45*, 105687. doi:10.1016/j.clsr.2022.105687

Fosso Wamba, S., Kala Kamdjoug, J. R., Epie Bawack, R., & Keogh, J. G. (2020). Bitcoin, Blockchain and Fintech: A systematic review and case studies in the supply chain. *Production Planning and Control, 31*(2–3), 115–142. doi:10.1080/09537287.2019.1631460

Giudici, P. (2018). Fintech Risk Management: A Research Challenge for Artificial Intelligence in Finance. *Frontiers in Artificial Intelligence, 1*(November), 1–6. doi:10.3389/frai.2018.00001 PMID:33733089

Gocer, B. D., & Bahtiyar, S. (2019). An Authorization Framework with OAuth for FinTech Servers. *UBMK 2019 - Proceedings, 4th International Conference on Computer Science and Engineering*, 536–541. 10.1109/UBMK.2019.8907182

Gomber, P., Kauffman, R. J., Parker, C., & Weber, B. W. (2018a). On the Fintech Revolution: Interpreting the Forces of Innovation, Disruption, and Transformation in Financial Services. *Journal of Management Information Systems, 35*(1), 220–265. doi:10.1080/07421222.2018.1440766

Gomber, P., Kauffman, R. J., Parker, C., & Weber, B. W. (2018b). On the Fintech Revolution: Interpreting the Forces of Innovation, Disruption, and Transformation in Financial Services. *Journal of Management Information Systems, 35*(1), 220–265. doi:10.1080/07421222.2018.1440766

Goyal, Bedi, Rajawat, & Shrivastava. (2022). Secure Authentication in Wireless Sensor Networks Using Blockchain Technology. In AI-Enabled Agile Internet of Things for Sustainable FinTech Ecosystems (p. 13). IGI Global. doi:10.4018/978-1-6684-4176-3.ch005

Hammood, W. A., Abdullah, R., Hammood, O. A., Mohamad Asmara, S., Al-Sharafi, M. A., & Muttaleb Hasan, A. (2020). A Review of User Authentication Model for Online Banking System based on Mobile IMEI Number. *IOP Conference Series. Materials Science and Engineering*, *769*(1), 012061. Advance online publication. doi:10.1088/1757-899X/769/1/012061

Helleiner, E. (1998). Electronic money: A challenge to the sovereign state? *Journal of International Affairs*, *51*(2), 387–409.

Hoofnagle, C. J., Van Der Sloot, B., Borgesius, F. Z., Jay, C., Van Der Sloot, B., & Zuiderveen, F. (2019). The European Union general data protection regulation : what it is and what it means The European Union general data protection regulation : what it is and what it means *. *Information & Communications Technology Law*, *28*(1), 65–98. doi:10.1080/13600834.2019.1573501

Hornuf, L., Klus, M. F., & Lohwasser, T. S. (2021). *How do banks interact with fintech startups?* Academic Press.

Https://www.idwatchdog.com. (2022). *Insider Threats Are Becoming More Frequent and More Costly: What Businesses Need to Know Now*. https://www.idwatchdog.com/insider-threats-and-data-breaches/

Hwang, Y., Park, S., & Shin, N. (2021). Sustainable development of a mobile payment security environment using fintech solutions. *Sustainability (Switzerland)*, *13*(15), 1–15. doi:10.3390u13158375

Ignatyuk, A., Liubkina, O., Murovana, T., & Magomedova, A. (2020). FinTech as an innovation challenge: From big data to sustainable development. *E3S Web of Conferences, 166*. doi:10.1051/e3s-conf/202016613027

Javaid, N. (2022). A Secure and Efficient Trust Model for Wireless Sensor IoTs Using Blockchain. *IEEE Access: Practical Innovations, Open Solutions*, *10*, 4568–4579. doi:10.1109/ACCESS.2022.3140401

Jibril, A. B., Kwarteng, M. A., Botchway, R. K., Bode, J., & Chovancova, M. (2020). The impact of online identity theft on customers' willingness to engage in e-banking transaction in Ghana: A technology threat avoidance theory. *Cogent Business and Management*, *7*(1), 1832825. Advance online publication. doi:10.1080/23311975.2020.1832825

Kabra, N., Bhattacharya, P., Tanwar, S., & Tyagi, S. (2020). MudraChain: Blockchain-based framework for automated cheque clearance in financial institutions. *Future Generation Computer Systems*, *102*, 574–587. doi:10.1016/j.future.2019.08.035

Kaur, G., Habibi Lashkari, Z., & Habibi Lashkari, A. (2021a). Cybersecurity Risk in FinTech BT - Understanding Cybersecurity Management in FinTech: Challenges, Strategies, and Trends. In G. Kaur, Z. Habibi Lashkari, & A. Habibi Lashkari (Eds.), *Understanding Cybersecurity Management in FinTech* (pp. 103–122). Springer International Publishing. doi:10.1007/978-3-030-79915-1_6

Kaur, G., Habibi Lashkari, Z., & Habibi Lashkari, A. (2021b). Cybersecurity Threats in FinTech BT - Understanding Cybersecurity Management in FinTech: Challenges, Strategies, and Trends (G. Kaur, Z. Habibi Lashkari, & A. Habibi Lashkari, Eds.). Springer International Publishing. doi:10.1007/978-3-030-79915-1_4

Kaur, G., Habibi Lashkari, Z., & Habibi Lashkari, A. (2021c). Cybersecurity Vulnerabilities in FinTech BT - Understanding Cybersecurity Management in FinTech: Challenges, Strategies, and Trends (G. Kaur, Z. Habibi Lashkari, & A. Habibi Lashkari, Eds.). Springer International Publishing. doi:10.1007/978-3-030-79915-1_5

Kerner, S. M. (2022). *34 Cybersecurity Statistics to Lose Sleep Over in 2022*. https://www.techtarget.com/whatis/34-Cybersecurity-Statistics-to-Lose-Sleep-Over-in-2020

Keshavarz, M., Gharib, M., Afghah, F., & Ashdown, J. D. (2020). UASTrustChain: A Decentralized Blockchain- Based Trust Monitoring Framework for Autonomous Unmanned Aerial Systems. *IEEE Access: Practical Innovations, Open Solutions*, 8, 226074–226088. doi:10.1109/ACCESS.2020.3044844

Kopp & Kaffenberger. (2017). Cyber Risks, Market Failures and Finanical Stability. *International Monetary Fund, 2017*(185), 36.

Kovalchuk, O., Shynkaryk, M., & Masonkova, M. (2021). Econometric Models for Estimating the Financial Effect of Cybercrimes. *2021 11th International Conference on Advanced Computer Information Technologies, ACIT 2021 - Proceedings*, 381–384. 10.1109/ACIT52158.2021.9548490

Kumari, A., & Devi, N. C. (2022). The Impact of FinTech and Blockchain Technologies on Banking and Financial Services. *Technology Innovation Management Review*, *12*(1/2). Advance online publication. doi:10.22215/timreview/1481

Lewis, J., & Baker, S. (2013). The Economic Impact of Cybercrime and Cyber Espionage Report Center for Strategic and International Studies. *McAfee*, 1–20.

Li, B., Liang, R., Zhou, W., Yin, H., Gao, H., & Cai, K. (2022). LBS Meets Blockchain: An Efficient Method with Security Preserving Trust in SAGIN. *IEEE Internet of Things Journal*, *9*(8), 5932–5942. doi:10.1109/JIOT.2021.3064357

Liao, C. H., Guan, X. Q., Cheng, J. H., & Yuan, S. M. (2022). Blockchain-based identity management and access control framework for open banking ecosystem. *Future Generation Computer Systems*, *135*, 450–466. doi:10.1016/j.future.2022.05.015

Liu, J., Yan, L., & Wang, D. (2021). A Hybrid Blockchain Model for Trusted Data of Supply Chain Finance. *Wireless Personal Communications*. Advance online publication. doi:10.100711277-021-08451-x PMID:33850344

Lu, Y. (2018). Blockchain and the related issues: A review of current research topics. *Journal of Management Analytics*, *5*(4), 231–255. doi:10.1080/23270012.2018.1516523

Lu, Z., Liu, W., Wang, Q., Qu, G., & Liu, Z. (2018). A privacy-preserving trust model based on blockchain for VANETs. *IEEE Access: Practical Innovations, Open Solutions*, 6, 45655–45664. doi:10.1109/ACCESS.2018.2864189

Lukonga, I. (2018). Fintech, Inclusive Growth and Cyber Risks: Focus on the MENAP and CCA Regions. *IMF Working Papers, 18*(201), 1. doi:10.5089/9781484374900.001

Matsuura, K. (2019). Token model and interpretation function for blockchain-based Fintech applications. *IEICE Transactions on Fundamentals of Electronics, Communications and Computer Science*, *1*(1), 3–10. doi:10.1587/transfun.E102.A.3

Mehrban, S., Khan, M. A., Nadeem, M. W., Hussain, M., Ahmed, M. M., Hakeem, O., Saqib, S., Kiah, M. L. M., Abbas, F., & Hassan, M. (2020). Towards secure FinTech: A survey, taxonomy, and open research challenges. *IEEE Access: Practical Innovations, Open Solutions*, *8*, 23391–23406. doi:10.1109/ACCESS.2020.2970430

Meng, S., He, X., & Tian, X. (2021). Research on Fintech development issues based on embedded cloud computing and big data analysis. *Microprocessors and Microsystems*, *83*(January), 103977. doi:10.1016/j.micpro.2021.103977

Moinet, A., Darties, B., & Baril, J.-L. (2017). *Blockchain based trust & authentication for decentralized sensor networks*. 1–6. https://arxiv.org/abs/1706.01730

Mosteanu, N. R., & Faccia, A. (2021). Fintech frontiers in quantum computing, fractals, and blockchain distributed ledger: Paradigm shifts and open innovation. *Journal of Open Innovation*, *7*(1), 1–19. doi:10.3390/joitmc7010019

Najaf, K., Mostafiz, M. I., & Najaf, R. (2021). Fintech firms and banks sustainability: Why cybersecurity risk matters? *International Journal of Financial Engineering*, *08*(02), 2150019. doi:10.1142/S2424786321500195

Najaf, K., Schinckus, C., Mostafiz, M. I., & Najaf, R. (2020). Conceptualising cybersecurity risk of fintech firms and banks sustainability. *International Conference on Business and Technology*, 1–16.

NavarettiG.B.CalzolariG.FrancoA.NumbersP.Mansilla-FernándezJ.M.DermineJ.VivesX.BofondiM.GobbiG.FerrariniG.XiangX.LinaZ.YunW.ChengxuanH. (2018). European economy banks, regulation, and the real sector fintech and banking. Friends or foes? https://www.econstor.eu/handle/10419/200276%0Ahttps://papers.ssrn.com/sol3/papers.cfm?abstract_id=3099337

Nayak, P. D. D. K., & Singh, P. (2021). Does Data Security and Trust Affect the Users of Fintech? *International Journal of Management*, *12*(1), 191–206. doi:10.34218/IJM.12.1.2021.016

Nikkel, B. (2020). Fintech forensics: Criminal investigation and digital evidence in financial technologies. *Forensic Science International: Digital Investigation*, *33*, 200908. doi:10.1016/j.fsidi.2020.200908

Ogbenika, G. (2000). The Seminarian and the Digital Age: Implications for Authentic Formation. *Acjol. Org*, 154–170. https://acjol.org/index.php/ekpoma/article/view/1750

Oladapo, I. A., Hamoudah, M. M., Alam, M. M., Olaopa, O. R., & Muda, R. (2021). Customers' perceptions of FinTech adaptability in the Islamic banking sector: Comparative study on Malaysia and Saudi Arabia. *Journal of Modelling in Management*. Advance online publication. doi:10.1108/JM2-10-2020-0256

Olalere, Ndunagu, & Abdulhamid. (2019). Performance Analysis of Security Information and Event Management Solutions for Detection of Web-Based Attacks. *Proceedings of the Cyber Secure Nigeria 2019 Conference*, 39–47.

Omarini, A. E. (2018). *Fintech and the Future of the Payment Landscape : The Mobile Wallet Ecosystem - A Challenge for Retail Banks?* doi:10.5430/ijfr.v9n4p97

Ometov, A., Bezzateev, S., Mäkitalo, N., Andreev, S., Mikkonen, T., & Koucheryavy, Y. (2018). Multi-factor authentication: A survey. *Cryptography*, *2*(1), 1–31. doi:10.3390/cryptography2010001

Phillip, A., Chan, J., & Peiris, S. (2018). A new look at Cryptocurrencies. *Economics Letters*, *163*, 6–9. doi:10.1016/j.econlet.2017.11.020

Pisano, G. (2006). Profiting from innovation and the intellectual property revolution. *Research Policy*, *35*(8), 1122–1130. doi:10.1016/j.respol.2006.09.008

Pompella, M., & Costantino, L. (2021). Fintech and Blockchain Based Innovation: Technology Driven Business Models and Disruption BT - The Palgrave Handbook of FinTech and Blockchain. In M. Pompella & R. Matousek (Eds.), *The Palgrave Handbook of FinTech and Blockchain* (pp. 403–430). Springer International Publishing. doi:10.1007/978-3-030-66433-6_18

Puschmann, T., Hoffmann, C. H., & Khmarskyi, V. (2020). How green fintech can alleviate the impact of climate change—The case of Switzerland. *Sustainability (Switzerland)*, *12*(24), 1–28. doi:10.3390u122410691

Rahmani, M. K. I., Shuaib, M., Alam, S., Siddiqui, S. T., Ahmad, S., Bhatia, S., & Mashat, A. (2022). Blockchain-Based Trust Management Framework for Cloud Computing-Based Internet of Medical Things (IoMT): A Systematic Review. *Computational Intelligence and Neuroscience*, *2022*, 1–14. doi:10.1155/2022/9766844 PMID:35634070

Rasheed, I., Asif, M., Khan, W. U., Ihsan, A., Ullah, K., & Ali, M. S. (2022). Blockchain-Based Trust Verification and Streaming Service Awareness for Big Data-Driven 5G and beyond Vehicle-to-Everything (V2X) Communication. *Wireless Communications and Mobile Computing*, *2022*, 1–13. Advance online publication. doi:10.1155/2022/7357820

Rauniyar, K., Komal, R., & Kumar, S. D. (2021). Role of fintech and innovations for improvising digital financial inclusion. *International Journal of Innovative Science and Research Technology*, *6*(5). https://ijisrt.com/assets/upload/files/IJISRT21MAY1089.pdf%0Awww.ijisrt.com

Ryle, P., Yan, J., & Gardiner, L. R. (2022). Gramm-Leach-Bliley gets a systems upgrade: What the ftc's proposed safeguards rule changes mean for small and medium american financial institutions. *EDPACS*, *65*(2), 6–17. doi:10.1080/07366981.2021.1911387

Saad, M., Spaulding, J., Njilla, L., Kamhoua, C., Shetty, S., Nyang, D. H., & Mohaisen, D. (2020). Exploring the Attack Surface of Blockchain: A Comprehensive Survey. *IEEE Communications Surveys and Tutorials*, *22*(3), 1977–2008. doi:10.1109/COMST.2020.2975999

Shin, D. D. H. (2019). Blockchain: The emerging technology of digital trust. *Telematics and Informatics*, *45*(June), 101278. Advance online publication. doi:10.1016/j.tele.2019.101278

Singh, M., Poongodi, M., Saurabh, P., Kumar, U., Bourouis, S., Alhakami, W., Osamor, J., & Hamdi, M. (2022). A novel trust-based security and privacy model for Internet of Vehicles using encryption and steganography ☆. *Computers & Electrical Engineering*, *102*(June), 108205. doi:10.1016/j.compeleceng.2022.108205

Sokolov, A. (2020). *How to mitigate fintech application threats*. https://www.itechart.com/blog/mobile-fintech-security-threats/

Song, Y., Sun, C., Peng, Y., Zeng, Y., & Sun, B. (2022). Research on Multidimensional Trust Evaluation Mechanism of FinTech Based on Blockchain. *IEEE Access: Practical Innovations, Open Solutions, 10*, 57025–57036. doi:10.1109/ACCESS.2022.3177275

Sorongan, F. A., Legowo, M. B., & Subanidja, S. (2021). FinTech as The Emerging Technologies in Banking Industry: Past, Present, and Future. *International Journal (Toronto, Ont.)*, 371–378. http://ijpsat.es/index.php/ijpsat/article/view/3550

Stoica, E. A., & Sitea, D. M. (2021).. . *Blockchain Disrupting Fintech and the Banking System, 24*, 24. Advance online publication. doi:10.3390/proceedings2021074024

Suprun, A., Petrishina, T., & Vasylchuk, I. (2020). *Competition and cooperation between fintech companies and*. Academic Press.

Suseendran, G., Chandrasekaran, E., Akila, D., & Sasi Kumar, A. (2020). Banking and FinTech (Financial Technology) Embraced with IoT Device. *Advances in Intelligent Systems and Computing, 1042*(February), 197–211. doi:10.1007/978-981-32-9949-8_15

Tang, K. L. (2021). *Behavioural Intention of Commercial Banks' Customers towards Financial Technology Services Related papers. Global Academy of Training & Research (GATR)* Enterprise.

Tapanainen, T. (2020). Toward Fintech Adoption Framework for Developing Countries -A Literature Review based on the Stakeholder Perspective. *Journal of Information Technology Applications & Management, 27*(October), 1–22.

Treleaven, P. (2015). Financial regulation of FinTech. *Journal of Financial Perspectives, 3*(3), 114–121.

Ullah, N., Al-Rahmi, W. M., Alfarraj, O., Alalwan, N., Alzahrani, A. I., Ramayah, T., & Kumar, V. (2022). Hybridizing cost saving with trust for blockchain technology adoption by financial institutions. *Telematics and Informatics Reports, 6*(April), 100008. doi:10.1016/j.teler.2022.100008

Universities, A. (2021). A Framework for Enhancing Cyber Security in Fintech Applications in India. *International Conference on Technological Advancements and Innovations (ICTAI)*.

Urien, P. (2021). A New IoT Trust Model Based on TLS-SE and TLS- IM Secure Elements : a Blockchain Use Case. *2021 IEEE 18th Annual Consumer Communications & Networking Conference (CCNC)*, 2021–2022.

Verma, G., & Adhikari, S. (2020). Cloud Computing Security Issues : A Stakeholder ' s Perspective. *SN Computer Science, 1*(6), 1–8. doi:10.100742979-020-00353-2

Wilson, J. D. (2017). Creating Strategic Value through Financial Technology. *Creating Strategic Value through Financial Technology*. doi:10.1002/9781119318682

Working, A., & Series, P. (2019). *Regulating fintech : Objectives, principles, and practices October 2019 Asian Development Bank Institute*. ADBI Working Paper Series, No. 1016, Asian Development Bank Institute (ADBI).

Wu, P. S. (2017). Fintech trends relationships research: A bibliometric citation meta-analysis. *Proceedings of the International Conference on Electronic Business (ICEB),* 99–105.

Wu, Y., Lu, X., & Wu, Z. (2021). Blockchain-Based Trust Model for Air Traffic Management Network. *2021 IEEE 6th International Conference on Computer and Communication Systems, ICCCS 2021,* 92–98. 10.1109/ICCCS52626.2021.9449156

Xavier, V. (2017). The Impact of Fintech on Banking. *European Economy, Banks, Regulation and the Real Sector - Fintechs and Banks: Friends or Foes?* 97–105. https://blog.iese.edu/xvives/files/2018/02/EE_2.2017.pdf

Yuen, T. H. (2020). PAChain: Private, authenticated & auditable consortium blockchain and its implementation. *Future Generation Computer Systems, 112,* 913–929. doi:10.1016/j.future.2020.05.011

Zhang, P., & Zhou, M. (2020). Security and Trust in Blockchains: Architecture, Key Technologies, and Open Issues. *IEEE Transactions on Computational Social Systems, 7*(3), 790–801. doi:10.1109/TCSS.2020.2990103

Chapter 10
Data Leakage in Business and FinTech

Usama Habib Chaudhry

Department of Computing, School of Electrical Engineering and Computer Sciences, National University of Sciences and Technology, Islamabad, Pakistan

Razi Arshad

Department of Computing, School of Electrical Engineering and Computer Sciences, National University of Sciences and Technology, Islamabad, Pakistan

Naveed Naeem Abbas

Department of Computing, School of Electrical Engineering and Computer Sciences, National University of Sciences and Technology, Islamabad, Pakistan

Adeel Ahmed Zeerak

Department of Computing, School of Electrical Engineering and Computer Sciences, National University of Sciences and Technology, Islamabad, Pakistan

ABSTRACT

With the advent of the internet and day-by-day advancement in technology, traditional services started to utilize technology to offer better, digitized, cutting-edge services. Financial services called FinTech are one such example of the adoption of cutting-edge technologies. On the other hand, with the adoption of technologies comes to the cybersecurity risks associated with them. Data leakage is one big issue in FinTech and business-related applications and services. The main aim of this chapter is to identify different ways and methods by which data leakage occurs and its adverse effects on organizations providing FinTech services. Furthermore, this chapter explores the various solutions and challenges in their implementation. It is concluded that no single solution can handle data leakage from all perspectives. Multiple solutions need to be combined and utilized to handle all scenarios.

DOI: 10.4018/978-1-6684-5284-4.ch010

INTRODUCTION

Fintech a term coined from the word financial technology is commonly used to describe financial services that leverage cutting-edge technologies such as blockchain (Du et al., 2019) (Dorfleitner & Braun, 2019) (Mahyuni et al., 2020), artificial intelligence (AI) (Ashta & Herrmann, 2021) (Pustokhina et al., 2021) (Bayramoğlu, 2021), big data (Awotunde et al., 2021; Ennouri & Mezghani, 2020; Meng et al., 2021), etc. to transform traditional financial and business services into more robust and cutting-edge services (Puschmann, 2017). In this advanced technological era, quick adaptability, iteration, and better management of financial operations are the need of the day for businesses and consumers. Fintech services, such as Peer-to-Peer (P2P), stimulate innovative products and increase market effectiveness while easing access to short-term cash for small and medium-sized businesses (Arner et al., 2017). FinTech by leveraging cutting-edge technologies offers a wide range of digital services to help accelerate traditional methods. FinTech services are enabled by IT–Infrastructure thus Fintech services by default inherit all the cybersecurity risks and threats associated with the IT–Infrastructure. FinTech services handle a lot of sensitive data related to businesses and consumers, thus such services are more prone to data leakages, providing secure and trustworthy service protection of data from leakage is one critical concern out of other cybersecurity concerns in this domain.

Data leakage (van der Kleij et al., 2020) is the unauthorized, intentional, or unintentional dissemination of sensitive data by an external or internal entity, and once data is leaked there is no way to contain it. One of the major threats to the organizations providing FinTech services is data leakage either by an external entity compromising their IT–Infrastructure and exposing sensitive data or by their employees. Employees having access to sensitive and critical data can leak it, intentionally or unintentionally. The most common ways of leaking sensitive data by employees are by email, USB, etc. Such events damage the reputation of the organizations and even threaten their existence (Huth et al., 2013). Different countries have implemented different laws for data protection. Examples of such laws are the Sarbanes-Oxley Act (SOX)-this law deals with the protection of financial data, HIPPA-this law with the protection of health records, GDPR-this law deals with the protection of personal data. Classification of data leakages in FinTech (Cheng et al., 2017) is presented in Figure 1.

Figure 1. Classification of data leakages in FinTech

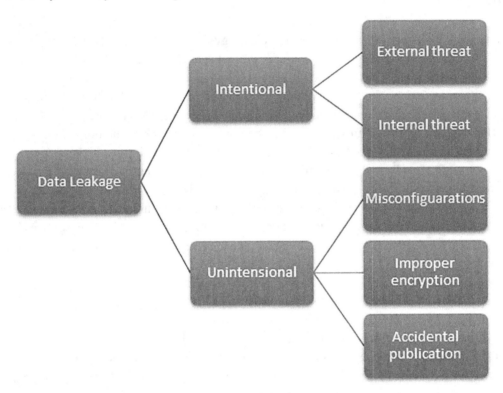

A detailed classification of data leakages in FinTech is given below

1. **Intentional data leakage:** In this type of data leakage, data is leaked by external threat actors such as hackers who exploit the system vulnerabilities, access sensitive information, and then either sell it on the black market, leak it or extort money from the FinTech service provider. External adversaries can also use phishing and social engineering techniques to fool employees into giving sensitive data to the adversary. Stolen or default credentials of employees can also be used to get sensitive data out of the organization.

   Data can also be leaked deliberately by internal threat actors referred to as employees of an organization, such attempts of data leakage by employees have the maximum impact and leaves little to no evidence (Alsuwaie et al., 2021).

2. **Unintentional data leakage:** In this type of data leakage, data is leaked unintentionally due to misconfigured systems and settings such as misconfigured authentication (Hassan et al., 2018) which can lead to granting a normal user a higher level of access to sensitive data. Improper or weak encryption of sensitive data at rest or in transit can also lead to the exposure of sensitive data. Data can be leaked unintentionally by employees, for example, employees sharing data internally without proper encryption and security measures (Prisca I. Okochi et al., 2021).

Data Leak Channels

To disseminate the stolen data either by employees of the organization or by notorious external entities, a channel of some form will be used. A classification of such channels is given below.

1. **Physical Channel:** This term refers to the leakage of data via physical mediums (Alneyadi et al., 2016a) such as laptops, HDDs, USB devices, etc. Notorious employees can save sensitive data in these devices, take them out of the organization and disseminate the stolen data. Similarly, even if an employee does not have any malicious intent but has possession of these devices with sensitive data on them, data can be leaked if someone stole these devices and retrieve data from them.
2. **Logical Channel:** This term refers to the leakage of data via a logical channel (Alneyadi et al., 2016b) such as the internet. A threat actor can publish stolen data online on web forums or file servers which are easy to access by the public, can send data to someone via methods such as email, instant message applications (WhatsApp, Skype, Messenger, etc.) or a notorious employee can use one of the logical channels to send data outside the organization or he/she can also upload data to a file server or a web forum.

Types of Data

Given below is a classification of types of data which is susceptible to leakage by insiders and external threats.

1. **Data in use:** Data in use (Gupta & Singh, 2022) means, the data which is currently being worked upon or which is currently under processing. This type of data is mostly stored in volatile storage such as Random Access Memory (RAM) or CPU registers. If sensitive data is being processed such as data of a FinTech service, proper security measures should be implemented for the secure processing of data to prevent it from being leaked. For example, a computer may be infected with malware that reads the data loaded in RAM and sends it to a malicious entity.
2. **Data in transit:** Data in transit (Ghouse et al., 2019) means, the motion of data from one location to another from one computer to another, and from one network to another. The most common example of data in transit is sending data via email. The FinTech service provider may communicate data with their stakeholders over the network, or they may leverage the cloud for processing data or data storage for such purposes data need to be sent over the network, without proper security measures applied, the data is prone to leakage. For example, if the data is being transferred over a non-secure network an attacker might intercept the data being transferred.
3. **Data at rest:** Data at rest (Shaik et al., 2022) means that the data is physically stored on a storage device. In terms of FinTech, it means that data related to FinTech service consumers is stored on a physical storage device. The storage device may be hosted in-house, hosted by the cloud service provider (ZAMFIR & SBUGHEA, 2020), hosted remotely, or hosted at a third-party storage service provider. Data at rest can be either structured or unstructured and is most easy to secure than the rest of the forms but vulnerabilities in security measures implemented can make this data susceptible to leakage also if sensitive data is stored at distributed places and is handled by multiple parties. It is more prone to leakage because the third-party storage service provider may not have implemented proper security and data leakage prevention measures.

Trust in security measures, implemented by FinTech service providers is one of the biggest factors in the adaptability of such services. Consumers and businesses put their trust in organizations providing FinTech services and if a data leakage happens, the organization loses the trust of consumers and businesses. Such incidents damage their reputation which in turn affects the overall adaptation of FinTech services. To increase the overall adaptability and maintain trust between consumers, FinTech services providers need to enforce data leakage prevention mechanisms.

LITERATURE REVIEW

In this section, we will review existing literature related to data leakage and its adverse effects on businesses and FinTech services.

According to a report by IMF (Bouveret, 2018) (Khan & Malaika, 2021), the FinTech industry has seen unprecedented levels of growth during the last decade. Due to their dependency on technology to provide services, hackers target vulnerable entry points in FinTech services to gain access to sensitive data and use it for defrauding. According to the report, the FinTech industry has lost 1450 million USD since 2013 due to such notorious activities of data theft and leakage by hackers.

(Hauer, 2015) conducted a study on data leakages in businesses. 1259 data points related to data leakages were characterized and analyzed. From the results gathered it was concluded that approximately 60% of data leakage incidents were caused by employees for their malicious agendas and financial motives.

In (Vimal M, 2019), a study was conducted which describes that inherent vulnerabilities of third-party service providers leveraging FinTech services can lead to data leakage, as well as external threat actors can use malware (Magableh, 2022) to compromise a FinTech service or a third-party service and gain access to sensitive data.

According to (Garvey et al., n.d.), FinTech has brought disruption to almost all aspects of the industry such as asset management (Fadhul & Hamdan, 2020), wealth management, lending, banking, etc. With unprecedented levels of growth, FinTech has its fair share of threats related to security and privacy. A lot of data is handled and recorded in digital formats by these FinTech service providers, which makes these services more susceptible to data breaches and leakages. The author identifies some key aspects that if not handled properly can lead to data breach or leakage, the key aspects described by the author are improper management and configuration of identities which if not configured correctly can lead to users having access to sensitive data, weak encryption of data, insecure coding practices and backdoor in FinTech services.

(Gai et al., 2017), provided a brief taxonomy of methods by which sensitive data can be accessed and leaked. The methods described in the taxonomy are

1. **Hacking**, notorious actors can exploit vulnerabilities in the system such as users using default usernames and passwords, exploiting flaws in authentication and access control mechanisms, performing sophisticated attacks such as SQL injections (Arashhhabibiilashkari, n.d.), cross-site scripting, or using social engineering techniques (Nikkel, 2020) to persuade employees of the organization into giving access credentials to organizations systems.
2. **Malware**, can be installed by a hacker after compromising the systems, can be installed by a notorious employee, or can be accidentally installed while surfing the unsafe web by employees. Malware can create a backdoor in the system for notorious actors to access sensitive data, it can

also record keystrokes and the recorded keystrokes to the malicious actor the keystrokes can have usernames, passwords, or other sensitive data.

3. **Physical access**, which includes physical access to devices that contains sensitive data devices such as laptops, hard drives, USBs, CD, etc.,

4. **Human error**, which includes mistakes or unintentional acts either by employees or software developers who designed the system. Software developers can accidentally leave a backdoor in the system which can be potentially used by a malicious actor to gain access to the system, or the employees can accidentally put sensitive data on storage media or servers which is available to access by anyone.

Out of many other service delivery methods cloud (Gai, 2014) is also being utilized by FinTech service providers to provide services to their consumers. But this leaves a great concern for the FinTech service providers as well as consumers, about sensitive data being stolen or leaked due to weak data controls in the cloud (Hernández et al., 2019).

According to (Ni et al., 2014), FinTech services of a FinTech service provider can be exploited to steal or leak data via vulnerabilities in cloud protocols, web services, misconfigured cloud configurations, and lack of proper data controls.

According to a report by (IBM, 2019) on data breaches and leakages in 2019, data leakages and breaches caused approximately damages of 3.92 million USD, the health sector sustained damages of 6.45 million USD in damages due to data breaches and leakages, and the business sector and industrial sector sustained damages of approximately 2.7 million USD.

According to another report (IBM, 2022), 550 data breaches and leakages happened which caused an estimated loss of 4.35 million USD. According to the report, most of the data leakages happened due to compromised, stolen, or default credentials. The report also states that organizations leveraging cloud technology also reported data leakage incidents about 16% of these incidents happened due to cloud misconfigurations.

Since the introduction of cloud technology, due to its inherent flexibility and scalability, service providers whether it be FinTech, movie streaming, EdTech startups, etc. all are leveraging the cloud for data processing and data storage. Data on the cloud is hosted inside virtual machines (Goli et al., 2020) running on bare hardware through hypervisors. These virtual machines communicate with each other for various purposes via a complex set of protocols. These protocols can result in complex vulnerabilities which can't be detected easily which can result in data leakage or theft in case they are found and exploited by a malicious entity (Gai et al., 2016)

Most organizations are mostly focused on protecting their data from external malicious entities and direct most of their efforts to implementing security solutions to protect them from external threats, but according to research (Padayachee, 2016) most data leakage incidents in organizations, happen from within organizations.

(al-Ain University et al., n.d.), states that data leakages by insiders such as employees are the most damaging ones. In the said research, the authors explored file formats and methods by which confidential data of organizations can be exfiltrated by insiders. The most common file formats used by insiders to save stolen data were PDF and word format. Some of the methods used to exfiltrate these files from the organization are such as changing file names and their extensions, encrypting the files, etc.

Most of the decision-makers in organizations are of the viewpoint that threats their organizations face in terms of cyber security and data leakages are from external threat actors but in most cases, according to (Lesnykh, 2011) insider threats are the major reason for data breaches and leakages.

With the advancement of technology now it has become possible to monitor the health vitals of patients via IoT devices (Shahid et al., 2022) These devices store their data on servers hosted by either the health care institution or over the cloud. Besides this data, the financial data of these institutes also reside on these servers. Malicious attackers or insiders can compromise these devices to access sensitive financial data of these institutes and the fintech service provider they are associated with.

Most of the businesses and Fintech service providers leverage cloud storage to store their data. The reason behind adopting cloud is due to its cost effectiveness which is a major benefit for credit crunch businesses. Cloud service provider achieves cost effectiveness via multi tenancy. If data segregation is not implemented correctly. A malicious entity on the cloud will end up accessing the stored sensitive financial data of the business and fintech service provider (Velumadhava Rao & Selvamani, 2015).

To understand the economic impact of data theft and leakage, (McAfee, 2020) sponsored a study according to which 0.5 million jobs and $100 billion were lost due to such attacks on FinTech and businesses. In a similar study by (Finance Nine, 2019), a bank named Westpac was breached by hackers who leaked the sensitive data of almost 0.1 million customers.

DATA LEAKAGE PREVENTION AND CHALLENGES

To protect confidential data from being leaked, there are Data Leakage Prevention (DLP) solutions that can be implemented to protect the data. These solutions come with their own set of challenges and for a solution to be implemented successfully these challenges must be addressed. In this section, we will review Data Leakage Prevention systems along with their challenges.

(Institute of Electrical and Electronics Engineers & PPG Institute of Technology, n.d.), proposed a solution called SeGate based on graph neural networks (GNN) to prevent text data, in transit from being leaked. According to the research, the proposed solution must be implemented in a network gateway (Unsal et al., 2020) to protect sensitive text data from flowing out of the organization's network. The proposed solution is only limited to the prevention of text data.

(Yu et al., 2018) proposed a solution for smart devices to protect sensitive text data by using a cluster graph structure model based on context. The proposed solution removes noise and redundant terms from text data and detects original confidential terms/text data as well as rephrased terms/text data. However, the challenge of preventing intentional data leaks remains unanswered in this research.

To prevent leakage of digital documents containing sensitive financial data. (Guha et al., 2021) proposed a solution based on artificial intelligence. The proposed solution uses Artificial Neural Network-based content classification, which determines patterns and identifies sensitive data from digital documents, and prevents data in rest or transit from being leaked.

Most of the data leakage prevention solutions are designed to prevent the leakage of electronic forms of data. But there is a very limited number of solutions to prevent the leakage of data in printed form. (Kozachok et al., 2019) proposed a watermarking technique based on the Gaussian mixture model and Radon transform. When a document containing sensitive information is to be printed, a watermark based on the proposed methodology is embedded before printing. The proposed solution is resistant to various image distortion transformations which makes this solution robust.

Data is classified into two types, structured and unstructured. Structured data such as credit card numbers follow a predefined format while unstructured data such as emails, documents, etc. do not have any kind of predefined format. A DLP solution must account for both types of data but most DLP solutions on focus on the prevention of structured data. (Alhindi et al., 2021) proposed a fingerprinting technique. The said technique tries to learn the semantics of information contained in the file and uses oncology to encode the learned semantic information. The proposed solution can detect data leakage with very high accuracy even if the data is modified or rewritten. The proposed solution currently focuses only on the semantic concepts learned not the relationship between those semantic concepts.

(Lu et al., 2018a), proposed a solution based on a model called Weighted Context Model. The said model is used to build semantic relations of data which is to be protected by referring to sensitive content as graph nodes and the edges between nodes represent the contextual association. To improve detection speed, the classification of data to be protected based on similarity features of the context graph is performed. To protect the privacy of sensitive content is the data, irreversible encryption is used to protect such content while maintaining the semantic association.

Communication via email is one of the most used modes of communication in electronic communication. Misuse of email can also lead to the leakage of sensitive information. (Kaur et al., 2018), proposed an Email Protection System (EPS). The proposed system is deployed on the network gateway whenever an email leaves the organization's network. EPS scans the content of the email as well as scans any attachment attached to the email and matches the scanned content using a pattern-matching algorithm with a database of known sensitive terms. If a match is found the network administrator is alerted and the email is stopped from leaving the network. The issue with the proposed methodology is that it relies on a simple pattern-matching algorithm, a smart employee can encrypt the file with sensitive data and send it via email, but the proposed solution will fail in this scenario. Moreover, this method handles data leakage via mail, a malicious employee can utilize other ways of leaking data such as posting data on online forums.

To date, numerous solutions have been proposed to prevent data leakages. Most of these solutions are based on traditional methods such as watermarking and steganography (Kadhim et al., 2019), both of these methods involve modification of original data. Businesses and FinTech service providers share information and their stakeholders, anyone from the mentioned can leak sensitive data, and tracking the main culprit is near to impossible in such cases. To solve this issue of tracking culprits in case of data leakage and to prevent data leakage. (Gupta & Singh, 2017) proposed a solution according to which when a data object is requested it is assigned via a data distributor and the association of the data object with the receiving client is recorded in a bigraph. To count the number of clients to whom the data object is assigned a matrix based on this bigraph is utilized. When a leakage happens the bigraph and matrix are used to identify the main culprit. The proposed solution is named as "Guilty Agent Identification Model", the proposed solution is for identifying who leaked the data, but it does not help in preventing data leakage.

For FinTech, organization complaints with regulations, laws, and regulatory bodies are obligatory, and implementing preventive measures against data loss is one of the conditions to comply with. FinTech service providers may utilize for cloud for data storage, but these storage services may have vulnerabilities that may lead to data loss to prevent this from happening. (Ong et al., 2017a) proposed a solution based on deep learning and machine learning algorithms. The proposed solution will detect sensitive stored data by learning semantic information with context via the said algorithms. When a user tries to access sensitive data an alert will be generated for the administrator and the access of the user will be blocked. The proposed solution is equally applicable to both in-house and cloud storage solutions.

Before the emergence of contextual semantic analysis-based data leakage prevention, old methods to prevent leakages were based on the syntactic analysis of documents and text data. Such methods relied upon extracting keywords from data and comparing the extracted keywords to a database of keywords representing sensitive data (Zdonik et al., n.d.). The drawback of this solution is that it is not resistant to rephrasing. (D. Du et al., 2015) proposed a contextual semantic analysis-based solution to overcome the flaws previously identified in syntactic analysis-based solutions. The proposed solution is based on latent semantic analysis utilizing singular value decomposition which will extract semantic features which represent the concept in the data to be protected. The proposed solution determines a threshold for sensitive data by semantic analysis and matches the threshold of data going out of the network with the given threshold. If the data has a higher threshold than the calculated threshold, the flow of data is stopped.

These days, most digital services such as online banking, and FinTech services are accessed via mobile apps. Hence proper security measures need to be taken into consideration and should be implemented appropriately to protect data from being leaked from mobile devices. (Continella et al., 2017) proposed a differential analysis-based black box technique to prevent data leakage. The proposed solution work in two steps. In the first step, it creates a baseline behavior of network traffic originating from the mobile device, and in the second step, it records the deviations in the network traffic behavior. If the deviation is higher than a certain threshold, the proposed solution will stop data from flowing out of the mobile device. Non-determinism is a key challenge that this solution still needs to address.

Data leaks by insider threats are the most difficult to detect and prevent. (Costante et al., 2016) proposed a hybrid framework for data leakage detection and prevention from insider threats. The proposed solution is composed of signature and anomaly-based solutions. The anomaly-based solution is used to learn the behavior of normal users by monitoring their activities, if a user deviates from their normal behavior, the anomaly detection system will flag the user and stop any activities being performed by the user. With the signature-based system, it generates the signature of the activity being performed and updates the database for future use in case any user repeats the same activity. The proposed framework is extendible to any kind of data e.g., network packets.

To protect organizations' sensitive data from being leaked and breached by external threat actors, Intrusion Detection Systems (IDS) (Liu et al., 2021) are also employed to detect a breach and before it is too late, stop the malicious actor from exfiltrating sensitive data. (C & Vijayalakshmi, 2022) proposed a machine learning-based solution which will work hand in hand with IDS to prevent data breaches. To classify malicious traffic the proposed solution employs gradient boost and rough set theory (RST). The proposed solution increased the overall accuracy of IDS and help detect data breaches much faster.

(Kiperberg et al., 2021a) proposed a data leakage prevention system based on a hypervisor. The proposed solution intercepts system calls such as inter-process communication calls (Will et al., 2021), network calls, file system calls, and calls related to copy-and-paste data commands. The solution makes sure that no sensitive data leaves the system. The solution can be made stricter to make sure that data does not even leave the specified directories.

For collaboration and sharing data among employees, organizations can utilize cloud storage. Most cloud storage solutions are browser-based. The users with their mouse can drag the files to the browser and drop them into cloud-based storage which will automatically upload the dropped data on cloud storage. With the usage of cloud storage, there comes the problem of data leakage. To tackle this problem (Han et al., 2020) proposed a data leak prevention solution called cloudDLP. The proposed solution is deployed at the network gateway and when data is about to be uploaded to cloud storage, the proposed solution captures the data being uploaded, checks it for sensitive data, sanitize it, and then allows it to be uploaded to the cloud storage. Also, to prevent text data from being leaked in the form of images, the proposed solution uses deep learning to detect text and checks for sensitive information if found the image is sanitized.

(Gu et al., 2022) proposed an encryption and blockchain based solution to store and transmit data. The proposed solution also provides a traceability feature, in case if data leakage happens it can be tracked to the entity who leaked it.

(Vukovic et al., n.d.) proposed a rule-based standalone solution. The proposed solution can be customized according to the need of the organization and applies to many scenarios. In the proposed system, detection of data leakage is achieved by using a strategy that intercepts possible threats as they leave the monitored system domain by using a set of predefined rules. But the main issue with rule-based systems is that they follow a predefined set of rules, and if they encounter something which does not match the rule set, it is allowed to pass through the system. Attackers can leverage this flaw and will exfiltrate sensitive data in such as way that will not trigger the system and hence will successfully leak the data.

RECOMMENDATIONS

Advancements in financial technologies and businesses attract cybercriminals and hence increase the risk of cyber-attacks on these organizations. Business and FinTech organizations generate and handle a lot of data related to their consumer and are always worried about the protection of their data from any kind of compromise, theft, or leakage. Not only do these organizations face data leakage and theft threats from malicious external entities but there is more likelihood of insider attacks than external entities. To protect these organizations from data leakage and theft, data leakage prevention methods described in the above section need to be implemented. No single solution will be able to protect data fully a combination of, the best of these solutions need to be implemented so that the data is fully protected. We will look from the perspective of both organizations and consumers what solutions need to be implemented at what side to prevent data leakage.

1. **Organizational perspective:** From an organization's perspective, we need to protect data in its all states i.e., data at rest, data in transit, and data in use. To protect data at rest from leakage, stored in the cloud or stored locally, we can implement solutions proposed by (Han et al., 2020) and (Ong et al., 2017b). Both of those solutions can be combined and used as one to protect data at rest. Both of these solutions are based on deep learning and machine learning algorithms. The benefit of the solution provided by (Han et al., 2020) is that it protects data at rest from leakage by insiders, and the solution provided by and (Ong et al., 2017b) protects it from external threats.

To protect data in use methodology proposed by (Kiperberg et al., 2021b), is recommended. The methodology proposed works at the operating system's kernel have a built-in protection mechanism from being turned off or being patched by a system update. Due to the execution of the proposed solution at the kernel level, the proposed solution easily intercepts system calls related to copy, paste, clipboard commands, etc. to protect data from being moved out or copied from the protected directories. To protect data in transit, solutions proposed by (Lu et al., 2018b), (Costante et al., 2016), (C & Vijayalakshmi,

2022), can be combined as one and utilized, the first two solutions are designed to protect against data leakage by insiders and the third solution provided, is excellent in detecting data breaches from external entities. All the mentioned solutions can detect data leakage at early stages with high accuracy and as soon a leakage attempt is detected, the solutions will kick in and halt the leakage activity being performed.

All the above-mentioned solutions are recommended to protect against data leakage via logical channels. For protection against data leakage via physical channels such as sensitive documents can be printed and then leaked, to prevent such a scenario. (Kozachok et al., 2019) proposed an excellent solution that watermarks documents before printing them or a solution provided by (Kiperberg et al., 2021b), which can also be used here to detect print calls and stop the printing of documents marked as sensitive. The same solution can also be utilized to prevent data from being copied to external storage media such as Hard drives, USBs, etc. Furthermore, policies should be enforced such as forcing employees to change their default credentials, changing credentials every 6 months, don't allow employees to take organizations' equipment home such as laptops, etc.

2. **Consumers perspective:** From the perspective of the consumer, a consumer of FinTech services expect that while they are utilizing services provided by the FinTech Service provider, their data is securely communicated without being leaked. Unfortunately, to handle this scenario, there aren't many solutions available. We found an excellent solution proposed by (Continella et al., 2017), this solution can be extended to any form of service delivery method to protect data from being leaked on the consumer's side.

CONCLUSION

Business and FinTech contribute a major share of Gross Domestic Production (GDP). Cybersecurity risks associated with FinTech are not merely technical issues, such risks can lead to serious implications, such as financial instability, damaged reputation and even running out of business. FinTech offers numerous benefits over traditional financial services such as cost-effective solutions, and faster-digitized services. With each passing day as technology advances, cybersecurity risks associated with Fintech are also increasing and attacks on FinTech have increased manifolds. As attacks on FinTech have become advanced and sophisticated so are the defensive measures. It is a known fact that nothing can be made 100% secure but we can make sure of maximum security by finding and fixing vulnerabilities at regular intervals. It is concluded in this chapter, that one of the major threats these FinTech organizations face is data leakage by insiders or external threats. To prevent data from being leaked researchers have proposed many solutions and techniques but it is observed that no single solution can handle data leakage from all perspectives. Multiple solutions need to be combined and utilized to handle all scenarios.

REFERENCES

al Ain University, Institute of Electrical and Electronics Engineers, Jordan Section, & Institute of Electrical and Electronics Engineers. (n.d.). *2019 International Arab Conference on Information Technology (ACIT) : proceedings : Al Ain, UAE, 03-05 Dec 2019*. Author.

Alhindi, H., Traore, I., & Woungang, I. (2021). Preventing Data Leak through Semantic Analysis. *Internet of Things, 14*, 100073.

Alneyadi, S., Sithirasenan, E., & Muthukkumarasamy, V. (2016). A survey on data leakage prevention systems. *Journal of Network and Computer Applications, 62*, 137–152. doi:10.1016/j.jnca.2016.01.008

Alsuwaie, M. A., Habibnia, B., & Gladyshev, P. (2021). Data Leakage Prevention Adoption Model DLP Maturity Level Assessment. *Proceedings - 2021 International Symposium on Computer Science and Intelligent Controls, ISCSIC 2021*, 396–405. 10.1109/ISCSIC54682.2021.00077

Arashhhabibiilashkari, G. Z. (n.d.). *Future of Business and Finance Understanding Cybersecurity Management in FinTech Challenges, Strategies, and Trends*. https://www.springer.com/series/16360

Arner, D. W., Barberis, J., Buckley, R. P., Arner, D., & Barberis, J. (2017). FinTech, RegTech, and the Reconceptualization of Financial Regulation. In *Northwestern Journal of International Law & Business* (Vol. 37, Issue 3). https://scholarlycommons.law.northwestern.edu/njilb/vol37/iss3/2

Ashta, A., & Herrmann, H. (2021). Artificial intelligence and fintech: An overview of opportunities and risks for banking, investments, and microfinance. *Strategic Change, 30*(3), 211–222. doi:10.1002/jsc.2404

Awotunde, J. B., Adeniyi, E. A., Ogundokun, R. O., & Ayo, F. E. (2021). Application of Big Data with Fintech in Financial Services. In P. M. S. Choi & S. H. Huang (Eds.), *Fintech with Artificial Intelligence, Big Data, and Blockchain* (pp. 107–132). Springer Singapore. doi:10.1007/978-981-33-6137-9_3

Bayramoğlu, G. (2021). An Overview of the Artificial Intelligence Applications in Fintech and Regtech. In S. Bozkuş Kahyaoğlu (Ed.), *The Impact of Artificial Intelligence on Governance, Economics and Finance* (Vol. I, pp. 291–298). Springer Singapore. doi:10.1007/978-981-33-6811-8_15

Bouveret, A. (2018). *WP/18/143 Cyber Risk for the Financial Sector: A Framework for Quantitative Assessment*. Academic Press.

C, A., & Vijayalakshmi, S. (2022). Prevention of Data Breach by Machine Learning Techniques. *2022 2nd International Conference on Advance Computing and Innovative Technologies in Engineering (ICACITE)*, 1819–1823. doi:10.1109/ICACITE53722.2022.9823523

Cheng, L., Liu, F., & Yao, D. D. (2017). Enterprise data breach: causes, challenges, prevention, and future directions. In Wiley Interdisciplinary Reviews: Data Mining and Knowledge Discovery (Vol. 7, Issue 5). Wiley-Blackwell. doi:10.1002/widm.1211

Continella, A., Fratantonio, Y., Lindorfer, M., Puccetti, A., Zand, A., Kruegel, C., & Vigna, G. (2017, May 13). *Obfuscation-Resilient Privacy Leak Detection for Mobile Apps Through Differential Analysis*. doi:10.14722/ndss.2017.23465

Costante, E., Fauri, D., Etalle, S., den Hartog, J., & Zannone, N. (2016). A Hybrid Framework for Data Loss Prevention and Detection. *Proceedings - 2016 IEEE Symposium on Security and Privacy Workshops, SPW 2016*, 324–333. 10.1109/SPW.2016.24

Dorfleitner, G., & Braun, D. (2019). Fintech, Digitalization and Blockchain: Possible Applications for Green Finance. In M. Migliorelli & P. Dessertine (Eds.), *The Rise of Green Finance in Europe: Opportunities and Challenges for Issuers, Investors and Marketplaces* (pp. 207–237). Springer International Publishing. doi:10.1007/978-3-030-22510-0_9

Du, D., Yu, L., & Brooks, R. R. (2015). Semantic similarity detection for data leak prevention. *ACM International Conference Proceeding Series*. 10.1145/2746266.2746270

Du, W., Pan, S. L., Leidner, D. E., & Ying, W. (2019). Affordances, experimentation and actualization of FinTech: A blockchain implementation study. *The Journal of Strategic Information Systems, 28*(1), 50–65.

Ennouri, M. F., & Mezghani, K. (2020). *Big Data Management in the Era of FinTech*. doi:10.4018/978-1-7998-7110-1.ch005

Fadhul, S., & Hamdan, A. (2020). The role of "fintech" on banking performance. *Proceedings of the European Conference on Innovation and Entrepreneurship, ECIE, 2020-September*, 911–914. 10.34190/EIE.20.230

Gai, K. (2014). A Review of Leveraging Private Cloud Computing in Financial Service Institutions: Value Propositions and Current Performances. *International Journal of Computers and Applications, 95*(3).

Gai, K., Qiu, M., Sun, X., & Zhao, H. (2017). Security and Privacy Issues: A Survey on FinTech. In M. Qiu (Ed.), *Smart Computing and Communication* (pp. 236–247). Springer International Publishing. doi:10.1007/978-3-319-52015-5_24

Gai, K., Qiu, M., Zhao, H., & Dai, W. (2016). Privacy-Preserving Adaptive Multi-channel Communications under Timing Constraints. *Proceedings - 2016 IEEE International Conference on Smart Cloud, SmartCloud 2016*, 190–195. 10.1109/SmartCloud.2016.50

Garvey, J., Burns, P., Alexander, O., & O'Hearn, S. (n.d.). *Crossing the lines: How fintech is propelling FS and TMT firms out of their lanes Contents*. Academic Press.

Ghouse, M., Nene, M. J., & VembuSelvi, C. (2019, December 1). Data Leakage Prevention for Data in Transit using Artificial Intelligence and Encryption Techniques. *2019 6th IEEE International Conference on Advances in Computing, Communication and Control, ICAC3 2019*. doi:10.1109/ICAC347590.2019.9036839

Goli, A., Hajihassani, O., Khazaei, H., Ardakanian, O., Rashidi, M., & Dauphinee, T. (2020). Migrating from monolithic to serverless: A fintech case study. *ICPE 2020 - Companion of the ACM/SPEC International Conference on Performance Engineering*, 20–25. 10.1145/3375555.3384380

Gu, B., Zou, Y., Cai, D., & Fan, H. (2022). A Method of Data Distribution and Traceability Based on Blockchain. In X. Sun, X. Zhang, Z. Xia, & E. Bertino (Eds.), *Artificial Intelligence and Security* (pp. 16–27). Springer International Publishing. doi:10.1007/978-3-031-06791-4_2

Guha, A., Samanta, D., Banerjee, A., & Agarwal, D. (2021). A Deep Learning Model for Information Loss Prevention from Multi-Page Digital Documents. *IEEE Access: Practical Innovations, Open Solutions, 9*, 80451–80465. doi:10.1109/ACCESS.2021.3084841

Gupta, I., & Singh, A. K. (2017). A probability based model for data leakage detection using Bigraph. *ACM International Conference Proceeding Series*, 1–5. 10.1145/3163058.3163060

Gupta, I., & Singh, A. K. (2022). *A Holistic View on Data Protection for Sharing, Communicating, and Computing Environments: Taxonomy and Future Directions*. https://arxiv.org/abs/2202.11965

Han, P., Liu, C., Cao, J., Duan, S., Pan, H., Cao, Z., & Fang, B. (2020). CloudDLP: Transparent and scalable data sanitization for browser-based cloud storage. *IEEE Access: Practical Innovations, Open Solutions, 8*, 68449–68459. doi:10.1109/ACCESS.2020.2985870

Hassan, M. M., Nipa, S. S., Akter, M., Haque, R., Deepa, F. N., Rahman, M. M., Siddiqui, M., & Sharif, M. H. (2018). Broken Authentication and Session Management Vulnerability: A Case Study of Web Application. *International Journal of Simulation: Systems, Science & Technology*. doi:10.5013/IJSSST.a.19.02.06

Hauer, B. (2015). Data and information leakage prevention within the scope of information security. *IEEE Access: Practical Innovations, Open Solutions, 3*, 2554–2565. doi:10.1109/ACCESS.2015.2506185

Hernández, E., Öztürk, M., Sittón, I., & Rodríguez, S. (2019). Data Protection on Fintech Platforms. In F. de La Prieta, A. González-Briones, P. Pawleski, D. Calvaresi, E. del Val, F. Lopes, V. Julian, E. Osaba, & R. Sánchez-Iborra (Eds.), *Highlights of Practical Applications of Survivable Agents and Multi-Agent Systems. The PAAMS Collection* (pp. 223–233). Springer International Publishing. doi:10.1007/978-3-030-24299-2_19

Huth, C. L., Chadwick, D. W., Claycomb, W. R., & You, I. (2013). Guest editorial: A brief overview of data leakage and insider threats. *Information Systems Frontiers, 15*(1), 1–4. doi:10.100710796-013-9419-8

IBM. (2019). *IBM security's cost of a data breach report 2019*. IBM.

IBM. (2022). *IBM security's cost of a data breach report 2022*. IBM.

Institute of Electrical and Electronics Engineers & PPG Institute of Technology. (n.d.). *Proceedings of the 5th International Conference on Communication and Electronics Systems (ICCES 2020) : 10-12, June 2020*. Author.

Kadhim, I. J., Premaratne, P., Vial, P. J., & Halloran, B. (2019). Comprehensive survey of image steganography: Techniques, Evaluations, and trends in future research. *Neurocomputing, 335*, 299–326. doi:10.1016/j.neucom.2018.06.075

Kaur, K., Gupta, I., & Singh, A. K. (2018). Data Leakage Prevention: E-Mail Protection via Gateway. *Journal of Physics: Conference Series, 933*, 012013. doi:10.1088/1742-6596/933/1/012013

Khan, A., & Malaika, M. (2021). Central Bank Risk Management, Fintech, and Cybersecurity. *IMF Working Papers, 2021*(105), A001. doi:10.5089/9781513582344.001.A001

Kiperberg, M., Amit, G., Yeshooroon, A., & Zaidenberg, N. J. (2021a). Efficient DLP-visor: An efficient hypervisor-based DLP. *Proceedings - 21st IEEE/ACM International Symposium on Cluster, Cloud and Internet Computing, CCGrid 2021*, 344–355. 10.1109/CCGrid51090.2021.00044

Kiperberg, M., Amit, G., Yeshooroon, A., & Zaidenberg, N. J. (2021b). Efficient DLP-visor: An efficient hypervisor-based DLP. *Proceedings - 21st IEEE/ACM International Symposium on Cluster, Cloud and Internet Computing, CCGrid 2021*, 344–355. 10.1109/CCGrid51090.2021.00044

Kozachok, A., Kopylov, S. A., Shelupanov, A. A., & Evsutin, O. O. (2019). Text marking approach for data leakage prevention. *Journal of Computer Virology and Hacking Techniques, 15*(3), 219–232. doi:10.100711416-019-00336-9

Lesnykh, A. (2011). Data loss prevention: A matter of discipline. *Network Security, 2011*(3), 18–19. doi:10.1016/S1353-4858(11)70028-9

Liu, D., Zhao, M., & Xu, H. (2021). Financial technology intelligent intrusion detection system based on financial data feature extraction and DNNs. *Proceedings of the 3rd International Conference on Intelligent Communication Technologies and Virtual Mobile Networks, ICICV 2021*, 89–93. 10.1109/ICICV50876.2021.9388459

Lu, Y., Huang, X., Ma, Y., & Ma, M. (2018a). A weighted context graph model for fast data leak detection. *IEEE International Conference on Communications, 2018-May*. 10.1109/ICC.2018.8422280

Lu, Y., Huang, X., Ma, Y., & Ma, M. (2018b). A weighted context graph model for fast data leak detection. *IEEE International Conference on Communications, 2018-May*. 10.1109/ICC.2018.8422280

Magableh, B. (2022). *Predictive Analytics for Malware Detection in FinTech using Machine Learning Classification Fiona Spelman Applied Research Project* [MSc dissertation]. Dublin Business School.

Mahyuni, L. P., Adrian, R., Darma, G. S., Krisnawijaya, N. N. K., Dewi, I. G. A. A. P., & Permana, G. P. L. (2020). Mapping the potentials of blockchain in improving supply chain performance. In Cogent Business and Management (Vol. 7, Issue 1). Cogent OA. doi:10.1080/23311975.2020.1788329

McAfee. (2020). *Study: $100 Billion Lost Annually to Cyber Attacks*. Author.

Meng, S., He, X., & Tian, X. (2021). Research on Fintech development issues based on embedded cloud computing and big data analysis. *Microprocessors and Microsystems, 83*, 103977. doi:10.1016/j.micpro.2021.103977

Ni, J., Yu, Y., Mu, Y., & Xia, Q. (2014). On the security of an efficient dynamic auditing protocol in cloud storage. *IEEE Transactions on Parallel and Distributed Systems, 25*(10), 2760–2761. doi:10.1109/TPDS.2013.199

Nikkel, B. (2020). Fintech forensics: Criminal investigation and digital evidence in financial technologies. *Forensic Science International: Digital Investigation, 33*, 200908.

Finance Nine. (2019). *Westpac security breach: Almost 100,000 customers exposed, cybersecurity news update*. Author.

Okochi, P. I., Okolie, S. A., & Odii, J. N. (2021). An improved data leakage detection system in a cloud computing environment. *World Journal of Advanced Research and Reviews, 11*(2), 321–328. doi:10.30574/wjarr.2021.11.2.0385

Ong, Y. J., Qiao, M., Routray, R., & Raphael, R. (2017). Context-Aware Data Loss Prevention for Cloud Storage Services. *IEEE International Conference on Cloud Computing, CLOUD, 2017-June*, 399–406. 10.1109/CLOUD.2017.58

Padayachee, K. (2016). An assessment of opportunity-reducing techniques in information security: An insider threat perspective. *Decision Support Systems, 92*, 47–56. doi:10.1016/j.dss.2016.09.012

Puschmann, T. (2017). Fintech. *Business & Information Systems Engineering, 59*(1), 69–76. doi:10.100712599-017-0464-6

Pustokhina, I., Pustokhin, D. A., Mohanty, S. N., García, P. A. G., & García-Díaz, V. (2021, November 13). Artificial intelligence assisted Internet of Things based financial crisis prediction in FinTech environment. *Annals of Operations Research*. Advance online publication. doi:10.100710479-021-04311-w

Shahid, J., Ahmad, R., Kiani, A. K., Ahmad, T., Saeed, S., & Almuhaideb, A. M. (2022). Data Protection and Privacy of the Internet of Healthcare Things (IoHTs). In Applied Sciences (Switzerland) (Vol. 12, Issue 4). MDPI. doi:10.3390/app12041927

Shaik, I., Chandran, N., & A, R. M. (2022). Privacy and data protection in the enterprise world. *CSI Transactions on ICT, 10*(1), 37–45. doi:10.1007/s40012-022-00348-9

Unsal, E., Oztekin, B., Cavus, M., & Ozdemir, S. (2020, October 20). Building a fintech ecosystem: Design and development of a fintech API gateway. *2020 International Symposium on Networks, Computers and Communications, ISNCC 2020*. 10.1109/ISNCC49221.2020.9297273

van der Kleij, R., Wijn, R., & Hof, T. (2020). An application and empirical test of the Capability Opportunity Motivation-Behaviour model to data leakage prevention in financial organizations. *Computers & Security, 97*, 101970. doi:10.1016/j.cose.2020.101970

Velumadhava Rao, R., & Selvamani, K. (2015). Data security challenges and its solutions in cloud computing. *Procedia Computer Science, 48*(C), 204–209. doi:10.1016/j.procs.2015.04.171

Vimal M. (2019). *Cybersecurity and fintech at a crossroads*. Academic Press.

Vukovic, M., Katusic, D., Soic, R., & Weber, M. (n.d.). *Rule-Based System for Data Leak Threat Estimation*. Academic Press.

Will, N. C., Heinrich, T., Viescinski, A. B., & Maziero, C. A. (2021, April 15). Trusted Inter-Process Communication Using Hardware Enclaves. *15th Annual IEEE International Systems Conference, SysCon 2021 - Proceedings*. 10.1109/SysCon48628.2021.9447066

Yu, X., Tian, Z., Qiu, J., & Jiang, F. (2018). A Data Leakage Prevention Method Based on the Reduction of Confidential and Context Terms for Smart Mobile Devices. *Wireless Communications and Mobile Computing, 5823439*, 1–11. Advance online publication. doi:10.1155/2018/5823439

Zamfir, C. G., & Sbughea, C. (2020). Phillips Curve: An Empirical Research on Romania. *Annals of Dunarea de Jos University of Galati. Fascicle I. Economics and Applied Informatics, 26*(2), 216–221. doi:10.35219/eai15840409129

Zdonik, S., Ning, P., Shekhar, S., Katz, J., Wu, X., Jain, L. C., Padua, D., Shen, X., Furht, B., & Subrahmanian, V. S. (n.d.). *SpringerBriefs in Computer Science*. https://www.springer.com/series/10028

Chapter 11
Enhancing Cybersecurity Through Blockchain Technology

Sriram V. P.
Acharya Bangalore B School, Bengaluru, India

Shouvik Sanyal
Dhofar University, Oman

Madan Mohan Laddunuri
Malla Reddy University, India

Mathiraj Subramanian
Alagappa University, India

Vijay Bose
Vaagdevi College of Engineering, India

Bharath Booshan
Acharya Institute of Graduate Studies, India

Chethan Shivaram
Acharya Institute of Graduate Studies, India

Manasa Bettaswamy
PES University, Bengaluru, India

Shabista Booshan
ISBR Business School, Bengaluru, India

Dhanabalan Thangam
 https://orcid.org/0000-0003-1253-3587
Presidency Business School, Presidency College, Bengaluru, India

ABSTRACT

Blockchain technology ensures data security through an integrated system whereby it collects, arranges, stores, and disseminates information in different blocks. This technology thus enables adding the data to the network. Once data has been added to the network, no one can alter the data set either by adding or deleting it. Further, this technology also helps to track and check the changes if anything is made to a blockchain, as the changes remain in the database forever. Since this technology uses lots of systems in a blockchain, it will regularly download its data, arranging, and keeping the copy locally. Locating the data errors and cyberattacks in advance by analyzing the data documented, it employs the consent of various participants and accomplishments in cryptography. With this backdrop, the chapter has attempted to disclose the basics of blockchain technology in data security, why blockchain in cybersecurity, how it ensures cybersecurity, its benefits, its innovative uses, and the future of cybersecurity in the online business platforms.

DOI: 10.4018/978-1-6684-5284-4.ch011

INTRODUCTION

The conventional economy has rejuvenated itself as a digital economy by incorporating the latest digital technology advancements in its business process. Its result transfer and so on. Hence the business houses have to understand deeply that now almost all the sectors such as manufacturing and services sectors have started to use the Information and Communication Technology (ICT) enabled digital gadgets into their business operations for designing, executing, supervising, and augmenting the business technologies have been supporting a lot to the business process, they are not free from data security issues such as cybercriminal and cyber attack, particularly in the operations by administering business and customers' data. Thus data has made a revolution in the recent business world, along with Internet technologies (Verma Mudit Kumar, 2020). Though the online business growing day-by-day, data security threats also have been growing along with the online business in various forms and distress the acuities of the way consumers are using online platforms for various purposes such as online purchasing, ticket booking, and money these threats will destroy their businesses which are operating on the online platform. Therefore the business houses need to take appropriate safety precautions to eliminate the data threats as possible as to increase consumers' self-confidence towards the online business, and thus it would be an option to maintain a tempo in online shopping (Liao and Fan, 2020). As these measures are used to secure the customer base, it is called cybersecurity, and it has been instituted to make sure the security of consumers' seclusion and data and thus it ensures a hassle-free shopping experience to the consumers. Hence there is a requirement for promoting cybersecurity measures at all levels of the online business to condense the impact of cybercrime and to promote the benefits connected with cybersecurity (Aboul-Enein, 2017).

Moreover Investing in cybersecurity has been increasing in recent times at all businesses to save customers' data. As far as the investment over cybersecurity has been concerned, it has been increased aggressively in the times of yore, with no sluggish. Further, it is also estimated that the business organizations planned to invest more than 1 trillion USD globally between 2017 and 2021 to protect their business houses and customers' data from online security threats (Morgan, 2019). Even though the business houses have invested a huge amount and efforts on cybersecurity, but still internet hackers prolong to assail business processes by hacking data and making the business units weak, interrupting data storage devices and their applications, and thus creating network errors or traffic. There was the worst experience in the past and they have insisted on the importance of developing cybersecurity systems. There were more than 4500 cyber assails have took place every day in the year 2016, and it is 300 percent more than the attacks that took place in 2015, while 1,000 assails were found approximately daily. In the case of Uber, around 60 million data of various drivers and riders have hacked in the year 2016. In the case of Facebook, about 5335 million users' details were hacked from 105 countries, of which 30 million users' records were from the USA, 11 million users from the UK, and 6.5 million were data from India (Holmes, 2021). Hacked data includes names, mobile numbers, user locations, birthdates, bios, and email addresses. Thus it is understood clearly that no industrial sectors are safe online, and hackers are continuously seeking new ways from new landscapes to the crook. CB Insights report has estimated that between 2017 and 2018 around 6 billion secret files were stolen one side. On the other side, the number of cyberattacks has also increased. These complicated attacks have collapsed the conventional data security methods, thus creating privacy challenges for business organizations. In the wake of the covid-19 outbreak, a large number of companies have insisted their employees work from home by connecting themselves with internet technology, and it is also created a new way of data threats to the company and employees (World Economic Forum, 2019). Therefore, instead of developing more potential tools, many business organizations have started to rethink the existing systems that formed these vulnerabilities in the primary place. As a result, there are technologies such as Artificial Intelligence (AI), Big-data analytics, Internet of things (IoT), and blockchain technology have been developed for strengthening the business process effectively, of which blockchain technology is one of the technologies that have played a major role and ensures smooth flow of the business process with adequate data security in the online business environment. Blockchain technology presents a diversified pathway towards better data and cybersecurity, one that is travelled a smaller amount and almost avoids the cybercriminals (Infosys, 2021). These moves trim down the susceptibility, present sturdy encryption, authenticate the ownership of the data and also assess the genuineness of the data. Still, this technology can reduce the requirement of some passwords, which are often making cybersecurity weak. The primary benefit of using blockchain in the business process is dispersed data ledger. A distributed communal key infrastructure model decreases numerous risks connected with the data stored in the centralized storage, by removing the most noticeable marks. Business transactions or dealings will be recording each node in the entire network, thus it ensures the data is secure and free from cyberattacks, hacking, data stealing, or meddling with data, unless the susceptibility exists at the platform level (Jamie Condliffe, 2016).

The combined consensus algorithm of the blockchain technology helps to remove the traditional data threats, by observing the malevolent activities, irregularities, and removing those problems by devoiding the requirement of the authority center. Thus this technology makes stronger the validation of the data and protects the data communications by maintaining a digital ledger. Even though blockchain technology holds various futuristic characteristics, it does not operate itself, and it is taking the support of cybersecurity technology called encryption (Mukundan, 2019). The dispersed data ledger can employ the public key platform to ensure data communication, by authenticating the devices, validating the changes in the configurations, and finding out secret devices in the IoT environment. Blockchain technology can protect various attached thermostats, security cameras, smart doorbells, and other susceptible technologies from side to side encryption and digital signatures. A report published by Palo Alto Networks reveals that 98 percent of the traffic of the IoT-enabled device was due to unencrypted and it paves a way for the cyberattack (Paloalto Networks, 2020). Thus blockchain technology act as a warhead against dispersed denial-of-service (DDoS) assails. Hence all the Industries irrespective of manufacturing or services require an excellent cybersecurity solution and depend on blockchain technology to distribute the goods and services without mistakes and fraud. Further, this technology also supports digitizing the business and customers' data. Hence all the industries, online business houses, in particular, are using this astonishing technology to make stronger their business processes by ensuring cybersecurity processes (Javaid, Haleem, Singh, Khan, & Suman, 2021).

This technology provides an essential as well as an effective platform to share the data securely, in relation to different financial, business transactions as well as contracts. In such process blockchain uses a technology called cryptography to transfer the data with utmost accuracy and safety. The data transfers happening in blockchains are just a transferring the assets and the assets are fundamentally data that may expose various personal as well as business data such as personal data, healthcare data, financial data or even companies data. One of the best applications of this technology is Bitcoin, where it has been using mostly for the secure transfer of bitcoins from one to another by executing the contract through blockchains. Further, this technology also used in smart contracts, for its safety. Etherium is a yet another application of blockchain, and it has been developed to execute smart contracts with predefined rules and regulations. Such type of smart contracts are having various application in different areas like Internet of Things (IoT), in which billions of devices need to function collectively, to build smart contracts for swapping data and carry out the process. Basically it is a peering technology without a centralised control of blockchains fundamentally deals with contracts and contracts involve data. Thus a huge volume of data will be collected, classified, processed, assessed and disseminated in different transactions. Since the data science technology is the heart of various business transactions, blockchain technology ensures a system to execute the transactions firmly (Thuraisingham, 2020). With this backdrop this present chapter will reveal about blockchain technology, its working structure, role of blockchain technology in data science and cybersecurity, how it ensures cybersecurity, blockchain technology and its benefits to cybersecurity, innovative uses of blockchain technology in cybersecurity, blockchain technology and future of cybersecurity subsequently. Finally this chapter concludes in the last part of the chapter.

WORKING STRUCTURE OF BLOCKCHAIN TECHNOLOGIES

Blockchain is a technology that works with group of blocks, which are linked with each other through chains. Each block will act as a file that restrains the data related to each transaction. Further the stored data can be transferred from one block to multiple blocks, in the same way one block also can collect the data from different blocks simultaneously. The data stored in the blocks will be permanent and irreversible. Thus the number of blocks can also be added to the chain depends upon the number of transactions, and each transaction will be verified to ensure the authenticity of the data. According to NIST technical publication, blocks can be used without permissions, it means anybody can use a block; on the other hand blocks can also be used with permissions, with the consent of centralized or decentralized authority (Kshetri, 2017). Thus in the blockchain there is an important component called cryptographic hash and it is playing major functions. Further it is a kind of data assimilates where multiple checks are calculated depends upon the content. It seems as one of the important component that ensures security for the blockchain. Notion of transaction is a yet another component of this technology that ensures the communication interface with two blocks or parties. Through this cryptocurrency transactions are passed between different users of this technology. This technology also uses asymmetric key method, as it is being an essential one in the public key cryptography. This blockchains also collects the network details which are derived from the communal key cryptography. The notion is considered as the central part of blockchain, as it is being a ledger of various transactions. Further these transactions are performed through a decentralized fashion, and hence this structural design supports blockchain as a distributed ledger. As the business transactions are performed, blocks will be added to the existing blockchain which have the data of authenticated business transactions and the metadata about those transactions. Each block will have the data, and the blocks are linked together to build the blockchain. Thus huge volume of relevant information available about the blockchains, it includes smart contracts and consensus model forks. With the help of these models, users can publish next block by showing the proof of completion of work. This model is also used in bitcoin transactions. In various cases blockchains required to do alteration and those alterations are called as forks (Casino, Dasaklis & Patsakis, 2019).

Blockchain is acting as a ledger of all the business transactions that have been performed, shared, and confirmed by various users in the blockchain system. Further, it is administered by a peer-to-peer network that is accountable for authenticating new-blocks and instituting inter-node communication. Whichever the changes need to do in the dataset in a blockchain will necessitate changes in all the consequent blocks in the chain, and it is making the assignment enormously as well as resource-extensive. Thus, blockchain technology is one of the most protected technologies for various types of business transactions, to date. The blockchain technology is a setup of linear association of blocks, in that such data is added sequentially on it. Thus the data is added to the chain by utilizing procedures that assist to evade faulty functioning of the system of blockchain. The requirement for unity protocol materialized from the thought of Hashcash, as a result of a poor working of cryptography methods like Elliptic Curve Digital Signature Algorithm (ECDSA) to alleviate the risks of dual expenditure and Sybil molests (Sankar, Sindhu & Sethumadhavan, 2017). Figure 1 explains the complete structure of stack of blockchain technology. This structure stack advocates how various layers of a blockchain work together with each other to get an operational blockchain.

Figure 1. Working structure of Blockchain Technology in the Data Security
Source: Mittal, Gupta, Chaturvedi, Chansarkar & Gupta (2021).

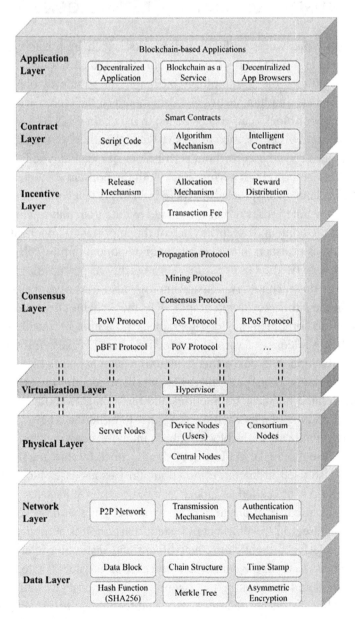

Homoliak et al., (2020) have proposed that the blockchain structure should contain seven layers right from Data layer, Network layer, Physical layer, Consensus layer, Incentive layer, Contract layer, and Application layer. Besides, they also have proposed the Virtualization layer to bridge the Physical layer to the Consensus layer. Yli-Huumo, Ko, Choi, Park, and Smolander (2016) revealed that in spite of the exposure of blockchain technology into different fields, the familiarity of the ordinary public about blockchain enabled systems has not highly developed, as research about it. Therefore, people must comprehend about blockchain technology and become skilled to promote the business applications to distribute their software applications and dealings across the network, and thus, afford enhanced cybersecurity to the developing cyber-infrastructure.

ROLE OF BLOCKCHAIN TECHNOLOGY

With the growth and development of internet technology, our entire life has been changed in all aspects. Computing systems have occupied the entire world, and it is spreading from mobile technology to autonomous vehicles. All these things are possible only because of the data and its related science. With the help of the data and its related science, it is easy to collect, accumulate, administer, and analyze a huge volume of data collected from various sensors and devices, with the help of IoT (Demirkan, Demirkan, & McKee, 2020). In this process, a huge number of self-functioning systems and devices are connected through internet technology and thereby synchronize their activities. Still, data security and solitude for the substantial number of data systems within the IoT have become a question mark. As, IoT collects huge volumes of assorted data from various sources with numerous devices, conventional data and cyber security methods such as encryption are not competent to safeguard the IoT and data systems. Hence to ensure efficient cybersecurity, more number of researches has been happening in recent times to examine the developments happening in data science for protecting such systems (Sarker, 2020). As a result, a new technology called blockchain has developed and it plays a major role as expected, in safeguarding data science and ensuring cybersecurity, and the same has been elucidated as follows;

In Data Science

Blockchain technology is an emerging one that ensures data safety and thus supports data science techniques also. It means this technology ensures the data collection in a highly secured environment, and it also helps to process the data, manage the data, analyze the data, and share the data in a secured manner. Yaga, Mell, Roby and Scarfone, (2018) mentioned in their work that data analysis is feasible in recent days due to blockchain technology, even from the basic individual devices. Furthermore, this technology also validated the data generated by it, in a planned and irreversible manner. Thus, blockchain technology ensures the genuineness of data, and thus improves big data. Tasnim, Omar, Rahman, Bhuiyan and Alam (2018) mentioned in his paper that blockchain is very much useful to data scientists to validate and verify the data at each block on a chain. As it is being immutable security, for this reason, it is treated as the main driver for its implementation. Further the decentralized ledger system available in blockchain shields data through manifold signatures, thus it helps to avoid data leaks and lacerates. As a result blockchain technology is ensuring and maintaining data security, and trust, helps to get better data quality, and firmly disseminates the data to the required parties. In several institutions, transaction or business trust is imposed by a centralized controlling authority; as a result, it is having the possibility to be a single point of the malfunctioning state. Where in the case of blockchain technology, it ensures the transactions trust in a decentralized manner, by utilizing a group of a system in the peer-to-peer network. In the same way, this technology also enables data sharing by enabling manifold parties to collect and disseminate the data firmly (Marr, 2018). This technology also helps to verify the reliability of the data at every transaction. The main component of blockchain technology called Distributed ledger is also playing a major role in deciding the derivation of the data, as it is an essential part of data science. The role of Blockchain technology in the supply chain is more significant as it is keep on tracking the data, and thus it is also helpful in the data supply chain process (Hamlen & Thuraisingham, 2013). This technology also invested a lot of effort in data science; especially in big data analytics for assessing private data, based on the hyper ledger framework (Lampropoulos, Georgakakos & Ioannidis, 2019). Data safety and solitude spread across all parts of data science and then converse with the help of blockchain with its decentralized system (Liu, Peng, Long, Wei, Liu, & Tian, 2020). Houben and Snyers (2018) have presented in their paper that blockchain-enabled cryptocurrencies will have transaction history and graphs to facilitate the public to access them. Thereby public can have detailed information about the impact of price on the underlying cryptocurrency. Further, a topological enabled data system helps to assess graph dimensions with the help of the data collected through blockchain, and it can be utilized to forecast the price structure of Bitcoin. Thuraisingham (2018) explained in their paper that blockchain technology ensures data safety and security in the whole data lifecycle process, right from data collection to data dissemination, and the same examined by (Thuraisingham, 2018) about different ways of combining cyber security process into the data science. The same data-driven approach has also suggested by (Thuraisingham et al, 2016).

In Cybersecurity

The ultimate objective of Blockchain technology is to ensure secured business transactions, especially in the case of the cryptocurrency business. As data security is at the forefront of this technology, it reached all the spheres of the business easily. With this backdrop, this section presents various applications of blockchain technology in cybersecurity (Zhuang, Zamir & Liang, 2020). There are four areas identified based on the blockchain-enabled security such as distributed ledger, IoT security, Domain Name System, and end-to-end encryption. As mentioned earlier, centralized data storage is not safe due to single point authorization, as it is having the possibility of massive errors. To replace the same issue, this technology uses the component called distributed ledger process, through this data can be managed in a decentralized manner and disseminated among numerous devices. With the help of distributed ledger architecture, blockchains enabled decentralized data storage, and also use Cryptographic checksums to make sure data security. The second area where this technology ensures security is IoT, as it is having association with numerous connected devices, and cybersecurity is a must for this case. Hence, blockchain technologies can be used to ensure secure data transfer between the systems and not have centralized control. Domain Name Systems (DNS) are typically functioning under a centralized controlling setup and it would be easy for the hackers to break the system and steal the data easily without complexity (Parizi, Dehghantanha, Azmoodeh & Choo, 2020). On the other hand blockchain technology facilitates distributed nature data storage, and it would be a challenge for the hackers to find out the place where the data is stored exactly, and it is more complicated to discover the point of entry. Thus the data can be safe and without any manipulation. In recent times all the applications are using more number of messaging services, for the same they are using the end-to-end encryption, to ensure secured data transfer. For the same, this end-to-end encryption system is started to use blockchain technology (Bansal, Panchal, Bassi, & Kumar, 2020). Where this technology enables a homogeneous way of communication in messaging systems, by utilizing distributed processing. Thus, there are researchers have discussed a lot of the uses of blockchain for security. Demirkan, Demirkan, and McKee (2020) presented in their work that blockchains technology has the potential to enhance the cybersecurity, and thus it acts as the safest platform to avoid deceitful activities through various consent mechanisms, and it also notices data corruption depending on its fundamental characteristics of functional resilience, data encryption, review, clearness, and immutability. Further, this technology also enhances security by removing human beings in the validation process, condensing the attacks happening through distributed denial of service (DDoS), affording data identifiably, and supporting scattered storage. Such parallel applications have also discussed in various research works including (Goldstein, 2020) where the author explained the extent to which blockchain technology improves cybersecurity, data privacy, and veracity are provided.

HOW THE BLOCKCHAIN TECHNOLOGY DOES ENSURES CYBERSECURITY

Blockchain Technology incorporates a system called decentralized distributed ledger on which business and other related transactions' data would be recorded with the help of diversified computer networks. The specialty of this technology is any type of data that can be stored on the blockchain, irrespective of the industries. This technology further assures absolute security against data breaches, cyber assails, and identifying potential data thefts. This technology also ensures that all our business transactions with fully protected and shielded from unlawful data access. With data hacking occurrences and this process reaching more concentrated and modernized over the years, and thus it moved the online business world securely and it had become a genuine concern. The conditions of the individual and business houses data security have become and no proper resolution was found until the arrival of blockchain technology in the cybersecurity field (Horbenko, 2017). Thus the application of blockchain technology in the industrial sectors has transformed various industries such as the IT industry, health sector, online business and banking, and financial sector from an unsecured zone to a well secure zone. Business experts from various industries state that this technology offers unconquerable safety from unlawful access of the customer and business data and avoid cyber-assail. Thus this technology can be used to keep the business process in the protected environment and thereby it enhances cybersecurity almost in all industries (IBM, 2021). The application of blockchain technology in business processes helps to deal with data in the protected environment by ensuring a scatter form of data storage. This method of data management helps individuals and business people to safeguard themselves from data threats, and it avoids hackers from the manipulation of the data storage. On the other side companies which are providing storage services are also evaluating the capability of blockchain technology in protecting data from hackers (Cloudtweaks, 2019). Thus this technology offers a secured environment for doing business in the following manner;

Ensures the Safety of the Private Messages

Due to the ICT developments, the usage of social media has popularized among the public, and the number of social and digital media platforms have also been increasing day by day, and the number of social media applications is also developed every day. Its a result online business is getting popular among the public. A huge volume of metadata would be collected during these transactions. Thereby it shields business accounts, transactions, and customers' data which have been used in social media. Many of the messaging companies have now started to use this technology than end-to-end encryption as it is being the best option for the collection of genuine data. Further, this technology also enables the security protocol consistently and it can be used to create a single Application Programming Interface (API) architecture to serve better communication capabilities among various messengers. It was experienced that numerous attacks have taken place recently against various social media platforms such as Facebook, Twitter, and Instagram. Crores of accounts were hacked as a result of these cyberattacks, as the users' data were into the erroneous points. These kinds of cyberattacks can be avoided easily if the social media platforms deployed this technology in their messaging systems, and it will also help these sectors to shun cyberattacks in the future (Arnold, 2019).

Ensuring the Safety of the Internet of Things

Due to the introduction of various edge devices like routing switches, Integrated Access Devices (IADs), thermostats, metropolitan area network (MAN), and routers, these are some of the devices used by the hackers progressively to access the data anonymously from a large number of networks. Increasing usage of AI and its enabling technologies make the hackers easy to get access to residence automation systems through these edge devices such as smart televisions, and smart switches. In many cases, the IoT-enabled gadgets are insecure, at this juncture, blockchain-enabled technologies can be an effective alternative to manage more systems, and thereby it secures those systems (Arnold, 2019). Thus this method will be helping to leverage the ability of the gadgets and make them do judge the security position of the systems. This technology also supports perceiving and reacting to various commands rose from the unidentified networks without depending upon the centralized systems; thereby it saves the edge devices from cyberattacks. As this technology deals with decentralized systems, it will make the hackers lose their control over the systems. Thus blockchain technology is operating with decentralized systems; it avoids cyberattacks and data threats and saves the entire network (Yatsenko and Sotnichek, 2021).

Protection From Domain Name System

In some cases, the users will be denied to access the resources from the target resource enters such as servers, networks, and websites when they have a DDoS attack, as a result, the system would be shutting down or slowing down. Another resource center called Domain Name System (DNS) would be monitored through a centralized system, however, it is having higher possibilities for hacking the sites, as it is monitored by the centralized system, and it is being a perfect place for the hackers to control the linkage between a website address and an IP address (Surajdeep Singh, 2021). This kind of assails will turn the websites into out of order, cashable, and even redirectable to various bogus websites. Fortunately, blockchain technology will avoid such issues by the distributed DNS entries, and it may also be used to diminish such assails in the future. Thus this technology would be removing the feeble points of the areas demoralized by hackers by distributed systems solutions (Sheikh, 2019).

Decentralization of Storage

Data contravene and thefts are common nowadays in the place of work, however it is a mounting issue for the business houses, as they are still using an integrated storage system. The integrated data storage system makes the hackers' job so easy, as they require only one vulnerable point to enter into the storage system and exploit the data easily (Underwood, 2016). Thus an illicit can get access to an organization's confidential and sensitive data, such as firms' financial records, customer databases, diplomacy, and another database. Hence the blockchain experts suggest using a blockchain-enabled decentralized data storage system, thereby the sensitive data can be stored and maintained without cyberattack or hacking threats. By this setup, the hacker will be finding it difficult to break the data storage systems and hack the data. Thus cloud storage service providers are started to use this blockchain technology to keep the data safe from cyberattacks (Arnold, 2019)

Helps to Verify the Cyber-Physical Infrastructure

The reliability of the data generated by the cyber-physical systems would be damaged by various factors such as corruption of data, wrong configuration of the systems, failure of the components, and so on. However, these problems can be rectified or avoided by incorporating blockchain technology into cyber-physical systems to generate reliable data. This technology ensures data integrity and authentication, and it can be used to authenticate the significance of various cyber-physical systems and their infrastructure. Thus the data developed by blockchain technology based on the components of the cyber-physical infrastructure would be more supportive to the whole chain of protection (Infosecurity magazine.com, 2018).

Enhances Data Diffusion Security

Blockchain technology would be used across various sectors in the future to limit unauthorized access to data while transiting the data. As a result, the transmission of Data can be shielded by incorporating this technology's widespread encryption technique to avert dreadful users from getting access to it, and the users may be organizations or individuals. This technique thus enhances the overall fidelity and veracity of data transmitted through blockchain technology. It also challenges the hackers having the intention to interrupt, change and erase the data transiting through this technology (Andrew, 2019).

BENEFITS OF ADOPTING BLOCKCHAIN IN CYBERSECURITY

A blockchain-enabled security structure will be performing in a decentralized environment, and it never compromises its operations and thus it is being a challenge for the hackers and the cyberattacks. This technology helps a lot across the sectors and users, especially for the internet users, it is offering huge benefits. Like that this technology offers various benefits in various ways, of which some of the benefits have been presented in the following manner;

It Ensures the Security of the Data Storage

Once the data has entered into blockchain it cannot be either changed or altered. If in case of any changes made in the data set on the blocks it would reveal the same transparently, as this technology has the feature of non-erasable, irreversible, and unchangeable. As a result, the saved data on the blockchain would be safe and sound than data maintained on conventional physical or digital records (Shrestha, Vassileva, & Deters, 2020).

Helps to Transfers the Data Securely

This emerging blockchain technology enables the users to accomplish the swift and secure data transit of various business and personal data such as banking and financial transactions, customer database, and information. It also supports executing Smart contracts by allowing the data safely and facilitating to implementation of the agreements among numerous parties automatically with cent percent data security (Sam Ingalls, 2021).

Minimize the Chances of Process Failure

As blockchain technology uses a decentralized storage system, it does not require permission for storing, and hence it is more flexible in its operations than the traditional system. Since it is using a decentralized storage system, its performance or safety will not be damaged even if a single node of the chain is compromised. It means though the storage system is subjected to cyberattacks, DDoS attacks, and hacking the system will prolong its performance usually without any data and speed loss, as it is having a huge number of copies in the data ledger (Shrimali, & Patel, 2021).

Augmenting Accuracy and Traceability of Data

Usually, all the business transactions will be stored in the blockchain with digitally encrypted technology along with time-stamped, and thus it keeps on recording the transactions as per the time it has collected. As a result, it records each and every transaction in different nodes. Thereby it helps network members to track various business, financial, personal transactions without any confusion along with the activity record. This way of data dealing ability aids business people to distribute the assets properly without any discrepancies, and all these benefits are possible only because of blockchain technology.

Protect Users' Privacy

Blockchain also supports a lot to increase users' privacy by employing public-key cryptography technology in its process. In that way, it authenticates the privacy of users' data, thus it also ensures the data secrecy of the users. Based on this privacy model some of the blockchain-based companies apply this technology in their business operations to move forward safely by leveraging its data privacy. One more advantage of this technology called Keyless Signature Infrastructure (KSI) enables the users to ensure the legality of their signs without using their keys (Shrimali, & Patel, 2021).

INNOVATIVE USES OF BLOCKCHAIN TECHNOLOGY

The growth and development of ICTs induce people to use internet technologies in all spheres of life and technologies keep on updating themselves on par with the developments in the ICTs. Thus the ICT-enabled technologies have changed the business landscape into more data-oriented. As a result all the industries now started to concentrate on various data such as business and customers. As the business houses need to forecast their business trend and customer base for the sustainability of the business (Business Insider Intelligence, 2020). Hence irrespective of the type of industries all the industries started to collect and use different types of data. Though the data have been collected and stored in a safe environment, they are not free from the threats such as cyberattacks, hackers, and so on. Millions of hackers are available throughout the world to steal business and customer data or try to corrupt the data. This is a great challenge to industries and business houses to safeguard the data and employ different technologies for the same, but they have attacked easily. At this juncture, blockchain technology has developed and started to deploy in business operations to safeguard the database (Sam Daley, 2021). Thus the technology served effectively for the purpose it has developed. This technology is also having a versatile application capable and providing more constructive and useful to the future of Internet technologies, helping users to secure the data from cyber threats. The groundbreaking application of blockchain technology has already been explored a lot in various fields such as banking and finance, online business, e-governance of government, further than bitcoin, cryptocurrency, and it thus has enhanced cybersecurity against cyber threats and hacking. Any industry can safeguard its data with the help of blockchain technology, as it is operating with precise encryption technology and well-established data circulation protocols. Thus this technology ensures data safety from various cyberattacks, and thus it keeps the data remain securely intact away from hackers (Ryo Takahashi, 2017). Thus blockchain technology has a striving feature in cybersecurity, and it may be implemented in the business houses for making numerous benefits to the business and customers.

BLOCKCHAIN AND THE FEATURE OF CYBERSECURITY

Cybersecurity is a major concern of all businesses nowadays and all industries have started to invest more in cybersecurity-related technologies. This tension has reduced now due to the arrival of blockchain technology. As this technology saves the data into different blocks from time to time, it is hard for hackers to attack the specific point. Moreover, this technology uses a decentralized data storage system, and thereby it saves the data in different blocks. By this means, even if the hackers try to attack the storage they have to get access to thousands of nodes, on a similar system (Neeraj, 2021). Even if we do any changes to the data stored in a block will consequence in the whole system will get alert of the same. Hacking or attacking a blockchain-based data system is equal to larcening hundreds of banks all at a time and makes sure that no alarm should be triggered while doing the same. This technology also helps to build a unanimity system and thereby it trims down deceptions and data corruptions by inculcating fresh blocks along with the various security features such as verifying and validating the data by the digital signature, recording the data from time to time with time-stamped, and connected the data to the preceding blocks, and compared the same with remaining blocks (Alex, 2019). Thus the blockchain would be a sound technology in the future for cybersecurity, and it can be possible through utilizing the available resources optimally and understanding this technology deeply. Further, this technology also trims down human involvement in the cybersecurity process, thereby it eliminates possible human error from the process, and thus it reduces the possibility of data violations as much as possible. However, there are chances for human error in the process, due to carelessness, and descends of operations will be the major threats to the data security in near future and it cannot solve these issues completely by the blockchains overnight. Hence, industries need to understand clearly about the blockchain and use it in their business operations appropriately to avoid cyberattacks in the future (Bansal, Panchal, Bassi, and Kumar, 2020).

CONCLUSION

For various reasons Blockchain technology has been used across industries, and it supports to avert cyber threats and attacks, data violence, individual data theft, and ensures the collected data is confidential and safe. As this technology is in the beginning phase, the developers need to build its advanced versions to manage the business operations and data in an enhanced manner. This technology can also supervise and forecast the cyberattacks with the help of AI and alarming the inward cyberattacks and threats, and thereby it helps the business and other organizations to minimize the cost incurred for data security and keep the data in a safe environment. Though blockchain technology ensures cybersecurity, it is not providing the solution for the global security requirements; however, it is an imperative tool for developing next-generation security systems. This technology also helps to build a reliable security system, well-designed storage system for recording business events, and it would be more helpful for various functions such as signing and tracking documents, individual data management, and tracking access. Further, this technology also empowers the data sharing process across the company and outside of the companies by establishing secured networks with no individual control over its process, but anybody can authenticate and validate it. Since millions of people use internet technologies globally, online-based business platforms have been growing every day. Since online-based businesses are more data-driven, millions of data have been generated every day from every business. On the other side, the number and type of hackers are also growing and they tried to attack, hack or corrupt that data sources. In many of the cases, hackers had already attacked social media such as Facebook and Twitter and hacked crores of users' data. All these issues have been rectified now with blockchain technology. As this technology has versatile and unbelievable safety features, it would be more useful for the Internet and internet-based businesses in the future, by establishing safety environment for the users and their data. The groundbreaking application of blockchain technology becoming an element of various business fields already beyond bitcoin business, cryptocurrencies and can also be used to boost cybersecurity further in the future. Thus any industry can ensure the cybersecurity environment comfortably and keep the business and users' data safely by deploying the blockchain technology into their business operations. Thus hack free and cyberattack-free business environment can be established for the smooth conduct of the business.

REFERENCES

Aboul-Enein, S. (2017). Cybersecurity challenges in the Middle East. *GCSP*, *17*, 5–49.

Arnold, A. (2019). Promising use cases of blockchain in cybersecurity. Forbes.

Bansal, P., Panchal, R., Bassi, S., & Kumar, A. (2020, April). Blockchain for cybersecurity: A comprehensive survey. In *2020 IEEE 9th International Conference on Communication Systems and Network Technologies (CSNT)* (pp. 260-265). IEEE. 10.1109/CSNT48778.2020.9115738

Benjamin, N. (2021, July 23). *Is Blockchain the Ultimate Cybersecurity Solution for My Applications?* https://www.isaca.org/resources/news-and-trends/isaca-now-blog/2021/is-blockchain-the-ultimate-cybersecurity-solution-for-my-applications

Business Insider Intelligence. (2020, March 2). *The growing list of applications and use cases of blockchain technology in business and life.* https://www.businessinsider.in/finance/news/the-growing-list-of-applications-and-use-cases-of-blockchain-technology-in-business-and-life/articleshow/74447275.cms

Casino, F., Dasaklis, T. K., & Patsakis, C. (2019). A systematic literature review of blockchain-based applications: Current status, classification and open issues. *Telematics and Informatics, 36,* 55–81. doi:10.1016/j.tele.2018.11.006

Cloudtweaks.com. (2019, February 26). *How Blockchain Is Transforming Cyber Security.* https://cloudtweaks.com/2019/04/how-blockchain-is-transforming-cyber-security/

Condliffe, J. (2016, July 28). *Massive Internet Outage Could Be a Sign of Things to Come.* https://www.technologyreview.com/2016/10/21/156505/massive-internet-outage-could-be-a-sign-of-things-to-come/

Daley, S. (2021, March 31). *30 Blockchain Applications and Real-World Use Cases Disrupting the Status Quo.* https://builtin.com/blockchain/blockchain-applications

Demirkan, S., Demirkan, I., & McKee, A. (2020). Blockchain technology in the future of business cyber security and accounting. *Journal of Management Analytics, 7*(2), 189–208. doi:10.1080/23270012.2020.1731721

Demirkan, S., Demirkan, I., & McKee, A. (2020). Blockchain technology in the future of business cyber security and accounting. *Journal of Management Analytics, 7*(2), 189–208. doi:10.1080/23270012.2020.1731721

Goldstein, K. (2020). Blockchain and Distributed Ledger Technology: Insurance Applications, Legal Developments, and Cybersecurity Considerations. *Conn. Ins. LJ, 27,* 511.

Hamlen, K. W., & Thuraisingham, B. (2013). Data security services, solutions and standards for outsourcing. *Computer Standards & Interfaces, 35*(1), 1–5. doi:10.1016/j.csi.2012.02.001

Holmes, A. (2021). *533 million Facebook users' phone numbers and personal data have been leaked online.* https://www.Businessinsider.com/stolen-data-of-533-million-facebook-users-leaked-online-2021-4

Homoliak, I., Venugopalan, S., Reijsbergen, D., Hum, Q., Schumi, R., & Szalachowski, P. (2020). The security reference architecture for blockchains: Toward a standardized model for studying vulnerabilities, threats, and defenses. *IEEE Communications Surveys and Tutorials, 23*(1), 341–390. doi:10.1109/COMST.2020.3033665

Horbenko, Y. (2017). *Using Blockchain Technology to Boost Cyber Security.* Retrieved from Steel Wiki: https://steelkiwi.com/blog/using-blockchain-technology-to-boost-cybersecurity

Houben, R., & Snyers, A. (2018). *Cryptocurrencies and blockchain: Legal context and implications for financial crime, money laundering and tax evasion.* https://www.europarl.europa.eu/cmsdata/150761/TAX3%20Study%20on%20cryptocurrencies%20and%20blockchain.pdf

IBM. (2021, August 16). *What is blockchain security?* https://www.ibm.com/in-en/topics/blockchain-security

Infosecurity magazine.com. (2018, August 7). *How Blockchain Is Revolutionizing Cybersecurity.* https://www.infosecurity-magazine.com/next-geninfosec/blockchain-cybersecurity

Infosys. (2021, July 29). *Assuring Digital-trust.* https://www.infosys.com/services/cyber-security/insights/assuring-digital-trust-cybersecurity.html

Ingalls, S. (2021, July 28). *The State of Blockchain Applications in Cybersecurity.* https://www.esecurityplanet.com/applications/cybersecurity-blockchain-applications/

Javaid, M., Haleem, A., Singh, R. P., Khan, S., & Suman, R. (2021). Blockchain technology applications for Industry 4.0: A literature-based review. *Blockchain: Research and Applications, 100027.*

Kshetri, N. (2017). Blockchain's roles in strengthening cybersecurity and protecting privacy. *Telecommunications Policy, 41*(10), 1027–1038. doi:10.1016/j.telpol.2017.09.003

Lampropoulos, K., Georgakakos, G., & Ioannidis, S. (2019, September). Using blockchains to enable big data analysis of private information. In *2019 IEEE 24th International Workshop on Computer Aided Modeling and Design of Communication Links and Networks (CAMAD)* (pp. 1-6). 10.1109/CAMAD.2019.8858468

Lampropoulos, K., Georgakakos, G., & Ioannidis, S. (2019, September). Using blockchains to enable big data analysis of private information. In *2019 IEEE 24th International Workshop on Computer Aided Modeling and Design of Communication Links and Networks (CAMAD)* (pp. 1-6). IEEE. 10.1109/CAMAD.2019.8858468

Liao, R., & Fan, Z. (2020, April). Supply chains have been upended. Here's how to make them more resilient. In *World Economic Forum* (Vol. 6). Academic Press.

Liu, J., Peng, S., Long, C., Wei, L., Liu, Y., & Tian, Z. (2020, March). Blockchain for data science. In *Proceedings of the 2020 The 2nd International Conference on Blockchain Technology* (pp. 24-28). 10.1145/3390566.3391681

Liu, J., Peng, S., Long, C., Wei, L., Liu, Y., & Tian, Z. (2020, March). Blockchain for data science. In *Proceedings of the 2020 The 2nd International Conference on Blockchain Technology* (pp. 24-28). 10.1145/3390566.3391681

Marr, B. (2018). How is AI used in education--Real world examples of today and a peek into the future? *Forbes Magazine*, 25.

Mathew. (2019). Cyber Security through Blockchain Technology. *International Journal of Engineering and Advanced Technology, 9*(1).

Morgan, S. (2019). Global cybersecurity spending predicted to exceed $1 trillion from 2017-2021. *Cybercrime Magazine, 10.*

Networks, P. (2020, August 6). *2020 Unit 42 IoT Threat Report.* https://unit42.paloaltonetworks.com/iot-threat-report-2020/

Ocampos. (2020). *Contribution of Blockchain to Cybersecurity.* Blockchain Land.

Parizi, R. M., Dehghantanha, A., Azmoodeh, A., & Choo, K. K. R. (2020). Blockchain in cybersecurity realm: An overview. *Blockchain Cybersecurity, Trust and Privacy*, 1-5.

Sankar, L. S., Sindhu, M., & Sethumadhavan, M. (2017, January). Survey of consensus protocols on blockchain applications. In *2017 4th international conference on advanced computing and communication systems (ICACCS)* (pp. 1-5). IEEE. 10.1109/ICACCS.2017.8014672

Sarker, I. H., Kayes, A. S. M., Badsha, S., Alqahtani, H., Watters, P., & Ng, A. (2020). Cybersecurity data science: An overview from machine learning perspective. *Journal of Big Data*, 7(1), 1–29. doi:10.118640537-020-00318-5

Sheikh, A., Kamuni, V., Urooj, A., Wagh, S., Singh, N., & Patel, D. (2019). Secured energy trading using byzantine-based blockchain consensus. *IEEE Access: Practical Innovations, Open Solutions*, 8, 8554–8571. doi:10.1109/ACCESS.2019.2963325

Shrestha, A. K., Vassileva, J., & Deters, R. (2020). A blockchain platform for user data sharing ensuring user control and incentives. *Frontiers in Blockchain, 48.*

Shrimali, B., & Patel, H. B. (2021). Blockchain state-of-the-art: architecture, use cases, consensus, challenges and opportunities. *Journal of King Saud University-Computer and Information Sciences.*

Singh, S. (2021, July 16). *Potential Use Cases of Blockchain Technology for Cybersecurity.* https://www.itbusinessedge.com/security/potential-use-cases-of-blockchain-technology-for-cybersecurity/

Takahashi, R. (2017, August 7). *How can creative industries benefit from blockchain?* https://www.mckinsey.com/industries/technology-media-and-telecommunications/our-insights/how-can-creative-industries-benefit-from-blockchain

Tasnim, M. A., Omar, A. A., Rahman, M. S., Bhuiyan, M., & Alam, Z. (2018, December). Crab: Blockchain based criminal record management system. In *International conference on security, privacy and anonymity in computation, communication and storage* (pp. 294-303). Springer.

Thuraisingham, B. (2020, October). Blockchain Technologies and Their Applications in Data Science and Cyber Security. In *2020 3rd International Conference on Smart BlockChain (SmartBlock)* (pp. 1-4). IEEE. 10.1109/SmartBlock52591.2020.00008

Thuraisingham, B., Kantarcioglu, M., Bertino, E., Bakdash, J. Z., & Fernandez, M. (2018, June). Towards a privacy-aware quantified self data management framework. In *Proceedings of the 23nd ACM on Symposium on Access Control Models and Technologies* (pp. 173-184). 10.1145/3205977.3205997

Thuraisingham, B., Kantarcioglu, M., Hamlen, K., Khan, L., Finin, T., Joshi, A., . . . Bertino, E. (2016, July). A data driven approach for the science of cyber security: Challenges and directions. In *2016 IEEE 17th International Conference on Information Reuse and Integration (IRI)* (pp. 1-10). IEEE.

Thuraisingham, B., Kantarcioglu, M., Hamlen, K., Khan, L., Finin, T., Joshi, A., . . . Bertino, E. (2016, July). A data driven approach for the science of cyber security: Challenges and directions. In *2016 IEEE 17th International Conference on Information Reuse and Integration (IRI)* (pp. 1-10). IEEE.

Underwood, S. (2016). Blockchain beyond bitcoin. *Communications of the ACM*, 59(11), 15–17. doi:10.1145/2994581

Verma, M. (2018). Artificial intelligence and its scope in different areas with special reference to the field of education. *Online Submission*, *3*(1), 5–10.

Vijayaraj, M. (2019). *Rethinking Security in IT by Incorporating Blockchain Technology*. https://www. relevance.com/rethinking-security-in-it-by-incorporating-blockchain-technology/

World Economic Forum. (2019). *World Economic Forum Annual Meeting 2019*. Davos: World Economic Forum.

Yaga, D., Mell, P., Roby, N., & Scarfone, K. (2019). *Blockchain technology overview*. arXiv preprint arXiv:1906.11078.

Yatsen, M., & Sotnichek, M. (2021, February 4). *Blockchain for Cybersecurity: Pros and Cons, Trending Use Cases*. https://www.apriorit.com/dev-blog/462-blockchain-cybersecurity-pros-cons

Yli-Huumo, J., Ko, D., Choi, S., Park, S., & Smolander, K. (2016). Where is current research on blockchain technology? A systematic review. *PLoS One*, *11*(10), e0163477. doi:10.1371/journal.pone.0163477 PMID:27695049

Zhuang, P., Zamir, T., & Liang, H. (2020). Blockchain for cybersecurity in smart grid: A comprehensive survey. *IEEE Transactions on Industrial Informatics*, *17*(1), 3–19. doi:10.1109/TII.2020.2998479

Chapter 12
Impact of Deepfake Technology on FinTech Applications

Naveed Naeem Abbas
National University of Sciences and Technology, Islamabad, Pakistan

Rizwan Ahmad
iD https://orcid.org/0000-0002-4758-7895
National University of Sciences and Technology, Islamabad, Pakistan

Shams Qazi
National University of Sciences and Technology, Islamabad, Pakistan

Waqas Ahmed
Pakistan Institute of Engineering and Applied Sciences, Islamabad, Pakistan

ABSTRACT

The distribution of fabricated disinformation through deliberate manipulation of audio/video content by imposters with the intent to affect organization is deepfake. The "infodemic" that spread alongside the COVID-19 pandemic also increased cyber risk in financial technology (FinTech) applications. The continuous evolution of cybercrime has culminated with deepfakes which severely magnify the threats of traditional frauds. Recent evidence indicates that deepfake videos are mainly created with the help of artificial intelligence (AI) or machine learning (ML) techniques. This results in creation of fake videos by merging, superimposing, and replacing actual video clips and images with other videos. There are a lot of people who accept deepfake videos as actual videos without any doubt. The use of AL and ML techniques have made video/image forgery difficult to identify with the help of existing deepfake detection techniques. Deepfake technology is becoming more and more sophisticated, and detection of fake videos is relatively challenged for quite some time.

DOI: 10.4018/978-1-6684-5284-4.ch012

INTRODUCTION

The term deepfake is derived from two words 'deep learning' and 'fake'. The deepfake was introduced in the year 2017 in the Reddit community discussion when a user posted a digitally altered video clip of a celebrity (Jones & Capstone, 2020). Since its inception, deepfake videos have been created by artificial intelligence (AI) or various machine learning (ML) techniques that look authentic. Deepfake content is generally produced using two different ML techniques: autoencoder and Generative Adversarial Networks (GANs). Artificial Neural Networks (ANNs) mimic the human brain in learning and recognizing patterns with the concept that the more real image samples that are fed into a dataset, the more accurate it can be replicated as a fake sample. A conventional GANs model comprises of two neural networks, a generator, and a discriminator. The generator is a convolutional neural network (CNN) that produces synthetic images creating fake videos from the original dataset. The discriminator is simply a classifier that tries to distinguish real data from the data created by the generator and attempts to analyze and distinguish the deepfake video from the real to synthesize for authenticity. The cycle continues with the two ML algorithms, with the generator network continuing to create fake videos until the discriminator network no longer can detect and authenticate the video forgery. With the increase of deepfake technology and easy-to-use sophisticated open-source applications in the market, individuals can manipulate images and videos by superimposing someone's face, mimicking facial expressions, and synthesizing their speech. In the start, it took days and required considerable knowledge and skills to create deepfake content, but now it is a matter of hours to create deepfake with extensively accessible free online applications (Zhao et al., 2021). It is practically impossible for a human to differentiate between genuine and forged content (Westerlund, 2019).

Additionally, cybercriminals have taken advantage of the technology to misinform and defraud businesses and individuals. As a countermeasure, FinTech was adopted, the term ''FinTech'' is a combination of ''financial technology'' and was first mentioned in the 1990s by Citicorp's chairman John Reed (Puschmann, 2017). It contains innovative financial solutions enabled by IT and includes the incumbent financial services providers like banks and insurers. Regardless, both audio and video deepfake can manifest multiple issues within financial services. There are many cases of fraudulent onboarding (criminal posing as someone else), fraudulent payment authorizations and transfers, synthetic identity, impersonation of business leaders for insider trading tricking employees into taking nefarious actions. Such as: -

1. Corporate Level Fraud

Corporate fraud refers to illegal activities undertaken by an individual or company that are done in a dishonest or unethical manner. Recently the most common method to implement corporate-level fraud is deepfake. As in the past, fraudsters try to convince an enterprise worker to send money via a fake email account, now they convince them through a fake call where the caller sounds like the CFO or CEO of the enterprise.

2. Extorting Money From Businesses or Individuals

Another method of fraudsters is, faces and voices transferred to media files with the help of deep learning that shows people making false statements (Khan et al., 2021). An attacker makes a video of a CEO making fake announcements and tries to blackmail an organization by threatening to post the video on social media (Weerawardana & Fernando, 2021).

3. False Information

Fake news or false information is used by attackers to mislead the public, misguide social activities, and disrupt business (Vaccari & Chadwick, 2020). Deepfake videos that describe the events or show the people doing things and saying, they never did, and can cause uncertainty. The fake news sector is already making an effort to do this (Qayyum et al., 2019). Other possible exploits in the financial sector through deepfake technology are:

- False allegations of malfeasance for the purpose of damaging the organization's reputation.
- Video backed HR complaints about a co-worker.
- Insurance fraud, supported by video proof.
- False news/information about the organizational CEO.
- Onboarding procedures were manipulated, and fake accounts were made.
- Identity theft through phishing attacks by using deepfake video to convince the worker to alter critical personal data.
- The distraction of shipments.
- Orders for unnecessary materials.
- Illegal funds transfer fraudulently authorized.

In summarizing, deepfake also be used to facilitate money laundering by enabling fraudsters to open bank accounts under false identities. Deepfakes could ruin an organization's reputation, trust, and undermine the confidence of customers, shareholders, and stakeholders in its capacity to secure their data and resources. Finally, all capital markets could be impacted by the unethical use of deepfakes (Bateman, 2020). On the other hand, deepfake technology can also be used in positive applications, like voice assistant technologies such as Window's Cortana and Apple's Siri (Neethirajan, 2021). It helps to recreate classic scenes in films and allows the use of special effects and face editing, it is also being used for dubbing voices in movies in different languages. Deepfake technology is also popular in the game industry to enhance the online interaction between players. The e-commerce industry might also see future advantages in using deepfake. According to researchers, the education department could also gain from deepfake technology by automating the process of producing educational content (Buo, 2020).

The rest of the chapter is structured as follows. Section 2 discusses the literature review. Section 3, and Section 4 present the techniques used for creating and detecting the deepfake. Section 5 contains the recommendations for countering and preventing the deepfake content. In the end, Section 6 concludes.

LITERATURE REVIEW

The rise of deepfake technology has become a major cybersecurity threat to our society and many businesses (Muna, 2020) (Atif et al., 2019). Cybercriminals have been targeting businesses through social engineering attacks for years using forms of malware, spamware, and launching various phishing campaigns to manipulate individuals by exposing confidential information and exploiting weaknesses

(Naeem et al., 2020) (H. Lin, 2019). The Trend Micro Security Predictions for 2020 report indicates that "deepfakes will be the next frontier for enterprise fraud" (Micro Research, 2020). Recently, the Federal Bureau of Information (FBI) warned about deepfake fraud being used to facilitate financial crime, called Business Identity Compromise (BIC). In a BIC different deepfake tools and techniques are deployed to create "synthetic corporate personas" that cause very significant financial and reputational impacts to victim organizations and businesses.

1. Classification of Deepfake Threat to Business

The deepfake threats can be classified into three main categories as shown in Figure 1. Further to this, the area is also classified as broadcast or narrowcast (Bateman, 2020). Where broadcast is designed for mass targets and disseminated through public social media channels, and narrowcast is designed for small individual targets and delivered through private channels.

a. Deepfake Vishing

Audio-based deepfake attacks are used to imitate high-level individuals over the phone for illegal financial transactions. In recent years, Symantec cyber security experts have reported three different cases of deepfakes vishing being deployed to steal millions from private organizations by imitating the voice of the Chief Executive Officer (CEO) (Huang et al., 2019). CEO fraud is not new in the market, but the use of machine learning-based voice manipulation software is a significant threat to business, with experts warning that the damage may not be limited to extorting cash only (Hartmann & Giles, 2020).

In the first known fraud case in 2019, attackers used AI to impersonate the voice of the CEO of a German parent company to scam $243,000 (Buo, 2020). Later in 2019, deepfake attackers were able to simulate the voice of a United Kingdom-based energy company's CEO to rip off nearly a quarter of a million dollars (Jones & Capstone, 2020). Recently in the United Arab Emirates, black hat hackers by using AI created a voice simulation of a prominent bank's CEO with a combination of emails to convince for illegal transactions of $35 million (Buo, 2020).

b. Fabricated Remarks

Deepfake video clips are manipulated to falsely depict a public figure making incriminating remarks (Ternovski et al., 2021). One of the most prominent deepfake videos that gained widespread attention in April 2018 was created by Buzzfeed CEO Jonah Peretti and actor/comedian Joran Peele depicting Barack Obama's misbehave to Donald Trump (Jones & Capstone, 2020). The purpose of the video clip was to make a warning about the dangers of deepfake technology and how easy it is to manipulate video content to spread misinformation. From 2015 to 2017, Israeli con artists pretended to be the French foreign minister over the skype to scam targets for an estimated $90 million stating, that it was used for secret operations and to pay a ransom for the release of Middle Eastern hostages. The con men created a replica of the foreign minister's office and hired makeup experts to disguise them to successfully extort money. According to the Daily Beast, in 2019, a woman from California was scammed out of about $300,000 after being led on by manipulated clips (Justin Rohrlich, 2020).

c. Synthetic Social Botnets

Social media contents can be fabricated from synthetic text and photographs aided by AI. This can lead to a range of financial harm to markets, regulators, and companies. In the future, with the improvements in AI, social botnets can become a bigger threat to society.

Table 1 lists the types of frauds and their corresponding financial harms these deepfake techniques cause. The US annually suffers $1.4 to $3.5 trillion worth of losses due to deepfake technology (Piper & Metcalfe, 2020). Many more cybercrimes might be using deepfake, but not all of them seem to be reported since victims might be embarrassed about being scammed.

2. Deepfake Literature Analysis

The study in this section retrieves articles from the Scopus database to build a systematic literature review (Burnham, 2006). The dataset was searched using the "Deepfake" keyword. The dataset was collected after manually verifying the documents and examining the completeness of the chosen research papers using various keyword combinations.

The main objective of this query is to fetch the articles that highlight the work in the deepfake area. Each bibliographic record includes the metadata of a published research article, including its abstract, authors, title, keywords, and references. Our analysis is based mainly on the Scopus dataset, which comprises about 450 unique records. The other parameters are set as follows. First, as most of the research on deepfake has appeared over recent years, so the analysis is performed on literature published within the last 10 years from the duration and set "Time Slicing" to 2012–2022. Second, Figure 2 shows documents classification by type of publication, including conference papers (56.4%), articles (36%), review papers (4.7%), and book chapters (2.9%).

a. Country-wise Contribution

As mentioned, research on the deepfake topic is increasing gradually. Figure 3 presents the top 10 contributing countries to deepfake research between 2012 and 2022. As evident in the figure, the major contributions to the deepfake field came from China and the United States of America. China is the largest contributor, publishing 106 papers. The United States and India are ranked second and third by publishing 104 and 45 papers, respectively.

b. Institution-wise Contributions

Figure 4 provides the institution-wise contribution to the field. It is evident that the Chinese Academy of Sciences provides the highest number of contributions. The Chinese Academy of Sciences is in the first place with 18 publications, followed by the Nanyang Technological University of Singapore and Sungkyunkwan University of South Korea with publications of 10 and 9 publications, respectively.

c. Author-wise Implications

It can be observed in Figure 5, S. Lyu from the State University of New York at Buffalo has 9 publications in the deepfake domain and S. S. Woo from the Department of Applied Data Science at Sungkyunkwan

University, South Korea has 8 publications followed by Y. Li from the Ocean University of China with 7 publications.

OVERVIEW OF ML AND AI TECHNIQUES USED FOR CREATING DEEPFAKE CONTENT

Deepfake technology is a type of synthetic media, which is operated by deep learning. AI neural networks are trained on a dataset of images and videos, learning to generate a person's similarity to another. The maximum data in a dataset can help to generate a similarity, match expressions and behaviors, and the more realistic the fake videos (Caldwell et al., 2020). Figure 6 indicates various tools and techniques that are used for creating deepfakes contents, but the most extensively used methods are autoencoder and GAN.

1. Deep Autoencoders

An autoencoder is a kind of neural network whose objective is to match the input. An algorithm that learns the given input data from different angles, and environments can replicate the same input content with more accuracy. As shown in Figure 7, pairs of encoder and decoder are necessary for generating deepfake content through autoencoder. In a training phase, the source image is first trained on one encoder and decoder then the targeted image is trained on the next encoder and decoder. Once the training phase is complete, the decoder of the source and targeted images are exchanged. The swapping is done so that the original encoder can generate the targeted image by generating the features from the original image.

In order to create a forged image that looks similar, supervised learning is employed throughout the process to reduce the difference between input and output. (K. Lin et al., 2021).

2. Generalized Adversarial Network (GAN)

In GAN deepfake generation technique, an adversarial process trained two models simultaneously. Figure 8 shows that the generator learns to generate images that seem to be real, while the main purpose of the discriminator is to learn to identify the real images apart from fake ones (Yadav, 2019). There are many types of GANs used to generate fake images from any dataset; some are used for specific deepfake content generation e.g. image to image translation, text-to-image generation, and style transfer (C. Li et al., 2022).

a. Deep Convolutional GAN

Deep Convolutional GAN (Radford et al., 2016) is an enhancement of GAN. In deep convolutional GAN, batch normalization is performed in two networks: - 1) generator network and 2) discriminator network. They can be applied to transfer styles.; style transfer describes the rendering of an image's semantic content as different artistic styles.

b. Conditional GAN

Extra label information has been used in conditional GAN (Dai et al., 2017) for generating good quality images, and it is capable of managing how generated images will appear. It learns to generate images by utilizing the information provided to the model.

c. StackGAN

StackGAN (Zhang et al., 2019) facilitates the creation of images from text descriptions and also enables image-to-image translation by creating a real image of an object using sketches (Kowalczyk, 2022).

d. InfoGAN

InfoGAN (Chen et al., 2016) is an extension to the GAN that can find out extricated representations in an unsupervised manner. InfoGAN is implemented to train a conditional GAN, where the dataset is not labeled and is very complex. Moreover, it also represents the most important features of images.

3. Tools Used to Generate Deepfake Content

There are many deepfake creation tools based on deep autoencoders and GANs.

a. FaceSwap

FaceSwap (*FaceSwap*, n.d.) is a free tool of deepfake technology with the functionality to operate each step of the deepfake process, from importing videos to creating a final deepfake video, but it requires a high processing speed for best performance.

b. Deepfakes Web β

Deepfakes web β (*DEEPFAKES WEB*, n.d.) is a web-based application for creating deepfake videos. Deep learning techniques are used to help it comprehend the many complexities of face properties. Deepfakes web β requires a powerful GPU on the cloud that takes about 4 hours and 30 minutes to learn, train and swap the face using an already trained model.

c. DeepFaceLab

DeepFaceLab (Perov et al., 2020) is a windows application that is developed for researchers of computer vision. It is the most advanced tool; the interface of the application is not user-friendly, and it's required a powerful PC and high-end GPU. It uses ML and human image synthesis to replace faces in videos.

d. Zao

Zao (*ZAO Application*, n.d.) is the latest android and iOS-based application which gained fame in a very short time by swapping users' faces with their favorite artists in short clips. Unlike powerful computers that may require hours to train to train and create a deepfake video, the Zao application can create a deepfake video within a few seconds which seems natural and indistinguishable from the original video.

ML AND AI TECHNIQUES FOR DETECTING DEEPFAKE

Detection of deepfake content has become very difficult, if not nearly impossible, to distinguish between a real video and a fake video alone with the human eye (Tariq et al., 2021). There are still flaws in the deep learning platform in detecting manipulated content; however, researchers have determined that there are some significant ways to detect AI-generated fake video content (Kim et al., 2021) (Y. Li & Lyu, 2018). Many methods that have been proposed to detect deepfake are based on deep learning and AI techniques (Stanciu & Ionescu, 2021). Researchers continue to explore potential technological solutions to detect and aid in the negative consequences of deepfake (Khadam et al., 2021) (Shende et al., 2021). (Almars, 2021) perform analysis of various technologies and their application for the identification of deepfakes videos or images in social content. (Shahzad et al., 2022) presents novel methods to detect face manipulation, deepfake identification, content, authentication, and deepfake prevention. Figure 9 depicts the deepfake detection techniques and tools based on these techniques.

1. Deepfake Image Detection

(Tariq et al., 2018) proposed a neural network-based method for identifying fake GAN videos that examines the statistical properties of the image and improves the recognition of deepfake images created by people. (Do et al., 2018) also introduced another approach in which the model first extracts face properties based on a face recognition network. After that, fine-tuning step is implemented to generate face features appropriate for image detection. In addition (Liu et al., 2019), (Hsu et al., 2020), (Zhou et al., 2017) introduced a hybrid deepfake detection approach for the effective detection of fake images. Hybrid approach results indicate that these approaches can overcome the limitations of fake image detectors (Chang et al., 2020).

2. Deepfake Video Detection

There are many deep learning methods for deepfake image detection, but it is not possible to directly implement these methods for fake videos detection, because it may cause a loss of frame

information after video compression (Pu et al., 2021). Deeptrace reported in 2018 that approximately 14,698 deepfake videos were circulating on the internet, 96% of which were pornographic and involved actors and politicians (Zeng & Olivera-Cintrón, 2019). (Y. Li et al., 2019) suggests that deepfake algorithms typically do not create video content with normal blinking patterns – blinking is a lot less, and it is easier to detect a 'fake' from 'real'. Most humans blink anywhere between every 2 to 10 seconds, with a single blink taking between one-tenth and four-tenths of a second with very few images found with an individual's eyes closed. Other biological indicators like heartbeat seem to be a trustworthy predictor for real video. (Ciftci et al., 2020b) has worked on GAN based model that analyzes the "heartbeat" of deep fakes for detection. The authors have used several datasets to verify the model performance. The result shows that the model can detect deepfake efficiently with 97.3% accuracy. (Dale et al., 2011) proposed a method that includes unnatural movements of the body between the face and head, a noticeable change of lighting in the background, and the skin tone of the video image considerably smooth. (Rathgeb et al., n.d.) introduced AI-based technology in video magnification techniques that could determine if an individual in a video was actual or computer-generated by detecting changes in the human pulse.

(Guera & Delp, 2019) worked on a temporally aware model for deepfake video detection. Recently, many researchers are examining the temporal arrangement between video frames that can help to differentiate a real video or the fake one (Ramadhani & Munir, 2020).

3. Tools Used to Detect Deepfake Content

There are many deepfake detection tools, mainly for deepfake videos and images. For deepfake videos, these are based on psychological measurements and unnatural body movements. For deepfake images, these are based on statistical properties and error level analysis. These tools are high-tech in their specifications and have been developed at high costs.

a. FotoForensics

FotoForensics tool (*FotoForensics*, n.d.) implements an algorithm to identify any photoshop images, and it implements the Error Level Analysis (ELA) technique to identify the portions of an image that are compressed at different levels (Sri et al., 2021). FotoForensics aims to identify artifacts and information that the human eye might not be able to recognize. Most people can easily understand how to identify deepfake images if they have the right tools and training.

b. JPEGSnoop

JPEGsnoop (*JPEGsnoop*, n.d.) is a windows program that identifies the deepfake images and finds out the information about any photoshop implementation. It can be used for authenticity by analyzing the source of the image. Every digital image has hidden information, and JPEGsnoop was created to find these specifics e.g., chroma subsampling, quantization table matrix, EXIF metadata, JPEG Quality setting, etc.

c. Ghiro

Ghiro (*Ghiro*, n.d.) is a free application for automated digital image forensics. It reports data that can be examined from various perspectives. It also implements the ELA technique to distinguish between the real or edited image (Rafique et al., 2021). Ghiro application is designed to analyze a huge number of images. Every image has a different level of compression, which is the main concept. After that, the analyzed image is saved again, and calculate the variations in compression levels if any difference is found the probability of edit is high.

D. Forensically

Forensically (*Forensically*, n.d.) is a free toolkit for digital image forensics. It has many features, such as error level analysis, clone detection, metadata extraction, and more. It also helps to identify the details that would otherwise be hidden. **a) Clone detector -** The copied areas of a picture are located using the clone detector. It can be a reliable sign that a photograph has been altered. **b) Error Level Analysis –**

This tool compares the original and the compressed versions of the image. This can make altered regions stand out in different ways. **c) Noise Analysis** – This tool is a reverse de-noising algorithm. It eliminates the rest of the image rather than just the noise. It can be helpful for spotting manipulations to the image like airbrushing, warping, deformations, and perspective corrected cloning. **d) PCA** – This tool provides a facility to view the image information from different angles which make determine certain manipulations and details. But it is quite slow when performing on big images.

e. FakeCatcher

FakeCatcher (Ciftci et al., 2020a) is a powerful tool for detecting fake video content in private media as well as social media. The detection is performed on the biological signals from the videos and applies different ML models to differentiate the real and fake content based on the heart-rate consistency or inconsistency.

f. DeepVision

DeepVision (Jung et al., 2020) is used to analyze deepfake video based on a significant change in the pattern of eye blinking. The integrity verification is performed through repeated numbers, and elapsed eye blink time when the eye blinks occurred repeatedly and continuously in a little amount of time. It has 87.5% successful detection accuracy.

g. DeepfakesON-Phys

DeepFakesON-Phys (Hernandez-Ortega et al., 2021) is worked on heart rate monitoring using remote photoplethysmography (rPPG). rPPG techniques investigate video sequences to identify subtle color changes in the human skin, revealing the presence of human blood under the tissues. It has two phases: 1) preprocessing step to normalize the video frames and 2) convolutional attention network that is composed of appearance and motion model for deepfake video detection.

Table 2 presents a comparison of the deepfake detection tools in terms of detection data type, environment, availability, and the technique used.

RECOMMENDATIONS FOR FINTECH TO COUNTER AND PREVENT DEEPFAKE

The development of technologies over the past few years, including AI, deep learning, and others, has had a significant impact on both enterprises and societies. It becomes more challenging to distinguish between actual and synthetic media due to the technological advancements. Deepfake is one of the technologies which heavily relies on the use of AI, deep learning etc. A deepfake use AI algorithms to replace and superimpose existing images and video clips to make fraudulent video and audio content that seem authentic. Deepfake used for fraud and extortion are now creating a landscape of threat for the financial systems. Academic researchers and IT companies are investigating methods to identify and delete such content from the internet to combat deepfake content. Giants like Facebook and Microsoft have partnered with colleges and universities to give incentives to scholars who create techniques to detect and stop the spread of deepfake content. Google has released deepfake samples to assist researchers in building detection technologies (Katarya & Lal, 2020). The commercial entities are contributing their part in terms of technology; however, they need legislative and regularity support from the governments to counter and prevent the consequences of deepfake. To this end, every country needs to clearly define the inappropriate use of deepfake technology and create legislations. This is because deepfake content is employed for both positive and negative purposes. It is challenging for the society to have a clear distinction of which uses are acceptable and which are not.

In 2019, the US took steps against deepfake growth where Texas was the first state to ban political deepfake. Later in 2019, the state of Virginia banned deepfake pornography by amending its laws. Additionally, California declared it unlawful "to produce or disseminate recordings, pictures, or audio of politicians" (O'Halloran, 2021). The World Intellectual Property Organization (WIPO) published the "Draft Issues Paper on Intellectual Property Policy and Artificial Intelligence" in December 2019. The draft holds problems of deepfake contents in terms of intellectual property rights (Drexl et al., 2020). The European Union (EU) has implemented the most innovative measures to combat deepfake and other types of purposeful misinformation by publishing a strategy for stopping disinformation. This contains relevant guidelines for defending against deepfake (Vizoso et al., 2021). In Germany, the Network Enforcement Act, which was enacted in 2017 to fight the dissemination of false information, may be invoked to ban deepfake content if it is used to circulate fake news. Spain and France also have enacted similar laws (Haciyakupoglu et al., 2018) (Claussen, 2018). China's Cyberspace Administration has published regulations that became effective on January 1, 2020, and prohibit the online publication of false information and relevant material that has been edited using AI or VR techniques (Pernot-Leplay, 2020).

To address all the issues related to deepfake technology, many developed countries have already introduced anti-deepfake legislation. However, it important to point out that this legislation is not specifically designed to address the deepfake threats in the FinTech sector. In the absence of proper legislation, implementing protective measures can reduce the deepfake threat in the FinTech sector to some extent. The protective measures have been categorized from the organizational and customer perspective.

1. Organizational Perspectives

While spreading false information is easy, combating malicious deepfakes could prove to be more difficult. As prior research has only recently begun to address digital disinformation in social media (Anderson, 2018), little is known about which techniques organizations should use to combat unethical and malicious deepfakes. In the light of the existing deepfake threat, businesses should take some simple and proactive measures to mitigate the risk of falling victim to deepfake-based scams (Hasan & Salah, 2019). These steps include:

- Enterprises, banks, and the FinTech groups should set up partnerships to combat the use of deepfake video and audio content by fraudsters. Recently a bank signed up to a biometric identification system, developed by technology firm Mitek and offered through a partnership with Adobe (Vincent, 2020).
- Training of staff, particularly those employees that are involved in the payment of money, also explaining the threats posed by deepfake and how they can be identified.
- Tightening the compliance guidelines for payment authorization.
- Enterprises must have a biometric identification system to check the identities of customers, and employees by using live images and electronic signatures.

- Media authentication and provenance tools must be used to verify the authenticity of the content, obtain its origins, and identify its creator.
- Encourage open communication: speaking and consulting with colleagues and others about anything that appears suspicious are effective tools to prevent fraud schemes.

2. Customer Perspectives

Fraudsters often use social engineering attacks to manipulate the customers by transferring funds or opening the door for future attacks. Social engineering is the psychological manipulation of people into performing actions or revealing confidential information. Following steps customers must adopt to prevent the scams:

- Delete any request for personal information or passwords.
- Reject requests for offers from unauthorized links.
- Set your spam filters to high.
- Secure the devices.
- Always be mindful of risks.
- Change all the passwords periodically.
- In case the malicious activity is detected report any fraudulent activity to your bank and Credit Card Company.

CONCLUSION

It is concluded that deepfake technology is observed as a major threat to businesses in the upcoming days. Technical solutions, and automated tools for deepfake detection are being used by many enterprises as the first line of defense against the prevention of deepfake. As deepfake technology is moving at a faster cadence, the automated detection tools will prove to be inefficient to counter the deepfake content, additional authentication techniques are required. The FinTech industry must be ripe with standardized security companies, such as iProov, that use AI with anti-spoofing technologies to detect both video and audio deepfake (*IProov*, n.d.). Recently, many security companies have also offered real-time detection to identify the deepfake representations of real clients. Apart from strengthening the technical side, the enterprises must educate their stakeholders on the powerful capabilities of deepfake. Regulation and legislation should more effectively protect individuals and organizations from deepfake attacks and offer victims a means to pursue cybercriminals. Criminal and civil penalties could deter the unethical use of deepfake technology. Since many developed countries like the United States of America and the United Kingdom have regulations against legal issues of deepfakes, it is now essential that underdeveloped countries should consider passing legislation against the use of deepfake with the intent to defame the character of individuals.

REFERENCES

Almars, A. M. (2021). Deepfakes Detection Techniques Using Deep Learning: A Survey. *Journal of Computer and Communications*, *09*(05), 20–35. doi:10.4236/jcc.2021.95003

Anderson, K. E. (2018). Getting acquainted with social networks and apps: Combating fake news on social media. *Library Hi Tech News*, *35*(3), 1–6. doi:10.1108/LHTN-02-2018-0010

Atif, M., Latif, S., Ahmad, R., Kiani, A. K., Qadir, J., Baig, A., Ishibuchi, H., & Abbas, W. (2019). Soft Computing Techniques for Dependable Cyber-Physical Systems. *IEEE Access: Practical Innovations, Open Solutions*, *7*, 72030–72049. doi:10.1109/ACCESS.2019.2920317

Bateman, J. (2020). *Deepfakes and Synthetic Media in the Financial System: Assessing Threat Scenarios.* https://www.jstor.org/stable/resrep25783

Buo, S. A. (2020). *The Emerging Threats of Deepfake Attacks and Countermeasures.* doi:10.13140/RG.2.2.23089.81762

Burnham, J. F. (2006). Scopus database: A review. *Biomedical Digital Libraries*, *3*(1), 1–8. doi:10.1186/1742-5581-3-1 PMID:16522216

Caldwell, M., Andrews, J. T. A., Tanay, T., & Griffin, L. D. (2020). AI-enabled future crime. *Crime Science*, *9*(1), 1–13. doi:10.118640163-020-00123-8

Chang, X., Wu, J., Yang, T., & Feng, G. (2020). DeepFake Face Image Detection based on Improved VGG Convolutional. *Neural Networks*, 7252–7256.

Chen, X., Duan, Y., Houthooft, R., Schulman, J., Sutskever, I., & Abbeel, P. (2016). InfoGAN: Interpretable Representation Learning. *Nips, Nips*, 2172–2180. https://arxiv.org/abs/1606.03657

Ciftci, U. A., Demir, I., & Yin, L. (2020a). FakeCatcher: Detection of Synthetic Portrait Videos using Biological Signals. *IEEE Transactions on Pattern Analysis and Machine Intelligence*, *X*(X), 1–1. doi:10.1109/TPAMI.2020.3009287 PMID:32750816

Ciftci, U. A., Demir, I., & Yin, L. (2020b). How do the hearts of deep fakes beat? deep fake source detection via interpreting residuals with biological signals. *IJCB 2020 - IEEE/IAPR International Joint Conference on Biometrics.* 10.1109/IJCB48548.2020.9304909

Claussen, V. (2018). Fighting hate speech and fake news. The Network Enforcement Act (NetzDG) in Germany in the context of European legislation. *Rivista Di Diritto Dei Media*, *3*, 1–27. www.reuters.com

Dai, B., Fidler, S., Urtasun, R., & Lin, D. (2017). Towards Diverse and Natural Image Descriptions via a Conditional GAN. *Proceedings of the IEEE International Conference on Computer Vision*, 2989–2998. doi:10.1109/ICCV.2017.323

Dale, K., Sunkavalli, K., Johnson, M. K., Vlasic, D., Matusik, W., & Pfister, H. (2011). Video face replacement. *ACM Transactions on Graphics*, *30*(6), 1–10. doi:10.1145/2070781.2024164

Deepfakes Web. (n.d.). https://deepfakesweb.com

Do, N., Na, I., & Kim, S. (2018). *Forensics Face Detection From GANs Using Convolutional Neural Network.* Academic Press.

Drexl, J., Hilty, R. M., Desaunettes-barbero, L., Globocnik, J., Kim, D., Kulhari, S., Richter, H., Scheuerer, S., Slowinski, P. R., & Wiedemann, K. (2020). Comments of the Max Planck Institute for Innovation and Competition of 11 February 2020: On the Draft Issues Paper of the World Intellectual Property Organization on Intellectual Property Policy and Artificial Intelligence. Max Planck Institute for Innovation and Competition, 1(December), 1–9.

FaceSwap. (n.d.). https://faceswap.dev

Forensically. (n.d.). https://29a.ch/photo-forensics/#forensic-magnifier

FotoForensics. (n.d.). http://fotoforensics.com

Ghiro. (n.d.). https://www.getghiro.org

Guera, D., & Delp, E. J. (2019). Deepfake Video Detection Using Recurrent Neural Networks. *Proceedings of AVSS 2018 - 2018 15th IEEE International Conference on Advanced Video and Signal-Based Surveillance.* 10.1109/AVSS.2018.8639163

Haciyakupoglu, G., Hui, J. Y., Suguna, V. S., Leong, D., Bin, M. F., & Rahman, A. (2018). *Countering Fake News a Survey of Recent Global Initiatives.* https://think-asia.org/bitstream/handle/11540/8063/PR180307_Countering-Fake-News.pdf?sequence=1

Hartmann, K., & Giles, K. (2020). The Next Generation of Cyber-Enabled Information Warfare. *International Conference on Cyber Conflict, CYCON,* 233–250. 10.23919/CyCon49761.2020.9131716

Hasan, H. R., & Salah, K. (2019). Combating Deepfake Videos Using Blockchain and Smart Contracts. *IEEE Access: Practical Innovations, Open Solutions,* 7, 41596–41606. doi:10.1109/ACCESS.2019.2905689

Hernandez-Ortega, J., Tolosana, R., Fierrez, J., & Morales, A. (2021). DeepFakesON-Phys: Deepfakes detection based on heart rate estimation. *CEUR Workshop Proceedings.*

Hsu, C. C., Zhuang, Y. X., & Lee, C. Y. (2020). Deep fake image detection based on pairwise learning. *Applied Sciences (Switzerland), 10*(1), 370. Advance online publication. doi:10.3390/app10010370

Huang, K., Siegel, M., Pearlson, K., & Madnick, S. E. (2019). Casting the Dark Web in a New Light: A Value-Chain Lens Reveals a Growing Cyber Attack Ecosystem and New Strategies for Combating It. SSRN *Electronic Journal, June.* doi:10.2139/ssrn.3459128

iProov. (n.d.). https://www.iproov.com

Jones, V. A., & Capstone, A. (2020). *The Emergence of a New Threat.* Academic Press.

JPEGsnoop. (n.d.). https://jpegsnoop.en.uptodown.com/windows

Jung, T., Kim, S., & Kim, K. (2020). DeepVision: Deepfakes Detection Using Human Eye Blinking Pattern. *IEEE Access: Practical Innovations, Open Solutions,* 8, 83144–83154. https://doi.org/10.1109/ACCESS.2020.2988660

Justin Rohrlich. (2020). *Romance Scammer Used Deepfakes to Impersonate a Navy Admiral and Bilk Widow Out of Nearly $300,000.* https://www.thedailybeast.com/romance-scammer-used-deepfakes-to-impersonate-a-navy-admiral-and-bilk-widow-out-of-nearly-dollar300000

Katarya, R., & Lal, A. (2020). A study on combating emerging threat of deepfake weaponization. *Proceedings of the 4th International Conference on IoT in Social, Mobile, Analytics and Cloud, ISMAC 2020,* 485–490. doi:10.1109/I-SMAC49090.2020.9243588

Khadam, U., Iqbal, M. M., Saeed, S., Dar, S. H., Ahmad, A., & Ahmad, M. (2021). Advanced security and privacy technique for digital text in smart grid communications. *Computers & Electrical Engineering, 93*(May), 107205. https://doi.org/10.1016/j.compeleceng.2021.107205

Khan, S. A., Artusi, A., & Dai, H. (2021). *Adversarially robust deepfake media detection using fused convolutional neural network predictions.* https://arxiv.org/abs/2102.05950

Kim, M., Tariq, S., & Woo, S. S. (2021). FReTAL: Generalizing deepfake detection using knowledge distillation and representation learning. *IEEE Computer Society Conference on Computer Vision and Pattern Recognition Workshops,* 1001–1012. doi:10.1109/CVPRW53098.2021.00111

Kowalczyk, P. (2022). *Detecting and Understanding Textual Deepfakes in Online Reviews.* doi:10.24251/HICSS.2022.184

Li, C., Wang, L., Ji, S., Zhang, X., Xi, Z., Guo, S., & Wang, T. (2022). *Seeing is Living? Rethinking the Security of Facial Liveness Verification in the Deepfake Era.* https://arxiv.org/abs/2202.10673

Li, Y., Chang, M. C., & Lyu, S. (2019). In Ictu Oculi: Exposing AI created fake videos by detecting eye blinking. *10th IEEE International Workshop on Information Forensics and Security, WIFS 2018.* doi:10.1109/WIFS.2018.8630787

Li, Y., & Lyu, S. (2018). *Exposing DeepFake Videos By Detecting Face Warping Artifacts.* https://arxiv.org/abs/1811.00656

Lin, H. (2019). The existential threat from cyber-enabled information warfare. *Bulletin of the Atomic Scientists, 75*(4), 187–196. https://doi.org/10.1080/00963402.2019.1629574

Lin, K., Han, W., Gu, Z., & Li, S. (2021). A Survey of DeepFakes Generation and Detection. *Proceedings - 2021 IEEE 6th International Conference on Data Science in Cyberspace, DSC 2021,* 474–478. doi:10.1109/DSC53577.2021.00076

Liu, F., Jiao, L., & Tang, X. (2019). Task-Oriented GAN for PolSAR Image Classification and Clustering. *IEEE Transactions on Neural Networks and Learning Systems, 30*(9), 2707–2719. https://doi.org/10.1109/TNNLS.2018.2885799

Micro Research. (2020). *The New Norm Trend Micro Security Predictions.* Author.

Muna, M. (2020). *Technological Arming: Is Deepfake the Next Digital Weapon?* https://www.researchgate.net/publication/341781104

Naeem, H., Ullah, F., Naeem, M. R., Khalid, S., Vasan, D., Jabbar, S., & Saeed, S. (2020). Malware detection in industrial internet of things based on hybrid image visualization and deep learning model. *Ad Hoc Networks, 105*, 102154. https://doi.org/10.1016/j.adhoc.2020.102154

Neethirajan, S. (2021). *Beyond Deepfake Technology Fear: On its Positive Uses for Livestock Farming* doi:10.20944/preprints202107.0326.v1

O'Halloran, A. (2021). *The Technical, Legal, and Ethical Landscape of Deepfake Pornography.* https://cs.brown.edu/research/pubs/theses/ugrad/2021/ohalloran.amelia.pdf

Pernot-Leplay, E. (2020). China's Approach on Data Privacy Law: A Third Way Between the U.S. and the E.U.? *Penn State Journal of Law & International Affairs, 8*(1), 49.

Perov, I., Gao, D., Chervoniy, N., Liu, K., Marangonda, S., Umé, C., Dpfks, M., Facenheim, C. S., RP, L., Jiang, J., Zhang, S., Wu, P., Zhou, B., & Zhang, W. (2020). *DeepFaceLab: Integrated, flexible and extensible face-swapping framework.* https://arxiv.org/abs/2005.05535

Piper, J., & Metcalfe, A. (2020). *Economic crime in a digital age.* www.accaglobal.com

Pu, J., Mangaokar, N., Kelly, L., Bhattacharya, P., Sundaram, K., Javed, M., Wang, B., & Viswanath, B. (2021). Deepfake videos in the wild: Analysis and detection. *The Web Conference 2021 - Proceedings of the World Wide Web Conference, WWW 2021, 2*, 981–992. doi:10.1145/3442381.3449978

Puschmann, T. (2017). Fintech. *Business & Information Systems Engineering, 59*(1), 69–76. https://doi.org/10.1007/s12599-017-0464-6

Qayyum, A., Qadir, J., Janjua, M. U., & Sher, F. (2019). Using Blockchain to Rein in the New Post-Truth World and Check the Spread of Fake News. *IT Professional, 21*(4), 16–24. https://doi.org/10.1109/MITP.2019.2910503

Radford, A., Metz, L., & Chintala, S. (2016). Unsupervised representation learning with deep convolutional generative adversarial networks. *4th International Conference on Learning Representations, ICLR 2016 - Conference Track Proceedings*, 1–16.

Rafique, R., Nawaz, M., Kibriya, H., & Masood, M. (2021). DeepFake Detection Using Error Level Analysis and Deep Learning. *Proceedings - 2021 IEEE 4th International Conference on Computing and Information Sciences, ICCIS 2021*, 0–3. doi:10.1109/ICCIS54243.2021.9676375

Ramadhani, K. N., & Munir, R. (2020). A Comparative Study of Deepfake Video Detection Method. *2020 3rd International Conference on Information and Communications Technology, ICOIACT 2020*, 394–399. doi:10.1109/ICOIACT50329.2020.9331963

Rathgeb, C., Tolosana, R., Vera-Rodriguez, R., & Busch, C. (n.d.). Advances in Computer Vision and Pattern Recognition. In *Handbook of Digital Face Manipulation and Detection From DeepFakes to Morphing Attacks.* https://link.springer.com/bookseries/4205

Shahzad, H. F., Rustam, F., Flores, E. S., Luís, J., Mazón, V., De, I., Diez, T., & Ashraf, I. (2022). *A Review of Image Processing Techniques for Deepfakes.* Academic Press.

Shende, A., Paliwal, S., & Mahay, T. K. (2021). Using deep learning to detect deepfake videos. *Turkish Journal of Computer and Mathematics Education Research Article, 12*(11), 5012–5017.

Sri, C. G., Bano, S., Deepika, T., Kola, N., & Pranathi, Y. L. (2021). Deep Neural Networks Based Error Level Analysis for Lossless Image Compression Based Forgery Detection. *2021 International Conference on Intelligent Technologies, CONIT 2021*, 1–8. doi:10.1109/CONIT51480.2021.9498357

Stanciu, D. C., & Ionescu, B. (2021). Deepfake Video Detection with Facial Features and Long-Short Term Memory Deep Networks. *ISSCS 2021 - International Symposium on Signals, Circuits and Systems*, 0–3. doi:10.1109/ISSCS52333.2021.9497385

Tariq, S., Lee, S., Kim, H., Shin, Y., & Woo, S. S. (2018). Detecting both machine and human created fake face images in the wild. *Proceedings of the ACM Conference on Computer and Communications Security*, 81–87. doi:10.1145/3267357.3267367

Tariq, S., Lee, S., & Woo, S. (2021). *One Detector to Rule Them All.* doi:10.1145/3442381.3449809

Ternovski, J., Kalla, J., & Aronow, P. M. (2021). *Deepfake Warnings for Political Videos Increase Disbelief but Do Not Improve Discernment: Evidence from Two Experiments.* https://osf.io/dta97/

Vaccari, C., & Chadwick, A. (2020). Deepfakes and Disinformation: Exploring the Impact of Synthetic Political Video on Deception, Uncertainty, and Trust in News. *Social Media and Society, 6*(1). doi:10.1177/2056305120903408

Vincent, M. (2020). Banks work with fintechs to counter 'deepfake' fraud. *Financial Times.* https://www.ft.com/content/8a5fa5b2-6aac-41cf-aa52-5d0b90c41840

Vizoso, Á., Vaz-álvarez, M., & López-García, X. (2021). Fighting deepfakes: Media and internet giants' converging and diverging strategies against hi-tech misinformation. *Media and Communication, 9*(1), 291–300. https://doi.org/10.17645/MAC.V9I1.3494

Weerawardana, M. C., & Fernando, T. G. I. (2021). Deepfakes Detection Methods: A Literature Survey. *2021 10th International Conference on Information and Automation for Sustainability, ICIAfS 2021*, 76–81. doi:10.1109/ICIAfS52090.2021.9606067

Westerlund, M. (2019). The emergence of deepfake technology: A review. *Technology Innovation Management Review, 9*(11), 39–52. doi:10.22215/TIMREVIEW/1282

Yadav, D. (2019). *Deepfake : A Survey on Facial Forgery Technique Using Generative Adversarial Network.* Academic Press.

ZAO Application. (n.d.). https://apps.apple.com/cn/app/id1465199127

Zeng, C., & Olivera-Cintrón, R. (2019). *Preparing for the World of a "Perfect" Deepfake.* https://czeng.org/classes/6805/Final.pdf

Zhang, H., Xu, T., Li, H., Zhang, S., Wang, X., Huang, X., & Metaxas, D. N. (2019). StackGAN++: Realistic Image Synthesis with Stacked Generative Adversarial Networks. *IEEE Transactions on Pattern Analysis and Machine Intelligence, 41*(8), 1947–1962. https://doi.org/10.1109/TPAMI.2018.2856256

Zhao, Z., Wang, P., & Lu, W. (2021). Multi-layer fusion neural network for deepfake detection. *International Journal of Digital Crime and Forensics, 13*(4), 26–39. https://doi.org/10.4018/IJDCF.20210701.oa3

Zhou, P., Han, X., Morariu, V. I., & Davis, L. S. (2017). Two-Stream Neural Networks for Tampered Face Detection. *IEEE Computer Society Conference on Computer Vision and Pattern Recognition Workshops,* 1831–1839. doi:10.1109/CVPRW.2017.229

Chapter 13
Organisational and Individual Behavioural Susceptibility and Protection Approach for Ransomware Attacks

Abubakar Bello
Western Sydney University, Australia

Queen Aigbefo
(iD) https://orcid.org/0000-0001-9358-2246
Macquarie University, Australia

ABSTRACT

Ransomware attacks have become complex due to the ability of networked-systems constantly used as attack-vectors for propagating the ransomware payload to victims. The threat is socially engineered, making it difficult for victims to protect their data. Confidential information resources and assets are lost and rarely recovered in an attack resulting in financial losses amounting to millions of dollars. Ongoing research is exploring avenues to solve this problem including cybersecurity awareness and training from a singularised perspective, not pluralistic, to educate users of the consequences of their actions. The purpose of this study is to gain perceptions of several industries to develop insights on how to protect organisations from becoming victims of socially engineered ransomware attacks. Using a qualitative approach, critical themes on behavioural susceptibility to socially engineered ransomware were obtained, as well as the demand for applying behavioural theories and technical controls to develop effective training and education initiatives for resisting these attacks.

DOI: 10.4018/978-1-6684-5284-4.ch013

INTRODUCTION

Ransomware attack is a cyber-epidemic affecting businesses and governments, and the effects of a ransomware attack has devastating consequences. A recent report claims that some organisations experience ransomware attacks on a weekly and monthly basis disrupting their business activities (Crowdstrike, 2019; Telstra, 2019). These ransomware attacks result in the loss of data and costing billions of dollars annually (Mansfield-Devine, 2016). Numerous resources have been developed to address the loss and consistency of ransomware attacks; however, the attacks remain persistent (Hull et al., 2019).

Cybersecurity is a growing concern and global issue. Reports of ransomware attacks feature prominent institutions, organisations, and government departments such as Maersk, United States government-several states and county, United Kingdom- NHS WannaCry, and Victoria health service in Australia (ABC News, 2019; National Audit, 2017; ZDNet, 2019). Ransomware figures reported between 2020 and 2022 show 23% increase in attacks on manufacturing companies and a 146% increase in Linux ransomware code affecting cloud environment (IBM, 2022). These attacks have become so prevalent with infrastructure such as Ransomware as a Service (RaaS) making it easy for would-be attackers to deploy ransomware payloads (O'Kane et al., 2018).

Ransomware attacks have been increasing at an alarming rate (Reshmi, 2021; Richardson & North, 2017). The attacks have tremendous effects on victims because a ransomware payload encrypts files and data, locks the device (such as computers or mobile phones), prevents the user from accessing it, and in extreme cases, makes computer systems unusable (Tailor & Patel, 2017). The United Kingdom's National Health Service (NHS) was hit with a ransomware infecting over 300,000 computer systems across 150 countries, showing that a ransomware could propagate widely over a short period of time (Akbanov et al., 2019).

Behavioural information security research has examined the behaviour of employees to understand how to increase security compliance and awareness(Anderson & Agarwal, 2010; Bulgurcu et al., 2010; Herath & Rao, 2009; Ifinedo, 2012; McGill & Thompson, 2017). One significant challenge in protecting employees against ransomware attacks is the lack of information regarding psychological factors that influence an employees' decision-making process, especially when attacks are socially engineered. With the use of social engineering techniques, attackers manipulate, instill intimidation, and extort money from the victim (Humayun et al., 2021; Kalaimannan et al., 2017). Cyber security analysts and professionals harden computer systems and networks, creating complex security processes they must depend on to ensure employees are protected. Humans are the first line of the cybersecurity defense system (Furnell et al., 2018). However, there is a dearth of empirical research that focuses on human-related ransomware solutions or frameworks for socially engineered ransomware prevention and mitigation.

The problem addressed in this research is socially engineered ransomware. These attack types and patterns are one of the significant challenges that individuals, businesses, and government departments encounter (Maurushat et al., 2019). Social engineering has provided an easy point of access for attackers to psychologically manipulate their victims to install destructive ransomware payloads (Al-rimy et al., 2018), leading to extortion, loss of sensitive data, and stored backups (FBI, 2018; IC3, 2020). As technology continues to dominate the lives of people; it is, therefore, imperative to understand how to empower individuals to protect themselves and mitigate against socially engineered ransomware attacks.

Purpose and Significance of the Study

The purpose of this qualitative study is to investigate the factors that make technology users susceptible to socially engineered ransomware attacks and to provide security control insights for addressing the ransomware threat. The information and analysis obtained in this study can be used to address the issue of socially engineered ransomware and prevent the resulting consequences of an attack, such as: loss of data and access to computer systems. Humans are often the first point of access and could facilitate easy entry for cybercriminals or form a line of defense for the protection of computer systems and sensitive data (Beaman et al., 2021; Furnell & Clarke, 2012).

Additionally, the data from this study could be used to expand behavioural and psychology theories and research around ransomware: predicting security behaviours, and cognitively influencing employees to enable them to identify and mitigate the risks of ransomware attacks. Thus, empowering individuals and organisations to better protect their confidential data and systems against socially engineered ransomware attacks.

Research Questions

The research question for this study explores the reasons behind users' susceptibility to socially engineered ransomware attacks. The questions serve to frame the primary subject matter of the study. Subsequently, semi-structured interviews questions are drawn from these research questions presented below:

1. What makes individuals' susceptible to ransomware attacks?
2. What can be done to prevent individuals from yielding to socially engineered ransomware attacks?

LITERATURE REVIEW

Ransomware is an extortion-base malware that exploits cryptography technology to encrypt data files on a computer system or device, locks, and prevents the victim from accessing their data until an anonymous ransom payment is made. The first ransomware reported in 1989 was called AIDS Trojan also known as the PC CYBORG, and used social engineering to manipulate victims to install an infected floppy disk on computer systems (Giri et al., 2006). Today, ransomware has become rampant and is now a global issue. The 2017 WannaCry ransomware attack that infected over 300,000 computer systems in 150 countries showed that ransomware propagation is fast, dangerous, and difficult to control (EY, 2017; Zimba & Mulenga, 2018). Ubiquitous information and communications technology (ICT) has changed the ransomware landscape, introducing infection vectors that could covertly spread ransomware payloads (Al-rimy et al., 2018; Humayun et al., 2021).

Several studies have examined individual's cybersecurity behaviour to profile users who might be more susceptible to cybersecurity attacks such as phishing (Rocha Flores et al., 2014), social engineering (Burns et al., 2013; Rocha Flores & Ekstedt, 2016), and ransomware (Gallegos-Segovia et al., 2017; Ophoff & Lakay, 2019). Given the significant problem of ransomware attacks, previous studies have examined ransomware families but often from a technical perspective (Ariffin et al., 2018; Hampton et al., 2018; Martin et al., 2018; Masum et al., 2022). These studies have increased our understanding of ransomware, providing classification and analysis of various ransomware families. However, there is a gap in the literature regarding the human aspects of ransomware mitigation and an understanding on how to enable individuals to resist socially engineered ransomware attacks.

Ransomware Evolution and Lifecycle

The emergence of ransomware has created a novel approach to cybercrime. The AIDS Trojan created in 1989 and distributed by floppy disks at the World Health Organisation's International Aids conference, used simple symmetric cryptography to encrypt data files (Richardson & North, 2017). Once installed, the virus remained dormant in a 90-reboot cycle incubation period, encrypting file, and system directory on the 90th reboot and demands a ransom of US$189 (Tailor & Patel, 2017). Advancement in cryptographic technology has created complex and sophisticated encryption methodologies in ransomware attacks. The rebirth of ransomware in 2005 (PGP Coder) led to the creation and spread of other ransomware families; additionally, emerging anonymous payment services led to large scale ransomware attack outbreak in 2011. Since 2011 to date, there has been significant growth in ransomware extortion-based attacks as technology progresses (Kumar & Ramlie, 2021). Modern ransomware variants and tools are readily available following the rise of cloud-based ransomware development (such as Ransomware-as-a-Service), providing an easy environment for the dissemination of ransomware payloads.

The ransomware lifecycle involves four major stages; ransomware infection, encryption of data files, demand for payment, and outcome. Figure 1 illustrates the ransomware lifecycle process.

Figure 1. Socially engineered ransomware lifecycle

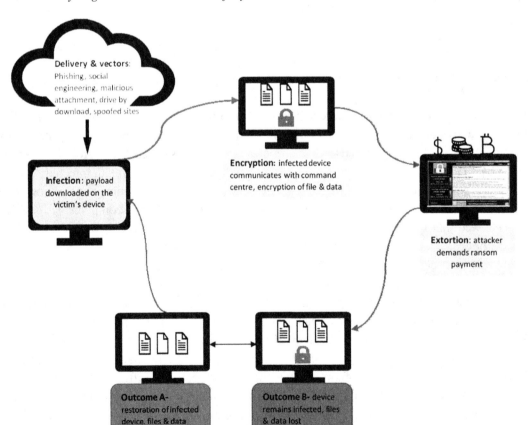

Stage 1: Ransomware Infection

In this phase, the ransomware payload is installed on the victim's device (such as a computer system or mobile device). Several actions are conducted in this first phase to ensure the malicious payload is successfully deployed and disseminated. A ransomware payload is made available to the victim through several attack vectors such as malicious email attachment, drive-by freeware application, and software, or botnet attack (Al-rimy et al., 2018; Bhardwaj et al., 2016). Exploiting human weakness to propagate the ransomware payload is often very effective as the majority of users may not be adequately skilled and knowledgeable about recognising social engineering techniques (Kumar & Ramlie, 2021). These techniques could manipulate the victim to install the ransomware payload from a malicious email attachment or spoofed websites. Social engineering refers to the exploit of human psychology using false interactions to convince a victim to grant access and give away sensitive information (Ferreira & Lenzini, 2015). A victim may be bombarded with targeted (spear) phishing emails, embedded with the ransomware payload. Spear phishing is a social engineering technique targeted at a specific victim, usually via electronic communications disguised as trustworthy and appealing, to coerce the target to divulge personal information (Lastdrager, 2014). Once the ransomware payload successfully infects the victim's device and spreads through the affected network, communication is established to the attacker's server to get the encryption key and report its progress.

Stage 2: Encryption

The encryption phase is a core process in the ransomware lifecycle. A locker ransomware payload on the infected device only initiates a lockdown preventing the victim from accessing the device typically without encrypting data stored on the device (Richardson & North, 2017). On the other hand, crypto ransomware utilises either the Symmetric or Asymmetric algorithm to encrypts files and data found on the device (Kumar & Ramlie, 2021). There is usually one key for both encryption and decryption in a symmetric encryption algorithm, while the asymmetric encryption algorithm encrypts using a public key requiring victims to pay for a decryption key (Kapoor et al., 2022). The crypto ransomware application contacts its command-and-control server to get the encryption key, searches through the victim's device, renaming, deleting, and encrypting targeted user files. The ransomware on the infected device may remain dormant after encrypting the data or spread through the network, encrypting other computer systems, shared network drives, and backup servers (Hampton et al., 2018). Crypto ransomware does not target system-critical files and data, allowing the system to function normally despite the infection.

Stage 3: Extortion

In this stage, the victim is prevented from accessing the lockdown system and device or the encrypted user files and data. A ransom notification is displayed, requesting the victim to make payment within a specified timeframe. Before the advent of bitcoin and anonymous online payment processes, victims were instructed to pay ransoms by mailing pre-paid cards, text messages, or call a premium rate telephone (Richardson & North, 2017). The creation of electronic and anonymous payment channels such as MoneyPak, DarkCoin, or BitCoin (Salvi & Kerkar, 2016) has advanced ransomware making it impossible to trace ransom paid.

Stage 4: Outcome

In this final stage, based on the actions of the victim, there are three possible outcomes: a) the victim is able to eliminate the ransomware application from their devices and restore all encrypted files, b) the victim succumb to the extortion and pays the ransom via the anonymous channels for restoration of the files and devices, or c) no payment is made, the ransomware is not eliminated, the victim's files are lost or destroyed and the device is permanently locked. However, there is no guaranty when dealing with cyber criminals, the victims may or may not get access to the encrypted files or devices after the ransom payment (Richardson & North, 2017).

Ransomware attacks are evolving as technology advances. Information and communications technology have made ordinary users easily accessible and susceptible to socially engineered ransomware attacks. Social engineering exploiting human weakness and error still account for the majority of data breaches in organisations (Verizon, 2019).

Socially Engineered Ransomware Prevention

Social engineering tactics are evolving with technology processes. Attackers can evade security perimeters, socially engineering the user to gain access to enterprise networks through social networks, email, and smart mobile devices. However, preventive and detection measures for social engineering and ransomware are usually evaluated in silos. There are numerous studies focused on social engineering prevention (Richardson, 2017; Saleem & Hammoudeh, 2018; Tailor & Patel, 2017), evaluating ransomware (Al-rimy et al., 2018; O'Kane et al., 2018), and ransomware detection (Azmoodeh et al., 2018; Scaife et al., 2016). The majority of the proposed solutions take a generic and technical approach to social engineering and ransomware prevention. There is no "silver bullet" solution, but perhaps a holistic approach is required to address social engineering and ransomware proposing a human and behavioural solution.

An automated approach for the detection and prevention of ransomware attacks is beneficial, but it has not proved effective because attacks are still pervasive. Ransomware "attack prevention" is the primary approach that has been adopted to deal with the ransomware problem. These approaches aim to prevent potential victims from being attacked in the first place. Table 1 presents preventive procedures proposed by previous studies. These preventive procedures are categorised into two types: proactive and reactive.

Proactive Ransomware Prevention

These proactive procedures primarily aim to avert a ransomware attack from an initial infiltration. Proactive procedure suggests the implementation of proper countermeasures to stop ransomware attacks by avoiding suspicious emails, URL, and disabling macros in office applications (Prakash et al., 2017), disabling remote service and file sharing (Mohurle & Patil, 2017). However, these procedures require the user's involvement in managing the security process, making it prone to human errors. The complexity of these procedures entails that users are skilled and knowledgeable in detecting ransomware attacks.

One proactive method of addressing socially engineered ransomware is training and awareness (Luo & Liao, 2007). In their study, Luo and Liao (2007) proposed a framework that suggests the awareness, education, and training of end-users, familiarising them with policy and procedures, access control and management, and exposure analysis and report. Organisations develop a set of rules that employees have to follow to combat security attacks such as phishing (Komatsu et al., 2013; Kumaraguru et al., 2010).

Previous research has found that such rule-based training methods are not sufficient to enable employees to resist ransomware attacks (Komatsu et al., 2013). Also, socially engineered ransomware attacks could employ dynamic tactics and attack vectors that stealthily elude security perimeter. Researchers are exploring the possibility of causing users to become more aware of social engineering techniques (Rocha Flores & Ekstedt, 2016) to make training more effective, making employees less susceptible to attacks.

Reactive Ransomware Prevention

Although proactive procedures intend to prevent ransomware attacks, reactive procedures aim at attenuating the effect of a ransomware infection. Ransomware victims can survive an attack by restoring a prior backup, reverting to older versions of the encrypted files (Bridges, 2008; Pathak & Nanded, 2016). Socially engineered ransomware victims are maybe naïve and less-skilled individuals, who may not be able to effect the simple proactive procedures. Besides, when users are socially engineered to propagate ransomware, proactive measures become obsolete. Some researchers propose techniques that allow the victim to decrypt their files. For example, Palisse et al. (2017) technique exploit a flaw in the ECB mode encryption, allowing the victim to decrypt the ciphertext using a replay attack. Lee et al. (2017) proposed a technique that backs-up encryption keys in a secure repository to enable victims to recover encrypted ransomware files and infected systems. A drawback to the ECB mode decryption, for ransomware utilising the CBC mode, the solution will likely fail. Similarly, if ransomware uses CAPI cryptographic library, the keys cannot be acquired.

Table 1. Ransomware prevention studies

Author	Luo and Liao (2007)	Bridges (2008)	Kumar and Kumar (2013)	Mustaca (2014)	Pathak and Nanded (2016)	Kolodenker et al. (2017)	Prakash et al. (2017)	Mohurle and Patil (2017)	Palisse et al. (2017)	Lee et al. (2017)	Gómez-Hernández et al. (2018)
Access control	*							*			
Regular Backup		*		*	*		*	*			
Security awareness	*										
Security patches and updates			*		*		*	*			
Deploying security products			*		*		*				
Resources monitoring			*					*			
Security precautions				*	*		*				*
Blocking Popups											
File Recovery						*			*		
Disabling Macros							*	*			
Disabling remote services											
Disabling or restricting file sharing							*				
Disabling unused wireless connections								*			
Key Vault						*				*	
Avoid suspicious emails and attachment							*	*			
Avoid suspicious and unreliable URLs							*	*			

Summary

There is no doubt that socially engineered ransomware presents a significant problem that affects individuals, businesses, and the government. Media reports and government statistics show that ransomware attacks and its associated impacts, such as loss of data, computer systems, devices, and associated financial costs, are increasing worldwide. Numerous studies have analysed and categorise ransomware families to provide solutions to detect and prevent the menace of ransomware attacks but to no avail.

Research has called for socio-technical approaches that incorporate humans as part of the solution to decrease the occurrence of a ransomware attack, ensuring that individuals are able to resist and mitigate socially engineered ransomware attacks.

This exploratory qualitative study addresses the issue of socially engineered ransomware attacks. Ransomware attacks could be socially engineered using phishing as a point of entry in the propagation of malicious payloads. The result of a socially engineered ransomware attack is devastating to the victim, from loss of sensitive data, extortion, and denied access to the infected device. Some victims whose computer systems were infected by the WannaCry ransomware paid the ransom but had no restoration of their data and computer systems (Bistarelli et al., 2018). The resulting themes from this study could provide the information required for security practitioners to develop cybersecurity methodologies and tools to prepare organisations and individuals to prevent socially engineered ransomware attacks.

METHODOLOGY

This study sought to answer questions around individuals, organisations and socially engineered ransomware attacks; and to gain insight about employees' standpoint about socially engineered ransomware. A qualitative method was appropriate to carry out a systematic inquiry about what? and how? aspects of socially engineered ransomware attacks (Teherani et al., 2015). Quantitative research methods are appropriate only when factual data are required to understand cause and effect among variables, test hypotheses, or when the research problem is known and unambiguous (Hammarberg et al., 2016). Therefore, qualitative research was found to be more suitable for this study because it enables the collection of rich and in-depth data around the ransomware phenomenon that is not fully understood and explored (Christensen et al., 2014). A semi-structured interview is deployed for data collection. The semi-structured interview enabled the listing of question themes that the interviewee can respond to, with follow up questions to promote further discussion and comments (Saunders et al., 2016). The study participants were selected from several organisations using non-random sampling (Robinson, 2014).

Participants

Theoretical and practical factors often influence the sample design in qualitative research. In this study, non-random criterion sampling techniques were used to select participants (Robinson, 2014). It was essential to identify study participants who made certain security decisions and functions about the research problem being explored. The study participants were senior and mid-level management employees responsible for end-user security at their organisations and based in Australia. All the participants (see Table 2) interviewed conformed to these criteria, ensuring the appropriateness of the sample.

The sample size in a qualitative study is relatively dependent on the research questions and objectives. Recommendation for sample size is in a qualitative range of 5 and 30 interviews (Creswell, 2013). However, a general recommendation is to conduct additional interviews until data saturation is reached (Saunders et al., 2016). Data saturation occurs when additional data collected brings no new information or incremental benefit to the study (Robinson, 2014). Consequently, in this study, interviews were conducted until thematic data saturation was achieved, resulting to 30 senior and mid-level management staff participants for the study.

Table 2. Summary of interview participants' role and industry

Industry	Respondent Job Role
Insurance	MD
Construction	CTO, CRO, IT Managers
Cryptocurrency-Tech	CTO
Technology (software and services)	Director, CIO, CTO, Solutions Architect, IT Managers
Finance	CIO, CTO, Solutions Architect, IT Project Managers
Hospitality	COO, CTO, IT Managers
Consulting	GM, IT Managers
Education	CIO, CTO
Transport	CTO, CRO, Technology Managers
Health	IT Managers

Materials and Procedures

Data gathering for the study consisted of four processes: (a) ethics approval to obtain the data (b) obtaining informed consents (c) semi-structured interviews data collection, and (d) transcribing recorded interviews for analysis. An email was sent to potential candidates for consent and participation in the study. The interview process was recorded to ensure the accuracy and reliability of the data rather than relying on the researcher's memory (Taylor et al., 2016). The audio recordings were transcribed into text; the researchers defined concepts, themes, and relationships using NVivo Qualitative Data Analysis (QDA) software package (Hilal & AlAbri, 2013).

The semi-structured interview guide comprised of open-ended questions to ensure consistency and efficiency of the interviews (Yin, 2018). The researchers presented the interview questions to a panel of experienced researchers and practitioners to ensure the validity of the questions. The interview sessions were carefully conducted, recorded, and transcribed to ensure the reliability of the data (Taylor et al., 2016). The data collected was professionally transcribed and further analysed. Several themes and patterns were derived from the data as reported in the results section below.

Results

The focus of this study was to understand organisational and individuals susceptibility to socially engineered ransomware attacks. Therefore, to address this key concern, Protection Motivation Theory (PMT) is employed in exploring the results of the study. PMT is a behavioural theory developed based on the expectancy-value theory (Rogers, 1983) to understand the behaviour of technology users and how to influence them to resist susceptibility to threats, such as socially engineered ransomware.

PMT theorise the use of fear appeals to motivate the individual's cognitive appraisal process to spur protective behaviours. The theory explains and predicts individuals' protection motivation action based on perceived fear appeals and cognitive mediating processes. Fear appeals are communications describing unfavorable consequences that may result from the failure to respond in an expected recommendation (Rogers, 1975). An effective fear appeal tends to heighten an individual's awareness and willingness to engage in protective behaviour. Researchers in psychology, information systems, criminology and other fields are continually exploring the effect of fear appeals in making users aware of the consequences of their actions (Johnston et al., 2015; Johnston & Warkentin, 2010). Ophoff and Lakay (2019) study showed that the variables of fear appeals could influence individual's protection motivation in the context of ransomware threats. Subsequently, it is necessary to understand how to influence employees' cognitively, in order to address the excesses in their behaviour and prevent the negative effects of a ransomware attack.

The protection motivation theory conceptualises that intrapersonal and environmental information sources mediated by fear will result in a threat and coping appraisal process. The threat appraisal process consists of threat severity; the extent to which an individual believes a threat is severe, and threat vulnerability; the extent to which they are exposed to a threat (Posey et al., 2014; Rogers, 1983). The coping appraisal refers of the evaluated response costs which an individual considers in preventing a threat (Rogers, 1983). Coping appraisal consists of the response efficacy: the belief that the coping behaviour will successfully eliminate the threat, and self-efficacy: the belief in the individual's ability to perform a protective response. PMT theory's focus in this study is to understand why organisations and individuals are susceptible to socially engineered ransomware attacks; to address the excesses in their behaviour; and prevent the negative effects of a ransomware attack.

The research questions explored why individuals are susceptible to socially engineered ransomware. Through the prism of the protection motivation theory, the results of the data analysis highlight several themes to empower individuals or organisational employees not to succumb to socially engineered ransomware attacks. The emerging themes show that the lack of knowledge on ransomware; lack of awareness on socially engineered ransomware attack vectors; and lack of knowledge on socially engineered ransomware may impede the cognitive appraisal of the perceived ransomware threat. On the other hand, the coping-appraisal evaluation of ransomware threats maybe hampered arising from an assumption of miscreant behaviour; equating IT savviness with susceptibility to ransomware attacks; and lack of training and awareness.

Figure 2 shows the final results of the interview analysis synthesised in the protection motivation theory framework. The central idea of socially engineered ransomware is to exploit the user's lack of knowledge and awareness to ensure ransomware propagation.

Figure 2. Ransomware protection motivation

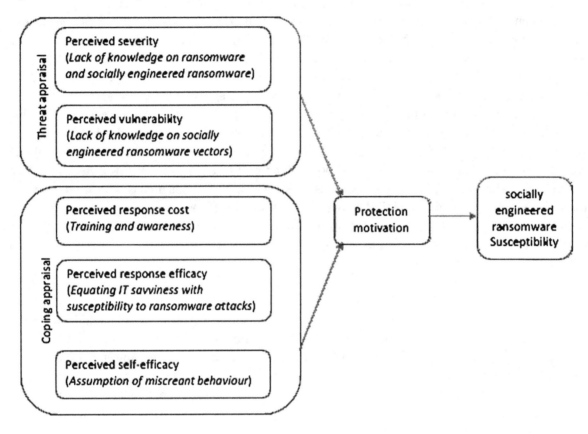

Ransomware Threat Appraisal

As depicted in Figure 2, the threat appraisal process triggers protection motivation if the individual adequately perceives the vulnerability and severity of the ransomware threats. The emerging themes in this study signals that user's knowledge on ransomware may be limited, preventing them from applying ransomware mitigation strategies to prevent propagation and spread.

Lack of Knowledge on Ransomware

As the world increasingly becomes interconnected, there is a significant number of people who are unfamiliar with ransomware attacks. Unfamiliarity about ransomware attack was a strong theme identified from the interview data. Evidently, if these individuals are unaware of what a ransomware attack entail, they are most likely vulnerable and unable to defend themselves against a ransomware attack. The majority of the participants were familiar with media reports or conference discussions on ransomware attacks (25%), while others had vague or no actual knowledge of what ransomware attacks entail (75%). The general perception gleaned from these responses is that only a small fraction of employees may be knowledgeable about ransomware attacks, and how it could potentially impact them.

Lack of Knowledge on Socially Engineered Ransomware

Several participants could not understand how cyberattacks differ from each other. Like the previous theme, employees are often not knowledgeable to discern that a ransomware attack could be socially engineered. The media and security vendors publish basic or highly technical information about ransomware attacks leaving the ordinary user with very little knowledge that ransomware could be socially engineered. Research shows that individuals who are technically knowledgeable and have tremendous insight into information technology processes and procedures may be less susceptible to socially engineered ransomware attacks (Musuva et al., 2019). However, knowledgeable users could fall prey to socially engineered ransomware because these attacks psychologically exploit and manipulate human weaknesses.

Lack of Awareness of Socially Engineered Ransomware Attack Vectors

The data revealed that users have very little information on the various types of socially engineered ransomware attack vectors. The majority of participants (80%) referred to only phishing emails or a compromised software as the ransomware attack vector, while others (20%) have no idea of what vectors could be used to propagate ransomware. However, further probe into the reference to phishing emails as an attack vector revealed that employees had little or no actual knowledge of how an email could potentially spread a ransomware payload. This finding shows that, as with most internet-connected devices, software or applications, they could become attack vectors for socially engineered propagation of ransomware applications.

Ransomware Coping Appraisal

Protection motivation results when users' response costs are low, and positive evaluations are deduced from response efficacy and self-efficacy as indicated in Figure 2. The results show that response costs (training and awareness) outweigh the users' efficacies hindering a protection motivation response.

Assumption of Miscreant Behaviour

A common misconception identified was that participants assume that miscreant user behaviour was a major cause for users to fall prey to socially engineered ransomware attacks. However, analysis of ransomware attacks shows that cybercriminals could exploit network vulnerabilities, use exploit kits, or brute force attacks to disseminate ransomware payload to their victims (Liao et al., 2016; Sahi, 2017). Additionally, about 30% of the participants believe that lack of technical security such as firewalls or antivirus accounts for users who may fall prey to ransomware attacks.

Equating IT Savviness With Susceptibility to Ransomware Attacks

Information technology (IT) savviness was a resounding response that 25% of participants equated to ransomware insusceptibility. Individuals who perceive themselves to be IT savvy are found to likely be vulnerable to socially engineered ransomware attacks due to overconfidence (Ament & Jaeger, 2017; Wang et al., 2016). Another 45% of the participants considered IT degrees, job role, or industry as factors responsible for users to resist socially engineered ransomware. Insusceptibility to socially engineered ransomware requires several components such as education, awareness, and training for individuals to become consciously accustomed to social engineering tactics behind a ransomware attack.

Training and Awareness

Training and awareness were referred to as a crucial method that could enable users to recognise and resist socially engineered ransomware attacks. Individuals and organisational employees need to be aware that their actions could trigger an infection and be knowledgeable about mitigating the spread of ransomware infection in the advert of an attack occurring. However, participants emphasised that basic and traditional training approaches alone may not help to increase users' insusceptibility to socially engineered ransomware attacks.

- **Lack of Pragmatic training approach**: The participants felt that basic training methods are not effective in enabling employees to resist socially engineered ransomware. This implies that training methods should be restructured and supported by research, real-life examples, and experiences from industries. Likewise, variation in training and awareness methods such as infographics, virtual labs, and simulations tests.
- **Lack of cybersecurity education that covers emerging threats**: While training and awareness are crucial for users to become attuned to socially engineered ransomware attacks, cybersecurity education is needed to equip users with the necessary skill and abilities to resist socially engineered ransomware. Cybersecurity education is a broad tool to show individuals "the big picture" about social engineering, ransomware, and staying cyber aware regarding security threats.
- **Lack of practical methodologies to mitigate socially engineered ransomware attacks**: The findings suggest that individuals and organisations need to employ more practical security measures that users can relate with to help mitigate the risk associated with socially engineered ransomware attacks. Consequently, employees require practical training methodologies to proactively ward against socially engineered ransomware rather than being reactive to attacks.

Overall, the summary of the themes and patterns from the semi-structured interviews findings show that users do not possess adequate knowledge about ransomware and attack vectors that could potentially propagate the ransomware threat. Additionally, training and awareness has stemmed as a key approach that could empower employees to be able to identify, protect, and mitigate against socially engineered ransomware attacks.

DISCUSSION

The analysis of the interviews through the PMT framework reveals several misconceptions and false perceptions of understanding socially engineered ransomware.

The protection motivation theory in the context of socially engineered ransomware, demonstrates that individuals and organisational employees may not always appraise security threats correctly. This is evident from the results of the interview, showing that the majority of respondents are unfamiliar with ransomware and unaware they could be socially engineered to propagate a ransomware payload (Al-rimy et al., 2018). The lack of knowledge on ransomware, especially socially engineered ransomware and its attack vectors may indicate the individuals' poor threat appraisal capacity affecting their perception on threat severity and vulnerability. This finding affirms previous research (Johnston & Warkentin, 2010; Ophoff & Lakay, 2019) which explains that users cognitive threat appraisal process motivates the user to perform a recommended protective or maladaptive behaviour. Users need to cognitively perceive and believe that their technology devices could become potential ransomware attack vectors exposing them to a socially engineered ransomware attack. Without a perception of security relevance (Johnston et al., 2019), users may remain susceptible to ransomware attacks.

Previous studies show that users self-efficacy is a vital factor in the ransomware coping appraisal process (Ophoff & Lakay, 2019). Although users may present a threat to security systems and networks due to their susceptibility to socially engineered ransomware attacks (Ferreira & Lenzini, 2015), the findings show that training and awareness is a potential method that could bolster the individuals cognitive appraisal and determine if a protective action will be initiated. This finding supports previous studies (Burns et al., 2013; Rocha Flores & Ekstedt, 2016), and demonstrates that training could empower users to identify and mitigate socially engineered ransomware attacks.

Socially engineered ransomware-based training and awareness program could potentially influence users provided they are presented with relevant information regarding how their social networks (such as colleagues, family members, customers) could be socially engineered in the ransomware propagation process. As socially engineered ransomware rely on human manipulation, practical training and awareness methodologies with languages suitable to the users efficacy levels (Johnston & Warkentin, 2010), are more appropriate to influence users cognitive threat and coping appraisal. An awareness about the intricacies of ransomware attacks could make users more cognisant of effective methods to mitigate socially engineered ransomware attacks (Martens et al., 2019) and initiate protective actions and behaviour when they encounter a socially engineered ransomware threat.

Protection motivation and coping behaviour is dependent on the cognitive mediating process of the individual regarding the threat perceived (Rogers, 1983). However, the costs of the adaptive behavioural responses that will lead to the user's insusceptibility to socially engineered ransomware needs to outweigh other factors presented. Training focused on improving employees' threat perception reinforces the user's self-efficacy and response efficacy motivation regarding socially engineered ransomware attacks.

In this study, the results show that protection motivation theory reflects the role of individuals or organisational employees cognitive mediating process, and the significant role in empowering their responses to not engage or engage in appropriate actions to protect their devices and information assets against socially engineered ransomware threats. The results show that the lack of knowledge on socially engineered ransomware, and potential attack vectors may contribute to employees not being able to adequately appraise socially engineered ransomware threats. However, pragmatic training methodologies and approaches could increase individuals' security awareness and knowledge on socially engineered ransomware and increase their self-efficacy to mitigate and combat socially engineered ransomware attacks. These findings expand previous studies (Ophoff & Lakay, 2019) and contribute to the ransomware body of knowledge regarding shaping employee's cognitive processes and behaviour to enable them resist socially engineered attacks (see Figure 2).

RECOMMENDATIONS

The findings from this qualitative study identified themes that provide a basis for commendation to practitioners and future studies. The themes and patterns originated from this study support the findings of previous studies such as the literature on security behaviour, and technology usage (Boss et al., 2015; Ophoff & Lakay, 2019; Rocha Flores & Ekstedt, 2016).

A key recommendation is that IT and security managers need to collaborate with other departments to classify employees based on their level of security knowledge and awareness. Creating these categories will help to identify training needs and make training programs more efficient and targeted to the various user categories. For example, skilled training to IT staff versus phishing training exercises to administrative staff.

Finally, training should incorporate relevant and practical scenarios based on the various categories of defined users. The design and implementation of training approaches should comprise of up-to-date real-life examples extracted from security logs or similar industries that highlight the various stages of propagation, infection, and impact of socially engineered ransomware attacks. These real-life examples will evoke the users' curiosity and protective response, which will result in employees being less susceptible to socially engineered ransomware attacks (Rocha Flores & Ekstedt, 2016).

LIMITATIONS AND FUTURE RESEARCH

The limitations of this study are centered on the use of qualitative interviews as common with most qualitative studies, making it difficult to generalise the findings. However, a qualitative study was most suitable to gain deeper insights into individuals and organisational perspectives about socially engineered ransomware. The study design employed a concise interview plan and guide for the interview process to ensure the reliability and validity of the qualitative data collected. Future research could provide a quantitative validation of the qualitative themes reported, evaluating how security and behavioural theories can be extended using the findings.

Another limitation lies in the scope of the sample context. Hence, it would be beneficial to conduct this study in more than one country. Previous studies show that culture (organisational and national) usually influences security behaviour, technology usage, and acceptance (Lowry et al., 2011; Menard et al., 2018). To determine if individuals' susceptibility to ransomware attacks varies in different context, future research should focus on conducting multicultural studies by exploring the role of culture in shaping users' perception towards socially engineered ransomware attacks across several geographical regions.

CONCLUSION

Ransomware attacks still remain a phenomenon that is not well understood, and a predicament that is not adequately addressed by the literature and practitioners. As ransomware continues to plague organisations, more research - academic and practitioner, is required to address this issue. Ransomware has been around since 1989 and became a persistent issue. The frequency of attacks has now made it a global issue.

Socially engineered ransomware leverages on technology advancement and explosion to ensure rapid propagation. Loss of data, downtime, and financial costs are some potential impacts. Previous studies conducted focus on analysing and categorising ransomware strains to propose technical solutions to detect, prevent, and mitigate ransomware attacks. However, attackers now socially engineer technology users to bypass security perimeters, deploying ransomware payload and infecting devices. The findings from this study show that employees form an integral part of the solution if provided with adequate security training and awareness to enable them to identify and mitigate socially engineered ransomware attacks. A significant contribution is that the findings established a pool of information that could expand theories such as PMT for researchers to employ in studying and predicting behaviour and factors that influence susceptibility to ransomware attack strains.

REFERENCES

Akbanov, M., Vassilakis, V. G., & Logothetis, M. D. (2019). Ransomware detection and mitigation using software-defined networking: The case of WannaCry. *Computers & Electrical Engineering*, *76*, 111–121. doi:10.1016/j.compeleceng.2019.03.012

Al-rimy, B. A. S., Maarof, M. A., & Shaid, S. Z. M. (2018). Ransomware threat success factors, taxonomy, and countermeasures: A survey and research directions. *Computers & Security*, *74*, 144–166. doi:10.1016/j.cose.2018.01.001

Ament, C., & Jaeger, L. (2017). Unconscious on their Own Ignorance:Overconfidence in Information Security. Association for Information Systems, 13.

Anderson, C. L., & Agarwal, R. (2010). Practicing Safe Computing: A Multimethod Empirical Examination of Home Computer User Security Behavioral Intentions. *Management Information Systems Quarterly*, *34*(3), 613–643. doi:10.2307/25750694

Ariffin, N., Zainal, A., Maarof, M. A., & Nizam Kassim, M. (2018). A Conceptual Scheme for Ransomware Background Knowledge Construction. *2018 Cyber Resilience Conference (CRC)*, 1–4. 10.1109/CR.2018.8626868

Azmoodeh, A., Dehghantanha, A., Conti, M., & Choo, K.-K. R. (2018). Detecting crypto-ransomware in IoT networks based on energy consumption footprint. *Journal of Ambient Intelligence and Humanized Computing*, *9*(4), 1141–1152. doi:10.1007/s12652-017-0558-5

Beaman, C., Barkworth, A., Akande, T. D., Hakak, S., & Khan, M. K. (2021). Ransomware: Recent advances, analysis, challenges and future research directions. *Computers & Security*, *111*, 102490. doi:10.1016/j.cose.2021.102490 PMID:34602684

Bhardwaj, A., Avasthi, V., Sastry, H., & Subrahmanyam, G. V. B. (2016). Ransomware digital extortion: A rising new age threat. *Indian Journal of Science and Technology*, *9*(14), 1–5. doi:10.17485/ijst/2016/v9i14/82936

Bistarelli, S., Parroccini, M., & Santini, F. (2018). Visualising Bitcoin Flows of Ransomware: WannaCry One Week Later. *ITASEc*, 8.

Boss, S. R., Galletta, D. F., Benjamin Lowry, P., Moody, G. D., & Polak, P. (2015). What Do Systems Users Have to Fear? Using Fear Appeals to Engender Threats and Fear That Motivate Protective Security Behaviors. *Management Information Systems Quarterly*, *39*(4), 837–864. doi:10.25300/MISQ/2015/39.4.5

Bridges, L. (2008). The changing face of malware. *Network Security*, *2008*(1), 17–20. doi:10.1016/S1353-4858(08)70010-2

Bulgurcu, B., Cavusoglu, H., & Benbasat, I. (2010). Information Security Policy Compliance: An Empirical Study of Rationality-Based Beliefs and Information Security Awareness. *Management Information Systems Quarterly*, *34*(3), 523–A7. doi:10.2307/25750690

Burns, M. B., Durcikova, A., & Jenkins, J. L. (2013). What Kind of Interventions Can Help Users from Falling for Phishing Attempts: A Research Proposal for Examining Stage-Appropriate Interventions. *2013 46th Hawaii International Conference on System Sciences*, 4023–4032. 10.1109/HICSS.2013.606

Christensen, L. B., Johnson, B., & Turner, L. A. (2014). *Research methods, design, and analysis* (12th ed.). Pearson.

Creswell, J. W. (2013). Qualitative Inquiry & Research Design: Choosing among Five Approaches (3rd ed.). SAGE Publications.

Crowdstrike. (2019). *2019 Global Threat Report: Adversary Tradecraft and the Importance of Speed*. https://crowdstrike.lookbookhq.com/web-global-threat-report-2019/crowdstrike-2019-gtr

EY. (2017). *'WannaCry' ransomware attack: Technical intelligence analysis*. Ernst & Young. https://www.ey.com/Publication/vwLUAssets/ey-wannacry-ransomware-attack/$FILE/ey-wannacry-ransomware-attack.pdf

FBI. (2018). *2018 Internet Crime Report*. Federal Bureau of Investigation. https://www.ic3.gov/media/annualreport/2018_IC3Report.pdf

Ferreira, A., & Lenzini, G. (2015). An analysis of social engineering principles in effective phishing. *2015 Workshop on Socio-Technical Aspects in Security and Trust*, 9–16. 10.1109/STAST.2015.10

Furnell, S., & Clarke, N. (2012). Power to the people? The evolving recognition of human aspects of security. *Computers & Security*, *31*(8), 983–988. doi:10.1016/j.cose.2012.08.004

Furnell, S., Khern-am-nuai, W., Esmael, R., Yang, W., & Li, N. (2018). Enhancing security behaviour by supporting the user. *Computers & Security*, *75*, 1–9. doi:10.1016/j.cose.2018.01.016

Gallegos-Segovia, P. L., Bravo-Torres, J. F., Larios-Rosillo, V. M., Vintimilla-Tapia, P. E., Yuquilima-Albarado, I. F., & Jara-Saltos, J. D. (2017). Social engineering as an attack vector for ransomware. *2017 CHILEAN Conference on Electrical, Electronics Engineering, Information and Communication Technologies (CHILECON)*, 1–6. 10.1109/CHILECON.2017.8229528

Gibbs, S. (2017). WannaCry: Hackers withdraw £108,000 of bitcoin ransom. *The Guardian*. https://www.theguardian.com/technology/2017/aug/03/wannacry-hackers-withdraw-108000-pounds-bitcoin-ransom

Giri, B. N., Jyoti, N., & Avert, M. (2006). *The emergence of ransomware*. AVAR.

Gómez-Hernández, J. A., Álvarez-González, L., & García-Teodoro, P. (2018). R-Locker: Thwarting ransomware action through a honeyfile-based approach. *Computers & Security, 73*, 389–398. doi:10.1016/j. cose.2017.11.019

Hammarberg, K., Kirkman, M., & de Lacey, S. (2016). Qualitative research methods: When to use them and how to judge them. *Human Reproduction (Oxford, England), 31*(3), 498–501. doi:10.1093/humrep/ dev334 PMID:26759142

Hampton, N., Baig, Z. A., & Zeadally, S. (2018). Ransomware behavioural analysis on windows platforms. *Journal of Information Security and Applications, 40*, 44–51. doi:10.1016/j.jisa.2018.02.008

Herath, T., & Rao, H. R. (2009). Protection motivation and deterrence: A framework for security policy compliance in organisations. *European Journal of Information Systems, 18*(2), 106–125. doi:10.1057/ ejis.2009.6

Hilal, A. H., & AlAbri, S. S. (2013). Using Nvivo for Data Analysis in Qualitative Research. *International Interdisciplinary Journal of Education, 2*(2), 181–186. doi:10.12816/0002914

Hull, G., John, H., & Arief, B. (2019). Ransomware deployment methods and analysis: Views from a predictive model and human responses. *Crime Science, 8*(1), 2. doi:10.118640163-019-0097-9

Humayun, M., Jhanjhi, N., Alsayat, A., & Ponnusamy, V. (2021). Internet of things and ransomware: Evolution, mitigation and prevention. *Egyptian Informatics Journal, 22*(1), 105–117. doi:10.1016/j. eij.2020.05.003

IC3. (2020, March 20). *FBI Sees Rise in Fraud Schemes Related to the Coronavirus (COVID-19) Pandemic.* https://www.ic3.gov/media/2020/200320.aspx

IBM. (2022). *X-Force Threat Intelligence Index 2022.* IBM. https://www.ibm.com/downloads/cas/ ADLMYLAZ

Ifinedo, P. (2012). Understanding information systems security policy compliance: An integration of the theory of planned behavior and the protection motivation theory. *Computers & Security, 31*(1), 83–95. doi:10.1016/j.cose.2011.10.007

Johnston, A. C., & Warkentin, M. (2010). Fear Appeals and Information Security Behaviors: An Empirical Study. *Management Information Systems Quarterly, 34*(3), 549–A4. doi:10.2307/25750691

Johnston, A. C., Warkentin, M., Dennis, A. R., & Siponen, M. (2019). Speak their Language: Designing Effective Messages to Improve Employees' Information Security Decision Making. *Decision Sciences, 50*(2), 245–284. doi:10.1111/deci.12328

Johnston, A. C., Warkentin, M., & Siponen, M. (2015). An Enhanced Fear Appeal Rhetorical Framework: Leveraging Threats to the Human Asset Through Sanctioning Rhetoric. *Management Information Systems Quarterly, 39*(1), 113–A7. doi:10.25300/MISQ/2015/39.1.06

Kalaimannan, E., John, S. K., DuBose, T., & Pinto, A. (2017). Influences on ransomware's evolution and predictions for the future challenges. *Journal of Cyber Security Technology, 1*(1), 23–31. doi:10.1 080/23742917.2016.1252191

Kapoor, A., Gupta, A., Gupta, R., Tanwar, S., Sharma, G., & Davidson, I. E. (2022). Ransomware Detection, Avoidance, and Mitigation Scheme: A Review and Future Directions. *Sustainability*, *14*(1), 8. doi:10.3390u14010008

Kolodenker, E., Koch, W., Stringhini, G., & Egele, M. (2017). PayBreak: Defense Against Cryptographic Ransomware. *Proceedings of the 2017 ACM on Asia Conference on Computer and Communications Security - ASIA CCS '17*, 599–611. 10.1145/3052973.3053035

Komatsu, A., Takagi, D., & Takemura, T. (2013). Human aspects of information security: An empirical study of intentional versus actual behavior. *Information Management & Computer Security*, *21*(1), 5–15. doi:10.1108/09685221311314383

Kumar, P. R., & Ramlie, H. R. E. B. H. (2021). Anatomy of Ransomware: Attack Stages, Patterns and Handling Techniques. *Computational Intelligence in Information Systems*, 205–214. doi:10.1007/978-3-030-68133-3_20

Kumar, S. M., & Kumar, M. R. (2013). Cryptoviral Extortion: A virus based approach. *International Journal of Computer Trends and Technology*, *5*(5), 1150–1153.

Kumaraguru, P., Sheng, S., Acquisti, A., Cranor, L. F., & Hong, J. (2010). Teaching Johnny not to fall for phish. *ACM Transactions on Internet Technology*, *10*(2), 1–31. doi:10.1145/1754393.1754396

Lastdrager, E. E. (2014). Achieving a consensual definition of phishing based on a systematic review of the literature. *Crime Science*, *3*(1), 9. Advance online publication. doi:10.118640163-014-0009-y

Lee, H.-K., Seong, J.-H., Kim, Y.-C., Kim, J.-B., & Gim, G.-Y. (2017). The Automation Model of Ransomware Analysis and Detection Pattern. *Journal of the Korea Institute of Information and Communication Engineering*, *21*(8), 1581–1588.

Liao, K., Zhao, Z., Doupe, A., & Ahn, G. (2016). Behind closed doors: Measurement and analysis of CryptoLocker ransoms in Bitcoin. *2016 APWG Symposium on Electronic Crime Research (ECrime)*, 1–13. 10.1109/ECRIME.2016.7487938

Lowry, P. B., Cao, J., & Everard, A. (2011). Privacy Concerns Versus Desire for Interpersonal Awareness in Driving the Use of Self-Disclosure Technologies: The Case of Instant Messaging in Two Cultures. *Journal of Management Information Systems*, *27*(4), 163–200. doi:10.2753/MIS0742-1222270406

Luo, X., & Liao, Q. (2007). Awareness Education as the Key to Ransomware Prevention. *Information Systems Security*, *16*(4), 195–202. doi:10.1080/10658980701576412

Mansfield-Devine, S. (2016). Ransomware: Taking businesses hostage. *Network Security*, *2016*(10), 8–17. doi:10.1016/S1353-4858(16)30096-4

Martens, M., De Wolf, R., & De Marez, L. (2019). Investigating and comparing the predictors of the intention towards taking security measures against malware, scams and cybercrime in general. *Computers in Human Behavior*, *92*, 139–150. doi:10.1016/j.chb.2018.11.002

Martin, A., Hernandez-Castro, J., & Camacho, D. (2018). An in-depth study of the jisut family of android ransomware. *IEEE Access: Practical Innovations, Open Solutions*, *6*, 57205–57218. Advance online publication. doi:10.1109/ACCESS.2018.2873583

Masum, M., Hossain Faruk, M. J., Shahriar, H., Qian, K., Lo, D., & Adnan, M. I. (2022). Ransomware Classification and Detection With Machine Learning Algorithms. *2022 IEEE 12th Annual Computing and Communication Workshop and Conference (CCWC)*, 316–322. 10.1109/CCWC54503.2022.9720869

Maurushat, A., Bello, A., & Bragg, B. (2019). Artificial Intelligence Enabled Cyber Fraud: A Detailed Look into Payment Diversion Fraud and Ransomware. *Indian Journal of Law and Technology*, *15*(2), 261–299.

McGill, T., & Thompson, N. (2017). Old risks, new challenges: Exploring differences in security between home computer and mobile device use. *Behaviour & Information Technology*, *36*(11), 1111–1124. doi :10.1080/0144929X.2017.1352028

Menard, P., Warkentin, M., & Lowry, P. B. (2018). The impact of collectivism and psychological ownership on protection motivation: A cross-cultural examination. *Computers & Security*, *75*, 147–166. doi:10.1016/j.cose.2018.01.020

Mohurle, S., & Patil, M. (2017). A brief study of Wannacry Threat: Ransomware Attack 2017. *International Journal of Advanced Research in Computer Science, 8*(5), 1938–1940.

Mustaca, S. (2014). Are your IT professionals prepared for the challenges to come? *Computer Fraud & Security*, *2014*(3), 18–20. doi:10.1016/S1361-3723(14)70472-5

Musuva, P. M. W., Getao, K. W., & Chepken, C. K. (2019). A new approach to modelling the effects of cognitive processing and threat detection on phishing susceptibility. *Computers in Human Behavior*, *94*, 154–175. doi:10.1016/j.chb.2018.12.036

National Audit. (2017). *Investigation-WannaCry-cyber-attack-and-the-NHS.pdf*. https://www.nao.org.uk/wp-content/uploads/2017/10/Investigation-WannaCry-cyber-attack-and-the-NHS.pdf

News, A. B. C. (2019, October 1). *Victorian hospitals lock down IT systems after ransomware attack*. ABC News. https://www.abc.net.au/news/2019-10-01/victorian-health-services-targeted-by-ransomware-attack/11562988

O'Kane, P., Sezer, S., & Carlin, D. (2018). Evolution of Ransomware. *IET Networks*, *7*(5), 321–327. doi:10.1049/iet-net.2017.0207

Ophoff, J., & Lakay, M. (2019). Mitigating the Ransomware Threat: A Protection Motivation Theory Approach. In H. Venter, M. Loock, M. Coetzee, M. Eloff, & J. Eloff (Eds.), *Information Security* (Vol. 973, pp. 163–175). Springer International Publishing. doi:10.1007/978-3-030-11407-7_12

Palisse, A., Le Bouder, H., Lanet, J.-L., Le Guernic, C., & Legay, A. (2017). Ransomware and the Legacy Crypto API. In F. Cuppens, N. Cuppens, J.-L. Lanet, & A. Legay (Eds.), *Risks and Security of Internet and Systems* (pp. 11–28). Springer International Publishing. doi:10.1007/978-3-319-54876-0_2

Pathak, P. B., & Nanded, Y. M. (2016). A Dangerous Trend of Cybercrime: Ransomware Growing Challenge. *International Journal of Advanced Research in Computer Engineering and Technology*, *5*(2), 371–373.

Posey, C., Roberts, T. L., Lowry, P. B., & Hightower, R. T. (2014). Bridging the divide: A qualitative comparison of information security thought patterns between information security professionals and ordinary organizational insiders. *Information & Management, 51*(5), 551–567. doi:10.1016/j.im.2014.03.009

Prakash, K. P., Nafis, T., & Biswas, S. S. (2017). Preventive Measures and Incident Response for Locky Ransomware. *International Journal of Advanced Research in Computer Science, 8*(5), 392–395.

Reshmi, T. R. (2021). Information security breaches due to ransomware attacks—A systematic literature review. *International Journal of Information Management Data Insights, 1*(2), 100013. doi:10.1016/j.jjimei.2021.100013

Richardson, R. (2017). Ransomware: Evolution. *Mitigation and Prevention., 13*(1), 13.

Richardson, R., & North, M. (2017). Ransomware: Evolution. *Mitigation and Prevention., 13*(1), 12.

Robinson, O. C. (2014). Sampling in Interview-Based Qualitative Research: A Theoretical and Practical Guide. *Qualitative Research in Psychology, 11*(1), 25–41. doi:10.1080/14780887.2013.801543

Rocha Flores, W., & Ekstedt, M. (2016). Shaping intention to resist social engineering through transformational leadership, information security culture and awareness. *Computers & Security, 59*, 26–44. doi:10.1016/j.cose.2016.01.004

Rocha Flores, W., Holm, H., Svensson, G., & Ericsson, G. (2014). Using phishing experiments and scenario-based surveys to understand security behaviours in practice. *Information Management & Computer Security, 22*(4), 393–406. doi:10.1108/IMCS-11-2013-0083

Rogers, R. W. (1975). A Protection Motivation Theory of fear appeals and attitude change. *The Journal of Psychology, 91*(1), 93–114. doi:10.1080/00223980.1975.9915803 PMID:28136248

Rogers, R. W. (1983). Cognitive and physiological processes in fear appeals and attitude change: A revised theory of protection motivation. In J. Cacioppo & R. Petty (Eds.), *Social Psychophysiology*. Guilford Press.

Sahi, S. K. (2017). A Study of WannaCry Ransomware Attack. *International Journal of Engineering Research in Computer Science and Engineering, 4*(9), 5–7.

Saleem, J., & Hammoudeh, M. (2018). Defense Methods Against Social Engineering Attacks. In K. Daimi (Ed.), *Computer and Network Security Essentials* (pp. 603–618). Springer International Publishing. doi:10.1007/978-3-319-58424-9_35

Salvi, M. H. U., & Kerkar, M. R. V. (2016). Ransomware: A cyber extortion. *Asian Journal for Convergence in Technology (AJCT), 2*.

Saunders, M., Lewis, P., & Thornhill, A. (2016). *Research Methods for Business Students* (7th ed.). Pearson.

Scaife, N., Carter, H., Traynor, P., & Butler, K. R. B. (2016). CryptoLock (and Drop It): Stopping Ransomware Attacks on User Data. *2016 IEEE 36th International Conference on Distributed Computing Systems (ICDCS)*, 303–312.

Tailor, J. P., & Patel, A. D. (2017). *A Comprehensive Survey: Ransomware Attacks Prevention, Monitoring and Damage Control.* Academic Press.

Taylor, S. J., Bogdan, R., & DeVault, M. L. (2016). *Introduction to Qualitative Research Methods* (4th ed.). John Wiley & Sons.

Teherani, A., Martimianakis, T., Stenfors-Hayes, T., Wadhwa, A., & Varpio, L. (2015). Choosing a Qualitative Research Approach. *Journal of Graduate Medical Education, 7*(4), 669–670. doi:10.4300/JGME-D-15-00414.1 PMID:26692985

Telstra. (2019). *Telstra Security Report 2019.* Telstra. https://www.telstra.com.au/content/dam/shared-component-assets/tecom/campaigns/security-report/TELE0394_Telstra_Security_Report_2019.pdf

Verizon. (2019). *2019 Data Breach Investigations Report* (Data Breach Investigations Report) [12th]. Verizon. https://www.key4biz.it/wp-content/uploads/2019/05/2019-data-breach-investigations-report.pdf

Wang, J., Li, Y., & Rao, H. R. (2016). Overconfidence in Phishing Email Detection. *Journal of the Association for Information Systems, 17*(11), 759–783. Advance online publication. doi:10.17705/1jais.00442

Yin, R. K. (2018). *Case Study Research: Design and Methods* (6th ed.). Sage.

ZDNet. (2019). *Georgia county pays a whopping $400,000 to get rid of a ransomware infection.* ZDNet. https://www.zdnet.com/article/georgia-county-pays-a-whopping-400000-to-get-rid-of-a-ransomware-infection/

Zimba, A., & Mulenga, M. (2018). A dive into the deep: demystifying WannaCry crypto ransomware network attacks via digital forensics. *International Journal on Information Technologies & Security, 4*(2).

Chapter 14
Prevention of Cryptojacking Attacks in Business and FinTech Applications

Subhan Ullah

Department of Cybersecurity, FAST School of Computing, Pakistan & FAST National University of Computer and Emerging Sciences, Islamabad, Pakistan

Tahir Ahmad

 https://orcid.org/0000-0001-8105-6791

Center for Cybersecurity, Bruno Kessler Foundation, Trento, Italy

Rizwan Ahmad

 https://orcid.org/0000-0002-4758-7895

School of Electrical Engineering and Computer Science, National University of Sciences and Technology, Islamabad, Pakistan

Mudassar Aslam

 https://orcid.org/0000-0003-3223-4234

Department of Cybersecurity, FAST School of Computing, Pakistan & FAST National University of Computer and Emerging Sciences, Islamabad, Pakistan

ABSTRACT

More than 2000 different cryptocurrencies are currently available in business and FinTech applications. Cryptocurrency is a digital payment system that does not rely on banks to verify their financial transactions and can enable anyone anywhere to send and receive their payments. Crypto mining attracts investors to mine and gets some coins as a reward for using the cryptocurrency. However, hackers can exploit the computing power without the explicit authorization of a user by launching a cryptojacking attack and then using it to mine cryptocurrency. The detection and protection of cryptojacking attacks are essential, and thus, miners are continuously working to find innovative ways to overcome this issue. This chapter provides an overview of the cryptojacking landscape. It offers recommendations to guide researchers and practitioners to overcome the identified challenges faced while realizing a mitigation strategy to combat cryptojacking malware attacks.

DOI: 10.4018/978-1-6684-5284-4.ch014

INTRODUCTION

There has been a rise in cryptocurrencies as an investment platform (Kamps & Kleinberg, 2018). According to the Statistica (Statistica., 2022) weekly report (from July 2010 to May 2022), the overall cryptocurrency market capitalization per week was around 1354.54 USD in May 2022. The most popular one is Bitcoin, a decentralized cryptocurrency that has become popular in the last decade. It is a peer-to-peer electronic currency that may be sent from one user to another without needing a trusted authority like a central bank or an administrator (Nakamoto, 2008; Toyoda et al., 2019). Unlike traditional currencies, bitcoin has two key features: 1) Transparency: a decentralized ledger (also termed Blockchain) stores publicly announced transactions, and 2) Pseudo-anonymity: the unlinkability between the pseudonyms (addresses) and the individuals (Nakamoto, 2008). The users can generate bitcoin addresses from the user's public keys at will (Toyoda et al., 2019). The users can create a unique address for each transaction. This flexibility increases privacy by creating an additional layer to keep the addresses from being linked to a specific owner (Nakamoto, 2008). Blockchain offers a broad collection of solutions synchronized by unique consensus processes, from installing public digital ledgers to supporting private and permissioned digital ledgers. Creating cryptographic communication among end-users and not deploying a centralized governance infrastructure promotes delicate interactions. Zero-knowledge proof and asymmetric key encryption prevent retroactive data change and improve individual authoritative ownership.

Figure 1. Cryptocurrencies ecosystem

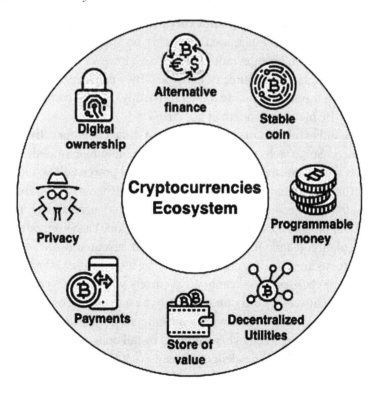

In the light of decentralized ledger technology, exclusive applications of cryptocurrencies are lead-ing toward an economic paradigm and a possible game-changer. In recent years, diversification in the investment opportunities in cryptocurrencies has sought new market alternatives for international stake-holders, policymakers, and regulators. The fine-tuned success of bitcoin ushered in a slew of innovative cryptocurrencies that use regulatory loopholes to create various financial bubbles. Even though these economic bubbles have the potential to spread highly contagious economic difficulties, their rate of financial return is at an all-time high. Because the market capitalization of these cryptocurrencies and their return rate depend on speculative projections and are very volatile, this instability exists (Vidal, 2020). The concept of Blockchain is at the heart of a significant number of cryptocurrencies because it enables peer-to-peer (P2P) fund transfers in a trustless, decentralized computing environment (Lohachab et al., 2021). Figure 1 shows the cryptocurrencies ecosystem; it is evident that emerging Blockchain and cryptocurrency-based technologies are redefining how we conduct business in cyberspace. Today, many crypto mining techniques and technologies are widely available to companies, end-users, and even malicious actors who want to exploit the computational resources of regular users through cryptojack-ing malware.

The process of mining, in which a group of users solves computational challenges to validate transac-tions and add them to the blockchain digital ledger, is the foundation of these cryptocurrencies (Stroud, 2018). Crypto mining draws investors, who are rewarded with coins for using cryptocurrencies. Dedicated hardware solutions, such as GPU and ASIC mining rigs have dominated cryptocurrency mining. This situation has begun to alter with the development of memory-bound cryptocurrencies like Monero, By-tecoin, and Ethereum. These currencies are based on memory-intensive computational puzzles, reducing the advantage of specialized hardware over commodity processors (Vries., 2018; Gohwong., 2019). As a result, the generated currencies may be mined profitably on standard computer systems, paving the way for cryptocurrency mining to become more ubiquitous. However, this rise has attracted criminals who have discovered bitcoins as a new source of earnings. They can leverage the available resources to generate revenue by fooling users into running a miner invisibly on their computers (a technique known as cryptojacking or drive-by mining) (Konoth et al., 2018).

Crypto mining is not unlawful, and many people opt to mine coins for a living by running files or scripts on their computers. Some websites may utilize coin mining to earn cash instead of advertising, which is fine as long as customers are informed that their CPU power will be used to mine cryptocur-rency while they are on the site. Mining a cryptocurrency such as Bitcoin requires more computing power because of the competitive and network-based activity for solving puzzles to get rewards. The resource usage for mining depends on hardware computing power, network hash rate, puzzles' complexity, and hardware's thermal regulation (Clark & Greanly., 2019). The resource usage of cryptojacking attacks also depends on the scenario in which it occurs. However, an attacker uses a low-energy device with ef-ficient mining capability or chooses a less competitive currency to mine. Cryptojacking attacks vary in sophistication and ability (Magazine., 2021), and generally, an increase in computational power increases the mining capability. Cryptojacking occurs when consumers are unaware that their computers are be-ing used to mine cryptocurrency or when cybercriminals install coin miners on victims' PCs or Internet of Things (IoT) devices without their knowledge. Mining cryptocurrency or creating new crypto coins often demands massive processing power, with the Bitcoin network calculating 71 quintillion hashes per second and requiring 7 Mwh. Cryptocurrency's growing popularity encourages hackers to deploy a specific type of malware (i.e., cryptojacking malware) to mine cryptocurrencies on victims' computers for profit. Arianna et al. (Arianna et al., 2022), Kaspersky (Robot., 2019), Symantec (Gorman., 2019), and Eset (Keeve., 2019) all claim an increase in the number of attacks that result in unauthorized mining on impacted systems.

More than 50 million cryptojacking attacks were detected in the first six months of 2019, up 450 percent over the same period in 2018 (Zorabedian., 2018). When a device is attacked with cryptojacking malware, the hacker gains control of its computing power and uses a portion to mine cryptocurrencies and send the coins to the hacker's wallet. By starting a cryptojacking attack and exploiting it to mine bitcoin, hackers can use processing resources without the user's explicit permission. Cryptojacking malware must be detected and protected; thus, miners are constantly attempting to develop new ways to combat the problem. Cryptojacking activity peaked in December 2017, when Symantec saw more than 8 million cryptojacking occurrences (Zorabedian., 2018). While there has been a minor decrease in action in 2018, it remains high, with total cryptojacking events prevented in July 2018 totaling slightly under 5 million. Monero (Li., 2019) is the primary cryptocurrency mined by these cryptojacking miners. It takes advantage of web browsers' ability to run code. The code in question is designed to "mine" bitcoins. The now-defunct website coinhive.com, for example, released browser-based crypto mining code that could mine Monero cryptocurrency bits. The initial concept was that users might reimburse a website provider by lending some of their browser's CPU cycles when visiting the site. This was a way to monetize 'free access' materials without relying on advertisements. Cryptojacking malware attacks are simple to launch but challenging to detect. They may be found on any Internet-connected device with a CPU, such as smartphones, computers, and the Internet of Things (Razali., 2019).

Most of the literature on cryptocurrencies lacks a comprehensive examination of its underlying monetization platform, i.e., crypto mining and how an attacker can exploit it using cryptojacking malware. Considering this, the motivation for conducting this study is threefold:

1. To understand the progressive development of mitigation strategies to counter cryptojacking malware attacks.
2. To analyze state-of-the-art for interwoven security issues that impact the current cryptocurrency monetizing model, i.e., the crypto mining paradigm.
3. To provide guidelines for researchers and practitioners in combating cryptojacking malware attacks.

The rest of the chapter is structured as follows: Section 2 presents the background information on the underlying technologies, i.e., crypto mining and cryptojacking. Section 3 surveys the existing literature on cryptojacking malware detection, prevention, and the challenges that hinder an appropriate attack-specific mitigation strategy. It also discusses the existing cryptojacking malware detection strategies. Section 4 lists recommendations to researchers (in the form of research directions) and practitioners (in the form of best practices). Finally, Section 5 concludes the chapter.

BACKGROUND

This section presents the necessary background information on crypto mining and cryptojacking.

Crypto Mining

Cryptocurrency mining (Ingalls., 2018)) is a vital component of the distributed blockchain ledger's upkeep and continuity, as it is how new cryptocurrencies enter circulation. The consensus mechanism, cryptocurrency mining, ensures the immutability of a blockchain network. Cryptocurrency mining is based on a problem based on cryptographic hash algorithms' primary properties. The Proof of Work (PoW) consensus model is the most common type of work-based consensus model. Cryptocurrency mining is a time-consuming, expensive activity in which one's payout is determined by luck. Work-based consensus techniques benefit from the hash algorithms' diffusion characteristic, which prevents miners from systematically anticipating hash values while preserving the luck factor. The miners are rewarded in cryptocurrencies for their efforts; it is an essential source of revenue for many cryptocurrency investors. However, the hardware investment increases with the complexity of solving the underlying mathematical problem (i.e., computing hash functions) (Tekiner et al., 2022).

While traditional cryptocurrency mining requires specialized hardware to be profitable, memory-bound currencies and new web standards have made it possible to mine in web browsers. Browser-based crypto mining exploded in popularity in the autumn of 2017 due to the advent of CPU-minable cryptocurrencies (such as Monero) and the rapid development of beneficial web standards (such as WebAssembly and the Stratum protocol). As an alternative to ads, Coinhive, a German firm, developed a simple browser-based mining tool (Coinhave2., 2018; Krebs., 2018). Developers can easily add a browser-based miner onto their website and let their visitors mine for Monero using a JavaScript library, an API, and a WebSocket proxy infrastructure. Coinhive keeps 30% of the mined Monero and gives 70% to the account owner. Similar miner applications, such as Cryptoloot (cryptoloot., 2018) and Coin-Have (Coinhave., 2018), sprung up shortly after Coinhive released theirs. Miner software comes and goes these days, with varying capacities and usage costs, but Coinhive remains a significant figure in the cryptojacking world.

Cryptojacking

Cryptojacking is the act of mining cryptocurrencies with the victim's computer capacity without their consent. This unlawful mining process consumes more electricity and significantly reduces the victim host's computational efficiency. As a result, the attacker converts the unlicensed computing power into cryptocurrency. Attackers can swiftly access many users through popular websites, especially after introducing service providers (e.g., Coinhive and CryptoLoot) offering ready-to-use implementations of in-browser mining scripts (Tekiner et al. 2021). Cryptojacking assaults on more powerful platforms, such as cloud servers (ESET., 2019), Docker engines (Chen., 2019), and IoT devices on large-scale Kubernetes clusters (Duan., 2018), have recently increased, according to security reports (Symantec., 2018; EternalBlue., 2019). The attackers use hardware vulnerabilities (Rüth., 2018), current CVEs (Vignau., 2019), poorly configured IoT devices (Matthews., 2021), Docker engines, and Kubernetes clusters (Duan., 2018) with inadequate security, and popular DDoS botnets for the side-profit (Saad., 2018) to hijack and obtain initial access (Rüth., 2018) to propagate the cryptojacking malware.

Cryptojacking's main effects include device slowdown, overheating batteries, higher energy consumption, unusable gadgets, and decreased productivity. Businesses invoiced based on CPU utilization may incur higher expenditures due to cryptojacking in the cloud. Cryptojacking increased in late 2017 due to the advent of the Coinhive service, which lowered the obstacles to entry and increased the value of various cryptocurrencies. The launch of Coinhive's new service in September 2017 sparked increased interest in browser-based mining. Coinhive, like most browser-based miners, mines Monero and was advertised as a revenue-generating alternative to website adverts. It advises users to make their presence known to site visitors, but that has not stopped unscrupulous operators from utilizing it to carry out cryptojacking in the hopes that users will not notice. There have been numerous allegations of it being used for cryptojacking without website visitors' awareness since its inception.

Cryptojacking software uses the victim's device's computing capabilities without the user's permission to mine bitcoins and gets rewards. In essence, the attacker utilizes as much CPU power as possible; however, the bandwidth consumption of a network is minimum for the mining behavior, e.g., the maximum consumption is approximately 3kb/s within instances (Clark & Greanly., 2019). Therefore, cryptojacking attacks appear relatively harmless compared to cyber threats in applications other than fintech and business applications. As pointed out by Vučinić and Luburic (Vučinić., 2022), the fintech and business application domain of the cryptocurrency's ecosystem is at a high risk of cryptojacking attacks. Cryptojacking attacks exploit vulnerabilities in internet-based systems such as web servers, VPNs, gateways, or cloud applications (Glover., 2022). It targets all those applications involving end-point devices such as smartphones, laptops, desktops, and even IoT devices because they are easy to attack (Masquelier., 2018; enterprise world., 2018; Chickowski., 2018). High-powered servers and data centers in an enterprise infrastructure can also attract cryptojacking attacks. Hence, cryptojacking can be a new threat to healthcare (Chouffani., 2018; Zilbiger., 2019) and power grids (Chickowski., 2018).

The lifetime of cryptojacking malware is divided into three stages: 1) script preparation, 2) script injection, and 3) the attack. For all cryptojacking malware varieties, the script preparation and attack phases are the same. However, the script injection step is carried out by injecting malicious scripts into webpages or embedding malware into other apps. There are broadly two types of cryptojacking malware: 1) web-based or in-browser cryptojacking and 2) host- or file-based cryptojacking. The following summarizes existing work on every kind of cryptojacking malware.

1. Web-based Cryptojacking

Web-based cryptojacking was first observed in websites, distinguishing them from CoinHive, CryptoLoot, and JSEcoin web-based mining (Eskandari et al., 2018). They detected the links of scripts of <u>coinhive.mine.js</u> within web pages and declared them malicious. However, their detection scheme gives false positives on security websites discussing malicious links or false negatives on the code obfuscation and running the scripts using proxies deployed by cybercriminals. A machine learning approach (Carlin et al. 2018) is used to detect crypto mining with a dynamic analysis of the opcode of non-executable subject files for the malware of web-based cryptojacking with a detection rate of 99% on 589 samples of the web-based cryptojackers. However, their approach could not detect the executable type of cryptojackers.

A semantic signature-matching system (Wang et al., 2018) detected and interrupted unauthorized web-based crypto mining as comparatively more robust than the detection scheme (Eskandari et al., 2018) of static code analysis and more susceptible to code obfuscation attacks. A cryptojacking detection technique (Tanana., 2020) is based on the CPU usage of applications applied to web-based and executable cryptojackings using a decision tree algorithm. They tested their techniques in a control VM environment. They achieved a detection rate of 82% from the selected 50 cryptojacking malware samples, 40 browser-based and ten executable-type from VirusShare, and some other legitimate applications of cryptojacking samples. Search the web for instances of the drive-by-mining approach (Konoth et al., 2018) first identified miners with the list of static keywords in JavaScript code and dynamically utilized the collected data in the form of a WebSocket and WebWorkers. They crawled the Alexa Top One Million front pages with three sub-pages for each and identified 1735 websites with a miner. They proposed a detection-based approach to identify cryptographic primitives inside the WebAssembly code (Haas et al., 2017; Naseem et al., 2021) and detected 744 miners in the one million web pages without including the sub-pages in April 2018. These techniques can sufficiently protect the known mining websites with static analysis; however ineffective against the various customized mining codes. Figure 2 shows an attack scenario of the web-based cryptojacking malware. The end-user has a powerful machine that sends a request to a web server for accessing Webpages. The attacker injects cryptojacking scripts into the requested Webpage to use the resources of the end-user device without his knowledge for crypto mining purposes. The attacker's script runs automatically on his machine and performs hashing on miners' transactions. The miners check the hashes, and if applied correctly, they send rewards to the attacker in Bitcoins.

Figure 2. Attack scenario of web-based cryptojacking malware.

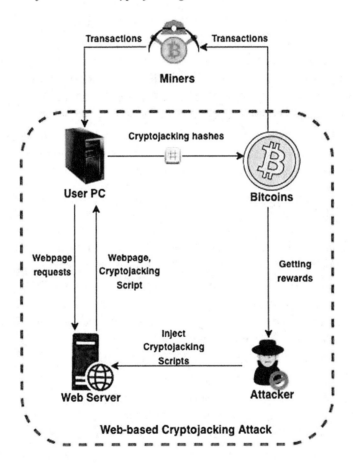

Run-time analysis is also required to track the mining activities reliably and detection based on the characteristics of the crypto mining code (Konoth et al., 2018). The approach is further extended (Musch et al., 2019) with static and dynamic indicators for the miner-based websites by using V8's profiler. They measure the utilization of the CPU on a per-function basis with an extended timeframe for the miner's presence. Moreover, they found 2506 websites having cryptojacking in the Alexa One Million websites without browsing any sub-pages. The emergence of mining scripts distributed by service providers (e.g., Coinhive) converted websites into crypto mining using the cryptocurrency paradigms. These scripts can be used by legitimate owners of a webpage or by malicious actors. However, all in-browser crypto mining is treated as malicious cryptojacking and blacklists them using browser extensions or antiviruses. This approach is empirically analyzed for the first time in a browser crypto mining process with permission (Tekiner & Uluagac., 2021). This approach created a dataset of 6269 unique websites and embedded crypto mining scripts for distinguishing the permission and permissionless crypto mining samples. They treated the permission-based in-browser crypto mining as legitimate if implemented without user interruption responsibly. The permission-based crypto mining adopted the legitimate crypto mining with the user's consent. A machine learning-based approach (Tahir et al., 2019) is also used on hardware-assisted profiling of a browser code in real-time and has analyzed the top 50K websites from Alexa. They determined that cryptojacking is often using obfuscated code. This approach achieved an accuracy of 99% for the classification of mining applications and provided flags for heavily obfuscated or encrypted mining codes. They also developed an extension that is comparatively good to the existing plugins. Their approach has less overhead and works for all common CPUs.

2. Host or File-based Cryptojacking

Host-based cryptojackings are malware that hides in a victim's computing device and performs crypto mining. They place cryptojacking malware on the victim's machine to profit, possibly for a long time. The attackers distribute and locate their host-based cryptojacking malware with third-party applications (Olennick., 2020), social engineering methods (McDonald., 2018), or exploit various vulnerabilities (Vignau., 2019) or botnets (McMillen., 2017) to access the host system. The host-based cryptojacking exploits the CPU and GPU of the victim host to generate cryptocurrency. The study (Darabian., 2020) used deep learning-based techniques to detect crypto-mining malware using static and dynamic analysis. In the case of dynamic analysis, they set up an environment to capture the system calls of around 1500 portable executable samples of the crypto mining malware. They also performed astatic analysis on the opcode sequences of the portable executables' files. They achieved 95% and 99% accuracy using static and dynamic analysis. Figure 3 shows the attack scenario of a host or file-based cryptojacking malware. In this scenario, the attacker comprises the file system of the end-user machine directly and exploits its resource for mining purposes without his knowledge. The resource can be used for hashing the miners' transactions and sending them back to the miners. In the response, the miners send a reward to the attacker in the form of Bitcoins to successfully verify a transaction.

Figure 3. Attack scenario of host or file-based cryptojacking malware.

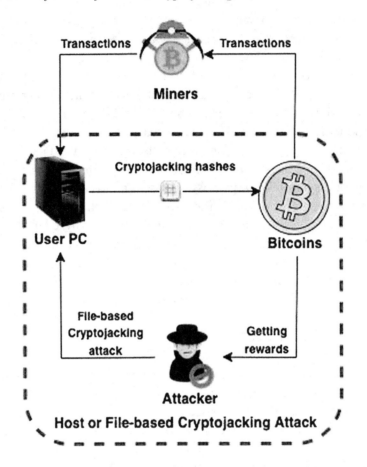

A network-based approach (Caprolu et al., 2020) is used to detect and identify crypto-clients from the normal or encrypted network traffic. They analyzed Bitcoin, Monero, and Bytecoin for normal and VPN-based traffic and proposed an ML-based framework called Crypto-Aegis to detect cryptocurrencies' related activities. They achieved a 0.96 F1 score and 0.99% AUC, greater than ROC curves. A cryptojacking detection mechanism (Tekiner et al. 2021) based on the analysis of network traffic features proposed for both in-browser and host-based cryptojacking and implemented in an Internet of Things (IoT) scenario. The approach used a 6.4M internet packets dataset with the network's traces and showed 99% accuracy in one hour. They also showed that the highest rate of 72% of malicious packets is less than the least generation rate of the benign datasets. They further observed comparatively high accuracy on servers rather than laptops or IoT-based victim devices. Their approach showed that the obfuscation methods of the attackers can still create differences during the detection phase.

CRYPTOJACKING DETECTION AND PREVENTION SYSTEMS

This section will discuss existing cryptojacking detection and prevention systems and highlight the challenges faced to combat cryptojacking malware.

Cryptojacking Detection

One of the essential tasks in information security is malware detection. A high level of detection reliability characterizes it. Static detection and dynamic detection are the two ways to solve this problem. Static detection typically searches for specific signatures in files and compares them to known malware signatures in their database. Dynamic detection, also known as behavioral analysis, investigates the behavior of an already running program. Both of these methods can be used to combat cryptojacking malware. The first is traditional executable malware, which runs as an application on the victim's computer and then delivers its payload via another method; the second, and more common, is browser-based JavaScript cryptojackers, which run within the victim's browser when they visit the infected website. Unfortunately, most antiviral programs' statistical signature analysis is inefficient against file-less malware, such as browser-based cryptojackers. It cannot be used to detect zero-day attacks by executable-type and browser-based cryptojackers.

Cryptojacking malware campaigns have targeted the banking industry, major commercial websites, government and military servers (e.g., US Department of Defense), online video sharing platforms (e.g., YouTube), gaming platforms (e.g., Nintendo), critical infrastructure resources (e.g., routers), and even recently popular remote video conferencing/meeting programs (e.g., Zoom during the Covid-19 pandemic). Attackers can get around them by employing obfuscation tactics or regularly changing their domains or scripts. As a result, most research in the literature has presented cryptojacking malware detection approaches based on various dynamic/ behavioral aspects. Detection solutions such as browser extensions that safeguard users with blacklist methods or antivirus applications that use various analytic methods can only be a partial solution to the cryptojacking problem. Furthermore, attackers try to merge the features of fileless (Kumar., 2020) and cryptojacking malware to make it invisible and riskier. Varlioglu et al. (Varlioglu et al. 2022) provide a detailed review of fileless cryptojacking attacks and present a novel approach for detecting the dangerous combo fileless malware (DFIR) and cryptojacking.

Cryptojacking Prevention

Most detection systems do not focus on preventing or interrupting cryptojacking malware; there are still many studies (Kelton., 2020; Naseem., 2021) that focus on both detection and prevention. The preventive approaches differ even for techniques that use similar dynamic traits to detect ongoing cryptojacking malware attacks. (Yulianto et al., 2019) raise a notification, Bian et al. (Kelton., 2020) put the mining process to sleep, and (Razali et al., 2019) kill the process immediately. There are various technologies available on the market to prevent cryptojacking. Proprietary antivirus products (Horn., 2018; Norton., 2022) are widely used to combat host-based cryptojacking malware.

Similarly, open-source browser extensions like No-Coin (Hosh., 2017) and MinerBlock (Ismail., 2021) are extensively used to combat in-browser cryptojacking malware. These open-source browser extensions work by blacklisting harmful domains, and the lists are updated as new ones are detected. When a user tries to access a website on the blacklist, the browser extension warns them. Because attackers can readily modify their domain using domain fluxing or other means to downshift the impact of blacklists, pure blacklisting-based prevention is ineffective in stopping cryptojacking software. Researchers offer several novel approaches (Ramanathan et al., 2020) for better and more optimal blacklisting, yet dynamic blacklisting methods are ineffective (Yadav et al., 2012) against domain fluxing strategies.

More recently, He et al. (He et al. 2022) proposed a Malware incident response (IR) lifecycle based on the NIST incident response lifecycle embedded with cyber threat intelligence (CTI). They examined different phases of the incident lifecycle and identified the main actions where CTI can be used in the IR processes. Then they presented a cryptojacking case study to demonstrate the use of the Malware IR lifecycle. They have categorized the malware into pre-incident, mid-incident, and post-incident phases. They focus on mid-incident and post-incident phases due to using the same prevention approaches across different organizations compared to pre-incident. They used these different phases and applied the best cybersecurity practices to secure healthcare systems from cryptojacking attacks.

CHALLENGES

Given the pervasiveness of cryptojacking malware, it is critical to detect and prevent unauthorized mining activities from abusing any computer platform's computational resources without the users' permission. Cryptojacking, despite its importance, is challenging to detect because it differs from typical malware in various ways. Following is a non-exhaustive list of challenges that hinder the development of cryptojacking malware detection and prevention system (Tekiner et al. 2021).

1. Traditional malware detection and prevention systems are designed to detect the malware's harmful behaviors. Unlike typical malware, they take advantage of their victims' computational capacity rather than damaging or controlling them. Cryptojacking malware only uses computing resources. It sends the calculated hash values back to the attacker, so malware detection systems treat cryptojacking malware as a heavy application that requires high performance.
2. They can be utilized or incorporated on legal websites, which makes them harder to detect because users do not expect nonconsensual mining on their computers from those websites.
3. Unlike traditional malware assaults, the attacker's goal in cryptojacking malware attacks is to remain undiscovered on the system for as long as possible because the attack's revenue is directly related to the amount of time it remains undetected. As a result, attackers employ filtering and obfuscation techniques to make their malware more difficult to detect and detectable by consumers.

Types of Cryptojacking Mitigation Strategies

Cryptojacking, as a new web security threat, has received extensive attention. Many researchers have proposed several mitigation strategies to safeguard users from cryptojacking while using the browser. We describe some studies related to cryptojacking mitigation strategies in the following.

- **In-browser-based mitigation:** The "miners" in the browser do, in most situations, impact the user's experience (Cimpanu., 2018). As a result, technicians continuously research protection strategies to combat these stealth attacks. For example, Google has long been interested in cryptocurrency mining systems (Cimpanu., 2018). In 2017, Google proposed a throttling system based on JavaScript. JavaScript services operating in the backstage tab will access less than 1% of the total CPU capacity. If a user switches to another tab, the script will not run as quickly and will not reach 100% CPU consumption. However, some websites, such as those for watching movies, are still attractive targets for attacks since users tend to open tabs and concentrate. However, limiting

CPU utilization may make it difficult for websites with large loads to function normally (Konoth et al., 2018). Persistent mining is also less likely to be found by consumers because it reduces computationally intensive activities.

- **Blacklist-based mitigation**: One of the most often used approaches in browsers is the blacklist (Keraf., 2021; NoCoin., 2020). Since frequent domain name or web address alterations can circumvent this detection mechanism, the blacklist should be updated regularly to lower the false-negative detection rate. Because NoCoin, one of the most popular mining interception extensions, no longer provides blacklist updates, developers have removed it. The majority of these techniques are implemented as browser extensions. When the user manually adds the matching text file to the blacklist, the Adblocks plugin adds a cryptojacking blocking mechanism. This type of detection works well for most simple mining scripts, especially when they interact with a big mining pool that maintains a nearly consistent domain.

- **Behavior-based mitigation**: CMTrack is a behavior-based dynamic detector proposed by (Hong et al., 2018). To detect cryptojacking assaults, they employed two run-time profilers and judged based on the two results. Tanana et al. (Tanana 2020) added network utilization and cryptography library calls to its malicious mining detection metrics. In addition, he developed a way for detecting browser-based or executable-type cryptojacking based on CPU load using an application (Tanana., 2020).

- **Machine learning-based mitigation**: Outguard, an automatic cryptojacking detection system, was proposed by (Kharraz et al., 2019). Their approach collects several features before settling on seven to use as the basis for a mining detection classifier model. The authors created a huge real-world data collection to train the Support Vector Machine (SVM) classification model with samples. Gomes et al. (Gomes & Correia., 2020) suggested a method for unsupervised detection that extracts and combines flow and performance counter-based information. They employed a machine-learning algorithm to group hosts with similar mining habits together. Nukala (Nukala., 2020) proposed detecting cryptojacking by monitoring cache activity and developed a multi-classification algorithm to detect the malicious miners' CPU percentage throttling. The author used five models, including random forest, decision tree, and SVM, to achieve superior detection in a comparative experiment.

- **Deep learning-based mitigation**: Deep learning could be an effective way to detect cryptojacking. The neural network application has achieved good results in various domains due to the development of deep learning. Pastor et al. (Rastor et al., 2020) investigated cryptomining detection techniques using deep learning and machine learning. They used a set of highly relevant network flow features for model learning. Ning et al. (Ning et al., 2019) presented CapJack, a malicious mining detection technology that uses a new network model called CapsNet with a high detection rate.

- **WASM module-based mitigation**: WebAssembly (WASM) is a web-compatible format that is compact and flexible. It is executed in a web browser to provide better performance. Researchers discovered that many rogue miners used WASM instead of JavaScript to initiate cryptojacking attacks. Konoth et al. (Konoth et al., 2018) proposed a Minesweeper tool based on the ability to execute hash functions. They performed static analysis after converting the WASM into linear assembly bytecode with a debugger. This method detects cryptojacking by looking for the existence of a hash, according to the encryption procedure used. Many academics have employed this technique to assess harmful mining in their investigations. Romano et al. presented MinerRay (Romano et al., 2020), which can detect cryptojacking in JavaScript and WebAssembly. SEISMIC, a dynamic analytic approach for identifying cryptojacking in WebAssembly, was proposed by Wang et al. (Wang et al., 2018). They could locate cryptojacking by dynamically counting the WASM byte-code instructions and determining the distribution features during script execution.

RECOMMENDATIONS

Based on the lessons learned from the extensive literature review of cryptojacking malware and prevention and detection systems, we recommend researchers and practitioners (computer or mobile phone users) combat cryptojacking attacks.

For Researchers

- More recently, the attacker's target devices with more processing power (such as cloud infrastructures and many inadequately protected IoT devices) than personal computers, as in the in-browser cryptojacking attacks (Tekiner., 2021). With this, the attackers' goal is to obtain more profit in a lesser time. In these attacks, the attackers used Coinhive's script and modified a non-malicious and open-source Monero miner called XMRig to perform the crypto mining in the background (Spring., 2018). Unlike in-browser cryptominers, the client does not come to the attacker; therefore, the attacker must deliver the malicious mining script to the victims. However, despite the decrease in the number of in-browser samples from active service providers and the potential trend shift in the attackers' behavior to host-based cryptojacking malware and techniques used to deliver the malware, host-based cryptojacking malware literature is not as rich as in-browser cryptojacking malware literature. Therefore, security researchers need more effort to find better solutions to detect and mitigate this continually evolving threat.
- According to the assault trends, the attackers prefer Monero to Bitcoin or other cryptocurrencies as a target cryptocurrency. Monero is the most widely used privacy coin for concealing transaction history. Even if the attackers used Bitcoin, it could track down the transactions even if the attack was noticed after a long time.
- In-browser cryptocurrency mining was created to give legitimate website owners an alternative source of revenue. Later, other service providers, such as Coinimp (CoinImp., 2018) and WebMinePool (Webmin., 2020), included explicit user permission procedures in their implementations. This usage of web-based crypto mining scripts is no longer possible because of the keyword-based automatic detection and prevention methods, which block websites hosting crypto mining scripts. Instead of prohibiting a website that attempts to upload a mining script, a feasible solution to this problem would be to ask for the user's explicit authorization. Furthermore, researchers should focus on utilizing legitimate crypto mining with user agreement and understanding as a funding model.
- There are two types of Bitcoins and blockchain-related malware: 1) those that use the Bitcoin and blockchain infrastructure to exploit the victim, and 2) those that use traditional malware attacks to exploit Bitcoin and blockchain users, such as key stealing, social engineering, or fake application attacks. Cryptojacking attacks take advantage of the Bitcoin and blockchain architecture to exploit the victim's computing capacity; nevertheless, Bitcoin and blockchain users are also vulnerable

to a wide range of classic malware attacks. Although these assaults (Acar., 2019; Celik., 2019; Acar.,2020) have been thoroughly explored in the literature (Heartfield, 2015), their influence on the Bitcoin and blockchain area has yet to be investigated, which could lead to new study directions.

For Practitioners

Cryptojacking can be a significant threat to cryptocurrency if a user is unaware that any mining script is running on their device (e.g., computer or mobile phone) by taking all the CPU power and slowing down the machine. Following best practices can help the users protect their devices from the threat of cryptojacking malware.

- Educate the user of a device or network, advising them to be wary of emails from unknown origins and opening attachments that have not been requested, as they may include file-based coin-mining malware.
- Educate personnel on the symptoms that their computer may be infected with a coinminer. Tell them to contact IT support immediately if they suspect a coinminer is present on a device connected to the company network.
- Consider installing ad-blocking or anti-coin-mining extensions on web browsers for an extra layer of security against potentially unwanted applications (PUAs).
- Cryptocurrency mining can also be done on mobile phones. Be cautious about clicking on adverts for strange websites while downloading apps and browser extensions to mobile phones.
- Monitor the device's battery usage, and scan it for file-based miners in case of an anomaly (i.e., a strange surge). If it does not work, list the websites visited when the battery usage spiked. Only visit trusted websites, and keep an eye out for any small print on the site that might indicate it is hosting a coin miner.
- Use secure passwords and keep personal gadgets up to date with the latest fixes. Similarly, update all personal devices with the latest patches, create secure passwords, and enable two-factor authentication. Also, ensure that surrounding routers and IoT devices are fully patched and have the most recent firmware.

CONCLUSION

Cryptojacking malware has become an indispensable tool for hackers. With the rapid ascent of cryptocurrencies, the attackers are enticed to the lucrative cryptocurrency ecosystem. The literature review hints at the lack of mitigation measures for the cryptomining sector. Most of the research is focused on proposing a cryptojacking malware detection investigation. This paper first reviewed the different types of cryptojacking malware and how they work. In addition, we conducted a comprehensive evaluation of existing detection and prevention research and the challenges faced while realizing appropriate mitigation strategies. Finally, we provided recommendations to assist researchers and practitioners in combating cryptojacking malware.

REFERENCES

Acar, A., Aksu, H., Uluagac, A. S., & Akkaya, K. (2020). A usable and robust continuous authentication framework using wearables. *IEEE Transactions on Mobile Computing*, *20*(6), 2140–2153.

Acar, A., Liu, W., Beyah, R., Akkaya, K., & Uluagac, A. S. (2019). A privacy-preserving multifactor authentication system. *Security and Privacy*, *2*(5), e88.

Ahmad, A., Shafiuddin, W., Kama, M. N., & Saudi, M. M. (2019). A new cryptojacking malware classifier model based on dendritic cell algorithm. In *Proceedings of the 3rd International Conference on Vision, Image and Signal Processing* (pp. 1-5). Academic Press.

Arianna, T., Kamps, J., Akartuna, E. A., Hetzel, F. J., Bennett, K., Davies, T., & Johnson, S. D. (2022). Cryptocurrencies and future financial crime. *Crime Science*, *11*(1).

Badawi, E., & Jourdan, G. V. (2020). Cryptocurrencies emerging threats and defensive mechanisms: A systematic literature review. *IEEE Access: Practical Innovations, Open Solutions*, *8*, 200021–200037.

Bartoletti, M., Pes, B., & Serusi, S. (2018). Data mining for detecting bitcoin ponzi schemes. In *2018 Crypto Valley Conference on Blockchain Technology (CVCBT)* (pp. 75-84). IEEE.

Caprolu, M., Cresci, S., Raponi, S., & Di Pietro, R. (2020). New Dimensions of Information Warfare: The Economic Pillar—Fintech and Cryptocurrencies. In *International Conference on Risks and Security of Internet and Systems* (pp. 3-27). Springer.

Caprolu, M., Raponi, S., Oligeri, G., & Di Pietro, R. (2019). *Crypto mining makes noise.* arXiv preprint arXiv:1910.09272.

Caprolu, M., Raponi, S., Oligeri, G., & Di Pietro, R. (2021). crypto mining makes noise: Detecting cryptojacking via Machine Learning. *Computer Communications*, *171*, 126–139.

Carlin, D., O'kane, P., Sezer, S., & Burgess, J. (2018). Detecting crypto mining using dynamic analysis. In *16th Annual Conference on Privacy, Security and Trust (PST)* (pp. 1-6). IEEE.

Celik, Z. B., Acar, A., Aksu, H., Sheatsley, R., McDaniel, P., & Uluagac, A. S. (2019). Curie: Policy-based secure data exchange. In *Proceedings of the Ninth ACM Conference on Data and Application Security and Privacy* (pp. 121-132). ACM.

Chen, J. (2019). *Graboid: First-Ever Cryptojacking Worm Found in Images on Docker Hub.* Unit42.

ChickowskiE. (2018). https://securityboulevard.com/2018/07/5-cryptojacking-consequences-cisos-cant-ignore/

Chickowski. (2018). https://securityboulevard.com/2018/07/5-cryptojacking-consequences-cisos-cant-ignore/

Cimpanu, C. (2018a). *Firefox working on protection against in-browser cryptojacking scripts.* Bleepingcomputer. Available at: https://www. bleepingcomputer. com/news/software/firefox-working-on-protection-against-inbrowser-cryptojacking-scripts/

Cimpanu, C. (2018b). *Tweak to chrome performance will indirectly stifle cryptojacking scripts*. https://www.bleeping-computer.com/news/software/firefox-working-on-protection-against-inbrowser-crypto-jacking-scripts

Clark, C. E., & Greenley, H. L. (2019). *Bitcoin, blockchain, and the energy sector*. Congressional Research Service.

Coinhav2. (2017). *First week status report*. https://coinhive.com/blog/en/status-report

Coinhave – monero javascript mining. (n.d.). https://coin-have.com/

Coinimp. (2018). *Coinnebula official webpage*. https://web.archive.org/

Cryptoloot - earn more from your traffic. (n.d.). https://crypto-loot.com/

Darabian, H., Homayounoot, S., Dehghantanha, A., Hashemi, S., Karimipour, H., Parizi, R. M., & Choo, K. K. R. (2020). Detecting crypto mining malware: A deep learning approach for static and dynamic analysis. *Journal of Grid Computing, 18*(2), 293–303.

De Vries, A. (2018). Bitcoin's growing energy problem. *Joule, 2*(5), 801–805.

DuanG. (2018). https://blog.neuvector.com/article/cryptojacking-crypto-mining-tesla-kubernetes-jenkins-exploits/

enterpriseitworld. (2018). https://www.enterpriseitworld.com/home-iot-devices-latest-targets-for-cryptojacking-fortinet/

ESET. (2019). *Cybersecurity Trends*. https://www.eset.com/us/trends-2019/

Eskandari, S., Leoutsarakos, A., Mursch, T., & Clark, J. (2018). A first look at browser-based cryptojacking. In *IEEE European Symposium on Security and Privacy Workshops (EuroS&PW)* (pp. 58-66). IEEE.

Glover. (2022). https://techmonitor.ai/technology/cybersecurity/cryptojacking

Gohwong, S. G. (2019). The State of the Art of Cryptography-based Cyber-attacks. *International Journal of Crime, Law and Social Issues, 6*(2).

Gomes, F., & Correia, M. (2020). Cryptojacking detection with cpu usage metrics. In *IEEE 19th International Symposium on Network Computing and Applications (NCA)* (pp. 1-10). IEEE.

Gorman, B. (2019). *Internet Security Threat Report*. Available at: https://www.symantec.com/content/dam/symantec/docs/reports/istr-24-2019-en.pdf

Haas, A., Rossberg, A., Schuff, D. L., Titzer, B. L., Holman, M., Gohman, D., ... Bastien, J. F. (2017). Bringing the web up to speed with WebAssembly. In *Proceedings of the 38th ACM SIGPLAN Conference on Programming Language Design and Implementation* (pp. 185-200). ACM.

He, Y., Inglut, E., & Luo, C. (2022). Malware incident response (IR) informed by cyber threat intelligence (CTI). *Science China. Information Sciences, 65*(7), 1–3.

Heartfield, R., & Loukas, G. (2015). A taxonomy of attacks and a survey of defence mechanisms for semantic social engineering attacks. *ACM Computing Surveys, 48*(3), 1–39.

Hong, G., Yang, Z., Yang, S., Zhang, L., Nan, Y., Zhang, Z., ... Duan, H. (2018). How you get shot in the back: A systematical study about cryptojacking in the real world. In *Proceedings of the ACM SIGSAC Conference on Computer and Communications Security* (pp. 1701-1713). ACM.

Hosh. (2017). *Nocoin: Block lists to prevent javascript miners.* https://github.com/hoshsadiq/adblock-nocoin-list

Hron, M. (2018). *Avast, Protect Yourself from Cryptojacking "Avastantimalware."* https://www.avast.com/c-protect-yourself-from-cryptojacking

Hu, X., Shu, Z., Song, X., Cheng, G., & Gong, J. (2021). Detecting Cryptojacking Traffic Based on Network Behavior Features. In *IEEE Global Communications Conference (GLOBECOM)* (pp. 1-6). IEEE.

Ingalls, S. (2018). *Cryptocurrency mining.* https://www.webopedia.com/TERM/C/cryptocurrency-mining.html

Ismail. (2021). *Minerblock: An efficient browser extension to block browser based cryptocurrency miners all over the web.* https://github.com/xd4rker/MinerBlock/blob/master/assets/filters.txt

Jayasinghe, K., & Poravi, G. (2020). A survey of attack instances of cryptojacking targeting cloud infrastructure. In *Proceedings of the 2nd Asia pacific information technology conference* (pp. 100-107). Academic Press.

Kamps, J., & Kleinberg, B. (2018). To the moon: Defining and detecting cryptocurrency pump-and-dumps. *Crime Science, 7*(1), 1–18. doi:10.118640163-018-0093-5 PMID:31984202

Keeve, A. (2019). *Cryptojacking shows no signs of slowing down in 2019, says ESET.* Available at: https://www.eset.com/us/about/newsroom/pressreleases/cryptojacking-shows-no-signs-of-slowing-down-in-2019-says-eset/

Kelton, C., Balasubramanian, A., Raghavendra, R., & Srivatsa, M. (2020). Browser-based deep behavioral detection of web crypto mining with coinspy. In *Workshop on Measurements, Attacks, and Defenses for the Web (MADWeb)* (pp. 1-12). Academic Press.

Keraf, NoCoin. (2018). https://github.com/keraf/NoCoin

Kerbs, B. (2018). *Krebs on security - who and what is coinhive.* https://krebsonsecurity.com/2018/03/who-and-what-is-coinhive/

Kharraz, A., Ma, Z., Murley, P., Lever, C., Mason, J., Miller, A., . . . Bailey, M. (2019). Outguard: Detecting in-browser covert cryptocurrency mining in the wild. In *The World Wide Web Conference* (pp. 840-852). Academic Press.

Konoth, R. K., Vineti, E., Moonsamy, V., Lindorfer, M., Kruegel, C., Bos, H., & Vigna, G. (2018). An in-depth look into drive-by mining and its defense. In *Proc. of ACM Conference on Computer and Communications Security (CCS)* (*Vol. 10*). Academic Press.

Konoth, R. K., Vineti, E., Moonsamy, V., Lindorfer, M., Kruegel, C., Bos, H., & Vigna, G. (2018). An in-depth look into drive-by mining and its defense. In *Proc. of ACM Conference on Computer and Communications Security (CCS)* (Vol. 10). ACM.

Konoth, R. K., Vineti, E., Moonsamy, V., Lindorfer, M., Kruegel, C., Bos, H., & Vigna, G. (2018). Minesweeper: An in-depth look into drive-by cryptocurrency mining and its defense. In *Proceedings of the ACM SIGSAC Conference on Computer and Communications Security* (pp. 1714-1730). Academic Press.

Kumar, S. (2020). An emerging threat Fileless malware: A survey and research challenges. *Cybersecurity, 3*(1), 1–12.

Lachtar, N., Elkhail, A. A., Bacha, A., & Malik, H. (2020). A cross-stack approach towards defending against cryptojacking. *IEEE Computer Architecture Letters, 19*(2), 126–129.

Li, Y., Yang, G., Susilo, W., Yu, Y., Au, M. H., & Liu, D. (2019). Traceable monero: Anonymous cryptocurrency with enhanced accountability. *IEEE Transactions on Dependable and Secure Computing, 18*(2), 679–691.

Lohachab, A. (2021). A perspective on using blockchain for ensuring security in smart card systems. In Research Anthology on Blockchain Technology in Business, Healthcare, Education, and Government (pp. 529-558). IGI Global.

Magazine. (2021). https://www.infosecurity-magazine.com/magazine-features/crypto-jacking-new-world-resource/

Mani, G., Pasumarti, V., Bhargava, B., Vora, F. T., MacDonald, J., King, J., & Kobes, J. (2020). Decrypto pro: Deep learning based crypto mining malware detection using performance counters. In *IEEE International Conference on Autonomic Computing and Self-Organizing Systems (ACSOS)* (pp. 109-118). IEEE.

MasquelierH. (2018). https://phys.org/news/2018-08-hackers-smartphones-cryptocurrencies.html

Matthews, R. (2021). *Analysis of System Performance Metrics Towards the Detection of Cryptojacking in IOT Devices.* Academic Press.

McDonald, C. (n.d.). *Cryptojacking malware hid into emails.* https://www.mailguard.com.au/blog/brandjacking-malware-hiding

McMillen, D., & Alvarez, M. (n.d.). *Mirai iot botnet: Mining for bitcoins?* https://securityintelligence.com/mirai-iot-botnet-mining-for-bitcoins/

Miner.Xmrig. (n.d.). *Symantec.* https://www.symantec.com/security-center/writeup/2018-061105-4627-99

MS-ISAC. (2019). *EternalBlue.* Technical Report #SP2019-0101. MS-ISAC.

Musch, M., Wressnegger, C., Johns, M., & Rieck, K. (2019). Thieves in the browser: Web-based cryptojacking in the wild. In *Proceedings of the 14th International Conference on Availability, Reliability and Security* (pp. 1-10). Academic Press.

Nakamoto, S. (2008). Bitcoin: A peer-to-peer electronic cash system. *Decentralized Business Review, 21260.*

Nakamoto, S. (2009). *Bitcoin: A peer-to-peer electronic cash system Bitcoin: A Peer-to-Peer Electronic Cash System.* https://bitcoin. org/en/bitcoin-paper

Naseem, F., Aris, A., Babun, L., Tekiner, E., & Uluagac, S. (2021). MINOS: A lightweight real-time cryptojacking detection system. *28th Annual Network and Distributed System Security Symposium, NDSS.*

Naseem, F., Aris, A., Babun, L., Tekiner, E., & Uluagac, S. (2021). MINOS: A lightweight real-time cryptojacking detection system. In *28th Annual Network and Distributed System Security Symposium, NDSS.* Academic Press.

Naseem, F., Aris, A., Babun, L., Tekiner, E., & Uluagac, S. (2021). MINOS: A lightweight real-time cryptojacking detection system. *28th Annual Network and Distributed System Security Symposium, NDSS.*

Ning, R., Wang, C., Xin, C., Li, J., Zhu, L., & Wu, H. (2019). Capjack: Capture in-browser cryptojacking by deep capsule network through behavioral analysis. In *IEEE INFOCOM-IEEE Conference on Computer Communications* (pp. 1873-1881). IEEE.

Norton. (n.d.). *Official site — norton™ - antivirus, anti-malware software.* https://us.norton.com/

Nukala, V. S. K. A. (2020). Website Cryptojacking Detection Using Machine Learning: IEEE CNS 20 Poster. In *IEEE Conference on Communications and Network Security (CNS)* (pp. 1-2). IEEE.

Olenick, D. (2019). *Miner into third party zoom.* https://www.trendmicro.com/en us/research/20/d/zoomed-in-a-look-into-a-coinminer-bundledwith-zoom-installer.html

Pastor, A., Mozo, A., Vakaruk, S., Canavese, D., López, D. R., Regano, L., ... Lioy, A. (2020). Detection of encrypted crypto mining malware connections with machine and deep learning. *IEEE Access: Practical Innovations, Open Solutions, 8,* 158036–158055.

Quamara, S., & Singh, A. K. (2022). A systematic survey on security concerns in cryptocurrencies: State-of-the-art and perspectives. *Computers & Security, 113,* 102548.

Ramanathan, S., Mirkovic, J., & Yu, M. (2020). Blag: Improving the accuracy of blacklists. *Network and Distributed Systems Security (NDSS) Symposium.*

Razali, M. A., & Mohd Shariff, S. (2019). Cmblock: In-browser detection and prevention cryptojacking tool using blacklist and behavior-based detection method. In *International Visual Informatics Conference* (pp. 404-414). Springer.

Razali, M. A., & Mohd Shariff, S. (2019). Cmblock: In-browser detection and prevention cryptojacking tool using blacklist and behavior-based detection method. In *International Visual Informatics Conference* (pp. 404-414). Springer.

Robot, M. (2019). *Rise of the cryptojackers.* Available at: https://www.kaspersky.com/blog/cryptojacking-rsa2019/25938/

Romano, A., Zheng, Y., & Wang, W. (2020). Minerray: Semantics-aware analysis for ever-evolving cryptojacking detection. In *35th IEEE/ACM International Conference on Automated Software Engineering (ASE)* (pp. 1129-1140). IEEE.

Rüth, J., Zimmermann, T., Wolsing, K., & Hohlfeld, O. (2018). Digging into browser-based crypto mining. In *Proceedings of the Internet Measurement Conference* (pp. 70-76). Academic Press.

Saad, M. (2018). *End-to-End Analysis of In-Browser Cryptojacking.* arXiv:1809.02152 [cs].

Sachan, R. K., Agarwal, R., & Shukla, S. K. (2022). *DNS based In-Browser Cryptojacking Detection.* arXiv preprint arXiv:2205.04685.

Spring, T. (2018). *Cryptominer, winstarnssmminer, has made a fortune by brutally hijacking computers.* https://blog.360totalsecurity.com/en/cryptominer-winstarnssmminer-made-fortune-brutally-hijacking-computer/

Statistia. (2022). Available online: https://www.statista.com/statistics/730876/cryptocurrency-maket-value/

Stroud, F. (2018). *Cryptocurrency mining.* https://www.webopedia.com/TERM/C/cryptocurrency-mining.html

Tahir, R., Durrani, S., Ahmed, F., Saeed, H., Zaffar, F., & Ilyas, S. (2019). The browsers strike back: countering cryptojacking and parasitic miners on the web. In *IEEE INFOCOM 2019-IEEE Conference on Computer Communications* (pp. 703-711). IEEE.

Tanana, D. (2020). Behavior-based detection of cryptojacking malware. In *Ural Symposium on Biomedical Engineering, Radioelectronics and Information Technology (USBEREIT)* (pp. 543-545). IEEE.

Tanana, D. (2020). Behavior-based detection of cryptojacking malware. In *Ural Symposium on Biomedical Engineering, Radioelectronics and Information Technology (USBEREIT)* (pp. 543-545). IEEE.

Tanana, D., & Tanana, G. (2020). Advanced behavior-based technique for cryptojacking malware detection. In *14th International Conference on Signal Processing and Communication Systems (ICSPCS)* (pp. 1-4). IEEE.

Tekiner, E., Acar, A., & Uluagac, A. S. (2021). *A Lightweight IoT Cryptojacking Detection Mechanism in Heterogeneous Smart Home Networks.* Academic Press.

Tekiner, E., Acar, A., Uluagac, A. S., Kirda, E., & Selcuk, A. A. (2021). In-Browser crypto mining for Good: *An Untold Story. In IEEE International Conference on Decentralized Applications and Infrastructures (DAPPS)* (pp. 20-29). IEEE.

Tesla, K., & Exploits, J. (2018). *Cryptojacking and Crypto Mining.* https://neuvector.com/containersecurity/cryptojacking-crypto-mining-tesla-kubernetesjenkins-exploits/

Toyoda, K., Mathiopoulos, P. T., & Ohtsuki, T. (2019). A novel methodology for hyip operators' bitcoin addresses identification. *IEEE Access: Practical Innovations, Open Solutions, 7,* 74835–74848. doi:10.1109/ACCESS.2019.2921087

Varlioglu, S., Elsayed, N., ElSayed, Z., & Ozer, M. (2022). The Dangerous Combo: Fileless Malware and Cryptojacking. *SoutheastCon, 2022,* 125–132.

Vasek, M., & Moore, T. (2015). There's no free lunch, even using Bitcoin: Tracking the popularity and profits of virtual currency scams. In *International conference on financial cryptography and data security* (pp. 44-61). Springer.

Vasek, M., & Moore, T. (2018). Analyzing the Bitcoin Ponzi scheme ecosystem. In *International Conference on Financial Cryptography and Data Security* (pp. 101-112). Springer.

Vidal, T. A. D. C. (2020). *How exchange platform attacks impact the cryptocurrency and traditional markets* (Doctoral dissertation).

Vignau, B., Khoury, R., & Hallé, S. (2019). 10 years of IoT malware: A feature-based taxonomy. In *2019 IEEE 19th International Conference on Software Quality, Reliability and Security Companion (QRS-C)* (pp. 458-465). IEEE.

Vignau, B., Khoury, R., & Hallé, S. (2019). 10 years of IoT malware: A feature-based taxonomy. In *2019 IEEE 19th International Conference on Software Quality, Reliability and Security Companion (QRS-C)* (pp. 458-465). IEEE.

Vučinić, M., & Luburić, R. (2022). Fintech, Risk-Based Thinking and Cyber Risk. *Journal of Central Banking Theory and Practice, 11*(2), 27–53.

Wang, W., Ferrell, B., Xu, X., Hamlen, K. W., & Hao, S. (2018). Seismic: Secure in-lined script monitors for interrupting cryptojacks. In *European Symposium on Research in Computer Security* (pp. 122-142). Springer.

Wang, W., Ferrell, B., Xu, X., Hamlen, K. W., & Hao, S. (2018). Seismic: Secure in-lined script monitors for interrupting cryptojacks. In *European Symposium on Research in Computer Security* (pp. 122-142). Springer.

Webmin. (2020). *The official webpage of webmine pool.* https://www.webminepool.com/page/documentation

xd4rker. (2021). *Minerblock.* https://github.com/xd4rker/MinerBlock

Xu, G., Dong, W., Xing, J., Lei, W., Liu, J., Gong, L., & Liu, S. (2022). *Delay-CJ: A novel cryptojacking covert attack method based on delayed strategy and its detection.* Digital Communications and Networks.

Yadav, S., Reddy, A. K. K., Reddy, A. N., & Ranjan, S. (2012). Detecting algorithmically generated domain-flux attacks with DNS traffic analysis. *IEEE/ACM Transactions on Networking, 20*(5), 1663–1677.

Yulianto, A. D., Sukarno, P., Warrdana, A. A., & Al Makky, M. (2019). Mitigation of cryptojacking attacks using taint analysis. In *4th International Conference on Information Technology, Information Systems and Electrical Engineering (ICITISEE)* (pp. 234-238). IEEE.

Yulianto, A. D., Sukarno, P., Warrdana, A. A., & Al Makky, M. (2019). Mitigation of cryptojacking attacks using taint analysis. In *4th International Conference on Information Technology, Information Systems and Electrical Engineering (ICITISEE)* (pp. 234-238). IEEE.

ZilbigerO. (2019). https://www.reliasmedia.com/articles/144339-cryptojacking-among-latest-cyber-threats-for-healthcare

Zimba, A., Wang, Z., & Mulenga, M. (2019). Cryptojacking injection: A paradigm shift to cryptocurrency-based web-centric internet attacks. *Journal of Organizational Computing and Electronic Commerce, 29*(1), 40–59.

Zimba, A., Wang, Z., & Mulenga, M. (2019). Cryptojacking injection: A paradigm shift to cryptocurrency-based web-centric internet attacks. *Journal of Organizational Computing and Electronic Commerce*, *29*(1), 40–59.

Zorabedian, J. (n.d.). *Cryptojacking Rises 450 Percent as Cybercriminals Pivot From Ransomware to Stealthier Attacks*. Available at:https://securityintelligence.com/cryptojacking-rises-450-percent-ascybercriminals-pivot-from-ransomware-to-stealthier-attacks/

Chapter 15

Privacy–Preserving Computing via Homomorphic Encryption:
Performance, Security, and Application Analysis

Noshaba Naeem

Department of Information Security, College of Signals, Pakistan & National University of Sciences and Technology, Islamabad, Pakistan

Tahreem Yaqoob

Department of Information Security, College of Signals, Pakistan & National University of Sciences and Technology, Islamabad, Pakistan

Fawad Khan

Department of Information Security, College of Signals, Pakistan & National University of Sciences and Technology, Islamabad, Pakistan

Shahzaib Tahir

Department of Information Security, College of Signals, Pakistan & National University of Sciences and Technology, Islamabad, Pakistan

ABSTRACT

In the era of IoT and big data, an enormous amount of data being generated by various sensors and handheld devices and for sectors not limited to healthcare, commerce, smart driving, smart grids, and fintech requires privacy and security. Although security can be ensured once the data is in transit or at rest, for certain application domains need to ensure privacy computations over encrypted data. Homomorphic encryption (HE) is one mechanism that allows parties to compute any arbitrary functions in an encrypted domain. Homomorphic encryption schemes have been employed in various applied sectors for privacy preservation; however, the limiting factor of these schemes is the computational and communication overhead and associated security. This chapter reviews the types of HE schemes, the application domains, and the associated costs for privacy preserving computing and discusses the underlying mathematical hardness problems, security in the classical and post quantum era, and challenges and recommendations for tradeoff in applied domains.

DOI: 10.4018/978-1-6684-5284-4.ch015

INTRODUCTION

The ever-increasing adoption of outsourced cloud computing and the Internet of Things (IoT) has led to the exponential growth of data with great velocity, volume, and variety. It has gained momentum with the introduction of actuators and sensors present in household devices, general infrastructure, and consumer electronics. Due to the resource-constrained nature of these devices, they are incapable of processing such a huge volume of data locally, therefore they end up uploading this bulk of data to a third party, generally the cloud for processing. To get the advantage of such big data, data analytics and mining are quite important as they help to gain insights and identify trends and patterns to make informed decisions. The role of cloud computing is quite important in this regard as it provides centralized storage for uploading data and performs heavy computation with great ease. However, the cloud used for processing bulks of data can be trustworthy, semi-honest, honest but curious, or not trustworthy at all. In other words, to use cloud services that are provided by companies such as file-sharing, file storing, and collaboration, end users have to sacrifice their privacy. Furthermore, un-trusted servers, cloud providers, and popular cloud operators can retain physical identifying elements, very long after the users have stopped using their services. For users, this poses a significant privacy concern. This endangers the privacy of individuals and ruins the reputation of an organization if an adversary successfully discloses confidential personal information and trade secrets. Hence, it is pivotal to encrypt this sensitive information before transmitting it to the cloud.

Generally, encryption plays a vital role in protecting any sensitive data, especially in cases where data has to be shared among multiple parties by storing it on some third party and providing access through this centralized storage. If this data is encrypted through conventional encryption algorithms like DES, AES, etc., all associated parties must have decryption keys to use such resources. Sharing deciphering keys breaches the privacy of individuals, healthcare organizations, business corporates, banks, insurance companies, and agriculture departments as most of these organizations hold sensitive data which they do not want to share. However, on the flip side, for improving the quality of offered services, they want to perform joint computations using datasets from other organizations to identify trends and customer preferences and perform predictive analysis based on the data imported to the cloud. Fig 1 indicates the various entities involved in an IoT and Big data analytics environment.

Figure 1. IoT and Bigdata Analytics

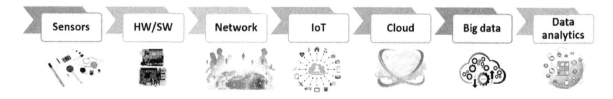

Homomorphic encryption plays a vital role in this regard as it allows computations over encrypted data while maintaining the confidentiality of users. Organizations employ homomorphic encryption schemes to encrypt their data before transmitting it to the cloud. This ensures the privacy of users as their sensitive data cannot be disclosed to unauthorized entities. Furthermore, it allows computations on the encrypted data. Thus, data can remain confidential throughout the processing process, allowing useful work to be done even with data that resides in untrusted environments.

Apart from HE, there exist several other encryption technologies that preserve the confidentiality of user data in an untrusted setting. These include:

- Multi-party computation approaches
- Differential privacy
- Trusted execution environments

All these techniques provide mechanisms to ensure secure outsourcing of data and perform joint computations for identifying trends and patterns that help in making accurate decisions. However, there are several limitations of these approaches including the incurrence of high computation and communication costs, complexity, information loss due to high noise factors, and vulnerability to side-channel attacks. Therefore, this chapter aims to investigate HE in detail, its structure, mathematical foundation, and hardness problem. The HE can be divided into three important categories including Partially Homomorphic Encryption (PHE), Somewhat Homomorphic Encryption (SHE), and Fully Homomorphic Encryption (FHE). Each of these techniques has different underlying schemes and algorithms which are discussed in detail in the subsequent section. To gain the advantage of these approaches, it has been widely employed in almost all domains of life including healthcare, fintech, banks, agriculture, food departments, transportation, and political institutions.

The chapter provides a holistic view of homomorphic encryption, application domains, security and performance discussion, and concludes by giving the future sights. In this chapter, the following points are covered.

- Present a comprehensive overview of homomorphic encryption, its construction, mathematical hardness problems, and computational complexities. It further discussed different types of homomorphic encryption and their underlying schemes and algorithms.
- Discuss different areas where homomorphic encryption has been applied by presenting a birds-eye view of existing literature.
- Argue about the communication, computation costs and post-quantum era security of discussed homomorphic encryption methodologies.
- Concludes the chapter by providing some future insights.

HOMOMORPHIC ENCRYPTION

In order to protect users' privacy, encryption is one of the most common techniques. However, traditional symmetric key cryptographic algorithms only allow users to encrypt data, and in order to perform any operations, one needs to decrypt the data for performing computation and finally re-encrypt it again. Moreover, users are sometimes required to disclose their secret encryption keys to third parties in order to process sensitive data. However, Homomorphic Encryption is a new research topic in the field of cryptography that has been introduced to make data more secure by allowing non-trusted parties to process calculations on encrypted data. HE technique is a special form of encryption that allows various computations to be performed on encrypted data, thereby producing the results in an encrypted form, which when decrypted match the result of operations performed on the underlying data. Fig 2 shows the working of Homomorphic Encryption Mechanism.

Figure 2. Working of Homomorphic Encryption

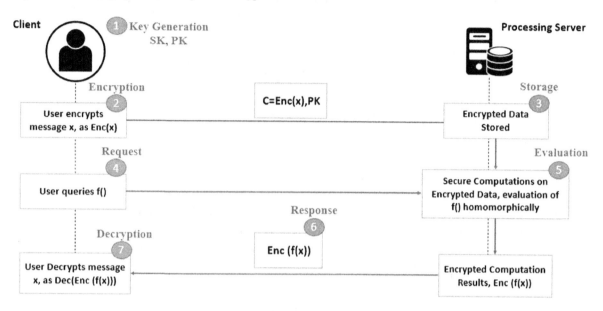

HE schemes often are based on four main algorithms that are Key Generation, Encryption, Decryption, and Evaluation. For HE's asymmetric version, Keygen creates a public and secret key pair, and for a symmetric version, it creates one key. Actually, Key Generation, Encryption and Decryption are not different from as they were in conventional schemes. Evaluation, on the other hand, is a HE specific operation that takes input a ciphertext to generate another ciphertext corresponding to a functional plaintext. Also, function f () is performed without seeing the messages (m_1, m_2) over the ciphertexts (c_1, c_2). In homomorphic encryption, the format of ciphertexts after an evaluation process must be preserved so that the ciphertexts can be decrypted correctly. In addition, the ciphertext size should be constant to ensure an unlimited number of operations, as a large ciphertext requires more resources, resulting in fewer homomorphic operations.

Three types of homomorphic encryption (HE) schemes exist, depending on how many computations are allowed on encrypted data. These schemes are PHE, SWHE and FHE. Fig 3 displays a tree diagram of existing homomorphic schemes that are categorized under various categories.

Figure 3. Homomorphic Encryption Algorithms Categories

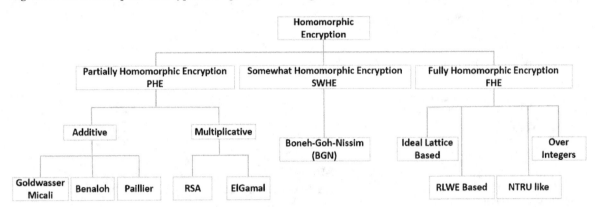

Among all HE schemes in the literature, PHE schemes support the Eval function only for multiplication or addition operations, SWHE schemes allow only some limited operation or circuit combinations, and FHE schemes allow arbitrary functions to be evaluated over ciphertexts indefinitely. Below is a summary and explanation of the well-known PHE, SWHE, and FHE schemes.

Partially Homomorphic Encryption Schemes

PHE only allows for a single operation yet it can be repeated unlimited times (no limit on usage). A number of useful PHE examples can be found in the literature. Each has made an important contribution to the PHE. However, this research focus primarily on the RSA, Goldwasser-Micali, El-Gamal, Benaloh, and Paillier PHE schemes.

Multiplicative Homomorphic

RSA

RSA is an early example of PHE and introduced by Rivest et al. (1978b) shortly after the invention of public key cryptography by Difie and Hellman (1976). RSA is the first feasible achievement of the public key cryptosystem. Moreover, the homomorphic property of RSA was shown by Rivest et al. (1978a) just after the seminal work of RSA. Indeed, the first attested use of the term "privacy homomorphism" was introduced in Rivest et al. (1978a). The security of the RSA cryptosystem is based on the hardness of the factoring problem of the product of two large prime numbers (Montgomery 1994).

RSA is an early example of PHE and introduced by Rivest et al. (1978b) shortly after the invention of public key cryptography by Difie and Hellman (1976). RSA is the first feasible

Rivest et al. (1978) created RSA. It is believed that the RSA Public Key Cryptosystem (PKC) was the first practical implementation of public key encryption. Soon after RSA's seminal work, (Rivest et al., 1978) demonstrated that RSA is homomorphic. The algorithms involved in the scheme are:

- Key Generation: Given a security parameter k, the key generation process produces the two primes p_A, q_A. Then $n = p_A . q_A$ and $\phi = (pA\_1)(qA\_1)$ is calculated. After that 'e' is chosen such that GCD (e, ϕ) and then by computing multiplicative inverse of 'e', d is calculated (ed^{o}1modϕ). A system's Private Key is sk=(d,n), and its Public Key is pk=(e,n).

- Encryption: To encryption of message 'x' is done as:

$$c = E(x) = x^e(\text{mod } n),$$

- Decryption: The message x can be recovered from the ciphertext using sk=(d,n) as:

$$x = D(c) = c^d(\text{mod } n).$$

- Homomorphic Property:

$$E\left(x_1\right) * E\left(x_2\right) = \left(x_1^e \bmod n\right) * \left(x_2^e \bmod n\right) = \left(x_1 * x_2\right)^e \bmod n = E\left(x_1 * x_2\right).$$

ElGamal

ElGamal (1985) devised a public key encryption system based on a discrete logarithmic hardness problem. This technique is typically used to encrypt the secret key for symmetric encryption systems as part of hybrid encryption systems. Algorithms involved in the scheme are:

- Key Generation: A cyclic group 'G' with order n using generator g is produced. Then, $h=g^y$ is computed for randomly chosen yÎZn*. System's Private Key is sk=a(aÎ{2,...,n–2}), and its Public Key is pk=(G,n,g,h).
- Encryption: The ciphertext pair c=(c_1,c_2) is produced by encrypting message x with g and a:

$$c = E\left(x\right) = \left(g^a, xh^a\right) = \left(g^a, xg^{ay}\right) = \left(c_1, c_2\right)$$

- Decryption: To decrypt c, first, $w=c_1^y$ is computed. Then, decryption of ciphertext c is as:

$$c_2 \cdot w^{-1} = xg^{ay} \cdot g^{-ay} = x.$$

- Homomorphic Property:

$$E\left(x_1\right) * E\left(x_2\right) = \left(g^{a_1}, x_1 h^{a_1}\right) * \left(g^{a_2}, x_2 h^{a_2}\right) = \left(g^{a_1+a_2}, x_1 * x_2 h^{a_1+a_2}\right) = E\left(x_1 * x_2\right).$$

Multiplicative homomorphic

Goldwasser Miceli

Probabilistic public key encryption approach was introduced by (Goldwasser and Miceli, 1984). Even though it is a probabilistic process, ciphertext can be encrypted bit by bit with this method. Quadratic-Residuosity Problem is a foundational aspect of GM cryptosystem. The algorithms involved are:

- Key Generation: Key generation algorithm generates two primes p_A, q_A given a security parameter k. After that $n=p_A.q_A$ is computed. Then a is chosen as one of the quadratics non-residue modulo n values with $\frac{a}{n} = 1$. System's Private Key is $sk=(p_A,q_A)$, and Public Key is $pk=(a,n)$.

- Encryption: Firstly, a string of bits representing message x is created. Then, a quadratic non-residue value y_i is generated for each bit of the message x_i such that $GCD(y_i,n)=1$. Each bit is then encrypted as follows:

$$c_i = E\left(x_i\right) = y_i^2 a^{x_i} \bmod n$$

where $x = x_0,x_1,\ldots,x_w$, $c = c_0,c_1,\ldots,c_w$, (where w denotes the block size used for the message space) and $a \hat{I} Z_n^*$. The multiplicative subgroup of integers modulo n in this case, referred to as Z_n^*, contains all the numbers that are smaller than and relatively prime to w.

- Decryption: Since $a \hat{I} Z_n^*$ ($1 < a £ n - 1$) is quadratic residue modulo n for only $x_i = 0$. To decrypt c_i, one needs to decides that whether c_i is a quadratic residue modulo n or not; if so, x_i returns 0, or else x_i it returns 1.

- Homomorphic Property: For each bit $x_i \hat{I} \{0, 1\}$,

$$E\left(x_1\right) * E\left(x_2\right) = \left(y_1^2 a^{x_1} \ mod \ n\right) * \left(y_2^2 a^{x_2} \ mod \ n\right) = \left(y_1 * y_2\right)^2 a^{x_1+x_2} \ mod \ n = E\left(x_1 + x_2\right)$$

Benaloh

Benaloh encryption was proposed to improve GM Cryptosystem's poor expansion factor. Instead of bit-by-bit encryption, the Benaloh (1995) scheme encrypts the ciphertext block-by-block at once with s-bits length, by employing a technique called "dense probabilistic encryption".

- Key Generation: Block size s and primes p_A, q_A are selected in a manner that s divides p_A-1 and s is relatively prime to $\frac{(p_A-1)}{s}$ and q_A-1 (i.e., $GCD\left(s,\frac{(p_A-1)}{s}\right) = 1$, $gcd(s(q_A-1))=1$). Then, $n_p A,q_A$ and $\phi=(pA\_1)(qA\_1)$ are computed. $y\hat{I}Zn^*$ is selected such that $y\phi^{11m}od \ n$ (Zn^* is multiplicative subgroup of integers modulo n that includes numbers relatively prime and smaller than s). Finally, (y,n) is published as public key and (pA, $_q$A) is kept as private key.

- Encryption: For message $x \hat{I} Zs$ (Zs$_=$ {0,1,...,s–1}), choose a random v (v$\hat{I}Zn$*). Then:

$$c = E(x) = y^x v^s \bmod n$$

- Decryption: Message x is retrieved by an exhaustive search for $i\hat{I}Z_s$, such that

$$\left(y^{-i} c\right)^{\phi/s} \equiv 1$$

where the message x is returned as the value of i, such that x=i.

- Homomorphic Property:

$$E\left(x_1\right) * E\left(x_2\right) = \left(y^{x_1} v_1^s \bmod n\right) * \left(y^{x_2} v_2^s \bmod n\right) = y^{x_1+x_2}\left(v_1 * v_2\right)^s \bmod n = E\left(x_1 + x_2\right)$$

Paillier

A probabilistic cryptographic scheme (Paillier, 1999) was introduced based on the composite residuosity problem. The system uses an asymmetric encryption approach to create homomorphic characteristics. The cryptosystem consists of three algorithms mentioned below:

- Key Generation: Key generation algorithm generates primes p_A, q_A given a security parameter k. After that, $n=p_A,q_A$ and λ=lcm(pA_1, qA_1) is calculated. Then, a function $L\left(u\right) = \dfrac{u-1}{n}$ is defined. Following the selection of generator $g \in Z_{n^2}^*$, μ=(L(gλ^{mo}d n2)$^)$-1 's calculated. A system's Private Key is sk=(λ,μ), and its Public Key is pk=(n,g).
- Encryption: Random $r\hat{I}Z$*n i$_s$ selected for message $x\hat{I}Zn$. $_T$he ciphertext can be calculated as:

$$C = E\left(x\right) = g^x \cdot r^n \bmod n^2.$$

- Decryption: Given a ciphertext C, the original message x can be recovered with sk=(λ,μ) as:

m = D(c) = L(cλ^{mo}d n2)$\cdot\mu$ mod n.

- Homomorphic Property:

$$E\left(m_1\right) * E\left(m_2\right) = \left(g^{m_1} r_1^n \bmod n^2\right) * \left(g^{m_2} r_2^n \bmod n^2\right) = g^{m_1+m_2}\left(r_1 * r_2\right)^n \bmod n^2 = E\left(m_1 + m_2\right)$$

Table 1 presents a comparison between different PHE Schemes where M, E and M^{-1} represent the modular multiplication, exponentiation, and inverse, respectively.

Table 1. Comparison of PHE Schemes

Factors		RSA	Goldwasser Miceli	ElGamal	Benaloh	Paillier
Developed year		1978	1982	1984	1994	1999
Cipher type		Asymmetric Deterministic	Asymmetric Probabilistic Encryption and Deterministic Decryption	Asymmetric Probabilistic	Asymmetric Probabilistic	Asymmetric Probabilistic
Computational Cost	Key Gen	$2M+M^{-1}$	M	E	$2M$	$2M+E_{MOD}$
	Encryption	E_{MOD}	$(2E+M)_{MOD}$	$2E+2M$	$(2E+M)_{MOD}$	$(2E+M)_{MOD}$
	Decryption	E_{MOD}	-	$3E+M$	$2E+M$	$(E+2M)_{MOD}$
	Total Cost	$2M+M^{-1}+2E_{MOD}$	$M+(2E+M)_{MOD}$	$6E+3M$	$3M+2E+(2E+M)_{MOD}$	$2M+(4E+3M)_{MOD}$
Security Assumption		Integer Factorization Problem	Quadratic Residuosity Problem	Discrete Log Problem	Higher Residuosity Problem	Decisional Composite Residuosity Assumption
Homomorphic Property		Multiplicative	Additive (Binary numbers, XOR)	Multiplicative	Additive	Additive

Somewhat Homomorphic Encryption Scheme

SWHE scheme refers to encryption systems that exhibit certain homomorphic properties but are not fully homomorphic. The schemes allow for a certain number of additions and only a single multiplication, but every time these operations are performed, the ciphertexts are put through too much "noise" that ultimately makes decryption impossible. Literature has a number of SWHE examples. We will primarily focus on Boneh-Goh-Nissim BGN, which was used as a steppingstone to the first plausible Fully Homomorphic Encryption Scheme.

BGN

Boneh et al. (2005) developed a semantically secure cryptosystem known as Boneh-Goh-Nissim (BGN). BGN introduced the FHE concept. In the BGN cryptosystem, arbitrary numbers of additions could be handled, but multiplication could only be performed once. To compute homomorphic multiplication of two ciphertexts, BGN cryptosystem uses bilinear pairings. By keeping ciphertext size constant, BGN evaluates 2DNF formulas on ciphertext, allowing any number of additions and one multiplication to be carried out.

- Key Generation: Public key is released as (n,G,G',e,g,i). Here e is a bilinear map such that $e:G\times G \circledR G'$, where G,G' are groups of order $n=q_A q_B$. g and v are the generators of G and set $i = v^{q_B}$ and i is the generator of G with order q_A, which is kept hidden as secret key.
- Encryption: To encrypt message x, a random r from set $\{0,1,\ldots,n-1\}$ is picked and encrypted as:

$c = E(m) = g^x i^r \bmod n$

- Decryption: To decrypt ciphertext c, one needs to first compute

$$c' = c^{q_A} = \left(g^x i^r\right)^{q_A} = \left(g^{q_A}\right)^x \left(i^{q_A} \equiv 1 \bmod n\right)$$

and $g' = g^{q_A}$ and finally decryption is proceeded as follows:

$$x = D\left(c\right) = \log_{g'} c'$$

- Homomorphic Property:

Over Addition: HE addition of plaintexts x_1 and x_2 using ciphertexts c_1 and c_2 is performed as

$$c = c_1 c_2 i^r = \left(g^{x_1} i^{r_1}\right)\left(g^{x_2} i^{r_2}\right) i^r = g^{x_1 + x_2} i^{r'},$$

where $r' = r_1 + r_2 + r$ and it can be seen that $x_1 + x_2$ can be easily recovered from resulting ciphertext c.

Over Multiplication: To perform homomorphic multiplication, use g_1 with order n and i_1 with order q_A and set $g_1 = e(g,g)$, $i_1 = e(g,i)$ and $i = g^{\alpha q_B} q_B$. Then, the homomorphic multiplication of messages x_1 and x_2 using the ciphertexts c_1 and c_2 are computed as follows:

$$c = e\left(c_1, c_2\right) i_1^r = e\left(g^{x_1} i^{r_1}, g^{x_2} i^{r_2}\right) i_1^r = g_1^{x_1 x_2} i_1^{x_1 r_2 + r_2 x_1 + \alpha q_B r_1 r_2 + r} = g_1^{x_1 x_2} i_1^{r'}$$

It is seen that r is uniformly distributed like r and so $x_1 x_2$ can be correctly recovered from resulting ciphertext c. However, c is now in the group G' instead of G. Therefore, another HE multiplication operation is not allowed in G' as there is no pairing in the target set G'. However, resulting ciphertext in G' still allows an unlimited number of homomorphic additions. Tab 2. presents BGN SWHE Scheme according to properties, categories, & security assumption.

Table 2. BGN SWHE Scheme Properties, Computational Cost and Security Assumption.

Factors		BGN
Developed year		2005
Cipher type		Based on pairing for elliptical curve
Computational Cost	Key Gen	$P+M+E$
	Encryption	$(2E+M)_{MOD}$
	Decryption	$2E+Log$
	Total Cost	$P+M+3E+Log+(2E+M)_{MOD}$
Security assumption		Subgroup decision problem
Homomorphic Property		Unlimited additions, but only one multiplication

Fully Homomorphic Encryption Schemes

FHE supports arbitrary multiplication and addition, allowing functions to be computed on the encrypted data. Although FHE uses public key encryption, its initial structure eluded cryptographer's attempts for a long time. Due to the difficulty in achieving FHE, its potential as a primitive for building and enhancing other cryptographic techniques was considered as a holy grail. Therefore, cryptographers have successfully obtained the holy grail with Gentry's innovative blueprint (Gentry, 2009). Gentry's work presented a plausible construction of FHE.

After Gentry's work, several researchers proposed the improved and efficient lattice-based schemes. Moreover, FHE scheme over integers was proposed. Thereafter, FHE scheme based on Ring Learning with Error (RLWE) problems was suggested. Lastly, an NTRU-like FHE was presented for its promising efficiency. Hence, these and similar concepts and attempts can be categorized into four main FHE families namely: (1) Ideal Lattice Based (2) Over Integers (3) RLWE Based (4) NTRU-like, as shown in Figure 2. Overview of some of the techniques proposed after Gentry's technique are summarized in Tab 3.

Table 3. Overview of FHE improvements after Gentry work

FHE Scheme		Scheme's Outline	Underlying Security Assumptions
Gentry's FHE		Seminal FHE scheme based on ideal-lattices	Sparse Subset Sum Problem (SSSP)
Gentry Optimizations	Stehle and Steinfeld	Faster FHE scheme	Sparse Subset Sum Problem-SSSP
	Gentry and Halevi	Gentry's scheme Implementation by a number of optimizations	The hardness of finding small principal ideal-lattice
	Gentry and Halevi	FHE without squashing	Decisional Diffie Hellman assumption, or SIVP problem over ideal lattices
	Smart and Vercauteren	Enabling SIMD operations	The decision variant of the Bounded Distance Decoding problem BDDP
Over LWE/ RLWE	Brakerski and Vaikuntanathan	FHE from RLWE	RLWE Problem
	Fourth, Lauter, Naehrig and Vaikuntanathan	Based on RLWE	RLWE Problem
	Gentry, Sahai, and Waters	Attribute based FHE scheme (GSW scheme)	LWE Problem
	Brakerski and Vaikuntanathan	Lattice based FHE	LWE Problem
Over Integers	Dijk, Gentry, Halevi, and Vaikuntanathan (DGHV)	FHE scheme using arithmetic over the integers	Approximate GCD Problem
	Coron, Mandal, Naccache, and Tibouchi	DGHV's improvement working over integers with smaller public keys	Approximate GCD Problem
	Coron, Naccache, and Tibouchi	Compression approach (to minimize the pk size used by DGHV scheme)	Approximate GCD Problem

Ideal Lattice-Based FHE Schemes

The first ever fully homomorphic encryption approach has been proposed by Gentry during his Ph.D. studies. Primarily, employed concepts of rings and ideals for designing and developing fully homomorphic schemes (Alkharji et al., 2016). Ideals can be defined as the property of conserving subsets of rings. Moreover, in this approach, each of the ideals is characterized by a lattice. Since this approach is a continuation of a somewhat homomorphic encryption technique therefore after reaching a specific threshold value the produced ciphertext becomes noisy. However, for proper decryption of a message, the noise must be minimized. To address this problem, Gentry used the concepts of bootstrapping and squashing so that noise can be reduced, and proper cipher text can be generated for executing homomorphic operations over the encrypted data. The description of bootstrapping and squashing is given below.

- **Bootstrapping**: To reduce the effect of noise, ciphertext needs to be refreshed using the concept of recryption. A homomorphic scheme can be bootstrappable if and only if it can assess the circuit of its decryption algorithm. First of all, with the help of squashing, the ciphertext is converted into bootstrapped ciphertext. Secondly, the refreshed ciphertext is determined using the bootstrapping process in which a noisy ciphertext is decrypted homomorphically using an encrypted secret key shared with a server already having a public key. The resultant is encrypted by another public key for introducing small new noise. The homomorphic operations can now be executed on this refreshed text until it reaches the threshold again.
- **Squashing**: This approach focuses on selecting a vector set whose summation must be equivalent to the multiplicative inverse of the private (secret) key. The degree of the circuit can be minimized

if the ciphertext gets multiplied by the elements of the selected vector set. The resultant ciphertext now becomes bootstrappable.

To enable computations over encrypted data, both techniques are applied repeatedly to maintain a certain threshold level of noise.

FHE Scheme Over Integers

Based on the bootstrapping approach proposed by Gentry, Van Dijk came up with another FHE. It is focused on the mathematical hardness difficulty of the Approximate Greatest Common Divisor (AGCD). It is a type of symmetric HE and is quite simple. This approach tries to retrieve an integer p by using its close multiples m_1 and m_2 where $m_i = q_i p + r_i$ and q_i can be defined as integers that are smaller than unknown error terms m_i and r_i. The homomorphic operations including addition and multiplication can be performed in this scheme and the resultant ciphertext maintains the format and homomorphic property. For decryption, the noise must remain half of the secret key. However, in the case of multiplication operation, this noise increases exponentially therefore the scheme puts more constraints on multiplicative homomorphic operations in comparison to addition (Dijk et al., 2010).

LWE FHE Scheme

Brakerski, Z. and Vaikuntanathan, V., (2011) proposed a FHE scheme that is based on a hard problem Learning with Error (LWE). This hardness approach is even secure for the post-quantum era. The worst-case lattice problem Shortest Vector Problem (SVP) is reduced to LWE, therefore if any algorithm can solve this then it can easily break SVP too. LWE based schemes are an ideal post quantum candidate.

NTRU Like FHE Scheme

It is considered the earliest effort to develop an encryption scheme based on lattices. In comparison to GGH and RSA cryptosystems, this technique improved performance both in the software and hardware implementations. However, there were some security issues that were minimized by modifying the key generation algorithm. Moreover, to make it fully homomorphic, the deterministic set used to select noise was converted into probabilistic along with selecting parameters that permit full homomorphism (Hoff stein et al, 1998) and (López-Alt et al., 2012)

APPLICATIONS OF HOMOMORPHIC ENCRYPTION

Homomorphic encryption has been employed by the research community for privacy preserving computations in various domains. Some of them are mentioned below.

Healthcare

Electronic Health Records (EHRs) are maintained and used in the healthcare sector to provide quality and timely healthcare facilities. This EHR entails sensitive information including medical reports, clinical data, medical history, and demographics that needs to be protected as disclosure of such critical information leads to regulatory penalties and affects the reputation of the healthcare organization. To preserve privacy, traditional encryption approaches simply encrypt this information using a secret key on which computations are not possible that again hinders the provision of quality healthcare facilities. Therefore, maintaining the confidentiality of patient records while permitting computations for improving efficiency and quality of care is a challenging task. Boomija and Raja (2022) in their research integrate a partially homomorphic encryption scheme and role-based user policy to prevent unauthorized disclosure and secure e-health records while allowing computations for decision making. The comparative analysis shows that this scheme outperforms Benaloh, ElGamal, and Paillier cryptosystems. Vengadapurvaja et al. (2017) in their research propose a modified RSA cryptosystem to develop a fully homomorphic encryption scheme to encrypt x-rays and other related scans as the image data from x-ray, CT scans, MRI, and other laboratory tests are important in diagnosing disease and providing treatment and reveals sensitive information about patients, therefore, it must be protected. Due to homomorphism, physicians, nurses, and other paramedical staff can perform operations on it and provide treatment without disclosing patient information. The statistical results demonstrate that the approach is effective and efficient. To perform computations over encrypted data, researchers (Raisaro et al., 2018) use an ElGamal-based partial homomorphic scheme on i2b2 demo datasets. The results exhibit that in the case of aggregated queries, a high homomorphic aggregation cost is incurred. The researcher concludes that although the storage cost is quite high, but not too much as it is only four times more than the unencrypted versions (Raisaro et al., 2018). Similarly, to secure ECG data, Shaikh et al. (2020) employ RSA based partial homomorphic encryption scheme. It is used to protect the ECG signals with an accuracy of 90%.

Moreover, to promote the well-being of society hospitals, laboratories, insurance companies, healthcare ministries, pharmacies, etc. need to share the health information of patients while preserving privacy and security for predicting disease patterns in different geographical locations so that necessary arrangements can be made. An et al. (2021) in their research secure location information of patients using Brakerski homomorphic encryption and proximity computation approaches to contain the covid-19 pandemic.

Apart from these, to predict the disease of a patient for prognosis and diagnosis using encrypted datasets, homomorphic encryption is of prime importance. In this regard, Girbov et al. (2019) in their research uses the ring-based FHE technique along with Recursive Least Squared (RLS) and time series analysis for computing models and predicting patients developing Parkinson's disease, diabetes, and cancer with great accuracy. Son et al., (2021) predicts the occurrence of breast cancer by employing a fully homomorphic CKKS scheme (Cheon et al., 2017) and Gated Recurrent Unit (GRU) with 89.3% accuracy. Another study (Kocabas et al., 2016) employs an additive pailler partial homomorphic encryption scheme to predict heart rate and Long QT syndrome by using THEW ECG monitoring dataset. The results demonstrate that detection via pailler is faster than BGV however encryption and decryption processes are slow in both cases. Similarly, privacy preserving computation can generally be employed over IoT based healthcare Ahmed et al. (2020) and for treating cancer disease as well AL Mansour et al. (2019).

Online Voting

Elections are considered the backbone of democracy and therefore they should be transparent and fair. Traditional voting systems required an individual to reach a polling station for casting his vote. In this setting, it becomes difficult for elders or people living in different places to come and cast vote. Moreover, the probability of rigging in such elections is quite high. Therefore, in this information age, the internet is considered a viable source to cast votes online from anywhere. This again brings lots of security and privacy challenges that must be addressed carefully for ensuring fair elections. Homomorphic encryption is of extreme importance in this regard as it ensures the security of data while allowing computations over it to get the maximum benefit of it.

Saproo et al. (2020) in their research propose an electronic voting system by employing a pailler-based partial homomorphic encryption technique. This system is secure and efficient as it stores a vote casted for a particular candidate in encrypted form whereas for the rest of the candidates it encrypts a null value and sets it for other candidates automatically in the database. In this way, admin, employees, or attackers cannot differentiate between the ballot saved for a particular candidate as an actual vote or a null value. With the help of the pailler additive property, total votes are computed. Another study by Jabbar and Alsaad (2017) employs ElGamal-based partial homomorphic cryptosystem to develop and implement a remote electronic voting system to ensure security, transparency, and fairness. The casted votes are counted by using the additive homomorphic property of ElGamal. However, computational cost is a major challenge in this scenario. Anggriane et al. (2016) in their research propose Paillier homomorphic cryptosystem to implement an e-voting system. The homomorphic property of this technique enables the determination of the sum of votes in encrypted form without even disclosing the selections of voters. The approach is probabilistic in nature as it generates different ciphertext for the same message to avoid guessing attacks.

Agriculture

The incorporation of communication technologies in agriculture revolutionized traditional practices by optimizing harvesting, irrigation, seeding, and fertilization. With the use of sensors and the Internet of Things (IoT), farmers easily manage variations in moisture level, nutrient availability, nutrient availability, field variability, soil type, etc. by providing accurate inputs remotely in a timely manner. Similarly, information gathered by different farms can be correlated to make informed decisions. However, this led to serious privacy concerns as this data is shared with third parties for analytics. Moreover, the disclosure of farm data including physical location can disclose physical locations, crop yield information, and planting strategies. Similarly, through several active attacks, adversaries can even tamper with the moisture level and nutrient supply that can destroy crops. To address these concerns, homomorphic encryption can play a significant role in maintaining the quality of crops by providing privacy-preserved monitoring and surveillance of agricultural data.

Zhaoliang et al. (2020) in their research propose a storage mechanism to accurately monitor the environment of crops in real-time. Since sensors generate a huge volume of data every day, storage in local space is infeasible. Therefore, this research stores data in the cloud in encrypted form using Paillier homomorphic scheme and blockchain. The results demonstrate that the scheme is efficient and secure. Similarly, Yan et al. (2021) in their research propose a Paillier homomorphic solution to secure the location of devices and determination of the distance between farms and sensors privately. In this scheme, servers can determine distance without having additional information about farms. Using the homomorphic property of the Paillier cryptosystem, servers can efficiently measure and compare distance on the encrypted locations. The results show that the proposed approach SPRIDE ensures privacy and improves performance.

Smart Grid

With the advancements in technology, smart meters have been installed to collect the electricity consumption of the entities so that utility suppliers can manage the load Khadam et al. (2021). However, this reveals the daily activities of individuals which impacts their privacy. Similarly, data analytics cannot be performed on this training data as users are reluctant to share their personal usage patterns which model training. In this scenario, homomorphic encryption is an optimal solution as it performs operations on encrypted data.

Syed et al. (2020) employs fully homomorphic encryption (based on matrix transformation) to train deep learning models using encrypted datasets for load forecasting, fault detection, and localization in smart grids. The results demonstrate the classification accuracy of 98% which is approximately equal to traditional model training using plain data. Similarly, Singh et al. (2021) present a privacy-preserving data aggregation model using homomorphic encryption for maintaining the confidentiality of real-time electricity usage patterns of consumers with minimum computational overhead. Regueiro et al. (2021) leverage blockchain and Paillier homomorphic schemes to aggregate smart metering data securely during storage and transmission. To overcome the falsification attacks on the collected power consumption data by smart meters, Joshi et al. (2022) propose Elliptic Curve Cryptography (ECC) based holomorphic mechanism. The analysis exhibits that the proposed mechanism ensures security with the least computational cost. The proposed approach is eighteen times faster than a common homomorphic scheme named CKKS.

Fintech

Like other sectors, data is of great value in the fintech sector and therefore requires mechanisms to ensure its confidentiality. With the proliferation of IT devices, business organizations nowadays have developed their own customized technical solutions and procedures for control and operation. Therefore, the information, control and operation variables, etc. that flow in those systems are the intellectual property that they do not want to share with others. However, on the other side, they do want business analytics and data mining for identifying customers' preferences, tailoring their marketing strategies, and improving bidding processes. In that scenario, homomorphic encryption plays a vital role as it operates on encrypted data so banks, corporates, insurance companies, and telecommunication companies share their data in encrypted form and leverage the benefits of additive and multiplicative homomorphic properties for getting meaningful insights into customers preferences that eventually improve their promotions and products.

Tebaa et al. (2015) propose a hybrid homomorphic system that incorporates Paillier and RSA cryptosystems to encrypt business data so that it can be shared on the cloud and different stakeholders can perform operations on it. Similarly, Alqarni (2021) employs Paillier homomorphic encryption mechanism to secure business data generated from various sensors, IoT, and software. For improving data mining in FinTech, Smilarubavathy et al. (2020) integrate homomorphic encryption with a k-means clustering algorithm to identify trends of customers' interests to tailor advertising and production policies. To deal with the problem of data transaction authentication in insurance companies, Xiao et al. (2019) proposes blockchain-based homomorphic approach for authenticating transactions so that a mutual account book in encrypted form can be shared for operations. The results demonstrate the effectiveness and security of the proposed scheme. Moreover, Chokparova and Urbas (2021) in their research employ the Paillier homomorphic mechanism to secure sensitive data that needs to be shared between the value provider and owner in the supply value chain. The experimental analysis ensures high security of shared information.

Transportation

The use of technology in transport systems has gained momentum in recent years due to its numerous advantages including convenience, reduced traffic accidents, improved traffic efficiency, traffic planning, traffic monitoring, road safety, and driver assistance. However, the provision of such services results in disclosing the privacy of users as these mechanisms require private information from the vehicles. Later on, such inputs are shared with insurance companies, car manufacturers, production companies and other related stakeholders that breach privacy of users. To address these problems, the role of homomorphic encryption is pivotal and researchers from academia and industry are now developing mechanisms for performing computations over encrypted data using homomorphic encryption.

Boudguiga et al. (2021) use CKKS homomorphic encryption with machine learning to secure sensitive data shared by vehicles in intelligent transportation systems while ensuring operations from different stakeholders. The experimentation results show an accuracy of 92%. Likewise, Ogundoyin (2022) presents a secure data aggregation mechanism for an intelligent transportation system by using a modified Paillier encryption technique, hashing, and Boneh signature scheme. The results exhibit that the proposed approach is secure and cost-effective. To protect communication between agents in ride-sharing services, Farokhi et al. (2020) use a Paillier-based homomorphic mechanism. It helps in preserving the privacy of individuals while using routing and sharing algorithms.

Figure 4 illustrates the various applications of homomorphic encryption in different domains including fintech, agriculture, smart grid, healthcare, e-voting and smart transportations.

Figure 4. Applications of Homomorphic Encryption

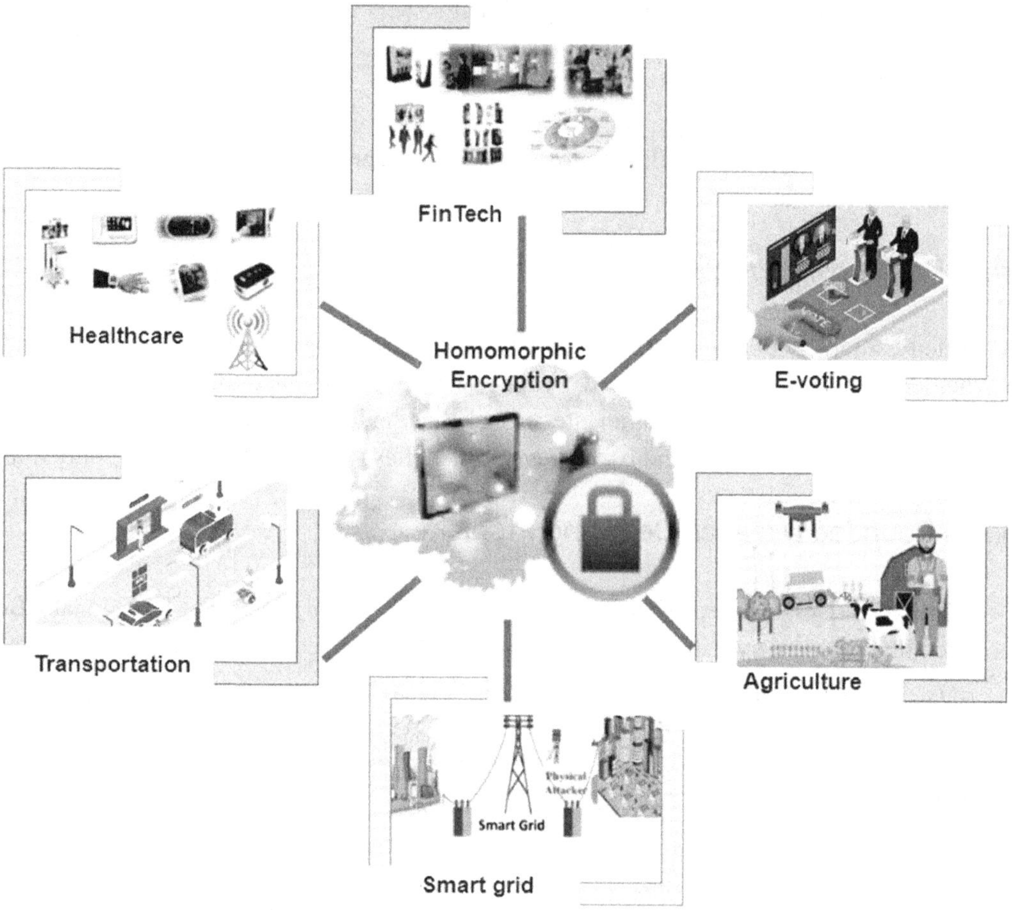

Security and Performance of Analysis

The security of any public key cryptosystem depends on the underlying mathematical hardness problem over which it is constructed. As RSA and Elgamal are based on the integer factorization hardness problem and discrete log problem respectively, hence as long as these mathematical hardness problems are hard to break or cannot be solved in polynomial time, the cryptosystem based on these problems are considered secure. Following this, we are going to revisit the definitions of some cryptographic hardness problems over which most of the types of homomorphic schemes are built.

Cryptographic Hardness Problems

Integer Factorization Problem

The difficulty of factoring large composite integers is the foundation of many cryptographic protocols. The integer factorization problem is defined as: Given a composite number Z, find two integers a and

b such that $a \cdot b = Z$, Montgomery, (1994). It can be demonstrated that RSA encryption is vulnerable if factoring can be done effectively, making it a significant issue.

Discrete Log Problem

Van Tilborg et al., (2014), given a cyclic group G or order n, where $g\hat{I}G$, and consider another element $y=g^x$, determine x given y and g.

Quadratic Residuosity Problem

The Quadratic Residuosity Problem (QRP) Van Tilborg et al., (2014) is defined as: Given Z and N, determine whether Z is a quadratic residue mod N or not, where N is assumed to be the product of two odd distinct prime numbers p_A and q_A, and Z is an integer such that the Jacobi symbol $(Z/N)=+1$. This problem is easy to solve given the factors p_A and q_A, however, it is believed to be difficult given only Z and N.

Decisional Bounded Distance Decoding Problem

Let $\gamma \hat{I} R+$ be a real positive and L be an N dimensional ideal lattice, and $\vec{v} \in Z^N$. The Decisional γ-Bounded Distance Decoding problem over ideal lattice (Decγ–BDDN) is to decide whether there exists a unique vector $\vec{u} \in L$ satisfying $\mathrm{Dist}(\vec{v},\vec{u}) \leq \gamma$ or not, given a basis of lattice L and $\vec{v}$, Lyubashevsky and Micciancio, (2009).

Sparse Subset Sum Problem

Given an integer set $A=\{a_1,a_2,\ldots,a_n\}$, and another target integer t, modulus $M\hat{I}Z$, an SSSP requires finding a sparse subset whose addition of elements sum up to t mod M. Lee, (2017) SSSP is generally considered to be hard like subset sum problem if n in large.

Approximate-Greatest Common Divisor (AGCD) Problem

Black (2014), Given a set of n integers of the form as $m_i = q_i p + r_i$ where $p,q_i,r_i \hat{I} Z$ and q_i,r_i are chosen randomly from different distributions, determine p.

Learning With Error Problem

Regev, (2009) LWE is described by parameters (N,M,q_A,χ) where N and qA are positive integers and are referred to as "dimension parameter" and "modulus parameter", respectively. χ is probability distribution over rational integers referred to as "error distribution". The following two probability distributions must be computationally indistinguishable in order to satisfy the LWE assumption:

Distribution 1. Choose a uniformly random matrix N×M matrix Q, a uniformly row vector r and s from vector space $Z_{q_A}^N$ and Z^M respectively. Each coordinate is chosen from error distribution χ. Compute $t=rQ+s$ (all computations are carried out modulo qA$_j$. Output (Q,t).

Distribution 2. Choose a uniformly random *N*×*M* matrix *Q*, and a uniformly row vector *x* from $Z_{q_A}^M$, Output (*Q*,*x*).

Ring Learning With Error Problem (RLWE)

Lyubashevsky et al. (2013) The RLWE is defined by parameters (N,M,q_A,χ) where N and qA are positive integers, referred to as "degree parameter" and "modulus parameter" respectively. χ is a probability distribution over the ring R=$Z[X]/(X^N+1)$, referred to as the "error distribution". The following two probability distributions must be computationally indistinguishable in order to satisfy the RLWE assumption:

Distribution 1. Choose random elements x and t from ring $\dfrac{R}{q_A R}$, and an element *f* from ring *R*,

chosen from error distribution χ. Compute y=*tx+f* (all computations are over ring $\dfrac{R}{q_A R}$. Output (*x*,*y*).

Distribution 2. Choose a uniformly random element *x* and *y* from the ring $\dfrac{R}{q_A R}$. Output (*x*,*y*).

Some of the above-mentioned hardness problems will no longer be secure in the near future once the practical quantum computers will be readily available in the near future. Quantum computers work on the principle of superposition and entanglement of Qubit (Quantum Bit) to achieve parallelism, and hence enhance the computational power to many folds (Mavroeidis et al., 2018). Moreover, there exists a post quantum Shor's algorithm (Shor, 1994) which can solve the mathematical hardness problems of integer factorization and discrete log (Jordan et al., 2018). Tab 4 lists the mathematical hardness problems which will be broken by Shor's algorithm executing on a quantum computer. The Pailliar scheme is based on the decisional composite residuosity hardness problem, but in fact this hardness is reduced to the integer factorization problem. Similarly, it applies to both Goldwasser Micali and the Benaloh homomorphic schemes. Hence, all partially homomorphic encryption mechanisms will no longer be secure in the post quantum era. Regarding BGN which belongs to a type of somewhat homomorphic scheme is also not secure in post quantum era because as seen from its key generation and decryption algorithms from above, retrieving the message from ciphertext without key translates to solving the integer factorization and discrete logarithm problem.

Table 4. Post Quantum Secure vs Non-Secure Homomorphic Encryption Schemes

Algorithms			Security Assumption	Quantum Secure
Partially Homomorphic	RSA		Integer Factorization Problem	Not Secure
	Goldwasser Micali		Quadratic Residuosity Problem (Integer Factorization Problem)	Not Secure
	Elgamal		Discrete Log Problem	Not Secure
	Benaloh		Higher Residuosity Problem (Integer Factorization Problem)	Not Secure
	Paillier		Decisional Composite Residuosity Assumption (Integer Factorization Problem)	Not Secure
Somewhat Homomorphic	BGN		Subgroup decision problem	Not Secure
Fully Homomorphic	Lattice Based	Gentry's FHE	The hardness assumption of SSSP, BDDP	Secure
	Over Integers	Dijk Gentry Halevi and Vaikuntanathan (DGHV)	Approximate-GCD Problem and SSSP	Secure
	LWE, R-LWE Based	Brakerski and Vaikuntanathan (BV)	The hardness of LWE Problem	Secure
		Fourth, Lauter, Naehrig and Vaikuntanathan	The hardness of R-LWE Problem	Secure
		Brakerski, Gentry and Vaikuntanathan (BGV)	R-LWE for an approximation factor exponential	Secure

Taking into consideration the Quantum computers and their ability to break certain mathematical hardness problems, the research community focused on developing the new hardness problems which are secure in the post quantum era. In fact, for some of the classical mathematical problems, there does not exist any quantum algorithm that can solve it in a reasonable amount of time. Some of the post quantum hard problems include sparse subset problem, shortest vector problem, bounded distance decoding, and Learning with Errors (LWE) based problems. As almost all of the fully homomorphic schemes are based on these quantum secure hardness problems, hence these are quantum resistant. A partial list of these FHE schemes includes Craig Gentry's original scheme based on ideal lattices, BGV (based on ring-LWE), and NTRU-based approach. These are all hard problems that are not breakable by Shor's method. Among these branches, lattice-based cryptography has the greatest potential.

Regarding the computation costs, the classical PHE schemes being based on simple group operations take a smaller number of operations to homomorphically compute over data. We can have arbitrary any number of computations either additive or multiplicative with retrieval of appropriate plaintext messages upon decryption. However, on the other hand, FHE schemes have associated noise which tends to increase with each homomorphic operation. Therefore, additional operational costs are incurred to limit the noise below the threshold after every homomorphic operation. Although FHE supports strong privacy guarantees, however, there is a significant cost associated with it in terms of computation and communication overhead. The FHE schemes have ciphertext expansion factor which leads to more communication overhead, often making the system too slow to be of practical usage. Also, FHE scheme's work underlying on Boolean circuits for evaluation of functions, where the complexity of function is directly related to the depth of circuit and the computation cost. Several optimizations and enhancements have been proposed by researchers to accelerate the FHE, thereby making it more practical for real life applications.

RECOMMENDATIONS

Computation over data in any application domain like healthcare, smart grid or fintech requires an underlying mathematical function which needs to be evaluated over that data in a privacy preserving manner. For example, in Smart grid, the various smart meters data needs to be aggregated/added and sent back to the control center of the smart grid for utility operations and better load management without breaching the privacy of any individual user/smart meter. In this case, the underlying function is simple addition of smart meters data, which can be attained by any additive PHE scheme. However, if we consider the case of privacy preserving Machine Learning (ML) model training or classification problem, then the underlying functions involve both addition and multiplication operations inherently obtained from the complex ML algorithms. In this case, FHE is the ideal candidate to attain privacy.

As computing over encrypted application domains require the involved entities to compute any arbitrary mathematical function, so if the underlying employed scheme is partially homomorphic (PHE), then it can perform either addition/subtraction and multiplication/division operations in a privacy preserving manner. However, FHE supports all mathematical operators at any instance of time, making it a good choice for complex mathematical functions. Regarding the choice of preferring either PHE, SHE, and FHE for any practical real-life application, we define it on the basis of three metrics: functional representation, performance and security. Functional representation indicates if a certain application function can be indicated by either additive or multiplicative operations, then we can proceed with any PHE scheme based on the context. However, if the application function can only be represented by an arbitrary number of both additive and multiplicative functions, then we must proceed with FHE. Similarly, for limited multiplicative operations with unbounded additive operations, the application can be proceeded by SHE. It is worth mentioning that FHE schemes can represent or implement functions represented by both PHE and SHE. Regarding performance in the resource constrained environment, PHE can be preferred over SHE and FHE. If privacy has highest priority, and post quantum security needs to be considered, then FHE schemes are deemed most appropriate for this case. Hence, according to the underlying functional representation in any application domain, the security versus performance tradeoff can be considered, and an appropriate type of HE schemes (amongst the three types) can be selected for privacy preserving computing.

CONCLUSION

With the development of the cloud computing paradigm, and the demand of various human and organization centric applications to outsource their data for better user experience and analytics in general, the privacy concerns are on the rise. Moreover, due to the pressing needs of various applications domains to perform computations over encrypted data while ensuring privacy is the dire need of this era. Homomorphic Encryption is one such mechanism which ensures computation over encrypted data with privacy preservation. In this chapter, the types of HE, their associated security and performance constraints, the application domains where these have been employed recently are reviewed. Finally, some recommendations for their usage based on the performance versus security tradeoff is suggested.

REFERENCES

Ahmed, L., Iqbal, M. M., Aldabbas, H., Khalid, S., Saleem, Y., & Saeed, S. (2020). Images data practices for semantic segmentation of breast cancer using deep neural network. *Journal of Ambient Intelligence and Humanized Computing*, 1–17.

Alkharji, M., Liu, H., & Washington, C. U. A. (2016). Homomorphic encryption algorithms and schemes for secure computations in the cloud. In *Proceedings of 2016 International Conference on Secure Computing and Technology* (p. 19). Academic Press.

AlMansour, N., & Saeed, S. (2019, April). IoT based healthcare infrastructure: A case study of Saudi Arabia. In *2019 International Conference on Computer and Information Sciences (ICCIS)* (pp. 1-7). IEEE.

Alqarni, A. (2021). *A Secure Approach for Data Integration in Cloud using Paillier Homomorphic Encryption*. Academic Press.

An, Y., Lee, S., Jung, S., Park, H., Song, Y., & Ko, T. (2021). Privacy-oriented technique for COVID-19 contact tracing (PROTECT) using homomorphic encryption: Design and development study. *Journal of Medical Internet Research*, 23(7), e26371.

Anggriane, S. M., Nasution, S. M., & Azmi, F. (2016, October). Advanced e-voting system using Paillier homomorphic encryption algorithm. In *2016 International Conference on Informatics and Computing (ICIC)* (pp. 338-342). IEEE.

Benaloh, J. (1994, May). Dense probabilistic encryption. In *Proceedings of the workshop on selected areas of cryptography* (pp. 120-128). Academic Press.

Black, N. D. (2014). *Homomorphic encryption and the approximate gcd problem* [Doctoral dissertation]. Clemson University.

Boneh, D., Goh, E. J., & Nissim, K. (2005, February). Evaluating 2-DNF formulas on ciphertexts. In *Theory of cryptography conference* (pp. 325–341). Springer. doi:10.1007/978-3-540-30576-7_18

Boomija, M. D., & Raja, S. V. (2022). Securing medical data by role-based user policy with partially homomorphic encryption in AWS cloud. *Soft Computing*, 1–10.

Boudguiga, A., Stan, O., Fazzat, A., Labiod, H., & Clet, P. E. (2021). Privacy Preserving Services for Intelligent Transportation Systems with Homomorphic Encryption. In ICISSP (pp. 684-693). Academic Press.

Brakerski, Z., & Vaikuntanathan, V. (2011, August). Fully homomorphic encryption from ring-LWE and security for key dependent messages. In *Annual cryptology conference* (pp. 505-524). Springer.

Cheon, J. H., Kim, A., Kim, M., & Song, Y. (2017, December). Homomorphic encryption for arithmetic of approximate numbers. In *International conference on the theory and application of cryptology and information security* (pp. 409-437). Springer.

Chokparova, Z., & Urbas, L. (2021, September). Utilization of Homomorphic Cryptosystems for Information Exchange in Value Chains. In *2021 26th IEEE International Conference on Emerging Technologies and Factory Automation (ETFA)* (pp. 1-7). IEEE.

Dijk, M. V., Gentry, C., Halevi, S., & Vaikuntanathan, V. (2010, May). Fully homomorphic encryption over the integers. In *Annual international conference on the theory and applications of cryptographic techniques* (pp. 24-43). Springer.

ElGamal, T. (1985). A public key cryptosystem and a signature scheme based on discrete logarithms. *IEEE Transactions on Information Theory*, *31*(4), 469–472. doi:10.1109/TIT.1985.1057074

Farokhi, F., Shames, I., & Johansson, K. H. (2020). Private routing and ride-sharing using homomorphic encryption. IET Cyber-Physical Systems. *Theory & Applications*, *5*(4), 311–320.

Gentry, C. (2009, May). Fully homomorphic encryption using ideal lattices. In *Proceedings of the forty-first annual ACM symposium on Theory of computing* (pp. 169-178). 10.1145/1536414.1536440

Goldwasser, S., & Micali, S. (1984). Probabilistic Encryption. *Journal of Computer and System Sciences*, *28*(2), 270–299. doi:10.1016/0022-0000(84)90070-9

Gribov, A., Horan, K., Gryak, J., Najarian, K., Shpilrain, V., Soroushmehr, R., & Kahrobaei, D. (2019, March). Medical diagnostics based on encrypted medical data. In *International Conference on Bio-inspired Information and Communication* (pp. 98-111). Springer.

Hoff stein, J., Pipher, J., & Silverman, J. H. (1998, June). NTRU: A ring-based public key cryptosystem. In *International algorithmic number theory symposium* (pp. 267-288). Springer.

Jabbar, I., & Alsaad, S. N. (2017). Design and Implementation of Secure Remote e-Voting System Using Homomorphic Encryption. *International Journal of Network Security*, *19*(5), 694–703.

Jordan, S. P., & Liu, Y. K. (2018). Quantum cryptanalysis: Shor, grover, and beyond. *IEEE Security and Privacy*, *16*(5), 14–21.

Joshi, S., Li, R., Bhattacharjee, S., Das, S. K., & Yamana, H. (2022, June). Privacy-Preserving Data Falsification Detection in Smart Grids using Elliptic Curve Cryptography and Homomorphic Encryption. In *2022 IEEE International Conference on Smart Computing (SMARTCOMP)* (pp. 229-234). IEEE.

Khadam, U., Iqbal, M. M., Saeed, S., Dar, S. H., Ahmad, A., & Ahmad, M. (2021). Advanced security and privacy technique for digital text in smart grid communications. *Computers & Electrical Engineering*, *93*, 107205.

Kocabas, O., Soyata, T., & Aktas, M.K. (2016). Emerging Security Mechanisms for Medical Cyber Physical Systems. *IEEE/ACM Trans Comput Biol Bioinf*, *13*(3), 401–416.

Lee, M. S. (2017). Sparse subset sum problem from Gentry–Halevi's fully homomorphic encryption. *IET Information Security*, *11*(1), 34–37.

López-Alt, A., Tromer, E., & Vaikuntanathan, V. (2012, May). On-the-fly multiparty computation on the cloud via multikey fully homomorphic encryption. In *Proceedings of the forty-fourth annual ACM symposium on Theory of computing* (pp. 1219-1234). ACM.

Lyubashevsky, V., & Micciancio, D. (2009, August). On bounded distance decoding, unique shortest vectors, and the minimum distance problem. In *Annual International Cryptology Conference* (pp. 577-594). Springer.

Lyubashevsky, V., Peikert, C., & Regev, O. (2013). On ideal lattices and learning with errors over rings. *Journal of the Association for Computing Machinery*, *60*(6), 1–35.

Mavroeidis, V., Vishi, K., Zych, M. D., & Jøsang, A. (2018). The impact of quantum computing on present cryptography. *International Journal of Advanced Computer Science and Applications*, *9*(3), 405–414.

Montgomery, P. L. (1994). A survey of modern integer factorization algorithms. *CWI Quarterly, 7*(4), 337-366.

Ogundoyin, S. O. (2022). A privacy-preserving multisubset data aggregation scheme with fault resilience for intelligent transportation system. *Information Security Journal: A Global Perspective*, 1-24.

Paillier, P. (1999, May). Public-key cryptosystems based on composite degree residuosity classes. In *International conference on the theory and applications of cryptographic techniques* (pp. 223-238). Springer. 10.1007/3-540-48910-X_16

Raisaro, J. L., Klann, J. G., Wagholikar, K. B., Estiri, H., Hubaux, J. P., & Murphy, S. N. (2018). Feasibility of homomorphic encryption for sharing I2B2 aggregate-level data in the cloud. *AMIA Joint Summits on Translational Science Proceedings AMIA Summit on Translational Science, 2018*, 176.

Regev, O. (2009). On lattices, learning with errors, random linear codes, and cryptography. *Journal of the Association for Computing Machinery, 56*(6), 1–40.

Regueiro, C., Seco, I., de Diego, S., Lage, O., & Etxebarria, L. (2021). Privacy-enhancing distributed protocol for data aggregation based on blockchain and homomorphic encryption. *Information Processing & Management, 58*(6), 102745.

Rivest, R. L., Shamir, A., & Adleman, L. (1978). A method for obtaining digital signatures and public-key cryptosystems. *Communications of the ACM, 21*(2), 120–126. doi:10.1145/359340.359342

Rivest, R. L., Adleman, L., & Dertouzos, M. L. (1978). On data banks and privacy homomorphisms. *Foundations of Secure Computation, 4*(11), 169-180.

Saproo, S., Warke, V., Pote, S., & Dhumal, R. (2020). Online voting system using homomorphic encryption. In *ITM Web of Conferences (Vol. 32*, p. 03023). EDP Sciences.

Shaikh, M. U., Adnan, W. A. W., & Ahmad, S. A. (2020). Secured electrocardiograph (ECG) signal using partially homomorphic encryption technique–RSA algorithm. *Pertanika Journal of Science & Technology, 28*(S2), 231–242.

Shor, P. W. (1994, November). Algorithms for quantum computation: discrete logarithms and factoring. In *Proceedings 35th annual symposium on foundations of computer science* (pp. 124-134). IEEE.

Singh, P., Masud, M., Hossain, M. S., & Kaur, A. (2021). Blockchain and homomorphic encryption-based privacy-preserving data aggregation model in smart grid. *Computers & Electrical Engineering*, *93*, 107209.

Smilarubavathy, G., Nidhya, R., Abiramy, N. V., & Dinesh Kumar, A. (2021). Paillier Homomorphic Encryption with K-Means Clustering Algorithm (PHEKC) for Data Mining Security in Cloud. In *Inventive Communication and Computational Technologies* (pp. 941–948). Springer.

Son, Y., Han, K., Lee, Y. S., Yu, J., Im, Y. H., & Shin, S. Y. (2021). Privacy-preserving breast cancer recurrence prediction based on homomorphic encryption and secure two party computation. *PLoS One*, *16*(12), e0260681.

Syed, D., Refaat, S. S., & Bouhali, O. (2020). Privacy preservation of data-driven models in smart grids using homomorphic encryption. *Information*, *11*(7), 357.

Tebaa, M., Zkik, K., & El Hajji, S. (2015). Hybrid homomorphic encryption method for protecting the privacy of banking data in the cloud. *International Journal of Security and Its Applications*, *9*(6), 61–70.

Van Tilborg, H. C., & Jajodia, S. (Eds.). (2014). *Encyclopedia of cryptography and security*. Springer Science & Business Media.

Vengadapurvaja, A. M., Nisha, G., Aarthy, R., & Sasikaladevi, N. (2017). An efficient homomorphic medical image encryption algorithm for cloud storage security. *Procedia Computer Science*, *115*, 643–650.

Xiao, L., Deng, H., Tan, M., & Xiao, W. (2019, December). Insurance block: A blockchain credit transaction authentication scheme based on homomorphic encryption. In *International Conference on Blockchain and Trustworthy Systems* (pp. 747-751). Springer.

Yan, Q., Lou, J., Vuran, M. C., & Irmak, S. (2021). Scalable Privacy-preserving Geo-distance Evaluation for Precision Agriculture IoT Systems. *ACM Transactions on Sensor Networks*, *17*(4), 1–30.

Zhaoliang, L., Huang, W., & Wang, D. (2021). Functional agricultural monitoring data storage based on sustainable block chain technology. *Journal of Cleaner Production*, *281*, 124078.

Chapter 16
Quantum and Post–Quantum Cybersecurity Challenges and Finance Organizations Readiness

Razi Arshad

Department of Computing, School of Electrical Engineering and Computer Science, National University of Sciences and Technology, Islamabad, Pakistan

Qaiser Riaz

Department of Computing, School of Electrical Engineering and Computer Science, National University of Sciences and Technology, Islamabad, Pakistan

ABSTRACT

Cryptography is used to protect sensitive information, but it is also required in many applications to ensure secure functionality and availability. The 100-year-old principles of physics are becoming industrially controllable, which leads to the era of the industrial quantum revolution. Products and applications such as quantum sensors, quantum simulators, quantum computers, and quantum cryptography are developing, which will affect the design of secure cryptographic systems. Post-quantum cryptography is a new field of research developing parallel to the progress in quantum technologies. Post-quantum cryptography deals with the development and investigation of algorithms that are assumed to be unbreakable even with quantum computers. This chapter will discuss the quantum and post-quantum cryptographic algorithms in detail and the migration strategies from classical asymmetric algorithms to post-quantum algorithms. This chapter also discusses the finance organization's readiness and recommendation for the replacement of vulnerable asymmetric algorithms with post-quantum algorithms.

DOI: 10.4018/978-1-6684-5284-4.ch016

1. INTRODUCTION

Financial technology (Fintech) is a new technology that improves and automates the usage of financial services. Fintech utilizes specialized software and algorithms, which help finance companies, business owners, and consumers to manage their financial operations more effectively. Fintech includes a variety of financial activities, such as online money transfers, online cheque deposits using a smartphone, and online investments management without the assistance of a bank person.

Government and finance companies around the world use cryptography to satisfy the CIA (confidentiality, Integrity, and Availability) triad of cybersecurity. The cryptographic system uses various types of communication protocols and secure infrastructure design where well-known cryptographic algorithms are employed. Cryptographic algorithms use complex mathematical functions as information transformation engines using a variable 'cryptographic based secret key' for the transformation of intelligible data into unintelligible data. The legitimate user can only transform back the unintelligible data into intelligible data with the help of a secret key. The authenticity of many cryptographic algorithms lies in the secrecy of the secret key.

There are two types of cryptographic algorithms: symmetric and asymmetric. In symmetric algorithms, legitimate users use the shared secret key for the protection of sensitive information. The security of the symmetric algorithms lies in the secrecy of the shared secret key. In an asymmetric algorithm, the sender uses one key and the receiver uses another key, which is related but completely different from each other. One key of asymmetric algorithm is always kept secret (usually called the private key) while the other key (usually called the public key) is publicly available without compromising the security of the cryptographic algorithm. Asymmetric algorithms are mainly used in financial services for user key distribution and digital signature procedures.

The revolution of quantum computing is underway. Quantum computing uses quantum physics principles to perform calculations that are not possible on most powerful supercomputers. Quantum computing has a lot of potential for the transformation of the financial sector and the global economy with accelerated scientific innovations. Quantum computers can greatly reduce the financial system time to analyze complex risk problems as well as increase their accuracy. The accelerated progress of quantum computing proposes an alarming cryptographic shift to more secure cryptographic algorithms. The financial system security algorithms, which include Internet communications protocols, mobile banking transactions, distributed ledger technologies, and digital currencies could become outdated or would require a significant upgrade. Shor's algorithm (Shor P., 1994) shows that nearly all the widely used asymmetric algorithms in financial sectors are theoretically vulnerable to large-scale quantum computers. Practical quantum computers will compromise the security of all modern asymmetric algorithms (Arute et al., 2019). Subsequently, all shared secret keys and private symmetric keys that are protected by asymmetric algorithms can be exposed. This may result in the leakage of all recorded sensitive communications. The availability of Shor's quantum algorithm requires that the stored secret keys and sensitive data will either be re-encrypted with quantum-resistant cryptographic algorithms or physical destruction of the backups of stored secret keys as well as sensitive data. The confidentiality and integrity of sensitive information will become unreliable unless they are encapsulated or processed with procedures that are not vulnerable to quantum-based attacks.

Many researchers have started contributing to algorithms development, which is not vulnerable to Shor's quantum-computing algorithm or other well-known quantum-computing algorithms which are referred to as post-quantum algorithms. The key establishment mechanism (i.e., secure key generation, and distribution) is the most important function of asymmetric algorithms. The replacement of quantum vulnerable algorithms (e.g. Diffie-Hellman (Diffie et al., 1976), RSA (Rivest et al., 1978)) is a vital need of time. There are several candidates for post-quantum algorithms but each candidate algorithm has certain advantages as well as disadvantages. For example, some post-quantum candidate algorithms have a large signature size that requires extensive processing time, some have very large public and private key sizes which require extensive computation powers at the sender and receiver end. The implementation of secure cryptographic algorithms requires addressing several issues such as asymmetric algorithm validation, re-usage of public keys, and implementation error which results in even incorrect input of parameters, the integration of auxiliary function (such as hash function in digital signature). The performance factors and scalability issues require a lot of modification in the existing protocol and communication infrastructure.

National Institute of Standards and Technology (NIST) is working on the standardization of post-quantum algorithms and the selection criteria of post-quantum algorithms will be completed within the next two to three years (Chen et al., 2016). However, finance organizations require significant implementation planning for the replacement of vulnerable asymmetric systems. The replacement of algorithms used in vulnerable asymmetric systems requires modifications in cryptographic libraries, hardware implementations, application source codes, communication device protocols, and user administration procedures. The main requirement of migration from the currently used asymmetric algorithms to the post-quantum algorithm is to identify the purpose of asymmetric cryptography usage in financial services such as e-commerce, mobile banking, Internet information exchange, and digital currencies. The examples of asymmetric cryptography usage in financial services include the following:

- Digital signatures can be used to provide non-repudiation of sender messages along with source authentication and integrity verification.
- Identity authentication for the establishment of a secure communication channel.
- Transport mechanism of symmetric keys.
- Authorization process of privileged entities.

Many information technology organizations and financial services providers are using asymmetric cryptography but still, a large number of small and medium-sized organizations have no information about cryptography usage. This makes the situation difficult the replacement of current asymmetric algorithms with post-quantum algorithms mainly due to lack of knowledge as well as the huge cost of replacement. There is a dire need for tools that can facilitate the discovery of asymmetric cryptography usage in currently available technology infrastructure. The cybersecurity standards and operational procedures are required for the migration from asymmetric cryptography to post-quantum cryptography. Once an organization has discovered the asymmetric cryptography usage then it can determine the use characteristics of asymmetric cryptographic algorithms which includes

- The key sizes of asymmetric algorithms.
- Throughput and latency threshold.
- Handshake protocol for key establishment schemes.
- Hardware and software limitations for key sizes.
- Supplier contractual and legal requirements
- Information sensitivity requirement.

Finance institutions should analyze future risks from a quantum computer. They need to prepare a list of their cryptographic algorithms (especially public keys) to make a transition to quantum secure algorithms and build cryptographic agility to improve their overall cybersecurity resilience.

2. BACKGROUND

Cryptography is used to keep information secret from unauthorized access which ensures information confidentially and integrity. Suppose Alice and Bob want to exchange messages over an insecure communication channel such that their messages are secured from eavesdropping. The communication channel is insecure, an eavesdropper Eve may capture the messages from this channel. Figure 1 illustrates this basic communication scenario. A mutually agreed secret key k is communicated via a secure method before the start of communication. Alice and Bob can use any cryptosystem for the secrecy of their information over insecure communication channel.

A cryptosystem is composed of two algorithms: encryption and decryption. An encryption algorithm transforms the plaintext message into an unintelligible message with the help of a secret key such that restoration of the actual plaintext message is very difficult or nearly impossible without the secret key. The unintelligible message is called ciphertext. Bob who has the secret key can easily transform Alice's ciphertext into her original plaintext message using the decryption algorithm.

Figure 1. Communication between Alice and Bob

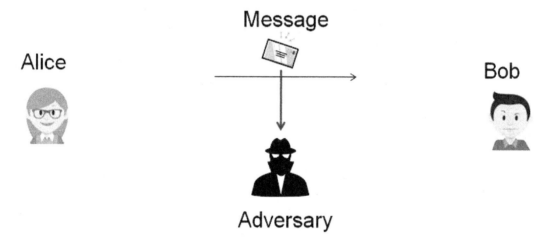

Cryptography can be classified into two types: Classical cryptography and modern cryptography.

2.1. Classical Cryptography

Classical cryptography is used for thousands of years to communicate messages securely. Around 400 years ago, Egyptians uses hieroglyphs to communicate secret messages. The coded message was the secret known only to the transcribers who used to transmit messages on behalf of the kings. Later, the cryptographers use simple mono-alphabetic substitution ciphers between 500 to 600 BC. In mono-alphabetic substitution, the secret rule is used to replace the alphabets of the message with other alphabets. The secret rule became a key to retrieving the message back from the unintelligible message. The Caesar Cipher is the earliest known cryptosystem used by Julius Caesar. The other well-known classical cryptosystems are given in (Stalling W., 2013).

Another example of a classical cryptosystem is the Vernam cryptosystem, see figure 2. It was introduced by Gilbert Vernam in 1918. Vernam cryptosystem works on binary data (bits) rather than alphabets.

Figure 2. Vernam cryptosystem

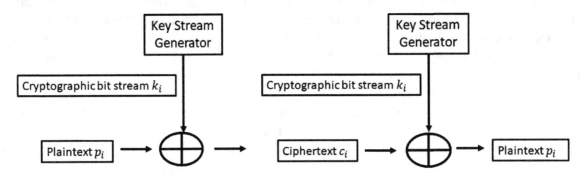

The security of the Vernam cryptosystem is based on the randomness of the secret key. Vernam proposed a running loop of tape which eventually repeated the key, so Vernam cryptosystem has a repeated but very long working key. Joseph Mauborgne proposed an improvement to the Vernam cryptosystem that provides ultimate security. Mauborgne proposed the use non repeated random key that is as long as the message. The key is only used for encryption and decryption of a single message. After it uses, it is discarded. Each new message needs a new key of the same length. This scheme is known as a one-time pad which is completely unbreakable. One-time pad security is dependent upon the randomness of a key.

2.2. Modern Cryptography

Modern cryptography is the foundation of computer and communications security. It is based on various mathematical concepts from number theory, algebraic number theory, computational complexity theory, and probability theory. The security of modern cryptosystems depends on the secrecy of the secret key that is used for encryption and decryption processes while the encryption and decryption algorithm is publicly available. All modern cryptosystems are based on the assumption that certain hard mathematical problems cannot be solved efficiently, or in practice, are "computationally infeasible". The modern cryptosystems can be classified into two types, namely symmetric and asymmetric cryptosystems (or public-key cryptosystems).

The Symmetric Cryptosystems use the same secret key for the encryption and decryption process. The most well-known symmetric cryptosystems include Data Encryption Standard (DES) (Menezes A., 1997), Advanced Encryption Standard (AES) (Nechvatal, J. et al., 2001), Blowfish (Schneier B., 1994), and Twofish (Schneier B., et al., 1999). The other well-known symmetric cryptosystems are given in (Menezes A. el al., 1997). Symmetric Cryptosystems have been demonstrated to be fast and efficient cryptosystems and encrypt/decrypt a bulk amount of data. Usually, the symmetric secret-key is exchanged among the communication parties using a public-key cryptosystem.

Asymmetric cryptosystems use different keys for encryption/decryption processes. In these cryptosystems, data is encrypted using a public key while a private key is used for decryption. Rivest-Shamir-Adleman (RSA) (Rivest R. et al., 1978) and ElGamal cryptosystems (ElGamal T., 1985) are the most well-known asymmetric cryptosystems. Asymmetric cryptosystems are used for generating digital signatures and distribution of symmetric keys.

The recent technological advancements suggest that some computationally hard mathematical problems might be feasible, endangering the security of today's digital world. The invention of Shor's Algorithm (Shor P., 1994) provides an efficient method to find the prime factors of an integer in a given polynomial time. The RSA cryptosystem is based on the assumption that it is computationally infeasible to compute the prime factors of very large composite numbers, the Shor's algorithm could be used to theoretically break this cryptosystem. However, the algorithm requires that it should be implemented on an ideal quantum computer.

The discovery of Shor's algorithm realized that most modern cryptosystems can be considered secure for a limited amount of time which arises a need for an efficient and more secure cryptosystem. Over the last few decades, cryptographers have tried to develop cryptosystems that are secure for at least a century. This leads to the discovery of quantum cryptography. Quantum cryptography uses quantum mechanical properties to perform cryptographic computation.

3. MAIN FOCUS OF THE CHAPTER

This chapter is focused on the following aspects of cybersecurity:

- Overview of classical cryptography
- Quantum computing
- Quantum key distribution.
- Quantum computing's impact on financial services
- Post Quantum cryptography
- Finance industry readiness for transition from classical to post-quantum cryptography

4. BASIC CONCEPTS OF QUANTUM COMPUTING

4.1. Heisenberg's Uncertainty Principle

In 1927, German physicist and Nobel laureate Werner Heisenberg discovered the uncertainty principle. This principle states that we cannot accurately measure both the speed and position of a particle (such as a photon or electron). The detailed tracking of a particle's position provides us with less information about its speed. It imposes a limitation on the measurement with some accuracy. In quantum physics, the Heisenberg uncertainty principle is used to study the objects having wave-like properties and quantum objects show wave-like properties due to quantum theory. Uncertainty is an integral aspect of any object having wave-like behavior.

4.2. Bits vs. Qubits

In the field of computer science, the information unit is usually represented by a bit. A bit has two possible states, "0" or "1". The states of bit can be represented in several possible ways, such as capacitor: it holds the 0 if not charged and it holds 1 if charged.

In quantum computing, a quantum bit or qubit is the analog of the bit. A qubit can take any of its two states, like the north and south pole of the sphere represented by $|0$ and $|1$ or a superposition of both, represented by $\alpha|0+\beta|1$, where α,β are complex numbers and $|\alpha|2$ and $|\beta|2$ are the probabilities that the qubit exists in the state $|0$ and $|1$. The superposition uses to represent any point on a sphere which is called the Bloch sphere, see figure 3. It is quite obvious that $|\alpha|2+|\beta|2=1$, where $|.|$ denotes the absolute value. Mathematically, the qubit state is completely described by a point on the Bloch sphere. This is the simplest example of a quantum state.

Figure 3. Bloch Sphere

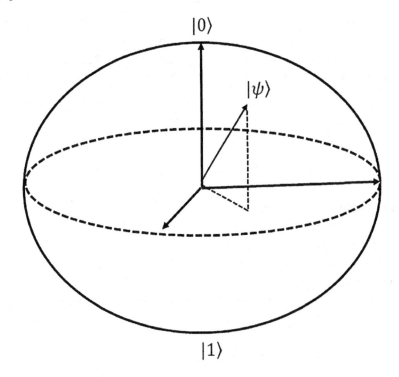

4.3. No Cloning Theorem

No Cloning Theorem was proposed by W. K. Wootters and W. H. Zurek in 1982. This theorem states that a perfect copy of the quantum state of a particle is not possible. In contrast, for a classical bit sequence, such as 10110101, it is quite easy to replicate it. This is in contrast to quantum states even in the simplest case of qubits states. It follows from the principles of quantum mechanics that there is no quantum mechanical operation that can create an independent identical copy of any given quantum state. This is known as the no-cloning theorem of quantum mechanics (Wootters et al., 1982). If an exact copy of arbitrary quantum states is not possible then an approximate copy of arbitrary quantum states can be created up to a certain degree. Moreover, in many contexts, it is sufficient to copy only selected quantum states as accurately as possible. There are numerous results on the conditions under which a certain quality of copied quantum states can be achieved. An overview of the results can be found in (Scarani et al., 2005).

4.4. Quantum Entanglement

Quantum entanglement refers to composite quantum physical systems. Two (or more) qubits are said to be entangled if the information stored in each qubit cannot be described solely by the individual information. For example, two qubits may be entangled such that a measurement of the first qubit assumes the state I0 and I1 with a probability of 50% in each case, and the second qubit is guaranteed to have assumed the same state as the first after this measurement. This means the first qubit measurement changes the state of the second qubit, even if the two entangled qubits are spatially far apart - a phenomenon Albert Einstein called "spooky action at a distance". In quantum computers, entanglement plays a central role. Quantum algorithms exploit quantum entanglement property to produce entangled states and thus encode information as densely as possible. The quantum entanglement principle is fundamental for quantum error correction and fault-tolerant mechanism with quantum computers.

4.5. Error Correction

In a classical computing system, a classical bit is either in state 0 or 1. The only unintended change that can occur in a single bit is the bit flip. This changes the bit 0 to bit 1 or bit 1 to bit 0. Classical error-correcting codes add redundancy to correct for individual bit flips. The state of a qubit is described by a point on the Bloch sphere. Thus, in contrast to the classical bit, a qubit can assume an infinite number of different states, which initially results in an infinite number of possible error cases, i.e. unintended changes of the original state. These errors are caused, for example, by decoherence of a quantum mechanical state, i.e. the interaction with the environment, or by imperfections in the technical realization of quantum gates operating on qubits. The error rate in classical systems is measured using the bit error rate, while in quantum systems, it is measured using the Quantum Bit Error Rate (QBER). The correction of arbitrary errors on a qubit can be reduced to the correction of only bit and phase flips (Knill et al., 1997).

4.6. Privacy Amplification

In quantum cryptographic protocols, privacy amplification is used to minimize the information exposure to a passive eavesdropper. Shannon's theorem (Shannon C.E., 1948) states Bob must have more information on Alice's bits to secure the communication between Alice and Bob. The information exposure can be further reduced to zero by incorporating privacy amplification techniques.

5. QUANTUM ALGORITHMS

The working mechanism of classical and quantum algorithms differs significantly. Classical algorithms perform computation on discrete bits on our modern computers. Quantum algorithms operate on qubits using quantum mechanical effects of entanglement and superposition. The main advantage of quantum algorithms is that they can solve some complex mathematical problems faster than classical algorithms. Some results suggest that quantum algorithms are not able to solve some complex mathematical problems faster than classical algorithms (see, for example, (Shor P., 1994), (Bennett et. al., 1997))

5.1. Shor's Algorithm

The security of public-key cryptography is based on the computational complexity of specific hard mathematical problems. For example, an algorithm that efficiently factors large natural numbers into their prime factors would break the widely used RSA scheme. In 1994, Shor published an efficient quantum algorithm for the large integer factorization problem (Shor P., 1994). Shor's factorization algorithm does not directly solve the integer factorization problem. Rather, it can first be reduced in a classical way to the problem of determining the period of a certain periodic function. Shor's factorization algorithm starts there and determines this period in polynomial runtime. In doing so, the superposition property of quantum states is used in a very clever way. Shor's factorization algorithm is probabilistic and gives the correct result with high probability. In practice, the correct integer factorization is obtained with few repetitions. In addition to the integer factorization problem, a large part of the modern public-key schemes is based on the discrete logarithm problem. There is no efficient polynomial-time classical algorithm to solve discrete logarithm problems in polynomial time. Shor also presents a quantum algorithm that computes discrete logarithms in polynomial runtime in the same publication. His two algorithms use similar techniques and are known as Shor's algorithms.

5.2. Grover's Algorithm

In 1996, L. Grover (Grover L., 1996) published a probabilistic search algorithm for quantum computers that finds an element in an unsorted list of N elements with a high probability in $\sqrt{N}$ steps. With classical algorithms, finding an element in an unsorted list can only be guaranteed after N steps. Grover's algorithm uses a superposition of quantum states in which each element in the list is contained with equal probability. The Grover transformation gradually increased the probability amplitude for the searched elements. An entry with the required property can be determined after only about $\sqrt{N}$ steps with high probability. Thus, Grover's algorithm does not provide an exponential speedup, but at least a quadratic one, which can make a significant difference for very large N. Grover's algorithm is relevant in many contexts where problems can be formulated as search problems. In symmetric-key cryptography, for keys of 128 bits in length, the keyspace can theoretically be searched in about 2^{64} quantum operations using Grover's algorithm. However, for a key length of 256 bits, an order of magnitude of 2^{128} quantum operations are required, which is not considered feasible with today's computational powers.

5.3. The HHL Algorithm

The Hassidim, Harrow, and Lloyd (HHL) algorithm (Harrow et al., 2008) is a quantum algorithm for solving systems of linear equations. The HHL algorithm provides an exponential speedup over the known classical algorithms for finding the solution of a system of linear equations under some conditions. In cryptographic applications, HHL may be used in the decryption of symmetric encryption algorithms such as AES. The practical implementation of HHL for cryptanalysis is very complex and these ideas are currently only theoretically relevant, see for example (Scherer et al., 2017)

5.4. Quantum and Classical Algorithms

Quantum algorithms can also be combined with classical algorithms to find the solution to certain complex problems. For example, the number field sieve is the fastest known classical factorization algorithm for large numbers, such as RSA numbers. Bernstein, Biasse, and Mosca (Bernstein et al., 2017) use the Grover algorithm to speed up an important step of the number field sieve. They do not achieve polynomial runtime like Shor's factorization algorithm but at least a speedup over the number field sieve. Moreover, this algorithm requires asymptotically fewer logical qubits than Shor's factorization algorithm. In (Martin D., 2018), it is shown that side-channel information about the keyspace can be included in the search for the key. The result of a side-channel analysis is usually a quantitative statement about the distribution of individual parts of the secret key.

6. QUANTUM KEY DISTRIBUTION

Quantum Key Distribution (QKD) is the communication method used to exchange cryptographic keys between Alice and Bob using quantum physical principles. The security of QKD protocols is based on quantum mechanical principles. Popular QKD protocols will now be discussed.

6.1. BB84 Protocol

Charles H. Bennett and Gilles Brassard (Bennett et al., 1984) proposed the first QKD protocol in 1984, commonly referred to as the BB84 protocol. This protocol is called prepare and measure protocol, see figure 4.

Figure 4. Systematic representation of prepare and measure QKD

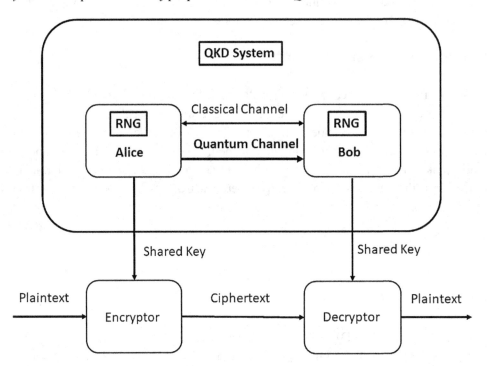

This protocol uses two channels of communication between Alice and Bob, an authenticated classical channel and a quantum channel. The classical channel communication does not have to be confidential, but Eve must not modify the communications. The protocol uses four quantum states with two different bases named the Rectilinear (R) and Diagonal (D) bases. By convention, the states $\mapsto$ and $\nearrow$ are used to represent '0' and the states $\uparrow$ and $\nwarrow$ are used to represent '1'. An example of the BB84 protocol can be found in (Kumar A. et al., 2021)

6.2. B92 Protocol

The B92 protocol was proposed by Charles H. Bennett in 1992 which is a revised version of the BB84 protocol (Bennett C.H., 1992.). Bennett found that four quantum states were unnecessary and two quantum states were sufficient. The B92 protocol uses two non-orthogonal states for each basis. The states $\mapsto$ and $\nearrow$ represent the bits '0' and '1' respectively. An example of the BB92 protocol can be found in (Kumar A. et al., 2021)

6.3. E91 Protocol

In 1992, Artur Ekert discovered the entanglement protocol. This protocol uses an entangled photon source to create pairs of entangled photons. This source could be located near Alice or Bob or it could even be a third party. The entangled pair generated by the source can be represented as

$$| \varnothing = \frac{1}{\sqrt{2}} \left(|\ 01 + |\ 10 \right)$$

The source sends one photon from this pair each to Alice and Bob says $|\ \varnothing_1$ and $|\ \varnothing_2$ respectively. Now, Alice measures the qubit in a direction chosen randomly from $\left\{ 0, \frac{\pi}{8}, \frac{2\pi}{8} \right\}$ and Bob measures the qubit in a direction chosen randomly from $\left\{ \frac{-\pi}{8}, 0, \frac{2\pi}{8} \right\}$. Once, they finished with the measurements, they broadcast the measurement bases they used for each photon. An example of the E91 protocol can be found in (Kumar A. et al., 2021)

6.4. Six State Protocol

In 1999, Six State Protocol (SSP) proposed by Bechmann-Pasquinucci, H. et. al. (Bechmann-Pasquinucci et al., 1999). This protocol uses three bases with a total of six states. The addition of a new basis changes the probability of Eve to uses a wrong basis for the measurement of the qubits from $\frac{1}{2}$ to $\frac{2}{3}$. Once all the qubits have been transmitted, Alice announces the bases she used to encode each qubit publicly to Bob. Bob then uses the respective bases to measure the qubits. If Eve was eavesdropping, she would have to send a qubit to Bob as a replacement after measuring the one from Alice. Since Eve only has a 33% chance of measuring each qubit correctly, her presence can easily be detected. However, since Bob is making measurements after the corresponding bases have been revealed by Alice, he needs access to quantum memory.

6.5. Other Protocols

There are several variations of the BB84 protocol. The most promising variation is the one proposed by H.K. Lo (Lo et al. (2005). In this variation, Alice or Bob do not have an equal probability of choosing the bases. This doubles the efficiency of the key distribution process. Now, Eve has a higher probability to gain more information along with the basis. However, a refined error analysis method was presented to detect Eve's presence. Another variation is BBM92 which was proposed by Bennett, C.H. et. al. (Bennett et al., 1992), an entanglement-based variation of BB84. It is similar to the E91 protocol such that there is a central entangled photon source. However, measurement by Alice and Bob is done on the regular rectilinear and diagonal bases. The process of comparing the bases, error detection, and correction remains the same as the B84 protocol.

SARG04 (Scarani et al., 2004) is a protocol that uses two non-orthogonal quantum states, much like B92. However, unlike B92, the bases used for measurement are not revealed. Using encoding the bases used in additional qubits and transmitting them, Alice and Bob can finalize a key, and also determine if there was an eavesdropper on the network. Coherent One-Way (COW) (Stucki et al., 2007) protocol can be used when high bit rates are needed. This protocol encodes information in time, using a combination of pulses of light in precise time slots. Moreover, it makes use of decoy states to offer additional security.

7. SECURITY OF QKD PROTOCOLS

There are several ways to attack a QKD protocol, which include side-channel attacks, authentication of QKD systems, and quantum random number generators.

7.1. Side-channel Attacks

Secure practical implementation of QKD must be ensured even if QKD is theoretically secure. Side-channel attacks exploit the weaknesses in the implementation of the cryptographic system. Over the past few years, numerous side-channel attacks have been demonstrated in practical QKD systems and intensive research is still being conducted in this area (Sajeed et al., 2017). Due to the high technical complexity of QKD devices, it is important to prevent all known side-channel attacks, advance research on yet unknown side channels, and thoroughly investigate the devices for their resistance to known side channels.

7.2. Authentication of QKD Systems

The authentication of the classic channel of the QKD system prevents a simple man-in-the-middle attack. One possible option for authentication is the use of Wegman-Carter authentication (Wegman et al., 1981), which provides information-theoretic security. For adequate security of authentication of QKD, Wegman-Carter authentication can be used together with post-quantum signature schemes. The security of the overall system against man-in-the-middle attacks is thus ultimately based on the security of post-quantum algorithms.

7.3. Quantum Random Number Generators

High-quality random numbers are an essential part of QKD protocols. Quantum random number generators (QRNGs) are a special type of physical random number generators. QRNGs provide random numbers based on natural laws and are therefore automatically secure. To date, there is no certified QRNG, the use of hybrid random number generators with cryptographic post-processing which, in addition to the information-theoretic security of the physical entropy source, also provide complexity-theoretic security (computational security).

8. LIMITATIONS OF QUANTUM CRYPTOGRAPHY

There are practical limitations of quantum cryptography that make this technology difficult to use. Some of these limitations are presented in this section.

8.1. Pre-distributed Keys

For the authentication of the classical channel, a secret shared key for communication must be shared at both ends before the start of the QKD protocol. It means the secret keys must be distributed between all pairs of QKD devices that wish to communicate with each other before use. This significantly limits the scalability of QKD networks or makes them costlier.

8.2. Limited Range

Loss in signals of optical fibers grows exponentially as the communication distance increases. It is currently not possible to transmit a key over a distance much larger than about 100km using fiber-based QKD. The no-cloning theorem of quantum mechanics states that there can be no signal amplifiers in the conventional sense where quantum states are copied and retransmitted. Thus, over long distances, "trusted nodes" must be introduced so that a key is agreed between neighboring nodes at the same time. Presently, end-to-end security cannot be achieved over fiber-based QKD and long distances. One possible solution is quantum repeaters based on quantum entanglement, which are currently the subject of intensive research. Another approach to guarantee end-to-end security over longer distances is satellite-based QKD, which is, relatively costly and raises questions about its availability.

8.3. QKD Costs and Manufacturer

QKD protocol requires specialized hardware in contrast to classical methods and post-quantum cryptography. Presently, the acquisition of this equipment represents a cost-intensive investment. Furthermore, no QKD manufacturer from the European Union has yet established itself. The digital sovereignty in encryption technologies is a necessary factor. This also applies in particular to quantum.

9. QUANTUM COMPUTING IMPACT ON FINANCIAL SERVICES

Quantum computers have several potential impacts on communication protocols used in financial institutional systems, which includes

- Online/Mobile Banking: An attacker may use a quantum computer to compromise public keys use in standard Internet communication protocols and eavesdrop on any secure communications between financial institutions and users. Moreover, an attacker may compromise the authorization and authentication schemes of a public-key based financial system to produce forged transactions. An attacker may obtain valid wallet keys from publicly available records of blockchain networks and central bank digital currencies (CBDC) to access the appropriate users' credits and tokens.
- Cash Withdrawals and Payment Transactions: Automated Teller Machines (ATMs) are operated in private networks. An attacker can tap into connections depending upon public-key encryption schemes and forge transactions of mobile or online banking.
- Business-to-Business Privacy: Public-key encryption is used in corporate point-to-point networks to build secure communication channels and allow authenticated data exchanges between different businesses. There are several communications and authentication protocols such as SSH, KERBEROS, etc. The attackers can compromise such communication protocols and gain full access to information by impersonating users or servers through *man-in-the-middle* attacks. The attackers would be able to add their resources to cooperate network by forging digital certificates. Another form of attack may be to store encrypted data now and decrypt it later after a quantum computer is available for computation, allowing them to expose current trade secrets in the future.
- VPN Communications: The staff of financial institutions often use VPN connections to work from home and to access organizational sensitive and internal resources. Public-key encryption

schemes are used in such connections to authenticate users and business workstations that would be vulnerable to the same issues as discussed in business-to-business connections.

The popular financial applications that use public-key cryptography are blockchain-based digital assets such as Bitcoin (Nakamoto S., 2009) or Ethereum (Wood G., 2014). and password-protected web applications. The ninety six percent of Internet websites (Google Report, 2020) use the best-known HTTPS protocols. Therefore, quantum computing is a major threat to several business organizations that rely on public-key cryptography for their daily routine operations (ETSI, 2020).

10. POST-QUANTUM CRYPTOGRAPHY

Post-quantum cryptography deals with the development and investigation of asymmetric cryptosystems which cannot be broken even with powerful quantum computers. These methods are based on quantum secure mathematical problems. Various approaches are being followed to recognize post-quantum cryptography. These include, among others:

- Code-based cryptography
- Lattice-based cryptography
- Hash-based cryptography
- Isogeny-based cryptography
- Multivariate cryptography

In the following section, all the classes of post-quantum cryptography will be discussed:

10.1. Code-based Cryptography

Code-based cryptography refers to encryption, key agreement, and signature algorithms whose security is based on a general error decoding problem. Its most prominent scheme is the McEliece cryptosystem, an asymmetric encryption scheme introduced in 1978 by Robert McEliece (McEliece R. J., 1978). Its security is based on two types of assumptions. The first assumption is that the binary goppa codes are indistinguishable from random linear codes. The second assumption is that random linear codes can only be decoded with exponential effort due to the general decoding problem on classical and quantum computers. Apart from an adaptation of the parameters originally proposed by McEliece (these have been attacked in the light of modern computing power in 2008 by Bernstein, Lange, and Peters in about 260 operations (Bernstein et al., 2008), after more than 40 years of research it has not been possible to find a structural weakness in the McEliece cryptosystem, where binary goppa codes are used. Thus, the McEliece cryptosystem can be considered to be one of the oldest unbroken quantum-safe proposals. A major disadvantage is the space requirement of the public key. This can be reduced by a variant of the McEliece cryptosystem described by Harald Niederreiter (Niederreiter H., 1986) in 1986, but remains in the megabyte range for high-security applications. On the other hand, however, the ciphertexts of code-based key agreement schemes are very small (about 200 bytes) and the encryption and decryption are much more efficient than RSA- or EC-based asymmetric encryption schemes. Traditional code-based signature schemes, e.g. (Courtois et al., 2001) have so far exhibited significant efficiency problems and are therefore only of theoretical interest. Alternative approaches for more efficient signature schemes which are based on coding theory are still at a very early stage.

10.2. Lattice-based Cryptography

Many cryptographic schemes' security is based on the hardness of lattice problems. This varies from basic primitives such as encryption, key agreement, and digital signatures, to advance cryptographic schemes such as fully homomorphic encryption. For cryptographic applications, the work of Ajtai (Ajtai M., 2004) is of fundamental theoretical importance, proving "worst to average-case" reductions for a certain type of lattice problem. The first lattice-based scheme is proposed by Ajtai and Dwork (Ajtai et al., 1997) which is relatively inefficient. In search of practical lattice schemes, the NTRU encryption scheme of Pipher, Hoffstein, and Silverman (Hoffstein et al., 1998) and the Ajtai-Dwork inspired cryptosystem of Goldwasser, Goldreich, and Halevi (Goldreich et al., 1997) were introduced. However, the standard version of the NTRU problem is currently not proven to be at least as hard as "worst-case" lattice problems. NTRU-based methods have not been broken to date given a suitable choice of parameters. Another milestone in lattice-based cryptography was the introduction of the so-called "Learning With Errors" (LWE) problem by Regev (Regev O., 2005) 2005. Many of today's lattice-based encryption and key agreement schemes are based on the LWE problem or one of its variants. These variants, such as ring LWE (Lyubashevsky et al., 2010) or module LWE (Brakerski et al., 2012) were introduced to increase efficiency and reduce key sizes. They are based on assumption that lattice problems are hard to solve even in lattices with additional (algebraic) structures. The NTRU cryptosystem mentioned above is also based on lattice problems in structured lattices. However, besides the increased efficiency, the additional structure in such lattice-based cryptosystems also carries the risk of potentially providing further attack vectors. Lattice-based cryptosystems received broader attention when the lattice-based method "New Hope" was experimentally tested in Google's Chrome browser. They have received a lot of attention in cryptographic research and make up a large part of the finalists in the current NIST standardization process

10.3. Hash-based Cryptography

Hash-based cryptography is a generic term for cryptographic constructions based on the security of hash functions. Essentially, the terminology refers to digital signatures that are constructed with the help of hash functions and one-time signature schemes. The construction of hash-based signatures goes back to Ralph Merkle (Merkle R., 1979), which is also referred to as Merkle signatures. The security properties of Merkle signatures are very well understood, and in their current form (LMS (Leighton et al., 1995), XMSS (Buchmann et al., 2011)) they are considered to be mature quantum-safe signature schemes. However, a key drawback is their statefulness, it means the signer must keep exact track of which one-time signature keys have already been used. Any error in this track-keeping procedure results in the loss of security and thus high requirements are imposed on the implementation and usage. In addition, the number of possible signatures is limited. When generating keys, a trade-off must be made between signature size and the number of signatures that can be created. Therefore, Merkle signatures, in addition to symmetric methods, are particularly suitable for future-proof software update concepts, where statefulness can be handled well and the maximum number of required signatures can be estimated. The hash-based signature schemes in the form of LMS are used in Cryptographic Message Syntax (CMS)

(Housley R., 2020) and Concise Binary Object Representation (COSE) (Housley R., 2020, RFC 8778). CMS and COSE are basic data formats that are used, for example, in S/ MIME and IoT, respectively. As a stateless variant of a hash-based signature scheme, SPHINCS (Bernstein et al., 2015) has been developed in recent years. It goes back to a design by Goldreich (Goldreich O., 1986). While it is no longer necessary to keep track of which signature keys have been used, this statelessness entails certain efficiency disadvantages (e.g., signature size) due to its design principles compared to LMS and XMSS. In a concrete application scenario, it must be assessed whether SPHINCS is a suitable solution despite the efficiency disadvantages

10.4. Multivariate Cryptography

Multivariate cryptography security is established upon the hardness of solving multivariate quadratic systems of equations over finite fields: At present, there is no efficient algorithm for finding solutions to random multivariate polynomial systems. The number of variables, the size of the finite field, and the degree of the system determine the hardness of solving a specific system of equations. A large number of equations and variables make an even system of quadratic equations defined over F_2 are hard to solve. Different algorithms are used to solve the multivariate polynomial system. In a brute force attack, the attacker tried all possible values until a correct solution is found. The computational complexity of a brute force attack requires exponential time depending upon the number of variables (Bouillaguet et al., 2013).

There are several algorithms to solve the system of equations numerically e.g. the extended linearization algorithm (XL) (Cheng et al., 2012) and F_4/F_5 family (Faugère J. C., 1999). Grover's algorithm gives square root speed up on exhaustive search (Schwabe et al., 2016) using quantum computers.

In the construction of the asymmetric public-key system, a set of multivariate quadratic polynomials is the public key, and trapdoor knowledge to compute the solution of the multivariate system is the private key. The signature scheme can be constructed with a multivariate system of equations with more variables than an equation. The solution of these multivariate systems of equations is a valid signature. The trust in signature schemes based on a multivariate system of equations is quite high. For instance, there is an agreement that the HFEv- signature scheme (Patarin J., 1996) can be considered secure. The primary drawback of HFEv- is its large public key. Research on secure parameters of post-quantum computing is still ongoing. It is assumed that systems of 200-256 variables over F_2 are the minimum number of variables to resist attacks by quantum computers and the public key size range between 500kB-1MB. The other important multivariate signature schemes are Rainbow (Ding et al., 2005) and MQDSS (Hülsing A., 2016). The construction of an efficient and secure multivariate encryption scheme is still an open challenge.

10.5. Super-Singular Elliptic-Curve Isogeny Cryptography

In Elliptic-Curve Cryptography (ECC), addition and scalar multiplication work on points of specific elliptic curves, and also coordinates of points are used to exchange data structures in cryptographic protocols. However, one can define operations among different elliptic curves instead of point computation on an elliptic curve. Operations that map one elliptic curve onto another elliptic curve have different kinds of properties. Mapping that satisfies a certain type of properties is called isogenies.

The construction of cryptographic schemes using isogenies between different elliptic curves is a relatively new approach. Isogenies-based Public-key cryptosystems were introduced by Stolbunov (Stolbunov

A., 2010). The long computation time for encryption and decryption is a major drawback of this kind of scheme. Jao and Soukharev (Childs et al., 2010) found a subexponential quantum computer attack on this scheme in 2010. In 2011 Jao and De Feo used the idea of isogenies on supersingular elliptic curves (Jao D., 2011) The Childs/Jao/Soukharev attack does not work on Child's scheme due to the special structure of supersingular elliptic curves. Furthermore, encryption/decryption efficiency is enhanced. Supersingular-based Isogenies cryptographic schemes are not yet matured enough. Therefore, they are not considered potential candidates for post-quantum public-key encryption.

11. FINANCE INDUSTRY READINESS

Quantum computers exist today but they require great technological evolution to deploy in a wide range of applications. Quantum computing relies on highly accurate hardware. The qubits can run basic operations with a 0.1% error rate but these errors propagate along with exponential growth over an entire system, which limits the size of a quantum computer. There is a need for around 20 million qubits to break the RSA-2048 cryptosystem, where 2048 is the most commonly used parameter size. We will discuss why we need to deploy post-quantum cryptography despite the engineering challenges. The new cryptographic primitives will maintain the security of information storage and communication in the aspect of quantum threats. Although quantum-based cryptographic techniques are also available that are secure against quantum computers, a major advantage of PQC is that they can be easily used in any modern devices and communication infrastructure.

12. TIMELINE FOR FINANCE INDUSTRY TRANSITION TO PQC

The timeline for the finance industry's transition to PQC consists of three parallel sequences of events. The first two sequences of events consist of the two most critical quantum threats. The first one is an active quantum threat known as a store now decrypt later (SNDL) attack. In this attack, the adversary stores the valuable encrypted information and decrypts it upon the availability of quantum computers. This attack assumes that encrypted information is still important in the future. To avoid this type of attack, finance organizations require clever strategic planning and technological experimentation. The second quantum attack discusses the breaking of two public key algorithms, RSA and ECC, with the help of Shor's algorithm. The vulnerable system includes zero trust architectures, secure web browsing, and cryptocurrency technologies. To avoid this type of attack, finance organizations require the effective implementation of PQC in production systems. The third sequence of events is the relevant government and finance industry bodies' standardization process. Finance organizations should implement PQC over quantum cryptography as their key quantum defense strategy.

13. GENERAL RECOMMENDATIONS TO FINANCE ORGANIZATIONS

The transition from quantum vulnerable algorithms to quantum resistance algorithms is not an easy task. The adversaries can exploit any unsecured system at any given time to start a devastating attack. We will discuss the general recommendation that helps the finance organization to make PQC transition easy to ensure a shorter transition time, optimizes costs, and minimizes security risks. The general recommendations include cryptographic agility, prioritization, and hybrid algorithms.

13.1. Cryptographic Agility

Finance organizations must adopt cryptographic agility to provide infrastructure security in the wake of migration to post-quantum algorithms. The changing of cryptographic algorithms needs a lot more work. There are differences in key sizes, encrypted file sizes, and signature lengths. The adoption of cryptographic agility at abstraction layers in particular important toolkits and services minimizes the effort on any successive changes. The finance organizations should implement centrally managed cryptographic services and libraries that hide in-use algorithms from infrastructure and application teams, identify size dependencies, and data fields and adjust data stores, databases, communication protocols, and other organization software that uses the latest fixed field sizes. The cryptographic agility should be incorporated in any financial standards, which are currently being under development. (ETSI, 2020) has outlined a framework of actions that finance organizations should take to enable migration to a quantum-safe cryptographic state. The critical financial system's regulators may start planning for cryptographic agility to reduce systemic risk.

13.2. Prioritization Strategy

The successful transition from classical to PQC requires prioritization. It means the identification of a task where the PQC transition is required in the first place. Firstly, we need to identify the high-risk cryptographic schemes. There is an urgent need for the up-gradation of confidentiality-based applications and key exchange algorithms. The output of key exchanged algorithms can be stored to be decrypted later i.e. SNDL attack. The digital signature requires an online attacker that forge the signatures at signing time. Certain other systems are difficult to upgrade but do not require the instant quantum-resistant confidentiality property such as autonomous vehicular communications.

13.3. Hybrid Algorithms

The post-quantum alternatives of existing classical cryptographic algorithms are comparatively less-studied. There is an approach that can combine traditional and post-quantum cryptographic algorithms into one application. This results in stronger security of the two cryptosystems. If any of the PQC algorithms are identified as flawed, then the security of the classical cryptographic scheme is still intact. In this technique, we can increase the security of the cryptographic system. In key exchange algorithms, we can use one classical and PQC algorithm to generate a shared single key. In this way, the adversary needs to break the classical as well as PQC schemes. The shared secrets can be combined by using the key derivation function (KDF) or bitwise XOR the values of the shared secrets. The KDF option provides minimal cost but maximum security. Moreover, several proposals can combine digital signature schemes in a hybrid manner approach.

The rapid pace of innovation in quantum computing and uncertainty in the availability of quantum-safe cryptographic standards leads finance institutions to build their cryptographic agility. This property allows smooth up-gradation of cryptographic algorithms to improve the overall cybersecurity poster of finance organizations in the future. In the longer term, there is a need to implement post-quantum cryptographic algorithms to reduce overall cybersecurity risks.

CONCLUSION

Classical cryptographic algorithms are used to provide confidentiality, integrity, and availability. Quantum cryptography is an emerging technology that uses quantum mechanical principles for performing cryptographic operations. The development of quantum cryptography has threatened the security of classical cryptographic algorithms in particular public-key cryptographic algorithms. Several quantum key distribution protocols have been proposed for the secure distribution of the shared secret key. Cryptographic researchers have thoroughly analyzed these protocols and proven them as secure algorithms. The invention of quantum algorithms that will break classical cryptographic algorithms leads to the development of quantum-resistant algorithms which are called post-quantum algorithms. Post-quantum algorithms are assumed to be unbreakable even in the presence of quantum computers. The probability of quantum computers breaking public-key cryptographic algorithms was more than 50% within the next 15 years so there is little transition time to the PQC. Hybrid cryptography without compromising security allows developers to securely deploy quantum-resistant schemes. The finance organizations can take the following steps to prevent quantum threat which includes building a public key cryptographic algorithms inventory that exists within the finance organization infrastructure, creating a PQC transition plan once PQC standards have been available, and performance measures for different PQC algorithms, such that transition to PQC takes minimum time and cost.

REFERENCES

Arute, F., Arya, K., Babbush, R., Bacon, D., Bardin, J. C., Barends, R., Biswas, R., Boixo, S., Brandao, F. G. S. L., Buell, D. A., Burkett, B., Chen, Y., Chen, Z., Chiaro, B., Collins, R., Courtney, W., Dunsworth, A., Farhi, E., Foxen, B., ... Martinis, J. M. (2019). Quantum supremacy using a programmable superconducting processor. *Nature*, *574*(7779), 505–510. doi:10.103841586-019-1666-5 PMID:31645734

Bechmann-Pasquinucci, H., & Gisin, N. (1999). Incoherent and coherent eavesdropping in the six-state protocol of quantum cryptography. *Physical Review A.*, *59*, 4238–4248.

Bennett, C. H. (1992). Quantum cryptography using any two non-orthogonal states. *Physical Review Letters*, *68*, 3121–3124.

Bennett, C. H., Bernstein, E., Brassard, G., & Vazirani, U. (1997). Strengths and Weaknesses of Quantum Computing. *SIAM Journal on Computing*, *26*(5), 1510–1523.

Bennett, C. H., & Brassard, G. (1984). Quantum cryptography: Public key distribution and coin tossing, *Proceedings of IEEE International Conference on Computers, Systems and Signal Processing*, 175, 8.

Bennett, C. H., Brassard, G., & Mermin, N. D. (1992). Quantum cryptography without Bell's theorem. *Physical Review Letters*, *68*, 557–559.

Bernstein, D., Biasse, J.-F., & Mosca, M. (2017). A low-resource quantum factoring algorithm. In *Post-Quantum Cryptography – 8th International Workshop, PQCrypto 2017, Utrecht, The Netherlands, 26-28. Juni, 2017, Proceedings, Lecture Notes in Computer Science* (vol. 10346, pp. 330-346). Springer.

Bernstein, D., Hopwood, D., Huelsing, A., Lange, T., Niederhagen, R., Papachristodoulou, L., Schneider, M., Schwabe, P., & Wilcox-O'Hearn, Z. (2015). *SPHINCS: Practical Stateless Hash-Based Signatures.* Lecture Notes in Computer Science. Advances in Cryptology -EUROCRYPT.

Bernstein, D., Lange, T., & Peters, C. (2008). Attacking and Defending the McEliece Cryptosystem. *Proceedings of the 2nd International Workshop on Post-Quantum Cryptography*, 31-46.

Bouillaguet, C., Cheng, C.-M., Chou, T., Niederhagen, R., & Yang, B.-Y. (2013). Fast Exhaustive Search for Quadratic Systems in F2 on FPGAs. In Selected Areas in Cryptography-SAC 2013. Springer.

Brakerski, Z., Gentry, C., & Vaikuntanathan, V. (2012). (Leveled) fully homomorphic encryption without bootstrapping. *ITCS, 2012*, 309–325.

Buchmann, J., Dahmen, E., & Huelsing, A. (2011). *XMSS – A Practical Forward Secure Signature Scheme Based on Minimal Security Assumptions.* Lecture Notes in Computer Science. Post-Quantum Cryptography.

Chen, L. (2016). *Report on Post-quantum Cryptography.* https://csrc.nist.gov/publications/detail/nistir/8105/final

Cheng, C.-M., Chou, T., Niederhagen, R., & Yang, B.-Y. (2012). Solving Quadratic Equations with XL on Parallel Architectures. In Cryptographic Hardware and Embedded Systems -CHES 2012. Springer.

Childs, A., Jao, D., & Soukharev, V. (2014). Constructing elliptic curve isogenies in quantum subexponential time. *Journal of Mathematical Cryptology, 8*(1). arXiv:1012.4019

Costello, C., Longa, P., & Naehrig, M. (2016). Efficient Algorithms for Supersingular Isogeny Diffie-Hellman. In Advances in Cryptology- CRYPTO 2016. Springer.

Courtois, N., Finiasz, M., & Sendrier, N. (2001). How to Achieve a McEliece-Based Digital Signature Scheme. *Advances in Cryptology - ASIACRYPT 2001*, 157-174.

Diffie, W., & Hellman, M. (1976). New directions in cryptography, Information Theory. *IEEE Transactions on, 22*(6), 644–654.

Ding, J., & Schmidt, D. (2005). Rainbow, a New Multivariable Polynomial Signature Scheme. In Applied Cryptography and Network Security — ACNS 2005. Springer.

ElGamal, T. (1985). A public key cryptosystem and a signature scheme based on discrete logarithms. *IEEE Transactions on Information Theory, IT-31*, 469–472.

ETSI. (2020). *CYBER; Migration strategies and recommendations to Quantum Safe schemes.* Available at: https://www.etsi.org/deliver/etsi_tr/103600_103699/103619/01.01.01_60/tr_103619v010101 p.pdf

Faugère, J.-C. (1999). A new efficient algorithm for computing Gröbner bases (F4). Journal of Pure and Applied Algebra, 139(1–3), 61–88.

Goldreich, O. (1986). *Two remarks concerning the Goldwasser-Micali-Rivest signature scheme, Advances in Cryptology CRYPTO '86* (Vol. 263). LNCS.

Goldreich, O., Goldwasser, S., & Halevi, S. (1997). Public-key cryptosystems from lattice reduction problems. *CRYPTO, 1997*, 112–131.

Grover, L. (1996). A fast quantum mechanical algorithm for database search. *Proceedings, 28th Annual ACM Symposium on the Theory of Computing*, 212.

Harrow, A., Hassidim, A., & Lloyd, S. (2008). Quantum algorithm for solving linear systems of equations. *Physical Review Letters, 103*(15).

Hoffstein, J., Pipher, J., & Silverman, J. H. (1998). NTRU: A Ring-Based Public Key Cryptosystem. *ANTS, 1998*, 267–288.

Housley, R. (2020a). *Use of the HSS/LMS Hash-Based Signature Algorithm in the Cryptographic Message Syntax (CMS), IETF RFC 8708*. Available at: https://tools.ietf.org/html/rfc8708

Housley, R. (2020b). *Use of the HSS/LMS Hash-Based Signature Algorithm with CBOR Object Signing and Encryption (COSE), IETF RFC 8778*. Available at: https://tools.ietf.org/html/rfc8778

Hülsing, A., Rijneveld, J., Samardjiska, S., & Schwabe, P. (2016). From 5-pass MQ-based identification to MQ-based signatures. In Advances in Cryptology-Asiacrypt 2016. Springer.

Jao, D., & De Feo, L. (2011). Towards Quantum-Resistant Cryptosystems from Supersingular Elliptic Curve Isogenies. In Post-Quantum Cryptography-PQCrypto 2011. Springer.

Knill, E., & Laflamme, R. (1997). Theory of quantum error-correcting codes. *Physical Review A., 55*, 900.

Kumar, A., & Garhwal, S. (2021). State-of-the-Art Survey of Quantum Cryptography. *Archives of Computational Methods in Engineering, 28*.

Leighton, T., & Micali, S. (1995). *Large provably fast and secure digital signature schemes from secure hash functions*. U.S. Patent 5,432,852.

Lo, H. K., Chau, H. F., & Ardehali, M. (2005). Efficient Quantum Key Distribution Scheme and a Proof of Its Unconditional Security. *Journal of Cryptology, 18*, 133–165.

Lyubashevsky, V., Peikert, C., & Regev, O. (2010). On Ideal Lattices and Learning with Errors over Rings. *EUROCRYPT, 2010*, 1–23.

Martin, D., Montanaro, A., Oswald, E., & Shepherd, D. (2018). Quantum Key Search with Side-Channel Advice. In. Lecture Notes in Computer Science: Vol. 10719. *Selected Areas in Cryptography – SAC 2017. SAC 2017*. Springer.

McEliece, R. J. (1978). *A public-key cryptosystem based on algebraic coding theory, Technical report*. NASA.

Menezes, A., Van Oorshot, J., & Vanstone, P. (1997). *Handbook of applied cryptography*. CRC Press.

Merkle, R. (1979). *Secrecy, Authentication, and Public Key Systems*. Stanford University Information Systems Laboratory Technical Report 1979-1.

Nakamoto, S. (2009). *Bitcoin: A Peer-to-Peer Electronic Cash System.* https://metzdowd.com

Nechvatal, J. (2001). Report on the development of the advanced encryption standard (AES). *Journal of Research of the National Institute of Standards and Technology, 106,* 511–577.

Carter. (1981). New Hash Functions and Their Use in Authentication and Set Equality. *Journal of Computer and System Sciences, 22.*

Niederreiter, H. (1986). Knapsack-type cryptosystems and algebraic coding theory. *Problems of Control and Information Theory, 15*(2), 159–166.

Patarin, J. (1996). Hidden Fields Equations (HFE) and Isomorphism's of Polynomials (IP): Two New Families of Asymmetric Algorithms. In Advances in Cryptology - EUROCRYPT '96. Springer.

Regev, O. (2005). On lattices, learning with errors, random linear codes, and cryptography. *STOC, 2005,* 84–93.

Report, G. (2020). *HTTPS encryption on the web.* Google Transparency Report. https://transparencyreport.google.com/https/overview?hl=en

Rivest, R. L., Shamir, A., & Adleman, L. (1978). A method for obtaining digital signatures and public-key cryptosystems. *Communications of the ACM, 21*(2), 120–126. doi:10.1145/359340.359342

Sajeed, S., Minshull, C., Jain, N., & Makarov, V. (2017). Invisible Trojan-horse attack. *Scientific Reports, 7.*

Scarani, V., Ac'ın, A., Ribordy, G., & Gisin, N. (2004). Quantum Cryptography Protocols Robust against Photon Number Splitting Attacks for Weak Laser Pulse Implementations. *Physical Review Letters, 92,* 057901.

Scarani, V., Iblisdir, S., Gisin, N., & Acín, A. (2005). Quantum cloning. *Reviews of Modern Physics, 77,* 1225.

Scherer, A., Valiron, B., Mau, S.-C., & Alexander, S., Berg, E. van den, & Chapuran, T. E. (2017). Concrete resource analysis of the quantum linear system algorithm used to compute the electromagnetic scattering cross-section of a 2D target. *Quantum Information Processing, 16,* 60.

Schneier, B. (1994). Description of a new variable-length key, 64- bit block cipher (Blowfish). In *Fast Software Encryption Second International Workshop, Leuven, Belgium, December 1993, Proceedings.* Springer-Verlag.

Schneier, B., Kelsey, J., Whiting, D., Wagner, D., Hall, C., & Ferguson, N. (1999). *The Twofish encryption algorithm: a 128-bit block cipher.* John Wiley & Sons, Inc.

Schwabe, P., & Westerbaan, B. (2016). Solving Binary MQ with Grover's Algorithm. In Security, Privacy, and Applied Cryptography Engineering —SPACE 2016. Springer.

Shannon, C. E. (1948). A mathematical theory of communication. *The Bell System Technical Journal, 27,* 379–423.

Shor, P. W. (1994): Polynomial-time algorithms for prime factorization and discrete logarithms on a quantum computer. *Proc. 35th Annual Symposium on Foundations of Computer Science, 124*–134. 10.1109/SFCS.1994.365700

Stallings, W. (2013). *Cryptography and Network Security Principles and Practice*. Pearson Education.

Stolbunov, A. (2010). Constructing public-key cryptographic schemes based on class group action on a set of isogenous elliptic curves. *Advances in Mathematics of Communications, 4*(2), 215–235.

Stucki, D., Fasel, S., Gisin, N., Thoma, Y., & Zbinden, H. (2007). Coherent one-way quantum key distribution. In Photon Counting Applications, Quantum Optics, and Quantum Cryptography. International Society for Optics and Photonics.

Wood, G. (2014). *Ethereum: A secure decentralised generalised transaction ledger*. Ethereum project yellow paper, 151, 1-32.

Wootters, W. K., & Zurek, W. H. (1982). A single quantum cannot be cloned. *Nature, 299*(5886), 802–803. doi:10.1038/299802a0

Chapter 17

A Secure Distributed System for the Electronic Voting System Using Blockchain Technology

Rana Muhammad Amir Latif

Department of Computer Science, COMSATS University Islamabad, Sahiwal, Pakistan

Muhammad Usama Riaz

BARANI Institute of Sciences, Pakistan

ABSTRACT

Traditionally, electronic voting has relied on a centralized method of administration. The database and the system are both under the jurisdiction of the system's central administration, which oversees the voting process. As a result, issues like database manipulation and duplicate voting may arise, whether accidentally or purposefully. Permissionless blockchain technology has helped overcome many of these issues; however, since the basic consensus technique of such blockchains demands particular computer resources for each voting operation, they are not ideal for new voting systems. Power consumption, efficiency, and system latency all suffer as a result. These issues may be alleviated in part if electronic voting technologies are used. By using corporate blockchain technology, this research presents an electronic voting system that is very reliable and secures the secret vote. It also discusses some of the frequent security and dependability challenges of electronic voting system solutions, such as a flexible network setup.

1. INTRODUCTION

Security is of the utmost importance in every election since it guarantees that every voter's right is respected. Computer applications may be used to ensure security while also lowering the expense of holding a nationwide poll. Pen and paper have always been the voting method used to choose any candidate (Roh & Lee, 2020). In the modern day, electronic voting machines (EVMs) are used instead of paper ballots, and the voter casts their vote by pushing a button that corresponds to the leader they

DOI: 10.4018/978-1-6684-5284-4.ch017

prefer. After hitting the button, the vote is added to the leader's account (Amir Latif, Hussain, Jhanjhi, Nayyar, & Rizwan, 2020).

The security community has seen electronic voting machines as vulnerable to manipulation because of worries about manual security. Anybody with physical access to the EVM can disrupt it, causing the election results to be impacted. It is where the Blockchain Mechanism enters the picture (Mukherjee, Boshra, Ashraf, & Biswas, 2020). A Blockchain is a public ledger that is distributed, irrefutable, and unchangeable. Decentralized databases, like the Blockchain, may be used to create trestles and distributed systems. There is no such thing as a "central coordinator" in this system. Instead, the data block is stored locally on each block on the Blockchain. Research in medicine, property resale, and carbon dating used this technology originally developed for money transfer applications (Latif et al., 2021).

Ethereum is one of several Blockchains that have been built throughout time. It comes with a Turing-complete programming language, and users on the Ethereum network may use it to construct their functions using smart contracts (Latif et al., 2019). Using a distributed system implies that computing is reliant on the Blockchain. To have a trustless system, all voters must trust each other and not any administration. This protocol establishes the system's accuracy and ensures voters' privacy by encrypting all votes. The final election outcome cannot be tampered with threshold encryption, even if an election administrator is malevolent (Priyadarshini et al., 2022). It is accomplished via the use of an asymmetric cryptographic approach. To ensure the integrity of the voting process, all parties participating in the election are given a public key, and the whole secret key is kept safe until the key reconstruction stage (Sharma et al., 2022). The secret key is reconstituted when n or more parties contribute their secrets.

Smart Contracts run the whole voting process on the Ethereum Blockchain. The outcome of a smart contract on the Blockchain may be relied upon as if it were the result of a trustworthy computer (Kok, Abdullah, & Jhanjhi, 2020). As soon as a Smart contract is performed, all parties are bound by the terms of the agreement. A smart contract written in the Ethereum programming language can implement voting functionality (Al-Madani, Gaikwad, Mahale, & Ahmed, 2020). This feature will require the generation of candidate data and procedures for adding votes to the appropriate candidates, among other things. To confirm the authenticity of the final result, the smart contract code will be run on every node of the Ethereum network. Consequently, the finished product is widely accepted by the public (Indapwar, Chandak, & Jain, 2020).

Voting is a method of selecting one alternative over another based on the voters' preferences; it is used in various contexts, including elections for public office, business meetings, and social gatherings (Negash, 2022). The implementer's requirements and resources will determine the voting system used. Important considerations must be made while choosing a voting method to ensure the integrity of the electoral process (Ali, Iqbal, Hussain, & Younas). Voting untraceability, which ensures that votes cannot be linked to a specific individual, is one such criterion; accuracy, or the ability of a system to count votes properly, is another; and verifiability, or the capacity to verify the results of an election, is yet another inflexibility (Goyal, Ahmed, & Gopalani, 2022), which prevents any side from gaming the system to their advantage; verifiability in order to ensure the legitimacy of the election, the system must be able to verify votes and detect any tampering (Wahab et al., 2022). ballot secrecy, since it is sometimes preferable that voters not be able to provide a paper trail indicating how they voted; dispute-freeness, to ensure that the protocol operates smoothly and that each voter acts following the norms of the protocol (Bonthu, Chakraverty, siva subrahmanya Varma, Ramani, & Karuppiah, 2022); accessibility, to guarantee that voters have easy access to casting their votes; and decentralization, which prevents any one party from manipulating the vote tally to change the result of an election. In elections, when information about voters' identities (Mookherji, Vanga, & Prasath, 2022), such as "who" voted for whom and why, is already available to the public, the voting untraceability characteristic is unnecessary.

When it comes to voting for a political candidate, legislation, or regulation, the security of the voting process is important to any firm, institution, or nation thinking about using it. To what extent, therefore, should we keep trusting centralized voting systems? Reducing the possibility of voter fraud is crucial and making the voting process traceable and verifiable when switching from a traditional system to a new one (Pranitha et al., 2022). What if a blockchain-based program existed that recorded each voter's choice, ensured that duplicate voting was impossible, and ensured that the results could not be tampered with?

As cryptocurrencies like Bitcoin and Ethereum continue to develop in popularity, more and more organizations and individuals are learning about the technology's numerous advantages (Malhotra, Kumar, Kumar, & Yadav, 2022). Benefits include the potential for the creation of decentralized applications that use cryptocurrencies and enable the management of supply networks, financial systems, games, and other businesses and situations. One case where scientists work to enhance integrity, anonymity, and non-repudiation is electronic voting (Majumder & Ray, 2022).

This paper's major contribution is a substitute for trust, transparency, and immutability in participatory management procedures like electronic voting. The article presents the architecture and proof of concept for a system built on Hyperledger Fabric that can be tailored to several voting scenarios and includes a technique to secure cryptographic artifacts against unauthorized access by users and network nodes.

2. LITERATURE REVIEW

Using business Blockchain technology, the method proposed in this research provides great dependability while maintaining the secrecy of the voting process. By eliminating the normal consensus processes used by public Blockchains, Blockchain increases efficiency and lowers system energy usage. To ensure vote results are accurate, smart contracts use a secure method that makes counting public and immune to manipulation (Denis González, Frias Mena, Massó Muñoz, Rojas, & Sosa-Gómez, 2022).

Data innovation, openness, and trust-ability are some of the most exciting aspects of Blockchain technology. Using Blockchain as a testing ground for electronic voting systems is the goal of this research. This study examines distributed ledger technologies' capabilities in political election decision-making by portraying a contextual analysis (Dong, Yu, Alharbi, & Ahmad, 2022).

Today's internet voting solutions offer security risks for public elections, while offline voting is more expensive. As a consequence, a Blockchain-powered electronic voting system is evolving. Because of the dispersed storage of individual voters and aggregate information, the system can provide openness and secrecy (Ahn, 2022).

Since its inception, Blockchain technology has emerged as a vital and widely recognized security countermeasure for online commerce, financial operations, networking systems, and Internet of Things-based smart systems (IoT). The private Blockchain approach offers immutability, prevents the alteration of records, and maintains the integrity and dependability of record transactions. Blockchain and electronic voting systems were tested using the Paillier homomorphic encryption technique with a false acceptance rate (FAR) of 0.2% and a false rejection rate (FRR) of 1% using bi-factors (Iris and Fingerprint) of certification and secrecy (Ajao, Umar, Olajide, & Misra, 2022).

If electronic voting is not adequately protected, it might open the door to electoral fraud. Vote-rigging, voter impersonation, and vote falsification are all addressed in this chapter's e-voting system. Electronic voting is safeguarded by a mix of MFA and Blockchain technologies. MFA prevents the tampering of voters' identities, while Blockchain technology ensures the integrity of the votes is not tampered with (Olaniyi et al., 2022).

By leveraging Blockchain technology, online voting might become more secure, private, and inexpensive. The goal of this research is to analyze the potential applications of Blockchain technology in the development of decentralized electronic voting systems. Some have just existed on paper, while others have been put into practice (Al-Maaitah, Qatawneh, & Quzmar, 2021).

There is a significant deal of promise for online voting to reduce expenses and improve voter participation. It's important to be cautious about internet voting due to the potential dangers. Massive voter fraud may be perpetrated by exploiting a single security flaw. Blockchain technologies may be able to alleviate some of the problems now plaguing voting systems, according to a new study (Jafar, Aziz, & Shukur, 2021).

Election-Block, a voting system featuring a biometric scanner and its Blockchain operating on a controlled network of nodes, is described in detail by the author. This system ensures the security and management of the user's vote while allowing data immutability. The system's capacity to manage a huge number of votes from numerous servers while retaining data integrity, performance, and security has been shown in experiments (Ibrahim, Ravindran, Lee, Farooqui, & Mahmoud, 2021).

Blockchain technology, e-voting may be done at any time and location, minimizing data fraud and providing real-time access to accurate and decentralized vote results. Covid-19 pandemic circumstance SUS trial analysis is used in this study technique. As a result, the SUS Score study demonstrates that the community may accept an E-Voting system that brings good and important benefits like efficiency and effectiveness to the table (Kamil, Bist, Rahardja, Santoso, & Iqbal, 2021).

It is one of the frameworks to reduce abstention and maintain security against manipulation that the e-voting system provides. Aadhar database biometrics and the voter's VID (Virtual ID) are used to cast a vote, and the digital signature is used as the key to encrypt the votes within the block (Roopak & Sumathi, 2020).

Voting is one of the most important governmental activities; thus, e-voting systems must be given greater attention and assurance regarding security and anonymity concerns. For many corporations and non-profit groups, it would be a cost-effective and easy-to-use solution that can be scaled up. A major goal of this study is to determine whether and how Blockchain technology may be used in electronic voting systems (Çabuk, Adiguzel, & Karaarslan, 2020).

Blockchain is a cutting-edge technology that has gained much traction in the cryptocurrency and financial markets. As a result of this research, Blockchain-based technologies, including the electronic voting system, are more accessible than ever before. According to the paper, voter data will be stored in a central database protected by the voter's private key and digital signature (Ahmed, Shamrat, Ali, Mia, & Khatun, 2020).

This research's author looks at several non-cryptocurrency-related uses for Blockchain technology. Verifiable electronic voting and healthcare records management are a few topics we'll discuss. For each, the author first examines the issue, the relevant requirements, and the potential benefits Blockchain technology can provide. "According to this list of relevant solutions, both from academia and industry, they conclude (Maesa & Mori, 2020).

Election voting may still be manipulated; however, research tackles the challenges associated with producing accurate results and authenticating the legitimacy of voting data. The research makes use of decentralized Blockchain technology to validate vote data. On the Blockchain, any server may join and play the same job, forming a peer-to-peer network, which is decentralized. Other servers can more easily execute backups and data tracking, and the troublesome server is temporarily withdrawn from the network to prevent more damage (Febriyanto, Rahayu, Pangaribuan, & Sunarya, 2020).

To effectively administer the constitution, a voting mechanism must be in place. Individual freedom of expression should be guaranteed in the voting process using fairness, independence, and unbiasedness. The author offers an application of Blockchain technology for the electronic voting system. A voting environment requires data integrity, which may be achieved via Blockchain technology (Bosri, Uzzal, Al Omar, Hasan, & Bhuiyan, 2019).

Decentralized and distributed public ledgers on a P2P network are becoming more popular thanks to Blockchain technology. Many interactive online systems may benefit from Blockchain, according to the author. These include supply chain systems, voting systems, and the Internet of Things. On the subject of e-voting and Blockchain security and privacy, this study aims to provide light on some recent developments (Abuidris, Kumar, & Wenyong, 2019).

An attempt is made in this research to conceive a distributed ledger architecture for the storing of election results that can be trusted, transparent, and immutable (DLT). In Ghana and other sub-Saharan African nations, faulty vote counting is a major problem. A cryptographic hash function ensures that the votes saved in the Blockchain cannot be tampered with, making the suggested architecture a viable solution to the problem of vote tampering (Agbesi & Asante, 2019).

EVM (Electronic Voting Machine) hacking, manipulating the election, and seizing polling stations are all big problems in today's voting system. The author of this research examines the flaws with current voting methods and makes a case for using an E-voting model to address them. Also, this research evaluates the use of Blockchain as a service to construct distributed electronic voting systems (Patil, Rathi, & Tribhuwan, 2018).

The author developed a decentralized electronic voting system using Blockchain technology and a complex Proof-Of-Voting consensus method. A major problem of a centralized electronic voting system is that it is less dependable than a distributed system due to the presence of a single point of failure. Legal issues that emerge with conventional methods are analyzed, along with possible solutions, including Blockchain technology (Chaudhari, 2018).

The author proposes a Blockchain-based electronic voting system. Any participant in a Blockchain system may see the whole ledger at any time. The author's Project combines double-envelope encryption with Blockchain technology. The distributed architecture eliminates the need for a central server, increasing reliability (Adiputra, Hjort, & Sato, 2018).

2.1. Summary

There are several limitations present in the existing systems. First, there is no transparency in the traditional voting systems, such as in signing ballot voting systems. The author has no guarantee that our vote is cast or not. Sometimes the author may face privacy issues during voting. Many people don't cast their votes due to their absence from the region of elections.

3. WHAT IS BLOCKCHAIN?

In the broadest sense, business Blockchain technology may be characterized as an information storage system that includes a registry distributed across various members (such as organizations) encrypted and arranged in blocks of related transactions. An irrevocable, unchangeable, and falsification-free decentralized global registry, a Blockchain stores a series of transactions in ordered blocks connected from a systemic perspective. Hashes are digitally signed using public-key cryptography, and each block has a unique block number and an alphanumeric code known as HASH digitally signed using public-key encryption, as shown in Figure 1.

Figure 1. Blocks committed in a ledger

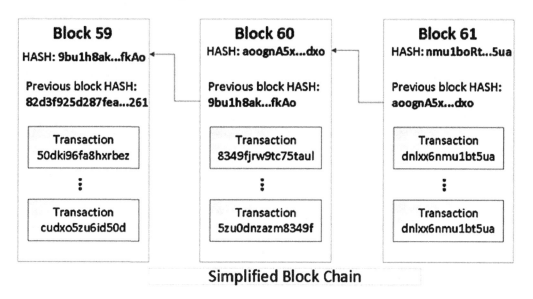

Figure 2 shows how a network of peer nodes communicates with each other and uses consensus procedures to create a decentralized architecture for the Blockchain. Each node holds a duplicate copy of the stored data in a network. Cryptographic methods (most notably hash functions) connect data blocks, making it possible to track every transaction. Blocks of transactions are kept in a consistent state across a time ledger; a database containing the blocks uses strong encryption to protect them. Transactions are added to the ledger in a distributed manner; For a new block to be added to the Blockchain, it must be agreed upon by all nodes (or a subset of nodes as indicated by the protocol in use), as shown in Figure 2.

Figure 2. The distributed network between peers

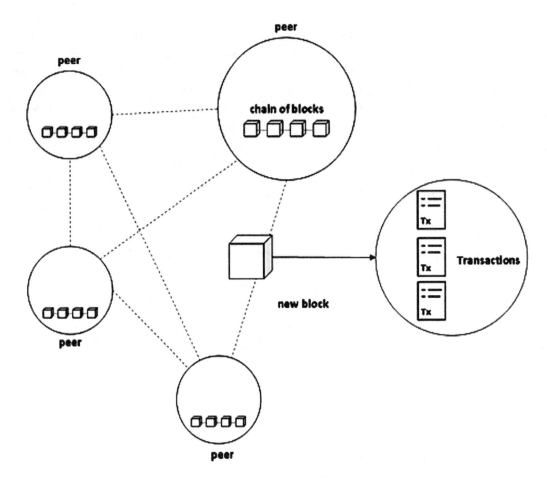

A variety of Blockchains are already available, each having a distinct set of capabilities and features that may be tailored to suit various purposes. Permissioned, permissionless, public, private, and hybrid are the most often used terminology to describe Blockchains in the literature.

3.1. Hyperledger Fabric (HF)

To set up a Hyperledger Fabric network, create channels for data exchange inside the network, and keep those channels up to date over the network's lifespan, this guide will walk you through the considerations businesses must make. Hyperledger Fabric's architecture and components are also discussed in depth.

3.2. Assets

Smart contracts may be used to alter assets on Hyperledger Fabric. Transactions in a ledger record changes in the state of a collection of key-value pairs, which may vary from physical (real estate and hardware) to intangible (intellectual property).

3.3. Chain Code or Smart Contract

Chain code has no natural language ambiguities since it is written in a general-purpose computer language. Verification of agreement compliance is automated by these tools, which are developed in executable code by the network (and because they are part of the network, they are unalterable). The distributed and decentralized Blockchain network contains the code and agreements included within. Trust may be built among members since transactions are both traceable and irrevocable. There are significant time and cost savings due to this and reduced risk. Software that describes an asset or assets, as well as the transaction instructions for updating the assets, is what we're talking about here.

3.4. Identities in Hyperledger Fabric

Participants in the Blockchain network, such as nodes (components) and users, must confirm their identity (authenticate) to function in the Blockchain network. Public Key Infrastructure (PKI) identities may be verified via a chain of trust. There is a CA network component for producing these public and private key pairs in HF.

3.5. Membership Service Provider (MSP)

An authentication method must be in place to ensure that a network participant's private key never leaves their wallet. Once the participant's identification has been validated, this process will have to select what rights they are granted in the system. How an MSP transforms its identity into a role is seen here. A network Blockchain's MSP is responsible for verifying members' identities and determining which individuals have rights.

3.6. Wallet

In a wallet, the voter will find a list of all the people who have access to the wallet. When a user's application joins the Blockchain network, it chooses one of these identities. An MSP and identity are used to decide access permissions to resources, such as the ledger.

4. THE CASE FOR A BLOCKCHAIN FOR VOTING SYSTEM

Voting is an excellent use for a Blockchain. Individual voting data is distributed among hundreds of computers worldwide, making it very difficult to change or remove votes once they have been cast. Protecting citizens' data and privacy is a key component of this strategy. Putting users in charge of their data fosters a sense of security and trust. Rather than waiting in line at voting locations, voters may vote using smartphone applications. There is no need for governments to re-engineer their systems to use a Blockchain; current platforms may be modified to suit. All indications indicate a trend away from conventional centralized polling locations toward decentralized, remote participation.

Blockchain technology directly solves one of the hardest aspects of confidence in elections. Distributing mistrust across a group of mutually suspicious parties means that all of them engage in preserving and administering the cryptographically secure digital trail of an election is possible thanks to Blockchain technology. Blockchains establish a trustless environment by spreading trust, reducing the trust necessary from individuals participating in an election. For most businesses, Blockchain is a non-starter since it can only store short strings of text that just record a balance transfer between two parties on its Blockchain.

In contrast, IPFS is an exciting initiative that might provide much of the infrastructure needed for Blockchain content storage by establishing a decentralized Web in which connections never expire and no one entity claims data ownership. It can store any kind of information and produce a unique hash for any business that uses it. IPFS is a content-addressed system, while the Web relies on IP addresses. In addition to facilitating complex programming interactions, it also empowers users with more control over the distributed ledger storage of their data. It has a lot of potential, but right now, it's only getting started.

- **Public Verifiability**: Voting results may be verified by anybody who participates since the voting process is recorded on a Blockchain and can be seen by everyone.
- **Individual Verifiability:** The final result may be checked by all voters to see whether their vote was counted. The election result must be accepted for the Blockchain to be reliable and consistent.
- **Auditability:** After the election, anybody with internet access or a third party may check the results of the vote on the Blockchain.
- **Anonymity:** No link exists between any ballot and its voter (but each voter can verify their cast vote).
- **Transparency:** The Blockchain's openness ensures that the general public may examine the operation.

5. ALGORITHM FOR ELECTRONIC VOTING SYSTEM

To ensure authentication and non-repudiation, we create a system-based user credential model. The following are the most significant changes, as shown in Figure 3:

- The ballot is marked with the person's signature to ensure that no one else may discover whom a voter is voting for.
- ECDSA signatures verify a vote's legitimacy by signing the vote's hash with the voter's private key.
- The identity element is denoted by O, while the base point of the elliptic curve is denoted by G. The letter n denotes the integer order in $n \times G = O$. It is customary to refer to n's bit length in terms of L_n.
- The creation of secret and public keys is required before a voter may sign their vote. An integer known as indicated by dA is the private key. $QA = dA \times G$, where dA is the elliptic curve point multiplication, is the public key.

Figure 3. User credentials based on

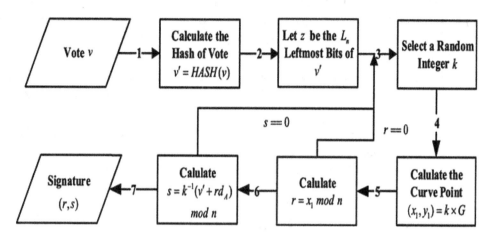

- "Compute v¢=HASH(v)."
- "Suppose that z is the Ln leftmost bit of v¢."
- "Select a random integer k from [1, n−1]."
- "Compute (x1, y1) =k×G"
- "Compute r=x1 mod n. If r==0, return to (3)"
- "Compute s=k−1(v¢+rdA) mod n. If s==0, return to (3)"
- "The signature of the vote is (r,s)."

5.1. Compute the Hash Value Based on SHA-256

Based on SHA-256, we calculate the hash value. When the hash value is compared to a known value, the integrity of the data is confirmed or denied. Hash values are usually computed by using SHA-256, as seen in Fig and explained in the following manner shown in Figure 4:

Figure 4. Computed hash value based on SHA-256

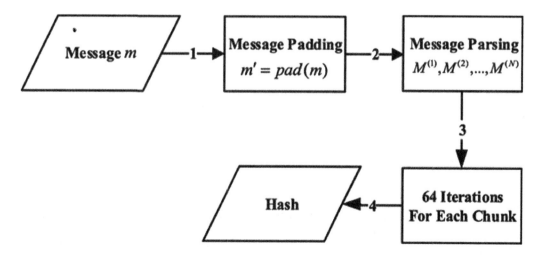

- "The message is denoted by m with the binary expression."
- "Pad m with 100...000 sequence and the length of m with 64-bit expression, i.e., m=pad(m)".
- "m¢ is broken into 512-bit chunks, i.e., M (1), M (2), ..., M(N)".
- "64 constants, denoted by W0, W1, ..., and W63, respectively, are used".
- "Eight working variables labeled A=0x6A09E667, B=0xBB67AE85, C=0x3C6EF372, D=0xA54FF53A, E=0x510E527F, F=0x9B05688C, G=0x1F83D9AB, and H=0x5BE0CD19 are used as the initial hash value".
- "Compute the 64-cycle cryptographic iterative computation for the first chunk, i.e., M(1). Repeat the iterative computation for the next chunk based on the result for the last chunk".
- "The result of the last iterative computation is the hash."

6. SCALABILITY AND PROCESSING OVERHEADS

Some users can profit from the Blockchain, but most people won't see any use in it at all. When utilized for widespread elections, the network experiences a dramatic increase in traffic that increases transaction costs and wait times. Scalability problems become worse as the number of nodes in the Blockchain network grows. In the current electoral climate, the system's scalability is already a major worry. Incorporating electronic voting into the Blockchain-based system would further improve its scalability. There is a comparison of several Blockchain-based systems, including Bitcoin, Ethereum, and Hyperledger Fabric, and an examination of the various measures or attributes common to all Blockchain frameworks. In order to increase the scalability of Blockchains, a kind of parallelization known as sharing is used. In a classic Blockchain network, nodes independently validate all transactions and new blocks. For high levels of parallelism, it is recommended that data be horizontally partitioned into shards.

6.1. User Identity

Pseudonyms are often used on the Blockchain as usernames. It's impossible to be anonymous using this approach. The user's identity may be found by reviewing and analyzing the transactions, which are open to the public. National elections are not well-suited to the operation of the Blockchain.

6.2. Transactional Privacy

Transactional anonymity and privacy are difficult to achieve using Blockchain technology. However, due to the transactions involved, election systems need transactional secrecy and anonymity. An independent third-party authority is essential for this purpose, but it should not be centralized and should serve as a check and balance for privacy-related issues.

6.3. Energy Efficiency

Protocols, consensus, peer-to-peer communication, and asymmetrical encryption are among the energy-intensive activities included in the Blockchain. The use of Blockchain-based electronic voting necessitates energy-efficient con sense mechanisms. Peer-to-peer protocols should be reworked to save energy, according to researchers.

6.4. Immatureness

With the advent of Blockchain, the internet will be completely decentralized. A business strategy, structure, operations, and culture benefit greatly. The present Blockchain implementation has several issues. A lack of public or professional knowledge of the technology makes it hard to predict its future potential. The immaturity of Blockchain technology is to blame for all of the current technical challenges with Blockchain adoption.

6.5. Acceptableness

For electronic voting on the Blockchain to work, people's trust and faith in the system must be high. Many people may be reluctant to embrace electronic voting on the Blockchain because of its complexity, which might substantially impede its widespread adoption. Big marketing campaigns are required to educate the public about the advantages of Blockchain voting systems, making it easier for them to embrace the technology.

6.6. Political Leaders' Resistance

Government organizations and electoral bodies will move away from Blockchain-based electronic voting. Political elites who have profited from the present electoral system are likely to reject Blockchain because it will empower public opposition through the decentralized autonomous organization.

7. RESULTS AND IMPLEMENTATION

In this research, a Blockchain was built on the Ethereum network to facilitate electronic voting. To put this notion to the test, we developed a website in Express.js. By using the Web3.js module in an RPC-based demonstration network, we successfully integrated the front end with the Blockchain system.

Blockchain-based smart contracts' voting system. A smart contract is deployed into the Ethereum Blockchain to begin a vote. Candidates (candidate list) and their respective vote totals are the two main components of a decentralized contract (votes received). When voters cast their ballot online, the smart contract's vote for candidate function is activated. If the voter has previously cast a ballot, the already voted method will return true, and the total number of votes will rise. The total vote is a function called after the votes have been counted.

Using a database, it is possible to ensure confidentiality, according to this study. The voter's member ID and password are used to produce a new account address during the registration process. We encoded the accounts and stored them in a database with the member ID values to protect their privacy. The Crypto-js API's AES encryption was applied for data security and eavesdropping protection. Due to its high level of security and speed, AES is one of the most used encryption methods today. The architecture of this system employs AES encryption to secure Blockchain-based transactions and prevent forgeries. Accessing the encryption key requires the usage of a password. After registering and logging in, voters may cast ballots. Logging in involves getting and decrypting the database value, which is then used to save the user's account address. The departure address of the transaction is set to the session value to vote. After that, a new block containing the smart contract is generated. For the relocation to a new block, a fee is needed, as shown in Figure 5.

Figure 5. The graphical user interface for the electronic voting result

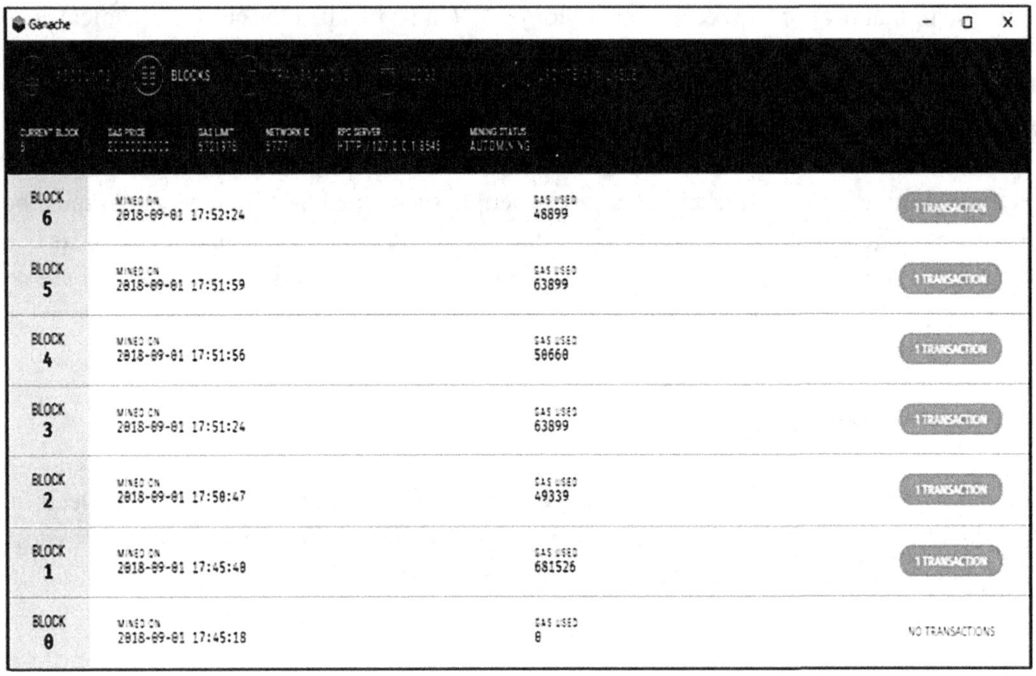

The functionalities of an online voting smart contract include voting (vote) and counting votes (vote-Count()). Voters must enter the candidate's Name into their voter account to record their vCount while casting a ballot. To prevent multiple votes from the same voter, the system marks the account of a voter who has already cast a ballot (msg.sender) as true. It is difficult to vote more than once due to the "true" value recorded in the contract kept by each account if the vote has already been finished (voteClosed()). If the candidate's Name is supplied into the input box, VoteCount() may return the current vote count (vCount). For visibility issues, the study's count status has been kept hidden; nevertheless, the verification may be made public, as shown in Figure 6.

Figure 6. Generated smart contract.

However, there are still concerns that must be solved when using Blockchain technology for electronic voting. This technique is consistent with the concept of universal and equal elections; however, the premise of direct election is flawed. Voters must submit an authentication code to participate in the election using their personal information (e-mail) following the principle of direct election, which mandates that voters cast their ballots without the intervention of a third party. Therefore, it is challenging for the monitoring agency to verify the voters engaged in voting operations at a non-designated site. Because each voter must use their communication device to vote, identity theft and coercion may result in a proxy vote.

7.1. Step by Step Working of Project

Blockchain voting is a decentralized system with no authority over anyone to control and change. But we see it can be used to follow some rules as government can start or end elections and show the result, but it will not change or control the elections. Let's see working how it works.

7.1.1. Starting

Blockchain vote Application has not started as the election has not started. It would only start as the admin or government start the election. As voters see in the diagram, the election has not started, and it would only be started if the admin can allow him to start, as shown in Figure 7.

Figure 7. Starting of the Election

7.1.2. Add Candidates

The government started the election, but before, it would select candidates for voters to vote for. The candidate could be started in different ways, and voters can allow voting for their candidate only. Voters can add candidates only once, which cannot change, as shown in Figure 8.

Figure 8. Add a new candidate

7.1.3. Confirmation

Confirmation is used as admin to start adding candidates and which candidates have been allowed to start in which position, as shown in Figure 9.

Figure 9. Confirmation through MetaMask

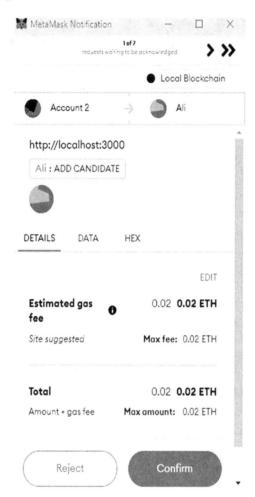

After Adding the desired Candidate, Government starts the election; Now election would be visible to the user as they can vote for their candidates for a specific time, as shown in Figure 10.

Figure 10. The screen of the new election

7.1.4. Register

Every user has a unique Hash id that can be used to register the voter as they can add their Name or Nickname. Only your hash can be used to register and always be used for logging in. Hash can be used as a session here. Your hash can create your session, and the voter can vote or see the result on your device. After the Voter registers, it shows your information. Your Name and number are your personal information, as shown in Figure 11.

Figure 11. The step for the registration

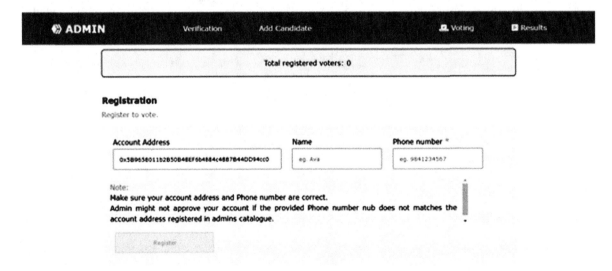

7.1.5. Register Verification and Voting

After a voter registration, the administrator may verify, validate, and approve the voter's registration id. Voters may register and vote if the administrator permits. In-App, your Status indicates whether voters have voted or not. If voters vote, it indicates that genuine voters are voting; otherwise, voters have not yet voted after Your vote. Voters may examine the outcome of all elections, as shown in Figure 12.

Figure 12. Verification of the registration

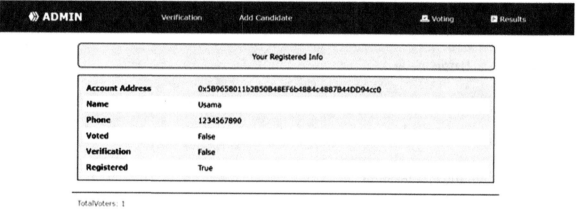

7.1.6. How to Vote Cast

It is an easy step to vote as voters see a list of candidates that allows them to choose their favorite candidates for vote. A voter can just click vote to submit his vote after her vote has been submitted. In the diagram, voters will see 3 candidates, and the voter can vote for your specific candidates by clicking on the vote. After the voter select it, it asks the voter to confirm, and then it casts a vote. After its user cannot change, as shown in Figure 13.

Figure 13. How to cast the vote

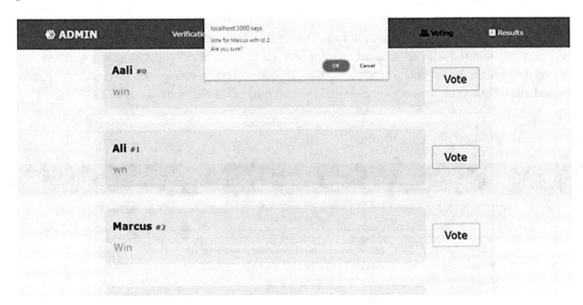

7.1.7. Voting Result Declaration

Voters can check the result in the system as to how many votes total cast. Who got more votes? Who wins, and every minor detail is shown in the results? In this testing, we only cast 1 vote, showing Marcus is a winner with 1 vote, and all other candidates get 0 votes, as shown in Figure 14.

Figure 14. The result of the election

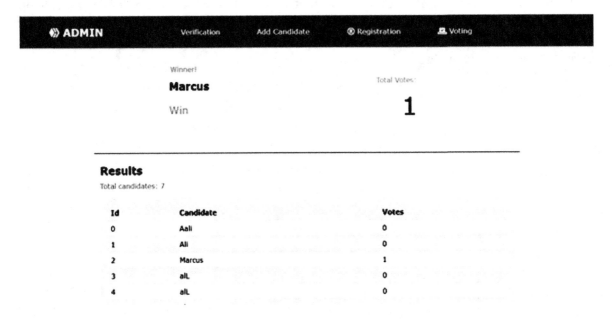

8. THE CASE OF ELECTRONIC VOTING

8.1. Challenges

It would seem that voting, counting, and the registration and authentication of voters all need to be refined. Vote manipulation and hacking of electronic voting machines are common problems in election systems. Some skepticism remains, however, despite the obvious advantages that blockchain technology can bring to the voting process; the most significant concern relates to accessibility, as voters are typically required to have a digital device with Internet access (Ahmad, Shaharuddin, Gunawan, & Arifin, 2022), such as a smartphone, tablet, or personal computer. While decentralization has helped alleviate some of these issues, it is not a foolproof solution.

The difficulty of scaling blockchain-based solutions is another issue. The Blockchain's need for decentralization makes achieving the primary attribute of conventional distributed systems scalability difficult. Consensus techniques, network size, and transaction verification are some elements that impact the speed of blockchain transactions. The transaction throughput of public blockchains such as Bitcoin and Ethereum 1.0 is capped at a certain number per second (Edwin, Christinal, & Chandy, 2022). Because of the potential impact on system performance, several studies have focused on permissioned Blockchain as a solution. Since the Hyperledger Consortium places a premium on speed and scalability, the Performance and Scalability Working Group (PSWG) was formed to investigate these issues and determine what metrics are most relevant to measuring the success of Blockchain and related technologies. Hyperledger Fabric's performance capabilities have been the subject of several academic studies. With the most recent upgrade, HF can process 20,000 transactions per second.

8.2. Why Hyperledger Fabric?

Hyperledger Fabric is a distributed ledger that stores blocks of network transactions in a chained fashion. Each block in the chain is further guaranteed authentic by sophisticated cryptographic methods. Each new block is committed to the global ledger by the members of the P2P network following the successful completion of the decentralized consensus mechanism, providing the system with an immutable audit trail of all transactions (Salman, Al-Janabi, & Sagheer, 2022).

Transactions in smart contracts are often performed after consensus or intertwined with it, and all participants execute all contracts following the sequential execution approach of conventional permissionless and permissioned blockchain systems. Scalability is an issue with Figure 15 order-execute design since it calls for sequential transactions and peer endorsement.

Figure 15. Methods used historically in the development of blockchain technology

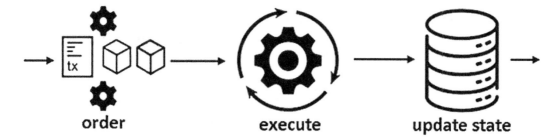

order   execute   update state

A new architecture for HF was developed that allows for scalability and adaptable trust assumptions. By offering a cutting-edge strategy that reworks how blockchains handle non-deterministic events and security challenges like resource depletion and Denial of Service (DoS) attacks, the concept of permissioned blockchains is being rethought (Rahman, Tripathi, & Noida). As seen in Figure 16, Hyperledger Fabric employs a novel architecture known as execute-order-validate, in which transactions are first performed and endorsed before being ordered and validated to ensure that they do not conflict.

Figure 16. How transactions are processed in Hyperledger Fabric

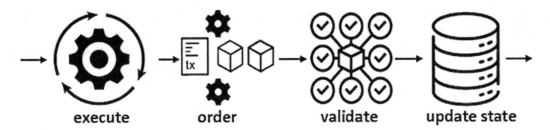

The transaction flow is broken down into modular building pieces in the execute-order-validate design, and it also incorporates features of scalable replicated databases, marking a significant departure from the order-execute paradigm. The flexibility of the platform's pluggable consensus mechanisms ensures it may be used with a wide variety of trust architectures. Consensus procedures may be used that don't use a central coin. By not using a cryptocurrency, several potentially disastrous attack vectors are eliminated, and the platform may be implemented with essentially the same operating costs as any other distributed system since no cryptographic mining activities are required (Adekeye). HF nodes may sign and verify transactions without disclosing their private keys by using a Hardware Security Module (HSM) to store private keys and execute cryptographic operations. To talk to an HSM, HF presently uses the PKCS11 standard.

It is one method in which HF facilitates cross-organizational cooperation in developing blockchain infrastructure. An organization may theoretically deploy an endless number of nodes, and each organization can use its own CA to produce the identities of its nodes since an organization is a security domain and a unit of identity and credentials. An organization may be structured with several subunits, or "affiliations," each responsible for a distinct set of tasks (PAVIČEVIĆ). The purpose of an OU is to facilitate access control, so think of it as a department inside your own company. Membership in a group or association gives access to the resources necessary to create a network architecture tailored to the needs of various clients and situations. Together, these characteristics make HF one of the best-performing platforms currently available in terms of transaction processing and confirmation latency (Kamath, Manikandan, Lamani, Shanbhag, & Srinivasa); it also allows for the use of smart contracts, privacy, and confidentiality of transactions, providing a flexible approach to solving many of the problems of the electoral system by providing an efficient architecture for the execution, ordering, validation, and committing of transactions (votes) in bulk.

9. DISCUSSION AND FUTURE WORK

In this study, we suggest a voting mechanism that meets several criteria. By implementing processes like vote counting in the chaincode, which does not need a central authority, Hyperledger Fabric technology ensures each vote's immutability, integrity, and traceability. The proposal also opens the door to integrate the solution with Hyperledger Explorer, a lightweight but robust and reliably updated open-source tool for exploring blockchain-related data and transactions. Also, the suggested network architecture provides additional configuration options and makes the network more versatile for use in different contexts. One or more intermediate certification authorities (ICAs) may be incorporated in SuffrageNet to lower the danger of the organization's CA (root) being hacked. For instance, the SUFFRAGE group may get support for a single ICA that represents both its MINTER and VOTER members. It's built into the structure of the network. Because the ballot is handled as NFT and a bitmap field is included in the ballot, the system may be easily adapted to support many voting methods.

The nodes of Hyperledger Fabric had their BCCSP (Blockchain Cryptographic Service Provider) configuration section changed and recompiled so that a SoftHSM could be used in the proposed system. Hyperledger Fabric nodes' cryptographic standards and algorithms are set up in this configuration for use with a Hardware Security Module (HSM). This add-on makes the solution safer to use. You should know that a SoftHSM is not safer than a real HSM. In contrast, real HSMs are built with hardened physical components. The HSM is fitted with tamper-detection circuitry to prevent a hacker from extracting keys from a hardware security module (HSM) by cracking open the casing and sniffing out the keys with a logic probe. Decoupling the CA's cryptographic identity authentication ensures that voters' activities are kept private. To ensure the security of each voter's identification, their credentials are encrypted inside a SoftHSM. Each vote is authenticated by inserting the voter's signature next to the transaction ID. The existing format of MSP certificates (X.509) was supposed to be replaced with Identity Mixer to increase the untraceability of votes. "Idemix is a cryptographic protocol suite that provides strong authentication and privacy-preserving features, such as anonymity, the ability to transact without revealing the transactor's identity, and unlinkability, the ability for a single identity to send multiple transactions without revealing that the same identity sent the transactions." In an X.509 certificate, all characteristics must be disclosed to validate the certificate signature, which raises questions about its unlinkability. It means that any certificate may be used to sign any transaction. Avoiding such linkability requires the usage of brand-new X.509 certificates each time, which adds complexity to the process of managing keys. Since not even the CA can connect proofs to the original credential, Idemix enables both the CA and verifiers to avoid linkability. No one, not even the issuer or verifier, can know whether two separate proofs originated from the same credential (or from two different ones).

Unfortunately, blockchain-based voting solutions are still in their early stages of development. While the blockchain network can ensure that votes are counted only once and only from approved devices, it cannot provide any assurance that the device used to cast a vote is free of malicious software. Direct recording electronic voting machines (DRE voting machines) have been widely adopted because of their accessibility and simplicity of use, and all signs point to blockchain technology being increasingly used in voting solutions like these. However, DREs are a regular target of cyberattackers. A blockchain may avoid or lessen the effects of some of these security flaws.

10. CONCLUSION

In this study, we look into and assess state of the art in Blockchain-based electronic voting systems. Recent studies have focused on the use of blockchain technology for electronic voting. Following a brief overview of Blockchain and its numerous applications, the various current electronic voting methods are discussed at length. The problems with current electronic voting methods are then identified, discussed, and addressed. The potential of the Blockchain to improve electronic voting underpins existing solutions for Blockchain-based electronic voting and future research paths for Blockchain-based electronic voting systems. Some industry leaders think Blockchain technology might improve a decentralized electronic voting system. All eligible voters and third-party observers have access to the electronic voting records kept by these systems. Most writing on electronic voting using the Blockchain has centered on the same problems. The present study on electronic voting has various holes that need to be filled by future research. We must deal with issues including scalability assaults, a lack of transparency, the use of faulty technology, and a lack of compliance with compulsion. The concerns associated with the security and scalability of Blockchain-based electronic voting systems are not yet fully understood, and additional study is required. There is a chance that users may be vulnerable to security issues and threats via blockchain voting processes. Improved knowledge of software engineering and project management is necessary for the widespread use of blockchain technology. From past experience, we know these issues must be addressed more comprehensively throughout the voting process. That's why it's important to test out electronic voting systems in a small number of jurisdictions first. Both the internet and voting machines may be compromised. Significant security enhancements are needed to enable electronic voting over a trusted and secure Internet. Even while the Blockchain system appeared like a perfect answer, these problems prevented it from completely fixing the electoral system. Since Blockchain technology is only getting started as an alternative to electronic voting, our inquiry found that there are still several technical hurdles that need to be resolved before the technology can be widely used.

REFERENCES

Abuidris, Y., Kumar, R., & Wenyong, W. (2019). *A survey of Blockchain based on e-voting systems.* Paper presented at the Proceedings of the 2019 2nd International Conference on Blockchain Technology and Applications. Adekeye, T. Securing the Electoral E-Voting System Using Blockchain Technology. 10.1145/3376044.3376060

Adiputra, C. K., Hjort, R., & Sato, H. (2018). *A proposal of blockchain-based electronic voting system.* Paper presented at the 2018 second world conference on smart trends in systems, security and sustainability (WorldS4). 10.1109/WorldS4.2018.8611593

Agbesi, S., & Asante, G. (2019). *Electronic voting recording system based on blockchain technology.* Paper presented at the 2019 12th CMI Conference on Cybersecurity and Privacy (CMI). 10.1109/CMI48017.2019.8962142

Ahmad, Y. A., Shaharuddin, M. F., Gunawan, T. S., & Arifin, F. (2022). *Implementation of an E-voting Prototype using Ethereum Blockchain in Ganache Network.* Paper presented at the 2022 IEEE 18th International Colloquium on Signal Processing & Applications (CSPA). 10.1109/CSPA55076.2022.9782016

Ahmed, M. R., Shamrat, F. J. M., Ali, M. A., Mia, M. R., & Khatun, M. A. (2020). The future of electronic voting system using Block chain. *International Journal of Scientific Technology Research*, *9*, 4131–4134.

Ahn, B. (2022). Implementation and Early Adoption of an Ethereum-Based Electronic Voting System for the Prevention of Fraudulent Voting. *Sustainability*, *14*(5), 2917. doi:10.3390u14052917

Ajao, L. A., Umar, B. U., Olajide, D. O., & Misra, S. (2022). Application of Crypto-Blockchain Technology for Securing Electronic Voting Systems. In *Blockchain Applications in the Smart Era* (pp. 85–105). Springer. doi:10.1007/978-3-030-89546-4_5

Al-Maaitah, S., Qatawneh, M., & Quzmar, A. (2021). *E-Voting System Based on Blockchain Technology: A Survey.* Paper presented at the 2021 International Conference on Information Technology (ICIT). 10.1109/ICIT52682.2021.9491734

Al-Madani, A. M., Gaikwad, A. T., Mahale, V., & Ahmed, Z. A. (2020). *Decentralized E-voting system based on Smart Contract by using Blockchain Technology.* Paper presented at the 2020 International Conference on Smart Innovations in Design, Environment, Management, Planning and Computing (ICSIDEMPC). 10.1109/ICSIDEMPC49020.2020.9299581

Amir Latif, R. M., Hussain, K., Jhanjhi, N., Nayyar, A., & Rizwan, O. (2020). A remix IDE: Smart contract-based framework for the healthcare sector by using Blockchain technology. *Multimedia Tools and Applications*, 1–24.

Bonthu, S. R., Chakraverty, S., Subrahmanya, S., Varma, N., Ramani, S., & Karuppiah, M. (2022). Blockchain for Electronic Voting System. In Data Analytics, Computational Statistics, and Operations Research for Engineers (pp. 61-88). CRC Press.

Bosri, R., Uzzal, A. R., Al Omar, A., Hasan, A. T., & Bhuiyan, M. Z. A. (2019). *Towards a privacy-preserving voting system through blockchain technologies.* Paper presented at the 2019 IEEE Intl Conf on Dependable, Autonomic and Secure Computing, Intl Conf on Pervasive Intelligence and Computing, Intl Conf on Cloud and Big Data Computing, Intl Conf on Cyber Science and Technology Congress (DASC/PiCom/CBDCom/CyberSciTech). 10.1109/DASC/PiCom/CBDCom/CyberSciTech.2019.00116

Çabuk, U. C., Adiguzel, E., & Karaarslan, E. (2020). *A survey on feasibility and suitability of blockchain techniques for the e-voting systems.* arXiv preprint arXiv:2002.07175.

Chaudhari, K. G. (2018). E-voting System using Proof of Voting (PoV) Consensus Algorithm using Block Chain Technology. *International Journal of Advanced Research in Electrical Electronics and Instrumentation Engineering*, *7*(11), 4051–4055.

Denis González, C., Frias Mena, D., Massó Muñoz, A., Rojas, O., & Sosa-Gómez, G. (2022). Electronic Voting System Using an Enterprise Blockchain. *Applied Sciences (Basel, Switzerland)*, *12*(2), 531. doi:10.3390/app12020531

Dong, Y., Yu, X., Alharbi, A., & Ahmad, S. (2022). AI-based production and application of English multimode online reading using multi-criteria decision support system. *Soft Computing*, *26*(20), 1–11. doi:10.100700500-022-07209-2 PMID:35668907

Edwin, K., Christinal, H., & Chandy, A. (2022). *Blockchain Based Online Voting System Using RSA Algorithm*. Academic Press.

Febriyanto, E., Rahayu, N., Pangaribuan, K., & Sunarya, P. A. (2020). *Using Blockchain Data Security Management for E-Voting Systems*. Paper presented at the 2020 8th International Conference on Cyber and IT Service Management (CITSM).

Goyal, J., Ahmed, M., & Gopalani, D. (2022). *A Privacy Preserving E-Voting System with Two-Phase Verification based on Ethereum Blockchain*. Academic Press.

Ibrahim, M., Ravindran, K., Lee, H., Farooqui, O., & Mahmoud, Q. H. (2021). *Electionblock: An electronic voting system using Blockchain and fingerprint authentication*. Paper presented at the 2021 IEEE 18th International Conference on Software Architecture Companion (ICSA-C). 10.1109/ICSA-C52384.2021.00033

Indapwar, A., Chandak, M., & Jain, A. (2020). E-voting system using Blockchain technology. *Int. J. of Advanced Trends in Computer Science and Engineering, 9*(3).

Jafar, U., Aziz, M. J. A., & Shukur, Z. (2021). Blockchain for electronic voting system—Review and open research challenges. *Sensors (Basel), 21*(17), 5874. doi:10.339021175874 PMID:34502764

Kamath, A., Manikandan, K., Lamani, K., Shanbhag, P. D., & Srinivasa, B. (n.d.). *Blockchain based solution for online voting system*. Academic Press.

Kamil, M., Bist, A. S., Rahardja, U., Santoso, N. P. L., & Iqbal, M. (2021). COVID-19: Implementation e-voting blockchain concept. *International Journal of Artificial Intelligence Research, 5*(1), 25–34. doi:10.29099/ijair.v5i1.173

Kok, S., Abdullah, A., & Jhanjhi, N. (2020). Early detection of crypto-ransomware using pre-encryption detection algorithm. *Journal of King Saud University-Computer and Information Sciences*.

Latif, R. M. A., Farhan, M., Rizwan, O., Hussain, M., Jabbar, S., & Khalid, S. (2021). Retail level Blockchain transformation for product supply chain using truffle development platform. *Cluster Computing, 24*(1), 1–16. doi:10.100710586-020-03165-4

Latif, R. M. A., Iqbal, S., Rizwan, O., Shah, S. U. A., Farhan, M., & Ijaz, F. (2019). *Blockchain transforms the retail level by using a supply chain rules and regulation*. Paper presented at the 2019 2nd International Conference on Communication, Computing and Digital systems (C-CODE).

Maesa, D. D. F., & Mori, P. (2020). Blockchain 3.0 applications survey. *Journal of Parallel and Distributed Computing, 138*, 99–114. doi:10.1016/j.jpdc.2019.12.019

Majumder, S., & Ray, S. (2022). Usage of Blockchain Technology in e-Voting System Using Private Blockchain. In *Intelligent Data Engineering and Analytics* (pp. 51–61). Springer. doi:10.1007/978-981-16-6624-7_6

Malhotra, M., Kumar, A., Kumar, S., & Yadav, V. (2022). Untangling E-Voting Platform for Secure and Enhanced Voting Using Blockchain Technology. In Transforming Management with AI, Big-Data, and IoT (pp. 51-72). Springer. doi:10.1007/978-3-030-86749-2_3

Mookherji, S., Vanga, O., & Prasath, R. (2022). Blockchain-based e-voting protocols. In *Blockchain Technology for Emerging Applications* (pp. 239–266). Elsevier. doi:10.1016/B978-0-323-90193-2.00006-5

Mukherjee, P. P., Boshra, A. A., Ashraf, M. M., & Biswas, M. (2020). *A hyper-ledger fabric framework as a service for improved quality e-voting system.* Paper presented at the 2020 IEEE Region 10 Symposium (TENSYMP). 10.1109/TENSYMP50017.2020.9230820

Negash, S. (2022). *Improving eGovernment Services with Blockchain: Restoring Trust in e-voting Systems.* Paper presented at the International Conference on Electronic Governance and Open Society: Challenges in Eurasia. 10.1007/978-3-031-04238-6_20

Olaniyi, O., Dogo, E., Nuhu, B., Treiblmaier, H., Abdulsalam, Y., & Folawiyo, Z. (2022). A Secure Electronic Voting System Using Multifactor Authentication and Blockchain Technologies. In *Blockchain Applications in the Smart Era* (pp. 41–63). Springer. doi:10.1007/978-3-030-89546-4_3

Patil, H. V., Rathi, K. G., & Tribhuwan, M. V. (2018). A study on decentralized e-voting system using blockchain technology. *Int. Res. J. Eng. Technol, 5*(11), 48–53.

Pranitha, G., Rukmini, T., Shankar, T., Sah, B., Kumar, N., & Padhy, S. (2022). *Utilization of Blockchain in E-Voting System.* Paper presented at the 2022 2nd International Conference on Intelligent Technologies (CONIT). 10.1109/CONIT55038.2022.9847995

Priyadarshini, I., Chatterjee, J. M., Sujatha, R., Jhanjhi, N., Karime, A., & Masud, M. (2022). Exploring Internet Meme Activity during COVID-19 Lockdown Using Artificial Intelligence Techniques. *Applied Artificial Intelligence, 36*(1), 2014218. doi:10.1080/08839514.2021.2014218

Roh, C.-H., & Lee, I.-Y. (2020). A study on electronic voting system using private Blockchain. *Journal of Information Processing Systems, 16*(2), 421–434.

Roopak, T., & Sumathi, R. (2020). *Electronic voting based on virtual id of aadhar using blockchain technology.* Paper presented at the 2020 2nd International Conference on Innovative Mechanisms for Industry Applications (ICIMIA). 10.1109/ICIMIA48430.2020.9074942

Salman, S. A.-B., Al-Janabi, S., & Sagheer, A. M. (2022). *A Review on E-Voting Based on Blockchain Models.* Academic Press.

Sharma, U., Nand, P., Chatterjee, J. M., Jain, V., Jhanjhi, N. Z., & Sujatha, R. (2022). *Cyber-Physical Systems: Foundations and Techniques.* John Wiley & Sons.

Wahab, Y. M., Ghazi, A., Al-Dawoodi, A., Alisawi, M., Abdullah, S. S., Hammood, L., & Nawaf, A. Y. (2022). *A Framework for Blockchain Based E-Voting System for Iraq.* Academic Press.

Chapter 18
Blockchain–Based Secure and Efficient Ride Sharing System

Rana Muhammad Amir Latif

Department of Computer Science, COMSATS University Islamabad, Sahiwal, Pakistan

Muhammad Ibtisam Asghar

BARANI Institute of Sciences, Pakistan

Muhammad Umer

Department of Computer Science, COMSATS University Islamabad, Sahiwal, Pakistan

Khalid Hussain

Department of Computer Science, Superior University, Islamabad, Pakistan

ABSTRACT

The attractive advantages of ridesharing include reduced traffic congestion and shared travel costs for users and drivers. However, most existing rideshare systems rely on an intermediary to coordinate the service, creating a single point of failure and raising privacy issues about exposure through internal and external assaults. The suggested approach allows drivers to provide ridesharing services directly to riders without needing a central hub or reliable intermediary. Sharing trips may teach passengers and drivers about transportation logistics without requiring them to change their plans or costs. The suggested system employs a time-locked technique to solve these problems. A membership deposit system for ridesharing services uses smart contracts and zero-knowledge evidence gathering. In short, the driver and the passenger need to put up some deposit to prove they are serious about using the blockchain. Later, a driver must show the blockchain that he or she was at the agreed-upon pick-up location at the appointed time.

DOI: 10.4018/978-1-6684-5284-4.ch018

1. INTRODUCTION

Over the last decade, the practice of drivers renting out spare seats in their cars to those in need has exploded in popularity. While this has helped alleviate traffic and vehicle emissions, the present state of ride-sharing systems relies on a centralized model in which a third party coordinates all interactions between passengers and drivers (Amir Latif et al., 2020). That creates a vulnerable, weak spot. This single point of failure leaves sensitive information exposed and may be used by bad actors (Latif et al., 2021). Moreover, because drivers pay for most petrol and vehicle maintenance, the central organization naturally gets a part of their earnings. The proposed solution, aptly named "Decentralized Trip Sharing," is an Ethereum Blockchain-based, distributed network for coordinating ride sharing (Latif et al., 2019).

Currently, the world is experiencing a fast transformation in which data increasingly plays a central role (Humayun, Jhanjhi, Niazi, Amsaad, & Masood, 2022). Data is becoming more qualitative, efficient, transparent, and responsible across many facets of society, including but not limited to government, logistics, electricity, health, traffic, and marketing (Humayun, Niazi, et al., 2020). To ensure that the information that makes up our increasingly connected world is not stored in insecure locations, it is essential to develop a system that ensures the continued operation of sound, efficient, and secure data systems (Humayun, Jhanjhi, Hamid, & Ahmed, 2020). One intriguing answer is Blockchain, which, thanks to its highly robust design and distributed nature, can easily adapt to the requirements of data-driven networks that are constantly changing and self-regulating systems (Kumar, Vimal, Jhanjhi, Dhanabalan, & Alhumyani, 2021). Since its first use with Bitcoin in 2009, many major industrial companies have investigated blockchain technology to diversify their offerings (A Almusaylim & Jhanjhi, 2020). Blockchain technology finds new uses in areas such as the public sector, healthcare, and transportation through smart contracts. After reaching an understanding, the parties establish several parameters used by the smart contract's interpretive lines of code to implement the conditions of the agreement (Q. Wang & Su, 2020). As a result, all financial dealings may be seen, tracked, and confirmed without question (Julie, Nayahi, & Jhanjhi, 2020). Blockchain has the potential to revolutionize many industries, but not until several hiccups in its implementation are ironed out. Education among sectors, standardized blockchain frameworks, cooperation across industries, and validating its public benefits are all crucial factors to consider (Xiong, Dalhaus, Wang, & Huang, 2020). As a result, we are advocating for the sharing economy, which has been a game-changer for many sectors.

Other companies using centralized ride-sharing are less secure and cost too much to maintain. Most importantly, it is less profitable for riders and users as riders do not get too much profit from the user because some profits also go to the company (Kakkar, Gupta, Tanwar, & Rodrigues, 2021). On the other hand, the user always pays extra fees to the company. Companies always get their profits and commissions, which is not beneficial for users and riders.

The promise of car-sharing to more sustainably meet individual transportation demand by reducing the need for passenger automobiles and, thus, potentially lowering emissions has given the concept significant support. Furthermore, emerging business models in car-sharing attempt to capitalize on these underused automobiles by replacing ownership with on-demand access to a fleet of shared or privately-owned vehicles, while 95% of private vehicles sit idle on average (D. Wang & Zhang, 2020). Moreover, shared mobility presents new prospects for the automotive industry, particularly in the automobile manufacturing sector, regarding software and hardware technology. It is estimated that a single car-sharing service might replace ten individual cars (Saad et al., 2019).

Original Equipment Manufacturers (OEMs) will refer to automakers like BMW, Volkswagen, and (OEMs) (Kakkar, Jadav, Gupta, Agrawal, & Tanwar, 2022). To lessen their environmental impact, original equipment manufacturers have begun investing money into car-sharing programs. Since OEMs already have the resources and experience necessary to impact the shared mobility movement significantly, they are in a prime position to contribute to this expanding trend. Automobile leasing gained popularity due to the trend away from car ownership, partly because it may still provide the consumer with the sensation of ownership (i.e., psychological ownership) (Kudva, Badsha, Sengupta, Khalil, & Zomaya, 2021). OEMs are more cognizant of the need to lessen their financial and environmental impact. To further car-sharing, however, original equipment manufacturers (OEMs) must keep developing new solutions.

In the automobile sector, blockchain technology has the potential to advance a wide range of mobility services by increasing trust and cooperation thanks to improved information traceability and transparency. In addition, Blockchain's advantages for IoT applications come from its secure data storage, authentication trust, and failure tolerance. In order to collect data about the vehicle, modern automobiles have Internet-of-Things (IoT) sensors and computer units installed (Pal & Ruj, 2019). With these enhancements, automobiles are a complicated combination of automotive hardware, software, and Internet of Things (IoT) devices that can perform various functions (L. Zhang et al., 2019). Today's state-of-the-art equipment (such as in-car telematics2) makes car-pooling and leasing a breeze, not to mention productive and cost-effective (offering a pay-as-you-go-based billing model). In addition, passengers may make specific model requests for their rental cars (Kakkar, Gupta, Alshehri, et al., 2022). Together, the increased customer happiness, less waste, and lessened carbon footprint that result from shared mobility constitute a novel business/service model.

However, the car-sharing and leasing markets have unique difficulties regarding trust and openness. The automobile's owner, for instance, is the only one who has any real interest in the outcome of private car ownership. In contrast, the car-sharing and leasing platform has many participants, including the original equipment manufacturer (OEM) (X. Zhang et al., 2019), leasing firm, insurance provider, renter, and lessee. The use cases may dictate the precise responsibilities of various stakeholders (Xu, Zhu, Yi, & Wang, 2020). However, regardless of the application, the platform's transactions will include several parties, which raises significant trust and transparency concerns.

Also, with a centralized car-sharing and leasing platform, the stakeholder that maintains the platform collects and retains the data on vehicle use and other telemetry data, leading to knowledge asymmetry among the stakeholders. Information asymmetry causes problems with trust and openness among stakeholders since not everyone has the same data access level (Gudymenko et al., 2020). This lack of information openness, particularly in conflicts, may lead to various trust difficulties among the stakeholders, harming the viability of car-sharing and leasing platforms (Baza et al., 2019). Decentralized systems, like blockchain technology, provide promising solutions in such cases. Vital data that must be disseminated to all parties is recorded in a distributed ledger that can be accessed by all parties involved with greater ease and reliability (Jeong, Youn, Jho, & Shin, 2020). In this article, we argue that Blockchain and IoT may be utilized to build an ecosystem for leased vehicles that allows keyless entry without interacting with the vehicle's owner.

1.1 Overview of Blockchain Technology

Coined by Satoshi Nakamoto in 2008, Bitcoin is the forerunner of the distributed ledger technology known as Blockchain. Distributed, decentralized, unchangeable, secured, and shareable are just a few of the reasons why Blockchain has become so popular. There is a public ledger where all transactions can be seen and verified by anybody on the network. Blockchain technology's decentralized, peer-to-peer structure makes intermediaries superfluous. Security, transparency, trust-lessness, and efficiency are just a few potential outcomes of using Blockchain technology in a smart city. An ICT-enabled "smart city" strives to improve residents" quality of life and build a more sustainable community (ICT) (Sedlmeir, Buhl, Fridgen, Keller, & Engineering, 2020). When used together, the Smart City and Blockchain have the potential to boost a city's smartness, efficiency, and security. Blockchain has quickly become the standard for distributed ledger applications. The information is structured into many chunks linked to one another (Shafiq, Jhanjhi, Abdullah, & Sciences, 2021). There are three distinct flavors of blockchain systems, with the others falling into the private and consortium categories. Anyone connected to a public blockchain has access to the shared ledger and may initiate transactions, verify them, and oversee the network without needing special authorization from anyone else (De Filippi, Mannan, Reijers, & Society, 2022). Some popular instances of public blockchains include Bitcoin and Ethereum. At the same time, a private blockchain is a network owned and operated by a single entity, even though it is decentralized. In the same way, a consortium blockchain is a private network; it also conducts transactions between companies.

1.2 What Is Ethereum?

Vitalik Buterin created Ethereum, the first decentralized open-source blockchain platform. Ether is written in a Turing-complete computer language, which addresses many of bitcoins' scripting language difficulties (Dutta, Choi, Somani, Butala, & review, 2020). Smart Contracts conduct trades on Ethereum. When specific criteria are satisfied, a smart contract act according to a predetermined set of rules. The instructions for Ethereum transactions are signed cryptographically. Typically, Ether is used to cover the cost of such deals. Ethereum's native currency is called "Ether." Ether is not only utilized as a means of exchange but also as a means of determining the cost of executing decentralized applications (Shafiq, Jhanjhi, Abdullah, & Alzain, 2021). Every operation on Ethereum has a fixed cost, measured in Gas. The Ethereum Virtual Machine (EVM) is a distributed computer that executes these instructions on every node in the network. Ethereum might be used in various industries, including finance, market forecasting, file storage, and insurance. This article, however, focuses on one of Ethereum's major use cases—the creation of decentralized applications (D-Apps) (Perera, Nanayakkara, Rodrigo, Senaratne, & Weinand, 2020).

1.3 Decentralized Applications (D-App)

A D-App is an application that runs on a blockchain without any central servers. Ethereum supported various D-Apps in various industries, such as insurance, energy, finance, healthcare, and more. The problem is that many D-Apps are not decentralized (Pan, Pan, Song, Ai, & Ming, 2020). The characteristics of a D-App are defined as follows.

- **Open Source:** The source code for D-Apps is publicly available so that an impartial party may audit them.
- **No single-point Failure:** There is no single point of failure since it is decentralized.
- **Consensus:** The nodes need to reach an agreement to provide transparency.

- **Currency Support:** Every decentralized application relies heavily on internal money as the primary element driving its ecosystem.

1.4 D-App Architecture

D-apps have a two-tier design, with the front-end client-side application communicating with the server-side back-end tier where the smart contract is implemented in the blockchain network. The client-server interface and overall architecture of the decentralized program. The next chapters discuss the software and frameworks used to create the ride-sharing D-app (Ali, Ally, & Dwivedi, 2020).

Assumedly a Truffle Suit There are many different parts to making a D-app, and the Truffle suite has them all. It helps in creating, compiling, deploying, and testing smart contracts. Moreover, it facilitates the development of the D-app's front ends. The Truffle suite consists of three main parts: The truffle framework, the development environment where the smart contracts are written, deployed, and tested; Truffle servers; and Truffle clients. Ganache, the D-app graphical user interface (GUI) testing simulator. Drizzle is the front-end library for creating decentralized applications. Web3.js The program runs on the client side and is similar to any other web app developed in HTML, CSS, and JavaScript. Web3.js is a library package that facilitates communication between the D-app browser and the Blockchain. It also facilitates transferring ethers between accounts and reading and writing data from smart contracts. Meta-mask's web3 provider in the browser is a key component of our project. Meta-mask is a Chrome add-on that provides a safe and convenient way to manage the Ethereum wallet and private keys. Sites built using web3.js are used to access the Ethereum accounts. Virtual Machine for Ethereum (EVM) Each node in an Ethereum network has its own Ethereum Virtual Machine (EVM), and they all work together to execute the same set of smart contract instructions.

2. LITERATURE REVIEW

This research proposes a secure and efficient blockchain-based data pricing mechanism for the ride-sharing business. Its principal objective is to safeguard the confidentiality of information transmitted between automobile owners and their customers. It leverages a communication network, namely 6G, to allow low-latency, high-throughput vehicle-to-consumer transmissions. Compared to more established networks such as 4G and 5G, the performance of the proposed system on a 6G communication network may be evaluated (Kakkar, Jadav, et al., 2022). People's perceptions of the car business have shifted with the introduction of the shared mobility idea. Authors have proposed the framework for a blockchain-based Internet of Things platform to encourage shared mobility via the integration of car-sharing and car-leasing services. This research shows that striking a good balance between security and privacy, authenticity, traceability, and dependability are crucial to the architecture of such an integrated platform (Auer, Nagler, Mazumdar, Mukkamala, & Applications, 2022).

People may use convenient, on-demand transportation services from the comfort of their smartphones, thanks to online ride-hailing services. The author employs a zone-based trip time estimate technique to securely compute sensitive data while masking each rider's position inside a zone region, preventing the service provider from learning the specific location of its riders. The author demonstrates that p-Share is a workable ride-sharing mechanism that can reliably discover the sharing riders with low ATT and no compromise in privacy (Huang, Luo, Xu, Hu, & Long, 2022).

There is a greater risk of data leakage and a single point of failure since the cab-sharing system relies so much on a centralized authority. The proposed system stores important data on drivers and passengers in a distributed ledger called a blockchain, including their identities, trip costs, pick-up and drop-off locations, and the times and dates of their respective trips. Without relying on a governing body, it uses a reputation system to provide ratings to drivers and passengers based on their past trips and subsequent actions (Namasudra & Sharma, 2022).

Many difficulties arise, particularly in terms of mobility, due to the rapid increase in urbanization and population. A conceptual model for a long-term smart transportation system is proposed in this research, including blockchain technology as a key component. The technology's main benefit is the ability to securely store information and defend against several security threats. This method allows TMCs to manage data from sensor networks more efficiently and safely (Traffic Monitoring Centers) (Dungan & Pop, 2022).

This piece suggests a safe and trustworthy optimum data pricing mechanism for ride-sharing based on blockchain technology and the principles of coalition game theory. Its primary goal is to ensure the privacy of information exchanged between car owners and their clients. Network latency, throughput, and car owners" profits are some of the many metrics examined (Kakkar et al., 2021).

The introduction of a consensus mechanism that is both effective and scalable remains an unsolved problem in computer science. This research proposes a novel method called Proof of Driving (PoD) to effectively generate blocks for blockchain-based VANET applications by randomly selecting honest miners. Proof-of-Stake (PoS), Proof-of-Work (PoW), and Practical Byzantine Fault Tolerant consensus all have inefficiencies that Proof-of-Discretion (PoD) aims to fix (PBFT) (Kudva et al., 2021).

With ride-sharing, drivers and passengers may split the cost of a journey and help alleviate traffic congestion, among other perks. Most ride-sharing systems are vulnerable to attack and lack transparency since they depend on a single, centralized, trusted entity to manage the service. In order to protect their personal information, drivers and passengers encrypt their offers and requests using a simple crypto-system, and the Blockchain matches these encrypted offers and requests without being able to decode them (Badr, Baza, Abdelfattah, Mahmoud, & Alasmary, 2021).

Because of the existing's security problems and centralization, the author proposes a technique based on a private Blockchain to assure safety. The leadership in traditional RSS had the power to alter or delete the report, including removing the riders" details. With our Hyperledger-based private blockchain solution, the author wants to end the immoral ease (Hossan, Khatun, Rahman, Reno, & Ahmed, 2021).

Intelligent connected vehicles (ICVs) are on the rise, indicating promising prospects for future intelligent traffic systems improving road safety and efficiency. Many obstacles, such as a lack of complete information to cope with a complex driving environment, stand in the way of ICVs that depend on data-driven perception and driving models. To improve the efficacy of information dissemination, the author presents a blockchain-based knowledge-sharing architecture that employs a distributed learning-based method (Chai, Leng, Wu, & He, 2021).

The author uses a consortium blockchain to offer a safe ride-sharing system that protects users" personal information and financial transactions. The information is first encrypted using attribute-based encryption by the traveler. Second, the controller node checks the car-pool log using a refined Delegated Proof-of-Stake (D-PoS) consensus. Third, following a rideshare transaction, drivers and riders may rate each other based on their trustworthiness. Also, a reliable source may expose the identities of malevolent users (D. Wang & Zhang, 2020).

Vehicle ownership may be shared via car sharing, resulting in frequent changes in who has legal title to a given vehicle. Single points of failure and a lack of mutual trust are two of the problems plaguing today's centralized car shearing control schemes. Therefore, the author proposes a blockchain and smart contract-based system for decentralized car-sharing administration (Zhou, Yang, Zhang, Zheng, & Liu, 2020).

The market for vehicle-sharing is expanding rapidly and has just surpassed the popularity of private car ownership. The central database server used by traditional car-sharing systems leaves them vulnerable to hacking and data leakage. The approach suggested here is to use Blockchain and smart contracts to facilitate a peer-to-peer model for short-term automobile sharing (Valaštín, Košt'ál, Bencel, & Kotuliak, 2019).

When using a ride-sharing service, customers trust the service's central providers to handle administrative tasks, including booking, monitoring, canceling, and determining fares. A nasty passenger might file a false complaint to get their money back and then rate the driver poorly. In order to guarantee that everyone on the journey pays their fair share, the author introduces BlockV, a blockchain-enabled solution. Anyride's creation, completion, dissatisfaction, or cancellation be recorded in the blockchain ledger and visible to all peer-to-peer network users. At the same time, this keeps the built-in reputation system functioning properly (Pal & Ruj, 2019).

For this reason, data and information transmission security is a primary problem in intelligent vehicle technologies. Data sent through intravenous lines may be protected and reliably transmitted when cTp is used in the surrounding communication environment. The author deploys blockchain technology in the ITS (Intelligent Transport System) to keep track of all the cars" records. Every car is accessible through IVs using ITS. As a case study, the author analyzes how our concept for better communication amongst intelligent cars works in an intersection setting (Singh & Kim, 2018).

The term "Internet of Vehicles" (IoV) refers to the network of interconnected vehicles and the services they provide, including navigation, entertainment, safety, and communication. Many accidents may be avoided and even lives saved if nodes communicate effectively. The nearest emergency agencies are alerted alongside the nodes when a traffic collision occurs. They are rerouted or forced to make way for emergency vehicles (Arora & Yadav, 2018).

Compared to other IoT network architectures, IoV requires additional edge computing to aid in content delivery because of the high mobility, constantly changing topology and open and diversified communication environment. Edge nodes might include the car and the roadside unit (RSU) (Javed et al., 2020). Decentralization, reduced latency, and idle resources are all made possible when users verify and transmit data directly amongst themselves rather than sending it to a central server in the cloud. Many experts in lightweight, efficiency and quality of service (QoS) improvement have studied the advantages of edge computing.

Edge computing in IoV may be implemented using Blockchain because of the features of decentralization, irreversibility, traceability, transparency, autonomy, and anonymity. A group of researchers has developed novel blockchain-based IoV application approaches based on validation, consensus, and reputation study paths to achieve security, scalability, and efficiency (Chai et al., 2021). This article applies the MPoR consensus algorithm suggested in it to a consortium blockchain-based IoV network, and the research includes both a consensus mechanism and an incentive mechanism based on reputation (Bhattacharjee, Badsha, & Sengupta, 2020).

A secure data sharing scheme based on the consortium blockchain, guaranteeing the confidentiality and privacy of data interaction via the attribute-based proxy re-encryption algorithm, and revealing the true identity of malicious users via the reputation rating, are all necessary components of a blockchain-based secure ride-sharing service model. Minimal matching algorithm for matching rideshare requests through a smart contract (Auer et al., 2022). When it comes to fog calculations and record-keeping for car pools, the Blockchain is an invaluable tool. A secure payment mechanism based on smart contracts may be used to prearrange pick-up points, routes, and prices. To safeguard the anonymity of the user's location and maximize the degree to which the user and the driver's feature vectors are the same, MinHash was developed. The preceding approaches have the drawback that the consensus relies on wasteful PoW (Kakkar, Gupta, Agrawal, et al., 2022) or PoS (Singh & Kim, 2018) procedures.

Proof of Driving (PoD) is a novel consensus technique implemented on the VANET (Zhou et al., 2020). Under the assumption that the penetration attacker is less than a third of the network and that the overall reputation of honest nodes is more than the total reputation of malicious nodes, this method may guarantee the system's security; nonetheless, it is vulnerable to collusive assaults (Baza, Mahmoud, Srivastava, Alasmary, & Younis, 2020). However, there is no incentive mechanism and no continuity in the system since reputation is reset to zero once each new block is generated.

A Proof of Travel (PoT) accreditation standard based on independently substantiated odometer readings (VVMT) (Namasudra & Sharma, 2022). The primary target audience is the first stages of an IoV network's rollout when relatively few benign automobiles are on the road. In order to increase the attack cost of malevolent cars, VVMT is obtained by interacting with RSU while driving, and only vehicles with reputation values over the threshold may participate in consensus (Gupta & Shanbhag, 2021). The insufficiency arises from the fact that cars keeping VVMT need a huge amount of communication overhead, and the viability of PoT relies on how densely dispersed the RSUs are.

A reputation assessment mechanism built on the Blockchain may address security flaws and privacy concerns in AVSN, encouraging lawful conduct and content delivery by cars. The evaluation of available past data determines the worth of a reputation (Y. Wang et al., 2021). PoW consensus was used by both systems, which is inefficient and has implementation challenges.

Incentives for miners to engage in the process of verifying blocks of secure data are implemented through smart contracts (Goel & Ghosh, 2021). To strengthen the DPoS consensus and decrease collusion between stakeholders and mining candidates, we offer a secure and efficient reputation management method using the weighted subjective logic model (Jani, Prakash, & Subramanian, 2021). There is a less-than-optimal chance that this technique will stop assaults from more than a third of malicious miners. This method does not consider how precisely weights are allocated, which is a drawback.

Use of a reputation system in ITS. Those seeking traffic data are seen as the primary actors in this setup. Data are checked for accuracy through crowdsourcing and then safely shared between certified individuals (Qin et al., 2020). Cluster-by-cluster, we confirm the consensus and establish the consensus threshold. The network's scalability is reduced, and the time it takes to reach a consensus grows steadily with the number of nodes.

3. METHODOLOGY OF RIDE SHARING SYSTEM

It is a flow of work of a Decentralized Ride sharing system that tells the behavior of the user and rider and their workflow. First of all, both riders and drivers need to log in through their Ethereum wallet address. If their wallet address is incorrect, the log-in process does not proceed, and an error occurs. However, after the successful log-in rider inputs its pick-up and drop-off locations and applies for a taxi.

In the meantime, drivers who are successfully logged in to their accounts see that ride requests in their area. If the driver is interested, he selects the ride, which notifies the rider, and their trip starts. During the ride, the rider has the authority to cancel the ride at any moment with the same authority the driver has. If both do not cancel their trip in the middle and reach the destination ride ends automatically, and all the fare is transferred into the driver's wallet, as shown in Figure 1.

Figure 1. The methodology diagram of a ride-sharing system

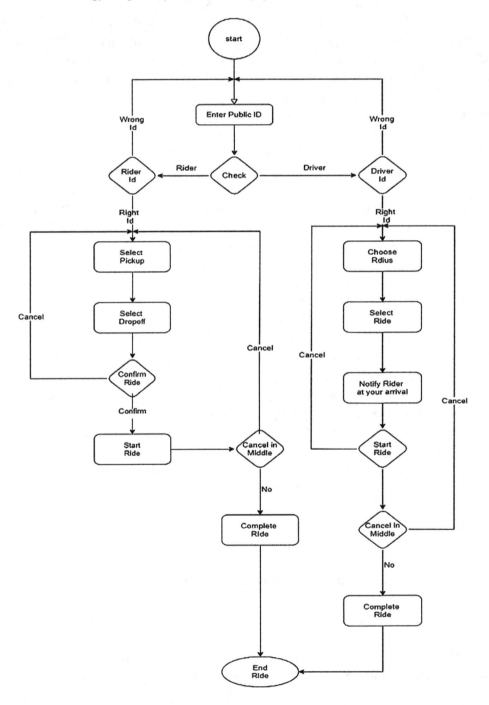

4. ALGORTHIMS

4.1 Algorithm 1: Pseudocode for Ride

See Figure 2.

Figure 2.

if Gclk [τ] ≥ t > Gclk [τ+1]	else
Broadcast REQUEST (Pid, Sp, Dp, t) to all	if Route Validation (Qt.REQ,"#, Pon) ≠ Φ
Tid ∈ Pnbr [after (τ +δ)]	Send CONFIRMATION 2 to Pid (for Qt.REQ)
L.append (REPLY message)	else
Sort L based on timed	Drop the passenger from the Qcon
Send CONFIRM 1 to the taxi with	Route Validation (Qt.REQ,"#, Pon) {
minimum timed	Qt.REQ = Dequeue head (Qt) //Request from
Wait for CONFIRM 2 from T until timer	Pid
expires	22. Route[k]=(Tloc, Qt.REQ.epick,
Pseudo Code at Taxi Tid	Qt.REQ.edrop,"# .epick,"# .edrop,
if Qt. ≠ Φ AND Nvac ≠ 0	Pon.edrop)
if Route Validation (Qt.REQ,"#, Pon)	for each k, (varying from 0-(k-1))
Send REPLY to Pid (for Qt.REQ)	for each passenger
else	If (time (Tloc, Dp)> (timed + Δ) – time already
Forward the Qt.REQ to neighboring taxis	travelled)
else if Nvac = 0	The route is NOT valid – drop it
Forward the Qt.REQ to neighboring taxis	if there are Valid Routes
if (Nvac = 0):	We choose the preferred route and return it
Drop the passenger from the Qcon	

4.2 Algorithm 2: Pseudocode for Payment Smart Contract

See Figure 3.

Figure 3.

contract Payment	trans f er (balance ∗ distance,driver)
address payable passenger	totalDistance ←this.totalDistance− distance
address payable driver	procedure GETFUNDS.Note{Return the
uint public distance	money to the passenger in case the waiting
procedure CONSTRUCTOR (driver,distance)	time runs out}
this.driver ← driver	if current.block.timestamp ≤ expirationTime
this.distance ← distance	return;
procedure PROOFOFDISTANCE (distance)	if current.block.owner != message.sender
if msg.sender 6= riderA return;	return;
while totalDistance ≤ distance do0020Note	transfer (balance, passenger) Send back the
{Pay only for distance traveled}	money to passenger

5. IMPLEMENTATION OF THE RIDE SHARING SYSTEM

5.1 Rider Log-in

In the initial stage, the rider logs into his account using the address of his Ethereum wallet. Afterward, he may see his profile, place orders, and share rides. The rider's log-in page uses his wallet address, as shown in Figure 2.

Figure 4. The address of the Ethereum wallet

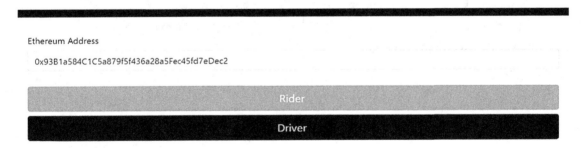

5.2 Driver Log-in

The driver also log-in into his account using his Ethereum wallet address, after which he can access all the rides near him, and he needs to decide which type of ride is suitable for him according to his route and fare, which are offered by riders to him. It all depends on whether the driver is available right now or not to any rider, as shown in Figure 3.

Figure 5. The log-in address of the driver

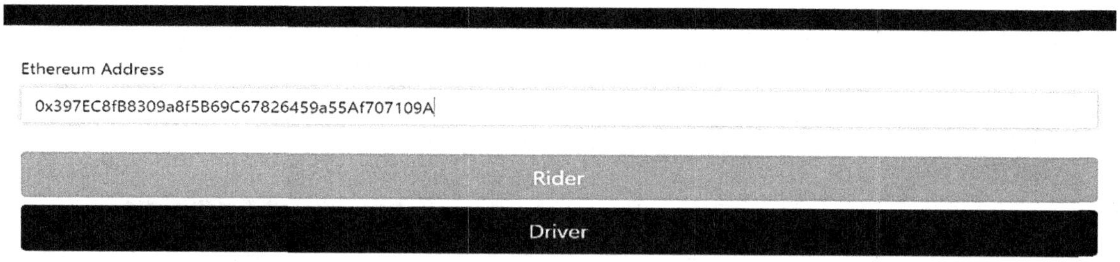

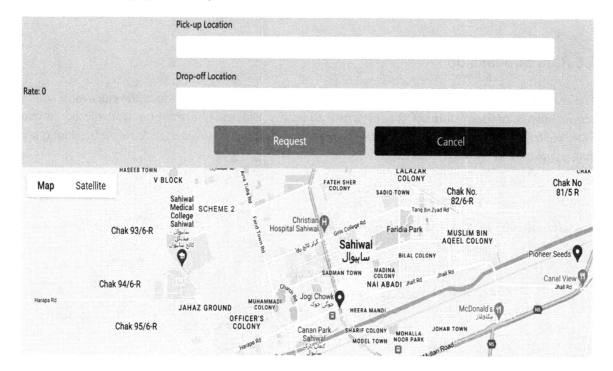

5.3 Rider Home Page

The screenshot below represents the rider's home page. Here the rider can choose his pick-up and drop-off locations using the map. After calculating the distance, the system also tells the rider about his total fare from pick-up to a drop-off location, as shown in Figure 4.

Figure 6. The home page screen of the rider

5.4 Ride Request

After entering the pick-up and drop-off locations, riders request the ride, and their ride information is uploaded into a map, which is now available to all active drivers at the time of request and where drivers have to accept or reject the ride, as shown in Figure 5.

Figure 7. The request for the ride

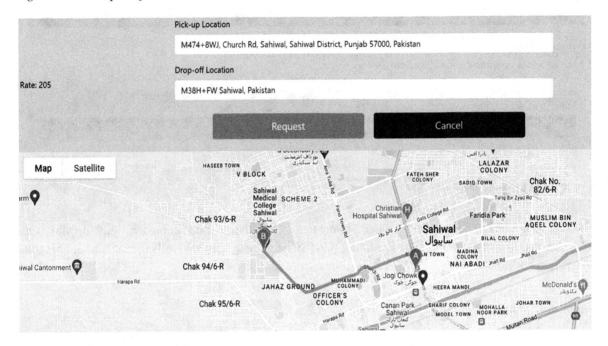

5.5 Ride Submission

The ride is posted to the map and uploaded to the Blockchain, following which the rider must wait a certain amount of time before offering his trip to all nearby vehicles. If no driver is available at a certain time, the trip is immediately canceled, and there are no expenses associated with this procedure other than gas prices, as shown in Figure 6.

Figure 8. The submission screen of the ride

Pick Up Location: M474+8WJ, Church Rd, Sahiwal, Sahiwal District, Punjab 57000, Pakistan   **Drop Off Location:** M38H+FW Sahiwal, Pakistan

Cancel

Ride Submitted! Waiting for a driver to accept your trip...

5.6 Driver Home Page

The screenshot below represents the driver's home page. Here the driver sets his location in the google map and updates his area of interest (radius). After entering the location and radius driver can see his area of interest covered in a red circle. The driver can now see all the ride requests from this area, as shown in Figure 7.

Figure 9. The home screen of the driver

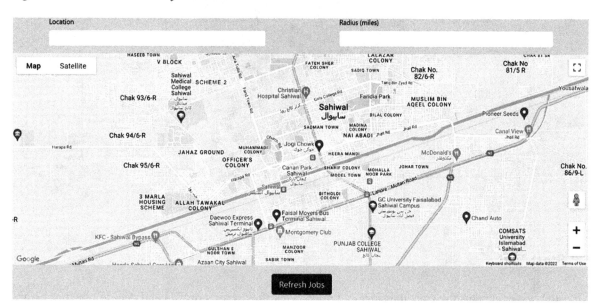

5.7 Ride Confirmation

Here the driver can see all the available rides near him; after checking the rides, request driver can confirm the ride he thinks is suitable according to his area of interest and fare; if he is not interested in the ride, he has not to accept the ride and the ride automatically vanish after a certain time as shown in Figure 8.

Figure 10. The confirmation of the ride

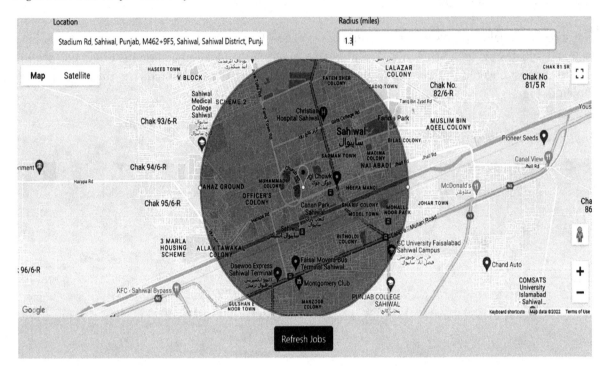

5.8 Start Trip

After the driver accepts the ride, the rider can now check the driver's profile and decide whether he has to ride with this driver or skip the driver. If he simply confirms the ride, the driver comes to pick up the rider, and if he cancels the offer, then the driver's request vanishes, as shown in Figure 9.

Figure 11. The trip starts on the screen

Pick Up Location: M38W+2HP, Sahiwal, Sahiwal District, Punjab 57000, Pakistan   **Drop Off Location:** M485+PG8, Sahiwal, Sahiwal District, Punjab 57000, Pakistan

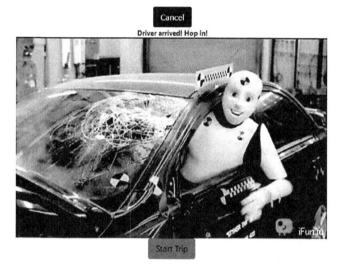

5.9 Drivers Arrival

After all the successful operations, the driver is on his way to the rider's place. Now the rider can see a window where he can see the live distance between him and the driver. With distance, he can also see another parameter of estimated time on his screen, as shown in Figure 10.

Figure 12. The notification of the driver's arrival

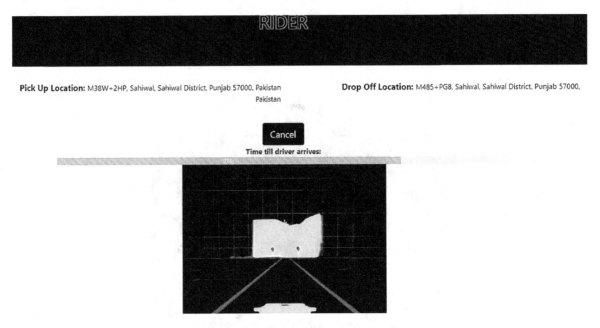

5.10 Riders Ride Progress

After the driver's arrival, the journey officially begins, and the rider may see the distance traveled as a progress bar on his home page. The money is also sent to the driver's wallets as the journey proceeds, as shown in Figure 11.

Figure 13. The history of the ride progress to the rider

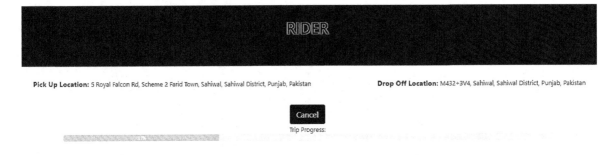

5.11 Drivers Ride Progress

The driver can also see the progress that he makes during the ride. The driver starts getting his trip payment while driving the car according to the distance he has covered at the current time of the ride, as shown in Figure 12.

Figure 14. The history of the ride progress to the driver

Pick Up Location: M39Q+2GC, Central Jail Ave, Central Jail Sahiwal, Sahiwal District, Punjab, Pakistan
Pakistan
Trip Progress:

Cancel

5.12 Ride Ends

After reaching the destination, trips cease immediately; the entire fare is removed from the passenger's account and sent to the driver's account. The driver and passenger may now submit another request after the conclusion of a successful journey, as shown in Figure 13.

Figure 15. The end screen of the ride

Pick Up Location: M38W+2HP, Sahiwal, Sahiwal District, Punjab 57000, Pakistan   Drop Off Location: M485+PG8, Sahiwal, Sahiwal District, Punjab 57000, Pakistan

Ride Complete!

Trip cost: 94

Back to login page

6. DISCUSSION

Our blockchain-based car-sharing network may be impacted by several things beyond the design above principles. These include the use of smart contracts, (ii) the use of immutable chains, (iii) the use of a central database, (iv) the use of decentralization, and (v) the formation of consortiums. Data immutability improves record traceability and dependability, which smart contracts focus on more than Blockchain Interoperability. The scalability and dependability are both improved by decentralization. Sharing databases may increase scalability and network throughput, and consortia have worked to solve problems of authenticity, interoperability, security, and privacy. We will talk briefly about each of these issues down below:

Smart contracts may improve confidence in the system while making it easier for various parties to cooperate. Due to the immutability of a smart contract, after it has been deployed, careful thought must be given to its logic design, interpretation, and legal status13 before it is put into action, with all applicable parties and their interests taken into account. However, the technical and legal growth of smart contracts will have significant implications for using blockchain-based shared mobility platforms, and this has to be developed in future studies.

Data immutability on the Blockchain is accomplished by hash references and an appropriate consensus mechanism, making it GDPR compliant. However, the viability and utility of implementing immutability in data storage must be assessed from various angles on a case-by-case basis. The proposed blockchain-based car-sharing network may collect personally identifiable (PII) data. The difficulty of erasing records/data from the Blockchain, which would leave the ledger in an inconsistent state, is compounded by the fact that people have the right to seek the deletion of their data (i.e., "Right to be Forgotten" (GDPR)). If the data is not removed, the Blockchain will violate GDPR. It has been shown by Faber et al. that storing personal data in off-chain repositories and then storing a hash reference on the Blockchain to that off-chain repository may make the data both immutable and GDPR-compliant (2019). Since the personal information in the off-chain repository can be confirmed using the hash value recorded in the hash pointer, the immutability characteristic of the Blockchain may be achieved by having a hash pointer on the Blockchain to the location of the personal data there. To further ensure compliance with GDPR, when an individual invokes their "Right to be Forgotten," all corresponding personal data stored in the off-chain repository must be deleted. In any case, the hash pointer saved on the Blockchain need not change, as the hash pointer without any identifying data on the off-chain repository exposes nothing. It solves the problem of how to store user data on the Blockchain.

Access rights may strike a balance between decentralization and power imbalance concerns like increased security but less oversight over data or the system (such as using permissioned Blockchain). For a permissioned blockchain, a group of stakeholders with the same influence oversees the consensus process and performs regular maintenance. An unbalanced distribution of power within the system might undermine the advantages of decentralized security. Therefore, OEM cooperation requires careful thought. When the validators utilize consensus to configure and fine-tune the network, certain consortium members may misuse their position of authority. They might base the terms of their deal on what is best for them individually (such as economic benefits). When implementing the planned high-level design, these details must be carefully evaluated.

According to Consortium Types, shared mobility on the Blockchain is still lacking in business use. We argue that a group of enterprises can work together to promote car sharing and other mobility services using blockchain technology. The mobility services consortium should be scalable and sustainable, and it should benefit all parties involved.14 The automotive industry's transformation through Blockchain and related technologies will be significant in the coming years, but the type of consortium that will lead the way is uncertain. Each consortium size has its advantages and disadvantages, comprising several enterprises or just one. It remains contingent upon factors like location, preexisting infrastructure, Blockchain tech advancements, and the availability of a dependable network.

The long-term objective will be to use blockchain technology's data- and resource-sharing capabilities to bring disparate car-sharing and other mobility services into a single, MaaS-style platform. Data and resource sharing can improve car sharing and leasing efficiency and effectiveness. Data silos on collaborative platforms would also be diminished by this method.

This shift toward platform and aggregation of services, which leads to the development of new value creation processes, is consistent with the ongoing transformation of the automotive industry, which is being propelled by digitalization. When combined with advanced Internet of Things (IoT) and digital twin, self-sovereign identity (SSI) technologies, car-sharing may gain new significance, especially once autonomous vehicles become safe for the road (e.g., earning money for renting out the car and paying for fuel). Therefore, to fully grasp the potential of acting autonomously in services, the proposed solution must be expanded to include careful consideration of cryptocurrencies and SSI. Finally, the end goal may be to centralize all mobility services on such a blockchain-based platform in the style of MaaS, shifting focus from the car to the passenger.

7. CONCLUSION

This research shows how blockchain technology, bitcoin, and smart contracts may be used to create a trustworthy, decentralized ride-hailing service that protects users' location data and personal information. The matching of drivers and ride requests is based on the Blockchain's consensus mechanism, making the system decentralized and independent of a central authority. In addition, the whole ride-sharing process (ride request, driver matching, and payment) takes place on the Blockchain. Only individuals who want to go on the journey learn its exact location; no personal information such as an email address, phone number, or payment card number is required. Here the driver sees his comforts and makes the rides suitable for him according to his route and fair. There is full control in the hands of the driver over whether he has to accept the ride; however, in some other centralized systems, if the driver does not accept a ride, he is fined for not accepting the ride. However, what is the matter is that they do not have any interest in that; they make sure that if a driver is online, he must take the requested ride. In this system, it is totally in the hands of the rider whether he has to take the full ride or cancel the ride in the middle, but this does not affect the driver's payment as he gets all his payments while progressing the trip.

8. FUTURE WORK

We will work on a new blockchain that works as proof of history and has a neglectable gas fee for deploying smart contracts, and we will also use its token to make financial transactions in this system.

REFERENCES

Ali, O., Ally, M., & Dwivedi, Y. (2020). *The state of play of blockchain technology in the financial services sector: A systematic literature review.* Academic Press.

Almusaylim, Z., & Jhanjhi, N. (2020). *Comprehensive review: Privacy protection of user in location-aware services of mobile cloud computing.* Academic Press.

Amir Latif, R. M., Hussain, K., Jhanjhi, N., Nayyar, A., & Rizwan, O. (2020). *A remix IDE: Smart contract-based framework for the healthcare sector by using Blockchain technology.* Academic Press.

Arora, A., & Yadav, S. K. (2018). Block chain based security mechanism for internet of vehicles (IoV). *Proceedings of 3rd international conference on internet of things and connected technologies (ICIoTCT).* 10.2139srn.3166721

Auer, S., Nagler, S., Mazumdar, S., & Mukkamala, R. (2022). *Towards blockchain-IoT based shared mobility: Car-sharing and leasing as a case study.* Academic Press.

Badr, M. M., Baza, M., Abdelfattah, S., Mahmoud, M., & Alasmary, W. (2021). *Blockchain-Based Ride-Sharing System with Accurate Matching and Privacy-Preservation.* Paper presented at the 2021 International Symposium on Networks, Computers and Communications (ISNCC). 10.1109/ISNCC52172.2021.9615661

Baza, M., Lasla, N., Mahmoud, M. M., Srivastava, G., & Abdallah, M. (2019). *B-ride: Ride sharing with privacy-preservation, trust and fair payment atop public blockchain.* Academic Press.

Baza, M., Mahmoud, M., Srivastava, G., Alasmary, W., & Younis, M. (2020). *A light blockchain-powered privacy-preserving organization scheme for ride sharing services.* Paper presented at the 2020 IEEE 91st Vehicular Technology Conference (VTC2020-Spring). 10.1109/VTC2020-Spring48590.2020.9129197

Bhattacharjee, A., Badsha, S., & Sengupta, S. (2020). *Blockchain-based secure and reliable manufacturing system.* Paper presented at the 2020 International Conferences on Internet of Things (iThings) and IEEE Green Computing and Communications (GreenCom) and IEEE Cyber, Physical and Social Computing (CPSCom) and IEEE Smart Data (SmartData) and IEEE Congress on Cybermatics (Cybermatics). 10.1109/iThings-GreenCom-CPSCom-SmartData-Cybermatics50389.2020.00052

Chai, H., Leng, S., Wu, F., & He, J. (2021). *Secure and Efficient Blockchain-Based Knowledge Sharing for Intelligent Connected Vehicles.* Academic Press.

De Filippi, P., Mannan, M., & Reijers, W. (2022). *The alegality of blockchain technology.* Academic Press.

Dungan, L., & Pop, M.-D. (2022). *Blockchain-based solutions for smart mobility sustainability assurance.* Paper presented at the IOP Conference Series: Materials Science and Engineering. 10.1088/1757-899X/1220/1/012057

Dutta, P., Choi, T.-M., Somani, S., & Butala, R. (2020). *Blockchain technology in supply chain operations: Applications, challenges and research opportunities.* Academic Press.

Goel, P., & Ghosh, M. (2021). Blockchain-Based Secure and Efficient Crowdsourcing Framework. In *Computer Networks and Inventive Communication Technologies* (pp. 391–406). Springer. doi:10.1007/978-981-15-9647-6_30

Gudymenko, I., Khalid, A., Siddiqui, H., Idrees, M., Clauß, S., Luckow, A., . . . Miehle, D. (2020). *Privacy-preserving blockchain-based systems for car sharing leveraging zero-knowledge protocols.* Paper presented at the 2020 IEEE international conference on decentralized applications and infrastructures (DAPPS). 10.1109/DAPPS49028.2020.00014

Gupta, R., & Shanbhag, S. (2021). *A Survey of Peer-to-Peer Ride Sharing Services using Blockchain.* Academic Press.

Hossan, M. S., Khatun, M. L., Rahman, S., Reno, S., & Ahmed, M. (2021). *Securing Ride-Sharing Service Using IPFS and Hyperledger Based on Private Blockchain.* Paper presented at the 2021 24th International Conference on Computer and Information Technology (ICCIT). 10.1109/ICCIT54785.2021.9689814

Huang, J., Luo, Y., Xu, M., Hu, B., & Long, J. (2022). pShare. *Privacy-Preserving Ride-Sharing System with Minimum-Detouring Route.* Academic Press.

Humayun, M., Jhanjhi, N., Hamid, B., & Ahmed, G. (2020). *Emerging smart logistics and transportation using IoT and blockchain.* Academic Press.

Humayun, M., Jhanjhi, N. Z., Niazi, M., Amsaad, F., & Masood, I. (2022). *Securing Drug Distribution Systems from Tampering Using Blockchain.* Academic Press.

Humayun, M., Niazi, M., Jhanjhi, N., Alshayeb, M., & Mahmood, S. (2020). *Cyber security threats and vulnerabilities: a systematic mapping study.* Academic Press.

Jani, K., Prakash, O., & Subramanian, C. B. (2021). *Developing Secured Peer to Peer Ride Sharing Services based on Blockchain Technology.* Academic Press.

Javed, M. U., Rehman, M., Javaid, N., Aldegheishem, A., Alrajeh, N., & Tahir, M. (2020). *Blockchain-based secure data storage for distributed vehicular networks.* Academic Press.

Jeong, B.-G., Youn, T.-Y., Jho, N.-S., & Shin, S. (2020). *Blockchain-based data sharing and trading model for the connected car.* Academic Press.

Julie, E. G., Nayahi, J. J. V., & Jhanjhi, N. Z. (2020). *Blockchain Technology: Fundamentals, Applications, and Case Studies.* CRC Press. doi:10.1201/9781003004998

Kakkar, R., Gupta, R., Agrawal, S., Tanwar, S., & Sharma, R. (2022). *Blockchain-based secure and trusted data sharing scheme for autonomous vehicle underlying 5G.* Academic Press.

Kakkar, R., Gupta, R., Alshehri, M. D., Tanwar, S., Dua, A., & Kumar, N. (2022). *Block-CPS: Blockchain and Non-Cooperative Game-based Data Pricing Scheme for Car Sharing.* Academic Press.

Kakkar, R., Gupta, R., Tanwar, S., & Rodrigues, J. (2021). *Coalition game and blockchain-based optimal data pricing scheme for ride sharing beyond 5g.* Academic Press.

Kakkar, R., Jadav, N. K., Gupta, R., Agrawal, S., & Tanwar, S. (2022). *Blockchain and Stackleberg Game-based Fair and Trusted Data Pricing Scheme for Ride Sharing.* Paper presented at the 2022 IEEE International Conference on Communications Workshops (ICC Workshops). 10.1109/ICCWorkshops53468.2022.9814704

Kudva, S., Badsha, S., Sengupta, S., Khalil, I., & Zomaya, A. (2021). *Towards secure and practical consensus for blockchain based VANET.* Academic Press.

Kumar, M. S., Vimal, S., Jhanjhi, N., Dhanabalan, S. S., & Alhumyani, H. (2021). *Blockchain based peer to peer communication in autonomous drone operation.* Academic Press.

Latif, R. M. A., Farhan, M., Rizwan, O., Hussain, M., Jabbar, S., & Khalid, S. (2021). *Retail level Blockchain transformation for product supply chain using truffle development platform.* Academic Press.

Latif, R. M. A., Iqbal, S., Rizwan, O., Shah, S. U. A., Farhan, M., & Ijaz, F. (2019). *Blockchain transforms the retail level by using a supply chain rules and regulation.* Paper presented at the 2019 2nd International Conference on Communication, Computing and Digital systems (C-CODE).

Namasudra, S., & Sharma, P. (2022). *Achieving a Decentralized and Secure Cab Sharing System Using Blockchain Technology*. Academic Press.

Pal, P., & Ruj, S. (2019). *BlockV: A blockchain enabled peer-peer ride sharing service*. Paper presented at the 2019 IEEE International Conference on Blockchain (Blockchain). 10.1109/Blockchain.2019.00070

Pan, X., Pan, X., Song, M., Ai, B., & Ming, Y. (2020). *Blockchain technology and enterprise operational capabilities: An empirical test*. Academic Press.

Perera, S., Nanayakkara, S., Rodrigo, M., Senaratne, S., & Weinand, R. (2020). *Blockchain technology: Is it hype or real in the construction industry?* Academic Press.

Qin, C., Guo, B., Shen, Y., Li, T., Zhang, Y., & Zhang, Z. (2020). *A secure and effective construction scheme for blockchain networks*. Academic Press.

Saad, M., Anwar, A., Ahmad, A., Alasmary, H., Yuksel, M., & Mohaisen, A. (2019). *RouteChain: Towards blockchain-based secure and efficient BGP routing*. Paper presented at the 2019 IEEE International Conference on Blockchain and Cryptocurrency (ICBC). 10.1109/BLOC.2019.8751229

Sedlmeir, J., Buhl, H. U., Fridgen, G., & Keller, R. (2020). *The energy consumption of blockchain technology: Beyond myth*. Academic Press.

Shafiq, D. A., Jhanjhi, N., & Abdullah, A. (2021). Load balancing techniques in cloud computing environment. *RE:view*.

Shafiq, D. A., Jhanjhi, N. Z., Abdullah, A., & Alzain, M. A. (2021). *A load balancing algorithm for the data centres to optimize cloud computing applications*. Academic Press.

Singh, M., & Kim, S. (2018). *Crypto trust point (cTp) for secure data sharing among intelligent vehicles*. Paper presented at the 2018 International Conference on Electronics, Information, and Communication (ICEIC). 10.23919/ELINFOCOM.2018.8330663

Valaštín, V., Košť'ál, K., Bencel, R., & Kotuliak, I. (2019). *Blockchain based car-sharing platform*. Paper presented at the 2019 International Symposium ELMAR. 10.1109/ELMAR.2019.8918650

Wang, D., & Zhang, X. (2020). *Secure ride-sharing services based on a consortium blockchain*. Academic Press.

Wang, Q., & Su, M. (2020). *Integrating blockchain technology into the energy sector—from theory of blockchain to research and application of energy blockchain*. Academic Press.

Wang, Y., Su, Z., Li, J., Zhang, N., Zhang, K., Choo, K.-K. R., & Liu, Y. (2021). *Blockchain-based secure and cooperative private charging pile sharing services for vehicular networks*. Academic Press.

Xiong, H., Dalhaus, T., Wang, P., & Huang, J. (2020). *Blockchain technology for agriculture: applications and rationale*. Academic Press.

Xu, C., Zhu, K., Yi, C., & Wang, R. (2020). *Data pricing for blockchain-based car sharing: A stackelberg game approach*. Paper presented at the GLOBECOM 2020-2020 IEEE Global Communications Conference. 10.1109/GLOBECOM42002.2020.9322221

Zhang, L., Luo, M., Li, J., Au, M. H., Choo, K.-K. R., Chen, T., & Tian, S. (2019). *Blockchain based secure data sharing system for Internet of vehicles: A position paper.* Academic Press.

Zhang, X., Liu, J., Li, Y., Cui, Q., Tao, X., & Liu, R. P. (2019). *Blockchain based secure package delivery via ridesharing.* Paper presented at the 2019 11th International Conference on Wireless Communications and Signal Processing (WCSP). 10.1109/WCSP.2019.8927952

Zhou, Q., Yang, Z., Zhang, K., Zheng, K., & Liu, J. (2020). *A decentralized car-sharing control scheme based on smart contract in internet-of-vehicles.* Paper presented at the 2020 IEEE 91st Vehicular Technology Conference (VTC2020-Spring). 10.1109/VTC2020-Spring48590.2020.9129439

Chapter 19
Open Governance in Budgeting and Financial Reporting:
A Case Study on the Local Governance of Bangladesh

Md. Abir Hasan Khan
Tampere University, Finland

Lasse O. Oulasvirta
Tampere University, Finland

Ari-Veikko Anttiroiko
Tampere University, Finland

ABSTRACT

This chapter discusses the adoption of open governance in public finance with a particular view to citizen-friendly budgeting and consistent financial reporting in local government in the developing country context. The authors are interested in how a concept that was developed in the Western world is adopted in developing countries. The objective is to shed light on local councilors' understanding of the conditions and development needs of open governance in budgeting and financial control in Bangladeshi municipalities. According to our survey conducted in 2018 with municipal managers and councilors, the key institutional actors consider that the conditions of open governance in local public finance are fairly good, financial information is provided systematically, and the competence level is sufficient among both citizens and representatives of local government. However, participatory methods and the utilization of digital tools in budgeting and financial reporting are still in their infancy.

DOI: 10.4018/978-1-6684-5284-4.ch019

1. INTRODUCTION

Public sector organizations are involved in various activities, which require the use of resources that must be planned and controlled. Among the most important aspects of this is public budgeting, which is essentially about the allocation of financial resources to government policies. Public financial management has been conceptualized primarily from the administrative and professional points of view, of which only a small proportion, mainly a budget and a balance sheet, has been open to political decision-making or public debates. In other words, the budget process has been kept firmly in the hands of leading politicians and public managers. We may, however, question this traditional view of public financial management, for it has its roots in elitism and competence issues that do not reflect today's realities. This issue is of vital importance in local government, which as a local democratic governmental jurisdiction has a close relationship with its citizens, who interact with local political-administrative systems as voters, inhabitants, workers, activists, and service users. Should they have better chances to have their say in public budgeting and financial management?

The approach to municipal financial management has been changing for some time. Among the most significant manifestations of this is the increased interest in participatory budgeting (Coleman and Sampaio 2017; Goldfrank, 2012; Brautigam, 2004; Souza, 2001). There is a good reason to assume that this gradual change is due to the increased demands for social inclusion and citizen engagement as well as to a generally perceived need for openness that reflects the idea of good governance. As in government functions in general, this also requires that budgeting and financial reporting overcomes its elitist, professional and administrative orientation and is opened to stakeholders from public, private and voluntary sectors.

Even if the demand for IAT (Integrity, Accountability, and Transparency) and other aspects of good governance is a widely accepted goal for public governance practically all over the world, the rhetoric does not match the reality (Porumbescu et al., 2022; Michener et al., 2021; Bauhr & Grimes, 2017; Matsiliza & Zonke, 2017; Hasan et al., 2014; Bergh, 2009). More often than not, governments claim to have adopted the principles of good governance, but the reality may be that public officials use their positions in an abusive way, information is not shared openly, and government units are not responsive enough. One of the root causes of such problems is the lack of openness and transparency, which are essential in striving for better public governance. This point has a heightened relevance at the time when digitalization is changing profoundly the way governments work and interact with their stakeholders.

The above challenges and opportunities are strongly context-dependent. This implies that advanced industrial democracies in the Western world with a long tradition of good governance have better preconditions for introducing financial management reforms than developing countries of the Global South (Blair, 2020). We focus on the latter country group and in this group especially on one case country, Bangladesh.

The issue is two-sided, for the first question is about the preconditions for municipalities in developing countries to improve the openness of their budgeting and financial reporting, while the second question is about the factual implementation of open and participatory budgeting and financial reporting in improving openness, transparency, and citizen-centred governance in municipalities. This discussion leads us to the issue of how the practices and arrangements designed originally in and for Western industrial democracies work in the developing country context (cf. Anttiroiko, 2017).

2. AIMS AND OBJECTIVES

In this chapter, we will discuss the role of openness in municipal budgeting and financial reporting with reference to the case of Bangladesh. What is of particular interest here is the developing country context in which the political, institutional, economic and societal structures are not sufficient in all respects for the realization of good governance, including public budgeting and financial management. Such challenges relate to all key actors of this setting, i.e. politicians, public managers, civil servants, the business community, and citizens.

At times developing and transitional countries perform better than is generally assumed, and they can be even pioneers in experimenting with new forms of governance, as with the role of Porto Alegre in the development of participatory budgeting and Belo Horizonte in e-participatory budgeting in Brazil (Baiocchi, 2001; Peixoto, 2008; Sintomer et al., 2008; Souza, 2001). In any case, it is worth scrutinizing to what extent the local governments of the Global South actually apply the principles of good governance to public finance.

To summarize, the objective of the chapter at hand is to assess the current state of development of the application of open governance in budgeting and financial management in local government in the developing country context, the empirical case being the local government in Bangladesh. The chapter focuses on the adoption of the open governance concept in municipalities to promote the scope of citizen participation in budgeting and financial reporting as seen by local councillors and public managers.

3. OPEN GOVERNANCE FRAMEWORK

3.1. Key Dimensions and Preconditions of Open Governance

In essence, open governance refers to a set of principles, policies, and practices that emphasize citizens' right to access public government information to allow for effective public oversight and democratic control.

Ruijer and Huff (2016) claim that open organizational culture is the precursor to effective open government. It affects both internal and external relations in the sense that it opens government information and engages key stakeholders in governance (OECD, 2016). This translates to a demand to remove barriers to participation and to make citizen involvement meaningful (Jetzek, Avital & Bjorn-Andersen, 2013). In this context, OECD (2016) emphasizes the need for understanding the dynamic nature of the open governance system and the need for proper change management, the latter including a transition from policy principles to policy catalysts and further to policy outcomes.

In the public financial management, IAT framework contains the core aspects of the integrity system that is designed to ensure the key institutional actors' commitment to the attainment of public good. Integrity is a fundamental category that brings into the picture the need for honesty and trustworthiness, which includes such requirements as making sure that financial reports are correct, consistent, and accurate. Accountability relates to responsibilities. Financial accountability requires that people holding political or administrative positions are kept accountable for their financial decisions and actions. Lastly, transparency refers to government's obligation to share relevant information with citizens. In financial management it implies an easy access to financial information about government and public policies. (Matsiliza & Zonke, 2017.)

In order for government to be truly open, certain conditions must be met. Among the most crucial are such as overcoming knowledge asymmetries, facilitating joint fact-finding, and enabling trust building (Kompella, 2017). Decreasing knowledge asymmetries helps not only to level the playing field between government and non-state stakeholders but also to empower citizens (Choi, Park, Rho & Zo, 2016; Karl, Susskind & Wallace, 2007)

Lastly, information and communication technologies (ICTs) have become among the most important factors behind the emergence of a new paradigm of public governance, the transformation of institutional and social organization of society, and the informatization that is essential in expanding citizens' knowledge and skills needed in smartening up governance (Ramos Chávez, 2015). Institutional arrangements must be supplemented by the utilization of new technologies that can significantly enhance IAT by providing new ways for information dissemination, government-society collaboration, and civic engagement and participation. Key components of the digital strategy for open governance are depicted in Figure 1.

Figure 1. Digital strategy in open governance concept.
(OECD, 2016).

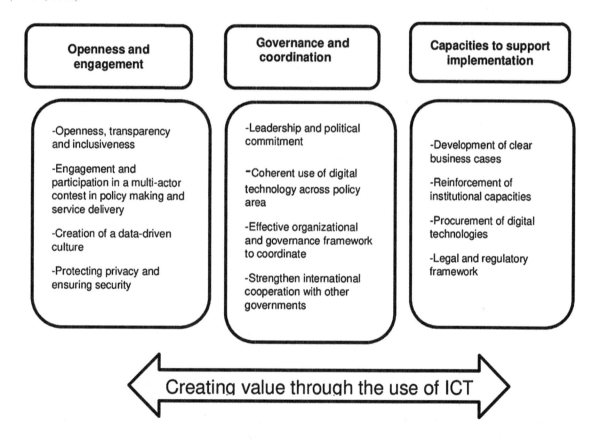

A particular aspect of openness in digital governance is open data, which has attracted increased attention in recent years in public sector reform discourses. The idea behind open data is to make government data freely accessible to the public for utilization, modification, and sharing (Chan, Johnson, & Shookner, 2016; Medina, Garcia, Juanes, Barrios & Yanes, 2014; Bartenberger & Grubmüller-Régent,

2014). It offers a range of economic, social and political benefits by enhancing service provision to meet individual and community demands and advancing citizen rights to access, modify, and share information, which both directly and indirectly increase IAT in public governance (Granickas, 2013; Zuiderwijk & Janssen, 2013; Veljković, Bogdanović-Dinić & Stoimenov, 2014). It paves the way for the building of a dynamic democratic polity (Beno, Figl, Umbrich & Polleres, 2017). It is worth emphasizing that this does not concern only developed countries. In most developing countries, governments have already embraced the idea of digitalization and have also utilized it in promoting open governance.

3.2. Open Governance in Budgeting and Financial Reporting

The principles and practices of IAT (Integrity, Accountability, and Transparency) will essentially improve the quality of budgeting and financial reporting in local governments. Budgets and financial reports are crucial elements of democratically steered public sector organizations. Budgetary reporting can be included in the broad concept of financial reporting (IPSASB, 2014). It can be separated from the concept of general purpose financial statements (GPFS) that consists of income statements, funds flow statements and balance sheets, which are all established statements in private sector accounting entities but are less frequently used by public sector entities. In the public sector and its tax-financed entities, budget and budgetary reporting form the core area of reporting, and provide the primary tool for accountable public entities to provide sufficient information to citizens and to show accountability.

Local self-government is a typical example of a commissioned economy that is run on behalf of citizens, who expect that they receive services organized by the local government as a return for their taxes and fees. They expect that activities are arranged in a cost-effective manner and produce "value-for-money" (Brusca, Manes Rossi & Aversano, 2015).

In this context of local government, a well-functioning chain of accountability runs from administration to the local council and further to citizens. Councillors are in charge of budget decision-making and steering the administration that implements the authoritative budgets decided by the council. Financial reporting should assist in fulfilling government's duty to be publicly accountable and should enable users to assess that accountability in a transparent way. Governmental financial reporting should provide information to assist users in (a) assessing accountability and (b) making economic, social, and political decisions. The duty to be publicly accountable in a many-sided way is more significant in governmental financial reporting than in business enterprise financial reporting (Mann, et.al. 2019; GASB, 1987, 22–23).

This accountability approach is connected to such reporting process outcomes as budget out-turn reports and other financial reports, including financial statement calculations, and to the citizens' right to know how the accountable public entities have succeeded. One of the main purposes of our article is to investigate such accountability in local governments in developing countries. Concerning the new tools associated with digital governance, we focus on such new tools and media that are feasible in developing countries, in which traditional paper formats of reporting may not be that accessible when compared with new media devices, most notably social media sites. These may offer not only new ways of reaching citizens after the budget year has passed, and of reporting for accountability purposes in order to grant discharge from liability, but also during the preparation of budgets. This turnsour interest to participatory budgeting in its several modes, both inside the public organizations and towards external stakeholders of which citizens form the most important category. This matter is addressed in the research, as illustrated in Figure 2.

Figure 2. Integrating the scheme into budgeting and reporting.

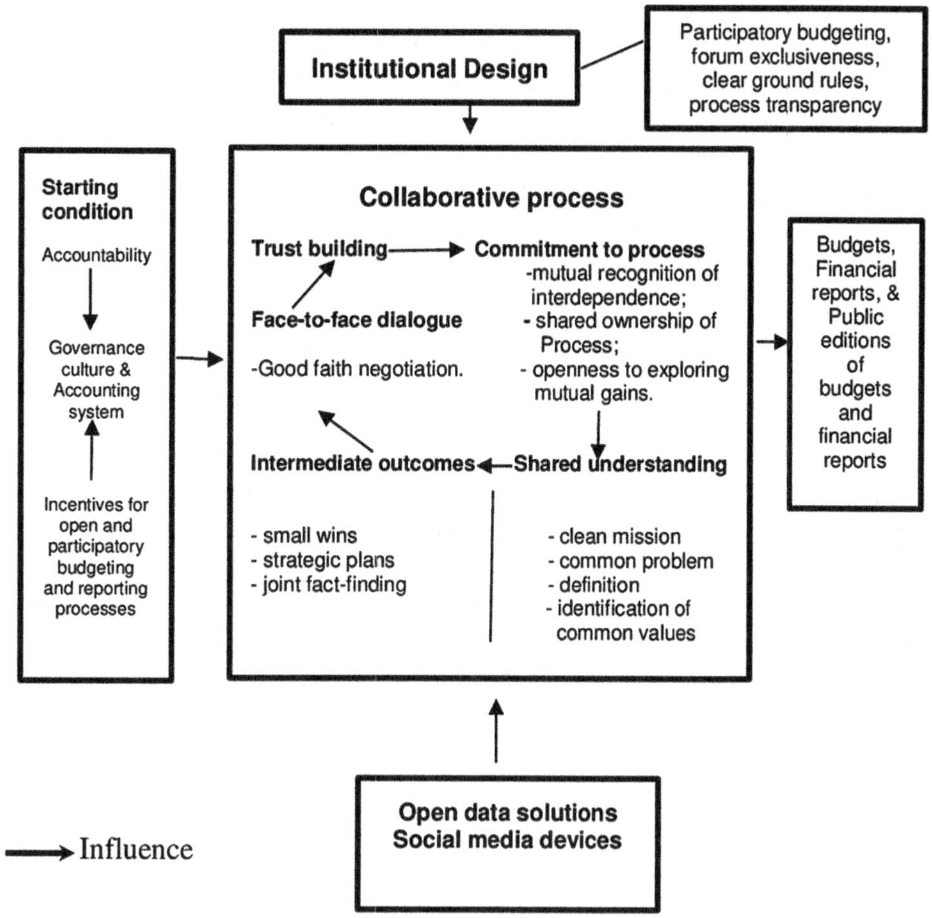

4. CONTEXT AND METHODOLOGY

4.1. Municipal Governance of Bangladesh

Bangladesh has two types of municipal corporations i.e., city corporations at the divisional level, while at district and sub-district levels the municipalities are named as Pourashavas. The eight largest cities have city corporation status in Bangladesh and the rest of the urban municipal corporations are known as *Pourashavas* (Khan, 2017).

City corporations and *Pourashavas* are led by mayors and councillors who are elected directly in local elections for the five-year term. Mayors are the heads of the city corporations and *Pourashavas*.

The budgeting systems in municipalities are monitored and financed by the Ministry of Local Government, Rural Development and Cooperatives. However, the mayor and councillors are responsible for preparing their budget on their own in order to allocate resources for a range of functions, such as public health and hospitals, education, and social welfare.

4.2. Research Methodology

The municipality is the area of focus of this research. The sample of the research is the councillors of the municipalities. The councillors form the elected body of the municipality. They are elected in direct elections of the respective area. Therefore, councillors both represent their voters and are accountable to them.

The data collection and analysis are based on conventional quantitative survey methodology. The primary data is collected using a questionnaire, which consists of closed-ended survey questions. In addition to this, there is also one open-ended question at the end of the questionnaire. The samples of the research have been selected based on the random selection process among the municipalities of Bangladesh. Eventually, in order to rationalize the research outcomes, multiple case areas have been considered and selected.

Three research assistants from different regions of Bangladesh assisted us in conducting the survey at the end of summer 2018. Among the 64 district municipalities, research assistants randomly selected eight case municipalities. In order to ensure research validity and reliability they contacted and reserved interview time with a few councillors from each municipality. Moreover, to broaden the view of local political and administrative leadership, research assistants also interviewed the mayor of each municipality, along with the chief executive officer (CEO) of the municipality. In each municipality the research had thus 4–6 respondents. Each interview session lasted from one to two hours.

5. FINDINGS

The open governance concept emphasizes openness, transparency and citizen engagement in a coordinativeway. . The first question addresses the very fundamental question of how the politicians and political and administrative leaders of Bangladeshi municipalities assess the current state of development. Is there enough openness in their governance system? The view of respondents on this issue are shown in Table 1.

Table 1. Bangladeshi municipalities included in this study. Open governance concept into the municipal governance system: Q2.2. Currently, we have enough openness and transparency in our municipality. (Councillor is 1, municipal secretary or CEO is 2).

Municipalities, Used for Empirical Data Collection	Description at a Glance
1. Lakshmipur	The Lakshmipur district municipality, with a population of 1,729,188 (according to the 2011 census), is situated in Chattagram division.
2. Chuadanga	The Chuadanga district municipality is situated in the Khulna division. According to the 2011 census, this district has a population of 1,129,015.
3. Netrokona	This district municipality is situated in northern Bangladesh under the Mymensingh division. Here, the total population is 2,229,642 (2011 census).
4. Dinajpur	This is another northern district municipality of Bangladesh, and is situated in the Rangpur division. 2,990,128 people populate this district (2011 census).
5. Naogaon	This district municipality is part of the Rajshahi division. This district's population is 2,600,157 people (2011 census).
6. Sylhet	Sylhet is a very old and famous district and divisional corporation of Bangladesh, and is the administrative centre of some other nearer districts. According to the 2016 census, the district has a population of 3,957,000.
7. Barishal	This district and divisional municipality is situated in the south-central part of Bangladesh. The total population of this district is 2,324,310 (2011 census).
8. Gazipur	This district is situated in the capital division of Dhaka. In many aspects, this is the most famous district of Bangladesh. This district has a total population of 3,403,912 (2011 census).

Municipal representatives emphasize that there is enough openness and transparency in their municipalities. Furthermore, it seems that CEOs agree strongly to a greater degree than elected representatives do. Among the 32 councillors only 25% strongly agreed with the statement, and on the other hand, 85.7% of CEOs were very positive and strongly agreed on the municipality's transparency and openness (see Table 1). What is understood as "enough" on sensitive issues like openness and transparency obviously varies between people. Therefore, the following detailed questions are supposed to help in elaborating this issue regarding various aspects of citizen involvement in municipal financial management..

In Table 2, councillors have answered about the feedback system from local people in the municipality's budgetary and financial matters. Among the total 39 respondents, only 3 (7.7%) have answered positively that there are established feedback mechanisms in municipalities' budgeting and financial affairs. This indicates that in the case of the municipality, the participation and collaboration processes are not satisfactory regarding internet feedback systems. If it is assumed that paid officials know the factual situation better than councillors, the majority of subject municipalities are not using internet feedback systems at all, which is a poor method of meeting the requirement of the modern concept of open governance.

Table 2. Open governance concept into the municipal governance system: Q2.2. Currently, we have enough openness and transparency in our municipality. (Councillor is 1, municipal secretary or CEO is 2). How much participatory opportunity do you have for local people in preparing the annual budget before it is formally accepted? Q4.2. Internet feedback system. (Councillor is 1, municipal secretary or CEO is 2).

		Currently, We Have Enough Openness and Transparency in Our Municipality				Total
		Barely Agree at All	Agree to Some Extent	Agree	Strongly Agree	
Councillors Municipal secretary or CEO	Count	2	6	16	8	32
	%	6.3%	18.8%	50.0%	25.0%	100.0%
	Count	0	0	1	6	7
	%	0.0%	0.0%	14.3%	85.7%	100.0%
Total	Count	2	6	17	14	39
	%	5.1%	15.4%	43.6%	35.9%	100.0%

Along with the feedback systems, budgetary and financial issues in local governance are in quite a poor state in terms of the utilization of various ICT tools and Internet. In Table3, it can be seen that in the case of using different methods of delivering financial reports to the mass of people, most of the respondents have shown that they do not have any way of delivering budgetary and financial matters to the mass of people via social media.

Table 3. How much participatory opportunity do you have for local people in preparing the annual budget before it is formally accepted? Q4.2. Internet feedback system. (Councillor is 1, municipal secretary or CEO is 2). Which of the following ways are used in your municipality? Q3.5. Use of social media, i.e. Facebook, YouTube, etc. to inform local people regarding the budget. (Councillor is 1, municipal secretary or CEO is 2).

		How Much Participatory Opportunity Do You Have for Local People in Preparing the Annual Budget Before It Is Formally Accepted?				Total
		Not Used at All in My Municipality	Sometimes, Not in an Established Way	Every Year, in an Established Way	I Do Not Know	
Councillors Municipal secretary or CEO	Count	16	6	3	7	32
	%	50.0%	18.8%	9.4%	21.9%	100.0%
	Count	6	1	0	0	7
	%	85.7%	14.3%	0.0%	0.0%	100.0%
Total	Count	22	7	3	7	39
	%	56.4%	17.9%	7.7%	17.9%	100.0%

In Table 4, in most cases the councillors have mentioned that their respective municipalities publish their annual report every year in an established way. On the other hand, the popular edition of the financial report has not been published in an established way but rather (Table 5) only on some particular occasion.

Table 4. Which of the following ways are used in your municipality? Q3.1. The annual report, after the budget year, is published as a whole as a paper format. (Councillor is 1, municipal secretary or CEO is 2).

		Ways of Delivering Financial Reporting Information to People: Use of Social Media, i.e. Facebook, YouTube etc. to Inform Local People Regarding Budget				Total
		Not Used at All in My Municipality	Sometimes, Not in an Established Way	Every Year, in an Established Way	I Do Not Know	
Councillors Municipal secretary or CEO	Count	19	7	2	4	32
	%	59.4%	21.9%	6.3%	12.5%	100.0%
	Count	5	1	1	0	7
	%	71.4%	14.3%	14.3%	0.0%	100.0%
Total	Count	24	8	3	4	39
	%	61.5%	20.5%	7.7%	10.3%	100.0%

Table 5. Which of the following ways are used in your municipality? Q3.1. The annual report, after the budget year, is published as a whole as a paper format. (Councillor is 1, municipal secretary or CEO is 2). Which of the following ways are used in your municipality? Q3.2. The annual report, after the budget year, is published as a popular edition. (Councillor is 1, municipal secretary or CEO is 2).

		Ways of Delivering Financial Reporting Information to People: The Annual Report, After the Budget Year, Is Published as a Paper Format			Total
		Sometimes, Not in an Established Way	Every Year, in an Established Way	I Do Not Know	
Councillors Municipal secretary or CEO	Count	2	29	1	32
	%	6.3%	90.6%	3.1%	100.0%
	Count	1	6	0	7
	%	14.3%	85.7%	0.0%	100.0%
Total	Count	3	35	1	39
	%	7.7%	89.7%	2.6%	100.0%

A confusing part of councillors' and officials' statements is shown in Table 6. They have answered in most cases that they need to learn to some extent about the financial statement.

Table 6. Which of the following ways are used in your municipality? Q3.2. The annual report, after the budget year, is published as a popular edition. (Councillor is 1, municipal secretary or CEO is 2). Q1.4. I would need to learn a lot in order to cope with the financial statement of my municipality. (Councillor is 1, municipal secretary or CEO is 2).

		Ways of Delivering Financial Reporting Information to people: The Annual Report, After the Budget Year, Is Published as a Popular Edition					Total
		Not Used at All in My Municipality	Sometimes, Not in an Established Way	Every Year, in an Established Way	I Do Not Know	5	
Councillors Municipal secretary or CEO	Count	4	18	5	4	1	32
	%	12.5%	56.3%	15.6%	12.5%	3.1%	100.0%
	Count	0	4	2	1	0	7
	%	0.0%	57.1%	28.6%	14.3%	0.0%	100.0%
Total	Count	4	22	7	5	1	39
	%	10.3%	56.4%	17.9%	12.8%	2.6%	100.0%

On the other hand, in defining the knowledge of citizens, councillors and officials have said that citizens are in most cases capable of understanding municipal financial reporting (Table 7). At first look, this is a confusing statement, if one assumes that in developing countries especially people may be for many reasons excluded from reading and understanding financial reporting text. However, one must notice that this is an opinion of the respondents about citizens' capabilities. Furthermore, respondents answered about their own need to learn and to cope with financial statements, which are difficult to understand for ordinary people without accounting training. Respondents' opinions about citizens' ability to read and understand make a reference to financial reporting, which also contains other financial reporting such as budgets and popular editions of budgets. Nonetheless, respondents did not have pessimistic opinions about people's ability to handle municipal financial reporting, and this result should then effect on municipal decision-makers in their responsibility for advancing open governance in public and transparent reporting to citizens, to whom they are accountable.

Table 7. Q1.4. I would need to learn a lot in order to cope with the financial statement of my municipality. (Councillor is 1, municipal secretary or CEO is 2). Q1.5. I think that citizens are able to read and understand the financial reporting of my municipality. (Councillor is 1, municipal secretary or CEO is 2)

		Reporting of My Municipality: I Would Need to Learn a Lot in Order to Cope With the Financial Statement of My Municipality					Total
		Do Not Agree at All	I Barely Agree at All	Agree to Some Extent	Agree	Strongly Agree	
Councillors Municipal secretary or CEO	Count	2	7	9	7	7	32
	%	6.3%	21.9%	28.1%	21.9%	21.9%	100.0%
	Count	0	1	3	2	1	7
	%	0.0%	14.3%	42.9%	28.6%	14.3%	100.0%
Total	Count	2	8	12	9	8	39
	%	5.1%	20.5%	30.8%	23.1%	20.5%	100.0%

Along with the aspects described above, this research also included other survey questions. Most of the respondents (59%) wanted accrual accounting rather than cash accounting in their municipalities. Most had quite a positive view about the status of open governance in their local governments. For instance, the respondents also believed (64.1%) that their respective municipality published financial statements in a timely manner, and that the financial statements were user-friendly (38.5% agreed and 48.7% strongly agreed) and were well-integrated (43.6% agreed and 38.5% strongly agreed). Moreover, the councillors and CEOs have acknowledged that they understand the open governance concept very well (20.5% agreed and 56.4% strongly agreed). In the case of the right of stakeholders to participate in budgeting and municipal financial matters, respondents have given positive feedback (i.e., 35.9% agreed and 41% strongly agreed). Besides, both councillors and CEOs have shown their strong positive attitude and trust towards the management of their respected municipalities (28.2% agreed and 66.7% strongly agreed). All this means that the decision-makers and those in power should also bring these thoughts into reality as much as possible. Regarding this, the survey shows that the opinions about the factual situation in some open governance matters are still immature, although in some matters they are well established. The following discussions give further evidence of this.

Table 8. Q1.5. I think that citizens are able to read and understand the financial reporting of my municipality. (Councillor is 1, municipal secretary or CEO is 2)

		Reporting of My Municipality: I Think That Citizens Are Able to Read and Understand Financial Reporting of My Municipality				Total
		I Barely Agree at All	**Agree to Some Extent**	**Agree**	**Strongly Agree**	
Councillors Municipal secretary or CEO is 2	Count	1	11	12	8	32
	%	3.1%	34.4%	37.5%	25.0%	100.0%
	Count	0	2	3	2	7
	%	0.0%	28.6%	42.9%	28.6%	100.0%
Total	Count	1	13	15	10	39
	%	2.6%	33.3%	38.5%	25.6%	100.0%

The survey questionnaire finally had some important questions on the availability of budgetary and financial information to the stakeholders. 64.1% of the respondents answered that the annual budget is published on the municipal website every year. In addition, 46.2% of respondents answered that public hearings on the budget and its outcomes happen every year, though not following a particular meeting format, whereas the same share of respondents (46.2%) said that the meeting was held every year in an established way. In the case of participatory opportunities for preparing the annual budget, 71.8% of respondents have agreed that the participatory budget meeting was held every year following an established procedure.

In order to define the role of local councillors, the researchers have asked the councillor's promptness in contacting local people and vice versa. Councillors demonstrated that they are quite communicative with local people (46.9% responded that they contact local people very often and 31.3% responded that they contact often). Moreover, local people also contact them often (28.1%) or very often (46.9%).

Beside the close-ended questions, there were also an open-ended question to identify the actual problems in municipal budgetary and financial matters. In the most common cases, the respondents pointed out that they needed skilled staff in building momentum for budgeting and public finance that is genuinely transparent and participatory. This is an important indication of the future needs of opening budgets and financial processes in Bangladeshi municipalities.

6. DISCUSSION

In the Western countries there are high hopes for building the culture of openness and transparency with the help of ICTs (Bertot et al., 2010; Bartenberger & Grubmüller-Régent, 2014; Chan et al., 2016; Jetzek et al., 2013; Veljković et al., 2016). This may not be the case in the developing countries, however, at least in the short term. Research results indicate that integrating ICTs in the financial and budgetary processes does not seem to provide the solution in the Bangladeshi context due to various political, cultural, societal, and technological reasons. Local conditions are seen to be fairly good even without the deployment of the new ICTs in budgeting and financial reporting. This entails that the development of openness in financial reporting and budgeting must be based on the specific preconditions of the given context.

Regarding large urban municipalities in Bangladesh, the preconditions for good governance are seen to be satisfactory. According to respondents, there is enough openness and transparency in budgeting and financial matters. Whether this is objectively true cannot be answered with an opinion survey only to councillors and managers. Such a positive view was balanced by equally critical remarks. Most notably, our survey shows that there is still much to do in developing modern new ways of transparency and of involving people in governance processes in budgeting and reporting. In the same vein the facilitation of participation in municipal budgeting and financial reporting is still in its infancy. This observation is in line with the findings of prior research on various aspects of good governance in developing countries (e.g. Krah & Mertens, 2020; Purwanto, Zuiderwijk & Janssen, 2020; Choi, Park, Rho & Zo, 2016; Khan & Anttiroiko, 2014).

Research surveys show that the annual financial reports are published every year in the way that fulfils local and national requirements. Financial statements are published in a timely manner and were assumed to be user-friendly. Politicians seem to trust in the financial administration of the municipality in this matter. They are also confident of their constituents' ability to understand sufficiently financial reports. In this sense the current situation contains a many encouraging signs.

On the other hand, there is still need to improve capacity and awareness of enhanced ways of transparent and participatory municipal budgeting and financial reporting.. Moreover, a true sense of openness and transparency as well as citizen engagement have their obvious challenges, too. Local political and administrative leaders are aware of the idea of 'open governance', but its realization is somewhat complex process that is conditioned by the underlying local realities.

This survey indicates that the local political elites have a fairly positive view of the overall functioning of the current budgeting and financial system, which implies that there is no particularly strong desire or urgent need for reforming the system towards greater openness and transparency. What would then be the drivers or pressures that might push open governance further? Let us discuss next three of the most prominent factors, i.e. participatory turn in democratic system, political leadership, and digital revolution (see Bergh, 2009; Bertot et al., 2020; Anttiroiko, 2017; Schnell, 2020).

To begin with, the rise of civil society and increased political participation within democratic system has its limits due to prevailing culture and political system in Bangladesh (Khan, 2017). In short, even if people are inspired by democratic ideals and the country has gone through democratic struggles for several decades, the path towards democracy continues to be cumbersome (Alam, 2019; cf. Bergh, 2009; Souza, 2001). An alternative route is paved with national political leadership, government intervention, and the introduction of administrative reforms. There are such tendencies in the central government, even though their impact on municipal government is varied and at times difficult to manage (Khan, 2017; 2018). The central government may also lead by example, as the government of Bangladesh has done with the development of e-government, for example (Khan & Anttiroiko, 2014).

Another external driver of change is the ICTs, which has an apparent potential to increase openness (Bertot et al., 2010). Could technological development overcome some hindrances associated with political culture, leadership and administrative reforms and thus provide a shortcut to open government (see e.g. Kompella, 2017; Choi et al., 2016; Khan, 2018; Veljković et al., 2014; Zuiderwijk & Janssen, 2013)? Currently it seems that even if Bangladesh supports many open governance initiatives, such as Bangladesh Open Data (http://data.gov.bd/), there is still no research findings of extent of factual transparency experienced by the people at the local level. In this regard the case of Bangladesh reflects the prevailing features of the global open government trend as portrayed by Schnell (2020). As concluded by Schnell (2020), technological tools for openness are not sufficient as such for ensuring systemic government openness.

Survey results confirm the assumption that in the given context digitalization may be more a promise than a factual impactful practice implemented in a consistent way. There are too many underdeveloped aspects in the use of ICTs in opening data, preparing and disseminating financial reports, and organizing feedback systems. There is actually a particular trap in such an ICT-based view of open government, for it may distance local government from rights-based view of openness and civil society involvement while at the same time being devoid of the blessings of the new technological advances that form the premise of global open government trend (Schnell, 2020). Such a trap may create technocrats without technological advancements that produce digital participatory feedback that also have an impact on budget decision making.

7. CONCLUSION

Municipalities in Bangladesh have developed budgeting and financial reporting systems that are seen to be sufficiently transparent. This is the view held especially by the chief executive officers. Yet, feedback systems are not particularly sophisticated, and the digital tools are still underutilized to a great extent. Against the high hopes of the role of ICTs in building open government, one of the future challenges is to assess how the traditional municipal system can be developed to enhance openness, while at the same time building better understanding of and preconditions for the greater utilization of digital tools in promoting openness in budgeting and financial reporting in developing countries.

REFERENCES

Alam, M. F. (2019). Democratization in Bangladesh: Past, Present and Future. *International Journal of Science and Business*, *3*(1), 156–166.

Anttiroiko, A.-V. (2017). Emulating models of good governance: Learning from the developments of the world's least corrupt countries. *International Journal of Public Policy*, *13*(1/2), 21–35. doi:10.1504/IJPP.2017.081043

Baiocchi, G. (2001). Participation, activism and politics: The Porto Alegre case and deliberative democratic theory. *Politics & Society*, *29*(1), 43–72. doi:10.1177/0032329201029001003

Bartenberger, M. & Grubmüller-Régent, V. (2014). The enabling effects of open government data on collaborative governance in smart city context. *The eJournal of eDemocracy and Open Government*, *6*(1), 36-48.

Bauhr, M., & Grimes, M. (2017). Transparency to curb corruption? Concepts, measures and empirical merit. *Crime, Law, and Social Change*, *68*(4), 431–458. doi:10.100710611-017-9695-1

Beno, M., Figl, K., Umbrich, J. & Polleres, A. (2017). Perception of key barriers in using and publishing open data. *The eJournal of eDemocracy and Open Government*, *9*(2), 134-165.

Bergh, S. I. (2009). Constraints to strengthening public sector accountability through civil society: The case of Morocco. *International Journal of Public Policy*, *4*(3/4), 344–365. doi:10.1504/IJPP.2009.023496

Bertot, J. C., Jaeger, P. T., & Grimes, J. M. (2010). Using ICTs to create a culture of transparency: E-government and social media as openness and anti-corruption tools for societies. *Government Information Quarterly*, *27*(3), 264–271. doi:10.1016/j.giq.2010.03.001

Blair, H. (2020). Accountability through participatory budgeting in India: Only in Kerala? In S. Cheema (Ed.), *Governance for urban services: Access, participation, accountability, and transparency* (pp. 57–76). Springer, Singapore. doi:10.1007/978-981-15-2973-3_3

Brautigam, D. (2004). The people's budget? politics, participation and pro-poor policy. *Development Policy Review*, *22*(6), 653–668. doi:10.1111/j.1467-7679.2004.00270.x

Brusca, I. Rossi, F.M. & Aversano, N. (2015). Drivers for the financial condition of local government: a comparative study between Italy and Spain. *Lex Localis - Journal of Local Self-Government*, *13*(2), 161-184.

Chan, M., Johnson, P.A. & Shookner, M. (2016). Assessing the use of government open data and the role of data infomediaries: The case of Nova Scotia's Community Counts Program. *The eJournal of eDemocracy and Open Government*, *8*(1), 1-27.

Choi, H., Park, M. J., Rho, J. J., & Zo, H. (2016). Rethinking the assessment of e-government implementation in developing countries from the perspective of the design-reality gap: Application in the Indonesian e-procurement system. *Telecommunications Policy*, *40*(7), 644–660. doi:10.1016/j.telpol.2016.03.002

GASB. (1987). *Objectives of Financial Reporting. Concepts Statement No. 1 of the Governmental Accounting Standards Board. NO. 037, MAY 1987*. Government Standard Accounting Board.

Goldfrank, B. (2012). The World Bank and globalization of participatory budgeting. *Journal of Public Deliberation, 8*(2), article,7.

Granickas, K. (2013). *Understanding the impact of releasing and re-using open government data.* Retrieved April 25, 2016 from https://www.epsiplatform.eu/content/understanding-impactreleasing-and-re-using-open-government-data

Hasan, B., Sultana, M., & Hasan, M. N. (2014). Good governance in Bangladesh: Problems and prospects. *UITS Journal, 3*(2), 22–44.

IPSASB. (2014). *The Conceptual Framework for General Purpose Financial Reporting by Public Sector Entities.* Retrieved from http://html5.epaperflip.com/?docid=9c3c49a0-9d06-49e1-b666-a5600137e9a9#page=1

Jetzek, T., Avital, M., & Bjorn-Andersen, N. (2013). Generating Value from Open Government Data. *Proceedings of Thirty Fourth International Conference on Information Systems.*

Karl, H. A., Susskind, L. E., & Wallace, K. H. (2007). A Dialogue, not a Diatribe: Effective Integration of Science and Policy through Joint Fact Finding. *Environment, 49*(1), 20–34. doi:10.3200/ENVT.49.1.20-34

Khan, M. A. H. & Anttiroiko, A. V. (2014). Democratizing digital Bangladesh: designing national web portal to facilitate government-citizen interaction. In L. G. Anthopoulos & C. G. Reddick (Eds.), Government e-strategic planning and management: Practices, patterns and roadmaps (pp. 245-261). New York, NY: Springer.

Khan, M. A. H. (2017). E-readiness of public administration in developing countries: A case study on Bangladesh public administration. Tampere University Press.

Khan, M. A. H. (2018). Administrative efficiency and effectiveness with the application of e-government: A study on Bangladesh public administration. In S. Saeed, T. Ramayah, & Z. Mahmood (Eds.), User centric e-government: Challenges and opportunities (pp. 105-116). New York, NY: Springer.

Kompella, L. (2017). E-governance systems as socio-technical transitions using multi-level perspective with case studies. *Technological Forecasting and Social Change, 123*, 80–94. doi:10.1016/j.techfore.2017.06.024

Krah, R., & Mertens, G. (2020). Democracy and financial transparency of local governments in Sub-Saharan Africa. *Meditari Accountancy Research, 28*(4), 681–699. doi:10.1108/MEDAR-08-2019-0539

Mann, B., Lorson, P. C., Oulasvirta, L., & Haustein, E. (2019). The Quest for a Primary EPSAS Purpose – Insights from Literature and Conceptual Frameworks. *Accounting in Europe, 16*(2), 195–218. doi:10.1080/17449480.2019.1632467

Matsiliza, N., & Zonke, N. (2017). Accountability and integrity as unique column of good governance. *Public and Municipal Finance, 6*(1), 75–82. doi:10.21511/pmf.06(1).2017.08

Medina, L.M.G., Garcia, J.L.R., Juanes, G.G., Barrios, A.R. & Yanes, P.G. (2014). Open data strategies and experiences to improve sharing and publication of public sector information. *The eJournal of eDemocracy and Open Government, 6*(1), 80-86.

Michener, G., Coelho, J., & Moreira, D. (2021). Are governments complying with transparency? Findings from 15 years of evaluation. *Government Information Quarterly*, *38*(2), 101565. doi:10.1016/j.giq.2021.101565

OECD. (2016). Open Government in Indonesia. OECD Public Governance Review. OECD Publishing.

Peixoto, T. (2008). e-Participatory Budgeting: e-Democracy from Theory to Success? SSRN *Electronic Journal*. doi:10.2139/ssrn.1273554

Porumbescu, G., Meijer, A., & Grimmelikhuijsen, S. (2022). *Government Transparency: State of the Art and New Perspectives (Elements in Public Policy)*. Cambridge University Press. doi:10.1017/9781108678568

Purwanto, A., Zuiderwijk, A., & Janssen, M. (2020). Citizen engagement with open government data: Lessons learned from Indonesia's presidential election. *Transforming Government: People, Process and Policy*, *14*(1), 1–30. doi:10.1108/TG-06-2019-0051

Ramos Chávez, H. A. (2015). Information and citizenship: A governance perspective. *Investigación Bibliotecológica: Archivonomía. Bibliotecología e Información*, *29*(67), 113–140. doi:10.1016/j.ibbai.2016.04.006

Ruijer, E. H. J. M., & Huff, R. F. (2016). Breaking through barriers: the impact of organizational culture on open government reform. *Transforming Government: People, Process and Policy*, *10*(2), 335–350.

Schnell, S. (2020). Vision, Voice, and Technology: Is There a Global "Open Government" Trend? *Administration & Society*, *52*(10), 1593–1620. doi:10.1177/0095399720918316

Sintomer, Y., Herzberg, C., & Röcke, A. (2008). From Porto Alegre to Europe: Potentials and Limitations of Participatory Budgeting (PDF). *International Journal of Urban and Regional Research*.

Souza, C. (2001). Participatory budgeting in Brazilian cities: Limits and possibilities in building democratic institutions. *Environment and Urbanization*, *13*(1), 159–184. doi:10.1177/095624780101300112

Veljković, N., Bogdanović-Dinić, S., & Stoimenov, L. (2014). Benchmarking open government: An open data perspective. *Government Information Quarterly*, *31*(2), 278–290. doi:10.1016/j.giq.2013.10.011

Zuiderwijk, A., & Janssen, M. (2013). Open data policies, their implementation and impact: A framework for comparison. *Government Information Quarterly*, *31*(1), 17–29. doi:10.1016/j.giq.2013.04.003

APPENDIX

1. Survey Questionnaire

Figure 3.

Q1. Do you think that it is necessary to have accrual accounting instead of cash accounting in your municipality?

Cash and accrual accounting: Under the cash accounting method, all revenues and expenses are recorded when cash is actually received or cash is actually paid. In accrual accounting, all revenues are recorded in the period when goods and services are performed, and all expenses are recorded in the period when goods and services are purchased.

☐ Yes   ☐ No   ☐ I do not know

	Do not agree at all 1	2	3	4	Strongly agree 5
1. I think that my municipality publishes financial statements timely.	☐	☐	☐	☐	☐
2. I think the financial statement of my municipality is user-friendly.	☐	☐	☐	☐	☐
3. I think the numerous information of the financial statement of my municipality are well integrated.	☐	☐	☐	☐	☐
4. I would need to learn a lot in order to cope with the financial statement of my municipality.	☐	☐	☐	☐	☐
5. I think that citizens are able to read and understand financial reporting of my municipality.	☐	☐	☐	☐	☐

Q2. Open governance concept into the municipal governance system:

Open governance concept is a combination of principles towards an inclusive government, through the citizen engagement, transparency, accountability and integrity, and to implement open data for all using ICTs applications into the system.

	Do not agree at all 1	2	3	4	Strongly agree 5	I cannot answer
1. I understand the concept 'open governance' very well.	☐	☐	☐	☐	☐	☐
2. Currently, we have enough openness and transparency in our municipality.	☐	☐	☐	☐	☐	☐
3. I think citizens and other stakeholders have right to participate budgeting and to oversight municipality's financial matters.	☐	☐	☐	☐	☐	☐

Figure 4.

| 4. I can trust upon the management of my municipality regarding budgeting and financial reporting, | ☐ | ☐ | ☐ | ☐ | ☐ | ☐ |

Ways of delivering financial reporting information to people:
Q3. What of following ways are used in your municipality?

	Not used at all in my municipality	Sometimes, not in an established way	Every year, in an established way	I do not know
1. The annual report, after the budget year, published as a whole in paper format.	☐	☐	☐	☐
2. The annual report after the budget year is published as a popular edition.	☐	☐	☐	☐
3. The annual report after the budget year is published in municipal website.	☐	☐	☐	☐
4. Open meetings and public hearing, in which the municipality officials tell about the budget and its outcomes.	☐	☐	☐	☐
5. Use of social media, i.e. Facebook, YouTube, etc. to inform local people regarding the budget.	☐	☐	☐	☐

Q4. How much participatory opportunity do you have for local people in preparing annual budget before it is formally accepted?

	Not used at all in my municipality	Sometime, not in an established way	Every year, in an established way	I do not know
1. Participatory budget meetings	☐	☐	☐	☐
2. Internet feedback system	☐	☐	☐	☐
3. Other channels for suggesting budget items and contents, if what?--------------- --- --	☐	☐	☐	☐

Local councilors role:

	Not contacts at all	Contacts seldom	Contacts often	Contacts very often
1. How active are you personally in taking contacts with local people.	☐	☐	☐	☐

Figure 5.

regarding the budget discussion and its processing.

2. How actively local people contact you regarding the budget and financial reporting.

☐ ☐ ☐ ☐

Open question:

What are the biggest problems regarding municipal budgetary and financial reporting in your municipality and how would you solve the problems?

Personal data

1.1. Group and number of respondent (filled by the researcher):

☐☐

e.g. In the first blank space municipality code (Name of the municipality or initials). In second blank space number of respondents (1, 2, 3 and so on)

1.2. Gender of respondent:

☐ Female   ☐ Male

1.3. Age of respondent:

☐☐

2. Professional background
2.1. Occupational group:

☐ Private sector employee   ☐ Public sector employee   ☐ Student

☐ Pensioner/retiree   ☐ Entrepreneur   ☐ self-employed/freelancer

☐ Unemployed/No, job

2.2. Does your work responsibility include financial and accounting matters?

☐ Yes   ☐ No

2.3. Job title:

Figure 6.

3. Educational background

3.1. Level of education:

☐ No formal education   ☐ O level/SSC   ☐ A level/ HSC
☐ University degree (Bachelor or Master)   ☐ Doctoral degree

☐ Other degree, What?---

3.2. Does your education include accounting training?

☐ Yes   ☐ No

4. Local council membership

4.1. Since when you have been member of the local/municipal council (year yyyy):

4.2. If applicable, interruption of membership:

4.3. I am a member of following committees in the local council:

☐ Steering committee   ☐ Financial committee   ☐ Audit committee

☐ Youth, social, school committee   ☐ Building/ construction committee   ☐ Committee on economic affair

☐ HR/staff committee   ☐ Cultural committee

☐ Other committee, what? _____

2. Survey Methods

Figure 7.

How we have completed our survey

Since the Questionnaire was closed ended, we have followed the interview method to complete the survey. Here we followed several steps to accomplish the survey.

Step-1: We contacted with the City Mayor, Chief Executive Officer, Secretary and Councilors of the respective City Corporations and Municipalities over phone and took a schedule for maximum 2hours for each interviewee.

Step-2: Then we went to each interviewee on the fixed schedule and took interviews. It took 75 minutes to 90 minutes to complete an interview. To make the questions easy to understand, we translated the questions into Bengali and gave a questionnaire to each interviewee. Besides we had kept a questionnaire which is written in English with us during the interview and filled up when they answered the questions.

It took 2 days to take interviews from each City Corporation or Municipality. Then we gathered all the questionnaires and completed the survey.

Chapter 20

The Role of Data Governance in Cybersecurity for E–Municipal Services:
Implications From the Case of Turkey

Ecem Buse Sevinç Çubuk

(iD) https://orcid.org/0000-0002-1679-1746

Adnan Menderes University, Turkey

Halim Emre Zeren

Aydın Adnan Menderes University, Turkey

Burcu Demirdöven

Pamukkale University, Turkey

ABSTRACT

The "e-Municipality Project" in Turkey has developed information systems (IS) for electronic municipal services since May 2017. This chapter discusses the role of data governance in relation to implementing an effective cybersecurity strategy for the project. Data were collected using a workshop with information technology (IT) officials of municipalities and semi-structured interviews with eight information IS managers about their experiences in the project. The research revealed that good data governance has been a prerequisite for any organization focused on its potential to transform processes, decision making and performance. Data governance delivers the insights that organizations need to identify their high-value and high-risk data sets and allocate additional or specific resources to protect this data. Good data governance for secured municipal services is related to a number of trade-offs between the different actors and their responsibilities. The dichotomy between centralization and decentralization of data governance can help to understand the management of cyber risks.

DOI: 10.4018/978-1-6684-5284-4.ch020

INTRODUCTION

Establishing safe information systems (IS), guaranteeing the proper operation of installed systems, and protecting them from external damage are all critical aspects of information system management. For this reason, besides the efforts to create systems that work correctly, what kind of environment the devices should be in, how a system can be used by information technology (IT) professionals and users, regular backups of programs and daily operations, what to do in case of data corruption due to a malfunction or a natural disaster should be considered for creating secure IS and maintaining their security.

New security dangers have evolved from the widespread use of the Internet and the transition to data-driven decision-making. Data is one of the most powerful assets in the world today. Technological innovations have drawn attention to the recognized value of data for both private sector enterprises and public organizations. The sectoral environment has been competitive, and dynamics have changed quite rapidly. Data has the potential to create a large market for businesses and government institutions.

The obvious societal benefits of big data, artificial intelligence, and machine learning have accelerated the transition to a data-driven public sector. Agbozo and Asamoah (2019) define data-driven e-government as "a collection of digital public services that channel previously stored data back to citizens as solutions, decisions, and reforms for accelerated national growth." The increasing penetration of data in public policies, legal regulations and government strategies has been altering operations and decision-making process within organizations. Digital advances are providing governments with unprecedented opportunities to improve rates of financial inclusion through financial technology (fintech) programs and solutions. Fintech solutions include the use of smart-phone technology for the distribution of government payments, and the digitization of financial transactions more broadly. But obstacles can range from infrastructure challenges such as mobile reception in rural areas; to cultural challenges such as a lack of trust in certain institutions; and technical or regulatory questions in areas such as data privacy and ID verification. Thus, data governance, security governance, and cyber governance have become increasingly prevalent as data has ingrained in the natural flow of daily life.

As a sense, using data alone is not an option. It should be viewed in its entirety. Data governance offers a cross-functional framework for managing data as a strategic organizational asset (Abraham, Schneider and Vom Brocke, 2019). Data governance, in its most general sense, is the allocation of authority and control over data and the power of decision-making regarding the data (Brackett and Earley, 2009; Plotkin, 2013). Data governance emerges as the sum of processes, roles, policies, standards, and criteria that ensure the effective and efficient use of information in order for an organization to achieve its goals (Benfeldt, Persson and Madsen, 2020). As a result, data governance establishes decision rights and duties for an organization's data-related decisions. Furthermore, data governance formalizes and oversees data policies, standards, and procedures.

Data privacy and data security are the most important considerations for data-driven systems. In data governance, the methods, and regulations for ensuring data privacy and security are still unclear. Data privacy and security issues can be caused by a variety of factors such as data leakages and illicit data disclosure. Laudon and Laudon (1996) identify security as the rules, processes, and technical measures that must be followed to prevent unauthorized access to or change of information, theft, and physical damage to IS. For computer hardware, software, networks and data, security refers to a range of strategies and technologies. External influence and disruption to IS is a real danger today since data can be corrupted, rendered unusable, stolen, or misappropriated. According to Laudon and Laudon (1996), data saved electronically is more vulnerable and destructive than data stored manually in the past.

As the volume of data grows, so does the risk of it being exploited and revealed. A data governance strategy is of great importance to any organization that works with huge volumes of data because it lays out how an organization benefits from consistent, common processes and responsibilities. Data governance strategy is a prerequisite for any organization, especially for those which has embraced fintech-related tools. Data governance strategy enables organizations to understand the value of data, where it is located, and who has access to it. In other words, data governance has a significant role in determining how best to allocate resources to protect the value of data, thus cyber security practices.

The main focus of this chapter is the role of data governance in improving cybersecurity protection of e-municipal initiatives. The volume of data produced, processed, and stored by municipalities is quite large. This volumetric size, which continues to increase day by day, creates significant benefits and gains for municipalities, while at the same time creating a security requirement. Municipalities store various data including sensitive data about citizens, in their own databases and at the same time generate new data by processing them. Considering the intensity of the transactions and the additional volume coming from smart city applications, it is of great importance to calculate the required capacity and to develop e-municipality initiatives in this direction.

The general objective of this research is to establish the level of cybersecurity within the e-municipality framework of Turkey. The chapter examines the extent to which the entire infrastructure of IS launched after the "e-Municipality Project" in 2014 to provide a plethora of services to the citizens of Turkish Republic is secure. An in-depth analysis of the various variables around the cybersecurity framework of e-municipal services is performed to identify areas of weakness. The following research questions have been formulated to achieve the specific objectives of this research:

- What are the areas of strength and weakness in the cybersecurity framework of the e-Municipality Project of Turkish Republic?
- What is the role of data governance to develop a cybersecurity framework for the e-Municipality Project of Turkish Republic?

In the following sections, first the conceptualization of data governance and cybersecurity is provided. Secondly, the chapter outlines the background of the e-Municipality Project in Turkey and discusses the initial developments in the practice of the project. The chapter then explains the research methodology and presents the results obtained from a workshop with IT officials of municipalities and the semi-structured interviews with eight IS managers about their experiences in the project, followed by a discussion of the potential solution to existing problems related to cybersecurity practices. The final section draws conclusions and makes suggestions for the upcoming policy-making process and future studies.

BACKGROUND AND RELATED WORK

This section presents the existing work and literature on the research topic and reviews the advancements and limitations of the main subjects linked to the research. First, it develops the research context by outlining the conceptualization of cybersecurity and data governance. Following that, it summarizes the role of data governance to furnish the adequate background on the case at hand.

CYBERSECURITY

Cybersecurity, as a term, has not yet reached sufficient maturity (Yılmaz, Ulus and Gönen, 2015). The term encompasses the protection of information resources as well as the protection of other assets, including the person himself (Karacı, Akyüz and Bilgici, 2017). Cybersecurity is defined as "the collection of tools, policies, security concepts, security guarantees, protocols, guidelines, risk management approaches, activities, trainings, practices, and technologies used to protect the assets of institutions, organizations, and users in the cyber environment" (Karacı, Akyüz and Bilgici, 2017). Hekim and Başbüyük (2013) define cybersecurity as a comprehensive concept that encompasses not just Internet security but also all communication infrastructures.

The generic term for the security of all virtual formations, as well as the information stored, published, and produced in the formations, is "cybersecurity". Individual, mass, regional, national, and even international security is all covered by cybersecurity to provide security of a cyber environment, space or network (Göçoğlu, 2018). It enters the life of the state, which is responsible for both the individual as a citizen and the individual's security, as well as being a policy maker and implementer in this regard.

The National Initiative for Cybersecurity Education (NICE) defines cybersecurity as an action or process that protects and defends information and communication systems, as well as the information contained inside them, against any damage, attack, or destruction. The collection of tools, policies, security concepts, security guidelines, risk management approaches, actions, courses, best practices, assurances, and technologies can be used to protect the assets of the cyber environment, institutions, and individuals. It is vital to protect the confidentiality, integrity, and availability of information in order for the cyber world to be secure (Hekim and Başbüyük, 2013).

Data is a critical enterprise asset that gives support to operations, drives decision-making, makes personalized end-to-end service delivery possible, unlocks competitive advantage, and more. On the other hand, all this data represents a highly desirable possession for cyber criminals looking to steal, hijack, or hold data to ransom. Institutions or organizations, whether public or private, need to store large amounts of data and develop an effective data governance strategy over them. This helps institutions and organizations maximize their value, manage risks, and reduce costs. In order to create framework and provide security, technology and innovation-based policies have been established, and are continuously developed. Since data governance considers the rules and limits that govern the generation, processing, and use of data, cyber security comes to the fore regarding risks such as misuse of the information in question and failure to protect it.

Salido (2010) suggests four principles to assist organizations in selecting strategies and actions for privacy and security of data assets. The first principle is a basic assumption that policies and standards must be followed throughout the validity of personal data. Data processing must adhere to existing laws and regulations. It is critical to protect consumers' privacy when it comes to their preferences, allowing them to re-establish the information as needed. The second principle reduces the chances of unauthorized access to or use of classified information. To ensure data confidentiality, integrity, and availability, a well-managed information system should provide suitable practical administrative protection. The third principle is to reduce the impact of losing essential data. The system must provide adequate safeguards (e.g. anonymization) to ensure data confidentiality against loss or theft. All users involved in the infringement response must be given appropriate plans and actions in the event of a data breach. The final principle specifies that the control sets should be recorded in order to verify its efficacy. This helps to ensure the organization's accountability and adherence to the privacy and confidentiality principles.

Furthermore, data must be demonstrated by meticulous monitoring, controls, and audits. Institutions must have systems in place to monitor non-compliance and clear alternatives (Salido, 2010).

Cybersecurity involves protecting the organization's infrastructure and data against attack, damage, or unauthorized access. These cyberattacks are usually aimed at accessing, changing, or destroying sensitive information; extorting money from users; or interrupting normal business processes. The goal of data governance, meanwhile, is to define what data assets the organization has, where data lives, who can take actions with it, when, and under what circumstances. This is why data governance plays such a critical role in the implementation of an organization's security strategy. In order to protect against threats, organizations need to know what data to protect and how best to protect it. Data governance allows an organization to identify its high value, high-risk datasets and allocate additional resources to protecting the data if necessary.

IT control frameworks are designed to promote effective IT governance (Ridley, G., Young, J., & Carroll, P., 2004). According to cybersecurity issues, it is possible to highlight standards as named of COBIT and ISO. COBIT known as a high- level IT governance framework. COBIT is an open and reliable standard used by many organizations around the world (Ridley, G., Young, J., & Carroll, P., 2004). The ISO 27000 series is a collection of information security management standards (Arora,2010). Generally, COBIT focuses on business orientation and IT governance, ISO covers implementation of security controls, stress on risk management approach (Arora,2010). While COBIT is more effective at the planning stage of the information and communication process, ISO is explained as the information technology management process (Arora,2010).

DATA GOVERNANCE

In the realm of IS, data governance is a new concept (Alhassan, Sammon and Daly, 2016). Data governance is defined as "an organization-wide framework for assigning decision-related rights and responsibilities in order to properly manage data as a company asset" (Otto, 2011). The definition of data governance identifies who has decision-making authority and accountability for an organization's data assets. The decision domains should be determined so that the appropriate responsibilities and obligations may be assigned (Alhassan, Sammon, and Daly, 2016).

Data governance is the sum of processes that contribute to the achievement of its objectives (Weber et al., 2009; Khatri and Brown, 2010). To manage risk and improve the quality and utility of selected data, data governance changes behavior linked to data definition, product, and usage (Seiner, 2014). High-quality data is a critical success factor in all functions of any organization. Proactive data management and a well-defined data governance program are essential to understanding the full value of the corporate asset.

The utilization of data poses challenges to organizations in terms of management, processing, and security. Because the huge volume of data in question is filtered from data sets that are too massive and complicated for present IS to handle.

As the volume of data grows, the majority of the information gleaned from data can be used to generate personal insight. Personal information is ubiquitous, and it may sometimes be found in the most surprising places. Even after realizing they must deal with a massive amount of data, an organization frequently underestimates the rules and legalities of data collection and processing. Users must have the right to know what information about them is being gathered. As a result, in data governance, user data privacy and security can be protected (Rosbach, 2019). Data privacy can be increased by encrypting data and preventing the content of personal information from being discovered by third parties. Furthermore, combining an individual's personal information with a huge range of external data allows the information to expand, resulting in fresh conclusions about the related individual. A judgment or inference about an individual should not be shared in most cases. A data analyst keeps it hidden from the data suppliers. Unfortunately, such sensitive data and information frequently leak with the source of the breach remaining unknown unless good data governance strategy is compromised (Singh, 2020).

One of the issues of data privacy and security addressed is data ownership (states, intuitions, businesses etc.). Ownership is a property that relates data with one or more entities that own or influence what can be done with the data. The ability to create, read, edit, and delete data is granted to database owners. Transparency in ownership promotes data owners' trust and control, as well as enterprise and community availability and utility. Unfortunately, data users frequently doubt the openness of data ownership. Although data provenance allows tracing through the system, an issue such as data leaking can be avoided from the start of the data privacy and security systems if it is correctly handled (Singh, 2020).

According to Abraham, Schneider, and Vom Brocke (2019) the components of data governance are grouped under three headings: 1) organizational bodies and policies, 2) standards and processes and 3) data governance technology. Organizational bodies and policies contain governance structure, data custodianship, user group charter, decision rights, issue escalation process. More components, data definition and standard (meta-data management), third party data extract, metrics development and monitoring, data profiling, data cleansing are introduced in the section on standards and processes. Metadata Repository, Data Profiling tool and Data Cleansing tool are the components of data governance technology.

E-MUNICIPALITY PROJECT IN TURKEY

In 2014, the Ministry of Interior, in Turkey intended to invest in municipal software in which municipalities can perform all business and transaction processes electronically and can provide local services to citizens in electronic environment. The Ministry submitted the project to the Ministry of Development (later transformed into the Presidency of Strategy and Budget under the Presidency of Turkey in 2018), with the aim of a rapid, safe and uninterrupted delivery of municipal services in accordance with the service-oriented local administration approach in 2014. As a result of the consultations with the Ministry of Development and the Ministry of Environment and Urbanization, the Ministry of Interior prepared a protocol in May 2017, and the Ministry of Development approved the project to support small-scale municipalities in need for IS.

The Law No. 7099 on the Amendment to Certain Laws for Improvement of the Investment Environment has been adopted on February 15, 2018 whereby all municipalities have been obliged to participate in the project. The Law has forced all municipalities regardless of their scales to use single municipal software for their digital services under the e-Municipality Project. Municipalities are, accordingly, required to complete the works related to the project within one year from the notification by the Ministry of the Interior. The e-Municipality Project has attracted the reaction of municipalities and non-governmental organizations (NGOs) in the IT sector. Local actors warned that the Project may cause problems related to cybersecurity practices.

The e-municipality system of Turkey is facing significant threats to cybersecurity leading to the requirement for a comprehensive cybersecurity framework. The case was modelled around the fact that the cybersecurity environment in the context of Turkey is significantly interconnected and interfaced with different stakeholders in technology. This chapter first identifies strengths and weaknesses of the Project regarding its cybersecurity environment and then explores data governance responds the weaknesses to boost cybersecurity. To make a comprehensive exploration, a workshop with 72 IT representatives of the municipalities and in-depth interviews with IS managers of local stakeholders. The details about the data collection process are explained below.

Methodology and Workshop on the E-Municipality Project

Workshops are an expedient research methodology to design authentic, domain-specific studies that meet the expectations of the participants in relation to their own interests (Ørngreen and Levinsen, 2017). They are intended for a research purpose to obtain "reliable and valid data" through "collaborative discussions" and "constructive feedbacks" (Ahmed and Asraf, 2018) about a sphere of activity or knowledge in question (Wakkary, 2007).

A workshop is a scientific meeting in which people with knowledge or expertise on the relevant subject participate and present their ideas in order to discuss a particular subject from a scientific point of view and with a broad perspective. The number of participants included in the workshop varies according to the topic to be discussed, the sub-topics of the topic and the time allocated for the workshop. Workshops are an important academic meeting, as they provide an in-depth information flow and discussion environment on a particular subject and present solutions for the subject or problem in a short time (George and Bennet, 2005).

Accordingly, the workshop titled "the E-Municipality Project: Problems and Proposed Solutions" was organized by the Information Technology Platform of the Marmara Municipalities Union (MMU) with 72 participants of IT representatives of the municipalities in the Marmara Region, on December 24, 2019. The workshop, designed as a one-day, two-session organization, identified the difficulties, areas of development and risks, and to share enhancement solutions based on knowledge and experiences of the participant municipalities.

Interviews with IS Managers of Local Stakeholders

Semi-structured interviews are well-suited for a research purpose, when researchers need to ask open-ended questions for further queries about uncharted territory to reinforce other data collection forms in mixed methods research (Adams, 2015).

The e-Municipality Project has introduced the implementation of arrangements dealt with at national level involving all the local actors concerned. To gain more precise insight into the cybersecurity environment, semi-structured online interviews with eight IS managers from the three related local authorities were conducted: municipalities, municipal software companies and NGOs. Eighteen IS managers, who are the stakeholders of municipal IS, were randomly invited to virtually participate in the study. The invitations were sent so as to increase the diversity among respondents. Eight of IS managers agreed to participate in an online interview.

The respondents were asked to evaluate the development of the e-Municipality Project and the potential threats related to cybersecurity after transition to the new system. The interviews also aimed to understand advantages and disadvantages of the new system, and the solutions to the risks faced or predicted by the IS managers. The interviews were conducted during the period August 19th to October

10th of 2020. Each interview was done by zoom cloud meeting and lasted approximately 75-90 minutes. Four of the respondents were IS managers in municipalities while two were from software companies and the last two represented NGOs. As a key principle to provide the confidentiality of personal information during this study, the anonymity of the participants was ensured.

The Areas of Strength and Weakness in the Cybersecurity Environment of the E-Municipality Project

The first question of the research was structured to discuss strengths and weaknesses of the e-Municipality Project in terms of cybersecurity. The respondents have primarily acknowledged five topics related to data governance and security as of great importance: archiving data on digital platforms, synchronization with the management information systems (MIS) and electronic document management system (EDMS), associating the existing archives of the institutions to access the history of the transactions, using documents as e-signed in legal proceedings, and compliance of the operations with the Law on the Protection of Personal Data and other legislation.

Strengths of the Cybersecurity Environment of the E-Municipality Project

A majority of the respondents of the research indicated that they viewed electronic services as prerequisite for effective public service delivery. However, not all municipalities have adequate sources to build the required infrastructure for e-services. Threats against computer-operated municipal infrastructure have become more sophisticated, yet they are difficult to detect due to the lack of visibility around users and applications. Unless municipalities provide technical and financial assistance, they will be vulnerable to cyber threats. The respondents believe that the government had taken enough measures to ensure the cybersecurity of e-municipal operations of small-scale municipalities in the long run. Therefore, the Project will reduce the digital gap between small and big municipalities.

To Identify Cybersecurity Weaknesses of the E-Municipality Project

Half of the respondents clearly expressed their concerns about security and data governance. None of the respondents found the cooperation with the project team sufficient to carry out their operations in terms of security and data governance sufficient. The lack of coordination between the central authority and local stakeholders paves the way for potential risks in the cybersecurity environment for the e-municipal infrastructure of the Project. These following risks were identified by the respondents:

- **Ownership:** The respondents highlighted the uncertainty in dealing with data ownership and responsibility. The main concern of the respondents about the Project is that municipalities as the producer, recorder and analyst of data on behalf of citizens would not be owners and responsible authorities of data. Although some municipalities have designated officers to the Project, the process is still pending since a project manager has not been appointed by the Ministry. There also seems a lack of precise legislation to determine who has authority and accountability for the collection and management of the municipalities' data.
- **Data preservation:** Since e-municipal services include users' sensitive data, they are prime targets for cybercriminals. Therefore, the respondents worry where sensitive data reside. They stated

that not knowing the storage and backup strategy and the capability to transfer previous data to the new system hampers the Ministry's ability to design an effective cybersecurity strategy. The primary concern of the respondents is the risk of a single point of failure (SPOF) because all municipalities' data would be kept in a centralized database.

- **Confidentiality:** The respondents stated that the system had vulnerabilities in controlling access levels of information internally and externally. They realized that insiders can have access to information that they do not need to perform their work. It is possible to access different municipalities' information with the password of one person. Although passwords are the most prevalent authentication strategy currently, the Project seems to have a risk of data breaches resulting in accidental distribution of sensitive information.

- **Quality:** The respondents raised their concerns about reliable and consistent data. Since there is no data storage in the local, the central government conducts so many workshops and surveys and purchases additional services to collect local data. Data is provided by someone regardless of his/ her competence.

- **Availability:** The respondents stated that the Project is missing to ensure that data is available and easy to consume by the e-municipality functions that require it. Municipalities cannot consume data and use reports in the system. They are dependent on the reports provided by the Ministry. When requested, special reports cannot be obtained because web services are not provided to the municipalities. Additionally, the respondents are concerned whether project-based modules in existing software that facilitate users' and citizens' transactions will be disabled, or not.

- **Integrity:** The early experiences with the system indicated that data coming in from a variety of sources needs to be combined. The Project team should provide a clearer picture of how different functions relate to each other within the system. For example, the title used for the term "head of department" by the municipalities and Central Registration System of the State Organization (DETSIS) is different. Therefore, different titles are used in official correspondences. Financial data, taxpayer information, personnel payroll information used in the existing systems (e.g. data for NetCad software widely used in the Geographic Information System [GIS]) should be transferred in a safe and secure way, without affecting its usability. Especially in small districts, the number of qualified personnel is very limited and they need support to transfer data to the new system.

- **Security posture and culture:** The respondents stated that the Project teams should clearly identify the collective security status of the system. Municipalities were not informed adequately about the set of values and standards adopted by the Project team that determine how to approach security. A majority of the respondents claimed that the Project has the problem related to the lack of appropriate staff specialized in data management. A staff shortage makes assessing its security posture difficult. The respondents further indicated that there is ambiguity in audit and certification. The municipalities which have many security and operational standards in their existing systems and setups will not be able to maintain these standards.

- **Service interruption:** The e-Municipality Project caused concern to the municipalities about the total or partial interruption, suspension, degradation or delay in the performance of the system. The main reason behind this concern is the lack a 24/7 contact center and slow server response times. The respondents also stated that there is no a disaster recovery plan of the Project that describes how the new system can quickly resume work after an unplanned incident.

The findings indicated that there is a need to frame the complex problem of cybersecurity in a way that the e-Municipality System can engage in. The e-Municipality Project is quite comprehensive that it is expectable to have various challenges during the implementations in the field. On the other hand, the weaknesses against strengths underlined the need to develop solutions services that enable both the Project team and municipalities to adopt cybersecurity strategies in compliance with the system objectives.

The Role of Data Governance to Develop an Effective Cybersecurity Framework for the E-Municipality Project

The cybersecurity concerns of the respondents revealed that the major obstacle to an effective cybersecurity framework for the Project is the inadequate conceptualization of the relationship between cyber security and data governance. The weaknesses of the project related to cybersecurity challenges are addressing the context of data governance "as the power relations between all the actors affected by, or having an effect on, the way data is accessed, controlled, shared and used, the various socio-technical arrangements set in place to generate value from data, and how such value is redistributed between actors" (Micheli et al., 2020: 3). The respondents implied a need for examining the enacting subjects and objects involved in the Project and considering how power relations affect the processes and the goals of particular governance strategy. To develop an effective cybersecurity framework, municipalities are expecting to be informed about the decisions made over data, who is able to make such decisions, and the way data is accessed, controlled, used and benefited from.

The research indicated that data governance is a fundamental part of security. It ensures that the right people have the right access, whilst data security makes sure that enterprise data is safeguarded. The weaknesses of the new system emphasized the essential requirement to answer the following questions:

1. Does the responsible Ministry know the value of data?
2. Who does have access to data (especially sensitive data)?
3. Where is the location of data?
4. Who is protecting data?
5. How is data protected?
6. What is the expertise level of the staff involved in the Project?
7. How much data quality is good enough?
8. Does the Project present security culture?
9. How well are the roles of stakeholders distributed?

Unless the Project provides well-formulated answers to these questions, it will remain weak to drive good data governance promising effective security measures for e-municipal services.

The respondents also discussed the role of good data governance in cybersecurity in relation to data governance model. The Project presented a tendency towards centralized data governance. Before the Project, data governance model of e-municipal services had the characteristics of decentralized execution. Because each municipality has different needs, objectives and administrative and financial capacities, individual municipality users were maintaining their own master data. The data has been created by the local users who were typically the consumers of this master data. Therefore, the development level of e-municipal services was dependent on each municipality's capabilities. This could create a service quality gap between the municipalities. The Project triggered centralized data governance characterized by the Ministry of Interior as a single unit centralizing the maintenance of master data. The Ministry acts as a central organization that owns setting up master data based on requests coming from the consumers of the master data. The respondents claimed that no single data governance model fits all municipalities due to the significant differences between municipalities' conditions (e.g. geography, population and administrative scale) and digital maturity level.

SOLUTIONS AND RECOMMENDATIONS

Although the implementation of the e-Municipality Project is at an advanced stage, the municipalities still remain uninformed about the details of the Project. The respondents stated that there is no clear explanation about the project planning, the required trainings, and the future directions. The ambiguity of security concerns is derived from the lack of interaction between the Project team and the municipalities. Therefore, there is a need for planning and coordination at the micro level organized by the Project team and the municipalities. Information sharing and collaboration with local governments creates an effective, whole-of-nation approach to enable enhanced cyber readiness of municipalities (Zabierek et al., 2021; Billingsley, 2020; Hoffman and Cseh, 2020).

As a result of the opportunities provided by the developing information and communication technologies, municipalities have been rapidly transferring their services to digital channels and improving their service quality. In other words, an e-municipality initiative is not a new concept for many municipalities. The e-Municipality Project should have a flexible structure in order to meet the different needs of the different municipalities. Especially for municipalities with advanced digital maturity level, possible service interruptions, possible disruptions, and problems in service quality with the transition to the e-Municipality Project were considered as serious risks by the respondents.

Many services have been provided to citizens by municipalities through digital channels with the principle of 24/7 operations. As the respondents stated, thanks to the capabilities acquired over the years, efficiency and productivity have been achieved in municipal operations, as well as increasing the satisfaction of the citizens. After the transition to the e-Municipality Platform, the established support operations should be well designed and operated in order to avoid service interruption.

The Project team should explain the legislative arrangement of the Project. Municipalities should be informed adequately about the set of values and standards that determine the Project team's approach to security. Municipalities are required to complete their harmonization process to the Personal Data Protection Law (KVKK) No. 6698 and the European Union General Data Protection Regulation (GDPR). The Ministry of Interior should provide the Information Security Management System (ISMS) standard. Municipalities use firewall and antivirus in their local systems. Within the scope of KVKK, necessary measures against data leakage and Distributed Denial of Service (DDoS) attacks should also be taken by the central system management.

The respondents recognized differences between the project objectives and the level of implementation in the field. Municipalities with higher digital maturity level and more competent software systems have difficulty in planning in the new system. This obstacle creates both administrative burdens (e.g. investment decisions) and security challenges (the maturity level of the Project is lower than the maturity level of some municipalities). Nelson and Madnick (2017) stated that in case of poor alignment between field operations and centralized cybersecurity unit, opportunities are lost due to conservative security policies and lack of appetite for more transformative digital development initiatives.

The principle of 24/7 operations have enabled the municipalities to provide services to citizens through digital channels. This has led to efficiency and productivity in municipal operations in return for helping keep citizens safe and satisfied. The transition to the e-Municipal Platform should guarantee to establish well designed and uninterrupted support services.

According to the findings, the issue of cybersecurity has been cast as the focal point of a fight between data governance operational models: centralized versus decentralized. The respondents stated that the project team should design data governance program that the Ministry needs to consider which operational model is best for the size and structure of the Project. The model should detail operational guidelines, establish oversight, and provide infrastructure for data ownership and decision-making. There is no single data governance model that is suitable for every organization. Trying to find information and resources that the Project receives from all units and stakeholders should help develop a customized data governance model that meets what the Project needs. A well-established data governance model will provide a robust framework that allows the project team to get the most value from data while maintaining data security.

Practical recommendations: the following steps are recommended to the Ministry of Interior and the e-Municipality Project team:

- By implementing data governance initiatives, the Project improves security and realizes other valuable business benefits.
- Since cybersecurity risks cannot be completely eliminated, they can be mitigated through cooperation, knowledge and timely communication between central and local stakeholders regarding the threats and how to face them.
- In order not to interrupt the services, it should be possible to exchange data bilaterally "from institution to e-Municipality" (I2eM) and "from e-Municipality to institution" (eM2I).
- Instead of centralized e-Municipality system, centralized backup can be used. The municipalities without enough resources can use the Ministry's system while those which have developed their own local system can be expected to back up their data in centralized system and add another layer of protection by encrypting them.
- Benefiting from the experiences and skills of the municipalities, the Ministry should promote a collaborative culture by providing consistent, accurate data across all stakeholders. Assigning deliverables, roles and responsibilities would provide foundational support for what is often a significant cultural and procedural shift for cybersecurity.

FUTURE RESEARCH DIRECTIONS

This initial research has discerned some interesting dynamics on the structure of current municipal e-governance arrangements in Turkey. Future work will more fully explore the development of a framework for cybersecurity needs assessment. Fintech-driven innovation has been accelerated worldwide during the global pandemic to help governments with the delivery of services and programs. The research indicated that governments have to be very careful given the increasing volume of transaction and personal data being generated. Municipal services include sensitive citizen data such as contact details, payment card industry data, credit card details and social security information. Although fintech solutions are very effective to help amplify access and usage of financial services as well as efficiency to the delivery of those financial services directly to citizens, without a well-established data governance model, it is hard to overcome an increasing number of cybersecurity challenges.

In the course of this research, the chapter identified various areas where further research was needed. The areas of further research include the following:

1. The research timeline did not allow full discussion of the differences between centralized, decentralized and hybrid data governance models in terms of the cybersecurity environment. The findings recommend that further work be done to elaborate these differences.

2. More methodological work is needed on how to robustly create a responsibility assignment matrix by involving all stakeholders of municipal e-governance systems for the development of a comprehensive cybersecurity framework.

3. Research to develop approaches and carry out a full cost–benefit analysis of municipalities' involvement in the Project would be beneficial. Despite methodological challenges, it would be very useful to conduct some longer-term studies which sought to quantify the impact of their involvement on such key indicators as service interruptions and recovery plans.

4. In-depth exploration of how fintech solutions become integrated into the new centralized system by the e-Municipality Project would be very helpful. Further research might compare, for example, experiences of different municipalities in digital financial services.

CONCLUSION

The rapid pace of technological innovation offers governments an unprecedented number of new value creation and service provision opportunities. As governments have digitized their operations, they have opened themselves to cyberattacks, resulting in harmful disruptions to government services. Cybersecurity at the municipal level has been more challenging since municipalities are tasked with providing critical services (e.g. digital financial services) at the local level. In case of Turkey, cybersecurity for municipal e-governance systems became a current issue with the e-Municipality Project of the Ministry of Interior. The Project has triggered the tension between the central government and local governments as it has expected the municipalities to abandon their own system to use new software developed by the Ministry.

As our findings make clear, the larger municipalities believed that the performance of the GIS, MIS, and business intelligence software they use have been meeting their needs and citizens' expectations. They stated that the involvement in the new system should be optional, and the Project should be matured with the participation of all municipalities and kept up with new technologies. The Project will be better prepared to welcome its stakeholders by consulting with local agencies and external experts on the risks and solutions. When dealing with highly sensitive, novel data, the level of comfort of all stakeholders can be helpful in assessing the legal, regulatory, and reputational cyber risks. Similarly, it is a good idea to seek input from municipalities on how municipal e-governance system should be developed through a good data governance framework to ensure data is not being stored, used or disclosed in a way that increases risk.

Finally, the Project team needs to formulate the "best fit" model of data governance for responding more effectively to cyberattacks against local governmental entities. Though technical measures have been adapted by the municipalities with greater experience and investments, without a fair data governance model, local governmental entities will be constrained in all kinds of ways when they seek to find solutions for the weaknesses of the Project.

ACKNOWLEDGMENT

The authors would like to thank eighty anonymous respondents for their insightful discussions and suggestions for the e-Municipality Project. This research was supported by the Marmara Municipalities Union and the 100/2000 Council of Higher Education (CoHE) Ph.D. Scholarship Program.

REFERENCES

Abraham, R., Schneider, J., & Vom Brocke, J. (2019). Data Governance: A Conceptual Framework, Structured Review, and Research Agenda. *International Journal of Information Management*, *49*, 424–438. doi:10.1016/j.ijinfomgt.2019.07.008

Agbozo, E., & Asamoah, B. K. (2019). Data-driven e-government: Exploring the Socio-economic Ramifications. *e-Journal of e-Democracy and Open Government, 11*(1), 81-90.

Alhassan, I., Sammon, D., & Daly, M. (2016). Data Governance Activities: an Analysis of the Literature. *Journal of Decision Systems, 25*(sup1), 64-75.

Arora, V. (2010). *Comparing Different Information Security Standards: COBIT v s. ISO 27001*. Carnegia Mellon University.

Benfeldt, O., Persson, J. S., & Madsen, S. (2020). Data Governance as a Collective Action Problem. *Information Systems Frontiers, 22*(2), 299–313. doi:10.100710796-019-09923-z

Billingsley, J. (2020, April 15). *State and Local Cybersecurity Collaboration* [Memorandum]. Legislative Council Staff. https://leg.colorado.gov/sites/default/files/r20_339_cybersecurity_state_local_memo_-_for_cathy.pdf

George, A. L., & Bennett, A. (2005). *Case Studies and Theory Development in the Social Sciences*. MIT Press.

Göçoğlu, V. (2018). *Türkiye'nin Siber Güvenlik Politikalarının Kamu Politikası Analizi Çerçevesinde Değerlendirilmesi* [Doctoral Dissertation]. University of Hacettepe, Ankara, Turkey.

Hekim, H., & Başıbüyük, O. (2013). Siber Suçlar ve Türkiye'nin Siber Güvenlik Politikaları. *Uluslararası Güvenlik ve Terörizm Dergisi, 4*(2), 135–158.

Hoffman, I., & Cseh, K. B. (2020). E-administration, Cybersecurity and Municipalities – the Challenges of Cybersecurity Issues for the Municipalities in Hungary. *Cybersecurity and Law, 2*(2), 199–211. doi:10.35467/cal/133999

Karacı, A., Akyüz, H. İ., & Bilgici, G. (2017). Üniversite Öğrencilerinin Siber Güvenlik Davranışlarının İncelenmesi. *Kastamonu Eğitim Dergisi, 25*(6), 2079–2094. doi:10.24106/kefdergi.351517

Khatri, V., & Brown, C. V. (2010). Designing Data Governance. *Communications of the ACM, 53*(1), 148–152. doi:10.1145/1629175.1629210

Laudon, K., & Laudon, J. (1996). *Management Information Systems*. Prentice Hall Inc.

Micheli, M., Ponti, M., Craglia, M., & Suman, A. B. (2020). Emerging Models of Data Governance in the Age of Datafication. *Big Data & Society, 7*(2), 1–15. doi:10.1177/2053951720948087

Mosley, M., Brackett, M., Earley, P. S., & Henderson, D. (2009). *The DAMA Guide to the Data Management Body of Knowledge (DAMA-DMBOK Guide)*. Technics Publications, LLC.

Nelson, N., & Madnick, S. (2017). *Trade-offs Between Digital Innovation and Cyber-security* [Working Paper]. MIT Sloan School of Management. https://cams.mit.edu/wp-content/uploads/2017-04.pdf

Otto, B. (2011). Organizing Data Governance: Findings from the Telecommunications Industry and Consequences for Large Service Providers. *Communications of the AIS, 29*, 45–66. doi:10.17705/1CAIS.02903

Plotkin, D. (2020). *Data Stewardship: An Actionable Guide to Effective Data Management and Data Governance*. Academic Press.

Ridley, G., Young, J., & Carroll, P. (2004). COBIT and its Utilization: A Framework from the Literature. In *Proceedings of the 37th Annual Hawaii International Conference on System Sciences*. IEEE. 10.1109/HICSS.2004.1265566

Rosbach, F. (2019). *The Top 3 Big Data Security and Compliance Challenges of 2019*. https://insights.comforte.com/big-data-analytics-the-top-3-security-and-compliance-challenges-of-2019

Salido, J. (2010). Data Governance for Privacy, Confidentiality and Compliance: A Holistic Approach. *Isaca Journal, 6*, 1–7.

Seiner, R. S. (2014). *Non-invasive Data Governance: The Path of Least Resistance and Greatest Success*. Technics Publications.

Singh, D. (2020). Toward Data Privacy and Security Framework in Big Data Governance. *International Journal of Software Engineering and Computer Systems, 6*(1), 41–51. doi:10.15282/ijsecs.6.1.2020.5.0068

Weber, K., Otto, B., & Oesterle, H. (2009). One Size does not Fit All: A Contingency Approach to Data Governance. *Journal of Data and Information Quality, 1*(1), 4. doi:10.1145/1515693.1515696

Yılmaz, E., Ulus, H., & Gönen, S. (2015). Bilgi toplumuna geçiş ve siber güvenlik. *Bilişim Teknolojileri Dergisi, 8*(3), 133.

Zabierek, L., Bueno, F., Kennis, G., Sady-Kennedy, A., & Kanyeka, N. (2021). *Toward a Collaborative Cyber Defense and Enhanced Threat Intelligence Structure*. The Cyber Project.

ADDITIONAL READING

AlDairi, A., & Tawalbeh, L. (2017). Cyber Security Attacks on Smart Cities and Associated Mobile Technologies. *Procedia Computer Science, 109*, 1086–1091. doi:10.1016/j.procs.2017.05.391

Caruson, K., MacManus, S. A., & McPhee, B. D. (2012). Cybersecurity Policymaking at the Local Government Level: An Analysis of Threats, Preparedness, and Bureaucratic Roadblocks to Success. *Journal of Homeland Security and Emergency Management, 9*(2), 1–22. doi:10.1515/jhsem-2012-0003

Falco, G., Noriega, A., & Susskind, L. (2019). Cyber Negotiation: A Cyber Risk Management Approach to Defend Urban Critical Infrastructure from Cyberattacks. *Journal of Cyber Policy, 4*(1), 90–116. doi :10.1080/23738871.2019.1586969

Lévy-Bencheton, C., & Darra, E. (2016). *Cyber security for smart cities: an architecture model for public transport.* European Network and Information Security Agency. https://op.europa.eu/en/publication-detail/-/publication/2e5c9aba-c8b3-11e5-a4b5-01aa75ed71a1/language-en

The World Bank. (2021). *World Development Report 2021: Data for Better Lives.* International Bank for Reconstruction and Development / The World Bank.

Velibeyoğlu, K. (2005). Urban information systems in Turkish local governments. In S. Marshall, W. Taylor, & X. Yu (Eds.), *Encyclopedia of Developing Regional Communities with Information and Communication Technology* (pp. 709–714). doi:10.4018/978-1-59140-575-7.ch127

Yaman, K., Aşgın, S., & Kaya, E. (2013). Comparative Analysis of the e-Municipality Applications in Turkey: The Case of Western Black Sea Region. *Yönetim ve Ekonomi, 20*(1), 207–220.

Chapter 21
Re–Thinking Cryptocurrencies as Safe–Haven Investment:
Evidence in the U.S. and Emerging Countries

Christy Dwita Mariana
Bina Nusantara University, Indonesia

Irwan Adi Ekaputra
Universitas Indonesia, Indonesia

Zaäfri Ananto Husodo
Universitas Indonesia, Indonesia

Dewi Tamara
iD https://orcid.org/0000-0002-8922-120X
Bina Nusantara University, Indonesia

ABSTRACT

This chapter investigates the global crisis's impact on the safe-haven role of the two most significant cryptocurrencies based on their market capitalizations: Bitcoin and Ethereum. This study compares the volatility transmission between the Bitcoin and stock markets in four emerging countries: Indonesia, Malaysia, Nigeria, and South Africa. This study follows the framework of volatility transmission of Diebold and Yilmas. This research also investigates the safe-haven role of cryptocurrencies using the safe-haven regression analysis and decoupling hypothesis. Overall results support the notion of cryptocurrencies as alternative investments. On average, the pairwise volatility spillover between Bitcoin and stock market in Indonesia, Malaysia, Nigeria, and South Africa reverted back to half of its mean in about 2-3 days. This result suggests on the choice of short-term investment for investors in the Bitcoin market. This study contributes to the discussion of cryptocurrencies as safe haven.

DOI: 10.4018/978-1-6684-5284-4.ch021

INTRODUCTION

In an increasingly developed economy with very diverse and broad investment possibilities, the characteristics of cryptocurrencies as an alternative investment have been widely studied. These studies are mostly about the pros and cons of managing this cryptocurrency. The Covid-19 pandemic has provided a natural laboratory to study the consistency and strength of cryptocurrencies as a hedging instrument or safe-haven in extreme economic conditions.

It is being stated that cryptocurrency has neither intrinsic value nor promised final payment (Geuder et al., 2019). However, cryptocurrencies' value highly depends on facilitating transactions and store value efficiently and effectively (Frankenfield, 2019). Therefore, the increasing price of Bitcoin could result from a price bubble, as being empirically detected from 2016 to 2018, with the critical point time at December 6, 2017 (Geuder et al., 2019). Market microstructure noise could affect Bitcoin's fluctuating price, in which the Bitcoin could be traded based on its noise.

During times of crisis or times with high volatility, financial markets tend to correlate significantly (Sandoval & Franca, 2012). The high correlation between asset classes during the crisis is extensively studied (see, for example(Forbes & Rigobon, 2016; Hartmann et al., 2004; Jang & Sul, 2002; Lin et al., 1994). The tendency of market behaviour as one during the crash shows the need for an asset that is uncorrelated during the crisis (Sandoval & Franca, 2012). The asset with related characteristics is further called the safe-haven asset (Baur & Lucey, 2010).

The lower returns of traditional financial investments during the low-interest-rate period lead the high-net-worth clients to invest in the "exotic" assets, i.e., wines, artworks, and collectable coins (Dimitriou et al., 2020). As a subset of the digital currency system, Bitcoin is initially developed as an online peer-to-peer payment system (Hong, 2017). Bitcoin has been accepted as a means of payment in Switzerland (Milutinovic, 2018) and Germany (Global Legal Research Center, 2018), also as both a payment method and legal tender in Canada (Global Legal Research Center, 2018). The Crypto Index (CRIX), a benchmark for the crypto market, and cryptocurrencies have low correlations with traditional assets from 2014 to 2017. Thus, it could be an excellent option to diversify portfolio risks (Lee et al., 2018). Therefore, cryptocurrency is considered an investment alternative (Hong, 2017; Lee et al., 2018).

It was widely studied how financial market tends to co-move during crisis. Therefore, there is a need of an asset that negatively correlated with other financial markets during crisis. This asset is later known as the safe-haven asset. The categorization of safe-haven asset has been revolting from the conventional assets (gold, bonds, land) into the alternative investments (hedge fund) (Wilcox & Fabozzi, 2013), and recently into the cryptocurrency. However, the empirical tests for safe-haven role of cryptocurrencies still have contradicting results (see, for example, (Baur & Lucey, 2010; Bouri et al., 2017, 2020; Shahzad et al., 2019; Stensås et al., 2019).

Despite all the research that has been done on cryptocurrencies, there is one question that the author tries to review through this chapter: *"Is cryptocurrency ready to become an investment instrument?"*.

To answer this, the authors need to review the news about Elon Musk's tweets and actions regarding Bitcoin. Starting from his investment of 1.5 billion US dollars in Bitcoin in February 2021, Elon Musk's actions have been highlighted by the public and became one of the causes of the surge in Bitcoin prices to reach a value of 900 million Indonesia Rupiah (IDR). However, other actions, such as the ban on the use of Bitcoin as a means of payment for Tesla cars in May 2021, contributed to the drastic fall in the value of this digital asset. Not only Bitcoin, but Elon Musk also causes the rise and fall of the price of other cryptocurrencies such as Dogecoin. This phenomenon is often known as "pom-pom investors", or investors who have a stake in "creating" the public perception of an asset.

Before looking further into cryptocurrency readiness, the authors need to revisit the definition of assets and investments. An asset is a thing of value that a person or company owns. Investment itself is a commitment of money to expect future benefit (Bodie et al., 2014). Referring to the two definitions, cryptocurrency can be categorized as an asset that becomes an investment instrument. This relates to how cryptocurrencies have exchange rates and are traded on a platform, and the goal of crypto players is to make profits in the future.

It has been extensively studied how "conventional" financial markets move together during a crisis, reflecting the inability of these conventional assets to act as asset-safe-haven or negatively correlated assets to financial markets especially during a crisis. The safe-haven categorization has grown from initially only conventional assets (gold, bonds, land or other tangible objects) to include alternative investment instruments (in the form of hedge funds and currently developing into cryptocurrencies).

BACKGROUND

Previous research has documented the safe-haven roles of different assets. A safe-haven asset is when it is uncorrelated with stocks during market turbulence (Baur & Lucey, 2010). Therefore, gold is a safe-haven asset. The notion is supported by Sandoval & Franca (2012), stating that the uncorrelated nature of an investment with stock is essential for a safe-haven investment. There are tendencies of the financial markets to co-move in financial crises, such as Black Monday in 1987, the Russian crisis in 1999, the dot-com bubble in 2001, and the global financial crisis in 2008 (Sandoval & Franca, 2012). In other words, an asset is a weak (strong) safe-haven if it is uncorrelated (or negatively correlated) with another asset during the market crash (Bouri et al., 2017).

In the previous studies, mainly gold and government bonds are considered the safe-haven assets of the equity investments (see, for example, (Baur & Lucey, 2010; Baur & Mcdermott, 2010; Hood & Malik, 2016; Joy, 2011). However, the results are somewhat to be mixed. The dependence between financial assets varies over time (Manner & Reznikova, 2012). Furthermore, each market's different features could also be made the safe-haven role of assets may vary across markets (Liu, 2018).

In the early empirical study of cryptocurrency, Bitcoin is considered a safe-haven against gold and the dollar (i.e., USD) (Dyhrberg, 2016). The notion of cryptocurrency as a safe-haven asset is supported using the wavelet analysis method (Bouri et al., 2020). and the cross-quantilogram approach (Bouri et al., 2020). However, Bitcoin's high volatility should be alleviated by another asset as a safe-haven against it, which is Tether (Baur & Hoang, 2020).

During the Covid-19 pandemic, there is a significant increase in the correlation between coins (Bitcoin and Etherum) and gold, also a negative correlation between currencies and stocks. This phenomenon could be an early indication of cryptocurrency as safe-haven assets for stocks (Bouri, Molnár, et al., 2017). Following the DCC model, as in Bouri et al. (2017), we could examine the dynamic correlation of cryptocurrency, gold, and stocks. An asset could be an investment if negatively correlated with another asset; and could be classified into a diversifier, a hedge, and a safe-haven (Bouri, Molnár, et al., 2017). As a diversifier, an asset has a weak positive correlation with another asset. Meanwhile, a weak (strong hedge is an asset that uncorrelated (negatively correlated) with another asset on average (Bouri, Molnár, et al., 2017). Furthermore, stablecoins such as Tether that act as safe-haven for both coins could alleviate the higher volatility of cryptocurrency than other assets (Baur & Hoang, 2020).

Whether an asset could be categorized as diversifier, hedge and safe-haven depends on the market conditions and investment horizons (see, for example, Bouri, Molnár, et al., 2017; Shahzad, Bouri, Roubaud, & Kristoufek, 2020; Shahzad et al., 2019; Smales, 2019). Precious metals, especially gold, are considered to be hedge or safe-haven for other volatile assets (stocks, bonds, crude oil) (see, for example, (Baur & Lucey, 2010; Peng, 2019). However, during the period of 1995 to 2010, the Volatility Index (VIX) performs better as safe-haven than gold for the U.S. stocks (Hood & Malik, 2016). Furthermore, during the recent Covid-19 pandemic crisis, cryptocurrencies shows better performance as safe-haven than gold for the U.S. stocks (Mariana, Ekaputra, & Husodo, 2021) and for the African equity markets (Omane-Adjepong & Alagidede, 2020).

The weak relation of cryptocurrency, especially Bitcoin, and other financial assets could have several explanations. First, Bitcoin's price determinants do not have much in common with other financial assets (Bouoiyour et al., 2016). Second, Bitcoin price tends to follow more on its unique characteristics, i.e., a) attractiveness (Kristoufek, 2015), user anonymity (Ober et al., 2013); and b) supported by computer programming enthusiasts and illegal activity (Yelowitz & Wilson, 2015). In short, Bitcoin price does not depend much on the economic and financial variables (Kristoufek, 2015), which also reflects bitcoin's exclusivity in abnormal market conditions while answering the wishes of bitcoin originators at the beginning of its formation.

To measure the value of Bitcoin, one could use the Network Value to Transactions (NVT) ratio of cryptocurrency. The NVT is similar to the Price to Earnings Ratio (PER) in stocks. The calculation of NVT is by dividing the network value or market cap of cryptocurrency with the daily USD transmitted through the Bitcoin transaction (Woonomic, 2017). The logical behind the equation is on the earnings as proxy for the underlying utility of the company. However, due to how cryptocurrencies do not have earnings, then the total value of transactions flowing through the network become the appropriate proxy of how much users derive from the chain (Kalichkin, 2018). NVT could also indicate the bubble territory or buying opportunities of Bitcoin. A high NVT means that the cryptocurrency's price is higher than its actual value.

The volatility co-movement of Bitcoin and Ethereum provides an opportunity to hedge these two cryptocurrencies (Katsiampa, 2019). However, using the cross-wavelet method, Dash has significant covariance throughout the sample period with Bitcoin, whereas Litecoin, Monero, and Ripple show sensitivity mostly over the high-frequency and 2014-2015 period (Mensi et al., 2019). Furthermore, by using the multi-resolution analysis and spillovers of seven leading cryptocurrencies, the level of connectedness and volatility causal linkages are found to be sensitive to the trading scales and the proxy for market volatility (Omane-adjepong & Alagidede, 2019).

There are two primary theoretical arguments on the volatility spillovers literature. Firstly, markets tend to co-move during crisis times and thus limit portfolio diversification benefits. This notion is further known as the contagion hypothesis. Secondly, the crisis effect is lower in emerging markets (Aggarwal, Inclan, & Leal, 1999). This notion is what is called the decoupling hypothesis. The hypothesis is built based on spillover direction reversal from the emerging to developed markets after the global financial crisis. In other words, the benefit of diversification still exists (see, for example, (Kenourgios et al., 2013; Yarovaya & Lau, 2016).

In short, prior studies already investigated the volatility transmission of cryptocurrency with other cryptocurrencies (see, for example, (Beneki et al., 2019; Mighri & Alsaggaf, 2019) or other assets (Bouri et al., 2018; Kurka, 2019). However, the study of volatility transmission between the same exchange across diverse countries or testing the emerging countries' contagion hypothesis is still relatively scarce.

Besides the contagion hypothesis, there is also the decoupling hypothesis in the study of volatility spillovers. This hypothesis's main argument is that portfolio diversification benefits accounted for decreasing volatility spillovers between one market with another, mainly related to the degree of vulnerability among the markets.

Although the volatility transmission of cryptocurrency is already being studied (e.g., (Katsiampa, 2019; Omane-adjepong & Alagidede, 2019), the study still focuses on the contagion hypothesis of volatility transmission. The empirical results show how the Bitcoin and Ethereum co-move, thus opening the hedging opportunity (Katsiampa, 2019). However, the connectedness and linkages of volatility causal among the seven leading cryptocurrencies are sensitive to the trading scales and market volatility proxy (Omane-adjepong & Alagidede, 2019).

Cryptocurrencies as Safe-Haven Instruments: Research Results

Through an article written by the authors in the Journal of Finance Research Letters Volume 38 in 2021 (see Mariana et al., 2021), cryptocurrencies (especially Bitcoin and Ethereum) are safe-haven investment instruments for the stock market in the United States. Furthermore, the author also found that the safe-haven role of cryptocurrencies is different for each country studied (the United States of America and developing countries) (Mariana, 2021).

For the first set of samples, the study uses data from July 1, 2019, until April 6, 2020. On July 1, 2019, the Internal Revenue Service (IRS) had begun to send letters to the taxpayers with virtual currency transaction that has a probability of failing to report the related transaction's income. The study also uses the data period to control Bitcoin's second halving potential impact on May 12, 2020 (Crawley, 2020), the date after the Covid-19 pandemic occurred in almost all parts of the world. The raw data consists of daily price data for Bitcoin (BTC), and Ethereum (ETH) retrieved from coindesk.com, Tether from CoinMarketCap.com S&P500, and gold spot prices data from DataStream. For the second set of samples, the research scope would be from January 2018 to October 2020. The study's starting period is due to the liquidity before 2018 in cryptocurrency markets was significantly lower (Makarov & Schoar, 2020). Alongside with the quantitative data analysis, this study also employs a comparative analysis between the legal context of countries being studied: United States, Indonesia, Malaysia, Nigeria and South Africa.

Overall, the volatility of assets tends to increase during the Covid-19 pandemic. There is also a tendency of increasing correlations between gold, Bitcoin and Ethereum during the pandemic. However, the correlations between cryptocurrencies and stock index turns negative during the pandemic. Thus, it could be an initial indication on how cryptos (especially Bitcoin and Ethereum) are possible safe-havens for stocks (Mariana et al., 2021)

The authors also investigate the possibility of safe-haven properties for Bitcoin in emerging stock markets (Indonesia, Malaysia, Nigeria, and South Africa). This research study the Luno Exchange due to its highest ranking (based on trading volume) among the cryptocurrency exchange established in emerging countries. Specifically, South Africa, Nigeria, Malaysia, and Indonesia are the research sample due to their highest Bitcoin volume traded in Luno Exchange.

The daily data of return for stocks and Bitcoin in four emerging countries, i.e., Indonesia, Malaysia, Nigeria, and South Africa, from January 2, 2018, until October 30, 2020, shows that Bitcoin returns are higher than the stock returns. Bitcoin in Malaysia holds the highest daily return standard deviation (denotes BTCMYR), then followed by Bitcoin in Indonesia (BTCIDR), Nigeria (BTCNGN), and South Africa (BTCZAR), respectively. However, the average returns of Bitcoin also higher than stocks, with the highest average return held by Bitcoin in Nigeria and South Africa. Bitcoin in Malaysia has the highest return (186.77%), then followed by Bitcoin in Nigeria (24.58%), South Africa (23.78%), and Indonesia (21.64%), correspondingly.

According to Table 1, Bitcoin in emerging countries could both correlates positively (Malaysia and South Africa) and negatively (Indonesia and Nigeria) with stocks in the related countries. Therefore, Bitcoin could be considered as a diversifier (hedge) for stocks in emerging countries due to its positive (negative) correlation during the research period, following the definitions in (Baur & Lucey, 2010).

The correlation between stocks and Bitcoin in Malaysia is positive both before (0.0217) and during the crisis (0.0863). Moreover, the correlation of stocks and Bitcoin in South Africa is positive both before (0.0434) and during the crisis (0.3434). On the other hand, the correlation between stocks and Bitcoin in Indonesia and Nigeria is negative before the crisis (-0.0362 and -0.0599) but turns positive during the crisis (0.0080 and 0.0679, respectively). Therefore, before (during) the crisis, Bitcoin in Indonesia and Nigeria could be a hedge (diversifier) for local stock markets. Meanwhile, Bitcoin in Malaysia and South Africa are considered diversifiers for stocks in related countries. Nevertheless, the increasing correlation between Bitcoin and emerging countries' stocks shows financial co-movement during the crisis.

Based on the safe-haven regression result, the cryptocurrencies (Bitcoin and Ethereum) are safe-havens for the U.S. stocks during the Covid-19 pandemic crisis (Mariana et al., 2021). This result is supported by the findings in (Gil-Alana et al., 2020), Stensås et al. (2019), and Bouri, Shahzad, et al. (2020). This study's result in line with how during the Brexit referendum in 2016, and the burst of Chinese market bubble in 2015, Bitcoin acted as safe-havens for both the U.S. and non-U.S. stocks (Stensås et al., 2019). These results are also supported by how Bitcoin, Ripple and Stellar (Ethereum, Dash and Nem) are safe-havens (hedges) for all U.S. equity indices (Bouri, Shahzad, et al., 2020).

However, this study's result is contrary to the findings on (Corbet et al., 2020) and (Conlon & McGee, 2020). During the Covid-19 market turbulence, the cryptocurrency (particularly Bitcoin) moves along with S&P500; and thus, does not act as safe-haven for stocks (Conlon & McGee, 2020). The different results could be due to how safe-haven role of cryptocurrencies depend on the stock market types, time horizons, and investment horizons (Bouri et al., 2017; Shahzad et al., 2019, 2020; Stensås et al., 2019).

The Time-Varying Volatility Transmission in Emerging Countries

The authors learn that daily standard deviations experienced a significant increase after the announcement of the Covid-19 pandemic for every asset class. The authors investigate the volatility transmission between Bitcoin and the local stock market in Indonesia, Malaysia, Nigeria, and South Africa.

There is a wide range of volatility spillover between stock markets analysis methods. To name a few, studies are using the cointegration tests (Harris et al., 1995), Multivariate GARCH models (Syllignakis & Kouretas, 2011), switching regression models (King & Wadhwani, 1990), and the Exponential-GARCH (EGARCH) models (Abbas et al., 2013). Following the study of connectedness in the cryptocurrency market (Ji et al., 2019), this study uses the connectedness methodology framework developed by Diebold & Yilmaz (2012). The Diebold-Yilmaz (further abbreviated as DY) method allows the decompositions of forecast-error variance invariant to the order of variables.

This study also uses the EGARCH model to account for the asymmetry effect on the markets to extend the DY method. This study employs the Exponential GARCH (EGARCH) due to its' ability to captures significant, stylized facts of the financial time-series, such as the leverage effect and volatility clustering (Hkiri et al., 2017). The time-varying volatility transmission of Bitcoin and the stock market in the emerging market would indicate the safe-haven role of Bitcoin. This research tests the notion of decoupling hypothesis, in which the reversal of volatility transmission direction in times of crises shows the existence of portfolio diversification benefit. By employing the framework of volatility spillovers between the emerging and emerged market, we would test the decoupling hypothesis between the Bitcoin and conventional stock index

Table 1 (a). Pairwise Correlation of Bitcoin and Stocks in Emerging Countries – Two Sub-Periods

	A. Before the Covid-19 Pandemic (January 2, 2018-March 10, 2020)							
	BTCIDR	**BTCMYR**	**BTCNGN**	**BTCZAR**	**JKSE**	**KLSE**	**NGSE**	**JSE**
BTCIDR	1.0000							
BTCMYR	0.3018***	1.0000						
BTCNGN	0.9185***	0.3104***	1.0000					
BTCZAR	0.9013***	0.2974***	0.9490***	1.0000				
JKSE	**-0.0362**	0.0360	-0.0030	-0.0340	1.0000			
KLSE	0.0304	**0.0217**	0.0221	0.0264	0.4240***	1.0000		
NGSE	-0.0504	-0.0328	**-0.0599***	-0.0757**	0.0931**	0.0819**	1.0000	
JSE	0.0715**	0.0398	0.0726**	**0.0434**	0.3380***	0.4306***	0.0562*	1.0000

Table 1 (b). Pairwise Correlation of Bitcoin and Stocks in Emerging Countries – Two Sub-Periods

B. During the Covid-19 Pandemic (March 11 2020-October 30, 2020)							
BTCIDR	**BTCMYR**	**BTCNGN**	**BTCZAR**	**JKSE**	**KLSE**	**NGSE**	**JSE**
1.0000							
0.9572***	1.0000						
0.9093***	0.8875***	1.0000					
0.9063***	0.9028***	0.8634***	1.0000				
0.0080	0.0813	0.0211	0.0140	1.0000			
0.0053	**0.0863**	0.0181	0.1097*	0.4461***	1.0000		
0.0650	0.0969	**0.0679**	0.0389	0.2117***	0.1866***	1.0000	
0.3628***	0.4008***	0.3594***	**0.3434***	0.4454***	0.5092***	0.0774	1.0000

Notes: The sample's basis is data retrieved from Bitcoincharts.com for Bitcoin spot price data and DataStream for the stock index in Indonesia, Malaysia, Nigeria, and South Africa. The second sample set data period is from January 2, 2018, until October 30, 2020. We divide the research data into two sub-periods, i.e., before the Covid-19 pandemic and during the Covid-19 pandemic. *, **, and *** indicates significances at the 10%, 5%, and 1% levels, respectively. Bold indicates the pairwise correlation between Bitcoin and the same country's stock index.

The conditional variance of EGARCH would be a proxy of daily volatility in both conventional stock and Bitcoin markets. The expression of log variance instead of the EGARCH model variance does not require restrictions on the estimated parameters. The perceived shock at time t-1 impacts the variance at time t, and thus, captured the leverage effect and volatility clustering. The conditional variance could be specified by an EGARCH (1,1) model as follows:

$$\ln\left(\sigma_t^2\right) = w + \alpha\left(\left|z_{t-1}\right| - E\left|z_{t-1}\right|\right) + \gamma z_{t-1} + \beta\ln\left(\sigma_{t-1}^2\right) \tag{1}$$

For a return time-series of $r_t = \mu + \varepsilon t$, whereas μ is the expected returns and εt is the zero-mean white noise.

Secondly, this study employs the DY (2012) approach in defining the volatility spillovers. This study uses the variance decomposition employed by Koop, Pesaran, & Potter (1996) (KPPS) and Pesaran & Shin (1998). In this method, two variances are being considered, i.e., (1) the own variance shares and (2) the cross variance shares (Diebold & Yilmaz, 2012). The own variance share defines as the fraction of the L-step-ahead error variances in the forecasting variable xi, $_d$ue to the common shocks variable for i=1,2,…,N. Meanwhile the cross variance defines as the L-step-ahead error variances that are due to shocks in another variable xj, $_f$or j=1,2,…,N and i1j. The KPPS L-step-ahead forecast error decomposition is as follows (for L=1,2,…)

$$\theta_{ij}^g = \frac{\sigma_{jj}^{-1}\sum_{l=0}^{L-1}(e_i A_l \sum e_j)^2}{\sum_{l=0}^{L-1}(e_i A_l \sum A_l e_j)} \tag{2}$$

Whereas å is the variance matrix for the error vector ε, σjj $_i$s the standard deviation of the error term for the jth ^{e}quation, and ei $_i$s the selection vector (one as the ith ^{e}lement, and zero otherwise).

In the generalized VAR framework, the shocks to every asset variable are not orthogonalized (Baruník et al., 2016). The element of the decomposition matrix could be normalized by the row sum as follows:

$$\tilde{\theta}_{ij}^g\left(L\right) = \frac{\theta_{ij}^g\left(L\right)}{\sum_{j=1}^{N}\theta_{ij}^g\left(L\right)} \tag{3}$$

Whereas, $\sum_{j=1}^{N}\tilde{\theta}_{ij}^g\left(L\right) = 1$ and $\sum_{i,j=1}^{N}\theta_{ij}^g\left(L\right) = N$.

Therefore, the total spillover index to measure how much of the shocks to volatility spills across the variables is given as follows:

$$S^g\left(L\right)=\frac{\sum_{\substack{i,j=1\\i\neq j}}^{N}\tilde{\theta}_{ij}^{g}\left(L\right)}{\sum_{j=1}^{N}\tilde{\theta}_{ij}^{g}\left(L\right)}.100=\frac{\sum_{\substack{i,j=1\\i\neq j}}^{N}\tilde{\theta}_{ij}^{g}\left(L\right)}{N}.100 \tag{4}$$

The following is the estimation of directional spillovers using the generalized variance decomposition matrix's normalized elements. The directional spillovers measure the total spillovers pending from or coming to particular assets. The estimation of directional spillovers is by employing the following equation:

$$S_{i.}^g\left(L\right)=\frac{\sum_{\substack{j=1\\j\neq i}}^{N}\tilde{\theta}_{ij}^{g}\left(L\right)}{\sum_{i,j=1}^{N}\tilde{\theta}_{ij}^{g}\left(L\right)}.100=\frac{\sum_{\substack{j=1\\j\neq i}}^{N}\tilde{\theta}_{ij}^{g}\left(L\right)}{N}.100 \tag{5}$$

Eq.(5) measure the directional spillovers from all indexes *j* received by index *i*. The directional volatility spillovers received by index *j* from index *i* could be measured by the following equation.

$$S_{.i}^g\left(L\right)=\frac{\sum_{\substack{j=1\\j\neq i}}^{N}\tilde{\theta}_{ji}^{g}\left(L\right)}{\sum_{i,j=1}^{N}\tilde{\theta}_{ji}^{g}\left(L\right)}.100=\frac{\sum_{\substack{j=1\\j\neq i}}^{N}\tilde{\theta}_{ji}^{g}\left(L\right)}{N}.100 \tag{6}$$

The next step is estimating net volatility spillover from index *i* to another index *j*. The net volatility spillover could be measured by the difference in the gross volatility shocks being broadcast to and received from other indexes. Therefore, the equation is as follows.

$$S_i^g\left(L\right)=S_{.i}^g\left(L\right)-S_{i.}^g\left(L\right) \tag{7}$$

Lastly, this study estimates the net pairwise volatility spillover following DY (2012), with the following equation:

$$S_{ij}^g\left(L\right)=\left(\frac{\tilde{\theta}_{ji}^{g}\left(L\right)}{\sum_{i,k=1}^{N}\tilde{\theta}_{ik}^{g}\left(L\right)}-\frac{\tilde{\theta}_{ij}^{g}\left(L\right)}{\sum_{j,k=1}^{N}\tilde{\theta}_{ik}^{g}\left(L\right)}\right).100=\frac{\tilde{\theta}_{ji}^{g}\left(L\right)-\tilde{\theta}_{ij}^{g}\left(L\right)}{N}.100 \tag{8}$$

On average, approximately 49.1% of the forecast error variance in Bitcoin and stock markets comes from the other Bitcoin and stock markets' volatility spillovers[1]. This number is higher than before the pandemic, which is 42.9%[2], and supports the existence of financial contagion during a time of crisis.

The positive (negative) value of net volatility spillovers indicates the market to be a net transmitter (receiver) of volatility. Before (during) the pandemic, BTCIDR, BTCNGN, and BTCZAR (BTCIDR and BTCNGN) are net volatility transmitters to other Bitcoin and stock markets. BTCMYR remains a net volatility receiver both before and during the pandemic. The negative or positive transmitted spillovers could indicate whether the market is dominated by the uninformed (when negative) and informed traders (when positive) (Mensi et al., 2020).

The authors then use the 60-day rolling window in full research period to estimate the total volatility spillovers between Bitcoin and stock market. The total volatility spillover plot before the pandemic starts slightly below 62.5% and fluctuates between 62.5% and 65%. This phenomenon could be due to increasing Bitcoin price during 2018 and half of 2019. The rapid increase in volatility spillover after the Covid-19 worldwide pandemic announcement further supports the existence of financial contagion during a crisis.

The directional volatility spillovers received by Bitcoin markets are higher during the pandemic than before the pandemic takes place. The authors learn that during the pandemic BTCIDR holds the most significant directional volatility to others at maximum level 120%. This number is significantly higher than the volatility being transmitted to other Bitcoin markets (74.3%). It shows how, during the pandemic, Bitcoin volatility spilled over more to their stock market counterparties than to other Bitcoin markets and" decouple" the local stock markets.

After calculated the net volatility spillovers, the authors then plot the net pairwise spillovers between Bitcoin and the local stock market during the research period in Figure 1 (using the framework developed by (Diebold & Yilmaz, 2012)). During the crisis period, Bitcoin in Nigeria became the most powerful transmitter at the maximum level of 30%, followed by Bitcoin in Indonesia (22.5%). On average, the pairwise spillovers between Bitcoin and stock markets (except in Nigeria) decreased during the crisis. It shows how the transmitter market is secluded from the other market during the crisis (Hkiri et al., 2017) and confirm the decoupling hypothesis.

Figure 1. Bitcoin and Stock market in Indonesia

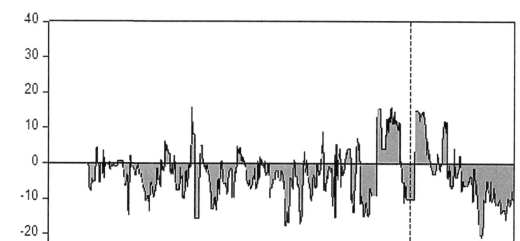

Figure 2. Bitcoin and Stock market in Malaysia

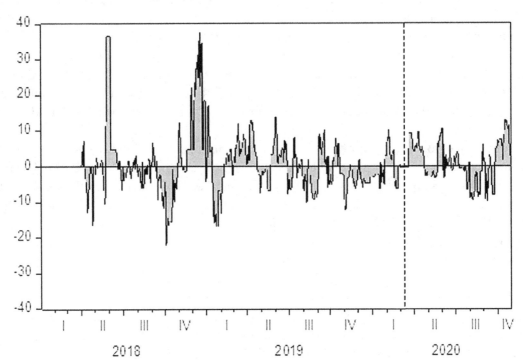

Figure 3. Bitcoin and Stock market in Nigeria

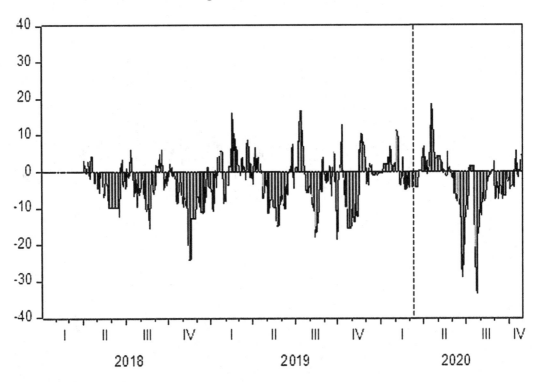

Figure 4. Bitcoin and Stock market in South Africa

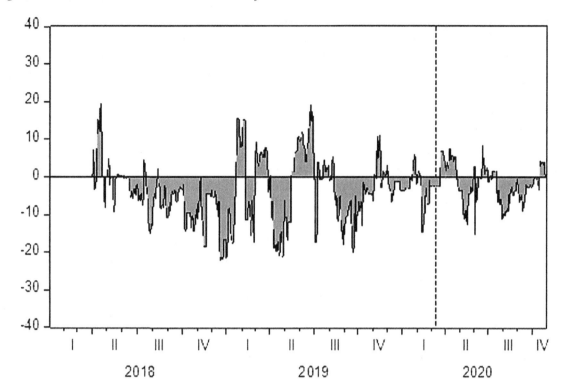

Figures 1-4. Net Pairwise Volatility Spillover – Bitcoin and Stock Market in Emerging Countries
Notes: The dashed line denotes March 11, 2020. The net pairwise volatility spillovers are calculated with the 60-day rolling window estimation

The Short-term Safe Haven Role During Crisis: Non-US Market

The authors also investigate the short-term safe-haven role of Bitcoin during crisis by considering the decoupling hypothesis (following (Hkiri et al., 2017)).. The dummy variable's estimated coefficient in Table 2 is negative (positive) and statistically significant for the stock and Bitcoin pair in Indonesia and Malaysia (Nigeria). However, Bitcoin and the stock market during the crisis in emerging countries correlates positively. Therefore, the authors consider Bitcoin as a hedge rather than a safe-haven for Indonesia's stocks during the Covid-19 pandemic crisis. These findings could have several explanations, i.e., (1) the Luno trading volume of each country, (2) the reverse trading activity between cryptocurrency and other financial markets, and (3) the cryptocurrency regulation.

The market caps of stocks from the highest to lowest is in South Africa (833.09 Billion USD)[3], Malaysia (448.60 Billion USD)[4], Indonesia (407.4 Billion USD)[5], and Nigeria (46.564 Billion USD). The trading volume of Bitcoin in South Africa (Nigeria) is 49.73% (17.62%) of Luno trading volume[6]. Bitcoin trade volumes in Indonesia (Malaysia) account for only 0.67% (6.63%) of the total Luno trading volume. Even though having the highest trading volume in the Luno exchange (16 Million USD), the stocks market in South Africa also significantly larger than the other countries. In Nigeria, the significantly smaller stock market caps compensate by the high trading volume of Bitcoin (12.3 Million USD).

In Indonesia, there were no government bonds issued until after the Asian Financial Crisis (AFC). The Indonesian stock market is also limited in size (account for 47% of GDP in 2015), liquidity (0.14% of market capitalization daily trading in 2015), and concentration (only 11 out of 532 companies account for 50% of the market capitalization) (Rowter, 2016). Meanwhile, In Malaysia, the bond market became a more feasible source of long-term financing for infrastructure projects. In Africa, the considerable safe-haven assets (Bitcoin, Gold, Silver, Palladium, and Platinum) does not provide a safety net for the emerging equity markets during the Covid-19 pandemic (Omane-Adjepong & Alagidede, 2020).

The legal status of cryptocurrency in a country could also be affecting its safe-haven role. In Indonesia, cryptocurrency is considered a legal commodity under Futures Trading Regulatory Agency (**Bappebti**), but not as a legal tender. In Malaysia, cryptocurrency is also a legal commodity, but only three coins are allowed to trade on regulated exchanges (Bitcoin, Ethereum, Litecoin, and Ripple) (Zhe, 2020). Contrasting to the regulation in Asia, there still no law in Africa which criminalized or legalized it (Infusion Lawyers, 2020).

To further examine the decoupling hypothesis, the authors analyze the net-volatility shifts behaviour around the Covid-19 pandemic crisis. This analysis could bring potential insights for investors and portfolio managers active in emerging countries' stock and Bitcoin markets.

This study employs a GARCH model in defining the dynamics of net volatility spillovers. Moreover, this study includes the dummy variables (in the mean and conditional variance equations) to express the crisis.

A changing sign on the dummy variable in both conditional and conditional variance models indicate the related crisis's impact on the net volatility spillovers across markets. The mean equation is as follows:

$$\rho_{ij,t} = \sum_{p=1}^{P} \psi_p \rho_{ij,t-p} + \beta COVID19_{Pandemic} + \eta_{ij,t} \qquad (9)$$

Whereas $\rho i_{j,t}$ is the net volatility spillovers between the Bitcoin market (i) and conventional stock index in related emerging countries (j). The mean equation's optimal lag length is estimated by the information criteria (AIC and SIC). For the dummy variable, this study employs the Covid-19 pandemic announcement on March 11, 2020, as the time of crisis

The coefficient of the dummy variable in both mean or variance equation models indicates the related crisis's impact on the net volatility spillover between the Bitcoin and stock markets in emerging countries. When the estimated coefficient is positive, there is an indication of the "contagion effect" between the stock and the Bitcoin market. Meanwhile, if the dummy variable's estimated coefficient is negative, it is suggested that the Bitcoin market moves against the stock market in emerging countries during the Covid-19 pandemic crisis. Moreover, it is implied that the Bitcoin market can be used as a hedge or safe haven for stock during the crisis period (e.g., Hkiri *et al.*, 2017).

On average, the pairwise volatility spillover between Bitcoin and stock market in Indonesia, Malaysia, Nigeria, and South Africa reverted back to half of its mean in about 2-3 days. This result suggests that investors of the Bitcoin market in Indonesia (Malaysia) must open a position at 0 days and must close on the 4th (5th) days if they want to utilize the safe-haven role of Bitcoin. In South Africa, although not statistically significant, the investors could consider the safe-haven role of Bitcoin by open a position at 0 days and close on the 4th days. Nevertheless, this results further supports the notion on the mean reversion process of Bitcoin market during the Covid-19 pandemic and suggests on the choice of short-term investment for investors in the Bitcoin market.

Table 2. Estimates of GARCH (1,1) of the net volatility for pairs of matching stocks and Bitcoin markets around the Covid-19 pandemic crisis

	Indonesia	Malaysia	Nigeria	South Africa
Panel A. The mean equation				
Constant	0.0007	0.0019	-0.0112	-0.0019
ρt_{-1}	-0.0451**	0.0012	-0.0533***	-0.0749***
Covid19_Pandemic$_t$	**-0.0496*****	**-0.0496****	0.0533***	-0.0002
Panel B. The variance equation				
Constant	0.0012***	0.0942***	5.26E-05***	0.0218***
η^2_{t-1}	0.1245***	0.1486**	0.0558***	0.1248***
h_{t-1}	0.5745***	0.5986***	0.9567***	0.5748***
Covid19_Pandemic$_t$	**-0.4124****	-0.0417	0.0427***	-0.0212
Panel C. Diagnostic tests				
Q(5)	0.7594	2.6622	7.5447	2.0634
ARCH(5)	1.0532	0.0183	0.3075	0.0073
Notes:	The sample's basis is data retrieved from Bitcoincharts.com for Bitcoin spot price data and DataStream for the stock index in Indonesia, Malaysia, Nigeria, and South Africa. The second sample set data period is from January 2, 2018, until October 30, 2020.			

THE REGULATION OF CRYPTOCURRENCIES IN UNITED STATES AND EMERGING COUNTRIES

Overall, there are two approaches to regulate cryptocurrencies and blockchain technology in the US. First, states promote innovative technology by exempting cryptocurrencies from the securities laws (Dewey, 2020). In Oklahoma, the state government issues a bill authorizing cryptocurrency to be used, offered, sold, and accepted as an instrument of monetary value (Dewey, 2020). However, there also states that issued the prohibition or warning about investment (for example, in Maryland and Hawaii) and accepting payment in cryptocurrencies (for example, Iowa).

The sale of cryptocurrency in the US is only regulated when the sale: (1) constitutes the security sale under state or federal law, or (2) considered as the money transmission under the state law under the Federal law (Dewey, 2020). Furthermore, the Securities and Exchange Commission (SEC) also has regulatory authority over the issuance of any token or digital asset that constitutes security (Dewey, 2020).

The legal status of cryptocurrency differs in Indonesia, Malaysia, Nigeria, and South Africa. In Indonesia, cryptocurrency is considered a legal commodity under Futures Trading Regulatory Agency (**Bappebti**), but not a legal tender. The Indonesian Law (Indonesian Law No.7 Year 2011) about currency prohibits any currency besides Indonesia Rupiah (IDR) as a medium of exchange. The regulatory authority in Indonesia, Bank Indonesia, also issue the BI regulation Number 19/12/PBI/2017 which prohibits financial technology (fintech) firms from processing payment transactions that use virtual currency. Therefore, the existence of Bitcoin is similar to a commodity, with the willingness of investors (Bitcoin holders) to bear their risks for things that do not meet their original expectations. In other words, every investor in the cryptocurrency market is at their own risk (Sanni, 2020).

In Malaysia, cryptocurrency also being a legal commodity but not recognized as legal tender by the Malaysian Central Bank (Moorthy, 2018). The cryptocurrencies allowed for trade on regulated exchanges are somewhat limited, i.e., Bitcoin, Ethereum, Litecoin, and Ripple (Zhe, 2020). The regulatory framework for the digital assets' offering and trading in Malaysia is regulated by the Securities Commission Malaysia (SC) and Bank Negara Malaysia (BNM). The relatively mature regulatory framework of cryptocurrency investment and a more developed capital market could make investors prefer the classical assets more as safe-haven assets.

Contrasting to Asia's regulation, Africa's cryptocurrency regulation is relatively undeveloped. There still no law in Nigeria, Kenya, or Ghana which criminalized or legalized it (Infusion Lawyers, 2020). Interestingly, the government in Nigeria has attempted to ban cryptocurrency indirectly. The government has emphasized how every cryptocurrency investment is not enforced by law in Nigeria. Nigeria has the Nigerian Cyber Crime (Prohibition, Prevention) Act 2015, and the Central Bank of Nigeria (CBN) Consumer Protection Framework keeps private consumers' data. However, cryptocurrency is beyond the consumers' data protection due to its non-traceable data, which implies investors' willingness to bear all risks (Sanni, 2020).

In South Africa, although cryptocurrencies could be traded on various platforms, they have not considered securities according to the Financial Markets Act, 2012 (Act No. 19 of 2012). Cryptocurrencies were also not regarded as legal tender due to only the South African Reserve Bank (SARB), which allowed to issue the legal tender for South Africa (IFWG - Crypto Assets Regulatory Working Group, 2014). Moreover, cryptocurrencies also do not consider as fiat currencies or virtual money in South Africa (Reddy & Lawack, 2019). However, SARS has announced continuing to apply the regular income tax rules to cryptocurrency transactions (SARS, 2018). The transaction includes mining, purchasing goods/service using, and the gains and losses from trading in cryptocurrencies (SARS, 2018).

SOLUTIONS AND RECOMMENDATIONS

This study utilizes sample sets of cryptocurrency, gold, and stocks daily price data around the Covid-19 pandemic. According to the dynamic conditional correlation analysis of cryptocurrency and traditional assets, cryptocurrency act as safe-havens for the US stocks during the pandemic. This finding is robust under the safe-haven regression and robust tests of safe-haven regression analysis.

The decoupling hypothesis test of the Bitcoin and stock markets in Indonesia, Malaysia, Nigeria, and South Africa align with the decreasing directional volatility spillover from the local stock markets. From the Covid-19 pandemic dummy variable coefficient, Bitcoin could act as safe-havens for stocks in Indonesia (statistically significant), Malaysia (statistically significant for mean model), and South Africa (not statistically significant). These findings could have several explanations, i.e., (1) the Luno trading volume of each country, (2) the reverse trading activity between cryptocurrency and other financial markets, (3) the economic outlook of each country, and (4) the cryptocurrency regulation.

This study could have several implications for government and investors in emerging countries, especially in Indonesia, Malaysia, Nigeria, and South Africa. First, the safe-haven role of cryptocurrency in a country could be related to its current capital market condition. When phase one agreement between the US and China occurred in December 2019, major equity markets in Asia achieved positive returns in the first three weeks of 2020 (Asian Development Bank, 2020). The Indonesian stock market is also limited in size (account for 47% of GDP in 2015, smaller than other ASEAN countries) and liquidity (0.14% of market capitalization daily trading in 2015), and concentration (only 11 out of 532 companies account for 50% of the market capitalization) (Rowter, 2016).

Meanwhile, In Malaysia, the bond market became a more viable source of long-term financing for infrastructure projects. In Africa, the considerable safe-haven assets (Bitcoin, Gold, Silver, Palladium, and Platinum) do not provide a safety net for the emerging equity markets during the Covid-19 pandemic (Omana-Adjepong and Alagidede, 2020). Therefore, the government or the local stock market authorities could consider issuing a finance or investment instrument backed up by the local authorities. To build better financial access for the business or organizations, government or financial market authorities could issue a law regulating organizations' requirements and mechanisms to invest in the cryptocurrency.

The legal status of cryptocurrencies in a country could also be affecting whether it is a safe-haven for local stock or not. This condition becomes important, especially since most countries in the world, even businesses themselves, view cryptocurrency as illegal. While in Indonesia, cryptocurrency is considered a legal commodity under Futures Trading Regulatory Agency (Bappebti), but not a legal tender. In Malaysia, cryptocurrency is also a legal commodity, but only three coins are allowed to trade on regulated exchanges (Bitcoin, Ethereum, Litecoin, and Ripple) (Zhe, 2020). Contrasting to Asia's regulation, Africa's cryptocurrency regulation is relatively undeveloped. There still no law in Nigeria, Kenya, or Ghana which criminalized or legalized it (Infusion Lawyers, 2020) and potentially to be used as a medium of illegal transactions.

To address the possibility of the higher Bitcoin price in few years ahead (Batabyal, 2020) and has been the case in recent times, local governments may consider using cryptocurrencies as investments. Indonesia recently has announced 229 cryptocurrencies (including Bitcoin, Ethereum, Tether), which could be traded legally in the Indonesian cryptocurrency exchange (Peraturan Badan Pengawas Perdagangan Berjangka Komoditi, 2020)However, the regulation should also be more advanced in regulating the investors' mechanisms and requirements to executing the investments.

The result also suggests the mean reversion of net pairwise spillover between Bitcoin and local stock market. On average, the pairwise volatility spillover between Bitcoin and stock market in Indonesia, Malaysia, Nigeria, and South Africa reverted back to half of its mean in about 2-3 days. This result suggests that investors of the Bitcoin market in Indonesia (Malaysia) must open a position at 0 days and must close on the 4th (5th) days if they want to utilize the safe-haven role of Bitcoin. Furthermore, this result also supports on the notion of Bitcoin as a short-term investment.

FUTURE RESEARCH DIRECTIONS

For further research, more variability in methodologies would allow us to identify the role of safe-haven cryptocurrencies in different situations. However, the test should remain in crisis corridors that often give rise to typical and interesting anomalies. Hence, crises could be treated as natural laboratories to deal with advanced crises predicted to become more frequent and immediate. One of the methodology variability is the future research could elaborate more on the determinant factors of lockdown (e.g., political stability, level of development; level of digitalization; degree of decentralization (Ferraresi et al., 2020) to the volatility transmissions among different countries. In addition, to test the existence of Mixture Distribution Hypothesis, further research could also incorporate the trading volume into the volatility models of cryptocurrencies.

To enrich the regulatory framework on cryptocurrency, there are several matters that could be done by the further research. First, the determination on how taxation level of cryptocurrency could affect the cryptocurrency transactions. In Indonesia, there are two main propositions on the appropriate tax level for cryptocurrency transaction: from the regulatory authority and from the Indonesian Crypto Asset Traders Association. The Directorate General of Taxation consider the cryptocurrency transactions are subject to income tax, i.e., 0.1% of the capital gain, similar to the transactions in stock markets. However, the Indonesian Crypto Asset Traders Association propose the level of tax to be a half from the income tax of stock market due to the high volatility of cryptocurrency investments. The high volatility and relatively new market of cryptocurrency could lead to the decrease in investors' participation when the taxation level is determined too high.

Second, the identification of market manipulation in the cryptocurrency market. In the case of cryptocurrency, this could relate to the parties of the upcoming cryptocurrency exchange. The market manipulation refers to the investors that conduct two or more securities transactions, either directly or indirectly, so that causing the price of securities on the stock Exchange to remain, increase, or decrease with the aim of influencing other parties to buy, sell or hold securities (Law No. 8 of 1995). Whether or not there is a market manipulation in the cryptocurrency market, could be a fruitful finding on the future cryptocurrency regulation.

Third, the identification of the relation between investors' financial literacy and the cryptocurrency transactions. This step relates to the notion of herding behavior in the cryptocurrency market. The further research could study the level of investors' financial literacy and the motivation of conducting cryptocurrency transactions. This finding could be an essential insight for the regulatory authority on including the financial literacy on the initial screening of investors in cryptocurrency market.

CONCLUSION

According to the DCC and safe-haven regression analysis, Bitcoin and Ethereum act as safe-havens for the US stocks during the Covid-19 pandemic. This finding is robust using the cDCC method[7] (Aielli, 2013). The result also robust after employing the safe-haven regression analysis on the London stock exchange and adding stablecoin to address the volatility issues[8] (Baur & Hoang, 2020).

This study also tested the contagion and decoupling hypothesis of Bitcoin and the local stock market during the pandemic. For the contagion hypothesis, this study follows the framework of Diebold & Yilmaz (2012). The results showed a spillover of higher total volatility between the Bitcoin market during the pandemic. Thus, it shows the Bitcoin market's financial contagion during the crisis. This research also discovered how before (after) the pandemic; informed (uninformed) traders dominated the Bitcoin market in South Africa. Transmission of positive volatility (negative) may indicate the dominance of informed (uninformed) traders in the market (Mensi et al., 2020). However, due to the information availability of the current data, this study still could not determine directly whether the market traders are informed or uninformed.

Overall, from an investor perspective, this study's results affirm the idea of cryptocurrencies as an alternative investment that the financial community at large has accepted. However, investors must also be aware of how cryptocurrencies' safe-haven properties depend on the research period's contextual settings (Bouri, Shahzad, et al., 2020; Bouri, Molnár, et al., 2017; Stensås et al., 2019). Because as modelling, there are still determining elements of the modelling feasibility. This research has sought to address the volatility issue by adding stablecoins to the safe-haven regression analysis of Bitcoin and Ethereum. Therefore, to ensure a crypto safe-haven for an investment portfolio, investors can also add stablecoins to the investment portfolio to balance the cryptocurrencies' volatilities.

This research limitation is a rather limited research period (from July 2019 for the first sample set and January 2018 for the second sample set) because it is related to the Covid-19 pandemic period that is difficult to predict will end. High volatility and dependence on the time and location of research lead to careful consideration before generalizing our findings. However, this research also attempts to address the bias caused by the limited research period. First, this research uses two multivariate methods such as GARCH DCC and cDCC, to accommodate the estimation dimension to achieve a more general result. Second, this study also attempted to address the small sample bias with several scenarios to achieve consistent results. For example, this research employs the rolling window estimation for both the correlation and standard deviation of Bitcoin and stock markets to see how the results are consistent for both research subperiods (before and during the pandemic).

The authors also note how the nature of this study's ex-post research also shows the Efficient Market Hypothesis (EMH) after publication. In other words, the same strategy cannot be implemented and generalized as a single strategy. Time factors, places, macro and micro situations are certainly important factors that must be considered before implementing the same strategy formula.

REFERENCES

Abbas, Q., Khan, S., & Shah, S. Z. A. (2013). Volatility transmission in regional Asian stock markets. *Emerging Markets Review*, *16*, 66–77. doi:10.1016/j.ememar.2013.04.004

Aielli, G. P. (2013). Dynamic Conditional Correlation: On Properties and Estimation. *Journal of Business & Economic Statistics*, *31*(3), 282–299. doi:10.1080/07350015.2013.771027

Baruník, J., Kočenda, E., & Vácha, L. (2016). Asymmetric connectedness on the U.S. stock market: Bad and good volatility spillovers. *Journal of Financial Markets*, *27*, 55–78. doi:10.1016/j.finmar.2015.09.003

Batabyal, A. (2020). *Bitcoin Price Prediction and Forecast 2020, 2022, 2025, 2030*. CoinSwitch. https://coinswitch.co/news/bitcoin-price-prediction-2020-2025-latest-btc-price-prediction-bitcoin-news-update

Baur, D. G., & Hoang, L. T. (2020). A crypto safe haven against Bitcoin. *Finance Research Letters*, *101431*(January). doi:10.1016/j.frl.2020.101431

Baur, D. G., & Lucey, B. M. (2010). Is gold a hedge or a safe haven? An analysis of stocks, bonds and gold. *Financial Review*, *45*(2), 217–229. doi:10.1111/j.1540-6288.2010.00244.x

Baur, D. G., & Mcdermott, T. K. (2010). Is gold a safe haven? International evidence. *Journal of Banking & Finance*, *34*(8), 1886–1898. doi:10.1016/j.jbankfin.2009.12.008

Beneki, C., Koulis, A., Kyriazis, N. A., & Papadamou, S. (2019). Investigating volatility transmission and hedging properties between Bitcoin and Ethereum. *Research in International Business and Finance, 48*(January), 219–227. doi:10.1016/j.ribaf.2019.01.001

Bodie, Z., Kane, A., & Marcus, A. J. (2014). *Investments* (10th ed.). McGraw-Hill Education.

Bouoiyour, J., Selmi, R., Tiwari, A. K., & Olayeni, O. (2016). What drives Bitcoin price? *Economic Bulletin, 36*(2).

Bouri, E., Das, M., Gupta, R., & Roubaud, D. (2018). Spillovers between Bitcoin and other assets during bear and bull markets. *Applied Economics, 50*(55), 5935–5949. doi:10.1080/00036846.2018.1488075

Bouri, E., Hussain Shahzad, S. J., & Roubaud, D. (2020). Cryptocurrencies as hedges and safe-havens for US equity sectors. *The Quarterly Review of Economics and Finance, 75*, 294–307. doi:10.1016/j.qref.2019.05.001

Bouri, E., Molnár, P., Azzi, G., Roubaud, D., & Hagfors, L. I. (2017). On the hedge and safe haven properties of Bitcoin: Is it really more than a diversifier? *Finance Research Letters, 20*, 192–198. doi:10.1016/j.frl.2016.09.025

Conlon, T., & McGee, R. (2020). Safe Haven or Risky Hazard? Bitcoin during the Covid-19 Bear Market. *Finance Research Letters, 101607*(April). doi:10.2139srn.3560361 PMID:32550843

Corbet, S., Hu, Y., Lucey, B. M., & Oxley, L. (2020). Aye Corona! The Contagion Effects of Being Named Corona during the COVID-19 Pandemic. *Finance Research Letters, 101591*. Advance online publication. doi:10.2139srn.3561866 PMID:32837362

Crawley, J. (2020, May 12). *Bitcoin halving: What does this mean and what will its effect be?* Finextra. Com. https://www.finextra.com/the-long-read/40/bitcoin-halving-what-does-this-mean-and-what-will-its-effect-be

Dewey, J. (2020). *Blockchain Laws and Regulations | USA | GLI.* Global Legal Insight. https://www.globallegalinsights.com/practice-areas/blockchain-laws-and-regulations/usa

Diebold, F. X., & Yilmaz, K. (2012). Better to give than to receive: Predictive directional measurement of volatility spillovers. *International Journal of Forecasting, 28*(1), 57–66. doi:10.1016/j.ijforecast.2011.02.006

Dimitriou, D., Kenourgios, D., & Simos, T. (2020). Are there any other safe haven assets? Evidence for "exotic" and alternative assets. *International Review of Economics & Finance, 69*, 614–628. Advance online publication. doi:10.1016/j.iref.2020.07.002

Dyhrberg, A. H. (2016). Bitcoin, gold and the dollar – A GARCH volatility analysis. *Finance Research Letters, 16*, 85–92. doi:10.1016/j.frl.2015.10.008

Ferraresi, M., Kotsogiannis, C., Rizzo, L., & Secomandi, R. (2020). The 'Great Lockdown' and its determinants. *Economics Letters, 197*, 109628. doi:10.1016/j.econlet.2020.109628 PMID:33100438

Forbes, K. J., & Rigobon, R. (2016). No Contagion, Only Interdependence : Measuring Stock Market Comovements. *The Journal of Finance, 57*(5), 2223–2261. doi:10.1111/0022-1082.00494

Frankenfield, J. (2019). *Do Cryptocurrencies Have Intrinsic Value? It Depends.* Investopedia Stock Analysis. https://www.investopedia.com/news/does-crypto-have-intrinsic-value-bitcoin-ethereum/#:~:text=Cryptocurrencies

Geuder, J., Kinateder, H., & Wagner, N. F. (2019). Cryptocurrencies as financial bubbles: The case of Bitcoin. *Finance Research Letters, 31*, 179–184. doi:10.1016/j.frl.2018.11.011

Gil-Alana, L. A., Abakah, E. J. A., & Rojo, M. F. R. (2020). Cryptocurrencies and stock market indices. Are they related? *Research in International Business and Finance, 51*, 101063. Advance online publication. doi:10.1016/j.ribaf.2019.101063

Global Legal Research Center. (2018). Regulation of Cryptocurrency Around the World. In *The Law Library of Congress* (Vol. 5080). https://www.loc.gov/law/help/cryptocurrency/regulation-of-cryptocurrency.pdf

Harris, F. H. deB., Mcinish, T. H., Shoesmith, G. L., Robert, A., The, S., Analysis, Q., Dec, N., Harris, F. H., Mclnish, T. H., Shoesmith, G. L., & Wood, R. A. (1995). Cointegration, Error Correction, and Price Discovery on Informationally Linked Security Markets. *Journal of Financial and Quantitative Analysis, 30*(4).

Hartmann, P., Straetmans, S., & de Vries, C. G. (2004). Asset Market Linkages in Crisis Periods. *Tinbergen Institute Discussion Paper, 71*(2).

Hkiri, B., Hammoudeh, S., Aloui, C., & Yarovaya, L. (2017). Are Islamic indexes a safe haven for investors? An analysis of total, directional and net volatility spillovers between conventional and Islamic indexes and importance of crisis periods. *Pacific-Basin Finance Journal, 43*, 124–150. doi:10.1016/j.pacfin.2017.03.001

Hong, K. H. (2017). Bitcoin as an alternative investment vehicle. *Information Technology Management, 18*(4), 265–275. doi:10.100710799-016-0264-6

Hood, M., & Malik, F. (2016). Is Gold the Best Hedge and a Safe Haven Under Changing Stock Market Volatility. *Review of Financial Economics*, (August). Advance online publication. doi:10.1016/j.rfe.2013.03.001

IFWG - Crypto Assets Regulatory Working Group. (2014). *Position Paper on Crypto Assets.* Author.

Infusion Lawyers. (2020). Nigeria : Deal Or No Deal, Cryptocurrency Transactions Remain Legal In Nigeria And Environs. Mondaq.Com.

Jang, H., & Sul, W. (2002). The Asian financial crisis and the co-movement of Asian stock markets. *Journal of Asian Economics, 13*(1), 94–104. doi:10.1016/S1049-0078(01)00115-4

Ji, Q., Bouri, E., Keung, C., Lau, M., & Roubaud, D. (2019). Dynamic connectedness and integration in cryptocurrency markets. *International Review of Financial Analysis, 63*(December), 257–272. doi:10.1016/j.irfa.2018.12.002

Joy, M. (2011). Gold and the US dollar : Hedge or haven? *Finance Research Letters, 8*(3), 120–131. doi:10.1016/j.frl.2011.01.001

Kalichkin, D. (2018). *Rethinking Network Value to Transactions (NVT) Ratio.* Medium.Com. https://medium.com/cryptolab/https-medium-com-kalichkin-rethinking-nvt-ratio-2cf810df0ab0

Katsiampa, P. (2019). Volatility co-movement between Bitcoin and Ether. *Finance Research Letters, 30*(June), 221–227. doi:10.1016/j.frl.2018.10.005

Kenourgios, D., Dimitriou, D., & Christopoulos, A. (2013). Asset Markets Contagion During the Global Financial Crisis. *Multinational Finance Journal, 17*(1/2), 49–76. doi:10.17578/17-1/2-2

King, M. A., & Wadhwani, S. (1990). Transmission of Volatility between Stock Markets. *Review of Financial Studies, 3*(1), 5–33. doi:10.1093/rfs/3.1.5

Koop, G., Pesaran, M. H., & Potter, S. M. (1996). Impulse response analysis in nonlinear multivariate models. *Journal of Econometrics, 74*(1), 119–147. doi:10.1016/0304-4076(95)01753-4

Kristoufek, L. (2015). What are the main drivers of the bitcoin price? Evidence from wavelet coherence analysis. *PLoS One, 10*(4), 1–15. doi:10.1371/journal.pone.0123923 PMID:25874694

Kurka, J. (2019). Do cryptocurrencies and traditional asset classes influence each other? *Finance Research Letters, 31*, 38–46. doi:10.1016/j.frl.2019.04.018

Lee, D. K. C., Guo, L., & Wang, Y. (2018). A New Investment Opportunity? *Journal of Alternative Investments.*

Lin, W., Engle, R. F., & Ito, T. (1994). Do Bulls and Bears Move Across Borders? International Transmission of Stock Returns and Volatility. *Review of Financial Studies, 7*(3), 507–538. doi:10.1093/rfs/7.3.507

Liu, W. (2018). Are Gold and Government Bond Safe-Haven Assets? An Extremal Quantile Regression Analysis. *International Review of Finance.* Advance online publication. doi:10.1111/irfi.12232

Makarov, I., & Schoar, A. (2020). Trading and arbitrage in cryptocurrency markets R. *Journal of Financial Economics, 135*(2), 293–319. doi:10.1016/j.jfineco.2019.07.001

Manner, H., & Reznikova, O. (2012, April). A Survey on Time-Varying Copulas: Specification, Simulations, and Application. *Econometric Reviews,* 37–41. doi:10.1080/07474938.2011.608042

Mariana, C. D. (2021). *Safe-haven dynamics of cryptocurrencies for the U.S. and emerging stock markets* [PhD dissertation].

Mariana, C. D., Ekaputra, I. A., & Husodo, Z. A. (2021). Are Bitcoin and Ethereum safe-havens for stocks during the COVID-19 pandemic? *Finance Research Letters, 38*, 101798. Advance online publication. doi:10.1016/j.frl.2020.101798 PMID:33100925

Mensi, W., Al-yahyaee, K. H., & Hoon, S. (2019). *Structural breaks and double long memory of cryptocurrency prices : A comparative analysis from Bitcoin and Ethereum.* Academic Press.

Mensi, W., Nekhili, R., Vo, X. V., Suleman, T., & Kang, S. H. (2020). Asymmetric volatility connectedness among U.S. stock sectors. *The North American Journal of Economics and Finance, 101327.* Advance online publication. doi:10.1016/j.najef.2020.101327

Mighri, Z., & Alsaggaf, M. I. (2019). *Volatility Spillovers among the Cryptocurrency Time Series.* Academic Press.

Milutinovic, M. (2018). Cryptocurrency. *Ekonomika (Nis), 64*(March), 95–104. doi:10.5937/ekonomika1801105M

Moorthy, D. (2018). A Study on Rising Effects of Cryptocurrency in the Regulations of Malaysian Legal System. *International Journal of Business, Economics and Law, 15*(4), 35–41.

Ober, M., Katzenbeisser, S., & Hamacher, K. (2013). Structure and anonymity of the bitcoin transaction graph. *Future Internet, 5*(2), 237–250. doi:10.3390/fi5020237

Omane-adjepong, M., & Alagidede, I. P. (2019). Multiresolution analysis and spillovers of major cryptocurrency markets. *Research in International Business and Finance, 49*(March), 191–206. doi:10.1016/j.ribaf.2019.03.003

Omane-Adjepong, M., & Alagidede, I. P. (2020). Exploration of safe havens for Africa's stock markets: A test case under COVID-19 crisis. *Finance Research Letters, 101877*(December). doi:10.1016/j.frl.2020.101877

Peng, X. (2019). Do precious metals act as hedges or safe havens for China's financial markets? *Finance Research Letters, 101353*. Advance online publication. doi:10.1016/j.frl.2019.101353

Pesaran, H. H., & Shin, Y. (1998). Generalized impulse response analysis in linear multivariate models. *Economics Letters, 58*(1), 17–29. doi:10.1016/S0165-1765(97)00214-0

Reddy, E., & Lawack, V. (2019). An Overview of the Regulatory Developments in South Africa Regarding the Use of Cryptocurrencies. *SA Mercantile Law Journal, 31*.

Rowter, K. (2016). Indonesia Capital Market Developments and Challenges. *Nomura Journal of Asian Financial Markets, 1*(1), 9–13. www.nomurafoundation.or.jp›2016/10›NJACM1-1AU16-05_Indonesia

Sandoval, L., & Franca, I. D. P. (2012). Correlation of financial markets in times of crisis. *Physica A, 391*(1–2), 187–208. doi:10.1016/j.physa.2011.07.023

Sanni, S. O. (2020). *Nigeria : Crypto Currency In Nigeria : Regulatory Framework & Related Issues.* Mondaq.Com. https://www.mondaq.com/nigeria/fin-tech/855410/crypto-currency-in-nigeria-regulatory-framework-related-issues?type=popular

SARS. (2018). *6 April 2018 - SARS's stance on the tax treatment of cryptocurrencies.* Sars.Gov.Za. https://www.sars.gov.za/Media/MediaReleases/Pages/6-April-2018---SARS-stance-on-the-tax-treatment-of-cryptocurrencies-.aspx

Shahzad, S. J. H., Bouri, E., Roubaud, D., Kristoufek, L., & Lucey, B. (2019). Is Bitcoin a better safe-haven investment than gold and commodities? *International Review of Financial Analysis, 63*(January), 322–330. doi:10.1016/j.irfa.2019.01.002

Stensås, A., Nygaard, M. F., Kyaw, K., & Treepongkaruna, S. (2019). Can Bitcoin be a diversifier, hedge or safe haven tool? *Cogent Economics and Finance, 7*(1), 1593072. Advance online publication. doi:10.1080/23322039.2019.1593072

Syllignakis, M. N., & Kouretas, G. P. (2011). Dynamic correlation analysis of financial contagion: Evidence from the Central and Eastern European markets. *International Review of Economics & Finance*, *20*(4), 717–732. doi:10.1016/j.iref.2011.01.006

Woonomic. (2017). *Bitcoin NVT Ratio: Woobull Charts*. Woobull.Com. http://charts.woobull.com/bitcoin-nvt-ratio/

Yarovaya, L., & Lau, M. C. K. (2016). Stock market comovements around the Global Financial Crisis: Evidence from the UK, BRICS and MIST markets. *Research in International Business and Finance*, *37*, 605–619. doi:10.1016/j.ribaf.2016.01.023

Yelowitz, A., & Wilson, M. (2015). Characteristics of Bitcoin users: An analysis of Google search data. *Applied Economics Letters*, *22*(13), 1030–1036. doi:10.1080/13504851.2014.995359

Zhe, K. S. K. (2020). *Cover Story: Are tighter cryptocurrency regulations needed?* The EdgeMarkets. Com. https://www.theedgemarkets.com/article/cover-story-are-tighter-cryptocurrency-regulations-needed

KEY TERMS AND DEFINITIONS

Co-Movement: The correlated or similar movement between two or more entities.

Crisis: A time of arising difficulties, financial crisis indicated by the rapid dropping value of assets.

Cryptocurrency: A type of digital currency in which transactions are verified and records maintained by a decentralized system using cryptography.

Decoupling: Relates to the condition the returns of an asset class that have been correlated with other assets in the past no longer move in similar movement.

Emerging Market: An economy that experiences considerable economic growth and possesses some characteristics of a developed economy.

Safe-Haven: A safe investment instrument, relates to the asset that negatively correlated with other financial assets during crisis.

Volatility Transmission: The degree to which price uncertainty in one market affects price uncertainty in the others.

ENDNOTES

[1]   The result is available upon request.
[2]   The result is available upon request.
[3]   Based on the data retrieved from www.african-markets.com as per 15 January 2021.
[4]   Based on the data retrieved from the CEIC Data Website as per 15 January 2021.
[5]   Based on the data retrieved from https://tradinghours.com as per 15 January 2021.
[6]   Based on the data retrieved from https://coinmarketcap.com/exchanges/luno/ as per 15 January 2021.
[7]   The result is available upon request.
[8]   The result is available upon request.

Chapter 22
Perceived Cyber Security Challenges in Adoption and Diffusion of FinTech Services in India

Pallavi Kudal

Dr. D.Y. Patil Institute of Management Studies, Pune, India

Sunny Dawar

Faculty of Management and Commerce, Manipal University Jaipur, India

Rashmi Rai

School of Business and Management, Christ University, Bangalore, India

Prince Dawar

Poornima Group of Colleges, Jaipur, India

ABSTRACT

FinTech is a term that refers to a new type of digital technology that intends to build up and automate the distribution and management of financial services. FinTech is an abbreviation for "financial technology." FinTech, or financial technology, assists companies, business holders, and consumers in managing their financial procedures and methods. The high adoption rate of fintech services creates a whole ecosystem of looters and hackers. This indeed is scary, and this chapter makes an attempt to understand the adoption rate of fintech services and diffusion challenges at the same time.

DOI: 10.4018/978-1-6684-5284-4.ch022

1.0 INTRODUCTION

FinTech is a term that refers to a new type of digital technology which intends to build up and automate the distribution and management of financial services. FinTech is an abbreviation for "financial technology."

Less than 1% (0.2%) people had mobile phones in 1990 (S.O'Dea, 2021). And now almost everyone owns a mobile phone in developed economies. If a technology can go from 0% to 100% adoption in nearly 3 decades, then that's fairly high adoption rate. If this is surprising, then fintech adoption rate is astonishing.

In the twenty-first century, the term FinTech was coined to explain the technology utilized in the back-end structures of recognized financial organisations. FinTech, on the other hand, now incorporates a comprehensive range of divisions and industries, involving education, nonprofit fundraising, investment management, retail banking, and much more.

FinTech, or financial technology, assists companies, business holders, and consumers in managing their financial procedures and methods through specialized software and algorithms. In today's world, FinTech has expanded to involve the creation and application of cryptocurrencies such as Bitcoin. Despite the fact that various sectors of FinTech maintain to gain grip today, a big portion related to FinTech however concentrates on the conventional worldwide banking sector and India is undoubtedly leading in the FinTech reforms worldwide.

To understand the FinTech landscape in India and identify the challenges and solutions related to Fintech in developing economy like India is the main objective of this chapter. The major challenges of FinTech remain the cybersecurity challenges as with increasing FinTech adoption the cybercrime is also increasing multifold.

2.0 LITERATURE REVIEW

Physical separation between the buyer and the seller, physical separation between the buyer and the product, environmental distance, and cybercrime risks are all serious challenges to the digital economy or businesses. Organizations must obtain techniques to initiate and develop this cyber connection, then the most efficient way is through reliable digital platforms (Shalhoub & Al Qasimi, 2010). Dynes, Goetz, & Freeman (2007) discovered the threats that for-profit entities face with increased FinTech adoption, the motivations and drivers that impact investment in cyber security actions, and exactly how policy programs may influence the cyber readiness of various business units. Concerns about cybersecurity are becoming more prevalent as blockchain technology is used more in accounting and other areas of the firm (Gordon et.al. 2008). Cyber security has emerged as a result of technological advancements and their impact on economic, geographical, and political development strategies (Hansen, Nissenbaum, 2009). All over the world policymakers, analysts, and international organizations are concerned about cybersecurity (Fischer, 2009).

A viable cybersecurity structure should strive to create a secure environment for IoT devices. As a result, it must include national and international collaborative efforts to develop standards, methodologies, procedures, and processes that align policy approaches to cybersecurity issues ranging from business to health to entertainment to education to technology (Teplinsky, 2013).

Cyber security, on the other hand, encompasses not only the protection of cyberspace, but also the protection of those who work in cyberspace and any assets that can be accessed via cyberspace (Von &

Van, 2013). Physical methods and human involvement are inadequate for observing and defending these structures; hence more modern cyber defense methods, capable of identifying a broad variety of risks and creating logical real-time decisions are required (Dilek et. Al., 2015).

The most pressing cybersecurity question for a company today is not whether to invest in cybersecurity, but how much to invest in cybersecurity to ensure the safety of not only their data, but their entire network (Gordon, Loeb, and Zhou, 2016). Because of the phenomenon's anonymity and border lessness, cybersecurity poses a security quandary for national and international governments in terms of how to secure their domain from cyberattack threats (Buchanan, 2016). Cyberattacks have impacted individuals, national governments, world governments, private enterprises, and public enterprises. This cyberthreat phenomenon primarily affects new emerging economies that are transitioning to digital economies and digital business activities (Antonucci, 2017).

Cybersecurity legislation is frequently associated with both punitive and protective measures, such as government surveillance and privacy legislation (Kosseff, 2017). Cybersecurity concerns the safeguarding of electronics, software, and data, as well as the procedures used to gain access to systems. In general, security goals include privacy, which means that information should not be inappropriately disclosed to unauthorized devices or individuals for modification or destruction (Furstenau et. al. 2020 & Gorog, 2018).

Furthermore, cyber-attacks on smart grids have a significant impact on citizen and government safety because critical infrastructure components are particularly vulnerable and expensive (Urquhart & McAuley (2018). Small businesses were able to anticipate the damage of both tangible and financial assets. Just a few companies, however, discovered intangible asset loss as a potential cyber risk. The majority of small-scale businesses had implemented necessary cybersecurity procedures to keep data entry and some core industry operations. Regrettably, they hardly take proactive steps to prevent and detect cyber threats (Yudhiyati, Putritama & Rahmawati (2021). Because many of our everyday objects can be connected to the Internet, cybersecurity has become a major concern in our daily lives and the present adoption of FinTech landscape is surely a challenge (Al et. al., 2021).

3.0 FINTECH LANDSCAPE IN INDIA

Fintech is not new in India. Even a simple ATM uses Fintech. Its impact on how we manage our finances has grown dramatically in recent years. The origins of the Fintech sector can be traced all the way back to the nineteenth century, when technology began to make its imprint on history, causing the fintech industry to develop. The key stages of fintech are classified into the following cycles Fintech 1.0, Fintech 2.0 and Fintech 3.0 (Arneris, Barberis & Ross, 2016). From the late twentieth century onwards, finance has been digitalized, first in an analogue setting, then in a digital context. In both the developed and developing worlds, a new era of FinTech has evolved since 2008. This age is defined not by the financial products or services provided, but by who provides them and how swiftly technology is evolving at the retail and wholesale levels. In the 1980s, banks began experimenting with online banking, and by the 1990s, they had mastered it and made it mainstream. In India, ICICI Bank was the first to enter the internet banking industry, offering very restricted financial services such as account access and intra-bank transfers. Other banks began to follow suit, rapidly altering the banking landscape. It's no surprise that banks have experienced difficulties such as technical difficulties, fraud, complex cross-border operations, payment methods, and so on.

Fintech 2.0 provided the fintech business a more modern appearance, and the events listed below sparked the emergence of fintech in India.

- The first Indian ATM launched in Mumbai by HSBC.
- Central Bank of India launched first credit card in 1980.
- PayPal launch in 1998.
- Global financial crisis in 2008.

In 21st century India emerged as an active player in FinTech verse with many smart improvements and innovations. With advent of bitcoin in 2009, Paytm in 2010, and UPI launch in 2016, the fintech landscape entered a exponential growth in India. The 2016 demonetization push drew a lot of attention from the finance community. The Indian government's push for Digital India, which aims to transform the country into a cashless economy with financial inclusion, provides significant support to fintech firms.

The fintech business has the ability to have the greatest impacts on the life cycles of unbanked of this world and which is indeed a magic in the making. The challenge of Fintech is not to make financial industry better but to make financial services serve the human life better. Tech is dead without people. Fintech can empower people and help the societies and more importantly help the unbanked. Financial technology (Fintech) and insurance technology (insurtech) has the power to serve the most vulnerable people around in the world. Financial technology (Fintech) services that make use of evolving technology like Internet of Things (IoT) are turning out to be more common (Lim, 2019).

From the perspective of consumers, the latest spread of the mobile payment segment, managed by innovative mobile Fintech payment services such as Google Pay, Paytm, Phone Pe and Amazon Pay, is extremely valuable and swiftly growing Fintech service. Even though businesses have made attempts to increase the application of services, security is critical in the spread of services. Fintech has its own set of challenges and majorly of those are digital literacy, awareness, and cyber security challenges (Pal, 2019).

India has certainly become one of the world's fastest developing FinTech hubs in present time, kudos to one of the world's speediest-rising economies. In India, mobile banking, paperless loaning, mobile wallets, secure payment accesses, and other models are already in use. More than the last couple of years, it's been a humongous acceptance of digital payment practices in India in recent couple of years, creating basic financial services far more convenient.

Several factors have assisted the continued growth of India's FinTech network, involving the rising accessibility of smartphones, high-speed connectivity, expanded internet access, and not to forget the cash crunch due to demonetization and lockdowns during Corona virus outbreak. Indeed, India is well-arranged to attain a FinTechs sector estimation of US$ 150-160 billion till 2025, indicating an incremental value creation capacity of US$ 100 billion (BCG and FICCI, March 2021). Not only have Indian consumers embraced Fintech across sectors, but financial institutions' adoption of FinTech products has also increased exponentially.

As a result, the number of FinTechs in India has increased dramatically. Of the 2100+ FinTech's in India today, 67 percent were originated in last five years. Investment into FinTechs has been likewise impressive, with India's FinTechs rising more than US$ 10 billion since 2016. Currently, 8 FinTechs have reached the coveted 'billion-dollar-valuation' milestone, with an additional 44 FinTechs valued at US$ 100 million or more (BCG and FICCI, March 2021).

Despite a drop in FinTech investment flows to India in 2020 India remains one of the Top 5 FinTech investment destinations (BCG and FICCI, March 2021). Furthermore, COVID-19 has hastened the rate of digitization through all categories. Even though certain FinTech segments (for instance, lending) may experience a short-term blip, there is a significant long-term behavioural shift toward digital subscriptions in financial services. Between March 2020 and May 2021, UPI payments (both by volume and value) increased to three times their pre-pandemic level, while the share of other payment methods decreased (Refer Fig 1). Similar increase of rate has been seen in virtual broking, where the shares of active customers with Fintech discount advisors (Zerodha, Upstox, 5paisa) increased from 43% to 57% (HDFC Securities, Oct 2021). Discount brokers account for an estimated 27% market share, despite accounting for only 49% active clients.

Figure 1. Comparison of Volumes of UPI and other Payment Modes from Dec 2019 to May 2021
Source: RBI data for Electronic Payment Systems (as published on NPCI website)

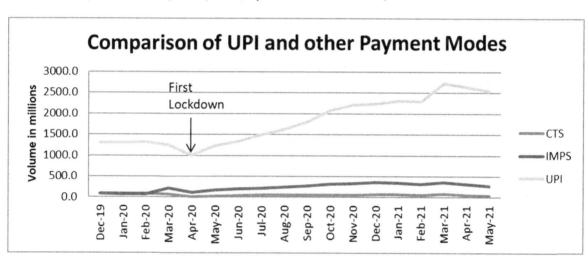

From 2015 to 2019, acceptance of consumer for fintech companies and products expanded dramatically around the world. As of 2019, 75% of users throughout the world have utilized a money transfer and/or compensation service. Insurance (insurtech) adoption has expanded substantially from 8% in 2015 to nearly 50% in 2019 (Norrestad, 2022).

Digital payment techniques indisputably have been the mark carriers of the India's FinTech business, with the introduction of innovative platforms like Paytm, MobiKwik, PhonePe, and others. Furthermore, the global relationship between Facebook and Reliance Jio is projected to have a huge impact on Indian digital payments division, along with special emphasis on hyperlocal digital business which will reach from tier 2 to 3 cities as well as rural regions.

Despite India's excellent diversity and residents, a large portion of the country stays underserved, unbanked, and susceptible to a continuously shifting governing environment. The country's economic situation and unexplained obstacles are no easy obstacles to conquer for these reasons. Fintech, with its capability and potential to profoundly alter and reorganize India's economic and investing services segment, comes into play here.

Fintech is democratizing financial services in India. FinTech directs the development of IT to all kinds of financial services, eliminating as much "inefficiency" as viable and responding the speed problem, allowing users to utilize the service for less money and more conveniently. The basic reasons of financial exclusion have been taken care of in new age Fintech.

Fintech doesn't differentiate in gender, geographical area, economic condition, and social status of an individual. During lock down (corona virus outbreak) when cash crunch was at its peak (due to un-availability of ready funds), small vegetable vendors, hawkers, house helps, and grocery shop owners all shifted to accepting Paytm and Google Pay accounts. Not only mobile payment systems but also the Insurtech saw a huge demand as people wanted to buy an affordable insurance plan for health coverage and fintech companies like Policy Bazaar became quite popular. Fintech has begun to have a direct and indirect impact on our lives. Everything from a company raising funds to a person obtaining a loan, obtaining information, transferring funds, and investing is undergoing significant change. But all that shines may not be gold. FinTech also comes with its own sets of challenges.

Fintech believes on technology and machines more than human. In a way its good but it surely brings in the technology related fears and insecurities into play. There are numerous incidences where bank accounts have been hacked and investors have been cheated by few unscrupulous individuals. The basic premise of financial technology is that the work previously performed by humans is automated and entirely de-intermediated using technology, the same results can be obtained at a very cheap cost. Technology supremacy of Fintech paves the way to disbelief in the system by a major part of the population.

4.0 CHALLENGES OF FINTECH

4.1 Technology Supremacy

Fintech has shaped significant transformation in recent years, impacting several corporate verticals, especially in the financial sector. Various sectors of finance, such as money lending and payments, have benefited from it. This transition has offered users with a seamless and distinctive experience, permitting them to certainly understand and embrace Fintech. Most of the customers, however, remain to prefer more conventional banking institutions. Fintech, while experiencing a technological transformation, faces some interests and obstacles. Security breaches, lack of transparency, lack of trust, etc. are some of the additional critical issues (Partasevitch, 2021). The number of cybercrimes reported in India expanded considerably in 2020 linked to the earlier year. More than fifty thousand cybercrime cases were registered in that year. At the same point found, Uttar Pradesh and Karnataka had the maximum percentage of cybercrime occurrences (Keelery, 2021).

Most of these complaints were recorded under the Information Technology Act with the intention of defrauding or sexually abusing victims. Indian consumers lost nearly 18 billion dollars in 2017 due to cybercrime, according to estimations. Due to lack of cybercrime awareness and classification methods in a country like India, the true figures of cyber fraud are likely to be under-informed. Phishing schemes, online harassment, identity theft scams, invasion of privacy and cyber stalking are the top five most frequent cybercrimes reported in India (Narnolia). As more people turn to digital transactions in the wake of the Covid outbreak, hundreds of people have been victims of financial cyber fraud. The sum of banking frauds in the nation has expanded as the figure of digital contracts has increased.

According to RBI data, India faced an average of 229 banking scams every day in fiscal year 2020-21 (Reserve Bank of India). In Financial year 2021, around were 83,638 cases of banking scam in India, with a total worth of Rs 1.38 lakh crore (www.businesstoday.com). According to statistics published by the

RBI in reply to a RTI (Right to Information) appeal accepted by India Today, only Rs 1,031.31 crore of cyber fraud amount has been recaptured so far. In Gujarat (one of the states in India) alone the number of such cases increased by 67 percent in 2020-21, as con artists cast a wider net to deceive people who were mostly at home due to the restrictions imposed by Covid-19.

In the fiscal year 2020-21, the state's scheduled commercial banks (SCBs) recorded 4,671 cases of cyber fraud, up from 2,803 in the previous fiscal year (Parikh, 2021). If in only one state, the cyber frauds increased 67 percent then one can imagine the magnitude in whole country. From FY08 to FY21, 3,14,270 incidences of financial fraud were registered, totaling Rs 5.31 lakh crore. But only Rs 56,502 crore had been recaptured so far (www.businesstoday.com). In 2020, the state of Telangana in India had the highest number banking frauds related to the One Time Password provision with approximately 525 cases registered with the authorities. Overall, there were over one thousand cases of OTP frauds that year across the country (Sandhya Keelery, 2021).

FinTech refers to the use of technology to deliver financial solutions in its broadest definition. This constant use of technology in finance is progressively placing pressure on the industry to move away from its regulations. Human behaviour is to treat regulations as hinderance to technology adoption. However, the rise of FinTech has necessitated the development of RegTech. The phrase 'RegTech' is a combination of the terms 'regulatory' and 'technology, and it implies to the usage of both in the context of regulation of technology, particularly information technology ('IT'), Monitoring, reporting, and compliance should all be a part of the process (Zetzsche, 2017). RegTech is not just confined to financial sectors however this is one sector where its demand is highest. Techfin on the other hand is a technology company that intends to provide financial solutions using existing technology. Unlike Fintech, these businesses aren't solely focused on providing financial services; it's just one of several services they offer. Techfin firms include companies like as Google, Facebook, Amazon, and Apple.

Around 19% of FinTech companies in India were in the digital payments industry as of August 2020. Digital lending came in second with 17 percent, and WealthTech came in third with 14 percent. In 2020, India had about 2,200 FinTech enterprises and start-ups, making it the world's second-largest FinTech hub behind the United States (Statista Research Department, 2021). Around 80% of respondents amongst the corporate finance leaders in India gave importance to improvement of existing ERP competences, real-time data analytics, robotic process automation and visualization tools as their desired emerging technologies for acceptance in a survey directed from September to October 2020 (Sun, 2021).

After 2008, while regulators struggled to come up with a new effective regulatory model, an explosion of Fintech development occurred, posing a tremendous challenge to regulators. Because the entire point of Fintech was to disrupt pre-existing models of markets, industries, and finance in general, it ran counter to the regulators' only goal of preventing market disruption. At the same time, there has been a considerable regulatory focus on supporting financial sector innovation and development. As a result, policymakers have to strike a balance between encouraging innovation and addressing the issues that come with adopting new technologies (Khan, 2018). To enforce this new vision the regulators adopted four major approaches:

1. **Doing Nothing** (Permissive or Restrictive): Prior to 2015, China was an example of this, as it took a permissive stance by not enforcing any restrictions, resulting in a meteoric rise in Fintech (and TechFin). However, as we have seen in the past, doing nothing comes with its own set of hazards and obstacles. As a result, China's priority has switched to developing a new legal framework for digital financial services since 2015. Other jurisdictions have taken a more restricted approach,

requiring new market entrants with innovative, technology-driven business models to adhere to the existing regulatory framework, which was created for traditional financial company models such as banks and insurance companies. As a result, the innovation spirit and growth prospects of these technologies are suffocated.

2. **Contact Points:** This strategy entailed regulators meeting with newcomers to learn about their business models and new technology in order to build appropriate regulatory responses.

3. **Sandboxes** - Some authorities have created what are known as sandboxes, which provide a platform for both the new company and the regulators to experiment with different types of regulations in a constrained market environment in the hopes of determining the optimal course of action.

4. **New Regulatory Frameworks**: With the rise of new business models such as peer-to-peer lending, alternative payment systems, and crowd funding platforms, countries such as India and China are trying to create totally new legal frameworks to meet the needs of these disruptive business models.

4.2 Consumer Concerns Regarding Digital Transactions

An online survey done by Statista.com for 13087 respondents from April 23- July 31, 2020, throws light on consumer concerns regarding digital transactions in India (Statista Research Department, 2021). Most of the respondents (31%) stated that they liked about the fundamental requirement to execute. In contrast, more than seven percent of the respondents chosen to get into digital operations to a trustable beneficiary that year. 28.49% respondents showed concerns regarding privacy and 28.4% respondents were worried about Security.

Only 13.72% were impressed with convenience of digital payments. 9.4% have trust in this system and only 8.04% have awareness about grievance redressal system. The above statistics clearly show that despite of the people's view that digital payments are basic requirement to transact now days but then also more than 50% respondents have concern regarding safety and privacy while making digital transactions.

Figure 2. Consumer interests about digital transactions India in 2020
Source: Statista.com

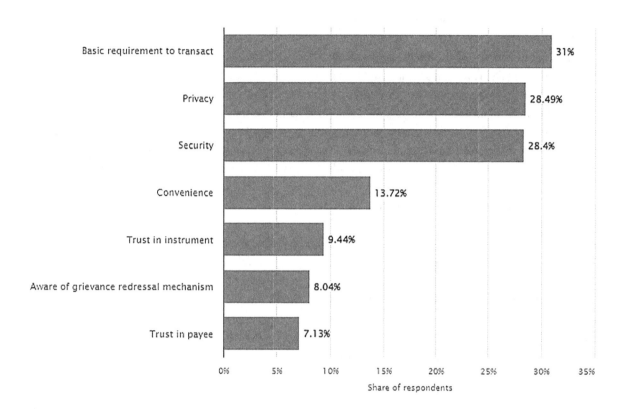

According to a study performed on digital payments throughout India in 2020, most of the respondents preferred to use UPI as the digital payment method (Statista Research Department, 2021). There is a growing need for rebuilding the trust in the Fintech landscape owing to increased number of cyber security related crimes. Cyber-attacks became far more widespread as the world adjusted to the WFH environment. Between 2020 and 2021, more than 92 percent of fintech applications were hacked. While uncertainties persist, it is critical that businesses, particularly those in the fintech sector, take preventative measures to protect themselves against ever-evolving cyber threats (Agarwal, 2022).

The more the governance develops, and Fintech possesses substantial personal records and assets, the additional probable crooks will notice. According to the IBM analysis, the average worldwide cost of a data breach in the banking sector is 4.9 million Euros per cyber-attack. According to ImmuniWeb, 98 percent of the world's top 100 financial start-ups are vulnerable to catastrophic cyber-attacks. According to BCG, Fintechs are 300 times more likely than previous businesses to be the target of a cyber-attack. Because start-ups in this field not have the human and financial sources to deal with safety issues, there is a danger of data being retrieved and violated by cybercriminals for improper purposes. In order to achieve total cybersecurity, Fintechs must protect crucial data and assets (Firdaus, 2020).

5.0 FINTECH CHALLENGES IN INDIA

However, the Fintech challenges are quite varied in India. The demographic divide of Indian population, lack of financial and digital literacy and financial exclusion are at the core of fintech challenges in India.

India's achievements in mobile penetration and financial inclusion have propelled the country into the era of fintech. The financial segment in India had made a substantial influence by emphasizing equal access to financial essential services through different strategies and practices like Pradhan Mantri Jan Dhan Yojana (PMJDY) and Direct Benefit Transfer (DBT) are few.

Regardless of many polices, a big segment of adult segment of population is not having access to conventional financial services because of country's massive population and the obvious disparity between rural and urban areas. Furthermore, the availability of cost saving and viable distribution processes to rural areas obscures matters.

Indian fintech sector is facing following challenges:

1. **A Lack of Trust:** Indian customers are traditionally conservative and choose to operate business in cash. In spite of an ever-escalating number of persons having approach to banking, individuals who are underbanked or unbanked continue to be unaware of banking services. As a result, it is difficult for FinTech companies to gain people's trust.

    Because the development and exponential evolution of fintech is a relatively new sector in the Indian marketplace, it has so far to gain the confidence of the general public as a reliable financial services alternative. To gain public approval, the fintech division must shift the way consumers identify and utilize financial essential services.

    Furthermore, fintech businesses would have to inform Indian consumers about the advantages of utilizing fintech to access financial facilities, as the FinTech sector would be responsible for streamlining learning and experiences of its services.

2. **Isolation due to Geography:** Rural India is home to roughly two-thirds of the population and 70 percent of the labour force. In spite of the expanding rural financial system and enhanced usage of financial services by rural residents, fintech companies are striving to pick up rural demand.

    Declining financial transaction margins, excessive operating capital and elevated operational expenditures, and a scarcity of financial knowledge are major barriers to the adoption of numerous financial products and services.

3. **Absence of Proper Control in the Fintech Sector:** Increased regulation may pose a threat to Indian fintech firms with suppressing originality and increasing operational costs. Though, controlling simplicity will help the segment in the potential by allowing it to gain client trust and attract more investment.

    The regulator bears the significant responsibility of fostering an environment conducive to innovation while sticking to customer safety, data protection, and secrecy matters. In reaction to the fast spurt of innovation, supervisors usually take action to some market activities in a specific manner.

4. **Age and Gender Differences in Demographics:** The Indian government has encouraged wide-spread growth in digitization across all sectors. The rise in digitization was primarily seen among Indian millennials, who made up a sizable portion of the country's consumer support and were open to innovative technologies and digital explanations.

However, older audiences faced difficulties in adopting fintech products and services due to a lack of financial and internet literacy. People's current capabilities, aspirations, and needs account for the gap in fintech practice.

To succeed in the rural financial sector, fintech firms require an omnichannel vigorous and efficient strategy to connect rural businesspersons and deliver them the right knowledge platform and support to deal many customer services economically and efficiently.

To deal with rural challenges, fintech enterprises must increase spread, enhance the customer knowledge of the rural meeting through relationship developing, reduce barriers to strategy execution, and foster adoption and use of the digital channel.

5. **Population Unbanked and Underbanked:** Even today, a large portion of the Indian population is unbanked and prefers cash operations over online purchases. To start with, Fintechs in India experienced slow growth due to poor structure, such as low internet access and literacy levels. Though the Indian government is addressing these concerns through substantial policies, the benefits will be apparent only in the long run.

Another barrier to Fintech growth in India is the country's low financial literacy. For example, in order to enhance financial inclusion in the country, India unveiled the Pradhan Mantri Jan Dhan Yojana. According to a World Bank report, after initiating a total of 180 billion bank accounts, more than 48% of them persisted unused without a single operation in a year. Regardless of all of its initiatives, India is still a long way from financial inclusion.

6. **The Government's Lack of Support:** Fintechs face a serious shortage of administration assistance and inducements to safeguard their interests in Indian financial marketplaces. This can be extremely discouraging for different Fintech participants. Fintechs play an important role in pushing economic growth and must be given every opportunity to succeed.
7. **Data safety:** Data security has emerged as a major point in the Internet circle, whether it is in the context of payment apps, mobile banking, or Fintech in usual. Conventional banking techniques, as we all understand, rely on safety shields, electronic vaults, CCTVs, and strong bulletproof entries to maintain their information secure and reliable. Vulnerabilities are considerably additional refined and potentially have a larger effect on clients.
8. **Customized services:** For a long time, personalized services had been the primary and fundamental factor of banking. Customization, in today's perspective, means cooperating with a user at the right moment, on their desired network, with a proper solution to their particular needs.

Furthermore, customers are eager to understand Fintech as financial well-being factor. Certain clients may feel amazed by a wide variety of alternatives, and efficient personalization provides them with only the limited choices they seek.

9. **A Lack of Mobile and Technological Expertise:** A few finance companies in the fintech business need proper or accessible mobile banking services. Several banks, however, struggle to imitate websites, but in this digital era, no one would prefer a mobile application. Every client needs a simple and accessible method of control.

So, a lack of knowledge in fintech mobile app growth facilities results in unfriendly functions which do not fully utilize mobile devices. Apps may not advance from NFC chips, fingerprint unlocking, geolocation features, and other elements, for example. Using these features and technologies, a fintech bank can provide incredible experiences.

10. **Customer Acquisition Marketing Strategies That Work:** In general, fintech companies do not know their niche, target consultation, or approaches. In modern times, where the majority of people still use conventional banking facilities, Fintech firms have struggled to defeat this challenge.
11. **User Retention and Usability:** User retention and Usability are major worries in fintech sector. A fintech app, on another side, must turn up an equilibrium between client understanding and protection. A company should analyze its competitors and use to gain a seamless user experience.

6.0 THE PRIMARY CYBER SECURITY CHALLENGES FOR FINTECH

In India financial literacy, financial awareness, and regulatory stability remain big concerns for the industry. Cybersecurity is a critical basic brick to Fintech's growth. Following are the cybersecurity challenges faced by fintech users:

1. **Susceptible and Complicated Cyber Security Algorithms:** Fintechs rely entirely on their installed Apps, which have access to users' profiles and essential data, especially through real-time operations. Applications are more susceptible to security threats than resources, and if a cybercriminal has access, it can obtain complete gain access to Fintech's current structure and system for services. (Firdaus, 2020)
2. **Excessive Reliance on Cloud Services:** Several Fintechs are transferring their functions to cloud services as a result of the introduction of cloud technologies, in order to be able to deliver smooth and high-value services at a lower price. Fintechs are unable to completely safeguard cloud operations as a result of this process, making it vulnerable in the same way that a traditional data centre is. It is challenging to guarantee security in the cloud environment due to the complexity and volume of data interactions. (Firdaus, 2020)
3. **Phishing Attacks due to Human Error**: Human error is a big cause for this kind of violation, and this is at ease of cybercriminals. The cause related to phishing attempts on lost or taken machines, and individual mistake is biggest cause meant for this kind of violation and margin to cybercriminals. (Firdaus, 2020)
4. **Convenience at the Expense of Security**: Fintech offers ease and simplicity of utilization to services, the difficulty is that it can sometimes undermine crucial security characteristics. (Firdaus, 2020)
5. **Failure to Comply with Regulations**: Fintechs must comply with compliance and regulatory standards, which include proper licenses, such as those for Specialized Banks, Electronic Money

Institutions, and Payment Institutions, as well as GDPR (EU General data protection regulation) and PSD2 (Payment Services Directive 2) compliance. Failure to achieve these and other critical criteria is a significant violation that puts you at greater risk (Firdaus, 2020).

6. **Excessive Association of Third Parties**: Currently, Fintechs are utilizing results from other companies to supplement delivering services from their functions. It turns out to be simpler for cybercriminals to hack Fintechs using third-party access (Firdaus, 2020).

7. **Digital threat related to Data:** Cybercriminals will have more opportunities as online transactions increase. Furthermore, companies that mine data, such as customer information, product analysis results, and standard market information, generate significant intellectual estate, which is a desired target in and of the situation.

8. **Supply Chain Interconnection:** Supply chains are becoming more interconnected. Companies are urging vendors and customers to become members of their networks. This weakens a company's security perimeter.

9. **Hacking:** This action involves breaking into someone's system without their permission in order to steal or destroy data, and it has increased hundreds of times in recent years. Because information is easily accessible online, even non-technical people can participate in hacking.

7.0 SOLUTIONS FOR CYBERSECURITY IN FINTECH BUSINESS

A business need to use following cybersecurity solutions to provide the cyber security to business which can help in maintaining protection in business operations.

1. **Detection software:** Businesses must invest additional in cyber defense and safety as hackers and cybercriminals develop more sophisticated, as do their tools and software. The main step toward cyber security is evaluating and realizing existing gaps in business security. Proactively identifying and eliminating vulnerabilities in business systems is preferable to anticipating for a cyberattack on IT structure and trading with the results (Dadhich, 2020).

2. **Antivirus software:** To provide better security against malware and viruses, a modern antivirus result, like Acronis Cyber Protect Cloud, should be used. This is an AI-powered solution for ransomware protection and malware. Acronis Cyber Protect Cloud also offers threat and exposure awareness, which can identify vulnerabilities in operational systems that a company may not update for weeks – a major access point for malware (Dadhich, 2020).

3. **Backup software on cloud:** Backups assist organizations recover missed or corrupted data triggered by system breakdowns, accidental removal, disasters, or stealing, and the more current the backup, the quicker and easier the retrieval. Cloud-based cybersecurity results backup records as well as involve security features that avoid unauthorized entry to it. Acronis, for example, takes a fusion approach, blending local and cloud backups to offer flexible hybrid backup security as well as full system support and recovery (Dadhich, 2020).

4. **Firewall:** The foundation of cybersecurity solutions is a firewall. This is the most valuable instrument that a business should be necessary. A firewall monitors network traffic to prevent those that may be harmful to a business web application or website from happening. Advanced cybercriminals have found how to create data or applications which bypass firewalls and gain entry (Dadhich, 2020).

5. **Public Key Infrastructure:** Public key infrastructure services are most commonly used in secure sockets layers, which protect an organisation and the event critical knowledge even as also increasing customer trust. It ensures the protection of all online communications in request to reduce the threat of phishing cheats. Because an SSL certificate cannot ever be duplicated, it makes the site less susceptible to phishing attacks (Dadhich, 2020).

In 2021, the mobile threat landscape has provided new and major security challenges. And, as we look ahead to 2022 and beyond, fintech product/service providers should consider the following themes as they design their security strategy for the year ahead:

1. **Secure Access Service Edge (SASE):** SASE is a new cybersecurity concept introduced by Gartner in 2019. SASE is based on SD-WAN (software defined WAN), which allows you to combine network security and network access management into a single platform. This will be a game-changer since it will allow enterprises to manage network security more efficiently while also giving user-based and least-privileged access based on granular identifiers like user role, device, and location, thus incorporating endpoint security (Agarwal, 2022).
2. **New Age RegTech:** RegTech is a type of cloud computing that helps financial companies comply with new rules and regulations. It assists in the monitoring, analysis, and identification of abnormalities such as vulnerabilities and gaps using big data and machine-learning technologies (Agarwal, 2022).
3. **AI based Fraud detection:** The use of artificial intelligence (AI) will be critical. For detecting and preventing financial crime, fintech companies must turn to powerful artificial intelligence and machine learning technology. Fraud detection AI systems analyze company and customer data to detect client risks and weaknesses based on the investigation's findings. It has the potential to play a significant part in supporting the financial domain's security as more and more breakthrough technologies join and disrupt the business (Agarwal, 2022).
4. **Reliance on Block chain Systems:** Going forward, the tendency in Fintech should be to increase reliance on blockchain systems. Blockchains have shown to be extremely decentralised data flow platforms with great security. In a link-node design, they provide cutting-edge security features such as storing vital data as cryptographic hashes. Because decrypting every node in the connection is extremely complex, hackers will have a difficult time breaking into the system.
5. **Financial Literacy:** The adoption of fintech without financial literacy is indeed scary as people are not cautious and don't understand the security challenges while using fintech apps. A lot of fintech related security issues challenges can be solved when financial literacy rates are higher.

8.0 CONCLUSION

In practically every area, pandemic has hastened the deployment of technology. Fintech, on the other hand, has experienced the most widespread acceptance. Digital payment has become the preferred method of payment for everyone from small businesses to individual customers. The threats that lie over Fintech as it expands to become one of the most dominating industries will tend to increase. With a significant growth in cyber-attack threats, particularly huge active threats of data access via mobile apps, the entire finance ecosystem is subject to security problems. To connect with their customers, all financial institutions, including banks, fintech firms, and small banking enterprises, rely on applications. In this instance, cybersecurity is crucial, and organizations must safeguard sensitive data (Agarwal, 2022).

A Fintech cyber-attack impact not just money but also erodes the trust of users and this is very crucial for further perceived usefulness and actual usage of fintech services. Fintech is indeed democratizing the financial services and can be a game changer to achieve the financial inclusion targets in a developing country like India. Fintech companies need to statutorily follow all compliance frameworks and implement an intrusion detection system. They should hire third parties with high reputation in the market and avoid any kind of data breaches. Fintech companies have a long way to go and customer safety and trust can take them to places.

REFERENCES

Agarwal, H. (2022, January 24). New & emerging Fintech Security Trends in 2022. *The Times of India*.

Al-Omari, M., Rawashdeh, M., Qutaishat, F., Alshira'H, M., & Ababneh, N. (2021). An intelligent tree-based intrusion detection model for cyber security. *Journal of Network and Systems Management, 29*(2), 1–18. doi:10.100710922-021-09591-y

Antonucci, D. (2017). *The cyber risk handbook: Creating and measuring effective cybersecurity capabilities*. John Wiley & Sons.

BCG & FICCI. (2021). *India FinTech: A USD 100 Billion Opportunity*. BCG.

Buchanan, B. (2016). *The cybersecurity dilemma: Hacking, trust, and fear between nations*. Oxford University Press.

Buckley, R., Arner, D., & Barberis, J. (2016). The evolution of Fintech: A new post-crisis paradigm. *Georgetown Journal of International Law, 47*(4), 1271–1319.

Dadhich, P. (2020). *5 powerful cybersecurity solutions every business needs*. Available: https://www.znetlive.com/blog/cybersecurity-solutions-business-needs/

Dilek, S., Çakır, H., & Aydın, M. (2015). *Applications of artificial intelligence techniques to combating cyber crimes: A review*. arXiv preprint arXiv:1502.03552.

Dynes, S., Goetz, E., & Freeman, M. (2007, March). Cyber security: Are economic incentives adequate? In *International Conference on Critical Infrastructure Protection* (pp. 15-27). Springer. 10.1007/978-0-387-75462-8_2

Firdaus, H. (2020, October 7). *13 Cybersecurity Challenges for Fintech Companies*. Retrieved March 31, 2022, from https://www.e2enetworks.com/13-cybersecurity-challenges-for-fintech-companies/

Fischer, E. A. (2009). *Creating a National Framework for Cybersecurity: An analysis of issues and options*. Nova Science Publishers.

Furstenau, L. B., Sott, M. K., Homrich, A. J. O., Kipper, L. M., Al Abri, A. A., Cardoso, T. F., . . . Cobo, M. J. (2020, March). 20 years of scientific evolution of cyber security: A science mapping. In *International Conference on Industrial Engineering and Operations Management* (pp. 314-325). IEOM Society International.

Gordon, L. A., Loeb, M. P., Sohail, T., Tseng, C. Y., & Zhou, L. (2008). Cybersecurity, capital allocations and management control systems. *European Accounting Review*, *17*(2), 215–241. doi:10.1080/09638180701819972

Gordon, L. A., Loeb, M. P., & Zhou, L. (2016). Investing in cybersecurity: Insights from the Gordon-Loeb model. *Journal of Information Security*, *7*(02), 49–59. doi:10.4236/jis.2016.72004

Gorog, C., & Boult, T. E. (2018, July). Solving global cybersecurity problems by connecting trust using blockchain. In *2018 IEEE International Conference on Internet of Things (iThings) and IEEE Green Computing and Communications (GreenCom) and IEEE Cyber, Physical and Social Computing (CPSCom) and IEEE Smart Data (SmartData)* (pp. 1425-1432). IEEE. 10.1109/Cybermatics_2018.2018.00243

Karake-Shalhoub, Z., & Al Qasimi, L. (2010). *Cyber law and cyber security in developing and emerging economies*. Edward Elgar Publishing. doi:10.4337/9781849803380

Keelery, S. (2021, Oct 25). Retrieved February 24, 2022, from https://www.statista.com/statistics/309435/india-cyber-crime-it-act/#:~:text=India%20saw%20a%20significant%20jump,during%20the%20measured%20time%20period

Keelery, S. (2021, Oct 20). Retrieved February 24, 2022, from https://www.statista.com/statistics/1097969/india-number-of-otp-frauds-recorded-by-leading-state/

Khan, F. (2018, August 17). *RegTech & its Challenges*. Retrieved March 29, 2022, from https://www.datadriveninvestor.com/2018/08/17/regtech-its-challenges/

Kosseff, J. (2017). Cyber-physical systems and national security concerns. *Security and Privacy in Cyber-Physical Systems: Foundations, Principles and Applications*, 77-91.

Lim, S. H., Kim, D. J., Hur, Y., & Park, K. (2019). An Empirical Study of the Impacts of Perceived Security and Knowledge on Continuous Intention to Use Mobile Fintech Payment Services. *International Journal of Human-Computer Interaction*, *35*(10), 886–898. doi:10.1080/10447318.2018.1507132

NakerN. (2021, Sep 28). Retrieved from https://www.ey.com/en_in/consulting/the-winds-of-change-trends-shaping-india-s-fintech-sector

NarnoliaN. (n.d.). Retrieved from https://www.legalserviceindia.com/legal/article-4998-cyber-crime-in-india-an-overview.html

Norrestad, F. (2022, January 11). Retrieved March 23, 2022, from https://www.statista.com/statistics/1055356/fintech-adoption-rates-globally-selected-countries-by-category/

O'Dea, S. (2021, December 9). Retrieved March 23, 2022, from Statista.com: https://www.statista.com/statistics/262950/global-mobile-subscriptions-since-1993/

Pal, A., De', R., Herath, T., & Rao, H. R. (2019). A review of contextual factors affecting mobile payment adoption and use. *Journal of Banking and Financial Technology*, *3*(1), 43–57. doi:10.100742786-018-00005-3

Parikh, K. D. (2021, Dec 8). Retrieved February 24, 2022, from https://timesofindia.indiatimes.com/city/ahmedabad/cyber-fraud-cases-in-state-grew-by-67-in-2020-21/articleshow/88152757.cms

Partasevitch, T. (2021, July 21). Retrieved February 24, 2022, from https://www.financemagnates.com/fintech/major-challenges-the-fintech-industry-faces-today-and-how-to-overcome-them/

HDFC Securities. (2021). *Fintech Playbook: Discount Brokers.* HDFC Securities.

Statista Research Department. (2021, June 8). *Consumer concerns regarding digital transactions India in 2020.* Retrieved March 29, 2022, from www.statista.com: https://www.statista.com/statistics/1242336/india-consumer-concerns-about-digital-transactions/#statisticContainer

Statista Research Department. (2021). *FinTech firms share in India 2020, by segment.* Statista Research Department.

Sun, S. (2021). *Preferred technologies in finance process digitalization in India 2020.* Statista Research Department.

Teplinsky, M. J. (2012). Fiddling on the roof: Recent developments in cybersecurity. *Am. U. Bus. L. Rev.*, *2*, 225.

Urquhart, L., & McAuley, D. (2018). Avoiding the internet of insecure industrial things. *Computer Law & Security Review*, *34*(3), 450–466. doi:10.1016/j.clsr.2017.12.004

Von Solms, R., & Van Niekerk, J. (2013). From information security to cyber security. *Computers & Security, 38*, 97-102.

Yudhiyati, R., Putritama, A., & Rahmawati, D. (2021). What small businesses in developing country think of cybersecurity risks in the digital age: Indonesian case. *Journal of Information, Communication and Ethics in Society*.

Zetsche, D. A., Buckley, R. P., Arner, D. W., & Barberis, J. N. (2017). From FinTech to TechFin: The regulatory challenges of data-driven finance. *NYUJL & Bus.*, *14*, 393.

Compilation of References

A Companion to Film Theory. (n.d.). Academic Press.

Aaron, M., Rivadeneyra, F., & Samantha, F. (2017). *Fintech: Is this time different? A framework for assessing risks and opportunities for central banks. Bank of Canada Staff Discussion Paper, No. 2017-1.* Bank of Canada. https://www.banqueducanada.ca/wp-content/uploads/2017/07/sdp2017-10.pdf

Abbas, Q., Khan, S., & Shah, S. Z. A. (2013). Volatility transmission in regional Asian stock markets. *Emerging Markets Review, 16*, 66–77. doi:10.1016/j.ememar.2013.04.004

Abdillah, L. A. (2020). *FinTech E-Commerce Payment Application User Experience Analysis during COVID-19 Pandemic.* doi:10.15294/sji.v7i2.26056

Aboul-Enein, S. (2017). Cybersecurity challenges in the Middle East. *GCSP, 17*, 5–49.

Abraham, R., Schneider, J., & Vom Brocke, J. (2019). Data Governance: A Conceptual Framework, Structured Review, and Research Agenda. *International Journal of Information Management, 49*, 424–438. doi:10.1016/j.ijinfomgt.2019.07.008

Abuhasan, F., & Moreb, M. (2021). The Impact of the Digital Transformation on Customer Experience in Palestine Banks. *2021 International Conference on Information Technology, ICIT 2021 - Proceedings*, 43–48. 10.1109/ICIT52682.2021.9491744

Abuidris, Y., Kumar, R., & Wenyong, W. (2019). *A survey of Blockchain based on e-voting systems.* Paper presented at the Proceedings of the 2019 2nd International Conference on Blockchain Technology and Applications. Adekeye, T. Securing the Electoral E-Voting System Using Blockchain Technology. 10.1145/3376044.3376060

Abulencia, J. (2021). Insider attacks: Human-factors attacks and mitigation. *Computer Fraud & Security, 2021*(5), 14–17. doi:10.1016/S1361-3723(21)00054-3

Acar, A., Aksu, H., Uluagac, A. S., & Akkaya, K. (2020). A usable and robust continuous authentication framework using wearables. *IEEE Transactions on Mobile Computing, 20*(6), 2140–2153.

Acar, A., Liu, W., Beyah, R., Akkaya, K., & Uluagac, A. S. (2019). A privacy-preserving multifactor authentication system. *Security and Privacy, 2*(5), e88.

Acar, O., & Çitak, Y. E. (2019). Fintech Integration Process Suggestion for Banks. *Procedia Computer Science, 158*, 971–978. doi:10.1016/j.procs.2019.09.138

Adam, D. (2022). The pandemic's true death toll: Millions more than official counts. *Nature, 601*(7893), 312–315. doi:10.1038/d41586-022-00104-8 PMID:35042997

Adiputra, C. K., Hjort, R., & Sato, H. (2018). *A proposal of blockchain-based electronic voting system.* Paper presented at the 2018 second world conference on smart trends in systems, security and sustainability (WorldS4). 10.1109/WorldS4.2018.8611593

Agarwal, H. (2022, January 24). New & emerging Fintech Security Trends in 2022. *The Times of India.*

Agarwal, M., Biswas, S., & Nandi, S. (2018). An efficient scheme to detect evil twin rogue access point attack in 802.11 Wi-Fi networks. *International Journal of Wireless Information Networks*, *25*(2), 130–145. doi:10.100710776-018-0396-1

Agbesi, S., & Asante, G. (2019). *Electronic voting recording system based on blockchain technology.* Paper presented at the 2019 12th CMI Conference on Cybersecurity and Privacy (CMI). 10.1109/CMI48017.2019.8962142

Agbozo, E., & Asamoah, B. K. (2019). Data-driven e-government: Exploring the Socio-economic Ramifications. *e-Journal of e-Democracy and Open Government, 11*(1), 81-90.

Ahmad, A., Shafiuddin, W., Kama, M. N., & Saudi, M. M. (2019). A new cryptojacking malware classifier model based on dendritic cell algorithm. In *Proceedings of the 3rd International Conference on Vision, Image and Signal Processing* (pp. 1-5). Academic Press.

Ahmad, Y. A., Shaharuddin, M. F., Gunawan, T. S., & Arifin, F. (2022). *Implementation of an E-voting Prototype using Ethereum Blockchain in Ganache Network.* Paper presented at the 2022 IEEE 18th International Colloquium on Signal Processing & Applications (CSPA). 10.1109/CSPA55076.2022.9782016

Ahmad, A. a. (2018). Towards blockchain-driven, secure and transparent audit logs. In *Proceedings of the 15th EAI International Conference on Mobile and Ubiquitous Systems: Computing, Networking and Services* (pp. 443-448). 10.1145/3286978.3286985

Ahmad, A. S., Saad, M., & Mohaisen, A. (2019). Secure and transparent audit logs with BlockAudit. *Journal of Network and Computer Applications*, *145*, 102406. doi:10.1016/j.jnca.2019.102406

Ahmed, L., Iqbal, M. M., Aldabbas, H., Khalid, S., Saleem, Y., & Saeed, S. (2020). Images data practices for semantic segmentation of breast cancer using deep neural network. *Journal of Ambient Intelligence and Humanized Computing*, 1–17.

Ahmed, M. R., Shamrat, F. J. M., Ali, M. A., Mia, M. R., & Khatun, M. A. (2020). The future of electronic voting system using Block chain. *International Journal of Scientific Technology Research*, *9*, 4131–4134.

Ahn, B. (2022). Implementation and Early Adoption of an Ethereum-Based Electronic Voting System for the Prevention of Fraudulent Voting. *Sustainability*, *14*(5), 2917. doi:10.3390u14052917

Ahuja, S., Mani, S., & Zambrano, J. (2012). A Survey of the State of Cloud Computing in Healthcare. *Network and Communication Technologies.*, *1*. Advance online publication. doi:10.5539/nct.v1n2p12

Aielli, G. P. (2013). Dynamic Conditional Correlation: On Properties and Estimation. *Journal of Business & Economic Statistics*, *31*(3), 282–299. doi:10.1080/07350015.2013.771027

Ajao, L. A., Umar, B. U., Olajide, D. O., & Misra, S. (2022). Application of Crypto-Blockchain Technology for Securing Electronic Voting Systems. In *Blockchain Applications in the Smart Era* (pp. 85–105). Springer. doi:10.1007/978-3-030-89546-4_5

Akbanov, M., Vassilakis, V. G., & Logothetis, M. D. (2019). Ransomware detection and mitigation using software-defined networking: The case of WannaCry. *Computers & Electrical Engineering*, *76*, 111–121. doi:10.1016/j.compeleceng.2019.03.012

Akcanca, N. (2020). An alternative teaching tool in science education: Educational comics. *International Online Journal of Education & Teaching, 7*(4), 1550–1570.

al Ain University, Institute of Electrical and Electronics Engineers, Jordan Section, & Institute of Electrical and Electronics Engineers. (n.d.). *2019 International Arab Conference on Information Technology (ACIT) : proceedings : Al Ain, UAE, 03-05 Dec 2019*. Author.

Al Obaidan, F., & Saeed, S. (2021). Digital Transformation and Cybersecurity Challenges: A Study of Malware Detection Using Machine Learning Techniques. In Handbook of Research on Advancing Cybersecurity for Digital Transformation (pp. 203-226). IGI Global. doi:10.4018/978-1-7998-6975-7.ch011

Alam, M. F. (2019). Democratization in Bangladesh: Past, Present and Future. *International Journal of Science and Business, 3*(1), 156–166.

Al-Ashban, A. A., & Burney, M. A. (2001). Customer adoption of tele-banking technology: The case of Saudi Arabia. *International Journal of Bank Marketing, 19*(5), 191–201. doi:10.1108/02652320110399683

AlGothami, S. S., & Saeed, S. (2021). Digital Transformation and Usability: User Acceptance of Tawakkalna Application During Covid-19 in Saudi Arabia. In *Pandemic, Lockdown, and Digital Transformation* (pp. 95–109). Springer. doi:10.1007/978-3-030-86274-9_6

Alhassan, I., Sammon, D., & Daly, M. (2016). Data Governance Activities: an Analysis of the Literature. *Journal of Decision Systems, 25*(sup1), 64-75.

Alhindi, H., Traore, I., & Woungang, I. (2021). Preventing Data Leak through Semantic Analysis. *Internet of Things, 14*, 100073.

Ali, F. (2021, February 19). *Ecommerce trends amid coronavirus pandemic in charts*. Digital Commerce 360. Available online: https://www.digitalcommerce360.com/2021/02/19/ecommerce-during-coronavirus-pandemic-in-charts/

Ali, N. I., Samsuri, S., Sadry, M., Brohi, I. A., & Shah, A. (2016, November). Online shopping satisfaction in Malaysia: A framework for security, trust and cybercrime. In *2016 6th International Conference on Information and Communication Technology for The Muslim World (ICT4M)* (pp. 194-198). IEEE. 10.1109/ICT4M.2016.048

Ali, O., Ally, M., & Dwivedi, Y. (2020). *The state of play of blockchain technology in the financial services sector: A systematic literature review*. Academic Press.

Ali, S., Hafeez, Y., Bilal, M., Saeed, S., & Kwak, K. S. (2022). Towards Aspect Based Components Integration Framework for Cyber-Physical System. *Computers Materials & Continua, 70*(1), 653–668. doi:10.32604/cmc.2022.018779

Al-Jaroodi, J., & Mohamed, N. (2019). Blockchain in industries: A survey. *IEEE Access: Practical Innovations, Open Solutions, 7*, 36500–36515. doi:10.1109/ACCESS.2019.2903554

Alkharji, M., Liu, H., & Washington, C. U. A. (2016). Homomorphic encryption algorithms and schemes for secure computations in the cloud. In *Proceedings of 2016 International Conference on Secure Computing and Technology* (p. 19). Academic Press.

Alladi, T., Chamola, V., Sahu, N., & Guizani, M. (2020). Applications of blockchain in unmanned aerial vehicles: A review. *Vehicular Communications, 23*, 100249. doi:10.1016/j.vehcom.2020.100249

Allen, F., Gu, X., & Jagtiani, J. (2022). Fintech, Cryptocurrencies, and CBDC: Financial Structural Transformation in China. *Journal of International Money and Finance, 124*, 102625. Advance online publication. doi:10.1016/j.jimonfin.2022.102625

Al-Maaitah, S., Qatawneh, M., & Quzmar, A. (2021). *E-Voting System Based on Blockchain Technology: A Survey.* Paper presented at the 2021 International Conference on Information Technology (ICIT). 10.1109/ICIT52682.2021.9491734

Al-Madani, A. M., Gaikwad, A. T., Mahale, V., & Ahmed, Z. A. (2020). *Decentralized E-voting system based on Smart Contract by using Blockchain Technology.* Paper presented at the 2020 International Conference on Smart Innovations in Design, Environment, Management, Planning and Computing (ICSIDEMPC). 10.1109/ICSIDEMPC49020.2020.9299581

AlMansour, N., & Saeed, S. (2019, April). IoT based healthcare infrastructure: A case study of Saudi Arabia. In *2019 International Conference on Computer and Information Sciences (ICCIS)* (pp. 1-7). IEEE.

Almars, A. M. (2021). Deepfakes Detection Techniques Using Deep Learning: A Survey. *Journal of Computer and Communications, 09*(05), 20–35. doi:10.4236/jcc.2021.95003

Almashhadani, A. O., Carlin, D., Kaiiali, M., & Sezer, S. (2022). MFMCNS: A multi-feature and multi-classifier network-based system for ransomworm detection. *Computers & Security, 121*, 102860. doi:10.1016/j.cose.2022.102860

Almuhaideb, A. M., & Saeed, S. (2020). Fostering sustainable quality assurance practices in outcome-based education: Lessons learned from ABET accreditation process of computing programs. *Sustainability, 12*(20), 8380. doi:10.3390u12208380

Almusaylim, Z., & Jhanjhi, N. (2020). *Comprehensive review: Privacy protection of user in location-aware services of mobile cloud computing.* Academic Press.

Alneyadi, S., Sithirasenan, E., & Muthukkumarasamy, V. (2016). A survey on data leakage prevention systems. *Journal of Network and Computer Applications, 62*, 137–152. doi:10.1016/j.jnca.2016.01.008

Al-Omari, M., Rawashdeh, M., Qutaishat, F., Alshira'H, M., & Ababneh, N. (2021). An intelligent tree-based intrusion detection model for cyber security. *Journal of Network and Systems Management, 29*(2), 1–18. doi:10.100710922-021-09591-y

Alouffi, Hasnain, Alharbi, Alosaimi, Alyami, & Ayaz. (2021). A systematic literature review on cloud computing security: Threats and mitigation strategies. *IEEE Access, 9*(57), 792–807.

Alqarni, A. (2021). *A Secure Approach for Data Integration in Cloud using Paillier Homomorphic Encryption.* Academic Press.

Al-Rakhami, M. S., & Al-Mashari, M. (2021). A blockchain-based trust model for the internet of things supply chain management. *Sensors (Basel), 21*(5), 1–15. doi:10.339021051759 PMID:33806319

Al-rimy, B. A. S., Maarof, M. A., & Shaid, S. Z. M. (2018). Ransomware threat success factors, taxonomy, and countermeasures: A survey and research directions. *Computers & Security, 74*, 144–166. doi:10.1016/j.cose.2018.01.001

Alsuwaie, M. A., Habibnia, B., & Gladyshev, P. (2021). Data Leakage Prevention Adoption Model DLP Maturity Level Assessment. *Proceedings - 2021 International Symposium on Computer Science and Intelligent Controls, ISCSIC 2021*, 396–405. 10.1109/ISCSIC54682.2021.00077

Alt, R., Beck, R., & Smits, M. T. (2018). FinTech and the transformation of the financial industry. In Electronic Markets (Vol. 28, Issue 3, pp. 235–243). Springer Verlag. doi:10.100712525-018-0310-9

Ament, C., & Jaeger, L. (2017). Unconscious on their Own Ignorance:Overconfidence in Information Security. Association for Information Systems, 13.

Amir Latif, R. M., Hussain, K., Jhanjhi, N., Nayyar, A., & Rizwan, O. (2020). *A remix IDE: Smart contract-based framework for the healthcare sector by using Blockchain technology.* Academic Press.

Amir Latif, R. M., Hussain, K., Jhanjhi, N. Z., Nayyar, A., & Rizwan, O. (2020). A remix IDE: Smart contract-based framework for the healthcare sector by using Blockchain technology. *Multimedia Tools and Applications*, 1–24. https://link.springer.com/article/10.1007/s11042-020-10087-1

Anderson, C. L., & Agarwal, R. (2010). Practicing Safe Computing: A Multimethod Empirical Examination of Home Computer User Security Behavioral Intentions. *Management Information Systems Quarterly*, *34*(3), 613–643. doi:10.2307/25750694

Anderson, K. E. (2018). Getting acquainted with social networks and apps: Combating fake news on social media. *Library Hi Tech News*, *35*(3), 1–6. doi:10.1108/LHTN-02-2018-0010

Anderson, R. E. (1992). ACM code of ethics and professional conduct. *Communications of the ACM*, *35*(5), 94–99. doi:10.1145/129875.129885

Anggriane, S. M., Nasution, S. M., & Azmi, F. (2016, October). Advanced e-voting system using Paillier homomorphic encryption algorithm. In *2016 International Conference on Informatics and Computing (ICIC)* (pp. 338-342). IEEE.

Antoniou, A., Vayanou, M., Katifori, A., Chrysanthi, A., Cheilitsi, F., & Ioannidis, Y. (2021). "Real Change Comes from Within!": Towards a Symbiosis of Human and Digital Guides in the Museum. *ACM Journal on Computing and Cultural Heritage*, *15*(1), 1–19.

Antonucci, D. (2017). *The cyber risk handbook: Creating and measuring effective cybersecurity capabilities*. John Wiley & Sons.

Anttiroiko, A.-V. (2017). Emulating models of good governance: Learning from the developments of the world's least corrupt countries. *International Journal of Public Policy*, *13*(1/2), 21–35. doi:10.1504/IJPP.2017.081043

An, Y., Lee, S., Jung, S., Park, H., Song, Y., & Ko, T. (2021). Privacy-oriented technique for COVID-19 contact tracing (PROTECT) using homomorphic encryption: Design and development study. *Journal of Medical Internet Research*, *23*(7), e26371.

Apau, R., & Koranteng, F. N. (2019). Impact of cybercrime and trust on the use of e-commerce technologies: An application of the theory of planned behavior. *International Journal of Cyber Criminology*, *13*(2), 228–254. doi:10.5281/zenodo.3697886

Arashhhabibiilashkari, G. Z. (n.d.). *Future of Business and Finance Understanding Cybersecurity Management in FinTech Challenges, Strategies, and Trends*. https://www.springer.com/series/16360

Arianna, T., Kamps, J., Akartuna, E. A., Hetzel, F. J., Bennett, K., Davies, T., & Johnson, S. D. (2022). Cryptocurrencies and future financial crime. *Crime Science*, *11*(1).

Ariffin, N., Zainal, A., Maarof, M. A., & Nizam Kassim, M. (2018). A Conceptual Scheme for Ransomware Background Knowledge Construction. *2018 Cyber Resilience Conference (CRC)*, 1–4. 10.1109/CR.2018.8626868

Arner, D. W., Barberis, J. N., & Buckley, R. P. (2018). FinTech and RegTech in a Nutshell, and the Future in a Sandbox. SSRN *Electronic Journal*. doi:10.2139/ssrn.3088303

Arner, D. W., Barberis, J., Buckley, R. P., Arner, D., & Barberis, J. (2017). FinTech, RegTech, and the Reconceptualization of Financial Regulation. In *Northwestern Journal of International Law & Business* (Vol. 37, Issue 3). https://scholarlycommons.law.northwestern.edu/njilb/vol37/iss3/2

Arnold, A. (2019). Promising use cases of blockchain in cybersecurity. Forbes.

Arora, A., & Yadav, S. K. (2018). Block chain based security mechanism for internet of vehicles (IoV). *Proceedings of 3rd international conference on internet of things and connected technologies (ICIoTCT)*. 10.2139srn.3166721

Arora, V. (2010). *Comparing Different Information Security Standards: COBIT vs. ISO 27001*. Carnegia Mellon University.

Artz, J. M. (1998). The role of stories in computer ethics. *ACM SIGCAS Computers and Society*, *28*(1), 11–13. doi:10.1145/277351.277354

Arute, F., Arya, K., Babbush, R., Bacon, D., Bardin, J. C., Barends, R., Biswas, R., Boixo, S., Brandao, F. G. S. L., Buell, D. A., Burkett, B., Chen, Y., Chen, Z., Chiaro, B., Collins, R., Courtney, W., Dunsworth, A., Farhi, E., Foxen, B., ... Martinis, J. M. (2019). Quantum supremacy using a programmable superconducting processor. *Nature*, *574*(7779), 505–510. doi:10.103841586-019-1666-5 PMID:31645734

Ashta, A., & Biot-Paquerot, G. (2018). FinTech evolution: Strategic value management issues in a fast changing industry. *Strategic Change*, *27*(4), 301–311. doi:10.1002/jsc.2203

Ashta, A., & Herrmann, H. (2021). Artificial intelligence and fintech: An overview of opportunities and risks for banking, investments, and microfinance. *Strategic Change*, *30*(3), 211–222. doi:10.1002/jsc.2404

Aste, T., Tasca, P., & Di Matteo, T. (2017). Blockchain technologies: The foreseeable impact on society and industry. *Computer*, *50*(9), 18–28. doi:10.1109/MC.2017.3571064

Atif, M., Latif, S., Ahmad, R., Kiani, A. K., Qadir, J., Baig, A., Ishibuchi, H., & Abbas, W. (2019). Soft Computing Techniques for Dependable Cyber-Physical Systems. *IEEE Access: Practical Innovations, Open Solutions*, *7*, 72030–72049. doi:10.1109/ACCESS.2019.2920317

Auer, S., Nagler, S., Mazumdar, S., & Mukkamala, R. (2022). *Towards blockchain-IoT based shared mobility: Carsharing and leasing as a case study*. Academic Press.

Awotunde, J. B., Adeniyi, E. A., Ogundokun, R. O., & Ayo, F. E. (2021). Application of Big Data with Fintech in Financial Services. In P. M. S. Choi & S. H. Huang (Eds.), *Fintech with Artificial Intelligence, Big Data, and Blockchain* (pp. 107–132). Springer Singapore. doi:10.1007/978-981-33-6137-9_3

Azmoodeh, A., Dehghantanha, A., Conti, M., & Choo, K.-K. R. (2018). Detecting crypto-ransomware in IoT networks based on energy consumption footprint. *Journal of Ambient Intelligence and Humanized Computing*, *9*(4), 1141–1152. doi:10.1007/s12652-017-0558-5

Badawi, E., & Jourdan, G. V. (2020). Cryptocurrencies emerging threats and defensive mechanisms: A systematic literature review. *IEEE Access: Practical Innovations, Open Solutions*, *8*, 200021–200037.

Badger, M. L., Grance, T., Patt-Corner, R., & Voas, J. M. (2012). Cloud computing synopsis and recommendations. National Institute of Standards & Technology.

Badr, M. M., Baza, M., Abdelfattah, S., Mahmoud, M., & Alasmary, W. (2021). *Blockchain-Based Ride-Sharing System with Accurate Matching and Privacy-Preservation*. Paper presented at the 2021 International Symposium on Networks, Computers and Communications (ISNCC). 10.1109/ISNCC52172.2021.9615661

Baiocchi, G. (2001). Participation, activism and politics: The Porto Alegre case and deliberative democratic theory. *Politics & Society*, *29*(1), 43–72. doi:10.1177/0032329201029001003

Bansal, P., Panchal, R., Bassi, S., & Kumar, A. (2020, April). Blockchain for cybersecurity: A comprehensive survey. In *2020 IEEE 9th International Conference on Communication Systems and Network Technologies (CSNT)* (pp. 260-265). IEEE. 10.1109/CSNT48778.2020.9115738

Barnet, B., & Bossio, D. (2020). Netflix's The Social Dilemma highlights the problem with social media, but what's the solution? *The Conversation, 6.*

Bartenberger, M. & Grubmüller-Régent, V. (2014). The enabling effects of open government data on collaborative governance in smart city context. *The eJournal of eDemocracy and Open Government, 6*(1), 36-48.

Bartoletti, M., Pes, B., & Serusi, S. (2018). Data mining for detecting bitcoin ponzi schemes. In *2018 Crypto Valley Conference on Blockchain Technology (CVCBT)* (pp. 75-84). IEEE.

Baruník, J., Kočenda, E., & Vácha, L. (2016). Asymmetric connectedness on the U.S. stock market: Bad and good volatility spillovers. *Journal of Financial Markets, 27,* 55–78. doi:10.1016/j.finmar.2015.09.003

Barzilay, O. (2017). *3 ways blockchain is revolutionizing cybersecurity.* Retrieved from www. forbes.com: https://www.forbes.com/sites/omribarzilay/2017/08/21/3-ways-blockchain-is-rev olutionizing-cybersecurity/#77dc34b12334

Basir, I. N., Alwi, S., Salleh, M. N. M., Aslam, S. N. A. M., & Abdullah, S. M. M. (2020). The occurrence of FinTech: The insight into the world of cryptocurrency from a Chinese investment perspective. *Test Engineering and Management, 83*(1089), 1089–1100. https://www.scopus.com/inward/record.uri?eid=2-s2.0-85082778628&partnerID=40&md5=b5 40e68af95d809171b94bd1e79a53d5

Batabyal, A. (2020). *Bitcoin Price Prediction and Forecast 2020, 2022, 2025, 2030.* CoinSwitch. https://coinswitch.co/news/bitcoin-price-prediction-2020-2025-latest-btc-price-prediction-bitcoin-news-update

Bateman, J. (2020). *Deepfakes and Synthetic Media in the Financial System: Assessing Threat Scenarios.* https://www.jstor.org/stable/resrep25783

Bátiz-Lazo, B. (2009). Emergence and evolution of ATM networks in the UK, 1967-2000. *Business History, 51*(1), 1–27. doi:10.1080/00076790802602164

Bauhr, M., & Grimes, M. (2017). Transparency to curb corruption? Concepts, measures and empirical merit. *Crime, Law, and Social Change, 68*(4), 431–458. doi:10.100710611-017-9695-1

Baur, D. G., & Hoang, L. T. (2020). A crypto safe haven against Bitcoin. *Finance Research Letters, 101431*(January). doi:10.1016/j.frl.2020.101431

Baur, D. G., & Lucey, B. M. (2010). Is gold a hedge or a safe haven? An analysis of stocks, bonds and gold. *Financial Review, 45*(2), 217–229. doi:10.1111/j.1540-6288.2010.00244.x

Baur, D. G., & Mcdermott, T. K. (2010). Is gold a safe haven? International evidence. *Journal of Banking & Finance, 34*(8), 1886–1898. doi:10.1016/j.jbankfin.2009.12.008

Bawack, R. E., Wamba, S. F., Carillo, K. D. A., & Akter, S. (2022). Artificial intelligence in E-Commerce: A bibliometric study and literature review. *Electronic Markets, 32*(1), 297–338. doi:10.100712525-022-00537-z PMID:35600916

Bayramoğlu, G. (2021). An Overview of the Artificial Intelligence Applications in Fintech and Regtech. In S. Bozkuş Kahyaoğlu (Ed.), *The Impact of Artificial Intelligence on Governance, Economics and Finance* (Vol. I, pp. 291–298). Springer Singapore. doi:10.1007/978-981-33-6811-8_15

Baza, M., Lasla, N., Mahmoud, M. M., Srivastava, G., & Abdallah, M. (2019). *B-ride: Ride sharing with privacy-preservation, trust and fair payment atop public blockchain.* Academic Press.

Baza, M., Mahmoud, M., Srivastava, G., Alasmary, W., & Younis, M. (2020). *A light blockchain-powered privacy-preserving organization scheme for ride sharing services.* Paper presented at the 2020 IEEE 91st Vehicular Technology Conference (VTC2020-Spring). 10.1109/VTC2020-Spring48590.2020.9129197

BCG & FICCI. (2021). *India FinTech: A USD 100 Billion Opportunity*. BCG.

Beaman, C., Barkworth, A., Akande, T. D., Hakak, S., & Khan, M. K. (2021). Ransomware: Recent advances, analysis, challenges and future research directions. *Computers & Security*, *111*, 102490. doi:10.1016/j.cose.2021.102490 PMID:34602684

Bechmann-Pasquinucci, H., & Gisin, N. (1999). Incoherent and coherent eavesdropping in the six-state protocol of quantum cryptography. *Physical Review A.*, *59*, 4238–4248.

Bellini, E., Iraqi, Y., & Damiani, E. (2020). Blockchain-Based Distributed Trust and Reputation Management Systems: A Survey. *IEEE Access: Practical Innovations, Open Solutions*, *8*, 21127–21151. doi:10.1109/ACCESS.2020.2969820

Bellovin, S. M. (2016). Attack Surfaces. *IEEE Security and Privacy*, *14*(3), 88. doi:10.1109/MSP.2016.55

Benaloh, J. (1994, May). Dense probabilistic encryption. In *Proceedings of the workshop on selected areas of cryptography* (pp. 120-128). Academic Press.

Bendiab, K., Kolokotronis, N., Shiaeles, S., & Boucherkha, S. (2018). WiP: A novel blockchain-based trust model for cloud identity management. *Proceedings - IEEE 16th International Conference on Dependable, Autonomic and Secure Computing, IEEE 16th International Conference on Pervasive Intelligence and Computing, IEEE 4th International Conference on Big Data Intelligence and Computing and IEEE 3, 2018*, 716–723. 10.1109/DASC/PiCom/DataCom/CyberSciTec.2018.00126

Beneki, C., Koulis, A., Kyriazis, N. A., & Papadamou, S. (2019). Investigating volatility transmission and hedging properties between Bitcoin and Ethereum. *Research in International Business and Finance*, *48*(January), 219–227. doi:10.1016/j.ribaf.2019.01.001

Benfeldt, O., Persson, J. S., & Madsen, S. (2020). Data Governance as a Collective Action Problem. *Information Systems Frontiers*, *22*(2), 299–313. doi:10.100710796-019-09923-z

Benjamin, N. (2021, July 23). *Is Blockchain the Ultimate Cybersecurity Solution for My Applications?* https://www.isaca.org/resources/news-and-trends/isaca-now-blog/2021/is-blockchain-the-ultimate-cybersecurity-solution-for-my-applications

Benjamin, S., Bhuvaneswari, R., & Rajan, P. (2007). Bhoomi:'E–governance'', or, an anti–politics machine necessary to globalize Bangalore? *CASUM–m Working Paper*.

Bennett, C. H. (1992). Quantum cryptography using any two non-orthogonal states. *Physical Review Letters*, *68*, 3121–3124.

Bennett, C. H., Bernstein, E., Brassard, G., & Vazirani, U. (1997). Strengths and Weaknesses of Quantum Computing. *SIAM Journal on Computing*, *26*(5), 1510–1523.

Bennett, C. H., & Brassard, G. (1984). Quantum cryptography: Public key distribution and coin tossing, *Proceedings of IEEE International Conference on Computers, Systems and Signal Processing*, 175, 8.

Bennett, C. H., Brassard, G., & Mermin, N. D. (1992). Quantum cryptography without Bell's theorem. *Physical Review Letters*, *68*, 557–559.

Beno, M., Figl, K., Umbrich, J. & Polleres, A. (2017). Perception of key barriers in using and publishing open data. *The eJournal of eDemocracy and Open Government*, *9*(2), 134-165.

Berg, G., Guadamillas, M., Natarajan, H., & Sarkar, A. (2020). Fintech in Europe and Central Asia. *Fintech in Europe and Central Asia*, *4*. Advance online publication. doi:10.1596/33591

Bergh, S. I. (2009). Constraints to strengthening public sector accountability through civil society: The case of Morocco. *International Journal of Public Policy*, *4*(3/4), 344–365. doi:10.1504/IJPP.2009.023496

Bernards, N. (2019). The poverty of fintech? Psychometrics, credit infrastructures, and the limits of financialization. *Review of International Political Economy, 26*(5), 815–838. doi:10.1080/09692290.2019.1597753

Bernstein, D., Biasse, J.-F., & Mosca, M. (2017). A low-resource quantum factoring algorithm. In *Post-Quantum Cryptography – 8th International Workshop, PQCrypto 2017, Utrecht, The Netherlands, 26-28. Juni, 2017, Proceedings, Lecture Notes in Computer Science (vol. 10346, pp. 330-346).* Springer.

Bernstein, D., Hopwood, D., Huelsing, A., Lange, T., Niederhagen, R., Papachristodoulou, L., Schneider, M., Schwabe, P., & Wilcox-O'Hearn, Z. (2015). *SPHINCS: Practical Stateless Hash-Based Signatures.* Lecture Notes in Computer Science. Advances in Cryptology -EUROCRYPT.

Bernstein, D., Lange, T., & Peters, C. (2008). Attacking and Defending the McEliece Cryptosystem. *Proceedings of the 2nd International Workshop on Post-Quantum Cryptography,* 31-46.

Bertot, J. C., Jaeger, P. T., & Grimes, J. M. (2010). Using ICTs to create a culture of transparency: E-government and social media as openness and anti-corruption tools for societies. *Government Information Quarterly, 27*(3), 264–271. doi:10.1016/j.giq.2010.03.001

Best practices for designing amazon api gateway private apis and private integration. (2021). Available: https://docs.aws.amazon.com/whitepapers/latest/best-practices-api-gateway-private-apis-integration/best-practices-api-gateway-private-apis-integration.html

Bhardwaj, A., Avasthi, V., Sastry, H., & Subrahmanyam, G. V. B. (2016). Ransomware digital extortion: A rising new age threat. *Indian Journal of Science and Technology, 9*(14), 1–5. doi:10.17485/ijst/2016/v9i14/82936

Bhargav-Spantzel, A., Squicciarini, A. C., Modi, S., Young, M., Bertino, E., & Elliott, S. J. (2007). Privacy preserving multi-factor authentication with biometrics. *Journal of Computer Security, 15*(5), 529–560. doi:10.3233/JCS-2007-15503

Bhatia, N. L., Shukla, V. K., Punhani, R., & Dubey, S. K. (2021, June). Growing Aspects of Cyber Security in E-Commerce. In *2021 International Conference on Communication information and Computing Technology (ICCICT)* (pp. 1-6). IEEE. 10.1109/ICCICT50803.2021.9510152

Bhatt, C. (2022, May 17). *10 Best Fintech Apps You Should Look Up to In.* Techtic Solutions. Available online: https://www.techtic.com/blog/best-fintech-apps/

Bhattacharjee, A., Badsha, S., & Sengupta, S. (2020). *Blockchain-based secure and reliable manufacturing system.* Paper presented at the 2020 International Conferences on Internet of Things (iThings) and IEEE Green Computing and Communications (GreenCom) and IEEE Cyber, Physical and Social Computing (CPSCom) and IEEE Smart Data (SmartData) and IEEE Congress on Cybermatics (Cybermatics). 10.1109/iThings-GreenCom-CPSCom-SmartData-Cybermatics50389.2020.00052

Bhowmik, A., & Karforma, S. (2021). Linear feedback shift register and integer theory: A state-of-art approach in security issues over e-commerce. *Electronic Commerce Research,* 1–21. doi:10.100710660-021-09477-w

Billingsley, J. (2020, April 15). *State and Local Cybersecurity Collaboration* [Memorandum]. Legislative Council Staff. https://leg.colorado.gov/sites/default/files/r20_339_cybersecurity_state_local_memo_-_for_cathy.pdf

Bistarelli, S., Parroccini, M., & Santini, F. (2018). Visualising Bitcoin Flows of Ransomware: WannaCry One Week Later. *ITASEc,* 8.

Black, N. D. (2014). *Homomorphic encryption and the approximate gcd problem* [Doctoral dissertation]. Clemson University.

Blair, H. (2020). Accountability through participatory budgeting in India: Only in Kerala? In S. Cheema (Ed.), *Governance for urban services: Access, participation, accountability, and transparency* (pp. 57–76). Springer, Singapore. doi:10.1007/978-981-15-2973-3_3

Bloom, B. (1970, July). Space/time Trade-offs in Hash Coding with Allowable Errors. *Communications of the ACM, 13*(7), 422–426. doi:10.1145/362686.362692

Blumenthal, R., & Blumenthal, J. (2020). Consider Visualizing Society within the ACM Code of Ethics. In *Proceedings of the 51st ACM Technical Symposium on Computer Science Education* (pp. 1292-1292). 10.1145/3328778.3372587

Bodie, Z., Kane, A., & Marcus, A. J. (2014). *Investments* (10th ed.). McGraw-Hill Education.

Bohnsack, R., Kurtz, H., & Hanelt, A. (2021). Re-examining path dependence in the digital age: The evolution of connected car business models. *Research Policy, 50*(9), 104328. Advance online publication. doi:10.1016/j.respol.2021.104328

Boiral, O., Brotherton, M.-C., Rivaud, L., & Guillaumie, L. (2021). Organizations' Management of the COVID-19 Pandemic: A Scoping Review of Business Articles. *Sustainability, 13*(7), 3993. doi:10.3390u13073993

Boneh, D., Goh, E. J., & Nissim, K. (2005, February). Evaluating 2-DNF formulas on ciphertexts. In *Theory of cryptography conference* (pp. 325–341). Springer. doi:10.1007/978-3-540-30576-7_18

Bonneau, J. (2012). The Science of Guessing: Analyzing an Anonymized Vorpus of 70 Million Passwords. *IEEE Symposium on Security and Privacy*. 10.1109/SP.2012.49

Bonthu, S. R., Chakraverty, S., Subrahmanya, S., Varma, N., Ramani, S., & Karuppiah, M. (2022). Blockchain for Electronic Voting System. In Data Analytics, Computational Statistics, and Operations Research for Engineers (pp. 61-88). CRC Press.

Boomija, M. D., & Raja, S. V. (2022). Securing medical data by role-based user policy with partially homomorphic encryption in AWS cloud. *Soft Computing*, 1–10.

Boratyńska, K. (2019). Impact of Digital Transformation on Value Creation in Fintech Services: An Innovative Approach. *Journal of Promotion Management, 25*(5), 631–639. Advance online publication. doi:10.1080/10496491.2019.1585543

Bosri, R., Uzzal, A. R., Al Omar, A., Hasan, A. T., & Bhuiyan, M. Z. A. (2019). *Towards a privacy-preserving voting system through blockchain technologies.* Paper presented at the 2019 IEEE Intl Conf on Dependable, Autonomic and Secure Computing, Intl Conf on Pervasive Intelligence and Computing, Intl Conf on Cloud and Big Data Computing, Intl Conf on Cyber Science and Technology Congress (DASC/PiCom/CBDCom/CyberSciTech). 10.1109/DASC/PiCom/CBDCom/CyberSciTech.2019.00116

Boss, S. R., Galletta, D. F., Benjamin Lowry, P., Moody, G. D., & Polak, P. (2015). What Do Systems Users Have to Fear? Using Fear Appeals to Engender Threats and Fear That Motivate Protective Security Behaviors. *Management Information Systems Quarterly, 39*(4), 837–864. doi:10.25300/MISQ/2015/39.4.5

Boudguiga, A., Stan, O., Fazzat, A., Labiod, H., & Clet, P. E. (2021). Privacy Preserving Services for Intelligent Transportation Systems with Homomorphic Encryption. In ICISSP (pp. 684-693). Academic Press.

Bouillaguet, C., Cheng, C.-M., Chou, T., Niederhagen, R., & Yang, B.-Y. (2013). Fast Exhaustive Search for Quadratic Systems in F2 on FPGAs. In Selected Areas in Cryptography-SAC 2013. Springer.

Bouoiyour, J., Selmi, R., Tiwari, A. K., & Olayeni, O. (2016). What drives Bitcoin price? *Economic Bulletin, 36*(2).

Bouri, E., Das, M., Gupta, R., & Roubaud, D. (2018). Spillovers between Bitcoin and other assets during bear and bull markets. *Applied Economics, 50*(55), 5935–5949. doi:10.1080/00036846.2018.1488075

Bouri, E., Hussain Shahzad, S. J., & Roubaud, D. (2020). Cryptocurrencies as hedges and safe-havens for US equity sectors. *The Quarterly Review of Economics and Finance, 75*, 294–307. doi:10.1016/j.qref.2019.05.001

Bouri, E., Molnár, P., Azzi, G., Roubaud, D., & Hagfors, L. I. (2017). On the hedge and safe haven properties of Bitcoin: Is it really more than a diversifier? *Finance Research Letters, 20*, 192–198. doi:10.1016/j.frl.2016.09.025

Bouveret, A. (2018). *WP/18/143 Cyber Risk for the Financial Sector: A Framework for Quantitative Assessment*. Academic Press.

Bowen, B. M. (2009). Baiting inside attackers using decoy documents. In *International Conference on Security and Privacy in Communication Systems* (pp. 51--70). Springer.

Brakerski, Z., Gentry, C., & Vaikuntanathan, V. (2012). (Leveled) fully homomorphic encryption without bootstrapping. *ITCS, 2012*, 309–325.

Brakerski, Z., & Vaikuntanathan, V. (2011, August). Fully homomorphic encryption from ring-LWE and security for key dependent messages. In *Annual cryptology conference* (pp. 505-524). Springer.

Branch, T. (2022). International Journal of Research in Industrial Engineering Paper Type : Original Article Identifying key indicators for developing the use of blockchain technology in financial systems 1 I Introduction 2 I Literature review. *International Journal of Research in Industrial Engineering, x*(x).

Brautigam, D. (2004). The people's budget? politics, participation and pro-poor policy. *Development Policy Review, 22*(6), 653–668. doi:10.1111/j.1467-7679.2004.00270.x

Bridges, L. (2008). The changing face of malware. *Network Security, 2008*(1), 17–20. doi:10.1016/S1353-4858(08)70010-2

Bronk, C. R., & Tikk-Ringas, E. (2013). The cyber attack on Saudi Aramco. *Survival, 55*(2), 81–96. doi:10.1080/00396338.2013.784468

Brusca, I. Rossi, F.M. & Aversano, N. (2015). Drivers for the financial condition of local government: a comparative study between Italy and Spain. *Lex Localis - Journal of Local Self-Government, 13*(2), 161-184.

Buchanan, B. (2016). *The cybersecurity dilemma: Hacking, trust, and fear between nations*. Oxford University Press.

Buchmann, J., Dahmen, E., & Huelsing, A. (2011). *XMSS – A Practical Forward Secure Signature Scheme Based on Minimal Security Assumptions*. Lecture Notes in Computer Science. Post-Quantum Cryptography.

Buckley, R., Arner, D., & Barberis, J. (2016). The evolution of Fintech: A new post-crisis paradigm. *Georgetown Journal of International Law, 47*(4), 1271–1319.

Buil-Gil, D., Miró-Llinares, F., Moneva, A., Kemp, S., & Díaz-Castaño, N. (2021). Cybercrime and shifts in opportunities during COVID-19: A preliminary analysis in the UK. *European Societies, 23*(S1), S47–S59. doi:10.1080/14616696.2020.1804973

Bulgurcu, B., Cavusoglu, H., & Benbasat, I. (2010). Information Security Policy Compliance: An Empirical Study of Rationality-Based Beliefs and Information Security Awareness. *Management Information Systems Quarterly, 34*(3), 523–A7. doi:10.2307/25750690

Bullock, M., & Sullivan, M. (2022). *Change Management During Digital Transformation Projects: How to Overcome Barriers Using an Agile Approach and Modern Change Models*. Academic Press.

Buo, S. A. (2020). *The Emerging Threats of Deepfake Attacks and Countermeasures*. doi:10.13140/RG.2.2.23089.81762

Burnham, J. F. (2006). Scopus database: A review. *Biomedical Digital Libraries*, *3*(1), 1–8. doi:10.1186/1742-5581-3-1 PMID:16522216

Burns, M. B., Durcikova, A., & Jenkins, J. L. (2013). What Kind of Interventions Can Help Users from Falling for Phishing Attempts: A Research Proposal for Examining Stage-Appropriate Interventions. *2013 46th Hawaii International Conference on System Sciences*, 4023–4032. 10.1109/HICSS.2013.606

Business Insider Intelligence. (2020, March 2). *The growing list of applications and use cases of blockchain technology in business and life.* https://www.businessinsider.in/finance/news/the-growing-list-of-applications-and-use-cases-of-blockchain-technology-in-business-and-life/articleshow/74447275.cms

Buterin, V. (2014). *A Next-Generation Smart Contract and Decentralized Application Platform.* Etherum. Available: http://buyxpr.com/build/pdfs/Ethe reumWhitePaper.pdf

Bu, Y., Li, H., & Wu, X. (2021). Effective regulations of FinTech innovations: The case of China. *Economics of Innovation and New Technology*. Advance online publication. doi:10.1080/10438599.2020.1868069

C, A., & Vijayalakshmi, S. (2022). Prevention of Data Breach by Machine Learning Techniques. *2022 2nd International Conference on Advance Computing and Innovative Technologies in Engineering (ICACITE)*, 1819–1823. doi:10.1109/ICACITE53722.2022.9823523

Çabuk, U. C., Adiguzel, E., & Karaarslan, E. (2020). *A survey on feasibility and suitability of blockchain techniques for the e-voting systems.* arXiv preprint arXiv:2002.07175.

Caldwell, M., Andrews, J. T. A., Tanay, T., & Griffin, L. D. (2020). AI-enabled future crime. *Crime Science*, *9*(1), 1–13. doi:10.118640163-020-00123-8

Callanan, G. A., & Perri, D. F. (2010). Teaching conflict management using a scenario-based approach. *Journal of Education for Business*, *81*(3), 131–139. doi:10.3200/JOEB.81.3.131-139

Caplan, J. (2021). *E-Commerce Has Been A Lifeline For Small Businesses During The Pandemic. Where Do They Go From Here?* Available at: https://www.forbes.com/sites/johncaplan/2021/05/03/ecommerce-has-been-a-lifeline-for-small-businesses-during-the-pandemic-where-do-they-go-from-here/?sh=45570e4a3587

Caprolu, M., Raponi, S., Oligeri, G., & Di Pietro, R. (2019). *Crypto mining makes noise.* arXiv preprint arXiv:1910.09272.

Caprolu, M., Cresci, S., Raponi, S., & Di Pietro, R. (2020). New Dimensions of Information Warfare: The Economic Pillar—Fintech and Cryptocurrencies. In *International Conference on Risks and Security of Internet and Systems* (pp. 3-27). Springer.

Caprolu, M., Raponi, S., Oligeri, G., & Di Pietro, R. (2021). crypto mining makes noise: Detecting cryptojacking via Machine Learning. *Computer Communications*, *171*, 126–139.

Carlin, D., O'kane, P., Sezer, S., & Burgess, J. (2018). Detecting crypto mining using dynamic analysis. In *16th Annual Conference on Privacy, Security and Trust (PST)* (pp. 1-6). IEEE.

Carter. (1981). New Hash Functions and Their Use in Authentication and Set Equality. *Journal of Computer and System Sciences*, 22.

Casino, F., Dasaklis, T. K., & Patsakis, C. (2019). A systematic literature review of blockchain-based applications: Current status, classification and open issues. *Telematics and Informatics*, *36*, 55–81. doi:10.1016/j.tele.2018.11.006

Celik, Z. B., Acar, A., Aksu, H., Sheatsley, R., McDaniel, P., & Uluagac, A. S. (2019). Curie: Policy-based secure data exchange. In *Proceedings of the Ninth ACM Conference on Data and Application Security and Privacy* (pp. 121-132). ACM.

Chai, H., Leng, S., Wu, F., & He, J. (2021). *Secure and Efficient Blockchain-Based Knowledge Sharing for Intelligent Connected Vehicles*. Academic Press.

Chan, M., Johnson, P.A. & Shookner, M. (2016). Assessing the use of government open data and the role of data infomediaries: The case of Nova Scotia's Community Counts Program. *The eJournal of eDemocracy and Open Government*, *8*(1), 1-27.

Chang, X., Wu, J., Yang, T., & Feng, G. (2020). DeepFake Face Image Detection based on Improved VGG Convolutional. *Neural Networks*, 7252–7256.

Chaudhari, K. G. (2018). E-voting System using Proof of Voting (PoV) Consensus Algorithm using Block Chain Technology. *International Journal of Advanced Research in Electrical Electronics and Instrumentation Engineering*, *7*(11), 4051–4055.

Chawla, D. S. (2021, April 15). *Research misconduct findings, 15-year publishing ban in graduate student suicide case.* Nature news. Retrieved August 16, 2022, from https://www.nature.com/nature-index/news-blog/research-misconduct-publishing-ban-graduate-student-suicide-case

Chen, F., & Chen, X. (2021). How Does FinTech Affect Consumer Non-cash Payment Satisfaction? The Moderating Role of Financial Knowledge. *South Asian Journal of Social Studies and Economics*, 217–231. doi:10.9734/sajsse/2021/v12i430329

Chen, J. (2019). *Graboid: First-Ever Cryptojacking Worm Found in Images on Docker Hub*. Unit42.

Chen, J., Chen, J., & Xue, Z. (n.d.). *Chinese e-commerce law: new challenges and new opportunities.* Spring 2019 Legal Briefing. Available at: https://www.inhouselawyer.co.uk/legal-briefing/chinese-e-commerce-law-new-challenges-and-new-opportunities/

Chen, L. (2016). *Report on Post-quantum Cryptography*. https://csrc.nist.gov/publications/detail/nistir/8105/final

Chen, X., Duan, Y., Houthooft, R., Schulman, J., Sutskever, I., & Abbeel, P. (2016). InfoGAN: Interpretable Representation Learning. *Nips, Nips*, 2172–2180. https://arxiv.org/abs/1606.03657

Chen, C. L., Lin, Y. C., Chen, W. H., Chao, C. F., & Pandia, H. (2021). Role of government to enhance digital transformation in small service business. *Sustainability (Switzerland)*, *13*(3), 1–26. doi:10.3390u13031028

Chen, C. M., Cai, Z. X., & Wen, D. W. M. (2021). Designing and Evaluating an Automatic Forensic Model for Fast Response of Cross-Border E-Commerce Security Incidents. *Journal of Global Information Management*, *30*(2), 1–19. doi:10.4018/JGIM.20220301.oa5

Cheng, C.-M., Chou, T., Niederhagen, R., & Yang, B.-Y. (2012). Solving Quadratic Equations with XL on Parallel Architectures. In Cryptographic Hardware and Embedded Systems -CHES 2012. Springer.

Cheng, L., Liu, F., & Yao, D. D. (2017). Enterprise data breach: causes, challenges, prevention, and future directions. In Wiley Interdisciplinary Reviews: Data Mining and Knowledge Discovery (Vol. 7, Issue 5). Wiley-Blackwell. doi:10.1002/widm.1211

Cheon, J. H., Kim, A., Kim, M., & Song, Y. (2017, December). Homomorphic encryption for arithmetic of approximate numbers. In *International conference on the theory and application of cryptology and information security* (pp. 409-437). Springer.

Chevers, D. A. (2019). The impact of cybercrime on e-banking: A proposed model. *International Conference on Information Resources Management*, 10.

Chickowski. (2018). https://securityboulevard.com/2018/07/5-cryptojacking-consequences-cisos-cant-ignore/

ChickowskiE. (2018). https://securityboulevard.com/2018/07/5-cryptojacking-consequences-cisos-cant-ignore/

Childs, A., Jao, D., & Soukharev, V. (2014). Constructing elliptic curve isogenies in quantum subexponential time. *Journal of Mathematical Cryptology, 8*(1). arXiv:1012.4019

Choi, H., Park, M. J., Rho, J. J., & Zo, H. (2016). Rethinking the assessment of e-government implementation in developing countries from the perspective of the design-reality gap: Application in the Indonesian e-procurement system. *Telecommunications Policy, 40*(7), 644–660. doi:10.1016/j.telpol.2016.03.002

Choi, Y., & Mai, D. Q. (2018). The sustainable role of the e-trust in the B2C e-commerce of Vietnam. *Sustainability, 10*(1), 291. doi:10.3390u10010291

Chokparova, Z., & Urbas, L. (2021, September). Utilization of Homomorphic Cryptosystems for Information Exchange in Value Chains. In *2021 26th IEEE International Conference on Emerging Technologies and Factory Automation (ETFA)* (pp. 1-7). IEEE.

Choo, K. K. R. (2011). The cyber threat landscape: Challenges and future research directions. *Computers & Security, 30*(8), 719–731. doi:10.1016/j.cose.2011.08.004

Chou, T.-S. (2013). Security threats on cloud computing vulnerabilities. *Inter-national Journal of Computer Science & Information Technology, 5*(3), 79–88. doi:10.5121/ijcsit.2013.5306

Christensen, L. B., Johnson, B., & Turner, L. A. (2014). *Research methods, design, and analysis* (12th ed.). Pearson.

Ciftci, U. A., Demir, I., & Yin, L. (2020b). How do the hearts of deep fakes beat? deep fake source detection via interpreting residuals with biological signals. *IJCB 2020 - IEEE/IAPR International Joint Conference on Biometrics*. 10.1109/IJCB48548.2020.9304909

Ciftci, U. A., Demir, I., & Yin, L. (2020a). FakeCatcher: Detection of Synthetic Portrait Videos using Biological Signals. *IEEE Transactions on Pattern Analysis and Machine Intelligence, X*(X), 1–1. doi:10.1109/TPAMI.2020.3009287 PMID:32750816

Cimpanu, C. (2018a). *Firefox working on protection against in-browser cryptojacking scripts.* Bleepingcomputer. Available at: https://www. bleepingcomputer. com/news/software/firefox-working-on-protection-against-inbrowser-cryptojacking-scripts/

Cimpanu, C. (2018b). *Tweak to chrome performance will indirectly stifle cryptojacking scripts.* https://www.bleepingcomputer.com/news/software/firefox-working-on-protection-against-inbrowser-cryptojacking-scripts

Clark, C. E., & Greenley, H. L. (2019). *Bitcoin, blockchain, and the energy sector.* Congressional Research Service.

Clark, K., Duckham, M., Guillemin, M., Hunter, A., McVernon, J., O'Keefe, C., Pitkin, C., Prawer, S., Sinnott, R., Warr, D., & Waycott, J. (2015). *Guidelines for the Ethical use of Digital Data in Human Research.* The University of Melbourne.

Claussen, V. (2018). Fighting hate speech and fake news. The Network Enforcement Act (NetzDG) in Germany in the context of European legislation. *Rivista Di Diritto Dei Media, 3*, 1–27. www.reuters.com

Clohessy, T., Acton, T., & Morgan, L. (2017). The Impact of Cloud-Based Digital Transformation on IT Service Providers. *International Journal of Cloud Applications and Computing, 7*(4), 1–19. doi:10.4018/IJCAC.2017100101

Cloudtweaks.com. (2019, February 26). *How Blockchain Is Transforming Cyber Security.* https://cloudtweaks.com/2019/04/how-blockchain-is-transforming-cyber-security/

Coinhav2. (2017). *First week status report.* https://coinhive.com/blog/en/status-report

Coinhave – monero javascript mining. (n.d.). https://coin-have.com/

Coinimp. (2018). *Coinnebula official webpage.* https://web.archive.org/

Cole, E. a. (2005). *Insider threat: Protecting the enterprise from sabotage, spying, and theft.* Elsevier.

COMTEX, A. N. (2022). *Global Fintech Market 2022 Industry Overview, New Market Opportunities and Statistics Research Report 2030.* Author.

Condliffe, J. (2016, July 28). *Massive Internet Outage Could Be a Sign of Things to Come.* https://www.technologyreview.com/2016/10/21/156505/massive-internet-outage-could-be-a-sign-of-things-to-come/

Conlon, T., & McGee, R. (2020). Safe Haven or Risky Hazard? Bitcoin during the Covid-19 Bear Market. *Finance Research Letters, 101607*(April). doi:10.2139srn.3560361 PMID:32550843

Conoscenti, M., Vetro, A., & De Martin, J. C. (2016, November). Blockchain for the Internet of Things: A systematic literature review. In *2016 IEEE/ACS 13th International Conference of Computer Systems and Applications (AICCSA)* (pp. 1-6). IEEE. https://ieeexplore.ieee.org/abstract/document/7973732

Conti, M., Dragoni, N., & Lesyk, V. (2016). A survey of man in the middle attacks. *IEEE Communications Surveys and Tutorials, 18*(3), 2027–2051. doi:10.1109/COMST.2016.2548426

Continella, A., Fratantonio, Y., Lindorfer, M., Puccetti, A., Zand, A., Kruegel, C., & Vigna, G. (2017, May 13). *Obfuscation-Resilient Privacy Leak Detection for Mobile Apps Through Differential Analysis.* doi:10.14722/ndss.2017.23465

Contributor, J. B. (n.d.). *Digitization, Digitalization, And Digital Transformation: Confuse Them At Your Peril I write and consult on digital transformation in the enterprise.* https://www.forbes.com/sites/jasonbloomberg/2018/04/29/digitization-digitalization-and-digital-transformation-confuse-them-at-your-peril/#78e677fd2f2c

Corbet, S., Hu, Y., Lucey, B. M., & Oxley, L. (2020). Aye Corona! The Contagion Effects of Being Named Corona during the COVID-19 Pandemic. *Finance Research Letters, 101591.* Advance online publication. doi:10.2139srn.3561866 PMID:32837362

Coronavirus pandemic changes how your privacy is protected - CNET. (n.d.). Retrieved February 27, 2022, from https://www.cnet.com/health/coronavirus-pandemic-changes-how-your-privacy-is-protected/

Costante, E., Fauri, D., Etalle, S., den Hartog, J., & Zannone, N. (2016). A Hybrid Framework for Data Loss Prevention and Detection. *Proceedings - 2016 IEEE Symposium on Security and Privacy Workshops, SPW 2016,* 324–333. 10.1109/SPW.2016.24

Costello, C., Longa, P., & Naehrig, M. (2016). Efficient Algorithms for Supersingular Isogeny Diffie-Hellman. In Advances in Cryptology- CRYPTO 2016. Springer.

Courtois, N., Finiasz, M., & Sendrier, N. (2001). How to Achieve a McEliece-Based Digital Signature Scheme. *Advances in Cryptology - ASIACRYPT 2001,* 157-174.

Crawley, J. (2020, May 12). *Bitcoin halving: What does this mean and what will its effect be?* Finextra.Com. https://www.finextra.com/the-long-read/40/bitcoin-halving-what-does-this-mean-and-what-will-its-effect-be

Creswell, J. W. (2013). Qualitative Inquiry & Research Design: Choosing among Five Approaches (3rd ed.). SAGE Publications.

Crone, E. A., & Konijn, E. A. (2018). Media use and brain development during adolescence. *Nature Communications*, *9*(1), 1–10. doi:10.103841467-018-03126-x PMID:29467362

Crowdstrike. (2019). *2019 Global Threat Report: Adversary Tradecraft and the Importance of Speed*. https://crowdstrike.lookbookhq.com/web-global-threat-report-2019/crowdstrike-2019-gtr

Crowell, C. R., Narvaez, D., & Gomberg, A. (2004). Moral psychology and information ethics. *Information Ethics: Privacy and Intellectual Property: Privacy and Intellectual Property*, 19.

Cryptoloot - earn more from your traffic. (n.d.). https://crypto-loot.com/

Cummings, A. a. (2012). *Insider threat study: Illicit cyber activity involving fraud in the US financial services sector*. Carnegie-Mellon Univ.

Cusumano, M. A. (2021). Section 230 and a tragedy of the commons. *Communications of the ACM*, *64*(10), 16–18. doi:10.1145/3481354

D'Adamo, I., González-Sánchez, R., Medina-Salgado, M. S., & Settembre-Blundo, D. (2021). E-commerce calls for cyber-security and sustainability: How european citizens look for a trusted online environment. *Sustainability*, *13*(12), 6752. doi:10.3390u13126752

Dadhich, P. (2020). *5 powerful cybersecurity solutions every business needs*. Available: https://www.znetlive.com/blog/cybersecurity-solutions-business-needs/

Dai, B., Fidler, S., Urtasun, R., & Lin, D. (2017). Towards Diverse and Natural Image Descriptions via a Conditional GAN. *Proceedings of the IEEE International Conference on Computer Vision*, 2989–2998. doi:10.1109/ICCV.2017.323

Dale, K., Sunkavalli, K., Johnson, M. K., Vlasic, D., Matusik, W., & Pfister, H. (2011). Video face replacement. *ACM Transactions on Graphics*, *30*(6), 1–10. doi:10.1145/2070781.2024164

Daley, S. (2021, March 31). *30 Blockchain Applications and Real-World Use Cases Disrupting the Status Quo*. https://builtin.com/blockchain/blockchain-applications

Dalziel, H. (2014). *Introduction to US Cybersecurity Careers*. Syngress.

Dapp, T. (2015). Fintech reloaded – Traditional banks as digital ecosystems With proven walled garden strategies into the future. *Deutsche Bank Research Management*, 1–27.

Darabian, H., Homayounoot, S., Dehghantanha, A., Hashemi, S., Karimipour, H., Parizi, R. M., & Choo, K. K. R. (2020). Detecting crypto mining malware: A deep learning approach for static and dynamic analysis. *Journal of Grid Computing*, *18*(2), 293–303.

Das, S. R. (2019). The future of fintech. *Financial Management*, *48*(4), 981–1007. doi:10.1111/fima.12297

Davidoff, J., Fonteneau, E., & Goldstein, J. (2008). Cultural differences in perception: Observations from a remote culture. *Journal of Cognition and Culture*, *8*(3-4), 189–209. doi:10.1163/156853708X358146

De Carvalho, A. F. P., Saeed, S., Reuter, C., Rohde, M., Randall, D., Pipek, V., & Wulf, V. (2022). Understanding Nomadic Practices of Social Activist Networks through the Lens of Infrastructuring: the Case of the European Social Forum. *Computer Supported Cooperative Work (CSCW)*, 1-39. 10.100710606-022-09442-7

De Filippi, P., Mannan, M., & Reijers, W. (2022). *The alegality of blockchain technology*. Academic Press.

De Filippi, P., Mannan, M., & Reijers, W. (2020). Blockchain as a confidence machine: The problem of trust & challenges of governance. *Technology in Society*, *62*, 101284. doi:10.1016/j.techsoc.2020.101284

De Vries, A. (2018). Bitcoin's growing energy problem. *Joule, 2*(5), 801–805.

Dean, B. (2021). *Etsy User and Revenue Stats: How Many People Shop on Etsy in 2022*. Available online: https://backlinko.com/etsy-users

Dean, V., & Nourbakhsh, I. (2022). Teaching Ethics by Teaching Ethics Pedagogy: A Proposal for Structural Ethics Intervention. In *Proceedings of the 53rd ACM Technical Symposium on Computer Science Education* (pp. 272-278). 10.1145/3478431.3499319

Deepfakes Web. (n.d.). https://deepfakesweb.com

Delamaire, Abdou, & Pointon. (2009). Credit card fraud and detection techniques: A review. *Banks and Bank Systems, 4*(2).

Demirkan, S., Demirkan, I., & McKee, A. (2020). Blockchain technology in the future of business cyber security and accounting. *Journal of Management Analytics, 7*(2), 189–208. doi:10.1080/23270012.2020.1731721

Denis González, C., Frias Mena, D., Massó Muñoz, A., Rojas, O., & Sosa-Gómez, G. (2022). Electronic Voting System Using an Enterprise Blockchain. *Applied Sciences (Basel, Switzerland), 12*(2), 531. doi:10.3390/app12020531

Dewey, J. (2020). *Blockchain Laws and Regulations | USA | GLI*. Global Legal Insight. https://www.globallegalinsights.com/practice-areas/blockchain-laws-and-regulations/usa

Dhanalakshmi, A., Prema Rajan, R. K., & Hui, X. (n.d.). *An Empirical Study on the Adoption Intention of Financial Technology (FinTech) Services among Bank Users*. Academic Press.

Dhar Dwivedi, A., Malina, L., Dzurenda, P., & Srivastava, G. (2019). *Optimized Blockchain Model for Internet of Things based Healthcare Applications*. arXiv e-prints, arXiv-1906.

Dias, M. D. O., & Vieira, P. (2022). Are the Russian Banks Threatened with Removal from SWIFT? A Multiple Case Study on Interbank Financial Messaging Systems. *International Journal of Scientific Research and Management, 10*(March), 3137–3144. Advance online publication. doi:10.18535/ijsrm/v10i3.em1

Diebold, F. X., & Yilmaz, K. (2012). Better to give than to receive: Predictive directional measurement of volatility spillovers. *International Journal of Forecasting, 28*(1), 57–66. doi:10.1016/j.ijforecast.2011.02.006

Diener, F., & Špaček, M. (2021). Digital transformation in banking: A managerial perspective on barriers to change. *Sustainability (Switzerland), 13*(4), 1–26. doi:10.3390u13042032

Diffie, W., & Hellman, M. (1976). New directions in cryptography, Information Theory. *IEEE Transactions on, 22*(6), 644–654.

Digital transformation in financial services A report from the Deloitte Center for Financial Services. (n.d.). www.deloittedigital.com

Dijk, M. V., Gentry, C., Halevi, S., & Vaikuntanathan, V. (2010, May). Fully homomorphic encryption over the integers. In *Annual international conference on the theory and applications of cryptographic techniques* (pp. 24-43). Springer.

Dilek, S., Çakır, H., & Aydın, M. (2015). *Applications of artificial intelligence techniques to combating cyber crimes: A review*. arXiv preprint arXiv:1502.03552.

Dimitriou, D., Kenourgios, D., & Simos, T. (2020). Are there any other safe haven assets? Evidence for "exotic" and alternative assets. *International Review of Economics & Finance, 69*, 614–628. Advance online publication. doi:10.1016/j.iref.2020.07.002

Ding, J., & Schmidt, D. (2005). Rainbow, a New Multivariable Polynomial Signature Scheme. In Applied Cryptography and Network Security — ACNS 2005. Springer.

Do, N., Na, I., & Kim, S. (2018). *Forensics Face Detection From GANs Using Convolutional Neural Network*. Academic Press.

Dongrie, V., Sharma, A., & Choudhary, R. (2020). *Workforce, workplace and HR reshaping - During COVID-19 Pandemic*. Academic Press.

Dong, Y., Yu, X., Alharbi, A., & Ahmad, S. (2022). AI-based production and application of English multimode online reading using multi-criteria decision support system. *Soft Computing, 26*(20), 1–11. doi:10.100700500-022-07209-2 PMID:35668907

Donnelly, R., & Fitzmaurice, M. (2005). Collaborative Project-based Learning and Problem-based Learning in Higher Education: a Consideration of Tutor and Student Role in Learner-Focused Strategies. In G. O'Neill, S. Moore, & B. McMullin (Eds.), *Emerging Issues in the Practice of University Learning and Teaching* (pp. 87–98). AISHE/HEA.

Dorfleitner, G., & Braun, D. (2019). Fintech, Digitalization and Blockchain: Possible Applications for Green Finance. In M. Migliorelli & P. Dessertine (Eds.), *The Rise of Green Finance in Europe: Opportunities and Challenges for Issuers, Investors and Marketplaces* (pp. 207–237). Springer International Publishing. doi:10.1007/978-3-030-22510-0_9

Drexl, J., Hilty, R. M., Desaunettes-barbero, L., Globocnik, J., Kim, D., Kulhari, S., Richter, H., Scheuerer, S., Slowinski, P. R., & Wiedemann, K. (2020). Comments of the Max Planck Institute for Innovation and Competition of 11 February 2020: On the Draft Issues Paper of the World Intellectual Property Organization on Intellectual Property Policy and Artificial Intelligence. Max Planck Institute for Innovation and Competition, 1(December), 1–9.

Du, W., Pan, S. L., Leidner, D. E., & Ying, W. (2019). Affordances, experimentation and actualization of FinTech: A blockchain implementation study. *The Journal of Strategic Information Systems, 28*(1), 50–65.

DuanG. (2018). https://blog.neuvector.com/article/cryptojacking-crypto-mining-tesla-kubernetes-jenkins-exploits/

Du, D., Yu, L., & Brooks, R. R. (2015). Semantic similarity detection for data leak prevention. *ACM International Conference Proceeding Series*. 10.1145/2746266.2746270

Dungan, L., & Pop, M.-D. (2022). *Blockchain-based solutions for smart mobility sustainability assurance*. Paper presented at the IOP Conference Series: Materials Science and Engineering. 10.1088/1757-899X/1220/1/012057

Dutta, P., Choi, T.-M., Somani, S., & Butala, R. (2020). *Blockchain technology in supply chain operations: Applications, challenges and research opportunities*. Academic Press.

Du, W., Pan, S. L., Leidner, D. E., & Ying, W. (2019). Affordances, experimentation and actualization of FinTech: A blockchain implementation study. *The Journal of Strategic Information Systems, 28*(1), 50–65. doi:10.1016/j.jsis.2018.10.002

Dyhrberg, A. H. (2016). Bitcoin, gold and the dollar – A GARCH volatility analysis. *Finance Research Letters, 16*, 85–92. doi:10.1016/j.frl.2015.10.008

Dynes, S., Goetz, E., & Freeman, M. (2007, March). Cyber security: Are economic incentives adequate? In *International Conference on Critical Infrastructure Protection* (pp. 15-27). Springer. 10.1007/978-0-387-75462-8_2

Ebert, C., & Duarte, C. H. C. (2018). Digital Transformation. *IEEE Software, 35*(4), 16–21. doi:10.1109/MS.2018.2801537

Eça, A., Ferreira, M., Prado, M., & Rizzo, A. E. (n.d.). *The Real Effects of FinTech Lending on SMEs: Evidence from Loan Applications*. www.cepr.org

Edwards, C. A. (2014). An analysis of a cyberattack on a nuclear plant: The stuxnet worm. *Critical Infrastructure Protection, 59*.

Edwin, K., Christinal, H., & Chandy, A. (2022). *Blockchain Based Online Voting System Using RSA Algorithm*. Academic Press.

Einhorn, F., Marnewick, C., & Meredith, J. (2019). Achieving strategic benefits from business IT projects: The critical importance of using the business case across the entire project lifetime. *International Journal of Project Management, 37*(8), 989–1002. doi:10.1016/j.ijproman.2019.09.001

Electronic Commerce (e-commerce). (2021, September 17). *Investopedia*. Available online: https://www.investopedia.com/terms/e/ecommerce.asp

ElGamal, T. (1985). A public key cryptosystem and a signature scheme based on discrete logarithms. *IEEE Transactions on Information Theory, 31*(4), 469–472. doi:10.1109/TIT.1985.1057074

ElGamal, T. (1985). A public key cryptosystem and a signature scheme based on discrete logarithms. *IEEE Transactions on Information Theory, IT-31*, 469–472.

Ellavarason, E. R., Guest, R., Deravi, F., Sanchez-Riello, R., & Corsetti, B. (2020). Touch-dynamics based behavioural biometrics on mobile devices–a review from a usability and performance perspective. *ACM Computing Surveys, 53*(6), 1–36. doi:10.1145/3394713

Elliott-Kingston, C., Doyle, O. P. E., & Hunter, A. (2016). Benefits of scenario-based learning in university education. *Acta Horticulturae*, (1126), 107–114. doi:10.17660/ActaHortic.2016.1126.13

Ellul, J., Galea, J., Ganado, M., Mccarthy, S., & Pace, G. J. (2020, October). Regulating Blockchain, DLT and Smart Contracts: a technology regulator's perspective. In *ERA Forum* (Vol. 21, No. 2, pp. 209-220). Springer Berlin Heidelberg. https://link.springer.com/article/10.1007/s12027-020-00617-7

Elsaid, H. M. (2021). *A review of literature directions regarding the impact of fintech firms on the banking industry*. Qualitative Research in Financial Markets. doi:10.1108/QRFM-10-2020-0197

Emme, M., Kirova, A., Kamau, O., & Kosanovich, S. (2006). Ensemble research: A means for immigrant children to explore peer relation- ships through fotonovela. *The Alberta Journal of Educational Research, 52*, 160–181.

Enisa, E. T. L. (2020). *Cyber Espionage; From January 2019 to April 2020*. Retrieved September 22, 2022, from https://www.enisa.europa.eu/topics/threat-risk-management/threats-and-trends/etl-review-folder/etl-2020-cyberespionage

Ennouri, M. F., & Mezghani, K. (2020). *Big Data Management in the Era of FinTech*. doi:10.4018/978-1-7998-7110-1.ch005

Enoch, S. Y., Moon, C. Y., Lee, D., Ahn, M. K., & Kim, D. S. (2022). A practical framework for cyber defence generation, enforcement and evaluation. *Computer Networks, 208*, 108878. doi:10.1016/j.comnet.2022.108878

enterpriseitworld. (2018). https://www.enterpriseitworld.com/home-iot-devices-latest-targets-for-cryptojacking-fortinet/

Epstein, R. G. (1995). Latest developments in the "killer robot" computer ethics scenario. *ACM SIGCSE Bulletin, 27*(1), 111–115. doi:10.1145/199691.199746

Epstein, R., & Robertson, R. E. (2015). The search engine manipulation effect (SEME) and its possible impact on the outcomes of elections. *Proceedings of the National Academy of Sciences of the United States of America, 112*(33), E4512–E4521. doi:10.1073/pnas.1419828112 PMID:26243876

Erica. (2022). Retrieved September 22, 2022, from https://promotions.bankofamerica.com/digitalbanking/mobilebanking/erica

ESET. (2019). *Cybersecurity Trends*. https://www.eset.com/us/trends-2019/

Eskandari, S. a. (2018). A first look at browser-based cryptojacking. In *2018 IEEE European Symposium on Security and Privacy Workshops (EuroS&PW)* (pp. 58--66). 10.1109/EuroSPW.2018.00014

Eskandari, S., Leoutsarakos, A., Mursch, T., & Clark, J. (2018). A first look at browser-based cryptojacking. In *IEEE European Symposium on Security and Privacy Workshops (EuroS&PW)* (pp. 58-66). IEEE.

Estay, B. (2022). *How to (Realistically) Start an Online Business That (Actually) Grows in 2022*. Available at: https://www.bigcommerce.com/blog/how-to-start-online-business/

ETSI. (2020). *CYBER; Migration strategies and recommendations to Quantum Safe schemes*. Available at: https://www.etsi.org/deliver/etsi_tr/103600_103699/103619/01.01.01_60/tr_103619v010101 p.pdf

Euromoney. (n.d.). *Learning*. Available at https://www.euromoney.com/learning/blockchain-explained/what-is-blockchain

EY. (2017). *'WannaCry' ransomware attack: Technical intelligence analysis*. Ernst & Young. https://www.ey.com/Publication/vwLUAssets/ey-wannacry-ransomware-attack/$FILE/ey-wannacry-ransomware-attack.pdf

Eyal, I. (2017). Blockchain Technology: Transforming Libertarian Cryptocurrency Dreams to Finance and Banking Realities. *Computer*, *50*(9), 38–49. doi:10.1109/MC.2017.3571042

Faccia, A., Narcisa, P., Moşteanu, R., Mintoff, T. D., Pio, L., Cavaliere, L., Foggia, U., Caggese, V. R., Fg, F., & Mataruna-dos-santos, L. J. (2020). Electronic Money Laundering, The Dark Side of Fintech. An Overview of the Most Recent Cases. *ICIME 2020: Proceedings of the 2020 12th International Conference on Information Management and Engineering*, 29–34. 10.1145/3430279.3430284

FaceSwap. (n.d.). https://faceswap.dev

Fadhul, S., & Hamdan, A. (2020). The role of "fintech" on banking performance. *Proceedings of the European Conference on Innovation and Entrepreneurship, ECIE, 2020-September*, 911–914. 10.34190/EIE.20.230

Fahlevi, M., Saparudin, M., Maemunah, S., Irma, D., & Ekhsan, M. (2019). Cybercrime Business Digital in Indonesia. *E3S Web of Conferences, 125*, 1–5. doi:10.1051/e3sconf/201912521001

Fairlie, R., & Fossen, F. M. (2022). The early impacts of the COVID-19 pandemic on business sales. *Small Business Economics*, *58*(4), 1853–1864. doi:10.100711187-021-00479-4

Faraz Mubarak, M., Zulfiqar Ali Bhutto, S., Ali Shaikh, F., Mubarik, M., Ahmed Samo, K., & Mastoi, S. (2019). The Impact of Digital Transformation on Business Performance A Study of Pakistani SMEs. In *Technology & []*. www.etasr.com]. *Applied Scientific Research*, *9*(6).

Farokhi, F., Shames, I., & Johansson, K. H. (2020). Private routing and ride-sharing using homomorphic encryption. IET Cyber-Physical Systems. *Theory & Applications*, *5*(4), 311–320.

Fatonah, S., Yulandari, A., & Wibowo, F. W. (2018). A Review of E-Payment System in E-Commerce. *Journal of Physics: Conference Series*, *1140*, 012033. doi:10.1088/1742-6596/1140/1/012033

Faugère, J.-C. (1999). A new efficient algorithm for computing Gröbner bases (F4). Journal of Pure and Applied Algebra, 139(1–3), 61–88.

FBI. (2018). *2018 Internet Crime Report*. Federal Bureau of Investigation. https://www.ic3.gov/media/annualreport/2018_IC3Report.pdf

Febriyanto, E., Rahayu, N., Pangaribuan, K., & Sunarya, P. A. (2020). *Using Blockchain Data Security Management for E-Voting Systems*. Paper presented at the 2020 8th International Conference on Cyber and IT Service Management (CITSM).

Fernández-Rovira, C., Álvarez Valdés, J., Molleví, G., & Nicolas-Sans, R. (2021). The digital transformation of business. Towards the datafication of the relationship with customers. *Technological Forecasting and Social Change, 162,* 120339. Advance online publication. doi:10.1016/j.techfore.2020.120339

Ferraresi, M., Kotsogiannis, C., Rizzo, L., & Secomandi, R. (2020). The 'Great Lockdown' and its determinants. *Economics Letters, 197,* 109628. doi:10.1016/j.econlet.2020.109628 PMID:33100438

Ferrari, M. V. (2022). The platformisation of digital payments: The fabrication of consumer interest in the EU FinTech agenda. *Computer Law & Security Review, 45,* 105687. doi:10.1016/j.clsr.2022.105687

Ferreira, A., & Lenzini, G. (2015). An analysis of social engineering principles in effective phishing. *2015 Workshop on Socio-Technical Aspects in Security and Trust,* 9–16. 10.1109/STAST.2015.10

Ferreira, R., & Vardi, M. Y. (2021). Deep tech ethics: an approach to teaching social justice in computer science. In *Proceedings of the 52nd ACM Technical Symposium on Computer Science Education* (pp. 1041-1047). 10.1145/3408877.3432449

Feyen, E., Frost, J., Gambacorta, L., Natarajan, H., & Saal, M. (2021). *BIS Papers No 117 Fintech and the digital transformation of financial services: Implications for market structure and public policy*. www.worldbank.org

Fianyi, I. (2016). *Curbing cyber-crime and Enhancing e-commerce security with Digital Forensics*. https://arxiv.org/abs/1610.08369

Fiesler, C., Garrett, N., & Beard, N. (2020, February). What do we teach when we teach tech ethics? a syllabi analysis. In *Proceedings of the 51st ACM Technical Symposium on Computer Science Education* (pp. 289-295). 10.1145/3328778.3366825

Finance Nine. (2019). *Westpac security breach: Almost 100,000 customers exposed, cybersecurity news update*. Author.

Firdaus, H. (2020, October 7). *13 Cybersecurity Challenges for Fintech Companies*. Retrieved March 31, 2022, from https://www.e2enetworks.com/13-cybersecurity-challenges-for-fintech-companies/

Fischer, E. A. (2009). *Creating a National Framework for Cybersecurity: An analysis of issues and options*. Nova Science Publishers.

Fischer, M., Imgrund, F., Janiesch, C., & Winkelmann, A. (2020). Strategy archetypes for digital transformation: Defining meta objectives using business process management. *Information & Management, 57*(5), 103262. Advance online publication. doi:10.1016/j.im.2019.103262

Forbes, K. J., & Rigobon, R. (2016). No Contagion, Only Interdependence : Measuring Stock Market Comovements. *The Journal of Finance, 57*(5), 2223–2261. doi:10.1111/0022-1082.00494

Forensically. (n.d.). https://29a.ch/photo-forensics/#forensic-magnifier

Fosso Wamba, S., Kala Kamdjoug, J. R., Epie Bawack, R., & Keogh, J. G. (2020). Bitcoin, Blockchain and Fintech: A systematic review and case studies in the supply chain. *Production Planning and Control, 31*(2–3), 115–142. doi:10.1080/09537287.2019.1631460

FotoForensics. (n.d.). http://fotoforensics.com

Frahim, J. (2015). *Securing the Internet of Things: A Proposed Framework*. Cisco White Paper.

Frankenfield, J. (2019). *Do Cryptocurrencies Have Intrinsic Value? It Depends*. Investopedia Stock Analysis. https://www.investopedia.com/news/does-crypto-have-intrinsic-value-bitcoin-ethereum/#:~:text=Cryptocurrencies

Fruhlinger, J. (2020). *What is phishing? How this cyber attack works and how to prevent it*. Retrieved from CSO Online: https://www.csoonline.com/article/2117843/what-is-phishing-how-this-cyber-attack-works-and-how-to-prevent-it.html

FTC. (2017). *Text of the Federal Trade Commission Enforcement Policy Statement*. https://www.ftc.gov/legal-library/browse/federal-trade-commission-enforcement-policy-statement-regarding-applicability-childrens-online

FTC. (2022). *Combatting Online Harms Through Innovation: A Report to Congress*. https://www.ftc.gov/reports/combatting-online-harms-through-innovation

FTC. (2022). *Policy Statement on Education Technology and the Children's Online Privacy Protection Act*. https://www.ftc.gov/legal-library/browse/policy-statement-federal-trade-commission-education-technology-childrens-online-privacy-protection

Fujimura, S., Watanabe, H., Nakadaira, A., Yamada, T., Akutsu, A., & Kishigami, J. J. (2015, September). BRIGHT: A concept for a decentralized rights management system based on blockchain. In *2015 IEEE 5th International Conference on Consumer Electronics-Berlin (ICCE-Berlin)* (pp. 345-346). IEEE. https://ieeexplore.ieee.org/abstract/document/7391275/

Furnell, S., & Clarke, N. (2012). Power to the people? The evolving recognition of human aspects of security. *Computers & Security*, *31*(8), 983–988. doi:10.1016/j.cose.2012.08.004

Furnell, S., Khern-am-nuai, W., Esmael, R., Yang, W., & Li, N. (2018). Enhancing security behaviour by supporting the user. *Computers & Security*, *75*, 1–9. doi:10.1016/j.cose.2018.01.016

Furstenau, L. B., Sott, M. K., Homrich, A. J. O., Kipper, L. M., Al Abri, A. A., Cardoso, T. F., . . . Cobo, M. J. (2020, March). 20 years of scientific evolution of cyber security: A science mapping. In *International Conference on Industrial Engineering and Operations Management* (pp. 314-325). IEOM Society International.

Fuscaldo, D. (2021, November 19). Everything You Need to Know About E-Commerce. *Business News Daily*. Available online: https://www.businessnewsdaily.com/15858-what-is-e-commerce.html

Gai, K., Qiu, M., Zhao, H., & Dai, W. (2016). Privacy-Preserving Adaptive Multi-channel Communications under Timing Constraints. *Proceedings - 2016 IEEE International Conference on Smart Cloud, SmartCloud 2016*, 190–195. 10.1109/SmartCloud.2016.50

Gai, K. (2014). A Review of Leveraging Private Cloud Computing in Financial Service Institutions: Value Propositions and Current Performances. *International Journal of Computers and Applications*, *95*(3).

Gai, K., Qiu, M., & Sun, X. (2018). A survey on FinTech. *Journal of Network and Computer Applications*, *103*, 262–273. doi:10.1016/j.jnca.2017.10.011

Gai, K., Qiu, M., Sun, X., & Zhao, H. (2017). Security and Privacy Issues: A Survey on FinTech. In M. Qiu (Ed.), *Smart Computing and Communication* (pp. 236–247). Springer International Publishing. doi:10.1007/978-3-319-52015-5_24

Galchenkova, E., & Chupsa, P. (2020). Introduction of fintech companies and their impact on the financial market. *Business Strategies*, *8*(6), 157–159. doi:10.17747/2311-7184-2020-6-157-159

Gallegos-Segovia, P. L., Bravo-Torres, J. F., Larios-Rosillo, V. M., Vintimilla-Tapia, P. E., Yuquilima-Albarado, I. F., & Jara-Saltos, J. D. (2017). Social engineering as an attack vector for ransomware. *2017 CHILEAN Conference on Electrical, Electronics Engineering, Information and Communication Technologies (CHILECON)*, 1–6. 10.1109/CHILECON.2017.8229528

Ganiyu, S. O. (2021). *Extended Risk-Based Context-Aware Model for Dynamic Access Control in Bring Your Own Device Strategy. In Machine Learning and Data Mining for Emerging Trend in Cyber Dynamics*. Springer.

Gao, F., Zhu, L., Shen, M., Sharif, K., Wan, Z., & Ren, K. (2018). A blockchain-based privacy-preserving payment mechanism for vehicle-to-grid networks. *IEEE Network*, *32*(6), 184–192. doi:10.1109/MNET.2018.1700269

Gardner, H. (1991). The tensions between education and development. *Journal of Moral Education*, *20*(2), 113–125. doi:10.1080/0305724910200201

Garvey, J., Burns, P., Alexander, O., & O'Hearn, S. (n.d.). *Crossing the lines: How fintech is propelling FS and TMT firms out of their lanes Contents*. Academic Press.

GASB. (1987). *Objectives of Financial Reporting. Concepts Statement No. 1 of the Governmental Accounting Standards Board. NO. 037, MAY 1987*. Government Standard Accounting Board.

Gazali, H. M., Hassan, R., Nor, R. M., & Rahman, H. M. (2017, May). Re-inventing PTPTN study loan with blockchain and smart contracts. In *2017 8th international conference on information technology (ICIT)* (pp. 751-754). IEEE. 10.1109/ICITECH.2017.8079940

General Data Protection Regulation (GDPR) Compliance Guidelines. (n.d.). Retrieved February 27, 2022, from https://gdpr.eu/

Gentry, C. (2009, May). Fully homomorphic encryption using ideal lattices. In *Proceedings of the forty-first annual ACM symposium on Theory of computing* (pp. 169-178). 10.1145/1536414.1536440

George, A. L., & Bennett, A. (2005). *Case Studies and Theory Development in the Social Sciences*. MIT Press.

Geuder, J., Kinateder, H., & Wagner, N. F. (2019). Cryptocurrencies as financial bubbles: The case of Bitcoin. *Finance Research Letters*, *31*, 179–184. doi:10.1016/j.frl.2018.11.011

Ghafir, I., Prenosil, V., Alhejailan, A., & Hammoudeh, M. (2016). Social Engineering Attack Strategies and Defence Approaches. *2016 IEEE 4th International Conference on Future Internet of Things and Cloud (FiCloud)*, 145–149. 10.1109/FiCloud.2016.28

Ghavifekr, S., & Fung, H. Y. (2021). Change Management in Digital Environment Amid the COVID-19 Pandemic: A Scenario from Malaysian Higher Education Institutions. In S. Saeed, M. P. R. Bolívar, & R. Thurasamy (Eds.), *Pandemic Lockdown, and Digital Transformation*. doi:10.1007/978-3-030-86274-9_8

Ghiro. (n.d.). https://www.getghiro.org

Ghouse, M., Nene, M. J., & VembuSelvi, C. (2019, December 1). Data Leakage Prevention for Data in Transit using Artificial Intelligence and Encryption Techniques. *2019 6th IEEE International Conference on Advances in Computing, Communication and Control, ICAC3 2019*. doi:10.1109/ICAC347590.2019.9036839

Gibbs, S. (2017). WannaCry: Hackers withdraw £108,000 of bitcoin ransom. *The Guardian*. https://www.theguardian.com/technology/2017/aug/03/wannacry-hackers-withdraw-108000-pounds-bitcoin-ransom

Gil-Alana, L. A., Abakah, E. J. A., & Rojo, M. F. R. (2020). Cryptocurrencies and stock market indices. Are they related? *Research in International Business and Finance*, *51*, 101063. Advance online publication. doi:10.1016/j.ribaf.2019.101063

Gill, S. H., Razzaq, M. A., Ahmad, M., Almansour, F. M., Haq, I. U., Jhanjhi, N. Z., . . . Masud, M. (2022). Security and Privacy Aspects of Cloud Computing: A Smart Campus Case Study. *Intelligent Automation & Soft Computing, 31*(1), 117-128. https://iopscience.iop.org/article/10.1088/1742-6596/1979/1/012035/meta

Gimpel, H., Rau, D., & Röglinger, M. (2018). Understanding FinTech start-ups – a taxonomy of consumer-oriented service offerings. *Electronic Markets, 28*(3), 245–264. doi:10.100712525-017-0275-0

Giri, B. N., Jyoti, N., & Avert, M. (2006). *The emergence of ransomware.* AVAR.

Giudici, P. (2018). Fintech Risk Management: A Research Challenge for Artificial Intelligence in Finance. *Frontiers in Artificial Intelligence, 1*(November), 1–6. doi:10.3389/frai.2018.00001 PMID:33733089

Global Legal Research Center. (2018). Regulation of Cryptocurrency Around the World. In *The Law Library of Congress* (Vol. 5080). https://www.loc.gov/law/help/cryptocurrency/regulation-of-cryptocurrency.pdf

Glover. (2022). https://techmonitor.ai/technology/cybersecurity/cryptojacking

Goagoses, N., Winschiers-Theophilus, H., & Zaman, T. (2020). Community protocols for researchers: Using sketches to communicate interaction guidelines. *AI & Society, 35*(3), 675–687. doi:10.100700146-019-00914-x

Gocer, B. D., & Bahtiyar, S. (2019). An Authorization Framework with OAuth for FinTech Servers. *UBMK 2019 - Proceedings, 4th International Conference on Computer Science and Engineering,* 536–541. 10.1109/UBMK.2019.8907182

Göçoğlu, V. (2018). *Türkiye'nin Siber Güvenlik Politikalarının Kamu Politikası Analizi Çerçevesinde Değerlendirilmesi* [Doctoral Dissertation]. University of Hacettepe, Ankara, Turkey.

Goel, P., & Ghosh, M. (2021). Blockchain-Based Secure and Efficient Crowdsourcing Framework. In *Computer Networks and Inventive Communication Technologies* (pp. 391–406). Springer. doi:10.1007/978-981-15-9647-6_30

Gohwong, S. G. (2019). The State of the Art of Cryptography-based Cyber-attacks. *International Journal of Crime, Law and Social Issues, 6*(2).

Goldfrank, B. (2012). The World Bank and globalization of participatory budgeting. *Journal of Public Deliberation, 8*(2), article,7.

Goldreich, O. (1986). *Two remarks concerning the Goldwasser-Micali-Rivest signature scheme, Advances in Cryptology CRYPTO '86* (Vol. 263). LNCS.

Goldreich, O., Goldwasser, S., & Halevi, S. (1997). Public-key cryptosystems from lattice reduction problems. *CRYPTO, 1997,* 112–131.

Goldstein, K. (2020). Blockchain and Distributed Ledger Technology: Insurance Applications, Legal Developments, and Cybersecurity Considerations. *Conn. Ins. LJ, 27,* 511.

Goldwasser, S., & Micali, S. (1984). Probabilistic Encryption. *Journal of Computer and System Sciences, 28*(2), 270–299. doi:10.1016/0022-0000(84)90070-9

Goli, A., Hajihassani, O., Khazaei, H., Ardakanian, O., Rashidi, M., & Dauphinee, T. (2020). Migrating from monolithic to serverless: A fintech case study. *ICPE 2020 - Companion of the ACM/SPEC International Conference on Performance Engineering,* 20–25. 10.1145/3375555.3384380

Golob, T., Makarovic, M., & Rek, M. (2021). Meta-reflexivity for resilience against disinformation. *Comunicar, 29*(66), 107–118. doi:10.3916/C66-2021-09

Gölzer, P., & Fritzsche, A. (2017). Data-driven operations management: Organisational implications of the digital transformation in industrial practice. *Production Planning and Control, 28*(16), 1332–1343. doi:10.1080/09537287.2017.1375148

Gomber, P., Kauffman, R. J., Parker, C., & Weber, B. W. (2018). On the Fintech Revolution: Interpreting the Forces of Innovation, Disruption, and Transformation in Financial Services. *Journal of Management Information Systems, 35*(1), 220–265. doi:10.1080/07421222.2018.1440766

Gomes, F., & Correia, M. (2020). Cryptojacking detection with cpu usage metrics. In *IEEE 19th International Symposium on Network Computing and Applications (NCA)* (pp. 1-10). IEEE.

Gómez-Hernández, J. A., Álvarez-González, L., & García-Teodoro, P. (2018). R-Locker: Thwarting ransomware action through a honeyfile-based approach. *Computers & Security, 73*, 389–398. doi:10.1016/j.cose.2017.11.019

Gong, C., & Ribiere, V. (2021). Developing a unified definition of digital transformation. *Technovation, 102*, 102217. Advance online publication. doi:10.1016/j.technovation.2020.102217

Gordon, L. A., Loeb, M. P., Sohail, T., Tseng, C. Y., & Zhou, L. (2008). Cybersecurity, capital allocations and management control systems. *European Accounting Review, 17*(2), 215–241. doi:10.1080/09638180701819972

Gordon, L. A., Loeb, M. P., & Zhou, L. (2016). Investing in cybersecurity: Insights from the Gordon-Loeb model. *Journal of Information Security, 7*(02), 49–59. doi:10.4236/jis.2016.72004

Gorman, B. (2019). *Internet Security Threat Report*. Available at: https://www.symantec.com/content/dam/symantec/docs/reports/istr-24-2019-en.pdf

Gorog, C., & Boult, T. E. (2018, July). Solving global cybersecurity problems by connecting trust using blockchain. In *2018 IEEE International Conference on Internet of Things (iThings) and IEEE Green Computing and Communications (GreenCom) and IEEE Cyber, Physical and Social Computing (CPSCom) and IEEE Smart Data (SmartData)* (pp. 1425-1432). IEEE. 10.1109/Cybermatics_2018.2018.00243

Gotterbarn, D., Bruckman, A., Flick, C., Miller, K., & Wolf, M. J. (2017). ACM code of ethics: A guide for positive action. *Communications of the ACM, 61*(1), 121–128. doi:10.1145/3173016

Goyal, Bedi, Rajawat, & Shrivastava. (2022). Secure Authentication in Wireless Sensor Networks Using Blockchain Technology. In AI-Enabled Agile Internet of Things for Sustainable FinTech Ecosystems (p. 13). IGI Global. doi:10.4018/978-1-6684-4176-3.ch005

Goyal, J., Ahmed, M., & Gopalani, D. (2022). *A Privacy Preserving E-Voting System with Two-Phase Verification based on Ethereum Blockchain*. Academic Press.

Granickas, K. (2013). *Understanding the impact of releasing and re-using open government data*. Retrieved April 25, 2016 from https://www.epsiplatform.eu/content/understanding-impactreleasing-and-re-using-open-government-data

Greitzer, F. L. (2014). *Analysis of unintentional insider threats deriving from social engineering exploits. IEEE Security and Privacy Workshops*. doi:10.1109/SPW.2014.39

Gribov, A., Horan, K., Gryak, J., Najarian, K., Shpilrain, V., Soroushmehr, R., & Kahrobaei, D. (2019, March). Medical diagnostics based on encrypted medical data. In *International Conference on Bio-inspired Information and Communication* (pp. 98-111). Springer.

Grobauer, B., Walloschek, T., & Stocker, E. (2010). Understanding cloud computing vulnerabilities. *IEEE Security and Privacy, 9*(2), 50–57. doi:10.1109/MSP.2010.115

Grosz, B. J., Grant, D. G., Vredenburgh, K., Behrends, J., Hu, L., Simmons, A., & Waldo, J. (2019). Embedded EthiCS: Integrating ethics across CS education. *Communications of the ACM, 62*(8), 54–61. doi:10.1145/3330794

Grover, L. (1996). A fast quantum mechanical algorithm for database search. *Proceedings, 28th Annual ACM Symposium on the Theory of Computing*, 212.

Gu, B., Zou, Y., Cai, D., & Fan, H. (2022). A Method of Data Distribution and Traceability Based on Blockchain. In X. Sun, X. Zhang, Z. Xia, & E. Bertino (Eds.), *Artificial Intelligence and Security* (pp. 16–27). Springer International Publishing. doi:10.1007/978-3-031-06791-4_2

Gudymenko, I., Khalid, A., Siddiqui, H., Idrees, M., Clauß, S., Luckow, A., . . . Miehle, D. (2020). *Privacy-preserving blockchain-based systems for car sharing leveraging zero-knowledge protocols.* Paper presented at the 2020 IEEE international conference on decentralized applications and infrastructures (DAPPS). 10.1109/DAPPS49028.2020.00014

Guera, D., & Delp, E. J. (2019). Deepfake Video Detection Using Recurrent Neural Networks. *Proceedings of AVSS 2018 - 2018 15th IEEE International Conference on Advanced Video and Signal-Based Surveillance.* 10.1109/AVSS.2018.8639163

Guha, A., Samanta, D., Banerjee, A., & Agarwal, D. (2021). A Deep Learning Model for Information Loss Prevention from Multi-Page Digital Documents. *IEEE Access: Practical Innovations, Open Solutions, 9*, 80451–80465. doi:10.1109/ACCESS.2021.3084841

Gull, H., Saeed, S., Iqbal, S. Z., Bamarouf, Y. A., Alqahtani, M. A., Alabbad, D. A., Saqib, M., al Qahtani, S. H., & Alamer, A. (2022). An Empirical Study of Mobile Commerce and Customers Security Perception in Saudi Arabia. *Electronics (Basel), 11*(3), 293. doi:10.3390/electronics11030293

Gunnarsson, B. R., vanden Broucke, S., Baesens, B., Óskarsdóttir, M., & Lemahieu, W. (2021). Deep learning for credit scoring: Do or don't? *European Journal of Operational Research, 295*(1), 292–305. doi:10.1016/j.ejor.2021.03.006 PMID:34955589

Gupta, I., & Singh, A. K. (2022). *A Holistic View on Data Protection for Sharing, Communicating, and Computing Environments: Taxonomy and Future Directions.* https://arxiv.org/abs/2202.11965

Gupta, R., & Shanbhag, S. (2021). *A Survey of Peer-to-Peer Ride Sharing Services using Blockchain.* Academic Press.

Gupta, I., & Singh, A. K. (2017). A probability based model for data leakage detection using Bigraph. *ACM International Conference Proceeding Series*, 1–5. 10.1145/3163058.3163060

Gupta, L., Salman, T., Das, R., Erbad, A., Jain, R., & Samaka, M. (2019). Hyper-vines: A hybrid learning fault and performance issues eradicator for virtual network services over multi-cloud systems. In *2019 International Conference on Computing, Networking and Communications (ICNC)*. IEEE.

Haas, A., Rossberg, A., Schuff, D. L., Titzer, B. L., Holman, M., Gohman, D., ... Bastien, J. F. (2017). Bringing the web up to speed with WebAssembly. In *Proceedings of the 38th ACM SIGPLAN Conference on Programming Language Design and Implementation* (pp. 185-200). ACM.

Haciyakupoglu, G., Hui, J. Y., Suguna, V. S., Leong, D., Bin, M. F., & Rahman, A. (2018). *Countering Fake News a Survey of Recent Global Initiatives.* https://think-asia.org/bitstream/handle/11540/8063/PR180307_Countering-Fake-News.pdf?sequence=1

Hami, A. N. R., & Cheng, A. Y. (2013). *A Risk Perception Analysis on the use of Electronic Payment Systems by Young Adult.* Academic Press.

Hamlen, K. W., & Thuraisingham, B. (2013). Data security services, solutions and standards for outsourcing. *Computer Standards & Interfaces, 35*(1), 1–5. doi:10.1016/j.csi.2012.02.001

Hammarberg, K., Kirkman, M., & de Lacey, S. (2016). Qualitative research methods: When to use them and how to judge them. *Human Reproduction (Oxford, England)*, *31*(3), 498–501. doi:10.1093/humrep/dev334 PMID:26759142

Hammood, W. A., Abdullah, R., Hammood, O. A., Mohamad Asmara, S., Al-Sharafi, M. A., & Muttaleb Hasan, A. (2020). A Review of User Authentication Model for Online Banking System based on Mobile IMEI Number. *IOP Conference Series. Materials Science and Engineering*, *769*(1), 012061. Advance online publication. doi:10.1088/1757-899X/769/1/012061

Hampton, N., Baig, Z. A., & Zeadally, S. (2018). Ransomware behavioural analysis on windows platforms. *Journal of Information Security and Applications*, *40*, 44–51. doi:10.1016/j.jisa.2018.02.008

Hanif, M., Ashraf, H., Jalil, Z., Jhanjhi, N. Z., Humayun, M., Saeed, S., & Almuhaideb, A. M. (2022). AI-Based Wormhole Attack Detection Techniques in Wireless Sensor Networks. *Electronics (Basel)*, *11*(15), 2324. doi:10.3390/electronics11152324

Han, P., Liu, C., Cao, J., Duan, S., Pan, H., Cao, Z., & Fang, B. (2020). CloudDLP: Transparent and scalable data sanitization for browser-based cloud storage. *IEEE Access: Practical Innovations, Open Solutions*, *8*, 68449–68459. doi:10.1109/ACCESS.2020.2985870

Hansman, S., & Hunt, R. (2004). A Taxonomy of Network and Computer Attacks. *Computers & Security*.

Harris, F. H. deB., Mcinish, T. H., Shoesmith, G. L., Robert, A., The, S., Analysis, Q., Dec, N., Harris, F. H., Mcinish, T. H., Shoesmith, G. L., & Wood, R. A. (1995). Cointegration, Error Correction, and Price Discovery on Informationally Linked Security Markets. *Journal of Financial and Quantitative Analysis*, *30*(4).

Harrow, A., Hassidim, A., & Lloyd, S. (2008). Quantum algorithm for solving linear systems of equations. *Physical Review Letters*, *103*(15).

Hartmann, P., Straetmans, S., & de Vries, C. G. (2004). Asset Market Linkages in Crisis Periods. *Tinbergen Institute Discussion Paper*, *71*(2).

Hartmann, K., & Giles, K. (2020). The Next Generation of Cyber-Enabled Information Warfare. *International Conference on Cyber Conflict, CYCON*, 233–250. 10.23919/CyCon49761.2020.9131716

Hasan, B., Sultana, M., & Hasan, M. N. (2014). Good governance in Bangladesh: Problems and prospects. *UITS Journal*, *3*(2), 22–44.

Hasan, H. R., & Salah, K. (2019). Combating Deepfake Videos Using Blockchain and Smart Contracts. *IEEE Access: Practical Innovations, Open Solutions*, *7*, 41596–41606. doi:10.1109/ACCESS.2019.2905689

Hassan, M. M., Nipa, S. S., Akter, M., Haque, R., Deepa, F. N., Rahman, M. M., Siddiqui, M., & Sharif, M. H. (2018). Broken Authentication and Session Management Vulnerability: A Case Study of Web Application. *International Journal of Simulation: Systems, Science & Technology*. doi:10.5013/IJSSST.a.19.02.06

Hassan, M. A., Shukur, Z., Hasan, M. K., & Al-Khaleefa, A. S. (2020). A Review on Electronic Payments Security. *Symmetry*, *12*(8), 1344. doi:10.3390ym12081344

Hassan, M. U., Rehmani, M. H., & Chen, J. (2019). Privacy preservation in blockchain-based IoT systems: Integration issues, prospects, challenges, and future research directions. *Future Generation Computer Systems*, *97*, 512–529. doi:10.1016/j.future.2019.02.060

Hassija, V., Chamola, V., Saxena, V., Jain, D., Goyal, P., & Sikdar, B. (2019). A survey on IoT security: Application areas, security threats, and solution architectures. *IEEE Access: Practical Innovations, Open Solutions*, *7*, 82721–82743. doi:10.1109/ACCESS.2019.2924045

Hauer, B. (2015). Data and information leakage prevention within the scope of information security. *IEEE Access: Practical Innovations, Open Solutions, 3*, 2554–2565. doi:10.1109/ACCESS.2015.2506185

HDFC Securities. (2021). *Fintech Playbook: Discount Brokers.* HDFC Securities.

Heartfield, R., & Loukas, G. (2015). A taxonomy of attacks and a survey of defence mechanisms for semantic social engineering attacks. *ACM Computing Surveys, 48*(3), 1–39.

Hekim, H., & Başıbüyük, O. (2013). Siber Suçlar ve Türkiye'nin Siber Güvenlik Politikaları. *Uluslararası Güvenlik ve Terörizm Dergisi, 4*(2), 135–158.

Helleiner, E. (1998). Electronic money: A challenge to the sovereign state? *Journal of International Affairs, 51*(2), 387–409.

Herath, T., & Rao, H. R. (2009). Protection motivation and deterrence: A framework for security policy compliance in organisations. *European Journal of Information Systems, 18*(2), 106–125. doi:10.1057/ejis.2009.6

Herian, R. (2017). Blockchain and the (re) imagining of trusts jurisprudence. *Strategic Change, 26*(5), 453-460.

Hernández, E., Öztürk, M., Sittón, I., & Rodríguez, S. (2019). Data Protection on Fintech Platforms. In F. de La Prieta, A. González-Briones, P. Pawleski, D. Calvaresi, E. del Val, F. Lopes, V. Julian, E. Osaba, & R. Sánchez-Iborra (Eds.), *Highlights of Practical Applications of Survivable Agents and Multi-Agent Systems. The PAAMS Collection* (pp. 223–233). Springer International Publishing. doi:10.1007/978-3-030-24299-2_19

Hernandez-Ortega, J., Tolosana, R., Fierrez, J., & Morales, A. (2021). DeepFakesON-Phys: Deepfakes detection based on heart rate estimation. *CEUR Workshop Proceedings.*

He, Y., Inglut, E., & Luo, C. (2022). Malware incident response (IR) informed by cyber threat intelligence (CTI). *Science China. Information Sciences, 65*(7), 1–3.

Hilal, A. H., & AlAbri, S. S. (2013). Using Nvivo for Data Analysis in Qualitative Research. *International Interdisciplinary Journal of Education, 2*(2), 181–186. doi:10.12816/0002914

Hkiri, B., Hammoudeh, S., Aloui, C., & Yarovaya, L. (2017). Are Islamic indexes a safe haven for investors? An analysis of total, directional and net volatility spillovers between conventional and Islamic indexes and importance of crisis periods. *Pacific-Basin Finance Journal, 43*, 124–150. doi:10.1016/j.pacfin.2017.03.001

Hoffstein, J., Pipher, J., & Silverman, J. H. (1998, June). NTRU: A ring-based public key cryptosystem. In *International algorithmic number theory symposium* (pp. 267-288). Springer.

Hoffman, I., & Cseh, K. B. (2020). E-administration, Cybersecurity and Municipalities – the Challenges of Cybersecurity Issues for the Municipalities in Hungary. *Cybersecurity and Law, 2*(2), 199–211. doi:10.35467/cal/133999

Hoffstein, J., Pipher, J., & Silverman, J. H. (1998). NTRU: A Ring-Based Public Key Cryptosystem. *ANTS, 1998*, 267–288.

Hollander, R., & Arenberg, C. R. (2009). *Ethics Education and Scientific and Engineering Research: What's Been Learned? What Should Be Done? Summary of a Workshop.* National Academy of Engineering. The National Academies Press.

Holmes, A. (2021). *533 million Facebook users' phone numbers and personal data have been leaked online.* https://www. Businessinsider.com/stolen-data-of-533-million-facebook-users-leaked-online-2021-4

Holotiuk, F., & Beimborn, D. (n.d.). *Critical Success Factors of Digital Business Strategy.* Academic Press.

Homoliak, I. E. (2018). *Insight into insiders and it: A survey of insider threat taxonomies, analysis, modeling, and countermeasures.* Academic Press.

Homoliak, I., Venugopalan, S., Reijsbergen, D., Hum, Q., Schumi, R., & Szalachowski, P. (2020). The security reference architecture for blockchains: Toward a standardized model for studying vulnerabilities, threats, and defenses. *IEEE Communications Surveys and Tutorials*, *23*(1), 341–390. doi:10.1109/COMST.2020.3033665

Hong, G., Yang, Z., Yang, S., Zhang, L., Nan, Y., Zhang, Z., ... Duan, H. (2018). How you get shot in the back: A systematical study about cryptojacking in the real world. In *Proceedings of the ACM SIGSAC Conference on Computer and Communications Security* (pp. 1701-1713). ACM.

Hong, K. H. (2017). Bitcoin as an alternative investment vehicle. *Information Technology Management*, *18*(4), 265–275. doi:10.100710799-016-0264-6

Hong, W., Zheng, C., Wu, L., & Pu, X. (2019). Analyzing the Relationship between Consumer Satisfaction and Fresh E-Commerce Logistics Service Using Text Mining Techniques. *Sustainability*, *11*(13), 3570. doi:10.3390u11133570

Hood, M., & Malik, F. (2016). Is Gold the Best Hedge and a Safe Haven Under Changing Stock Market Volatility. *Review of Financial Economics*, (August). Advance online publication. doi:10.1016/j.rfe.2013.03.001

Hoofnagle, C. J., Van Der Sloot, B., Borgesius, F. Z., Jay, C., Van Der Sloot, B., & Zuiderveen, F. (2019). The European Union general data protection regulation : what it is and what it means The European Union general data protection regulation : what it is and what it means *. *Information & Communications Technology Law*, *28*(1), 65–98. doi:10.1080/13600834.2019.1573501

Horbenko, Y. (2017). *Using Blockchain Technology to Boost Cyber Security*. Retrieved from Steel Wiki: https://steelkiwi.com/blog/using-blockchain-technology-to-boost-cybersecurity

Horgan, D., Hackett, J., Westphalen, C. B., Kalra, D., Richer, E., Romao, M., Andreu, A. L., Lal, J. A., Bernini, C., Tumiene, B., Boccia, S., & Montserrat, A. (2020). Digitalisation and COVID-19: The Perfect Storm. *Biomedicine Hub*, *5*(3), 1–23. doi:10.1159/000511232 PMID:33564668

Hornuf, L., Klus, M. F., & Lohwasser, T. S. (2021). *How do banks interact with fintech startups?* Academic Press.

Hosh. (2017). *Nocoin: Block lists to prevent javascript miners.* https://github.com/hoshsadiq/adblock-nocoin-list

Hossan, M. S., Khatun, M. L., Rahman, S., Reno, S., & Ahmed, M. (2021). *Securing Ride-Sharing Service Using IPFS and Hyperledger Based on Private Blockchain.* Paper presented at the 2021 24th International Conference on Computer and Information Technology (ICCIT). 10.1109/ICCIT54785.2021.9689814

Houben, R., & Snyers, A. (2018). *Cryptocurrencies and blockchain: Legal context and implications for financial crime, money laundering and tax evasion.* https://www.europarl.europa.eu/cmsdata/150761/TAX3%20Study%20on%20cryptocurrencies%20and%20blockchain.pdf

House, W. (n.d.). *The national strategy for pandemic influenza.* Academic Press.

Housley, R. (2020a). *Use of the HSS/LMS Hash-Based Signature Algorithm in the Cryptographic Message Syntax (CMS), IETF RFC 8708.* Available at: https://tools.ietf.org/html/rfc8708

Housley, R. (2020b). *Use of the HSS/LMS Hash-Based Signature Algorithm with CBOR Object Signing and Encryption (COSE), IETF RFC 8778.* Available at: https://tools.ietf.org/html/rfc8778

Hron, M. (2018). *Avast, Protect Yourself from Cryptojacking "Avastantimalware."* https://www.avast.com/c-protect-yourself-from-cryptojacking

Hsu, C. C., Tsaih, R. H., & Yen, D. C. (2018). The evolving role of IT Departments in digital transformation. *Sustainability (Switzerland)*, *10*(10), 3706. Advance online publication. doi:10.3390u10103706

Hsu, C. C., Zhuang, Y. X., & Lee, C. Y. (2020). Deep fake image detection based on pairwise learning. *Applied Sciences (Switzerland)*, *10*(1), 370. Advance online publication. doi:10.3390/app10010370

Https://www.idwatchdog.com. (2022). *Insider Threats Are Becoming More Frequent and More Costly: What Businesses Need to Know Now*. https://www.idwatchdog.com/insider-threats-and-data-breaches/

Hu, X., Shu, Z., Song, X., Cheng, G., & Gong, J. (2021). Detecting Cryptojacking Traffic Based on Network Behavior Features. In *IEEE Global Communications Conference (GLOBECOM)* (pp. 1-6). IEEE.

Huang, K., Siegel, M., Pearlson, K., & Madnick, S. E. (2019). Casting the Dark Web in a New Light: A Value-Chain Lens Reveals a Growing Cyber Attack Ecosystem and New Strategies for Combating It. SSRN *Electronic Journal, June*. doi:10.2139/ssrn.3459128

Huang, J., Kong, L., Chen, G., Wu, M. Y., Liu, X., & Zeng, P. (2019). Towards secure industrial IoT: Blockchain system with credit-based consensus mechanism. *IEEE Transactions on Industrial Informatics*, *15*(6), 3680–3689. doi:10.1109/TII.2019.2903342

Huang, J., Luo, Y., Xu, M., Hu, B., & Long, J. (2022). pShare. *Privacy-Preserving Ride-Sharing System with Minimum-Detouring Route*. Academic Press.

Huckle, S., Bhattacharya, R., White, M., & Beloff, N. (2016). Internet of things, blockchain and shared economy applications. *Procedia Computer Science*, *98*, 461–466. doi:10.1016/j.procs.2016.09.074

Hull, G., John, H., & Arief, B. (2019). Ransomware deployment methods and analysis: Views from a predictive model and human responses. *Crime Science*, *8*(1), 2. doi:10.118640163-019-0097-9

Hülsing, A., Rijneveld, J., Samardjiska, S., & Schwabe, P. (2016). From 5-pass MQ-based identification to MQ-based signatures. In Advances in Cryptology-Asiacrypt 2016. Springer.

Humayun, M., Jhanjhi, N. Z., Hamid, B., & Ahmed, G. (2020). Emerging smart logistics and transportation using IoT and blockchain. *IEEE Internet of Things Magazine, 3*(2), 58-62. https://ieeexplore.ieee.org/abstract/document/9125435

Humayun, M., Jhanjhi, N., Hamid, B., & Ahmed, G. (2020). *Emerging smart logistics and transportation using IoT and blockchain*. Academic Press.

Humayun, M., Niazi, M., Jhanjhi, N., Alshayeb, M., & Mahmood, S. (2020). *Cyber security threats and vulnerabilities: a systematic mapping study*. Academic Press.

Humayun, M., Jhanjhi, N. Z., Niazi, M., Amsaad, F., & Masood, I. (2022). *Securing Drug Distribution Systems from Tampering Using Blockchain*. Academic Press.

Humayun, M., Jhanjhi, N., Alsayat, A., & Ponnusamy, V. (2021). Internet of things and ransomware: Evolution, mitigation and prevention. *Egyptian Informatics Journal*, *22*(1), 105–117. doi:10.1016/j.eij.2020.05.003

Huth, C. L., Chadwick, D. W., Claycomb, W. R., & You, I. (2013). Guest editorial: A brief overview of data leakage and insider threats. *Information Systems Frontiers*, *15*(1), 1–4. doi:10.100710796-013-9419-8

Hwang, Y., Park, S., & Shin, N. (2021). Sustainable development of a mobile payment security environment using fintech solutions. *Sustainability (Switzerland)*, *13*(15), 1–15. doi:10.3390u13158375

Hydara, I., Sultan, A. B. M., Zulzalil, H., & Admodisastro, N. (2015). Current state of research on cross-site scripting (XSS)–A systematic literature review. *Information and Software Technology*, *58*, 170–186. doi:10.1016/j.infsof.2014.07.010

IBM. (2019). *IBM security's cost of a data breach report 2019*. IBM.

IBM. (2021, August 16). *What is blockchain security?* https://www.ibm.com/in-en/topics/blockchain-security

IBM. (2022). *IBM security's cost of a data breach report 2022.* IBM.

IBM. (2022). *X-Force Threat Intelligence Index 2022.* IBM. https://www.ibm.com/downloads/cas/ADLMYLAZ

Ibrahim, M., Ravindran, K., Lee, H., Farooqui, O., & Mahmoud, Q. H. (2021). *Electionblock: An electronic voting system using Blockchain and fingerprint authentication.* Paper presented at the 2021 IEEE 18th International Conference on Software Architecture Companion (ICSA-C). 10.1109/ICSA-C52384.2021.00033

IC3. (2020, March 20). *FBI Sees Rise in Fraud Schemes Related to the Coronavirus (COVID-19) Pandemic.* https://www.ic3.gov/media/2020/200320.aspx

Ifinedo, P. (2012). Understanding information systems security policy compliance: An integration of the theory of planned behavior and the protection motivation theory. *Computers & Security, 31*(1), 83–95. doi:10.1016/j.cose.2011.10.007

IFWG - Crypto Assets Regulatory Working Group. (2014). *Position Paper on Crypto Assets.* Author.

Ignatyuk, A., Liubkina, O., Murovana, T., & Magomedova, A. (2020). FinTech as an innovation challenge: From big data to sustainable development. *E3S Web of Conferences, 166.* doi:10.1051/e3sconf/202016613027

Imgrund, F., Fischer, M., & Winkelmann, A. (2018). *Approaching Digitalization with Business Process Management.* https://www.researchgate.net/publication/323665985

Indapwar, A., Chandak, M., & Jain, A. (2020). E-voting system using Blockchain technology. *Int. J. of Advanced Trends in Computer Science and Engineering, 9*(3).

Infosecurity magazine.com. (2018, August 7). *How Blockchain Is Revolutionizing Cybersecurity.* https://www.infosecurity-magazine.com/next-geninfosec/blockchain-cybersecurity

Infosys. (2021, July 29). *Assuring Digital-trust.* https://www.infosys.com/services/cyber-security/insights/assuring-digital-trust-cybersecurity.html

Infusion Lawyers. (2020). Nigeria : Deal Or No Deal, Cryptocurrency Transactions Remain Legal In Nigeria And Environs. Mondaq.Com.

Ingalls, S. (2018). *Cryptocurrency mining.* https://www.webopedia.com/TERM/C/cryptocurrency-mining.html

Ingalls, S. (2021, July 28). *The State of Blockchain Applications in Cybersecurity.* https://www.esecurityplanet.com/applications/cybersecurity-blockchain-applications/

Ingle, G. B. (2021). *Adversarial Deep Learning Attacks—A Review.* Information and Communication Technology for Competitive Strategies. doi:10.1007/978-981-16-0882-7_26

Insiders, C. (2019). *Insider Threat Report, 2019.* Retrieved September 21, 2022, from https://www.cybersecurity-insiders.com/portfolio/insider-threat-report/

Insiders, C. (2020). *Insider Threat Report.* Retrieved September 22, 2022, from https://www.cybersecurity-insiders.com/wp-content/uploads/2019/11/2020-Insider-Threat-Report-Gurucul.pdf

Insiders, C. (2021). *2021 Insider Threat Report.* Retrieved September 21, 2022, from https://www.cybersecurity-insiders.com/portfolio/2021-insider-threat-report-gurucul/

Institute of Electrical and Electronics Engineers & PPG Institute of Technology. (n.d.). *Proceedings of the 5th International Conference on Communication and Electronics Systems (ICCES 2020) : 10-12, June 2020.* Author.

iProov. (n.d.). https://www.iproov.com

IPSASB. (2014). *The Conceptual Framework for General Purpose Financial Reporting by Public Sector Entities*. Retrieved from http://html5.epaperflip.com/?docid=9c3c49a0-9d06-49e1-b666-a5600137e9a9#page=1

ISACA. (2018). *Introduction and Methodology*. http://linkd.in/ISACAOfficial

ISACA. (n.d.). *ISACA Survey Cybersecurity Attacks Are Rising During COVID 19*. Retrieved April 25, 2022, from https://www.isaca.org/why-isaca/about-us/newsroom/press-releases/2020/isaca-survey-cybersecurity-attacks-are-rising-during-covid-19

Ishmaev, G. (2017). Blockchain technology as an institution of property. *Metaphilosophy, 48*(5), 666-686.

Ismail. (2021). *Minerblock: An efficient browser extension to block browser based cryptocurrency miners all over the web*. https://github.com/xd4rker/MinerBlock/blob/master/assets/filters.txt

ISO 22313:2020(en), Security and resilience — Business continuity management systems — Guidance on the use of ISO 22301. (n.d.). Retrieved February 27, 2022, from https://www.iso.org/obp/ui/#iso:std:iso:22313:en

Jabbar, I., & Alsaad, S. N. (2017). Design and Implementation of Secure Remote e-Voting System Using Homomorphic Encryption. *International Journal of Network Security, 19*(5), 694–703.

Jafar, U., Aziz, M. J. A., & Shukur, Z. (2021). Blockchain for electronic voting system—Review and open research challenges. *Sensors (Basel), 21*(17), 5874. doi:10.339021175874 PMID:34502764

Jang, H., & Sul, W. (2002). The Asian financial crisis and the co-movement of Asian stock markets. *Journal of Asian Economics, 13*(1), 94–104. doi:10.1016/S1049-0078(01)00115-4

Jani, K., Prakash, O., & Subramanian, C. B. (2021). *Developing Secured Peer to Peer Ride Sharing Services based on Blockchain Technology*. Academic Press.

Jan, S. U., Abbasi, I. A., & Algarni, F. (2021). A key agreement scheme for IoD deployment civilian drone. *IEEE Access: Practical Innovations, Open Solutions, 9*, 149311–149321. doi:10.1109/ACCESS.2021.3124510

Jao, D., & De Feo, L. (2011). Towards Quantum-Resistant Cryptosystems from Supersingular Elliptic Curve Isogenies. In Post-Quantum Cryptography-PQCrypto 2011. Springer.

Javaid, M., Haleem, A., Singh, R. P., Khan, S., & Suman, R. (2021). Blockchain technology applications for Industry 4.0: A literature-based review. *Blockchain: Research and Applications, 100027*.

Javaid, N. (2022). A Secure and Efficient Trust Model for Wireless Sensor IoTs Using Blockchain. *IEEE Access: Practical Innovations, Open Solutions, 10*, 4568–4579. doi:10.1109/ACCESS.2022.3140401

Javed, M. U., Rehman, M., Javaid, N., Aldegheishem, A., Alrajeh, N., & Tahir, M. (2020). *Blockchain-based secure data storage for distributed vehicular networks*. Academic Press.

Jayasinghe, K., & Poravi, G. (2020). A survey of attack instances of cryptojacking targeting cloud infrastructure. In *Proceedings of the 2nd Asia pacific information technology conference* (pp. 100-107). Academic Press.

Jeong, B.-G., Youn, T.-Y., Jho, N.-S., & Shin, S. (2020). *Blockchain-based data sharing and trading model for the connected car*. Academic Press.

Jetzek, T., Avital, M., & Bjorn-Andersen, N. (2013). Generating Value from Open Government Data. *Proceedings of Thirty Fourth International Conference on Information Systems*.

Ji, Q., Bouri, E., Keung, C., Lau, M., & Roubaud, D. (2019). Dynamic connectedness and integration in cryptocurrency markets. *International Review of Financial Analysis, 63*(December), 257–272. doi:10.1016/j.irfa.2018.12.002

Jibril, A. B., Kwarteng, M. A., Botchway, R. K., Bode, J., & Chovancova, M. (2020). The impact of online identity theft on customers' willingness to engage in e-banking transaction in Ghana: A technology threat avoidance theory. *Cogent Business and Management, 7*(1), 1832825. Advance online publication. doi:10.1080/23311975.2020.1832825

John the Ripper password cracker. (n.d.). Retrieved September 22, 2022, from https://www.openwall.com/john/

Johnston, A. C., & Warkentin, M. (2010). Fear Appeals and Information Security Behaviors: An Empirical Study. *Management Information Systems Quarterly, 34*(3), 549–A4. doi:10.2307/25750691

Johnston, A. C., Warkentin, M., Dennis, A. R., & Siponen, M. (2019). Speak their Language: Designing Effective Messages to Improve Employees' Information Security Decision Making. *Decision Sciences, 50*(2), 245–284. doi:10.1111/deci.12328

Johnston, A. C., Warkentin, M., & Siponen, M. (2015). An Enhanced Fear Appeal Rhetorical Framework: Leveraging Threats to the Human Asset Through Sanctioning Rhetoric. *Management Information Systems Quarterly, 39*(1), 113–A7. doi:10.25300/MISQ/2015/39.1.06

Jones, V. A., & Capstone, A. (2020). *The Emergence of a New Threat.* Academic Press.

Joo, M. H. (2019). Cryptocurrency, a successful application of blockchain technology. *Managerial Finance*.

Jordan, S. P., & Liu, Y. K. (2018). Quantum cryptanalysis: Shor, grover, and beyond. *IEEE Security and Privacy, 16*(5), 14–21.

Joshi, S., Li, R., Bhattacharjee, S., Das, S. K., & Yamana, H. (2022, June). Privacy-Preserving Data Falsification Detection in Smart Grids using Elliptic Curve Cryptography and Homomorphic Encryption. In *2022 IEEE International Conference on Smart Computing (SMARTCOMP)* (pp. 229-234). IEEE.

Joy, M. (2011). Gold and the US dollar : Hedge or haven? *Finance Research Letters, 8*(3), 120–131. doi:10.1016/j.frl.2011.01.001

JPEGsnoop. (n.d.). https://jpegsnoop.en.uptodown.com/windows

JRana, P., & Baria,. (2015). A Survey on Fraud Detection Techniques in Ecommerce. *International Journal of Computers and Applications, 113*(14), 5–7. doi:10.5120/19892-1898

Julie, E. G., Nayahi, J. J. V., & Jhanjhi, N. Z. (2020). *Blockchain Technology: Fundamentals, Applications, and Case Studies.* CRC Press. doi:10.1201/9781003004998

Junadi & Sfenrianto. (2015). A Model of Factors Influencing Consumer's Intention To Use E-payment System in Indonesia. *Procedia Computer Science, 59*, 214–220. doi:10.1016/j.procs.2015.07.557

Jung, T., Kim, S., & Kim, K. (2020). DeepVision: Deepfakes Detection Using Human Eye Blinking Pattern. *IEEE Access: Practical Innovations, Open Solutions, 8*, 83144–83154. https://doi.org/10.1109/ACCESS.2020.2988660

Justin Rohrlich. (2020). *Romance Scammer Used Deepfakes to Impersonate a Navy Admiral and Bilk Widow Out of Nearly $300,000.* https://www.thedailybeast.com/romance-scammer-used-deepfakes-to-impersonate-a-navy-admiral-and-bilk-widow-out-of-nearly-dollar300000

Kabra, N., Bhattacharya, P., Tanwar, S., & Tyagi, S. (2020). MudraChain: Blockchain-based framework for automated cheque clearance in financial institutions. *Future Generation Computer Systems, 102*, 574–587. doi:10.1016/j.future.2019.08.035

Kadhim, I. J., Premaratne, P., Vial, P. J., & Halloran, B. (2019). Comprehensive survey of image steganography: Techniques, Evaluations, and trends in future research. *Neurocomputing, 335*, 299–326. doi:10.1016/j.neucom.2018.06.075

Kakkar, R., Gupta, R., Agrawal, S., Tanwar, S., & Sharma, R. (2022). *Blockchain-based secure and trusted data sharing scheme for autonomous vehicle underlying 5G*. Academic Press.

Kakkar, R., Gupta, R., Alshehri, M. D., Tanwar, S., Dua, A., & Kumar, N. (2022). *Block-CPS: Blockchain and Non-Cooperative Game-based Data Pricing Scheme for Car Sharing*. Academic Press.

Kakkar, R., Gupta, R., Tanwar, S., & Rodrigues, J. (2021). *Coalition game and blockchain-based optimal data pricing scheme for ride sharing beyond 5g*. Academic Press.

Kakkar, R., Jadav, N. K., Gupta, R., Agrawal, S., & Tanwar, S. (2022). *Blockchain and Stackleberg Game-based Fair and Trusted Data Pricing Scheme for Ride Sharing*. Paper presented at the 2022 IEEE International Conference on Communications Workshops (ICC Workshops). 10.1109/ICCWorkshops53468.2022.9814704

Kalaimannan, E., John, S. K., DuBose, T., & Pinto, A. (2017). Influences on ransomware's evolution and predictions for the future challenges. *Journal of Cyber Security Technology, 1*(1), 23–31. doi:10.1080/23742917.2016.1252191

Kalichkin, D. (2018). *Rethinking Network Value to Transactions (NVT) Ratio*. Medium.Com. https://medium.com/cryptolab/https-medium-com-kalichkin-rethinking-nvt-ratio-2cf810df0ab0

Kamath, A., Manikandan, K., Lamani, K., Shanbhag, P. D., & Srinivasa, B. (n.d.). *Blockchain based solution for online voting system*. Academic Press.

Kamil, M., Bist, A. S., Rahardja, U., Santoso, N. P. L., & Iqbal, M. (2021). COVID-19: Implementation e-voting blockchain concept. *International Journal of Artificial Intelligence Research, 5*(1), 25–34. doi:10.29099/ijair.v5i1.173

Kamps, J., & Kleinberg, B. (2018). To the moon: Defining and detecting cryptocurrency pump-and-dumps. *Crime Science, 7*(1), 1–18. doi:10.118640163-018-0093-5 PMID:31984202

Kapoor, A., Gupta, A., Gupta, R., Tanwar, S., Sharma, G., & Davidson, I. E. (2022). Ransomware Detection, Avoidance, and Mitigation Scheme: A Review and Future Directions. *Sustainability, 14*(1), 8. doi:10.3390u14010008

Karacı, A., Akyüz, H. İ., & Bilgici, G. (2017). Üniversite Öğrencilerinin Siber Güvenlik Davranışlarının İncelenmesi. *Kastamonu Eğitim Dergisi, 25*(6), 2079–2094. doi:10.24106/kefdergi.351517

Karafiloski, E., & Mishev, A. (2017, July). Blockchain solutions for big data challenges: A literature review. In *IEEE EUROCON 2017-17th International Conference on Smart Technologies* (pp. 763–768). IEEE. doi:10.1109/EUROCON.2017.8011213

Karake-Shalhoub, Z., & Al Qasimi, L. (2010). *Cyber law and cyber security in developing and emerging economies*. Edward Elgar Publishing. doi:10.4337/9781849803380

Karl, H. A., Susskind, L. E., & Wallace, K. H. (2007). A Dialogue, not a Diatribe: Effective Integration of Science and Policy through Joint Fact Finding. *Environment, 49*(1), 20–34. doi:10.3200/ENVT.49.1.20-34

Katarya, R., & Lal, A. (2020). A study on combating emerging threat of deepfake weaponization. *Proceedings of the 4th International Conference on IoT in Social, Mobile, Analytics and Cloud, ISMAC 2020,* 485–490. doi:10.1109/ISMAC49090.2020.9243588

Katsiampa, P. (2019). Volatility co-movement between Bitcoin and Ether. *Finance Research Letters, 30*(June), 221–227. doi:10.1016/j.frl.2018.10.005

Kaur, G., Habibi Lashkari, Z., & Habibi Lashkari, A. (2021b). Cybersecurity Threats in FinTech BT - Understanding Cybersecurity Management in FinTech: Challenges, Strategies, and Trends (G. Kaur, Z. Habibi Lashkari, & A. Habibi Lashkari, Eds.). Springer International Publishing. doi:10.1007/978-3-030-79915-1_4

Kaur, G., Habibi Lashkari, Z., & Habibi Lashkari, A. (2021c). Cybersecurity Vulnerabilities in FinTech BT - Understanding Cybersecurity Management in FinTech: Challenges, Strategies, and Trends (G. Kaur, Z. Habibi Lashkari, & A. Habibi Lashkari, Eds.). Springer International Publishing. doi:10.1007/978-3-030-79915-1_5

Kaur, G. Z. (2021). *Understanding Cybersecurity Management in FinTech. Springer International Publishing, 2021.* Springer International Publishing.

Kaur, G., Habibi Lashkari, Z., & Habibi Lashkari, A. (2021a). Cybersecurity Risk in FinTech BT - Understanding Cybersecurity Management in FinTech: Challenges, Strategies, and Trends. In G. Kaur, Z. Habibi Lashkari, & A. Habibi Lashkari (Eds.), *Understanding Cybersecurity Management in FinTech* (pp. 103–122). Springer International Publishing. doi:10.1007/978-3-030-79915-1_6

Kaur, K., Gupta, I., & Singh, A. K. (2018). Data Leakage Prevention: E-Mail Protection via Gateway. *Journal of Physics: Conference Series*, *933*, 012013. doi:10.1088/1742-6596/933/1/012013

Kaur, S., Gupta, S., Singh, S., & Arora, T. (2021). A Review on Natural Disaster Detection in Social Media and Satellite Imagery Using Machine Learning and Deep Learning. *International Journal of Image and Graphics*, 2250040. Advance online publication. doi:10.1142/S0219467822500401

Keelery, S. (2021, Oct 20). Retrieved February 24, 2022, from https://www.statista.com/statistics/1097969/india-number-of-otp-frauds-recorded-by-leading-state/

Keelery, S. (2021, Oct 25). Retrieved February 24, 2022, from https://www.statista.com/statistics/309435/india-cyber-crime-it-act/#:~:text=India%20saw%20a%20significant%20jump,during%20the%20measured%20time%20period

Keeve, A. (2019). *Cryptojacking shows no signs of slowing down in 2019, says ESET.* Available at: https://www.eset.com/us/about/newsroom/pressreleases/cryptojacking-shows-no-signs-of-slowing-down-in-2019-says-eset/

Keith, K. D. (Ed.). (2019). *Cross-cultural psychology: Contemporary themes and perspectives.* John Wiley & Sons. doi:10.1002/9781119519348

Kelton, C., Balasubramanian, A., Raghavendra, R., & Srivatsa, M. (2020). Browser-based deep behavioral detection of web crypto mining with coinspy. In *Workshop on Measurements, Attacks, and Defenses for the Web (MADWeb)* (pp. 1-12). Academic Press.

Kenourgios, D., Dimitriou, D., & Christopoulos, A. (2013). Asset Markets Contagion During the Global Financial Crisis. *Multinational Finance Journal*, *17*(1/2), 49–76. doi:10.17578/17-1/2-2

Keraf, NoCoin. (2018). https://github.com/keraf/NoCoin

Kerbs, B. (2018). *Krebs on security - who and what is coinhive.* https://krebsonsecurity.com/2018/03/who-and-what-is-coinhive/

Kerner, S. M. (2022). *34 Cybersecurity Statistics to Lose Sleep Over in 2022.* https://www.techtarget.com/whatis/34-Cybersecurity-Statistics-to-Lose-Sleep-Over-in-2020

Keshavarz, M., Gharib, M., Afghah, F., & Ashdown, J. D. (2020). UASTrustChain: A Decentralized Blockchain-Based Trust Monitoring Framework for Autonomous Unmanned Aerial Systems. *IEEE Access: Practical Innovations, Open Solutions*, *8*, 226074–226088. doi:10.1109/ACCESS.2020.3044844

Kewell, B., Adams, R., & Parry, G. (2017). Blockchain for good? *Strategic Change, 26*(5), 429-437.

Khadam, U., Iqbal, M. M., Saeed, S., Dar, S. H., Ahmad, A., & Ahmad, M. (2021). Advanced security and privacy technique for digital text in smart grid communications. *Computers & Electrical Engineering, 93*, 107205. doi:10.1016/j.compeleceng.2021.107205

Khan, A., & Malaika, M. (2021). Central Bank Risk Management, Fintech, and Cybersecurity. *IMF Working Papers, 2021*(105), A001. doi:10.5089/9781513582344.001.A001

Khan, F. (2018, August 17). *RegTech & its Challenges*. Retrieved March 29, 2022, from https://www.datadriveninvestor.com/2018/08/17/regtech-its-challenges/

Khan, M. A. H. & Anttiroiko, A. V. (2014). Democratizing digital Bangladesh: designing national web portal to facilitate government-citizen interaction. In L. G. Anthopoulos & C. G. Reddick (Eds.), Government e-strategic planning and management: Practices, patterns and roadmaps (pp. 245-261). New York, NY: Springer.

Khan, M. A. H. (2017). E-readiness of public administration in developing countries: A case study on Bangladesh public administration. Tampere University Press.

Khan, M. A. H. (2018). Administrative efficiency and effectiveness with the application of e-government: A study on Bangladesh public administration. In S. Saeed, T. Ramayah, & Z. Mahmood (Eds.), User centric e-government: Challenges and opportunities (pp. 105-116). New York, NY: Springer.

Khan, S. A., Artusi, A., & Dai, H. (2021). *Adversarially robust deepfake media detection using fused convolutional neural network predictions*. https://arxiv.org/abs/2102.05950

Khan, M. A., & Salah, K. (2018). IoT security: Review, blockchain solutions, and open challenges. *Future Generation Computer Systems, 82*, 395–411. doi:10.1016/j.future.2017.11.022

Kharraz, A., Ma, Z., Murley, P., Lever, C., Mason, J., Miller, A., . . . Bailey, M. (2019). Outguard: Detecting in-browser covert cryptocurrency mining in the wild. In *The World Wide Web Conference* (pp. 840-852). Academic Press.

Khatri, V., & Brown, C. V. (2010). Designing Data Governance. *Communications of the ACM, 53*(1), 148–152. doi:10.1145/1629175.1629210

Kim, M., Tariq, S., & Woo, S. S. (2021). FReTAL: Generalizing deepfake detection using knowledge distillation and representation learning. *IEEE Computer Society Conference on Computer Vision and Pattern Recognition Workshops*, 1001–1012. doi:10.1109/CVPRW53098.2021.00111

Kim, S. S. (2020). Purchase intention in the online open market: Do concerns for e-commerce really matter? *Sustainability, 12*(3), 773. doi:10.3390u12030773

Kim, Y., Choi, J., Park, Y., & Yeon, J. (2016). The Adoption of Mobile Payment Services for "Fintech". *International Journal of Applied Engineering Research: IJAER, 11*(2), 1058–1061.

King, M. A., & Wadhwani, S. (1990). Transmission of Volatility between Stock Markets. *Review of Financial Studies, 3*(1), 5–33. doi:10.1093/rfs/3.1.5

Kiperberg, M., Amit, G., Yeshooroon, A., & Zaidenberg, N. J. (2021a). Efficient DLP-visor: An efficient hypervisor-based DLP. *Proceedings - 21st IEEE/ACM International Symposium on Cluster, Cloud and Internet Computing, CCGrid 2021*, 344–355. 10.1109/CCGrid51090.2021.00044

Kirkpatrick, K. (2020). Deceiving the masses on social media. *Communications of the ACM, 63*(5), 33–35. doi:10.1145/3386375

Kitsios, F., Giatsidis, I., & Kamariotou, M. (2021). Digital transformation and strategy in the banking sector: Evaluating the acceptance rate of e-services. *Journal of Open Innovation*, *7*(3), 204. Advance online publication. doi:10.3390/joitmc7030204

Knill, E., & Laflamme, R. (1997). Theory of quantum error-correcting codes. *Physical Review A.*, *55*, 900.

Kocabas, O., Soyata, T., & Aktas, M.K. (2016). Emerging Security Mechanisms for Medical Cyber Physical Systems. *IEEE/ACM Trans Comput Biol Bioinf, 13*(3), 401–416.

Koetsier, J. (2021). *Fintech 2021 top 100 apps: who's winning, emerging players, where it's all going*. Singular. https://www.singular.net/blog/top-fintech-apps-2021/

Kok, S., Abdullah, A., & Jhanjhi, N. (2020). Early detection of crypto-ransomware using pre-encryption detection algorithm. *Journal of King Saud University-Computer and Information Sciences*.

Kolodenker, E., Koch, W., Stringhini, G., & Egele, M. (2017). PayBreak: Defense Against Cryptographic Ransomware. *Proceedings of the 2017 ACM on Asia Conference on Computer and Communications Security - ASIA CCS '17*, 599–611. 10.1145/3052973.3053035

Komatsu, A., Takagi, D., & Takemura, T. (2013). Human aspects of information security: An empirical study of intentional versus actual behavior. *Information Management & Computer Security*, *21*(1), 5–15. doi:10.1108/09685221311314383

Kompella, L. (2017). E-governance systems as socio-technical transitions using multi-level perspective with case studies. *Technological Forecasting and Social Change*, *123*, 80–94. doi:10.1016/j.techfore.2017.06.024

Konoth, R. K., Vineti, E., Moonsamy, V., Lindorfer, M., Kruegel, C., Bos, H., & Vigna, G. (2018). An in-depth look into drive-by mining and its defense. In *Proc. of ACM Conference on Computer and Communications Security (CCS)* (*Vol. 10*). Academic Press.

Konoth, R. K., Vineti, E., Moonsamy, V., Lindorfer, M., Kruegel, C., Bos, H., & Vigna, G. (2018). Minesweeper: An in-depth look into drive-by cryptocurrency mining and its defense. In *Proceedings of the ACM SIGSAC Conference on Computer and Communications Security* (pp. 1714-1730). Academic Press.

Konoth, R. K., Vineti, E., Moonsamy, V., Lindorfer, M., Kruegel, C., Bos, H., & Vigna, G. (2018). An in-depth look into drive-by mining and its defense. In *Proc. of ACM Conference on Computer and Communications Security (CCS)* (Vol. 10). ACM.

Koop, G., Pesaran, M. H., & Potter, S. M. (1996). Impulse response analysis in nonlinear multivariate models. *Journal of Econometrics*, *74*(1), 119–147. doi:10.1016/0304-4076(95)01753-4

Kopp & Kaffenberger. (2017). Cyber Risks, Market Failures and Finanical Stability. *International Monetary Fund, 2017*(185), 36.

Korhonen, A., & Vivitsou, M. (2019). Digital storytelling and group work. *Annual Conference on Innovation and Technology in Computer Science Education*. 10.1145/3304221.3325528

Kosseff, J. (2017). Cyber-physical systems and national security concerns. *Security and Privacy in Cyber-Physical Systems: Foundations, Principles and Applications*, 77-91.

Kostić, Z. (2018). Innovations and digital transformation as a competition catalyst. *Ekonomika (Nis)*, *64*(1), 13–23. doi:10.5937/ekonomika1801013K

Kovalchuk, O., Shynkaryk, M., & Masonkova, M. (2021). Econometric Models for Estimating the Financial Effect of Cybercrimes. *2021 11th International Conference on Advanced Computer Information Technologies, ACIT 2021 - Proceedings*, 381–384. 10.1109/ACIT52158.2021.9548490

Kowalczyk, P. (2022). *Detecting and Understanding Textual Deepfakes in Online Reviews.* doi:10.24251/HICSS.2022.184

Kozachok, A., Kopylov, S. A., Shelupanov, A. A., & Evsutin, O. O. (2019). Text marking approach for data leakage prevention. *Journal of Computer Virology and Hacking Techniques, 15*(3), 219–232. doi:10.100711416-019-00336-9

Krah, R., & Mertens, G. (2020). Democracy and financial transparency of local governments in Sub-Saharan Africa. *Meditari Accountancy Research, 28*(4), 681–699. doi:10.1108/MEDAR-08-2019-0539

Krishnaveni, S., Prabakaran, S., & Sivamohan, S. (2016). Automated vulnera-bility detection and prediction by security testing for cloud saas. *Indian Journal of Science and Technology, 9*(1).

Kristoufek, L. (2015). What are the main drivers of the bitcoin price? Evidence from wavelet coherence analysis. *PLoS One, 10*(4), 1–15. doi:10.1371/journal.pone.0123923 PMID:25874694

Kshetri, N. (2017). Blockchain's roles in strengthening cybersecurity and protecting privacy. *Telecommunications Policy, 41*(10), 1027–1038. doi:10.1016/j.telpol.2017.09.003

Kudva, S., Badsha, S., Sengupta, S., Khalil, I., & Zomaya, A. (2021). *Towards secure and practical consensus for blockchain based VANET.* Academic Press.

Kugler, L. (2022). Technology's impact on morality. *Communications of the ACM, 65*(4), 15–16. doi:10.1145/3516516

Kumar, M. S., Vimal, S., Jhanjhi, N., Dhanabalan, S. S., & Alhumyani, H. (2021). *Blockchain based peer to peer communication in autonomous drone operation.* Academic Press.

Kumar, P. R., & Ramlie, H. R. E. B. H. (2021). Anatomy of Ransomware: Attack Stages, Patterns and Handling Techniques. *Computational Intelligence in Information Systems*, 205–214. doi:10.1007/978-3-030-68133-3_20

Kumar, A., & Garhwal, S. (2021). State-of-the-Art Survey of Quantum Cryptography. *Archives of Computational Methods in Engineering, 28.*

Kumaraguru, P., Sheng, S., Acquisti, A., Cranor, L. F., & Hong, J. (2010). Teaching Johnny not to fall for phish. *ACM Transactions on Internet Technology, 10*(2), 1–31. doi:10.1145/1754393.1754396

Kumari, A., & Devi, N. C. (2022). The Impact of FinTech and Blockchain Technologies on Banking and Financial Services. *Technology Innovation Management Review, 12*(1/2). Advance online publication. doi:10.22215/timreview/1481

Kumar, M. S., Vimal, S., Jhanjhi, N. Z., Dhanabalan, S. S., & Alhumyani, H. A. (2021). Blockchain based peer to peer communication in autonomous drone operation. *Energy Reports, 7*, 7925–7939. doi:10.1016/j.egyr.2021.08.073

Kumar, S. (2020). An emerging threat Fileless malware: A survey and research challenges. *Cybersecurity, 3*(1), 1–12.

Kumar, S. M., & Kumar, M. R. (2013). Cryptoviral Extortion: A virus based approach. *International Journal of Computer Trends and Technology, 5*(5), 1150–1153.

Kurka, J. (2019). Do cryptocurrencies and traditional asset classes influence each other? *Finance Research Letters, 31*, 38–46. doi:10.1016/j.frl.2019.04.018

Lachtar, N., Elkhail, A. A., Bacha, A., & Malik, H. (2020). A cross-stack approach towards defending against cryptojacking. *IEEE Computer Architecture Letters, 19*(2), 126–129.

Lampropoulos, K., Georgakakos, G., & Ioannidis, S. (2019, September). Using blockchains to enable big data analysis of private information. In *2019 IEEE 24th International Workshop on Computer Aided Modeling and Design of Communication Links and Networks (CAMAD)* (pp. 1-6). 10.1109/CAMAD.2019.8858468

Lastdrager, E. E. (2014). Achieving a consensual definition of phishing based on a systematic review of the literature. *Crime Science*, *3*(1), 9. Advance online publication. doi:10.118640163-014-0009-y

Latif, R. M. A., Farhan, M., Rizwan, O., Hussain, M., Jabbar, S., & Khalid, S. (2021). *Retail level Blockchain transformation for product supply chain using truffle development platform.* Academic Press.

Latif, R. M. A., Iqbal, S., Rizwan, O., Shah, S. U. A., Farhan, M., & Ijaz, F. (2019). *Blockchain transforms the retail level by using a supply chain rules and regulation.* Paper presented at the 2019 2nd International Conference on Communication, Computing and Digital systems (C-CODE).

Latif, R. M. A., Farhan, M., Rizwan, O., Hussain, M., Jabbar, S., & Khalid, S. (2021). Retail level Blockchain transformation for product supply chain using truffle development platform. *Cluster Computing*, *24*(1), 1–16. doi:10.100710586-020-03165-4

Laudon, K., & Laudon, J. (1996). *Management Information Systems.* Prentice Hall Inc.

Leão, P., & da Silva, M. M. (2021). Impacts of digital transformation on firms' competitive advantages: A systematic literature review. *Strategic Change*, *30*(5), 421–441. doi:10.1002/jsc.2459

Lee, J., Jung, O., Lee, Y., Kim, O., & Park, C. (2021). A Comparison and Interpretation of Machine Learning Algorithm for the Prediction of Online Purchase Conversion. *Journal of Theoretical and Applied Electronic Commerce Research*, *16*(5), 1472–1491. doi:10.3390/jtaer16050083

Lee, S. H., & Yang, C. S. (2018). Fingernail analysis management system using microscopy sensor and blockchain technology. *International Journal of Distributed Sensor Networks*, *14*(3).

Lee, B., & Lee, J. H. (2017). Blockchain-based secure firmware update for embedded devices in an Internet of Things environment. *The Journal of Supercomputing*, *73*(3), 1152–1167. doi:10.100711227-016-1870-0

Lee, C. H., Liu, C. L., Trappey, A. J. C., Mo, J. P. T., & Desouza, K. C. (2021). Understanding digital transformation in advanced manufacturing and engineering: A bibliometric analysis, topic modeling and research trend discovery. *Advanced Engineering Informatics*, *50*, 101428. Advance online publication. doi:10.1016/j.aei.2021.101428

Lee, D. K. C., Guo, L., & Wang, Y. (2018). A New Investment Opportunity? *Journal of Alternative Investments*.

Lee, H.-K., Seong, J.-H., Kim, Y.-C., Kim, J.-B., & Gim, G.-Y. (2017). The Automation Model of Ransomware Analysis and Detection Pattern. *Journal of the Korea Institute of Information and Communication Engineering*, *21*(8), 1581–1588.

Lee, I., & Shin, Y. J. (2018). Fintech: Ecosystem, business models, investment decisions, and challenges. *Business Horizons*, *61*(1), 35–46. doi:10.1016/j.bushor.2017.09.003

Lee, M. S. (2017). Sparse subset sum problem from Gentry–Halevi's fully homomorphic encryption. *IET Information Security*, *11*(1), 34–37.

Lee, S. J., Ahn, C., Song, K. M., & Ahn, H. (2018). Trust and distrust in e-commerce. *Sustainability*, *10*(4), 1015. doi:10.3390u10041015

Leighton, T., & Micali, S. (1995). *Large provably fast and secure digital signature schemes from secure hash functions.* U.S. Patent 5,432,852.

Le, N. B. V., & Huh, J. H. (2021). Applying Sentiment Product Reviews and Visualization for BI Systems in Vietnamese E-Commerce Website: Focusing on Vietnamese Context. *Electronics (Basel)*, *10*(20), 2481. doi:10.3390/electronics10202481

Leong, K. (2018). FinTech (Financial Technology): What is it and how to use technologies to create business value in fintech way? *International Journal of Innovation, Management and Technology*, 74–78. doi:10.18178/ijimt.2018.9.2.791

Lesnykh, A. (2011). Data loss prevention: A matter of discipline. *Network Security*, *2011*(3), 18–19. doi:10.1016/S1353-4858(11)70028-9

Leuprecht, C. D., Skillicorn, D. B., & Tait, V. E. (2016). Beyond the Castle Model of cyber-risk and cyber-security. *Government Information Quarterly*, *33*(2), 250–257. doi:10.1016/j.giq.2016.01.012

Lewis, J., & Baker, S. (2013). The Economic Impact of Cybercrime and Cyber Espionage Report Center for Strategic and International Studies. *McAfee*, 1–20.

Li, C., Wang, L., Ji, S., Zhang, X., Xi, Z., Guo, S., & Wang, T. (2022). *Seeing is Living? Rethinking the Security of Facial Liveness Verification in the Deepfake Era*. https://arxiv.org/abs/2202.10673

Li, Y., & Lyu, S. (2018). *Exposing DeepFake Videos By Detecting Face Warping Artifacts*. https://arxiv.org/abs/1811.00656

Li, Y., Chang, M. C., & Lyu, S. (2019). In Ictu Oculi: Exposing AI created fake videos by detecting eye blinking. *10th IEEE International Workshop on Information Forensics and Security, WIFS 2018*. doi:10.1109/WIFS.2018.8630787

Liao, R., & Fan, Z. (2020, April). Supply chains have been upended. Here's how to make them more resilient. In *World Economic Forum* (Vol. 6). Academic Press.

Liao, C. H., Guan, X. Q., Cheng, J. H., & Yuan, S. M. (2022). Blockchain-based identity management and access control framework for open banking ecosystem. *Future Generation Computer Systems*, *135*, 450–466. doi:10.1016/j.future.2022.05.015

Liao, H.-T., Zhao, M., & Sun, S.-P. (2020). *A Literature Review of Museum and Heritage on Digitization*. Digitalization, and Digital Transformation.

Liao, K., Zhao, Z., Doupe, A., & Ahn, G. (2016). Behind closed doors: Measurement and analysis of CryptoLocker ransoms in Bitcoin. *2016 APWG Symposium on Electronic Crime Research (ECrime)*, 1–13. 10.1109/ECRIME.2016.7487938

Li, B., Liang, R., Zhou, W., Yin, H., Gao, H., & Cai, K. (2022). LBS Meets Blockchain: An Efficient Method with Security Preserving Trust in SAGIN. *IEEE Internet of Things Journal*, *9*(8), 5932–5942. doi:10.1109/JIOT.2021.3064357

Li, H., Wu, Y., Cao, D., & Wang, Y. (2021). Organizational mindfulness towards digital transformation as a prerequisite of information processing capability to achieve market agility. *Journal of Business Research*, *122*, 700–712. doi:10.1016/j.jbusres.2019.10.036

Lim, S. H., Kim, D. J., Hur, Y., & Park, K. (2019). An Empirical Study of the Impacts of Perceived Security and Knowledge on Continuous Intention to Use Mobile Fintech Payment Services. *International Journal of Human-Computer Interaction*, *35*(10), 886–898. doi:10.1080/10447318.2018.1507132

Lin, K., Han, W., Gu, Z., & Li, S. (2021). A Survey of DeepFakes Generation and Detection. *Proceedings - 2021 IEEE 6th International Conference on Data Science in Cyberspace, DSC 2021*, 474–478. doi:10.1109/DSC53577.2021.00076

Lin, H. (2019). The existential threat from cyber-enabled information warfare. *Bulletin of the Atomic Scientists*, *75*(4), 187–196. https://doi.org/10.1080/00963402.2019.1629574

Lin, W., Engle, R. F., & Ito, T. (1994). Do Bulls and Bears Move Across Borders? International Transmission of Stock Returns and Volatility. *Review of Financial Studies*, *7*(3), 507–538. doi:10.1093/rfs/7.3.507

Littell, J. (2019). *Don't Believe Your Eyes or Ears: The Weaponization of Artificial Intelligence, Machine Learning, and Deepfakes*. Retrieved from War on the Rocks: https://warontherocks.com/2019/10/dont-believe-your-eyes-or-ears-the-weaponization-of-artificial-intelligence-machine-learning-and-deepfakes/

Liu, D., Zhao, M., & Xu, H. (2021). Financial technology intelligent intrusion detection system based on financial data feature extraction and DNNs. *Proceedings of the 3rd International Conference on Intelligent Communication Technologies and Virtual Mobile Networks, ICICV 2021*, 89–93. 10.1109/ICICV50876.2021.9388459

Liu, F., Jiao, L., & Tang, X. (2019). Task-Oriented GAN for PolSAR Image Classification and Clustering. *IEEE Transactions on Neural Networks and Learning Systems*, *30*(9), 2707–2719. https://doi.org/10.1109/TNNLS.2018.2885799

Liu, J., Peng, S., Long, C., Wei, L., Liu, Y., & Tian, Z. (2020, March). Blockchain for data science. In *Proceedings of the 2020 The 2nd International Conference on Blockchain Technology* (pp. 24-28). 10.1145/3390566.3391681

Liu, J., Yan, L., & Wang, D. (2021). A Hybrid Blockchain Model for Trusted Data of Supply Chain Finance. *Wireless Personal Communications*. Advance online publication. doi:10.100711277-021-08451-x PMID:33850344

Liu, S., & Kuhn, R. (2010). Data loss prevention. *IT Professional*, *12*(2), 10–13. doi:10.1109/MITP.2010.52

Liu, W. (2018). Are Gold and Government Bond Safe-Haven Assets? An Extremal Quantile Regression Analysis. *International Review of Finance*. Advance online publication. doi:10.1111/irfi.12232

Li, X., Jiang, P., Chen, T., Luo, X., & Wen, Q. (2020). A survey on the security of blockchain systems. *Future Generation Computer Systems*, *107*, 841–853. doi:10.1016/j.future.2017.08.020

Li, Y., Yang, G., Susilo, W., Yu, Y., Au, M. H., & Liu, D. (2019). Traceable monero: Anonymous cryptocurrency with enhanced accountability. *IEEE Transactions on Dependable and Secure Computing*, *18*(2), 679–691.

Lo, H. K., Chau, H. F., & Ardehali, M. (2005). Efficient Quantum Key Distribution Scheme and a Proof of Its Unconditional Security. *Journal of Cryptology*, *18*, 133–165.

Lohachab, A. (2021). A perspective on using blockchain for ensuring security in smart card systems. In Research Anthology on Blockchain Technology in Business, Healthcare, Education, and Government (pp. 529-558). IGI Global.

Loonam, J., Eaves, S., Kumar, V., & Parry, G. (2018). Towards digital transformation: Lessons learned from traditional organizations. *Strategic Change*, *27*(2), 101–109. doi:10.1002/jsc.2185

López-Alt, A., Tromer, E., & Vaikuntanathan, V. (2012, May). On-the-fly multiparty computation on the cloud via multikey fully homomorphic encryption. In *Proceedings of the forty-fourth annual ACM symposium on Theory of computing* (pp. 1219-1234). ACM.

Los Angeles Times. (2013). *Six people fired from Cedars-Sinai over patient privacy breaches*. Retrieved September 22, 2022, from https://www.latimes.com/local/la-xpm-2013-jul-12-la-me-hospital-security-breach-20130713-story.html

Lowry, P. B., Cao, J., & Everard, A. (2011). Privacy Concerns Versus Desire for Interpersonal Awareness in Driving the Use of Self-Disclosure Technologies: The Case of Instant Messaging in Two Cultures. *Journal of Management Information Systems*, *27*(4), 163–200. doi:10.2753/MIS0742-1222270406

Luk, M. (2007). MiniSec: A Secure Sensor Network Communication Architecture. *International Conf. on Information Processing in Sensor Networks*. 10.1109/IPSN.2007.4379708

Lukonga, I. (2018). Fintech, Inclusive Growth and Cyber Risks: Focus on the MENAP and CCA Regions. *IMF Working Papers*, *18*(201), 1. doi:10.5089/9781484374900.001

Luo, X., & Liao, Q. (2007). Awareness Education as the Key to Ransomware Prevention. *Information Systems Security*, *16*(4), 195–202. doi:10.1080/10658980701576412

Lu, Y. (2018). Blockchain and the related issues: A review of current research topics. *Journal of Management Analytics*, *5*(4), 231–255. doi:10.1080/23270012.2018.1516523

Lu, Y., Huang, X., Ma, Y., & Ma, M. (2018a). A weighted context graph model for fast data leak detection. *IEEE International Conference on Communications, 2018-May*. 10.1109/ICC.2018.8422280

Lu, Z., Liu, W., Wang, Q., Qu, G., & Liu, Z. (2018). A privacy-preserving trust model based on blockchain for VANETs. *IEEE Access: Practical Innovations, Open Solutions*, *6*, 45655–45664. doi:10.1109/ACCESS.2018.2864189

Lyubashevsky, V., & Micciancio, D. (2009, August). On bounded distance decoding, unique shortest vectors, and the minimum distance problem. In *Annual International Cryptology Conference* (pp. 577-594). Springer.

Lyubashevsky, V., Peikert, C., & Regev, O. (2010). On Ideal Lattices and Learning with Errors over Rings. *EUROCRYPT*, *2010*, 1–23.

Lyubashevsky, V., Peikert, C., & Regev, O. (2013). On ideal lattices and learning with errors over rings. *Journal of the Association for Computing Machinery*, *60*(6), 1–35.

M. (2020). *The History of Ecommerce: How Did It All Begin?* Miva Blog. Available online: https://blog.miva.com/the-history-of-ecommerce-how-did-it-all-begin

Maesa, D. D. F., & Mori, P. (2020). Blockchain 3.0 applications survey. *Journal of Parallel and Distributed Computing*, *138*, 99–114. doi:10.1016/j.jpdc.2019.12.019

Magableh, B. (2022). *Predictive Analytics for Malware Detection in FinTech using Machine Learning Classification Fiona Spelman Applied Research Project* [MSc dissertation]. Dublin Business School.

Magazine. (2021). https://www.infosecurity-magazine.com/magazine-features/crypto-jacking-new-world-resource/

Mahmood, Z. (2013). *Software engineering frameworks for the cloud computing paradigm* (S. Saeed, Ed.). Springer.

Mahyuni, L. P., Adrian, R., Darma, G. S., Krisnawijaya, N. N. K., Dewi, I. G. A. A. P., & Permana, G. P. L. (2020). Mapping the potentials of blockchain in improving supply chain performance. In Cogent Business and Management (Vol. 7, Issue 1). Cogent OA. doi:10.1080/23311975.2020.1788329

Majumder, S., & Ray, S. (2022). Usage of Blockchain Technology in e-Voting System Using Private Blockchain. In *Intelligent Data Engineering and Analytics* (pp. 51–61). Springer. doi:10.1007/978-981-16-6624-7_6

Makarov, I., & Schoar, A. (2020). Trading and arbitrage in cryptocurrency markets R. *Journal of Financial Economics*, *135*(2), 293–319. doi:10.1016/j.jfineco.2019.07.001

Makers, P. (2021). *Artificial Intelligence, Machine Learning and Big Data in Finance*. OECD.

Malenkov, Y., Kapustina, I., Kudryavtseva, G., Shishkin, V., & Shishkin, V. I. (2021). Digitalization and strategic transformation of retail chain stores: Trends, impacts, prospects. *Journal of Open Innovation*, *7*(2), 108. Advance online publication. doi:10.3390/joitmc7020108

Malhotra, M., Kumar, A., Kumar, S., & Yadav, V. (2022). Untangling E-Voting Platform for Secure and Enhanced Voting Using Blockchain Technology. In Transforming Management with AI, Big-Data, and IoT (pp. 51-72). Springer. doi:10.1007/978-3-030-86749-2_3

Mani, G., Pasumarti, V., Bhargava, B., Vora, F. T., MacDonald, J., King, J., & Kobes, J. (2020). Decrypto pro: Deep learning based crypto mining malware detection using performance counters. In *IEEE International Conference on Autonomic Computing and Self-Organizing Systems (ACSOS)* (pp. 109-118). IEEE.

Man, K. a. (2020). Dns cache poisoning attack reloaded: Revolutions with side channels. *Proceedings of the 2020 ACM SIGSAC Conference on Computer and Communications Security*, 1337-1350. 10.1145/3372297.3417280

Mann, B., Lorson, P. C., Oulasvirta, L., & Haustein, E. (2019). The Quest for a Primary EPSAS Purpose – Insights from Literature and Conceptual Frameworks. *Accounting in Europe*, *16*(2), 195–218. doi:10.1080/17449480.2019.1632467

Mannebäck, E., & Padyab, A. (2021). Challenges of Managing Information Security during the Pandemic. *Challenges*, *12*(2), 30. doi:10.3390/challe12020030

Manner, H., & Reznikova, O. (2012, April). A Survey on Time-Varying Copulas: Specification, Simulations, and Application. *Econometric Reviews, 37*–41. doi:10.1080/07474938.2011.608042

Manser Payne, E. H., Dahl, A. J., & Peltier, J. (2021). Digital servitization value co-creation framework for AI services: A research agenda for digital transformation in financial service ecosystems. *Journal of Research in Interactive Marketing*, *15*(2), 200–222. doi:10.1108/JRIM-12-2020-0252

Mansfield-Devine, S. (2016). Ransomware: Taking businesses hostage. *Network Security*, *2016*(10), 8–17. doi:10.1016/S1353-4858(16)30096-4

Mariana, C. D. (2021). *Safe-haven dynamics of cryptocurrencies for the U.S. and emerging stock markets* [PhD dissertation].

Mariana, C. D., Ekaputra, I. A., & Husodo, Z. A. (2021). Are Bitcoin and Ethereum safe-havens for stocks during the COVID-19 pandemic? *Finance Research Letters*, *38*, 101798. Advance online publication. doi:10.1016/j.frl.2020.101798 PMID:33100925

Marr, B. (2018). How is AI used in education--Real world examples of today and a peek into the future? *Forbes Magazine*, 25.

Martens, M., De Wolf, R., & De Marez, L. (2019). Investigating and comparing the predictors of the intention towards taking security measures against malware, scams and cybercrime in general. *Computers in Human Behavior*, *92*, 139–150. doi:10.1016/j.chb.2018.11.002

Martin, A., Hernandez-Castro, J., & Camacho, D. (2018). An in-depth study of the jisut family of android ransomware. *IEEE Access: Practical Innovations, Open Solutions*, *6*, 57205–57218. Advance online publication. doi:10.1109/ACCESS.2018.2873583

Martin, D., Montanaro, A., Oswald, E., & Shepherd, D. (2018). Quantum Key Search with Side-Channel Advice. In. Lecture Notes in Computer Science: Vol. 10719. *Selected Areas in Cryptography – SAC 2017. SAC 2017*. Springer.

Masihuddin, M., Islam Khan, B. U., Islam Mattoo, M. M. U., & Olanrewaju, R. F. (2017). A Survey on E-Payment Systems: Elements, Adoption, Architecture, Challenges and Security Concepts. *Indian Journal of Science and Technology*, *10*(20), 1–19. doi:10.17485/ijst/2017/v10i20/113930

MasquelierH. (2018). https://phys.org/news/2018-08-hackers-smartphones-cryptocurrencies.html

Masterson, V. (2020). *6 ways the pandemic has changed businesses*. Available at: https://www.weforum.org/agenda/2020/11/covid-19-innovation-business-healthcare-restaurants/

Masum, M., Hossain Faruk, M. J., Shahriar, H., Qian, K., Lo, D., & Adnan, M. I. (2022). Ransomware Classification and Detection With Machine Learning Algorithms. *2022 IEEE 12th Annual Computing and Communication Workshop and Conference (CCWC)*, 316–322. 10.1109/CCWC54503.2022.9720869

Mathew. (2019). Cyber Security through Blockchain Technology. *International Journal of Engineering and Advanced Technology, 9*(1).

Matsiliza, N., & Zonke, N. (2017). Accountability and integrity as unique column of good governance. *Public and Municipal Finance, 6*(1), 75–82. doi:10.21511/pmf.06(1).2017.08

Matsuura, K. (2019). Token model and interpretation function for blockchain-based Fintech applications. *IEICE Transactions on Fundamentals of Electronics, Communications and Computer Science, 1*(1), 3–10. doi:10.1587/transfun.E102.A.3

Matt, C., Hess, T., & Benlian, A. (2015). Digital Transformation Strategies. In Business and Information Systems Engineering (Vol. 57, Issue 5, pp. 339–343). Gabler Verlag. doi:10.100712599-015-0401-5

Matthews, R. (2021). *Analysis of System Performance Metrics Towards the Detection of Cryptojacking in IOT Devices.* Academic Press.

Mattoo, A., & Meltzer, J. P. (2018). International data flows and privacy: The conflict and its resolution. *Journal of International Economic Law, 21*(4), 769–789. doi:10.1093/jiel/jgy044

Matuszelański, K., & Kopczewska, K. (2022). Customer Churn in Retail E-Commerce Business: Spatial and Machine Learning Approach. *Journal of Theoretical and Applied Electronic Commerce Research, 17*(1), 165–198. doi:10.3390/jtaer17010009

Maurushat, A., Bello, A., & Bragg, B. (2019). Artificial Intelligence Enabled Cyber Fraud: A Detailed Look into Payment Diversion Fraud and Ransomware. *Indian Journal of Law and Technology, 15*(2), 261–299.

Mavlutova, I., & Volkova, T. (n.d.). *Digital Transformation Of Financial Sector And Challengies For Competencies Development.* Academic Press.

Mavroeidis, V., Vishi, K., Zych, M. D., & Jøsang, A. (2018). The impact of quantum computing on present cryptography. *International Journal of Advanced Computer Science and Applications, 9*(3), 405–414.

McAfee. (2020). *Study: $100 Billion Lost Annually to Cyber Attacks.* Author.

McDonald, C. (n.d.). *Cryptojacking malware hid into emails.* https://www.mailguard.com.au/blog/brandjacking-malware-hiding

McEliece, R. J. (1978). *A public-key cryptosystem based on algebraic coding theory, Technical report.* NASA.

McGill, T., & Thompson, N. (2017). Old risks, new challenges: Exploring differences in security between home computer and mobile device use. *Behaviour & Information Technology, 36*(11), 1111–1124. doi:10.1080/0144929X.2017.1352028

McKinsey & Company. (2020). *How COVID-19 has pushed companies over the technology tipping point—and transformed business forever.* Available at: https://www.mckinsey.com/business-functions/strategy-and-corporate-finance/our-insights/how-covid-19-has-pushed-companies-over-the-technology-tipping-point-and-transformed-business-forever

McMillen, D., & Alvarez, M. (n.d.). *Mirai iot botnet: Mining for bitcoins?* https://securityintelligence.com/mirai-iot-botnet-mining-for-bitcoins/

McVicker, C. J. (2007). Comic strips as a text structure for learning to read. *The Reading Teacher, 61*(1), 85–88. doi:10.1598/RT.61.1.9

Medina, L.M.G., Garcia, J.L.R., Juanes, G.G., Barrios, A.R. & Yanes, P.G. (2014). Open data strategies and experiences to improve sharing and publication of public sector information. *The eJournal of eDemocracy and Open Government*, *6*(1), 80-86.

Mehrban, S., Khan, M. A., Nadeem, M. W., Hussain, M., Ahmed, M. M., Hakeem, O., Saqib, S., Kiah, M. L. M., Abbas, F., & Hassan, M. (2020). Towards secure FinTech: A survey, taxonomy, and open research challenges. *IEEE Access: Practical Innovations, Open Solutions*, *8*, 23391–23406. doi:10.1109/ACCESS.2020.2970430

Menard, P., Warkentin, M., & Lowry, P. B. (2018). The impact of collectivism and psychological ownership on protection motivation: A cross-cultural examination. *Computers & Security*, *75*, 147–166. doi:10.1016/j.cose.2018.01.020

Mendhurwar, S., & Mishra, R. (2021). Integration of social and IoT technologies: Architectural framework for digital transformation and cyber security challenges. *Enterprise Information Systems*, *15*(4), 565–584. doi:10.1080/1751757 5.2019.1600041

Menezes, A., Van Oorshot, J., & Vanstone, P. (1997). *Handbook of applied cryptography*. CRC Press.

Meng, S., He, X., & Tian, X. (2021). Research on Fintech development issues based on embedded cloud computing and big data analysis. *Microprocessors and Microsystems*, *83*(January), 103977. doi:10.1016/j.micpro.2021.103977

Mensi, W., Al-yahyaee, K. H., & Hoon, S. (2019). *Structural breaks and double long memory of cryptocurrency prices : A comparative analysis from Bitcoin and Ethereum*. Academic Press.

Mensi, W., Nekhili, R., Vo, X. V., Suleman, T., & Kang, S. H. (2020). Asymmetric volatility connectedness among U.S. stock sectors. *The North American Journal of Economics and Finance*, *101327*. Advance online publication. doi:10.1016/j.najef.2020.101327

Merkle, R. (1979). *Secrecy, Authentication, and Public Key Systems*. Stanford University Information Systems Laboratory Technical Report 1979-1.

Mhlungu, N. S. M., Chen, J. Y. J., & Alkema, P. (2019). The underlying factors of a successful organisational digital transformation. *South African Journal of Information Management*, *21*(1). Advance online publication. doi:10.4102ajim. v21i1.995

Micheli, M., Ponti, M., Craglia, M., & Suman, A. B. (2020). Emerging Models of Data Governance in the Age of Datafication. *Big Data & Society*, *7*(2), 1–15. doi:10.1177/2053951720948087

Michelin, R. A., Dorri, A., Steger, M., Lunardi, R. C., Kanhere, S. S., Jurdak, R., & Zorzo, A. F. (2018, November). SpeedyChain: A framework for decoupling data from the blockchain for smart cities. In *Proceedings of the 15th EAI international conference on mobile and ubiquitous systems: Computing, networking and services* (pp. 145-154). 10.1145/3286978.3287019

Michener, G., Coelho, J., & Moreira, D. (2021). Are governments complying with transparency? Findings from 15 years of evaluation. *Government Information Quarterly*, *38*(2), 101565. doi:10.1016/j.giq.2021.101565

Micro Research. (2020). *The New Norm Trend Micro Security Predictions*. Author.

Mićunović, N., & Srića, V. (n.d.). *Digital Transformation in Montenegro-opportunities, challenges, and recommendations for improvement? Building elite (excellence in leadership, innovattion and technology) network*. doi:10.9790/0661-2301021018

Mighri, Z., & Alsaggaf, M. I. (2019). *Volatility Spillovers among the Cryptocurrency Time Series*. Academic Press.

Miglani, A., Kumar, N., Chamola, V., & Zeadally, S. (2020). Blockchain for Internet of Energy management: Review, solutions, and challenges. *Computer Communications*, *151*, 395–418. doi:10.1016/j.comcom.2020.01.014

Mihai, I.-C. D. (2014). Cyber kill chain analysis. *Int'l J. Info. Sec. & Cybercrime*, *3*, 37.

Miklosik, A., & Evans, N. (2020). Impact of Big Data and Machine Learning on Digital Transformation in Marketing: A Literature Review. In *IEEE Access* (Vol. 8, p. 101284–101292). Institute of Electrical and Electronics Engineers Inc. doi:10.1109/ACCESS.2020.2998754

Milutinovic, M. (2018). Cryptocurrency. *Ekonomika (Nis)*, *64*(March), 95–104. doi:10.5937/ekonomika1801105M

Miner.Xmrig. (n.d.). *Symantec*. https://www.symantec.com/security-center/writeup/2018-061105-4627-99

Ministry of Education Malaysia. (2015). Malaysia education blueprint 2015–2025 (higher education). *Ministry of Education Malaysia*, *2025*, 40.

Mir, F. A. (2011). Emerging Legal Issues Of E-Commerce In India. *International Journal of Electronic Commerce Studies*. Available at: http://academic-pub.org/ojs/index.php/ijecs/article/view/976

MoC, Ministry of Commerce, Pakistan. (2019). *E-Commerce Policy of Pakistan*. https://www.commerce.gov.pk/content/uploads/2019/11/e-Commerce_Policy_of_Pakistan_Web.pdf

Mohurle, S., & Patil, M. (2017). A brief study of Wannacry Threat: Ransomware Attack 2017. *International Journal of Advanced Research in Computer Science*, *8*(5), 1938–1940.

Moinet, A., Darties, B., & Baril, J.-L. (2017). *Blockchain based trust & authentication for decentralized sensor networks*. 1–6. https://arxiv.org/abs/1706.01730

Montgomery, P. L. (1994). A survey of modern integer factorization algorithms. *CWI Quarterly*, *7*(4), 337-366.

Mookherji, S., Vanga, O., & Prasath, R. (2022). Blockchain-based e-voting protocols. In *Blockchain Technology for Emerging Applications* (pp. 239–266). Elsevier. doi:10.1016/B978-0-323-90193-2.00006-5

Moore. (2016). *The Critical role of positive incentives for reducing insider threats*. Carnegie Mellon University.

Moor, J. H. (1985). What is computer ethics? *Metaphilosophy*, *16*(4), 266–275. doi:10.1111/j.1467-9973.1985.tb00173.x

Moorthy, D. (2018). A Study on Rising Effects of Cryptocurrency in the Regulations of Malaysian Legal System. *International Journal of Business, Economics and Law*, *15*(4), 35–41.

Morgan, S. (2019). Global cybersecurity spending predicted to exceed $1 trillion from 2017-2021. *Cybercrime Magazine*, *10*.

Mosley, M., Brackett, M., Earley, P. S., & Henderson, D. (2009). *The DAMA Guide to the Data Management Body of Knowledge (DAMA-DMBOK Guide)*. Technics Publications, LLC.

Mosteanu, N. R., & Faccia, A. (2021). Fintech frontiers in quantum computing, fractals, and blockchain distributed ledger: Paradigm shifts and open innovation. *Journal of Open Innovation*, *7*(1), 1–19. doi:10.3390/joitmc7010019

MS-ISAC. (2019). *EternalBlue*. Technical Report #SP2019-0101. MS-ISAC.

Mukherjee, P. P., Boshra, A. A., Ashraf, M. M., & Biswas, M. (2020). *A hyper-ledger fabric framework as a service for improved quality e-voting system*. Paper presented at the 2020 IEEE Region 10 Symposium (TENSYMP). 10.1109/TENSYMP50017.2020.9230820

Muna, M. (2020). *Technological Arming: Is Deepfake the Next Digital Weapon?* https://www.researchgate.net/publication/341781104

Musch, M., Wressnegger, C., Johns, M., & Rieck, K. (2019). Thieves in the browser: Web-based cryptojacking in the wild. In *Proceedings of the 14th International Conference on Availability, Reliability and Security* (pp. 1-10). Academic Press.

Mustaca, S. (2014). Are your IT professionals prepared for the challenges to come? *Computer Fraud & Security, 2014*(3), 18–20. doi:10.1016/S1361-3723(14)70472-5

Musuva, P. M. W., Getao, K. W., & Chepken, C. K. (2019). A new approach to modelling the effects of cognitive processing and threat detection on phishing susceptibility. *Computers in Human Behavior, 94*, 154–175. doi:10.1016/j.chb.2018.12.036

Muzammal, S. M., Murugesan, R. K., & Jhanjhi, N. Z. (2021, March). Introducing mobility metrics in trust-based security of routing protocol for internet of things. In *2021 National Computing Colleges Conference (NCCC)* (pp. 1-5). IEEE. https://ieeexplore.ieee.org/abstract/document/9428799

Muzammal, S. M., Murugesan, R. K., & Jhanjhi, N. Z. (2020). A comprehensive review on secure routing in internet of things: Mitigation methods and trust-based approaches. *IEEE Internet of Things Journal, 8*(6), 4186–4210. doi:10.1109/JIOT.2020.3031162

Nabi, F., Tao, X., & Yong, J. (2021). Security aspects in modern service component-oriented application logic for social e-commerce systems. *Social Network Analysis and Mining, 11*(1), 1–19. doi:10.100713278-020-00717-9

Nachreiner, C. (2003). *Anatomy of an ARP poisoning attack.* Academic Press.

Naeem, H., Ullah, F., Naeem, M. R., Khalid, S., Vasan, D., Jabbar, S., & Saeed, S. (2020). Malware detection in industrial internet of things based on hybrid image visualization and deep learning model. *Ad Hoc Networks, 105*, 102154. doi:10.1016/j.adhoc.2020.102154

Najaf, K. M. (2021). *Fintech firms and banks sustainability: Why cybersecurity risk matters?* Academic Press.

Najaf, K., Mostafiz, M. I., & Najaf, R. (2021). Fintech firms and banks sustainability: Why cybersecurity risk matters? *International Journal of Financial Engineering, 08*(02), 2150019. doi:10.1142/S2424786321500195

Najaf, K., Schinckus, C., Mostafiz, M. I., & Najaf, R. (2020). Conceptualising cybersecurity risk of fintech firms and banks sustainability. *International Conference on Business and Technology*, 1–16.

Nakamoto, S. (2008). Bitcoin: A peer-to-peer electronic cash system. *Decentralized Business Review, 21260.*

Nakamoto, S. (2009). *Bitcoin: A peer-to-peer electronic cash system Bitcoin: A Peer-to-Peer Electronic Cash System.* https://bitcoin. org/en/bitcoin-paper

Nakamoto, S. (2009). *Bitcoin: A Peer-to-Peer Electronic Cash System.* https://metzdowd.com

NakerN. (2021, Sep 28). Retrieved from https://www.ey.com/en_in/consulting/the-winds-of-change-trends-shaping-india-s-fintech-sector

Namasudra, S., & Sharma, P. (2022). *Achieving a Decentralized and Secure Cab Sharing System Using Blockchain Technology.* Academic Press.

NarnoliaN. (n.d.). Retrieved from https://www.legalserviceindia.com/legal/article-4998-cyber-crime-in-india-an-overview.html

Naseem, F., Aris, A., Babun, L., Tekiner, E., & Uluagac, S. (2021). MINOS: A lightweight real-time cryptojacking detection system. In *28th Annual Network and Distributed System Security Symposium, NDSS.* Academic Press.

Naseem, F., Aris, A., Babun, L., Tekiner, E., & Uluagac, S. (2021). MINOS: A lightweight real-time cryptojacking detection system. *28th Annual Network and Distributed System Security Symposium, NDSS.*

Naser, H. (2020). The Impact Of Cloud Computing In Fintech. *VEXXHOST.* https://vexxhost.com/blog/cloud-computing-in-fintech/

National Audit. (2017). *Investigation-WannaCry-cyber-attack-and-the-NHS.pdf.* https://www.nao.org.uk/wp-content/uploads/2017/10/Investigation-WannaCry-cyber-attack-and-the-NHS.pdf

NavarettiG. B.CalzolariG.FrancoA.NumbersP.Mansilla-FernándezJ. M.DermineJ.VivesX.BofondiM.GobbiG.FerrariniG.XiangX.LinaZ.YunW.ChengxuanH. (2018). European economy banks, regulation, and the real sector fintech and banking. Friends or foes? https://www.econstor.eu/handle/10419/200276%0Ahttps://papers.ssrn.com/sol3/papers.cfm?abstract_id=3099337

Nayak, P. D. D. K., & Singh, P. (2021). Does Data Security and Trust Affect the Users of Fintech? *International Journal of Management, 12*(1), 191–206. doi:10.34218/IJM.12.1.2021.016

Naz, F., Karim, S., Houcine, A., & Naeem, M. A. (2022). Fintech Growth during COVID-19 in MENA Region: Current Challenges and Future prospects. *Electronic Commerce Research.* Advance online publication. doi:10.100710660-022-09583-3

Nechvatal, J. (2001). Report on the development of the advanced encryption standard (AES). *Journal of Research of the National Institute of Standards and Technology, 106,* 511–577.

Neethirajan, S. (2021). *Beyond Deepfake Technology Fear: On its Positive Uses for Livestock Farming* doi:10.20944/preprints202107.0326.v1

Negash, S. (2022). *Improving eGovernment Services with Blockchain: Restoring Trust in e-voting Systems.* Paper presented at the International Conference on Electronic Governance and Open Society: Challenges in Eurasia. 10.1007/978-3-031-04238-6_20

Nelson, N., & Madnick, S. (2017). *Trade-offs Between Digital Innovation and Cyber-security* [Working Paper]. MIT Sloan School of Management. https://cams.mit.edu/wp-content/uploads/2017-04.pdf

Networks, P. (2020, August 6). *2020 Unit 42 IoT Threat Report.* https://unit42.paloaltonetworks.com/iot-threat-report-2020/

News, A. B. C. (2019, October 1). *Victorian hospitals lock down IT systems after ransomware attack.* ABC News. https://www.abc.net.au/news/2019-10-01/victorian-health-services-targeted-by-ransomware-attack/11562988

Nguyen, D. C., Pathirana, P. N., Ding, M., & Seneviratne, A. (2020). Integration of blockchain and cloud of things: Architecture, applications and challenges. *IEEE Communications Surveys and Tutorials, 22*(4), 2521–2549. doi:10.1109/COMST.2020.3020092

Niederreiter, H. (1986). Knapsack-type cryptosystems and algebraic coding theory. *Problems of Control and Information Theory, 15*(2), 159–166.

Ni, J., Yu, Y., Mu, Y., & Xia, Q. (2014). On the security of an efficient dynamic auditing protocol in cloud storage. *IEEE Transactions on Parallel and Distributed Systems, 25*(10), 2760–2761. doi:10.1109/TPDS.2013.199

Nikkel, B. (2020). Fintech forensics: Criminal investigation and digital evidence in financial technologies. *Forensic Science International: Digital Investigation, 33,* 200908.

Nikkel, B. (2020). Fintech forensics: Criminal investigation and digital evidence in financial technologies. *Forensic Science International: Digital Investigation, 33,* 200908. doi:10.1016/j.fsidi.2020.200908

Ning, R., Wang, C., Xin, C., Li, J., Zhu, L., & Wu, H. (2019). Capjack: Capture in-browser crypto-jacking by deep capsule network through behavioral analysis. In *IEEE INFOCOM-IEEE Conference on Computer Communications* (pp. 1873-1881). IEEE.

Nisbett, R. E., & Miyamoto, Y. (2005). The influence of culture: Holistic versus analytic perception. *Trends in Cognitive Sciences, 9*(10), 467–473. doi:10.1016/j.tics.2005.08.004 PMID:16129648

Norrestad, F. (2022, January 11). Retrieved March 23, 2022, from https://www.statista.com/statistics/1055356/fintech-adoption-rates-globally-selected-countries-by-category/

Norton. (n.d.). *Official site — norton™ - antivirus, anti-malware software.* https://us.norton.com/

Nukala, V. S. K. A. (2020). Website Cryptojacking Detection Using Machine Learning: IEEE CNS 20 Poster. In *IEEE Conference on Communications and Network Security (CNS)* (pp. 1-2). IEEE.

O'Dea, S. (2021, December 9). Retrieved March 23, 2022, from Statista.com: https://www.statista.com/statistics/262950/global-mobile-subscriptions-since-1993/

O'Halloran, A. (2021). *The Technical, Legal, and Ethical Landscape of Deepfake Pornography.* https://cs.brown.edu/research/pubs/theses/ugrad/2021/ohalloran.amelia.pdf

O'Kane, P., Sezer, S., & Carlin, D. (2018). Evolution of Ransomware. *IET Networks, 7*(5), 321–327. doi:10.1049/iet-net.2017.0207

O'Leary, K., O'Reilly, P., Feller, J., Gleasure, R., Li, S., & Cristoforo, J. (2017, August). Exploring the application of blockchain technology to combat the effects of social loafing in cross functional group projects. In *Proceedings of the 13th International Symposium on Open Collaboration* (pp. 1-8). 10.1145/3125433.3125464

Ober, M., Katzenbeisser, S., & Hamacher, K. (2013). Structure and anonymity of the bitcoin transaction graph. *Future Internet, 5*(2), 237–250. doi:10.3390/fi5020237

Ocampos. (2020). *Contribution of Blockchain to Cybersecurity.* Blockchain Land.

OECD. (2016). Open Government in Indonesia. OECD Public Governance Review. OECD Publishing.

Office for Civil Rights, T., Department of Health, U., & Services, H. (2020). *COVID-19 & HIPAA Bulletin Limited Waiver of HIPAA Sanctions and Penalties During a Nationwide Public Health Emergency.* Author.

Ogbenika, G. (2000). The Seminarian and the Digital Age: Implications for Authentic Formation. *Acjol.Org*, 154–170. https://acjol.org/index.php/ekpoma/article/view/1750

Ogundoyin, S. O. (2022). A privacy-preserving multisubset data aggregation scheme with fault resilience for intelligent transportation system. *Information Security Journal: A Global Perspective*, 1-24.

Okochi, P. I., Okolie, S. A., & Odii, J. N. (2021). An improved data leakage detection system in a cloud computing environment. *World Journal of Advanced Research and Reviews, 11*(2), 321–328. doi:10.30574/wjarr.2021.11.2.0385

Okolica, J. S. (2007). Using Author Topic to detect insider threats from email traffic. *Digital Investigation, 4*, 158–164.

Oladapo, I. A., Hamoudah, M. M., Alam, M. M., Olaopa, O. R., & Muda, R. (2021). Customers' perceptions of FinTech adaptability in the Islamic banking sector: Comparative study on Malaysia and Saudi Arabia. *Journal of Modelling in Management*. Advance online publication. doi:10.1108/JM2-10-2020-0256

Olagunju, T., Oyebode, O., & Orji, R. (2020). Exploring Key Issues Affecting African Mobile eCommerce Applications Using Sentiment and Thematic Analysis. *IEEE Access: Practical Innovations, Open Solutions*, *8*, 114475–114486. doi:10.1109/ACCESS.2020.3000093

Olalere, Ndunagu, & Abdulhamid. (2019). Performance Analysis of Security Information and Event Management Solutions for Detection of Web-Based Attacks. *Proceedings of the Cyber Secure Nigeria 2019 Conference*, 39–47.

Olaniyi, O., Dogo, E., Nuhu, B., Treiblmaier, H., Abdulsalam, Y., & Folawiyo, Z. (2022). A Secure Electronic Voting System Using Multifactor Authentication and Blockchain Technologies. In *Blockchain Applications in the Smart Era* (pp. 41–63). Springer. doi:10.1007/978-3-030-89546-4_3

Olenick, D. (2019). *Miner into third party zoom*. https://www.trendmicro.com/en us/research/20/d/zoomed-in-a-look-into-a-coinminer-bundledwith-zoom-installer.html

Omane-adjepong, M., & Alagidede, I. P. (2019). Multiresolution analysis and spillovers of major cryptocurrency markets. *Research in International Business and Finance*, *49*(March), 191–206. doi:10.1016/j.ribaf.2019.03.003

Omane-Adjepong, M., & Alagidede, I. P. (2020). Exploration of safe havens for Africa's stock markets: A test case under COVID-19 crisis. *Finance Research Letters*, *101877*(December). doi:10.1016/j.frl.2020.101877

Omarini, A. E. (2018). *Fintech and the Future of the Payment Landscape : The Mobile Wallet Ecosystem - A Challenge for Retail Banks?* doi:10.5430/ijfr.v9n4p97

Ometov, A., Bezzateev, S., Mäkitalo, N., Andreev, S., Mikkonen, T., & Koucheryavy, Y. (2018). Multi-factor authentication: A survey. *Cryptography*, *2*(1), 1–31. doi:10.3390/cryptography2010001

O'Neil, C. (2016). *Weapons of math destruction: How big data increases inequality and threatens democracy*. Broadway Books.

Ong, Y. J., Qiao, M., Routray, R., & Raphael, R. (2017). Context-Aware Data Loss Prevention for Cloud Storage Services. *IEEE International Conference on Cloud Computing, CLOUD, 2017-June*, 399–406. 10.1109/CLOUD.2017.58

Ophoff, J., & Lakay, M. (2019). Mitigating the Ransomware Threat: A Protection Motivation Theory Approach. In H. Venter, M. Loock, M. Coetzee, M. Eloff, & J. Eloff (Eds.), *Information Security* (Vol. 973, pp. 163–175). Springer International Publishing. doi:10.1007/978-3-030-11407-7_12

Osmundsen, K., Iden, J., & Bygstad, B. (2018). *Association for Information Systems AIS Electronic Library (AISeL) Digital Transformation: Drivers, Success Factors, and Implications Recommended Citation*. https://aisel.aisnet.org/mcis2018/37

Otto, B. (2011). Organizing Data Governance: Findings from the Telecommunications Industry and Consequences for Large Service Providers. *Communications of the AIS*, *29*, 45–66. doi:10.17705/1CAIS.02903

Owen, R., Macnaghten, P., & Stilgoe, J. (2020). Responsible research and innovation: From science in society to science for society, with society. In *Emerging technologies: ethics, law and governance* (pp. 117–126). Routledge. doi:10.4324/9781003074960-11

Özkan, E., Azizi, N., & Haass, O. (2021). Leveraging smart contract in project procurement through dlt to gain sustainable competitive advantages. *Sustainability*, *13*(23), 13380. doi:10.3390u132313380

Ozyılmaz, K. R., & Yurdakul, A. (2017, October). Integrating low-power iot devices to a blockchain-based infrastructure: work-in-progress. In *Proceedings of the thirteenth acm international conference on embedded software* (p. 13). ACM.

Pabian, A., Pabian, B., & Reformat, B. (2020). E-Customer Security as a Social Value in the Sphere of Sustainability. *Sustainability*, *12*(24), 10590. doi:10.3390u122410590

Padayachee, K. (2016). An assessment of opportunity-reducing techniques in information security: An insider threat perspective. *Decision Support Systems*, *92*, 47–56. doi:10.1016/j.dss.2016.09.012

Paillier, P. (1999, May). Public-key cryptosystems based on composite degree residuosity classes. In *International conference on the theory and applications of cryptographic techniques* (pp. 223-238). Springer. 10.1007/3-540-48910-X_16

Pal, P., & Ruj, S. (2019). *BlockV: A blockchain enabled peer-peer ride sharing service*. Paper presented at the 2019 IEEE International Conference on Blockchain (Blockchain). 10.1109/Blockchain.2019.00070

Pal, A., De', R., Herath, T., & Rao, H. R. (2019). A review of contextual factors affecting mobile payment adoption and use. *Journal of Banking and Financial Technology*, *3*(1), 43–57. doi:10.100742786-018-00005-3

Palisse, A., Le Bouder, H., Lanet, J.-L., Le Guernic, C., & Legay, A. (2017). Ransomware and the Legacy Crypto API. In F. Cuppens, N. Cuppens, J.-L. Lanet, & A. Legay (Eds.), *Risks and Security of Internet and Systems* (pp. 11–28). Springer International Publishing. doi:10.1007/978-3-319-54876-0_2

Pan, X., Pan, X., Song, M., Ai, B., & Ming, Y. (2020). *Blockchain technology and enterprise operational capabilities: An empirical test*. Academic Press.

Pardoux, É. (2022). Ethical Design for AI in Medicine. In *Proceedings of the 2022 AAAI/ACM Conference on AI, Ethics, and Society* (pp. 907-907). 10.1145/3514094.3539564

Parikh, K. D. (2021, Dec 8). Retrieved February 24, 2022, from https://timesofindia.indiatimes.com/city/ahmedabad/cyber-fraud-cases-in-state-grew-by-67-in-2020-21/articleshow/88152757.cms

Parizi, R. M., Dehghantanha, A., Azmoodeh, A., & Choo, K. K. R. (2020). Blockchain in cybersecurity realm: An overview. *Blockchain Cybersecurity, Trust and Privacy*, 1-5.

Partasevitch, T. (2021, July 21). Retrieved February 24, 2022, from https://www.financemagnates.com/fintech/major-challenges-the-fintech-industry-faces-today-and-how-to-overcome-them/

Pastor, A., Mozo, A., Vakaruk, S., Canavese, D., López, D. R., Regano, L., ... Lioy, A. (2020). Detection of encrypted crypto mining malware connections with machine and deep learning. *IEEE Access: Practical Innovations, Open Solutions*, *8*, 158036–158055.

Patarin, J. (1996). Hidden Fields Equations (HFE) and Isomorphism's of Polynomials (IP): Two New Families of Asymmetric Algorithms. In Advances in Cryptology - EUROCRYPT '96. Springer.

Pathak, P. B., & Nanded, Y. M. (2016). A Dangerous Trend of Cybercrime: Ransomware Growing Challenge. *International Journal of Advanced Research in Computer Engineering and Technology*, *5*(2), 371–373.

Patil, H. V., Rathi, K. G., & Tribhuwan, M. V. (2018). A study on decentralized e-voting system using blockchain technology. *Int. Res. J. Eng. Technol*, *5*(11), 48–53.

Pawłowski, M. (2021a). Machine Learning Based Product Classification for eCommerce. *Journal of Computer Information Systems*, 1–10. doi:10.1080/08874417.2021.1910880

Peixoto, T. (2008). e-Participatory Budgeting: e-Democracy from Theory to Success? SSRN *Electronic Journal*. doi:10.2139/ssrn.1273554

Pelletier, C., & Martin Cloutier, L. (n.d.). *Challenges of Digital Transformation in SMEs: Exploration of IT-Related Perceptions in a Service Ecosystem*. https://hdl.handle.net/10125/59934

Peng, X. (2019). Do precious metals act as hedges or safe havens for China's financial markets? *Finance Research Letters*, *101353*. Advance online publication. doi:10.1016/j.frl.2019.101353

Pereira, C. S., Durão, N., Moreira, F., & Veloso, B. (2022). The Importance of Digital Transformation in International Business. *Sustainability (Switzerland)*, *14*(2), 834. Advance online publication. doi:10.3390u14020834

Perera, S., Nanayakkara, S., Rodrigo, M., Senaratne, S., & Weinand, R. (2020). *Blockchain technology: Is it hype or real in the construction industry?* Academic Press.

Pernot-Leplay, E. (2020). China's Approach on Data Privacy Law: A Third Way Between the U.S. and the E.U.? *Penn State Journal of Law & International Affairs*, *8*(1), 49.

Perov, I., Gao, D., Chervoniy, N., Liu, K., Marangonda, S., Umé, C., Dpfks, M., Facenheim, C. S., RP, L., Jiang, J., Zhang, S., Wu, P., Zhou, B., & Zhang, W. (2020). *DeepFaceLab: Integrated, flexible and extensible face-swapping framework*. https://arxiv.org/abs/2005.05535

Pesaran, H. H., & Shin, Y. (1998). Generalized impulse response analysis in linear multivariate models. *Economics Letters*, *58*(1), 17–29. doi:10.1016/S0165-1765(97)00214-0

PF, E., P, A., & MJ, H. (2018). Health Insurance Portability and Accountability Act. Encyclopedia of Information Assurance, 1299–1309. doi:10.1081/E-EIA-120046838

Phillip, A., Chan, J., & Peiris, S. (2018). A new look at Cryptocurrencies. *Economics Letters*, *163*, 6–9. doi:10.1016/j.econlet.2017.11.020

Piper, J., & Metcalfe, A. (2020). *Economic crime in a digital age*. www.accaglobal.com

Pisano, G. (2006). Profiting from innovation and the intellectual property revolution. *Research Policy*, *35*(8), 1122–1130. doi:10.1016/j.respol.2006.09.008

Plotkin, D. (2020). *Data Stewardship: An Actionable Guide to Effective Data Management and Data Governance*. Academic Press.

Poerjoto, J. I., Gui, A., & Deniswara, K. (2021, February 16). Identifying Factors Affecting the Continuance Usage Intention of Digital Payment Services among Millennials in Jakarta. *2021 25th International Conference on Information Technology, IT 2021*. 10.1109/IT51528.2021.9390125

Pompella, M., & Costantino, L. (2021). Fintech and Blockchain Based Innovation: Technology Driven Business Models and Disruption BT - The Palgrave Handbook of FinTech and Blockchain. In M. Pompella & R. Matousek (Eds.), *The Palgrave Handbook of FinTech and Blockchain* (pp. 403–430). Springer International Publishing. doi:10.1007/978-3-030-66433-6_18

Ponemon Institute. (2022). *Cost of insider threats global report*. Retrieved September 21, 2022, from https://www.bloomberg.com/press-releases/2022-01-25/global-cybersecurity-study-insider-threats-cost-organizations-15-4-million-annually-up-34-percent-from-2020

Porumbescu, G., Meijer, A., & Grimmelikhuijsen, S. (2022). *Government Transparency: State of the Art and New Perspectives (Elements in Public Policy)*. Cambridge University Press. doi:10.1017/9781108678568

Posey, C., Roberts, T. L., Lowry, P. B., & Hightower, R. T. (2014). Bridging the divide: A qualitative comparison of information security thought patterns between information security professionals and ordinary organizational insiders. *Information & Management*, *51*(5), 551–567. doi:10.1016/j.im.2014.03.009

Prakash, K. P., Nafis, T., & Biswas, S. S. (2017). Preventive Measures and Incident Response for Locky Ransomware. *International Journal of Advanced Research in Computer Science*, *8*(5), 392–395.

Pranitha, G., Rukmini, T., Shankar, T., Sah, B., Kumar, N., & Padhy, S. (2022). *Utilization of Blockchain in E-Voting System.* Paper presented at the 2022 2nd International Conference on Intelligent Technologies (CONIT). 10.1109/CONIT55038.2022.9847995

PricewaterhouseCooper (PwC). (2019). *Study on the Scale and Impact of Industrial Espionage and Theft of Trade Secrets through Cyber.* Retrieved September 22, 2022, from https://www.pwc.com/it/it/publications/docs/study-on-the-scale-and-Impact.pdf

Priyadarshini, I., Chatterjee, J. M., Sujatha, R., Jhanjhi, N., Karime, A., & Masud, M. (2022). Exploring Internet Meme Activity during COVID-19 Lockdown Using Artificial Intelligence Techniques. *Applied Artificial Intelligence*, *36*(1), 2014218. doi:10.1080/08839514.2021.2014218

Pu, J., Mangaokar, N., Kelly, L., Bhattacharya, P., Sundaram, K., Javed, M., Wang, B., & Viswanath, B. (2021). Deepfake videos in the wild: Analysis and detection. *The Web Conference 2021 - Proceedings of the World Wide Web Conference, WWW 2021, 2*, 981–992. doi:10.1145/3442381.3449978

Purwanto, A., Zuiderwijk, A., & Janssen, M. (2020). Citizen engagement with open government data: Lessons learned from Indonesia's presidential election. *Transforming Government: People, Process and Policy*, *14*(1), 1–30. doi:10.1108/TG-06-2019-0051

Puschmann, T. (2017). Fintech. *Business & Information Systems Engineering*, *59*(1), 69–76. doi:10.100712599-017-0464-6

Puschmann, T., Hoffmann, C. H., & Khmarskyi, V. (2020). How green fintech can alleviate the impact of climate change—The case of Switzerland. *Sustainability (Switzerland)*, *12*(24), 1–28. doi:10.3390u122410691

Pustokhina, I., Pustokhin, D. A., Mohanty, S. N., García, P. A. G., & García-Díaz, V. (2021, November 13). Artificial intelligence assisted Internet of Things based financial crisis prediction in FinTech environment. *Annals of Operations Research*. Advance online publication. doi:10.100710479-021-04311-w

Qatawneh, A. M., Aldhmour, F. M., & Aldmour, L. T. (2016). The Impact of Applying the Electronic Cheque Clearing System on Employees' Satisfaction in Accounting Departments' of Jordanian Islamic Banks. *International Business Research*, *9*(2), 137. doi:10.5539/ibr.v9n2p137

Qayyum, A., Qadir, J., Janjua, M. U., & Sher, F. (2019). Using Blockchain to Rein in the New Post-Truth World and Check the Spread of Fake News. *IT Professional*, *21*(4), 16–24. https://doi.org/10.1109/MITP.2019.2910503

Qiao, Z. a. (2014). Survey of attribute based encryption. *15th IEEE/ACIS International Conference on Software Engineering, Artificial Intelligence, Networking and Parallel/Distributed Computing (SNPD)*, 1-6.

Qin, C., Guo, B., Shen, Y., Li, T., Zhang, Y., & Zhang, Z. (2020). *A secure and effective construction scheme for blockchain networks.* Academic Press.

Quamara, S., & Singh, A. K. (2022). A systematic survey on security concerns in cryptocurrencies: State-of-the-art and perspectives. *Computers & Security*, *113*, 102548.

Radford, A., Metz, L., & Chintala, S. (2016). Unsupervised representation learning with deep convolutional generative adversarial networks. *4th International Conference on Learning Representations, ICLR 2016 - Conference Track Proceedings*, 1–16.

Rafique, R., Nawaz, M., Kibriya, H., & Masood, M. (2021). DeepFake Detection Using Error Level Analysis and Deep Learning. *Proceedings - 2021 IEEE 4th International Conference on Computing and Information Sciences, ICCIS 2021*, 0–3. doi:10.1109/ICCIS54243.2021.9676375

Rahmani, M. K. I., Shuaib, M., Alam, S., Siddiqui, S. T., Ahmad, S., Bhatia, S., & Mashat, A. (2022). Blockchain-Based Trust Management Framework for Cloud Computing-Based Internet of Medical Things (IoMT): A Systematic Review. *Computational Intelligence and Neuroscience, 2022*, 1–14. doi:10.1155/2022/9766844 PMID:35634070

Raisaro, J. L., Klann, J. G., Wagholikar, K. B., Estiri, H., Hubaux, J. P., & Murphy, S. N. (2018). Feasibility of homomorphic encryption for sharing I2B2 aggregate-level data in the cloud. *AMIA Joint Summits on Translational Science Proceedings AMIA Summit on Translational Science, 2018*, 176.

Ramadhani, K. N., & Munir, R. (2020). A Comparative Study of Deepfake Video Detection Method. *2020 3rd International Conference on Information and Communications Technology, ICOIACT 2020*, 394–399. doi:10.1109/ICOIACT50329.2020.9331963

Ramanathan, S., Mirkovic, J., & Yu, M. (2020). Blag: Improving the accuracy of blacklists. *Network and Distributed Systems Security (NDSS) Symposium.*

Ramos Chávez, H. A. (2015). Information and citizenship: A governance perspective. *Investigación Bibliotecológica: Archivonomía. Bibliotecología e Información, 29*(67), 113–140. doi:10.1016/j.ibbai.2016.04.006

Rangwala, M. e., Zhang, P., Zou, X., & Li, F. (2014). A taxonomy of privilege escalation attacks in Android applications. *International Journal of Security and Networks, 9*(1), 40–55. doi:10.1504/IJSN.2014.059327

Rasheed, I., Asif, M., Khan, W. U., Ihsan, A., Ullah, K., & Ali, M. S. (2022). Blockchain-Based Trust Verification and Streaming Service Awareness for Big Data-Driven 5G and beyond Vehicle-to-Everything (V2X) Communication. *Wireless Communications and Mobile Computing, 2022*, 1–13. Advance online publication. doi:10.1155/2022/7357820

Rathgeb, C., Tolosana, R., Vera-Rodriguez, R., & Busch, C. (n.d.). Advances in Computer Vision and Pattern Recognition. In *Handbook of Digital Face Manipulation and Detection From DeepFakes to Morphing Attacks.* https://link.springer.com/bookseries/4205

Rauniyar, K., Komal, R., & Kumar, S. D. (2021). Role of fintech and innovations for improvising digital financial inclusion. *International Journal of Innovative Science and Research Technology, 6*(5). https://ijisrt.com/assets/upload/files/IJISRT21MAY1089.pdf%0Awww.ijisrt.com

Ravi, N., Verma, S., Jhanjhi, N. Z., & Talib, M. N. (2021, August). Securing VANET Using Blockchain Technology. In *Journal of Physics: Conference Series* (Vol. 1979, No. 1, p. 012035). IOP Publishing. https://iopscience.iop.org/article/10.1088/1742-6596/1979/1/012035/meta

Rawat, A., & Matter Expert, S. (2016). *Achieving Customer-Centricity Through Digital Transformation Anubhav RawaT Subject Matter Expert.* www.cmo.com

Ray, B. C., Chowdhury, S. D., & Khatun, A. (2019). Productive performance and cost effectiveness of broiler using three different probiotics in the diet. *Bangladesh Journal of Animal Science, 48*(2), 85–91. doi:10.3329/bjas.v48i2.46761

Razali, M. A., & Mohd Shariff, S. (2019). Cmblock: In-browser detection and prevention cryptojacking tool using blacklist and behavior-based detection method. In *International Visual Informatics Conference* (pp. 404-414). Springer.

Reddy, E., & Lawack, V. (2019). An Overview of the Regulatory Developments in South Africa Regarding the Use of Cryptocurrencies. *SA Mercantile Law Journal, 31.*

Regev, O. (2005). On lattices, learning with errors, random linear codes, and cryptography. *STOC, 2005*, 84–93.

Regev, O. (2009). On lattices, learning with errors, random linear codes, and cryptography. *Journal of the Association for Computing Machinery, 56*(6), 1–40.

Regueiro, C., Seco, I., de Diego, S., Lage, O., & Etxebarria, L. (2021). Privacy-enhancing distributed protocol for data aggregation based on blockchain and homomorphic encryption. *Information Processing & Management, 58*(6), 102745.

Reich, R., Sahami, M., Weinstein, J. M., & Cohen, H. (2020, February). Teaching computer ethics: A deeply multidisciplinary approach. In *Proceedings of the 51st ACM Technical Symposium on Computer Science Education* (pp. 296-302). 10.1145/3328778.3366951

Report, G. (2020). *HTTPS encryption on the web.* Google Transparency Report. https://transparencyreport.google.com/https/overview?hl=en

ResearchGate. (n.d). Available at https://www.researchgate.net/figure/Overview-of-the-blockchain-working-principle_fig1_319128148

Reshmi, T. R. (2021). Information security breaches due to ransomware attacks—A systematic literature review. *International Journal of Information Management Data Insights, 1*(2), 100013. doi:10.1016/j.jjimei.2021.100013

Restoy, F. (n.d.). *Regulating fintech: what is going on, and where are the challenges?* Bank for International Settlements. www.suerf.org/policynotes

Reuvid, J. (Ed.). (2018). *Managing Cybersecurity Risk: Cases Studies and Solutions.* Legend Press Ltd.

Richardson, R. (2017). Ransomware: Evolution. *Mitigation and Prevention., 13*(1), 13.

Ridley, G., Young, J., & Carroll, P. (2004). COBIT and its Utilization: A Framework from the Literature. In *Proceedings of the 37th Annual Hawaii International Conference on System Sciences.* IEEE. 10.1109/HICSS.2004.1265566

Rishabh, K., & Schäublin, J. (n.d.). *Fintech Lending and Sales Manipulation.* Academic Press.

Rivest, R. L., Adleman, L., & Dertouzos, M. L. (1978). On data banks and privacy homomorphisms. *Foundations of Secure Computation, 4*(11), 169-180.

Rivest, R. L., Shamir, A., & Adleman, L. (1978). A method for obtaining digital signatures and public-key cryptosystems. *Communications of the ACM, 21*(2), 120–126. doi:10.1145/359340.359342

Robinson, O. C. (2014). Sampling in Interview-Based Qualitative Research: A Theoretical and Practical Guide. *Qualitative Research in Psychology, 11*(1), 25–41. doi:10.1080/14780887.2013.801543

Robot, M. (2019). *Rise of the cryptojackers.* Available at: https://www.kaspersky.com/blog/cryptojacking-rsa2019/25938/

Rocha Flores, W., & Ekstedt, M. (2016). Shaping intention to resist social engineering through transformational leadership, information security culture and awareness. *Computers & Security, 59*, 26–44. doi:10.1016/j.cose.2016.01.004

Rocha Flores, W., Holm, H., Svensson, G., & Ericsson, G. (2014). Using phishing experiments and scenario-based surveys to understand security behaviours in practice. *Information Management & Computer Security, 22*(4), 393–406. doi:10.1108/IMCS-11-2013-0083

Rodríguez-Abitia, G., & Bribiesca-Correa, G. (2021). Assessing digital transformation in universities. *Future Internet, 13*(2), 1–17. doi:10.3390/fi13020052

Rogers, R. W. (1975). A Protection Motivation Theory of fear appeals and attitude change. *The Journal of Psychology, 91*(1), 93–114. doi:10.1080/00223980.1975.9915803 PMID:28136248

Rogers, R. W. (1983). Cognitive and physiological processes in fear appeals and attitude change: A revised theory of protection motivation. In J. Cacioppo & R. Petty (Eds.), *Social Psychophysiology.* Guilford Press.

Roh, C.-H., & Lee, I.-Y. (2020). A study on electronic voting system using private Blockchain. *Journal of Information Processing Systems*, *16*(2), 421–434.

Rolfe, G., Freshwater, D., & Jasper, M. (2001). *Critical reflection for nursing and the helping professions: a user's Guide*. Palgrave Macmillan.

Romano, A., Zheng, Y., & Wang, W. (2020). Minerray: Semantics-aware analysis for ever-evolving cryptojacking detection. In *35th IEEE/ACM International Conference on Automated Software Engineering (ASE)* (pp. 1129-1140). IEEE.

Roopak, T., & Sumathi, R. (2020). *Electronic voting based on virtual id of aadhar using blockchain technology*. Paper presented at the 2020 2nd International Conference on Innovative Mechanisms for Industry Applications (ICIMIA). 10.1109/ICIMIA48430.2020.9074942

Rosbach, F. (2019). *The Top 3 Big Data Security and Compliance Challenges of 2019*. https://insights.comforte.com/big-data-analytics-the-top-3-security-and-compliance-challenges-of-2019

Rowter, K. (2016). Indonesia Capital Market Developments and Challenges. *Nomura Journal of Asian Financial Markets*, *1*(1), 9–13. www.nomurafoundation.or.jp›2016/10›NJACM1-1AU16-05_Indonesia

Ruijer, E. H. J. M., & Huff, R. F. (2016). Breaking through barriers: the impact of organizational culture on open government reform. *Transforming Government: People, Process and Policy*, *10*(2), 335–350.

Rüth, J., Zimmermann, T., Wolsing, K., & Hohlfeld, O. (2018). Digging into browser-based crypto mining. In *Proceedings of the Internet Measurement Conference* (pp. 70-76). Academic Press.

Ryle, P., Yan, J., & Gardiner, L. R. (2022). Gramm-Leach-Bliley gets a systems upgrade: What the ftc's proposed safeguards rule changes mean for small and medium american financial institutions. *EDPACS, 65*(2), 6–17. doi:10.1080/07366981.2021.1911387

Saad, M. (2018). *End-to-End Analysis of In-Browser Cryptojacking*. arXiv:1809.02152 [cs].

Saad, M., Anwar, A., Ahmad, A., Alasmary, H., Yuksel, M., & Mohaisen, A. (2019). *RouteChain: Towards blockchain-based secure and efficient BGP routing*. Paper presented at the 2019 IEEE International Conference on Blockchain and Cryptocurrency (ICBC). 10.1109/BLOC.2019.8751229

Saad, M., Spaulding, J., Njilla, L., Kamhoua, C., Shetty, S., Nyang, D. H., & Mohaisen, D. (2020). Exploring the Attack Surface of Blockchain: A Comprehensive Survey. *IEEE Communications Surveys and Tutorials*, *22*(3), 1977–2008. doi:10.1109/COMST.2020.2975999

Saarikko, T., Westergren, U. H., & Blomquist, T. (2020). Digital transformation: Five recommendations for the digitally conscious firm. *Business Horizons*, *63*(6), 825–839. doi:10.1016/j.bushor.2020.07.005

Sachan, R. K., Agarwal, R., & Shukla, S. K. (2022). *DNS based In-Browser Cryptojacking Detection*. arXiv preprint arXiv:2205.04685.

Saeed, S., Bamarouf, Y. A., Ramayah, T., & Iqbal, S. Z. (2016). Design Solutions for User-Centric Information Systems. *Design Solutions for User-Centric Information Systems*. doi:10.4018/978-1-5225-1944-7

Saeed, S., Jhanjhi, N. Z., Naqvi, M., Humayun, M., & Ahmed, S. (2020, October). Ransomware: A framework for security challenges in internet of things. In *2020 2nd International Conference on Computer and Information Sciences (ICCIS)* (pp. 1-6). IEEE. https://ieeexplore.ieee.org/abstract/document/9257660

Saeed, S., Rodríguez Bolívar, M. P., & Thurasamy, R. (Eds.). (2021). Pandemic, Lockdown, and Digital Transformation. doi:10.1007/978-3-030-86274-9

Saeed, S. (2019). Digital Business adoption and customer segmentation: An exploratory study of expatriate community in Saudi Arabia. *ICIC Express Letters*, *13*, 133–139.

Saeed, S. (Ed.). (2013). *Knowledge-based processes in software development*. IGI Global.

Saeed, S., Almuhaideb, A. M., Bamarouf, Y. A., Alabaad, D. A., Gull, H., Saqib, M., Iqbal, S. Z., & Salam, A. A. (2021). Sustainable Program Assessment Practices: A Review of the ABET and NCAAA Computer Information Systems Accreditation Process. *International Journal of Environmental Research and Public Health*, *18*(23), 12691. doi:10.3390/ijerph182312691 PMID:34886417

Saeed, S., Khan, M. A., & Ahmad, R. (Eds.). (2013). *Business strategies and approaches for effective engineering management*. IGI Global. doi:10.4018/978-1-4666-3658-3

Saeed, S., Wahab, F., Cheema, S. A., & Ashraf, S. (2013). Role of usability in e-government and e-commerce portals: An empirical study of Pakistan. *Life Science Journal*, *10*(1), 8–13.

Sahi, S. K. (2017). A Study of WannaCry Ransomware Attack. *International Journal of Engineering Research in Computer Science and Engineering*, *4*(9), 5–7.

Sajeed, S., Minshull, C., Jain, N., & Makarov, V. (2017). Invisible Trojan-horse attack. *Scientific Reports*, *7*.

Saleem, J., & Hammoudeh, M. (2018). Defense Methods Against Social Engineering Attacks. In K. Daimi (Ed.), *Computer and Network Security Essentials* (pp. 603–618). Springer International Publishing. doi:10.1007/978-3-319-58424-9_35

Salido, J. (2010). Data Governance for Privacy, Confidentiality and Compliance: A Holistic Approach. *Isaca Journal*, *6*, 1–7.

Salloum, S., Gaber, T., Vadera, S., & Shaalan, K. (2021). Phishing email detection using natural language processing techniques: A literature survey. *Procedia Computer Science*, *189*, 19–28. doi:10.1016/j.procs.2021.05.077

Salman, S. A.-B., Al-Janabi, S., & Sagheer, A. M. (2022). *A Review on E-Voting Based on Blockchain Models*. Academic Press.

Salvi, M. H. U., & Kerkar, M. R. V. (2016). Ransomware: A cyber extortion. *Asian Journal for Convergence in Technology (AJCT)*, *2*.

Sandoval, L., & Franca, I. D. P. (2012). Correlation of financial markets in times of crisis. *Physica A*, *391*(1–2), 187–208. doi:10.1016/j.physa.2011.07.023

Sankar, L. S., Sindhu, M., & Sethumadhavan, M. (2017, January). Survey of consensus protocols on blockchain applications. In *2017 4th international conference on advanced computing and communication systems (ICACCS)* (pp. 1-5). IEEE. 10.1109/ICACCS.2017.8014672

Sanni, S. O. (2020). *Nigeria : Crypto Currency In Nigeria : Regulatory Framework & Related Issues*. Mondaq. Com. https://www.mondaq.com/nigeria/fin-tech/855410/crypto-currency-in-nigeria-regulatory-framework-related-issues?type=popular

Saproo, S., Warke, V., Pote, S., & Dhumal, R. (2020). Online voting system using homomorphic encryption. In *ITM Web of Conferences* (Vol. 32, p. 03023). EDP Sciences.

Sarkar, K. R. (2010). Assessing insider threats to information security using technical, behavioural and organisational measures. *Information Security Technical Report*, *15*(3), 112–133. doi:10.1016/j.istr.2010.11.002

Sarker, I. H., Kayes, A. S. M., Badsha, S., Alqahtani, H., Watters, P., & Ng, A. (2020). Cybersecurity data science: An overview from machine learning perspective. *Journal of Big Data*, *7*(1), 1–29. doi:10.118640537-020-00318-5

SARS. (2018). *6 April 2018 - SARS's stance on the tax treatment of cryptocurrencies.* Sars.Gov.Za. https://www.sars.gov.za/Media/MediaReleases/Pages/6-April-2018---SARS-stance-on-the-tax-treatment-of-cryptocurrencies-.aspx

Saunders, M., Lewis, P., & Thornhill, A. (2016). *Research Methods for Business Students* (7th ed.). Pearson.

Scaife, N., Carter, H., Traynor, P., & Butler, K. R. B. (2016). CryptoLock (and Drop It): Stopping Ransomware Attacks on User Data. *2016 IEEE 36th International Conference on Distributed Computing Systems (ICDCS)*, 303–312.

Scarani, V., Ac'ın, A., Ribordy, G., & Gisin, N. (2004). Quantum Cryptography Protocols Robust against Photon Number Splitting Attacks for Weak Laser Pulse Implementations. *Physical Review Letters*, *92*, 057901.

Scarani, V., Iblisdir, S., Gisin, N., & Acín, A. (2005). Quantum cloning. *Reviews of Modern Physics*, *77*, 1225.

Scherer, A., Valiron, B., Mau, S.-C., & Alexander, S., Berg, E. van den, & Chapuran, T. E. (2017). Concrete resource analysis of the quantum linear system algorithm used to compute the electromagnetic scattering cross-section of a 2D target. *Quantum Information Processing*, *16*, 60.

Schneier, B. (1994). Description of a new variable-length key, 64- bit block cipher (Blowfish). In *Fast Software Encryption Second International Workshop, Leuven, Belgium, December 1993, Proceedings.* Springer-Verlag.

Schneier, B., Kelsey, J., Whiting, D., Wagner, D., Hall, C., & Ferguson, N. (1999). *The Twofish encryption algorithm: a 128-bit block cipher.* John Wiley & Sons, Inc.

Schnell, S. (2020). Vision, Voice, and Technology: Is There a Global "Open Government" Trend? *Administration & Society*, *52*(10), 1593–1620. doi:10.1177/0095399720918316

Schreider, T., & Noakes-Fry, K. (2017). *The manager's guide to cybersecurity law: essentials for today's business.* Academic Press.

Schwabe, P., & Westerbaan, B. (2016). Solving Binary MQ with Grover's Algorithm. In Security, Privacy, and Applied Cryptography Engineering —SPACE 2016. Springer.

Schwertner, K. (2017). Digital transformation of business. *Trakia Journal of Sciences*, *15*(Suppl.1), 388–393. doi:10.15547/tjs.2017.s.01.065

Sedlmeir, J., Buhl, H. U., Fridgen, G., & Keller, R. (2020). *The energy consumption of blockchain technology: Beyond myth.* Academic Press.

Seiner, R. S. (2014). *Non-invasive Data Governance: The Path of Least Resistance and Greatest Success.* Technics Publications.

Sengupta, J., Ruj, S., & Bit, S. D. (2020). A comprehensive survey on attacks, security issues and blockchain solutions for IoT and IIoT. *Journal of Network and Computer Applications*, *149*, 102481. doi:10.1016/j.jnca.2019.102481

Senturk, M., & Simsek, U. (2021). Educational comics and educational cartoons as teaching material in the social studies course. *American Educational Research Journal*, *9*(2), 515–525. doi:10.30918/AERJ.92.21.073

Senyo, P. K., Gozman, D., Karanasios, S., Dacre, N., & Baba, M. (2022). Moving away from trading on the margins: Economic empowerment of informal businesses through <scp>FinTech</scp>. *Information Systems Journal*, isj.12403. Advance online publication. doi:10.1111/isj.12403

Services, A. W. (2021). *Ferpa and student data privacy compliance on aws.* Available: https://d1.awsstatic.com/whitepapers/compliance/AWS-ferpa-whitepaper.pdf

Setiawan, N., Emia Tarigan, V. C., Sari, P. B., Rossanty, Y., Putra Nasution, M. D. T., & Siregar, I. (2018). Impact of cybercrime in e-business and trust. *International Journal of Civil Engineering and Technology*, *9*(7), 652–656.

Shafi, A., Saeed, S., Bamarouf, Y. A., Iqbal, S. Z., Min-Allah, N., & Alqahtani, M. A. (2019). Student outcomes assessment methodology for ABET accreditation: A case study of computer science and computer information systems programs. *IEEE Access: Practical Innovations, Open Solutions*, *7*, 13653–13667. doi:10.1109/ACCESS.2019.2894066

Shafiq, D. A., Jhanjhi, N. Z., Abdullah, A., & Alzain, M. A. (2021). *A load balancing algorithm for the data centres to optimize cloud computing applications*. Academic Press.

Shafiq, D. A., Jhanjhi, N., & Abdullah, A. (2021). Load balancing techniques in cloud computing environment. *RE:view*.

Shah, A., & Nagree, P. (n.d.). *Legal Issues in E-Commerce*. Nishith Desai Associates. Available at: http://www.nishith-desai.com/fileadmin/user_upload/pdfs/Legal_issues_in_eCommerce.pdf

Shah, I. A. (2022). Cybersecurity Issues and Challenges for E-Government During COVID-19: A Review. *Cybersecurity Measures for E-Government Frameworks*, 187-222. https://www.igi-global.com/chapter/cybersecurity-issues-and-challenges-for-e-government-during-covid-19/302729

Shah, I. A., Wassan, S., & Usmani, M. H. (2022). E-Government Security and Privacy Issues: Challenges and Preventive Approaches. In *Cybersecurity Measures for E-Government Frameworks* (pp. 61-76). IGI Global. https://www.igi-global.com/chapter/the-influence-of-cybersecurity-attacks-on-e-governance/302722

Shah, I. A., Habeeb, R. A. A., Rajper, S., & Laraib, A. (2022). The Influence of Cybersecurity Attacks on E-Governance. In *Cybersecurity Measures for E-Government Frameworks* (pp. 77–95). IGI Global. doi:10.4018/978-1-7998-9624-1.ch005

Shah, I. A., & Rajper, S., & ZamanJhanjhi, N. (2021). Using ML and Data-Mining Techniques in Automatic Vulnerability Software Discovery. *International Journal (Toronto, Ont.)*, *10*(3).

Shahid, J., Ahmad, R., Kiani, A. K., Ahmad, T., Saeed, S., & Almuhaideb, A. M. (2022). Data protection and privacy of the internet of healthcare things (IoHTs). *Applied Sciences (Basel, Switzerland)*, *12*(4), 1927. doi:10.3390/app12041927

Shahzad, H. F., Rustam, F., Flores, E. S., Luís, J., Mazón, V., De, I., Diez, T., & Ashraf, I. (2022). *A Review of Image Processing Techniques for Deepfakes*. Academic Press.

Shahzad, S. J. H., Bouri, E., Roubaud, D., Kristoufek, L., & Lucey, B. (2019). Is Bitcoin a better safe-haven investment than gold and commodities? *International Review of Financial Analysis*, *63*(January), 322–330. doi:10.1016/j.irfa.2019.01.002

Shaik, I., Chandran, N., & A, R. M. (2022). Privacy and data protection in the enterprise world. *CSI Transactions on ICT*, *10*(1), 37–45. doi:10.1007/s40012-022-00348-9

Shaikh, M. U., Adnan, W. A. W., & Ahmad, S. A. (2020). Secured electrocardiograph (ECG) signal using partially homomorphic encryption technique–RSA algorithm. *Pertanika Journal of Science & Technology*, *28*(S2), 231–242.

Shakya, V., Chatterjee, J. M., & Thakur, R. N. (2021). Network Security and Its Impact on Business Strategy: A Case Study on E-Commerce Site Daraz. Com. *Network Security*, *3*(1).

Shannon, C. E. (1948). A mathematical theory of communication. *The Bell System Technical Journal*, *27*, 379–423.

Sharma, P. K., Kumar, N., & Park, J. H. (2020). Blockchain technology toward green IoT: Opportunities and challenges. *IEEE Network*, *34*(4), 263–269. doi:10.1109/MNET.001.1900526

Sharma, U., Nand, P., Chatterjee, J. M., Jain, V., Jhanjhi, N. Z., & Sujatha, R. (2022). *Cyber-Physical Systems: Foundations and Techniques*. John Wiley & Sons.

Sheikh, A., Kamuni, V., Urooj, A., Wagh, S., Singh, N., & Patel, D. (2019). Secured energy trading using byzantine-based blockchain consensus. *IEEE Access: Practical Innovations, Open Solutions, 8*, 8554–8571. doi:10.1109/AC-CESS.2019.2963325

Shende, A., Paliwal, S., & Mahay, T. K. (2021). Using deep learning to detect deepfake videos. *Turkish Journal of Computer and Mathematics Education Research Article, 12*(11), 5012–5017.

Sherman, L. E., Greenfield, P. M., Hernandez, L. M., & Dapretto, M. (2018). Peer influence via Instagram: Effects on brain and behavior in adolescence and young adulthood. *Child Development, 89*(1), 37–47. doi:10.1111/cdev.12838 PMID:28612930

Shin, D. D. H. (2019). Blockchain: The emerging technology of digital trust. *Telematics and Informatics, 45*(June), 101278. Advance online publication. doi:10.1016/j.tele.2019.101278

Shor, P. W. (1994): Polynomial-time algorithms for prime factorization and discrete logarithms on a quantum computer. *Proc. 35th Annual Symposium on Foundations of Computer Science, 124*–134. 10.1109/SFCS.1994.365700

Shor, P. W. (1994, November). Algorithms for quantum computation: discrete logarithms and factoring. In *Proceedings 35th annual symposium on foundations of computer science* (pp. 124-134). IEEE.

Shrestha, A. K., Vassileva, J., & Deters, R. (2020). A blockchain platform for user data sharing ensuring user control and incentives. *Frontiers in Blockchain, 48*.

Shrimali, B., & Patel, H. B. (2021). Blockchain state-of-the-art: architecture, use cases, consensus, challenges and opportunities. *Journal of King Saud University-Computer and Information Sciences.*

Shrivastava, A., Sondhi, J.S., & Kumar, B. (2017). *Machine learning technique for product classification in e-commerce data using Microsoft Azure cloud.* Academic Press.

Shukla, B., Khatri, S. K., & Kapur, P. K. (n.d.). *2017 6th International Conference on Reliability, Infocom Technologies and Optimization (ICRITO) (Trends and Future Directions).* Amity University.

Siegfried, N., Rosenthal, T., & Benlian, A. (2020). Blockchain and the Industrial Internet of Things: A requirement taxonomy and systematic fit analysis. *Journal of Enterprise Information Management.*

Singer, A. a. (2014). *Keep it Simple, Stupid: Why the Usual Password Policies Don't Work, and What to Do About It.* Academic Press.

Singh, D. (1999). *Electronic Commerce: Issues for the South.* Trade-related Agenda, Development and Equity. Working Paper, South Centre.

Singh, M., & Kim, S. (2018). *Crypto trust point (cTp) for secure data sharing among intelligent vehicles.* Paper presented at the 2018 International Conference on Electronics, Information, and Communication (ICEIC). 10.23919/ELINFO-COM.2018.8330663

Singh, S. (2021, July 16). *Potential Use Cases of Blockchain Technology for Cybersecurity.* https://www.itbusinessedge.com/security/potential-use-cases-of-blockchain-technology-for-cybersecurity/

Singh, A. P., Pradhan, N. R., Luhach, A. K., Agnihotri, S., Jhanjhi, N. Z., Verma, S., Kavita, Ghosh, U., & Roy, D. S. (2020). A novel patient-centric architectural framework for blockchain-enabled healthcare applications. *IEEE Transactions on Industrial Informatics, 17*(8), 5779–5789. doi:10.1109/TII.2020.3037889

Singh, D. (2020). Toward Data Privacy and Security Framework in Big Data Governance. *International Journal of Software Engineering and Computer Systems, 6*(1), 41–51. doi:10.15282/ijsecs.6.1.2020.5.0068

Singh, M., Poongodi, M., Saurabh, P., Kumar, U., Bourouis, S., Alhakami, W., Osamor, J., & Hamdi, M. (2022). A novel trust-based security and privacy model for Internet of Vehicles using encryption and steganography ☆. *Computers & Electrical Engineering*, *102*(June), 108205. doi:10.1016/j.compeleceng.2022.108205

Singh, P., Masud, M., Hossain, M. S., & Kaur, A. (2021). Blockchain and homomorphic encryption-based privacy-preserving data aggregation model in smart grid. *Computers & Electrical Engineering*, *93*, 107209.

Sintomer, Y., Herzberg, C., & Röcke, A. (2008). From Porto Alegre to Europe: Potentials and Limitations of Participatory Budgeting (PDF). *International Journal of Urban and Regional Research*.

Sironi, P. (2016). *FinTech innovation: from robo-advisors to goal based investing and gamification*. John Wiley & Sons. doi:10.1002/9781119227205

Slager, K., Nunez, R., Short, W., & Doore, S. A. (2021, March). Computing Ethics Starts on 'Day One' Ethics Narratives in Introductory CS Courses. In *Proceedings of the 52nd ACM Technical Symposium on Computer Science Education* (pp. 1282-1282). 10.1145/3408877.3439648

Smilarubavathy, G., Nidhya, R., Abiramy, N. V., & Dinesh Kumar, A. (2021). Paillier Homomorphic Encryption with K-Means Clustering Algorithm (PHEKC) for Data Mining Security in Cloud. In *Inventive Communication and Computational Technologies* (pp. 941–948). Springer.

Smith, K. T. (2011). An Analysis of E-Commerce: E-Risk, Global Trade, and Cybercrime. SSRN *Electronic Journal*. doi:10.2139/ssrn.1315423

Smith, S. (2022). Out of Gas: A Deep Dive Into the Colonial Pipeline Cyberattack. In *SAGE Business Cases*. SAGE Publications.

Sokolov, A. (2020). *How to mitigate fintech application threats*. https://www.itechart.com/blog/mobile-fintech-security-threats/

Song, Y., Sun, C., Peng, Y., Zeng, Y., & Sun, B. (2022). Research on Multidimensional Trust Evaluation Mechanism of FinTech Based on Blockchain. *IEEE Access: Practical Innovations, Open Solutions*, *10*, 57025–57036. doi:10.1109/ACCESS.2022.3177275

SonicWall. (2022). *SonicWall Cyber Threat Report*. Available at: https://www.sonicwall.com/2022-cyber-threat-report/

Son, Y., Han, K., Lee, Y. S., Yu, J., Im, Y. H., & Shin, S. Y. (2021). Privacy-preserving breast cancer recurrence prediction based on homomorphic encryption and secure two party computation. *PLoS One*, *16*(12), e0260681.

Sorongan, F. A., Legowo, M. B., & Subanidja, S. (2021). FinTech as The Emerging Technologies in Banking Industry: Past, Present, and Future. *International Journal (Toronto, Ont.)*, 371–378. http://ijpsat.es/index.php/ijpsat/article/view/3550

Souza, C. (2001). Participatory budgeting in Brazilian cities: Limits and possibilities in building democratic institutions. *Environment and Urbanization*, *13*(1), 159–184. doi:10.1177/095624780101300112

Spence, S. (2003). Social skills training with children and young peo- ple: Theory, evidence and practice. *Child and Adolescent Mental Health*, *8*(2), 84–96. doi:10.1111/1475-3588.00051 PMID:32797550

Spring, T. (2018). *Cryptominer, winstarnssmminer, has made a fortune by brutally hijacking computers*. https://blog.360totalsecurity.com/en/cryptominer-winstarnssmminer-made-fortune-brutally-hijacking-computer/

Sri, C. G., Bano, S., Deepika, T., Kola, N., & Pranathi, Y. L. (2021). Deep Neural Networks Based Error Level Analysis for Lossless Image Compression Based Forgery Detection. *2021 International Conference on Intelligent Technologies, CONIT 2021*, 1–8. doi:10.1109/CONIT51480.2021.9498357

Stallings, W. (2013). *Cryptography and Network Security Principles and Practice*. Pearson Education.

Stallings, W., & Brown, L. (2018). *Computer security: principles and practice* (4th ed.). Pearson Education Limited.

Stanciu, D. C., & Ionescu, B. (2021). Deepfake Video Detection with Facial Features and Long-Short Term Memory Deep Networks. *ISSCS 2021 - International Symposium on Signals, Circuits and Systems*, 0–3. doi:10.1109/ISS-CS52333.2021.9497385

Statista Research Department. (2021). *FinTech firms share in India 2020, by segment*. Statista Research Department.

Statista Research Department. (2021, June 8). *Consumer concerns regarding digital transactions India in 2020*. Retrieved March 29, 2022, from www.statista.com: https://www.statista.com/statistics/1242336/india-consumer-concerns-about-digital-transactions/#statisticContainer

Statista. (2022). *Fintech – Worldwide*. Retrieved September 21, 2022, from https://www.statista.com/outlook/dmo/fintech/worldwide

Statistia. (2022). Available online: https://www.statista.com/statistics/730876/cryptocurrency-maket-value/

Stensås, A., Nygaard, M. F., Kyaw, K., & Treepongkaruna, S. (2019). Can Bitcoin be a diversifier, hedge or safe haven tool? *Cogent Economics and Finance*, 7(1), 1593072. Advance online publication. doi:10.1080/23322039.2019.1593072

Stewart, H., & Jürjens, J. (2018). *Data security and consumer trust in FinTech innovation in Germany*. Information & Computer Security. doi:10.1108/ICS-06-2017-0039

Stoica, E. A., & Sitea, D. M. (2021).. . *Blockchain Disrupting Fintech and the Banking System, 24*, 24. Advance online publication. doi:10.3390/proceedings2021074024

Stolbunov, A. (2010). Constructing public-key cryptographic schemes based on class group action on a set of isogenous elliptic curves. *Advances in Mathematics of Communications*, 4(2), 215–235.

Stroud, F. (2018). *Cryptocurrency mining*. https://www.webopedia.com/TERM/C/cryptocurrency-mining.html

Stucki, D., Fasel, S., Gisin, N., Thoma, Y., & Zbinden, H. (2007). Coherent one-way quantum key distribution. In Photon Counting Applications, Quantum Optics, and Quantum Cryptography. International Society for Optics and Photonics.

Sun, S. (2021). *Preferred technologies in finance process digitalization in India 2020*. Statista Research Department.

Sun, X., Chung, S., & Ma, H. (2020). Operational Risk in Airline Crew Scheduling: Do Features of Flight Delays Matter? *Decision Sciences*, 51(6), 1455–1489. doi:10.1111/deci.12426

Suprun, A., Petrishina, T., & Vasylchuk, I. (2020). *Competition and cooperation between fintech companies and*. Academic Press.

Suryateja, P. S. (2018). Threats and vulnerabilities of cloud computing: A review. *International Journal on Computer Science and Engineering*, 6(3), 297–302.

Suryono, R. R., Budi, I., & Purwandari, B. (2020). Challenges and trends of financial technology (Fintech): A systematic literature review. In Information (Switzerland) (Vol. 11, Issue 12, pp. 1–20). MDPI AG. doi:10.3390/info11120590

Suseendran, G., Chandrasekaran, E., Akila, D., & Sasi Kumar, A. (2020). Banking and FinTech (Financial Technology) Embraced with IoT Device. *Advances in Intelligent Systems and Computing*, 1042(February), 197–211. doi:10.1007/978-981-32-9949-8_15

Swanson, M., Bowen, P., Phillips, A. W., Gallup, D., & Lynes, D. (2010). *Contingency planning guide for federal information systems*. doi:10.6028/NIST.SP.800-34r1

Swanson, M., Wohl, A., Pope, L., Grance, T., Hash, J., & Thomas, R. (2002). *Contingency planning guide for information technology systems.* doi:10.6028/NIST.SP.800-34

Syed, D., Refaat, S. S., & Bouhali, O. (2020). Privacy preservation of data-driven models in smart grids using homomorphic encryption. *Information, 11*(7), 357.

Syllignakis, M. N., & Kouretas, G. P. (2011). Dynamic correlation analysis of financial contagion: Evidence from the Central and Eastern European markets. *International Review of Economics & Finance, 20*(4), 717–732. doi:10.1016/j.iref.2011.01.006

Tabrizchi, H., & Rafsanjani, M. K. (2020). A survey on security challenges in cloud computing: Issues, threats, and solutions. *The Journal of Supercomputing, 76*(12), 9493–9532.

Tahir, R., Durrani, S., Ahmed, F., Saeed, H., Zaffar, F., & Ilyas, S. (2019). The browsers strike back: countering cryptojacking and parasitic miners on the web. In *IEEE INFOCOM 2019-IEEE Conference on Computer Communications* (pp. 703-711). IEEE.

Tahir, S., & Rajarajan, M. (2018). Privacy-preserving searchable encryption framework for permissioned blockchain networks. In *2018 IEEE International Conference on Internet of Things (iThings) and IEEE Green Computing and Communications (GreenCom) and IEEE Cyber, Physical and Social Computing (CPSCom) and IEEE Smart Data (SmartData).* IEEE.

Tahir, S., Tahir, H., Sajjad, A., Rajarajan, M., & Khan, F. (2021). Privacy-preserving COVID-19 contact tracing using blockchain. *Journal of Communications and Networks (Seoul), 23*(5), 360–373. doi:10.23919/JCN.2021.000031

Tailor, J. P., & Patel, A. D. (2017). *A Comprehensive Survey: Ransomware Attacks Prevention, Monitoring and Damage Control.* Academic Press.

Takahashi, R. (2017, August 7). *How can creative industries benefit from blockchain?* https://www.mckinsey.com/industries/technology-media-and-telecommunications/our-insights/how-can-creative-industries-benefit-from-blockchain

Tanana, D. (2020). Behavior-based detection of cryptojacking malware. In *Ural Symposium on Biomedical Engineering, Radioelectronics and Information Technology (USBEREIT)* (pp. 543-545). IEEE.

Tanana, D., & Tanana, G. (2020). Advanced behavior-based technique for cryptojacking malware detection. In *14th International Conference on Signal Processing and Communication Systems (ICSPCS)* (pp. 1-4). IEEE.

Taneja, B. (2021). The Digital Edge for M-Commerce to Replace E-Commerce. In Emerging Challenges, Solutions, and Best Practices for Digital Enterprise Transformation (pp. 299-318). IGI Global.

Tang, K. L. (2021). *Behavioural Intention of Commercial Banks' Customers towards Financial Technology Services Related papers.* Global Academy of Training & Research (GATR) Enterprise.

Tapanainen, T. (2020). Toward Fintech Adoption Framework for Developing Countries -A Literature Review based on the Stakeholder Perspective. *Journal of Information Technology Applications & Management, 27*(October), 1–22.

Tariq, S., Lee, S., & Woo, S. (2021). *One Detector to Rule Them All.* doi:10.1145/3442381.3449809

Tariq, S., Lee, S., Kim, H., Shin, Y., & Woo, S. S. (2018). Detecting both machine and human created fake face images in the wild. *Proceedings of the ACM Conference on Computer and Communications Security,* 81–87. doi:10.1145/3267357.3267367

Tarutė, A., Duobienė, J., Klovienė, L., Vitkauskaitė, E., & Varaniūtė, V. (2018). Identifying factors affecting digital transformation of SMEs. ICEB.

Tasnim, M. A., Omar, A. A., Rahman, M. S., Bhuiyan, M., & Alam, Z. (2018, December). Crab: Blockchain based criminal record management system. In *International conference on security, privacy and anonymity in computation, communication and storage* (pp. 294-303). Springer.

Taylor, S. J., Bogdan, R., & DeVault, M. L. (2016). *Introduction to Qualitative Research Methods* (4th ed.). John Wiley & Sons.

Tebaa, M., Zkik, K., & El Hajji, S. (2015). Hybrid homomorphic encryption method for protecting the privacy of banking data in the cloud. *International Journal of Security and Its Applications, 9*(6), 61–70.

Techcrunch. (2019). *Binance pledges to 'significantly' increase security following $40M Bitcoin hack*. Retrieved September 22, 2022, from https://techcrunch.com/2019/05/10/binance-security-hack/

Teherani, A., Martimianakis, T., Stenfors-Hayes, T., Wadhwa, A., & Varpio, L. (2015). Choosing a Qualitative Research Approach. *Journal of Graduate Medical Education, 7*(4), 669–670. doi:10.4300/JGME-D-15-00414.1 PMID:26692985

Tekiner, E., Acar, A., & Uluagac, A. S. (2021). *A Lightweight IoT Cryptojacking Detection Mechanism in Heterogeneous Smart Home Networks*. Academic Press.

Tekiner, E., Acar, A., Uluagac, A. S., Kirda, E., & Selcuk, A. A. (2021). In-Browser crypto mining for Good: *An Untold Story. In IEEE International Conference on Decentralized Applications and Infrastructures (DAPPS)* (pp. 20-29). IEEE.

Telstra. (2019). *Telstra Security Report 2019*. Telstra. https://www.telstra.com.au/content/dam/shared-component-assets/tecom/campaigns/security-report/TELE0394_Telstra_Security_Report_2019.pdf

Teplinsky, M. J. (2012). Fiddling on the roof: Recent developments in cybersecurity. *Am. U. Bus. L. Rev., 2*, 225.

Ternovski, J., Kalla, J., & Aronow, P. M. (2021). *Deepfake Warnings for Political Videos Increase Disbelief but Do Not Improve Discernment: Evidence from Two Experiments*. https://osf.io/dta97/

Tesla, K., & Exploits, J. (2018). *Cryptojacking and Crypto Mining*. https://neuvector.com/containersecurity/cryptojacking-crypto-mining-tesla-kubernetesjenkins-exploits/

The Coronavirus is Already Taking Effect on Cyber Security– This is How CISOs Should Prepare | Threatpost. (n.d.). Retrieved February 27, 2022, from https://threatpost.com/cynet-the-coronavirus-is-already-taking-effect-on-cyber-security-this-is-how-cisos-should-prepare/153758/

The Fintech 50 2021. (n.d.). *Forbes*. Retrieved May 30, 2022, from https://www.forbes.com/fintech/2021/#170f1f1f31a6

The impact of cloud computing in fintech. (2021). *TELEHOUSE*. https://www.telehouse.net/blog/the-impact-of-cloud-computing-in-fintech/

The One Brief. (n.d.). *2021's Top 10 Risks: The Pandemic Shines a Spotlight on Interconnected Risks - The One Brief*. Retrieved April 25, 2022, from https://theonebrief.com/2021s-top-10-risks-the-pandemic-shines-a-spotlight-on-interconnected-risks/

Thuraisingham, B. (2020, October). Blockchain Technologies and Their Applications in Data Science and Cyber Security. In *2020 3rd International Conference on Smart BlockChain (SmartBlock)* (pp. 1-4). IEEE. 10.1109/SmartBlock52591.2020.00008

Thuraisingham, B., Kantarcioglu, M., Hamlen, K., Khan, L., Finin, T., Joshi, A., . . . Bertino, E. (2016, July). A data driven approach for the science of cyber security: Challenges and directions. In *2016 IEEE 17th International Conference on Information Reuse and Integration (IRI)* (pp. 1-10). IEEE.

Thuraisingham, B., Kantarcioglu, M., Bertino, E., Bakdash, J. Z., & Fernandez, M. (2018, June). Towards a privacy-aware quantified self data management framework. In *Proceedings of the 23nd ACM on Symposium on Access Control Models and Technologies* (pp. 173-184). 10.1145/3205977.3205997

Toh, T. L., Cheng, L. P., Ho, S. Y., Jiang, H., & Lim, K. M. (2017). Use of comics to enhance students'' learning for the development of the twenty-first-century competencies in the mathematics classroom. *Asia Pacific Journal of Education*, *37*(4), 437–452. doi:10.1080/02188791.2017.1339344

Tosh, D. K., Shetty, S., Liang, X., Kamhoua, C. A., Kwiat, K. A., & Njilla, L. (2017, May). Security implications of blockchain cloud with analysis of block withholding attack. In *2017 17th IEEE/ACM International Symposium on Cluster, Cloud and Grid Computing (CCGRID)* (pp. 458-467). IEEE. 10.1109/CCGRID.2017.111

Touchton, M. R. (2020). Whistleblowing or leaking? Public opinion toward Assange, Manning, and Snowden. *Research & Politics, 7*(1).

Toyama, K. (2017). Geek Heresy: Rescuing Social Change from the Cult of Technology. *Innovations in Teaching & Learning Conference Proceedings,* (9). 10.13021/itlcp.2017

Toyoda, K., Mathiopoulos, P. T., & Ohtsuki, T. (2019). A novel methodology for hyip operators' bitcoin addresses identification. *IEEE Access: Practical Innovations, Open Solutions, 7,* 74835–74848. doi:10.1109/ACCESS.2019.2921087

Treleaven, P. (2015). Financial regulation of FinTech. *Journal of Financial Perspectives, 3*(3), 114–121.

Uddin, M. A., Stranieri, A., Gondal, I., & Balasubramanian, V. (2019, February). An efficient selective miner consensus protocol in blockchain oriented IoT smart monitoring. In *2019 IEEE International Conference on Industrial Technology (ICIT)* (pp. 1135-1142). IEEE. 10.1109/ICIT.2019.8754936

Uddin, M. A., Stranieri, A., Gondal, I., & Balasubramanian, V. (2021). A survey on the adoption of blockchain in iot: Challenges and solutions. *Blockchain: Research and Applications, 2*(2), 100006. doi:10.1016/j.bcra.2021.100006

Ujjan, R. M. A., Khan, N. A., & Gaur, L. (2022). E-Government Privacy and Security Challenges in the Context of Internet of Things. In *Cybersecurity Measures for E-Government Frameworks* (pp. 22–42). IGI Global. doi:10.4018/978-1-7998-9624-1.ch002

Ullah, A., Azeem, M., Ashraf, H., Jhanjhi, N. Z., Nkenyereye, L., & Humayun, M. (2021). Secure Critical Data Reclamation Scheme for Isolated Clusters in IoT enabled WSN. *IEEE Internet of Things Journal.* https://ieeexplore.ieee.org/abstract/document/9491079

Ullah, N., Al-Rahmi, W. M., Alfarraj, O., Alalwan, N., Alzahrani, A. I., Ramayah, T., & Kumar, V. (2022). Hybridizing cost saving with trust for blockchain technology adoption by financial institutions. *Telematics and Informatics Reports, 6*(April), 100008. doi:10.1016/j.teler.2022.100008

Underwood, S. (2016). Blockchain beyond bitcoin. *Communications of the ACM, 59*(11), 15–17. doi:10.1145/2994581

Universities, A. (2021). A Framework for Enhancing Cyber Security in Fintech Applications in India. *International Conference on Technological Advancements and Innovations (ICTAI).*

Unsal, E., Oztekin, B., Cavus, M., & Ozdemir, S. (2020, October 20). Building a fintech ecosystem: Design and development of a fintech API gateway. *2020 International Symposium on Networks, Computers and Communications, ISNCC 2020.* 10.1109/ISNCC49221.2020.9297273

Urien, P. (2021). A New IoT Trust Model Based on TLS-SE and TLS- IM Secure Elements : a Blockchain Use Case. *2021 IEEE 18th Annual Consumer Communications & Networking Conference (CCNC),* 2021–2022.

Urquhart, L., & McAuley, D. (2018). Avoiding the internet of insecure industrial things. *Computer Law & Security Review, 34*(3), 450–466. doi:10.1016/j.clsr.2017.12.004

Vaccari, C., & Chadwick, A. (2020). Deepfakes and Disinformation: Exploring the Impact of Synthetic Political Video on Deception, Uncertainty, and Trust in News. *Social Media and Society, 6*(1). doi:10.1177/2056305120903408

Valaštín, V., Košt'ál, K., Bencel, R., & Kotuliak, I. (2019). *Blockchain based car-sharing platform.* Paper presented at the 2019 International Symposium ELMAR. 10.1109/ELMAR.2019.8918650

van der Kleij, R., Wijn, R., & Hof, T. (2020). An application and empirical test of the Capability Opportunity Motivation-Behaviour model to data leakage prevention in financial organizations. *Computers & Security, 97*, 101970. doi:10.1016/j.cose.2020.101970

van Dyk, R., & van Belle, J. P. (2019). Factors influencing the intended adoption of digital transformation: A South African case study. *Proceedings of the 2019 Federated Conference on Computer Science and Information Systems, FedCSIS 2019*, 519–528. 10.15439/2019F166

Van Gevelt, T., Holzeis, C. C., George, F., & Zaman, T. (2017). Indigenous community preferences for electricity services: Evidence from a choice experiment in Sarawak, Malaysia. *Energy Policy, 108*, 102–110. doi:10.1016/j.enpol.2017.05.054

Van Tilborg, H. C., & Jajodia, S. (Eds.). (2014). *Encyclopedia of cryptography and security.* Springer Science & Business Media.

Varlioglu, S., Elsayed, N., ElSayed, Z., & Ozer, M. (2022). The Dangerous Combo: Fileless Malware and Cryptojacking. *SoutheastCon, 2022*, 125–132.

Vasek, M., & Moore, T. (2018). Analyzing the Bitcoin Ponzi scheme ecosystem. In *International Conference on Financial Cryptography and Data Security* (pp. 101-112). Springer.

Vasek, M., & Moore, T. (2015). There's no free lunch, even using Bitcoin: Tracking the popularity and profits of virtual currency scams. In *International conference on financial cryptography and data security* (pp. 44-61). Springer.

Veljković, N., Bogdanović-Dinić, S., & Stoimenov, L. (2014). Benchmarking open government: An open data perspective. *Government Information Quarterly, 31*(2), 278–290. doi:10.1016/j.giq.2013.10.011

Velumadhava Rao, R., & Selvamani, K. (2015). Data security challenges and its solutions in cloud computing. *Procedia Computer Science, 48*(C), 204–209. doi:10.1016/j.procs.2015.04.171

Vengadapurvaja, A. M., Nisha, G., Aarthy, R., & Sasikaladevi, N. (2017). An efficient homomorphic medical image encryption algorithm for cloud storage security. *Procedia Computer Science, 115*, 643–650.

Verizon, B. (2022). *2022 Data Breach Investigations.* Retrieved September 21, 2022, from https://www.verizon.com/business/resources/reports/dbir/2022/financial-services-data-breaches

Verizon. (2018). *Data Breach Investigations Report.* Available online: https://www.verizon.com/about/sites/default/files/2018-Verizon-Annual-Report.pdf

Verizon. (2019). *2019 Data Breach Investigations Report* (Data Breach Investigations Report) [12th]. Verizon. https://www.key4biz.it/wp-content/uploads/2019/05/2019-data-breach-investigations-report.pdf

Verma, G., & Adhikari, S. (2020). Cloud Computing Security Issues : A Stakeholder ' s Perspective. *SN Computer Science, 1*(6), 1–8. doi:10.100742979-020-00353-2

Verma, M. (2018). Artificial intelligence and its scope in different areas with special reference to the field of education. *Online Submission, 3*(1), 5–10.

Vidal, T. A. D. C. (2020). *How exchange platform attacks impact the cryptocurrency and traditional markets* (Doctoral dissertation).

Vignau, B., Khoury, R., & Hallé, S. (2019). 10 years of IoT malware: A feature-based taxonomy. In *2019 IEEE 19th International Conference on Software Quality, Reliability and Security Companion (QRS-C)* (pp. 458-465). IEEE.

Vijayaraj, M. (2019). *Rethinking Security in IT by Incorporating Blockchain Technology.* https://www.relevance.com/rethinking-security-in-it-by-incorporating-blockchain-technology/

Villalón-Fonseca, R. (2022). The nature of security: A conceptual framework for integral-comprehensive modelling of IT security and cybersecurity. *Computers & Security, 120*, 102805. doi:10.1016/j.cose.2022.102805

Vimal M. (2019). *Cybersecurity and fintech at a crossroads.* Academic Press.

Vincent, M. (2020). Banks work with fintechs to counter 'deepfake' fraud. *Financial Times.* https://www.ft.com/content/8a5fa5b2-6aac-41cf-aa52-5d0b90c41840

Vinoth, S., Vemula, H. L., Haralayya, B., Mamgain, P., Hasan, M. F., & Naved, M. (2022). Application of cloud computing in banking and e-commerce and related security threats. *Materials Today: Proceedings, 51*, 2172–2175. doi:10.1016/j.matpr.2021.11.121

Vizoso, Á., Vaz-álvarez, M., & López-García, X. (2021). Fighting deepfakes: Media and internet giants' converging and diverging strategies against hi-tech misinformation. *Media and Communication, 9*(1), 291–300. https://doi.org/10.17645/MAC.V9I1.3494

von Leipzig, T., Gamp, M., Manz, D., Schöttle, K., Ohlhausen, P., Oosthuizen, G., Palm, D., & von Leipzig, K. (2017). Initialising Customer-orientated Digital Transformation in Enterprises. *Procedia Manufacturing, 8*, 517–524. doi:10.1016/j.promfg.2017.02.066

Von Solms, R., & Van Niekerk, J. (2013). From information security to cyber security. *Computers & Security, 38*, 97-102.

Vučeković, M., & Gavrilović, K. (n.d.). *Digital Transformation and Evolution of Business Models.* Academic Press.

Vučinić, M., & Luburić, R. (2022). Fintech, Risk-Based Thinking and Cyber Risk. *Journal of Central Banking Theory and Practice, 11*(2), 27–53.

Vukovic, M., Katusic, D., Soic, R., & Weber, M. (n.d.). *Rule-Based System for Data Leak Threat Estimation.* Academic Press.

Wahab, Y. M., Ghazi, A., Al-Dawoodi, A., Alisawi, M., Abdullah, S. S., Hammood, L., & Nawaf, A. Y. (2022). *A Framework for Blockchain Based E-Voting System for Iraq.* Academic Press.

Wang, D., & Zhang, X. (2020). *Secure ride-sharing services based on a consortium blockchain.* Academic Press.

Wang, Q., & Su, M. (2020). *Integrating blockchain technology into the energy sector—from theory of blockchain to research and application of energy blockchain.* Academic Press.

Wang, Y., Su, Z., Li, J., Zhang, N., Zhang, K., Choo, K.-K. R., & Liu, Y. (2021). *Blockchain-based secure and cooperative private charging pile sharing services for vehicular networks.* Academic Press.

Wang, J., Li, Y., & Rao, H. R. (2016). Overconfidence in Phishing Email Detection. *Journal of the Association for Information Systems, 17*(11), 759–783. Advance online publication. doi:10.17705/1jais.00442

Wang, M., & Choi, J. (2022). How Web Content Types Improve Consumer Engagement through Scarcity and Interactivity of Mobile Commerce? *Sustainability, 14*(9), 4898. doi:10.3390u14094898

Wang, W., Ferrell, B., Xu, X., Hamlen, K. W., & Hao, S. (2018). Seismic: Secure in-lined script monitors for interrupting cryptojacks. In *European Symposium on Research in Computer Security* (pp. 122-142). Springer.

Warner, K. S. R., & Wäger, M. (2019). Building dynamic capabilities for digital transformation: An ongoing process of strategic renewal. *Long Range Planning, 52*(3), 326–349. doi:10.1016/j.lrp.2018.12.001

Waseem, A. (2020). Analysis of Factor Affecting e-Commerce Potential of any Country using Multiple Regression. *Jinnah Business Review, 8*(1), 1–17. doi:10.53369/YONH5168

Weber, F., & Schütte, R. (2019). A Domain-Oriented Analysis of the Impact of Machine Learning—The Case of Retailing. *Big Data and Cognitive Computing, 3*(1), 11. doi:10.3390/bdcc3010011

Weber, K., Otto, B., & Oesterle, H. (2009). One Size does not Fit All: A Contingency Approach to Data Governance. *Journal of Data and Information Quality, 1*(1), 4. doi:10.1145/1515693.1515696

Webmin. (2020). *The official webpage of webmine pool.* https://www.webminepool.com/page/documentation

Webroot Inc. (2021). *Webroot BrightCloud Threat Report 2021.* Available at: https://community.webroot.com/news-announcements-3/the-2021-webroot-brightcloud-threat-report-54-of-phishing-sites-use-https-to-trick-users-347178

Weerawardana, M. C., & Fernando, T. G. I. (2021). Deepfakes Detection Methods: A Literature Survey. *2021 10th International Conference on Information and Automation for Sustainability, ICIAfS 2021,* 76–81. doi:10.1109/ICIAfS52090.2021.9606067

Werth, O., Schwarzbach, C., Rodríguez Cardona, D., Breitner, M. H., & Graf von der Schulenburg, J. M. (2020). Influencing factors for the digital transformation in the financial services sector. *Zeitschrift Fur Die Gesamte Versicherungswissenschaft, 109*(2–4), 155–179. doi:10.100712297-020-00486-6

Westerlund, M. (2019). The emergence of deepfake technology: A review. *Technology Innovation Management Review, 9*(11), 39–52. doi:10.22215/TIMREVIEW/1282

Westerman, G. (n.d.). *The Questions Leaders Should Ask in the New Era of Digital Transformation.* Academic Press.

What Is Cybersecurity? (2022, May 12). Cisco.

WHO. (2022). *COVID-19 Weekly Epidemiological Update.* WHO.

Widia, F., Rosanensi, M., & Rahmawati, L. (2021). Netflix's Strategy to Dominate the World's Entertainment Media Market After the Death of Blockbuster. *JBTI : Jurnal Bisnis : Teori Dan Implementasi, 12*(3), 155–171. doi:10.18196/jbti.v12i3.13396

Will, N. C., Heinrich, T., Viescinski, A. B., & Maziero, C. A. (2021, April 15). Trusted Inter-Process Communication Using Hardware Enclaves. *15th Annual IEEE International Systems Conference, SysCon 2021 - Proceedings.* 10.1109/SysCon48628.2021.9447066

Wilson, J. D. (2017). Creating Strategic Value through Financial Technology. *Creating Strategic Value through Financial Technology.* doi:10.1002/9781119318682

Winschiers-Goagoses, N., Winschiers-Theophilus, H., Rodil, K., Kapuire, G., & Jensen, K. (2012). Design democratization with communities: Drawing toward locally meaningful design. *International Journal of Sociotechnology and Knowledge Development, 4*(4), 32–43. doi:10.4018/jskd.2012100103

Winschiers-Theophilus, H., Zaman, T., & Yeo, A. (2015, June). Reducing "white elephant" ICT4D projects: a community-researcher engagement. In *Proceedings of the 7th International Conference on Communities and Technologies* (pp. 99-107). 10.1145/2768545.2768554

Wood, G. (2014). *Ethereum: A secure decentralised generalised transaction ledger*. Ethereum project yellow paper, 151, 1-32.

Woonomic. (2017). *Bitcoin NVT Ratio: Woobull Charts*. Woobull.Com. http://charts.woobull.com/bitcoin-nvt-ratio/

Wootters, W. K., & Zurek, W. H. (1982). A single quantum cannot be cloned. *Nature, 299*(5886), 802–803. doi:10.1038/299802a0

Working, A., & Series, P. (2019). *Regulating fintech : Objectives, principles, and practices October 2019 Asian Development Bank Institute*. ADBI Working Paper Series, No. 1016, Asian Development Bank Institute (ADBI).

World Economic Forum. (2019). *World Economic Forum Annual Meeting 2019*. Davos: World Economic Forum.

Wu, Y., Lu, X., & Wu, Z. (2021). Blockchain-Based Trust Model for Air Traffic Management Network. *2021 IEEE 6th International Conference on Computer and Communication Systems, ICCCS 2021*, 92–98. 10.1109/ICCCS52626.2021.9449156

Wu, K., Chou, S., Chen, S., Tsai, C., & Yuan, S. (2018). Application of machine learning to identify Counterfeit Website. *Proceedings of the 20th International Conference on Information Integration and Web-Based Applications & Services*. 10.1145/3282373.3282407

Wu, P. S. (2017). Fintech trends relationships research: A bibliometric citation meta-analysis. *Proceedings of the International Conference on Electronic Business (ICEB)*, 99–105.

Xavier, V. (2017). The Impact of Fintech on Banking. *European Economy, Banks, Regulation and the Real Sector - Fintechs and Banks: Friends or Foes?* 97–105. https://blog.iese.edu/xvives/files/2018/02/EE_2.2017.pdf

xd4rker. (2021). *Minerblock*. https://github.com/xd4rker/MinerBlock

Xiang, S., Rasool, S., Hang, Y., Javid, K., Javed, T., & Artene, A. E. (2021). The Effect of COVID-19 Pandemic on Service Sector Sustainability and Growth. *Frontiers in Psychology, 12*, 1178. doi:10.3389/fpsyg.2021.633597 PMID:34025507

Xiao, L., Deng, H., Tan, M., & Xiao, W. (2019, December). Insurance block: A blockchain credit transaction authentication scheme based on homomorphic encryption. In *International Conference on Blockchain and Trustworthy Systems* (pp. 747-751). Springer.

Xiong, H., Dalhaus, T., Wang, P., & Huang, J. (2020). *Blockchain technology for agriculture: applications and rationale*. Academic Press.

Xu, C., Zhu, K., Yi, C., & Wang, R. (2020). *Data pricing for blockchain-based car sharing: A stackelberg game approach*. Paper presented at the GLOBECOM 2020-2020 IEEE Global Communications Conference. 10.1109/GLOBECOM42002.2020.9322221

Xu, G., Dong, W., Xing, J., Lei, W., Liu, J., Gong, L., & Liu, S. (2022). *Delay-CJ: A novel cryptojacking covert attack method based on delayed strategy and its detection*. Digital Communications and Networks.

Xu, Y. Z., Zhang, J. L., Hua, Y., & Wang, L. Y. (2019). Dynamic Credit Risk Evaluation Method for E-Commerce Sellers Based on a Hybrid Artificial Intelligence Model. *Sustainability, 11*(19), 5521. doi:10.3390u11195521

Yadav, D. (2019). *Deepfake : A Survey on Facial Forgery Technique Using Generative Adversarial Network*. Academic Press.

Yadav, S., Reddy, A. K. K., Reddy, A. N., & Ranjan, S. (2012). Detecting algorithmically generated domain-flux attacks with DNS traffic analysis. *IEEE/ACM Transactions on Networking, 20*(5), 1663–1677.

Yaga, D., Mell, P., Roby, N., & Scarfone, K. (2019). *Blockchain technology overview*. arXiv preprint arXiv:1906.11078.

Yan, Q., Lou, J., Vuran, M. C., & Irmak, S. (2021). Scalable Privacy-preserving Geo-distance Evaluation for Precision Agriculture IoT Systems. *ACM Transactions on Sensor Networks*, *17*(4), 1–30.

Yaokumah, W., Kumah, P., & Okai, E. S. A. (2017). Demographic Influences on E-Payment Services. *International Journal of E-Business Research*, *13*(1), 44–65. doi:10.4018/IJEBR.2017010103

Yarovaya, L., & Lau, M. C. K. (2016). Stock market comovements around the Global Financial Crisis: Evidence from the UK, BRICS and MIST markets. *Research in International Business and Finance*, *37*, 605–619. doi:10.1016/j.ribaf.2016.01.023

Yatsen, M., & Sotnichek, M. (2021, February 4). *Blockchain for Cybersecurity: Pros and Cons, Trending Use Cases.* https://www.apriorit.com/dev-blog/462-blockchain-cybersecurity-pros-cons

Yelowitz, A., & Wilson, M. (2015). Characteristics of Bitcoin users: An analysis of Google search data. *Applied Economics Letters*, *22*(13), 1030–1036. doi:10.1080/13504851.2014.995359

Yılmaz, E., Ulus, H., & Gönen, S. (2015). Bilgi toplumuna geçiş ve siber güvenlik. *Bilişim Teknolojileri Dergisi*, *8*(3), 133.

Yin, R. K. (2018). *Case Study Research: Design and Methods* (6th ed.). Sage.

Yli-Huumo, J., Ko, D., Choi, S., Park, S., & Smolander, K. (2016). Where is current research on blockchain technology? A systematic review. *PLoS One*, *11*(10), e0163477. doi:10.1371/journal.pone.0163477 PMID:27695049

Yucel, S. (2018). Estimating the benefits, drawbacks and risk of digital transformation strategy. *Proceedings - 2018 International Conference on Computational Science and Computational Intelligence, CSCI 2018*, 233–238. 10.1109/CSCI46756.2018.00051

Yudhiyati, R., Putritama, A., & Rahmawati, D. (2021). What small businesses in developing country think of cybersecurity risks in the digital age: Indonesian case. *Journal of Information, Communication and Ethics in Society*.

Yuen, T. H. (2020). PAChain: Private, authenticated & auditable consortium blockchain and its implementation. *Future Generation Computer Systems*, *112*, 913–929. doi:10.1016/j.future.2020.05.011

Yulianto, A. D., Sukarno, P., Warrdana, A. A., & Al Makky, M. (2019). Mitigation of cryptojacking attacks using taint analysis. In *4th International Conference on Information Technology, Information Systems and Electrical Engineering (ICITISEE)* (pp. 234-238). IEEE.

Yu, X., Tian, Z., Qiu, J., & Jiang, F. (2018). A Data Leakage Prevention Method Based on the Reduction of Confidential and Context Terms for Smart Mobile Devices. *Wireless Communications and Mobile Computing*, *5823439*, 1–11. Advance online publication. doi:10.1155/2018/5823439

Yu, Y., Li, Y., Tian, J., & Liu, J. (2018). Blockchain-based solutions to security and privacy issues in the internet of things. *IEEE Wireless Communications*, *25*(6), 12–18. doi:10.1109/MWC.2017.1800116

Zabierek, L., Bueno, F., Kennis, G., Sady-Kennedy, A., & Kanyeka, N. (2021). *Toward a Collaborative Cyber Defense and Enhanced Threat Intelligence Structure*. The Cyber Project.

Zachariadis, M., & Ozcan, P. (2017). *The API economy and digital transformation in financial services: The case of open banking*. Academic Press.

Zaki, M. (2019). Digital transformation: Harnessing digital technologies for the next generation of services. *Journal of Services Marketing*, *33*(4), 429–435. doi:10.1108/JSM-01-2019-0034

Zaman, T., Winschiers-Theophilus, H., George, F., Wee, A. Y., Falak, H., & Goagoses, N. (2016a). Using sketches to communicate interaction protocols of an indigenous community. In *Proceedings of the 14th Participatory Design Conference: Short Papers, Interactive Exhibitions, Workshops-Volume 2* (pp. 13-16). 10.1145/2948076.2948088

Zaman, T., Yeo, A. W., & Jengan, G. (2016b). Designing digital solutions for preserving Penan sign language: A reflective study. *Advances in Human-Computer Interaction, 2016*, 1–9. Advance online publication. doi:10.1155/2016/4174795

Zamfir, C. G., & Sbughea, C. (2020). Phillips Curve: An Empirical Research on Romania. *Annals of Dunarea de Jos University of Galati. Fascicle I. Economics and Applied Informatics, 26*(2), 216–221. doi:10.35219/eai15840409129

ZAO Application. (n.d.). https://apps.apple.com/cn/app/id1465199127

ZDNet. (2019). *Georgia county pays a whopping $400,000 to get rid of a ransomware infection.* ZDNet. https://www.zdnet.com/article/georgia-county-pays-a-whopping-400000-to-get-rid-of-a-ransomware-infection/

Zdonik, S., Ning, P., Shekhar, S., Katz, J., Wu, X., Jain, L. C., Padua, D., Shen, X., Furht, B., & Subrahmanian, V. S. (n.d.). *SpringerBriefs in Computer Science.* https://www.springer.com/series/10028

Zeng, C., & Olivera-Cintrón, R. (2019). *Preparing for the World of a "Perfect" Deepfake.* https://czeng.org/classes/6805/Final.pdf

Zetsche, D. A., Buckley, R. P., Arner, D. W., & Barberis, J. N. (2017). From FinTech to TechFin: The regulatory challenges of data-driven finance. *NYUJL & Bus., 14*, 393.

Zhang, L., Luo, M., Li, J., Au, M. H., Choo, K.-K. R., Chen, T., & Tian, S. (2019). *Blockchain based secure data sharing system for Internet of vehicles: A position paper.* Academic Press.

Zhang, X., Liu, J., Li, Y., Cui, Q., Tao, X., & Liu, R. P. (2019). *Blockchain based secure package delivery via ridesharing.* Paper presented at the 2019 11th International Conference on Wireless Communications and Signal Processing (WCSP). 10.1109/WCSP.2019.8927952

Zhang, F., Huang, Y., Wang, H., Chen, H., & Zang, B. (2008). Palm: security preserving vm live migration for systems with vmm-enforced protec-tion. In *2008 Third Asia-Pacific Trusted Infrastructure Technologies Conference.* IEEE.

Zhang, H., Xu, T., Li, H., Zhang, S., Wang, X., Huang, X., & Metaxas, D. N. (2019). StackGAN++: Realistic Image Synthesis with Stacked Generative Adversarial Networks. *IEEE Transactions on Pattern Analysis and Machine Intelligence, 41*(8), 1947–1962. https://doi.org/10.1109/TPAMI.2018.2856256

Zhang, M., Lin, L., & Chen, Z. (2021). Lightweight security scheme for data management in E-commerce platform using dynamic data management using blockchain model. *Cluster Computing*, 1–15. doi:10.100710586-021-03373-6

Zhang, P., & Zhou, M. (2020). Security and Trust in Blockchains: Architecture, Key Technologies, and Open Issues. *IEEE Transactions on Computational Social Systems, 7*(3), 790–801. doi:10.1109/TCSS.2020.2990103

Zhang, Q., Lu, J., & Jin, Y. (2020). Artificial intelligence in recommender systems. *Complex & Intelligent Systems, 7*(1), 439–457. doi:10.100740747-020-00212-w

Zhao, J. L., Fan, S., & Yan, J. (2016). Overview of business innovations and research opportunities in blockchain and introduction to the special issue. *Financial innovation, 2*(1), 1-7.

Zhaoliang, L., Huang, W., & Wang, D. (2021). Functional agricultural monitoring data storage based on sustainable block chain technology. *Journal of Cleaner Production, 281*, 124078.

Zhao, M., Liao, H.-T., & Sun, S.-P. (2020). *An Education Literature Review on Digitization.* Digitalization, Datafication, and Digital Transformation.

Zhao, Z., Wang, P., & Lu, W. (2021). Multi-layer fusion neural network for deepfake detection. *International Journal of Digital Crime and Forensics*, *13*(4), 26–39. https://doi.org/10.4018/IJDCF.20210701.oa3

Zharikov, E., Telenyk, S., & Bidyuk, P. (2020). Adaptive workload forecasting in cloud data centers. *Journal of Grid Computing*, *18*(1), 149–168.

Zhe, K. S. K. (2020). *Cover Story: Are tighter cryptocurrency regulations needed?* The EdgeMarkets.Com. https://www.theedgemarkets.com/article/cover-story-are-tighter-cryptocurrency-regulations-needed

Zheng, Z., Xie, S., Dai, H., Chen, X., & Wang, H. (2017). An overview of blockchain technology: architecture, consensus, and future trends. *2017 IEEE International Congress on Big Data (BigData Congress)*. 10.1109/BigDataCongress.2017.85

Zhou, P., Han, X., Morariu, V. I., & Davis, L. S. (2017). Two-Stream Neural Networks for Tampered Face Detection. *IEEE Computer Society Conference on Computer Vision and Pattern Recognition Workshops,* 1831–1839. doi:10.1109/CVPRW.2017.229

Zhou, Q., Yang, Z., Zhang, K., Zheng, K., & Liu, J. (2020). *A decentralized car-sharing control scheme based on smart contract in internet-of-vehicles.* Paper presented at the 2020 IEEE 91st Vehicular Technology Conference (VTC2020-Spring). 10.1109/VTC2020-Spring48590.2020.9129439

Zhuang, P., Zamir, T., & Liang, H. (2020). Blockchain for cybersecurity in smart grid: A comprehensive survey. *IEEE Transactions on Industrial Informatics*, *17*(1), 3–19. doi:10.1109/TII.2020.2998479

ZilbigerO. (2019). https://www.reliasmedia.com/articles/144339-cryptojacking-among-latest-cyberthreats-for-healthcare

Zimba, A., & Mulenga, M. (2018). A dive into the deep: demystifying WannaCry crypto ransomware network attacks via digital forensics. *International Journal on Information Technologies & Security*, *4*(2).

Zimba, A., Wang, Z., & Mulenga, M. (2019). Cryptojacking injection: A paradigm shift to cryptocurrency-based web-centric internet attacks. *Journal of Organizational Computing and Electronic Commerce*, *29*(1), 40–59.

Zimmermann, A., Schmidt, R., Sandkuhl, K., Wißotzki, M., Jugel, D., & Möhring, M. (2015). Digital enterprise architecture-transformation for the internet of things. *Proceedings of the 2015 IEEE 19th International Enterprise Distributed Object Computing Conference Workshops and Demonstrations, EDOCW 2015*, 130–138. 10.1109/EDOCW.2015.16

Zorabedian, J. (n.d.). *Cryptojacking Rises 450 Percent as Cybercriminals Pivot From Ransomware to Stealthier Attacks.* Available at:https://securityintelligence.com/cryptojacking-rises-450-percent-ascybercriminals-pivot-from-ransomware-to-stealthier-attacks/

Zottola, A. J. (2014). *Legal Considerations for E-Commerce Businesses.* Available at: https://www.venable.com/insights/publications/2014/04/legal-considerations-for-ecommerce-businesses

Zou, P., Huo, D., & Li, M. (2020). The impact of the COVID-19 pandemic on firms: A survey in Guangdong Province, China. *Global Health Research and Policy*, *5*(1), 1–10. doi:10.118641256-020-00166-z PMID:32885048

Zuiderwijk, A., & Janssen, M. (2013). Open data policies, their implementation and impact: A framework for comparison. *Government Information Quarterly*, *31*(1), 17–29. doi:10.1016/j.giq.2013.04.003

Zulkifl, Z., Khan, F., Tahir, S., Afzal, M., Iqbal, W., Rehman, A., Saeed, S., & Almuhaideb, A. M. (2022). FBASHI: Fuzzy and Blockchain-Based Adaptive Security for Healthcare IoTs. *IEEE Access: Practical Innovations, Open Solutions*, *10*, 15644–15656. doi:10.1109/ACCESS.2022.3149046

About the Contributors

Saqib Saeed is an Associate Professor with the Department of Computer Information Systems, Imam Abdulrahman Bin Faisal University, Dammam, Saudi Arabia. He received the B.Sc. degree (Hons.) in computer science from International Islamic University Islamabad, Pakistan, in 2001, the M.Sc. degree in software technology from the Stuttgart Technology University of Applied Sciences, Germany, in 2003, and the Ph.D. degree in information systems from the University of Siegen, Germany, in 2012. He is also a Certified Software Quality Engineer from the American Society of Quality. His research interests include human-centered computing, data visualization and analytics, software engineering, information systems management, and digital business transformation. He is also an Associate Editor of IEEE Access and International Journal of Public Administration in the Digital Age, besides being member of the advisory boards of several international journals.

Abdullah M. Almuhaideb received the B.S. degree (Hons.) in computer information systems from King Faisal University, Saudi Arabia, in 2003, and the M.S. (Hons.) and Ph.D. degrees in network security from Monash University, Melbourne, Australia, in 2007 and 2013, respectively. He is currently an Associate Professor in information security, a Supervisor with the Saudi Aramco Cybersecurity Chair, and the Dean of the College of Computer Science and Information Technology, Imam Abdulrahman Bin Faisal University, Saudi Arabia. He received several honors, including the Imam Abdulrahman Bin Faisal University President's Award for the highest research publications at the college level and sixth place on the university's list of distinguished researchers for the year 2021. He has published two patents and more than 50 scientific articles in peer reviewed international journals and premier ACM/ IEEE/Springer conferences. His research interests include mobile security, ubiquitous wireless access, authentication, and identification.

Noor Zaman received the Ph.D. degree in IT from UTP, Malaysia. He has great international exposure in academia, research, administration, and academic quality accreditation. He was with ILMA University, KFU for a decade, and currently with Taylor's University, Malaysia. He has 19 years of teaching & administrative experience. He has an intensive background of academic quality accreditation in higher education besides scientific research activities, he had worked a decade for academic accreditation and earned ABET accreditation twice for three programs at CCSIT, King Faisal University, Saudi Arabia. Dr. Noor Zaman has awarded as top reviewer 1% globally by WoS/ISI (Publons) recently. He has edited/authored more than 11 research books with international reputed publishers, earned several research grants, and a great number of indexed research articles on his credit. He has supervised several postgraduate students including masters and Ph.D. Dr. Jhanjhi is an Associate Editor of IEEE ACCESS,

Guest editor of several reputed journals, member of the editorial board of several research journals, and active TPC member of reputed conferences around the globe.

Yousaf Bin Zikria (Senior Member, IEEE) is currently working as an Assistant Professor with the Department of Information and Communication Engineering, Yeungnam University, South Korea. He authored more than 100 refereed articles, conference papers, book chapters, and patents. He published papers at the top venue, including IEEE COMMUNICATIONS SURVEYS & TUTORIALS, IEEE Wireless Communications Magazine, IEEE Network, Future Generation Computer Systems (Elsevier), and Sustainable Cities and Society (Elsevier). He has managed numerous FT/SI in SCI/E indexed journals. His research interests include the IoT, 5G, machine learning, wireless communications and networks, WSNs, routing protocols, CRAHN, CRASN, transport protocols, VANETs, embedded systems, and network and information security. He also held the prestigious CISA, JNCIS-SEC, JNCIS-ER, JNCIA-ER, JNCIAEX, and Advance Routing Switching and WAN Technologies certifications. He has been listed in the world's top 2% researchers/scientists published by Stanford University and Elsevier.

* * *

Zainab Abaid is an Assistant Professor in the Department of Cybersecurity in the FAST School of Computing, National University of Computer and Emerging Sciences, Islamabad, Pakistan. She completed her Ph.D. in machine learning and cybersecurity from the University of New South Wales, Sydney, Australia, in 2017, and has worked in teaching and research roles in Australia and Pakistan since. Her areas of interest are insider attacks, adversarial machine learning and network security.

Naveed Naeem Abbas is a Ph.D. Computer Science scholar at the National University of Sciences and Technology (NUST) Pakistan. He holds M.S. in Computer Sciences from The Islamia University of Bahawalpur, Pakistan. His main area of interest is Machine Learning, Cyber Security and Scientometrics.

Rizwan Ahmad received the M.Sc. degree in communication engineering and media technology from the University of Stuttgart, Stuttgart, Germany, in 2004, and the Ph.D. degree in electrical engineering from Victoria University, Melbourne, Australia, in 2010. From 2010 to 2012, he was a Postdoctoral Research Fellow with Qatar University on a QNRF Grant. He is currently working as an Associate Professor with the School of Electrical Engineering and Computer Science, National University of Sciences and Technology, Pakistan. His research interests include medium access control protocols, spectrum and energy efficiency, energy harvesting, and performance analysis for wireless communication and networks.

Tahir Ahmad received his Master's degree in Computer and Communication Security from the School of Electrical Engineering and Computer Science (SEECS), National University of Science & Technology (NUST) Islamabad, Pakistan, in 2013. He obtained his Ph.D. with European Ph.D. Label in Computer Science and Systems Engineering from Department of Computer Science, Bioengineering, Robotics and Systems Engineering (DIBRIS), University of Genova, Italy, in 2020. Currently, he is working in the Security & Trust Unit, Foundation Bruno Kessler, Trento, Italy as a Researcher. His research interests are in distributed systems security, with particular emphasis on understanding the security issues in the current data-driven Internet-connected world and exploring practical solutions for improving their security and privacy.

Waqas Ahmad received the Ph.D. degree in electrical engineering from Victoria University, Melbourne, VIC, Australia, in 2012. He is currently a Professor with the Department of Electrical Engineering, Pakistan Institute of Engineering and Applied Sciences, Islamabad, Pakistan. His research interests include cognitive radios, cooperative communication, and physical layer aspects of wireless communication and networks.

Queen Aigbefo is a doctoral candidate at Macquarie University, Sydney Australia. She has a master's degree in Information Technology, Management and Organizational Change from Lancaster University. Her research interest includes evaluating users' cyber security behaviors, security strategy and risk assessment.

Dina A. Alabbad received the B.S degree in Computer Science from Imam Abdulrahman bin Faisal University, Saudi Arabia in 2002, and the MSc and PhD degrees in Artificial Intelligence from the University of Manchester, in UK in 2012 and 2019 respectively. She is currently an Assistant Professor at Computer Engineering department at the College of Computer Science and Information Technology (CCSIT), Imam Abdulrahman bin Faisal University. She is currently the chair of Computer Information Systems at CCSIT, and the director of the Data Management Office at Imam Abdurlahman bin Faisal University. Her research interest includes machine learning, natural language processing, and BioHealth informatics. [Biography pulled from the Profile]

Ari-Veikko Anttiroiko, PhD, is a Senior Lecturer and an Adjunct Professor at the Faculty of Management and Business, Tampere University, Finland. His main research interests lie in the areas of local governance and local economic development. Anttiroiko has collaborated with academics and government agencies in different parts of the world. He has memberships in several editorial boards of international journals. He has published extensively on various topics in internationally distributed publications, including Encyclopedia of Digital Government vols. I-III (Idea Group Reference, 2007) and Electronic Government vols. I-VI (IGI Global, 2008). His latest books include The Political Economy of City Branding (Routledge 2014), New Urban Management (Palgrave 2015), Wellness City (Palgrave 2018) and The Inclusive City (Palgrave 2020).

Razi Arshad is working as Assistant Professor at department of information security, School of Electrical Engineering and Computer Sciences, National University of Sciences and Technology, Islamabad, Pakistan. Dr. Razi Arshad has extensive experience in the field of cybersecurity over the span of 18 years. He worked in several reputable US based cybersecurity firms. He holds a Ph.D. degree in information security from Otto-Von-Guericke University, Magdeburg, Germany, an MS degree in information security from Sichuan University, China, and a BS degree in Mathematics and Computer Science from Quaid-i-Azam University and international Islamic University, Islamabad, Pakistan respectively.

Mudassar Aslam has over 16 years of experience in academia and industry. He is currently working in NUCES-FAST as Assistant Professor. Previously, he worked as a Senior Researcher in the Cybersecurity Unit at RISE Research Institutes of Sweden, where he worked on the EU-funded project "nIoVe". His other experiences include working at COMSATS University Islamabad for over 9 years; and working in the industry as a researcher together with companies like Ericsson, Telia, and Saab. His main research interests include IoT, Edge, and Cloud security with expertise in platform security mechanisms provided by Trusted Execution Environments (TEEs) such as Trusted Platform Module (TPM), ARM Trustzone, Intel SGX. He did his post-doctorate under ERCIM fellowship program at RISE, Sweden (2018); Ph.D. in an industrial setup at Swedish Institute of Computer Sciences (now RISE Sweden) and Mälardalen University Sweden. Earlier, he did his Masters in Security from KTH, Sweden in 2009, and completed his BCS/MCS in 2002 from International Islamic University, Islamabad.

Neda Azizi has received her PhD in the School of ICT at Griffith University, studying A Process Theory of IT Risk Management Implementation. She holds a B. Sc. degree in Physics (Solid State) and also a M. Sc. degree in Industrial Engineering (System and Productivity Management). Dr Neda has been active as a project management consultant in some companies and is currently lecturing Microservice Architecture and Cybersecurity at Torrens University. She is passionate about how people interact with technology and ultimately how people and communities can benefit from their interaction, particularly from the application of new and emerging technology. Her seminars, publications and regular involvement in conferences, journals and industry projects highlight her main research interests in the field of Business and Technology. Orcid number: 0000-0001-5651-4869.

Manasa Bettaswamy is currently working as Assistant Professor in RNS First Grade College, She has presented Best Paper Award and papers published - Title of the Paper 'A Comparative Study on Management Conditions of Pre and Post Merger of SBM with SBI'. She has 5 Years of Experience in the field of Commerce and Management. She has participated in Various Workshops, Seminars, Conferences and Orientation programs conducted by Bangalore University.

Bharath Booshan has a PhD from University of Mysore on the thesis title "Impact of Experiential Marketing for Brand Building of Luxury Hotels in Select Metropolitan Cities of India" MBA from Bangalore University.

Shabista Booshan has a PhD in HRM from Sri Satya Sai University of Medical Science and Technology.

Vijay Bose is currently working as Assistant Professor in the Department of Business Management, in Vaagdevi College of Engineering at Warangal, Telangana state. He is having Five years of teaching, Four years of Research and Three years of Industry experience. He has published three papers in International Journals, and two Papers in National Journal. His areas of interest are Marketing and Human Resources Management.

Usama Habib Chaudhry is M.S. Information Security scholar at the National University of Sciences and Technology (NUST) Pakistan. He holds a BS in Computer Sciences from Bahria University Islamabad, Pakistan. His main area of interest is Cyber Security, Blockchain and Artificial Intelligence.

Prince Dawar is working in Poornima Group of Colleges, Jaipur. He is also pursuing his doctoral research from MNIT, Jaipur. He has more than 16 years of research and teaching experience. He has published several research papers in national and international journals.

Sunny Dawar holds Ph.D., MBA and M.COM degress. Dr. Sunny Dawar is working at Faculty of Management & Commerce, Manipal University Jaipur,Rajasthan, India. Dr. Dawar is having 12 years experience of teaching and research. He has published many research papers in refereed journals. He has also presented several research papers in national and international conferences.

Burcu Demirdöven is a researcher in the Department of Political Science and Public Administration of Pamukkale University, Turkiye. Her PhD research focuses on digital signage technologies in the case of emergencies. She was awarded the 100/2000 CoHE Ph.D. Scholarship Program.

Irwan Adi Ekaputra is a professor of finance and Head of the Management Department in the Faculty of Economics and Business, Universitas Indonesia. His research interests are in investments, market microstructure, and corporate finance.

Hina Gull is working as lecturer in Department of Computer Information Systems, Imam Abdulrahman Bin Faisal University Dammam Saudi Arabia. She has earned her MS (CSE) degree from NUST Pakistan.

Omid Haass is a Lecturer at the RMIT University, School of Property, Construction and Project Management based in Melbourne, Australia. His research interests entails Information system Development, Project, Knowledge and Risk management. Omid is a member of Project Management Institute (PMI) and PMI Melbourne chapter since 2014 and have been certified as a Project Management Professional (PMP) by PMI since 2015. Omid is also a Certified Scrum Master (CSM) with Scrum Alliance since July 2019. ORCID: https://orcid.org/0000-0002-1561-4561.

Anum Hasan did her MS in Information Security from Bahria University Islamabad, Pakistan with a gold medal. She did her MSc from Quaid-i-Azam University, Islamabad. She is a lecturer at the Department of Computer Science, National University of Modern languages(NUML), Rawalpindi, Pakistan. She enjoys working in the domains of cyber security and AI/ ML.

Zaäfri Ananto Husodo is a lecturer in Finance and Banking at Department of Management, Faculty of Economics and Business, Universitas Indonesia since 2000. He holds Ph.D. in Finance and Banking from Australian School of Business, University of New South Wales, Australia. His current research covers topics on Digital Business, Analytics in Finance, Frictions in Financial Markets, Financial System Stability, and Islamic Finance. Courses taught are Seminar on Asset Pricing, Applied Financial Econometrics, Risk Modelling, and Investment. He has been securing competitive research grants from the Central Bank of Indonesia, the Debt Management Office of the Republic of Indonesia and the World Bank. He serves as invited reviewer in many reputable academic journals.

Sardar Zafar Iqbal received the M.S. (C.S.) degree in computer science from IQRA University, Karachi. He is currently a Lecturer with the College of Computer Science and Information Technology, Imam Abdualrahman Bin Faisal University. His research interests include educational research, big data, software process modeling, algorithms, and software quality assurance.

Fawad Khan is a cyber security expert and an academician with several years of experience. He specializes in Cryptography & Information security and has worked on several cyber security projects. He is presently an Assistant Professor at Department of Information Security in National University of Sciences and Technology (NUST), Islamabad, Pakistan. He received PhD Degree in Information Security from School of Cyber Engineering, Xidian University, Xi'an, China in 2018 and Masters' and Bachelors' degrees in Electrical (Communication) Engineering from CECOS University, Peshawar and University of Engineering & Technology, Peshawar in 2014 and 2010, respectively. His research interest and expertise include Attribute-based Encryption, Searchable Encryption, Homomorphic Encryption, Multi party computation, Authentication, Blockchain and Privacy preserving Machine Learning. He has also served as a Lab Engineer at the Department of Electrical Engineering, FAST – NUCES, Peshawar Campus from 2011-2015. Fawad has a passion for industry-oriented teaching and seeks to provide solutions to address the industry related problems. His professional services include Technical Program Committee Member and reviewer for several international journals and conferences. He is a Senior Member of IEEE.

Md. Abir Hasan Khan has completed his doctoral degree from the School of Management under the University of Tampere, Finland. Besides of his PhD monograph, Dr. Khan has published several articles in international peer-reviewed scientific journals. He has accomplished post-doctoral research from the same School of his doctoral studies. At present, Dr. Khan is jointly working with the professors of the Faculty of Management and Business under the Tampere University, Finland, on local government's budgetary and financial aspects of developed, developing and under-developed countries.

Sohaib Khan did his bachelor's in Telecommunication engineering and master's in Information Security from the National University of Sciences and Technology, Pakistan. He has been teaching various core subjects related to information security since 2017. His active area of interest includes computer security, Network Security, Digital forensics, and Cryptography. Apart from research activities he has also conducted various practical workshops related to vulnerability assessment and penetration testing.

Pallavi Kudal is a certified Data Analyst and Data Science Trainer with 12+ years of experience in academics and training and 3+ years of experience in interpreting and analyzing data in order to drive successful business solutions. She holds a BSc. in Statistics, an MBA in Finance and Marketing and Ph.D. in Finance. She has Proficient knowledge in statistics, mathematics, and analytics. Dr. Pallavi is at present associated DYPIMS, Pune as Faculty- Business Analytics. In the past she has been associated with prestigious universities like Christ University, Bangalore and Amity University, Noida.

Madan Mohan Laddunuri is from India. He has been working at several universities in India and abroad. His research papers have appeared in many peer-reviewed international journals. More over He published several books related to Social Sciences.

Areeba Laraib is an associate with the Shah Abdul Latif University, Khair pur Pakistan.

Adrian Lau Hui Yi is currently an undergraduate student pursuing a degree in Bachelor of Computer Science in University of Technology Sarawak (UTS).

Christy Dwita Mariana is a faculty member in Bina Nusantara University. She obtained her doctoral degree from University of Indonesia as the best, fastest, and youngest graduate from the Graduate School of Management, Faculty of Economics and Business, University of Indonesia. Her dissertation is the first dissertation in Indonesia that discussed about cryptocurrencies, which entitled "The Safe-Haven Dynamics of Cryptocurrencies for the U.S. and Emerging Stock Markets". Her research interests are about Investment, FinTech, Cryptocurrencies, and Corporate Finance.

Baria Mirza is a Master's student in the Artificial Intelligence at the School of Electrical Engineering and Computer Science (SEECS), National University of Science and Technology (NUST). She has a BSc. in Computer Science from COMSATS University Islamabad (2020). Her current research interests include Cybersecurity, Information Systems, Internet of Things (IoT), Artificial Intelligence, text mining and HCI.

Noshaba Naeem received the B.S. degree in Computer Engineering from College of Electrical and Mechanical Engineering, NUST, Islamabad in 2019. Currently, she is pursuing the Master's Degree in Information Security from College of Signals, NUST, Islamabad, Pakistan. Her research interests includes Information Security and Quantum Cryptography.

Tooba Nasir is Assistant Professor in CS Miss Nasir Miss Nasir is a computer scientist. She did her first Masters in CS from Bahria University Islamabad with Communication Networks for majors. Her second [research] Masters is from the University of Kent at Canterbury, England, where researched on multimodal visualisation and converted image-based datasets to sound. Miss Nasir has been in academia since 2004. She has taught at the School of Computing at the University of Kent among other places in England. She also worked for the IT Services at Kent as a Web Programmer and Developer. She has worked as a researcher at FBK in Italy at their I3 Research Unit and worked on several projects on Interactive Interface and Interaction Design, Cognitive Science, and Social Engagement. She's published several papers over the years. In Pakistan she has taught at Bahria University Islamabad, COMSATS Islamabad, and Iqra University Islamabad Campus. Miss Nasir has been installed at Beaconhouse International College since Feb 2022.

Lasse Oulasvirta, PhD, M.A. in business economics, is professor at the Tampere University, in the field of public sector accounting. He has been holding board memberships of the Finnish Government Accounting Board, the Scientific Council of the National Audit Office of Finland, the Central Accounting Board of the Church, the Finnish EPSAS group in the Ministry of Finance, the Finnish auditor oversight body and one leading audit firm in Finland. His research focus has been broadly on public sector financing, accounting, and auditing.

Mathiraj P. is a professor in the Department of Corporate Secretaryship at Alagappa University in Karaikudi. He has more than 26 years of Teaching and Research Experience. His research work was published in more than 150 articles in reputed journals and also published books, Chapters. He also got a patent in the area of Blockchain Technology. He also got the Best Faculty Award. He serves as a Research advisor to many scholars, academicians, and Industrialists. He co-directs the academic activities at the University. He serves as knowledge in the department of commerce and under his guidance,

14 research scholars were awarded their Ph.D. degrees. He had completed projects and been funded by USC, RUSA 2.0, etc.

Shams Qazi has completed his PhD in 2016 from University of Wollongong, Australia. At present, he is teaching in NUST as an Assistant Professor and his main research areas are Wireless Network Security, Security in routing protocols, IOTs, Software Systems, Secure applications.

Rashmi Rai is a Ph.D. in Management. She works as an Associate Professor and Head of the Department at the School of Business and Management, CHRIST (Deemed to be) University. She has 20 years of experience, her primary area of interest is Human Resourcesand Organisational Behaviour. She has curated many unique courses for her universities. Her Core Competencies are good communication and writingskills, profound knowledge of the subject areas, and teaching students using various methods. Having a keen research interest has helped her develop around thirty-five research papers and six Book Chapters published nationally and internationally in reputed journals and books, and the quest is still on. She has also published a book on "Quality of Life" by Routledge. She has conducted several workshops on various subjects in management and had an opportunity to present papers at several conferences and attend FDP programs to widen her horizon.

Qaiser Riaz (Senior Member, IEEE) received the M.S. degree in autonomous systems from the Bonn-Rhein-Sieg University of Applied Sciences, Sankt Augustin, Germany, in 2011, and the Ph.D. (Dr. rer. nat.) degree in computer science from the University of Bonn, Germany, in 2016. Since 2016, he has been an Assistant Professor with the Department of Computing, School of Electrical Engineering and Computer Science, National University of Sciences and Technology, Islamabad, Pakistan. His research interests include motion capturing, human motion analysis and synthesis, information security, and machine and deep learning.

Chethan S. is currently working as an Assistant professor in the Department of Management Studies at Acharya Institute of Graduate Studies for the past 3 Years expertise in the area of Finance and Accounting and published several articles in reputed Journals and also attended various conferences at National and International level and attended Webinar and FDP's at National and International level.

Ahsan Saadat is currently working as an assistant professor at School of Electrical Engineering and Computer Science, NUST, Islamabad. Dr Ahsan completed his PhD from Macquarie University Sydney Australia in 2017 and has worked in multiple Australian universities. Prior to PhD, he completed his MS Electrical Engineering from NUST in 2013 and BS Computer Engineering from COMSATS in 2009 where he secured two gold medals.

Shouvik Sanyal is an MBA and Ph.D in Marketing and has more than two decades of teaching in undergraduate and postgraduate levels. He has taught at several prestigious institutions in India and the Sultanate of Oman. Dr. Sanyal is an active researcher and has published several articles in leading journals. He has also published several book chapters and presented his research at conferences in five countries. Dr. Sanyal is currently an Assistant Professor of Marketing at Dhofar University, Oman.

Madeeha Saqib is a lecturer at department of computer information systems, Imam Abdulrahman Bin Faisal University, Dammam, Saudi Arabia. She has a Masters degree in engineering management. Her research interests include organizational communication, technology management and digital transformation.

Ecem Buse Sevinç Çubuk is a research associate in the Department of Public Administration at the Faculty of Business Administration of Adnan Menderes University, Turkiye. She graduated from Bilkent University, Turkey with a Bachelor of International Relations in 2006. She received her PhD from Pamukkale University, Turkey. She was a guest researcher at Delft University of Technology between January 2020 and November 2021. Her research focuses on public policy, public value(s), digital transformation of public services, policy & practice of innovation management, Big Data and Smart Cities.

Imdad Ali Shah is an associate with the School of Computer Science at Taylor's University Malaysia.

Hasan Tahir is an Associate Professor and Head of Department Information Security at School of Electrical Engineering and Computer Science (SEECS), NUST. He holds a PhD in Information Security from the University of Essex UK. He obtained his BE in Software Engineering from Bahria University, Islamabad, Pakistan and MS in Software Engineering from College of E&ME, NUST. Dr Hasan was the recipient of the University of Essex Doctoral Scholarship award. He specializes in Computer Security and IoT. He actively researches applications of cryptography in one to one and group settings. His primary area of research is the use of Physically Unclonable Functions for securing group of devices. Dr Hasan Tahir teaches courses related to applied cryptography, cyber security, information security management, cloud computing security, software engineering, software requirements analysis and design. Dr Hasan has served as a committee member in many renowned IEEE conferences. He is a Senior Member of IEEE.

Shahzaib Tahir received his PhD in Information Engineering from City, University of London, UK in January 2019. He received his B.E. degree in Software Engineering from Bahria University, Islamabad, Pakistan, in 2013. In 2015, he received his MS degree in Information Security from NUST, Islamabad, Pakistan. From 2020 till 2021, Shahzaib was a Postdoctoral Research Fellow at the City, University of London, UK. Currently, he is an Assistant Professor in the Department of Information Security, NUST. He is also the founder and the Chief Technical Officer of CityDefend Limited, UK. His research interest include applied cryptography and cloud security. Dr Shahzaib is a Senior Member of IEEE. He is a reviewer of many high impact journals including IEEE Transactions on Dependable and Secure Computing, IEEE Journal of Biomedical and Health Informatics, IEEE ICC, Elsevier FGCS, Springer Cluster Computing, Springer Sadhna, Springer Science China Information Sciences, Springer Neural Computing and Applications. He has been a TPC member of many international IEEE conferences. Dr. Shahzaib Tahir is also an alumni of InnovateUK CyberASAP.

Dewi Tamara is Associate Professor at Binus Business School, Indonesia. She is also responsible for master's program for executive education. She holds PhD and MBA qualifications and has published more than 20 business cases and multiple research papers.

Dhanabalan Thangam presently working as Assistant Professor in Commerce and Management at Acharya Institute of Graduate Studies, Bangalore, India. Earlier he was worked as Post - Doctoral researcher in Konkuk School of Business, Konkuk University, Seoul, Korea South. He received his Ph.D. degree in Management from Alagappa University, Tamilnadu, India. His current research interests are marketing, small business management and Industry 4.0 Technologies and its application in Business and Management.

Subhan Ullah is Assistant Professor in Department of Computer Networks and Cyber Security, FAST School of Computing, National University of Computer & Emerging Sciences Islamabad, Pakistan. He received his Ph.D. degree in Computer Science/IT (April 2019) from the University of Klagenfurt, Austria, collaboration with the University of Genoa, Italy, under Erasmus Mundus Joint Doctorate Program for Interactive and Cognitive Environments (EMJD-ICE). As the recipient of European Union IDEAS scholarship, Subhan Ullah also studied two semesters of Joint International Master (JIM) in Computer Science (Dec, 2014) at the University of Applied Science, Darmstadt, Germany. He received MS (Computer Science) degree from International Islamic University Islamabad (March 2013) and BS (Computer Science) degree from the University of Malakand, Dir (Lower), Pakistan (August 2008). His research interests include lightweight crypto-based security and data protection techniques for IoT applications, security/privacy of smart cameras, embedded devices, malware detection and prevention in cybersecurity.

Sriram V. P. is currently working as a Professor of Acharya Bangalore B School, Bengaluru, Karnataka, India. His breadth of experience includes 12 years of Academic Teaching Experience in University Level and 4 years of Industry Experience. In addition to that, he had completed International Certification on SAP Business One and worked as a Senior Functional Consultant in various projects of India. His Area of Expertise includes Retail Management; Consumer Behaviour; Services Marketing; Sales and Marketing Management. He had participated and published research articles in both National and International Conferences of Reputed Organizations in India and Overseas. He had acted as Reviewer cum Scientific Committee Member for several IEEE International Conferences and also he's been currently acting as a senior reviewer in many of reputed national and International Journals. Recently He was honored by the Central Programme Committee of NPTEL (Supported by MHRD) along with Indian Institute of Madras (IIT) by issuing the certificate of Appreciation for being as the mentor for Consumer Behaviour and Human Resource Management.

Tahreem Yaqoob has received her B.S. degree in Computer Science with emphasis in Security of cloud network from Fatima Jinnah Women University, Pakistan. She did M.S. in Information Security from the Department of Information Security, National University of Sciences and Technology, Islamabad, H-12, Pakistan in 2018. Her research interests include security issues in privacy preservation in healthcare environment and medical devices.

Tariq Zaman earned his Ph.D. from the Faculty of Computer Science and Information Technology, Univeristi Malaysia Sarawak, Malaysia. He is an associate professor at the School of Computing and Creative Media, University of Technology Sarawak.

Adeel Ahmed Zeerak is M.S. Information Security scholar at the National University of Sciences and Technology (NUST) Pakistan. He holds B.S. in Computer Sciences from Punjab University College of Information Technology, Lahore, Pakistan. His key areas of interest are Cyber Security and Cloud Engineering.

Halim Emre Zeren is an Associate Professor and the head of the Department of Public Administration at the Faculty of Business Administration of Adnan Menderes University, Turkiye. His research interests are public policy, public institutions, and local governments.

Index

A

Accountability 28, 32, 100, 114, 139, 144, 283, 389-390, 392, 402-403, 413-414, 417
Artificial Intelligence 2, 4-5, 7, 12, 50, 85-86, 88-89, 106, 109, 111, 114, 123, 141, 175, 181, 184-185, 193, 198, 203-204, 207, 210, 224-226, 235, 238, 263, 362-363, 411, 462-463
Autoencoders 225, 230-231

B

Behavioural Intention 190, 243
Big Data 2-5, 7, 14-15, 18, 61, 64, 109, 111, 117, 127, 178, 181, 184, 186, 188, 193, 203-204, 206, 213-214, 222-223, 288-289, 361, 411, 424, 462
Bitcoin 2, 9, 50, 55, 57, 89, 175, 185, 210-211, 214, 219-220, 223, 247, 259-260, 262, 267-269, 274, 278-281, 283, 285, 328, 336, 340, 348, 357, 365-367, 383, 426-448, 450, 452
Blockchain 1-2, 5, 7, 12-13, 15, 49-64, 84-85, 88, 90, 111, 139, 145, 173-176, 178-179, 182-191, 193, 201, 203-204, 206, 208, 210-224, 238, 240, 267-268, 270, 278-281, 283, 302-303, 312-313, 327, 338-343, 345-346, 348-349, 351-352, 357-371, 376, 381-387, 439, 444, 450, 462, 464
Budgeting 388-390, 392-393, 395, 399-404
Business 1-5, 7-8, 10, 12-19, 21, 23, 29, 33-34, 48-51, 53, 55-60, 64, 66, 69, 72, 78, 84, 88-89, 91-92, 95-105, 107-111, 125, 132-134, 138, 140-142, 144, 154, 158, 160-163, 165, 172, 178, 184, 186, 188-189, 191-193, 197-198, 201-203, 206-208, 210-211, 213-216, 218-221, 226-228, 240, 244, 264, 266, 268, 271, 283, 289, 303, 313, 315, 328, 339-340, 343, 346, 349, 365-366, 368, 382, 390, 392, 402, 414-415, 421-422, 441, 443-445, 447-453, 456, 458, 460-463
Business Activities 49, 51, 55, 100, 244, 451

C

Cloud 1, 5, 7, 12, 14-16, 52, 61-63, 101, 110-111, 133, 138, 144, 147-173, 178-181, 184, 188-190, 195, 197-201, 204-207, 217, 231, 239, 244, 270-271, 278, 282, 289, 302-303, 309-310, 312-313, 361, 370, 383, 386, 417, 460-462
Cloud Computing 1, 5, 7, 12, 61, 111, 146-148, 150, 153-154, 156-157, 159-173, 178-180, 188, 190, 204, 206-207, 289, 309, 383, 386, 462
Cloud Vulnerabilities 146-147
Collaboration 62, 124, 161, 163, 165, 178, 182, 200, 289, 388, 391, 395, 420, 423
Comics 112, 115, 119, 121, 124, 127
Co-Movement 429, 431, 445-446, 448
Computer Security 21, 23, 36, 40, 44, 46, 48, 110, 146, 184, 262, 264, 286
Computing 1, 5, 7, 12, 16, 20, 27, 31, 36, 47, 61-63, 86-87, 89, 96, 106, 111-114, 116, 124-125, 127-129, 146-150, 153-154, 156-157, 159, 161-173, 178-180, 184, 188-190, 192, 203-207, 213, 223, 237, 240, 259, 263-264, 266, 268-271, 273, 276, 278, 280-281, 283, 286-289, 293, 301, 309-312, 314-315, 319-321, 327-328, 330-335, 339, 361-362, 370, 383-386, 462, 464
Conflicting Scenarios 112, 119, 121
Consumer Perspective 192
Coronavirus 106, 130-131, 135, 139, 144-145, 261
COVID-19 7, 17, 19, 63, 66, 91, 99, 106-107, 109, 130-132, 135-136, 139-141, 143-145, 162, 183, 209, 225, 261, 275, 301, 310, 341, 362-363, 426-431, 433, 435, 437-444, 446-447, 452, 455
Crisis 175, 207, 426-429, 431, 434-435, 437-439, 441-442, 445-448, 452
Crypto Mining 266, 268-273, 278, 280-285
Cryptocurrency 8-9, 51, 67, 85-86, 88, 94, 180, 184-185, 211, 214, 219, 266-271, 273, 276, 278-279, 282-283, 285-286, 331, 341, 358, 386, 427-431, 437-442, 445-448

Cryptojacking Malware 266, 268-276, 278-280, 283, 285
Cyber Attack Countermeasures 21, 32
Cyber Behaviour 112
Cyber Security 18, 22, 57, 60, 65, 80, 97, 106, 112-113, 116-117, 132-133, 135-136, 138, 140, 145-146, 162, 174, 182, 190, 198, 208, 213-214, 221-223, 228, 244, 261, 385, 412-413, 419, 424-425, 449-450, 452, 457, 460-461, 463-465
Cyber Threats and Attacks 21, 24, 46, 220
Cybercrimes 68, 91, 95-97, 99, 104, 178, 187, 229, 454
Cybersecurity 13-14, 21-23, 28-29, 33, 35, 41, 44, 46-50, 53-55, 57, 59-60, 63-64, 67-70, 80, 83, 88, 91, 95-96, 104, 107, 144, 186-188, 192-193, 202-203, 205-211, 213-215, 217, 219-224, 227, 243-245, 251, 256, 266, 276, 281, 283, 314-317, 319, 332-333, 360, 410, 412-414, 416-423, 425, 450-451, 457, 460-465

D

Data Availability 410
Data Confidentiality 410, 413
Data Governance 51, 410-417, 419-424
Data Integrity 5, 157, 217, 341-342, 410
Data Leakage 82, 159, 167, 192-207, 369-370, 420
Data Quality 213, 410, 419
Data Security 105, 110, 117, 159, 161, 163, 166-167, 176, 179, 188, 207-210, 212-215, 218-221, 285, 349, 362, 411, 419, 421, 424, 459
Decentralized Applications (D-App) 364, 367
Decoupling 62, 359, 426, 429-430, 432, 435, 437-438, 440, 442, 448
Deepfake 225-242
Detection 21, 36, 41, 46-47, 82-83, 89, 96, 100, 102, 104, 107-109, 150, 172, 180-181, 188, 199-201, 203-206, 225, 232-242, 248, 259, 262-263, 265-266, 269, 271-272, 274-279, 281-286, 301, 303, 311, 325, 362, 461-463
Digital Transformation 1-20, 46, 91, 106, 145
Digitization 1-4, 6, 16, 18, 20, 66, 162, 175, 411, 453, 459

E

E-Commerce 91-111, 141, 183, 227, 316
Election 338-342, 345-346, 348, 351-354, 356-357, 404
Emerging Market 432, 448
E-Municipality 412, 415-423, 425
Encryption 24, 29, 36-39, 43, 75, 81, 89, 150, 162, 167, 173, 176, 179, 182-183, 189, 194, 196, 199, 201, 204, 210, 213-217, 219, 246-247, 249, 267, 277, 288-296, 298-308, 310-313, 317-319, 322, 327-331, 334-336, 339-340, 342-343, 348-349, 369
Epidemic 130-131, 133, 142-143
Ethereum 9, 268, 328, 337-340, 348-349, 357, 360, 362, 364-365, 367-368, 371, 374, 426, 429-431, 438, 440-444, 446
Ethics 44-45, 112-119, 121, 123-129, 252, 465
External Threats 67, 150, 153-155, 192, 195, 197, 201-202

F

Finance 2, 5, 8, 10, 15, 65-66, 69, 71, 76-78, 88, 109, 163, 175, 178, 185, 187, 198, 203-204, 206, 219, 221, 314-317, 319, 331, 333, 367, 388, 390, 400, 403, 430, 441, 443-448, 451-452, 454-455, 460, 462, 465
Financial Reporting 96, 388-390, 392, 398-403
Financial Transactions Security 49
FinTech 1-2, 4-5, 7-10, 12, 15-19, 65-67, 76-78, 84-91, 93-95, 106, 108, 110-111, 146, 161-162, 172-207, 225-226, 234-236, 240, 266, 271, 280, 286, 288, 290, 303-304, 309, 315, 411, 421-422, 440, 449-455, 457-465

G

GANs 225-226, 230-231, 238

H

Hardness Problems 290, 305, 307-308
Healthcare 5, 22, 48, 60, 63, 65-67, 71-72, 76, 99, 110-111, 115, 132-133, 139, 141, 143, 145-146, 163-165, 172, 207, 210, 271, 276, 283, 288-290, 300-301, 304, 309-310, 341, 361, 365, 367, 383
Homomorphic 167, 288-302, 304-305, 307-308, 310-313, 329, 334, 340
Hyperledger 338, 340, 344-345, 348, 357-359, 384

I

Information Security 22, 29, 39, 49, 59, 89, 103, 130, 140, 144, 146, 162, 176, 205, 207, 243-244, 259-264, 275, 288, 311-312, 414, 420, 423, 425, 464-465
Insider 24, 65-79, 81-90, 174, 177, 186, 198, 200-201, 205, 207, 218, 221, 226
Insider Attack 65, 68-69, 75-76, 78, 83, 90
Insur Tech 449

Internal Threats 103, 146, 192

Internet of Things 1, 6, 12, 20, 47, 60-64, 109, 144, 173, 178-179, 183, 185, 187, 203, 207, 210, 216, 240, 261, 268-269, 274, 289, 302, 342, 366, 368, 382-384, 452, 464

IT Management 132, 138

IT Security Planning 130

IT Systems 33-34, 36, 130-132, 138, 140-141, 143, 263

L

Local Governance 388, 396

M

Machine Learning 5, 7, 12, 14, 18, 46, 50, 83, 85, 87-88, 91, 95, 100-101, 108-111, 139, 181, 199, 201, 203, 206, 223, 225-226, 263, 271, 277, 280, 284, 288, 304, 309, 411, 462

Marmara Municipalities Union 416, 423

Ministry of Interior 415, 420-422

Mitigation 27, 32, 41, 62, 72, 84, 86, 142, 172, 244, 246, 254, 259, 261-262, 264, 266, 269, 276-277, 279, 286

Monero 266, 268-271, 274, 278, 281, 283, 429

N

Network 6, 10, 18, 22, 24, 26-28, 30-32, 38, 41, 47, 50, 52-53, 55-58, 61, 63, 68-71, 73-75, 81, 85-87, 90, 95, 99, 102, 108-110, 135, 140-141, 148-150, 152-156, 159-161, 168-169, 172, 179-180, 182, 191, 195, 198-201, 203, 206, 208-211, 213-214, 216, 218, 220, 226, 230, 232, 234-235, 237-239, 241-242, 247, 255, 260, 262, 264-265, 268, 270-271, 274, 277, 279, 281-282, 284, 310-311, 325, 327, 334, 337-345, 348-349, 357-360, 365, 367-371, 381-382, 413, 425, 429, 446, 451-452, 459, 461-463

O

Open Governance 388, 390-392, 394-396, 398-401

Organizational Perspective 201

P

Pandemic 7, 17, 65-66, 92, 98, 106-107, 109, 130-145, 183, 225, 261, 275, 301, 341, 421, 426-431, 433-435, 437-444, 446, 462

Participation 91, 114, 123, 252, 341, 345, 388, 390-391, 395, 400-402, 422, 442

Phishing 24, 28, 69, 71, 73, 76, 85, 87, 89-90, 95-97, 103-104, 135-136, 174, 177, 194, 227, 245, 247-248, 251, 255, 258, 260, 262-265, 454, 460, 462

Post Quantum Security 288, 309

Post-Quantum Cryptography 314, 316, 319, 327-328, 331, 334

Prevention 28, 65, 67, 82, 86, 88, 96, 99-100, 104-105, 167, 178, 182, 195-196, 198-201, 203-207, 232, 236, 244, 248-250, 261-262, 264-265, 269, 274-276, 278-279, 284, 361, 440

Privacy 14, 44, 47, 59, 61, 63-67, 72, 86-88, 95, 97, 99-100, 103, 107-110, 125, 130, 134, 139-140, 142, 144-147, 159, 163-164, 166, 172, 174, 179, 181-182, 184, 189, 196, 199, 203-204, 207, 209, 215, 218, 222-223, 239-240, 262, 267, 278, 280-281, 288-290, 292, 300-304, 308-313, 321, 327, 336, 339, 342, 345, 348-349, 358, 360, 362, 364, 368-371, 381, 383, 411, 413, 415, 424, 451, 454, 456, 464

Privilege-Escalation 90

Professionalism 112-114, 116

Protection Motivation 243, 252-257, 261, 263-264

Public Ledger 53, 338-339, 367

Public-Key Cryptography 218, 314, 322, 328, 343

Q

Quantum Cryptography 314, 319, 326, 331, 333, 335-337

Quantum Key Distribution 314, 319, 323, 333, 335, 337

Qubits 320-321, 323, 325, 331

R

Ransomware 24, 63, 67, 71, 85, 99, 177, 243-265, 287, 461

Real-Time Cyber Threat Detection and Mitigation 21, 41

Reg Tech 449

Riders and Drivers 364, 371

Ridesharing 364, 387

Risk Management 32-34, 104, 130, 132-133, 138, 142, 185, 205, 413-414, 425

S

Safe-Haven 426-432, 437-438, 440-443, 446-448

Security 14-15, 18, 21-36, 39-49, 51, 53-54, 57-67, 69-72, 77-80, 84-91, 95-99, 102-113, 116-117, 130-136, 138-142, 144-150, 152, 154-155, 157-169,

171-174, 176-191, 194-198, 200, 202-224, 228, 236, 239, 241, 243-245, 248-249, 251, 255-265, 269-271, 275-276, 278-286, 288, 290, 292, 294-295, 297-298, 300-305, 309-313, 315, 318-319, 322-323, 325-342, 345, 349, 358-360, 362, 367-371, 381-383, 385, 411-415, 417-421, 423-425, 439, 445, 449-452, 454, 456-457, 459-465

Security and Privacy 47, 61, 63-64, 66-67, 72, 86-87, 103, 108, 130, 139, 144, 146-147, 164, 172, 179, 189, 196, 203-204, 239, 280-281, 302, 311, 342, 368, 464

Smart Contract 47, 60, 338-339, 345, 349-351, 361, 365, 367-368, 371, 373, 381, 387

Social Engineering 67, 73, 75-76, 79, 87, 90, 135, 144, 166, 194, 196, 227, 236, 243-245, 247-249, 256, 260, 264, 273, 278, 281

Systems 4-6, 10, 14, 17-29, 31, 33-34, 36, 38-40, 44, 46, 48, 51-52, 56, 59-62, 66, 69-73, 80, 83, 86, 90-91, 93-94, 96-97, 99, 101, 104, 107-111, 123-124, 129-132, 136-138, 140-141, 143-145, 147-148, 150, 157, 165, 167, 172-173, 176, 178, 184-187, 189-191, 194, 196, 198, 200-201, 203-210, 213-217, 220, 223, 234, 237, 239-241, 244-245, 247, 249-251, 253, 257, 259-265, 268-269, 271, 274-276, 278, 280, 283-286, 293, 296, 301, 303-304, 310-311, 313-314, 316, 321-322, 326-327, 330-335, 338-342, 345, 348-349, 357,

360-367, 369-371, 383-385, 389, 393, 395-396, 401, 403, 410-411, 413-415, 417-418, 420, 422-425, 451, 453-454, 456, 461-464

T

Tech Fin 449

Transmission 27, 104, 164, 179, 217, 303, 370, 426, 429-432, 439, 442-444, 446, 448

Transparency 5, 59, 83-84, 100, 267, 302, 336, 340, 342, 346, 360, 366-367, 369-370, 389-390, 392, 394-396, 400-404, 415, 454

Truffle 362, 364, 368, 385

Trust Model 174, 178-184, 186-187, 190-191

V

Virtual Machine for Ethereum (EVM) 368

Volatility 426-435, 437-448

Volatility Transmission 426, 429-432, 443-444, 448

Voting System 302, 312, 338-342, 345-346, 349, 360-363

W

WebAssembly 266, 270, 272, 277-278, 281

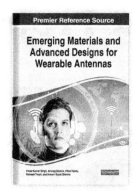

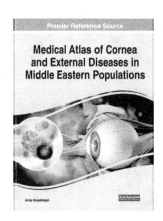

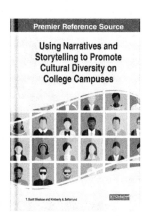

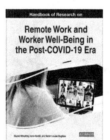

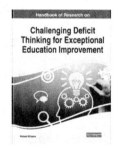

Printed in the United States
by Baker & Taylor Publisher Services